William Wilson, Nicholas Surrey Garland

A Compilation of the Laws and Amendments Thereto

Relating to Building Societies, loan companies, joint stock companies, and interest on mortgages and other acts

William Wilson, Nicholas Surrey Garland

A Compilation of the Laws and Amendments Thereto
Relating to Building Societies, loan companies, joint stock companies, and interest on mortgages and other acts

ISBN/EAN: 9783337152314

Printed in Europe, USA, Canada, Australia, Japan

Cover: Foto ©Suzi / pixelio.de

More available books at **www.hansebooks.com**

A COMPILATION

—OF THE—

LAWS AND AMENDMENTS THERETO

—RELATING TO—

Building Societies, Loan Companies,

JOINT STOCK COMPANIES,

—AND—

INTEREST ON MORTGAGES AND OTHER ACTS

PERTAINING TO MONETARY INSTITUTIONS,

—AS PASSED BY—

THE DOMINION PARLIAMENT

—AND THE SEVERAL—

PROVINCIAL LEGISLATURES;

TO WHICH IS APPENDED A COMPLETE REFERENCE TABLE TO PRIVATE ACTS AND AMENDMENTS

BY

N. SURREY GARLAND,

Clerk of Statistics, Finance Department.

ALSO THE LAWS RELATING TO

BANKS AND BANKING.

COMPILED BY

WILLIAM WILSON,

Assistant Law Clerk, House of Commons.

OTTAWA
PUBLISHED BY A. S. WOODBURN.
1882.

ENTERED according to Act of Parliament of Canada, in the year 1882, by A. S. WOODBURN, in the Office of the Minister of Agriculture.

PREFACE.

In preparing and classifying for the *Canada Gazette* the returns rendered to the Finance Department by the Building Societies, the compiler had frequent occasion to refer to the laws governing those Institutions, and as they were scattered here and there through the Statute Books of the several Provinces both before and after Confederation, and have also a place in the legislation of the Dominion, it seemed to the compiler desirable for purposes of reference to bring these laws together into one volume ; hence this compilation.

In addition to placing before the public the laws governing Building Societies, it may not perhaps be deemed out of place to give also a brief review of the history of the rise and progress of these institutions as far as they form part of the trade of the country.

The earliest legislation appears to have been passed by the Legislature of the old Province of Canada in 1846, to encourage the establishment of Building Societies in that part of Canada formerly consisting of Upper Canada. Shortly after an Act was passed having the same object in view for Lower Canada. In 1847 a similar Act was passed in New Brunswick, and in 1849 an Act was passed by Nova Scotia to the like effect. The above four Acts are so similar that they appear to have had one common origin, and seem from the returns rendered to the Dominion Government to be—especially in the Maritime Provinces—the Acts under which the Building Societies are chiefly incorporated. The Acts passed since the above dates, with the exception of the Consolidating Act of the Province of Canada, seem chiefly to provide for the continuance of the original Acts as the amendments and additions are not extensive in character.

The Act calling for returns in the late Province of Canada was passed by the Legislature of 1865, and the first returns under that Act were prepared in the following year. But in the Municipal returns for the year 1863 for some reason were included the returns relating to Building Societies. Looking at the returns of 1863 from eleven Societies it is difficult to comprehend how in the short space of eighteen years the business has grown to such large dimensions. In that year the capital

Preface.

of these eleven Societies was under one million and a quarter dollars and the Liabilities and Assets were in proportion. For the information of readers the figures are subjoined:

		Capital
1	Quebec Permanent Building Society	$90,799 95
2	Montreal " " "	120,403 07
*3	Kingston " " "	60,784 61
*4	Freehold Building Society, Toronto	133,570 82
5	Commercial Building and Investment Society, Toronto	62,746 90
*6	Canada Permanent Building Society, Toronto	664,428 00
7	Metropolitan Building Society, Toronto	32,129 65
*8	Western Canada Permanent Building Society, Toronto	6,503 49
9	Toronto Permanent Building Society, Toronto	11,928 51
10	Wellington " " " Guelph	10,836 00
11	London " " " London	13,941 26
	Total	$1,208,072 26

LIABILITIES.

Capital stock paid up	$1,208,072 26
Deposits	365,825 46
Dividends unpaid	36,669 93
Advance payments on Morgtages	31,589 80
Interest due	13,818 06
Balance Profits	179,366 52
Miscellaneous	11,614 36
Total	$1,846,956 39

ASSETS.

Amount secured by Stockholders Mortgages	$1,537,226 71
" " " other Mortgages	45,709 96
" " " Loans with Collaterals	16,077 65
" of Stock in Banks	17,485 60
" " Municipal debentures City of Toronto	4,400 00
" " " " " Quebec	700 00
" " Cash in Banks or in hand	84,035 73
" " instalments in arrear	47,310 19
" " fines and fees	76,480 73
Miscellaneous	17,529 82
Total	$1,846,956 39

* Transacting Savings Bank Business.

Preface. 5

In addition to the above there were in existence what were called Terminable Building Societies, the Capital of which amounted to $873,872 45, which with the Building Societies before enumerated amounted to $2,720,828 84—a strange contrast to the last returns to the Dominion Government, where the capital alone of the Companies who made statements was twelve times as great as in 1863.

Small as the capital was, the business appeared so important to the then Clerk of Statistics, Mr. Arthur Harvey, that he drew attention to it and he also had published a communication from Mr. Charles Robertson, at that time Secretary to the Freehold Society, with such forboding of evil as would follow the measure of valuation, that even although the danger has apparently long since passed, it is as well that it should be recorded, as the opinion of an expert as to what might happen—" It will afford me great pleasure at any time to give you all infor-
" mation in my power relating to Building Societies, being particularly
" anxious to have them all placed on a uniform basis, and subject to the
" Parliamentary supervision with fixed rules for valuing their securities,
" as I feel convinced much evil is likely to arise at no distant day
" from the fallacious mode of valuing their mortgages adopted by some
" of these institutions. * * * It is to be feared some of them have
" divided larger profits among the stockholders than they have earned, a
" system which must ultimately result in ruin to innocent parties." To repeat here the yearly statements rendered to the Finance Department since 1863 would be too prolix, and for the purpose of showing the progress of these institutions it will suffice to show the results exhibited in the year 1873, the more so as up to that time no permission seems to have been accorded to Building Societies to issue debentures. By the returns then rendered from twenty-three Societies the business seems to have grown nearly five-fold, and is as follows:

Total Capital Stock paid up..................	$6,376,281 58
Deposits....................................	2,869,381 51
Dividends unpaid............................	171,264 21
Interest on deposits unpaid..................	119,972 71
Miscellaneous	159,959 04
Balance Profits of year last past............	340,666 85
" " " previous years	916,962 26
Total...........................	$10,954,482 16

ASSETS.

Cash value of Stockholders Mortgages........	$9,224,160 91
" " other "	346,288 59
" " Loans with collateral securities..	267,832 86

Amount of Stock in Banks, viz:

Merchants Bank	10,182 50
Canadian Bank of Commerce	93,362 50
Banque Ville-Marie	4,250 00
Other Banks	28,903 50
Municipal Debentures, viz:	
City of Toronto	9,948 20
" Quebec	34,400 00
Other Municipalities	29,560 00
Board Trustees Common Schools	8,069 61
Cash in Banks and on hand	193,277 13
Real Estate	332,362 86
Instalments of Mortgages in arrear	181,524 19
Fees and Fines in arrear	57,062 53
Miscellaneous	133,296 78
Balance—Loss	
Total	$10,954,482 16

In 1874, by an Act of the Dominion Parliament power was given to issue Debentures, and the impetus given to Building Societies, thereby, as shown by returns lately rendered by the eighty Societies seems to have been marvellous. For purposes of comparison the figures are subjoined:

LIABILITIES.

Capital Stock	$24,495,975 26	
Accumulating Stock	1,176,759 80	
Reserve Fund	4,617,832 83	
Dividends declared and unpaid	688,680 26	
Profits on accumulating shares	318,403 85	
Contingent fund and unappropriated profits	644,754 47	
Liabilities to Shareholders		$31,942,406 47
Deposits	$11,713,633 37	
Debentures payable in Canada	244,659 60	
" " " Britain or elsewhere	22,968,108 74	
Interest on Deposits	184,997 87	
" " Debentures	158,906 35	
Owing to Banks in Canada	227,945 80	
" " " elsewhere	85,102 60	
Other Liabilities	994,707 71	
		36,575,062 04
Total Liabilities		$68,517,468 51

Preface.

ASSETS.

Loans secured on Real Estate...............	$56,612,200	46
" " County Securities............	52,000	97
" " City "	73,149	14
" " Township, Town and Village Securities...............................	74,998	56
Loans secured on School Sections..............	7,550	00
" " shareholders on their Stock....	768,976	12
" otherwise secured....................	904,161	83

    Total Loans................... **$58,493,037 08**

Property owned consisting of Real Estate............	$4,352,439	63
Do Dominion Securities.......	250,472	73
Do Provincial Securities......	116,785	26
Do County Securities.........	536,695	19
Do City Securities............	173,819	00
Do Township, Town and Village Securities...............	536,061	29
Do School Sections...........	9,540	08
Office Furniture and Fixtures.................	38,276	13
Do Cash on hand.............	71,870	47
Do Cash in Banks...........	4,454,207	06
Other property consisting of (descriptions specified in return)...	955,431	34

                                 11,495,598 18

    Total Assets.................... **$69,988,635 26**

Value of Real Estate under Mortgage.
    Ontario......... $112,612,157 32
    Quebec......... 3,756,132 04
                       $116,368,289 36

Amount invested and secured by Mortgage Deeds.
    Ontario......... $45,910,756 00
    Quebec......... 2,389,929 98
                       $48,200,675 98

Value of Mortgaged property held for sale.
    Ontario......... $2,720,293 22
    Quebec......... 652,227 01
                       $3,372,520 23

Amount chargeable against such property.
    Ontario......... $2,645,820 88
    Quebec......... 217,032 98
                       $2,862,853 76

Present Cash value of Investments on Mortgages and other Securities.

Ontario........	$59,001,694 56	
Quebec........	5,797,738 95	
		$64,799,433 51

The compiler regrets that the returns last rendered, although much more in volume than those previously published, are so far incomplete, through many Companies not having forwarded statements, it is further very probable that the names of many Companies have been inadvertently overlooked, although the compiler searched through the Directories of almost all the Counties in Ontario to complete the list. The result shown however even with the statements of those published is so important as to show that against a total value in Real Estate in Ontario alone, amounting as by the last official statements to $509,294,610 50, (as per Ontario sessional papers Vol. 13, Part 4, 1881,) Real Estate of the value $112,612,157 32 is under assignment to these fifty-eight Companies. This factor is of itself so important in considering the future of Canada as to justify to the mind of the compiler the preparation of this volume which he trusts may be useful as a handy book to those connected with such Societies.

TABLE OF CONTENTS:

UPPER CANADA.

	PAGE.	YEAR.	VIC. CAP.
A brief review of the progress of Building Societies and Loan Companies for the past eighteen years.	4	1882	
A table of all private and other Acts and amendments passed in Dominion Parliament and Quebec and Ontario Legislatures, relating to Building Societies, Loan Companies and Joint Stock Companies, alphabetically arranged...............	408		
An Act to encourage the establishment of certain Societies commonly called Building Societies in that part of the Province of Canada formerly constituting Upper Canada. The provisions of this Act are substantially incorporated in Cap. 53, Con. Stat., but the original act is retained in its entirety it being the first passed in Canada relating to Building Societies	9	1846	9 90
An Act respecting Building Societies	16	1859	22 53
An Act to make further provisions for the management of Permanent Building Societies in Upper Canada................................	23	1865	29 38

LOWER CANADA.

An Act respecting Building Societies..............	25	Con.Stat.,L. C.	69

DOMINION OF CANADA.

	PAGE.	YEAR.	VIC. CAP.
An Act to make further provision for the management of Permanent Building Societies carrying on business in the Province of Ontario........	34	1874	37 50
An Act to amend the Act Thirty-seventh Victoria, chapter Fifty, respecting Permanent Building Societies in Ontario..........	41	1877	40 48
An Act to amend the Act to make further provision for the management of Permanent Building Societies carrying on business in the Province of Ontario	42	1877	40 49
An Act to amend the Law respecting Building Societies carrying on business in the Province of Ontario	43	1878	41 22
An Act respecting Building Societies carrying on business in the Province of Ontario	44	1879	42 49
An Act for the relief of Permanent Building Societies and Loan Companies.....................	47	1880	43 43
An Act to make further provision respecting the			

[CONTENTS.]

	PAGE	YEAR	VIC.	CAP
constituting and management of Building Societies in the Province of Quebec.	52	1877	40	50
An Act to provide for the liquidation of the affairs of Building Societies in the Province of Quebec	62	1879	42	48
An Act to amend the Law respecting the incorporation of Joint Stock Companies by Letters Patent	66	1877	40	43
An Act to authorize Corporations and Institutions incorporated without the limits of Canada to lend and invest money in Canada.	91	1874	37	49
An Act relating to Interest and Moneys secured by mortgage on Real Estate.	93	1880	43	42
An Act to enlarge and extend the powers of the Credit Foncier Franco-Canadian.	113	1881	44	58
An Act to incorporate the Credit Foncier of the Dominion of Canada.	117	1881	44	59
An Act respecting the Canadian Pacific Railway.	300	1881	44	1
An Act to amend "An Act relating to Banks and Banking," and to continue for a limited time the charters of certain Banks to which this Act applies.	367	1880	43	22
An Act to amend and consolidate the law respecting Duties imposed on Promissory Notes and Bills of Exchange.	400	1879	42	17
An Act to repeal the duty on Promissory Notes, Drafts and Bills of Exchange.	325	1882	45	1
An Act to further amend the law respecting Building Societies and Loan and Saving Companies carrying on business in the Province of Ontario	349	1882	45	24
An Act respecting insolvent Banks, Insurance Companies, Loan Companies, Building Societies and Trading Corporations	326	1882	45	23

PROVINCE OF ONTARIO, L.

	PAGE			
An Act to authorize Corporations and Institutions incorporated out of Ontario to lend and invest moneys therein.	94	R. Stat., Ont.		163
An Act respecting Building Societies.	97	"	"	164
An Act respecting Mortgages and Sales of Personal Property.	260	"	"	119
An Act containing general provisions applicable to Joint Stock Companies incorporated by special Act and for certain purposes	141	"	"	149
An Act respecting the incorporation of Joint Stock Companies by Letters Patent.	150	"	"	150

	PAGE	YEAR	VIC.	CAP.
An Act to amend the Law respecting Building Societies.	134	1878	41	7

[CONTENTS.]

	PAGE.	YEAR.	VIC.	CAP.
An Act respecting the winding up of Joint Stock Companies...	266	1878	41	5
An Act to give Mortgagees certain powers now commonly inserted in Mortgages...	284	1879	42	20
An Act to amend the Building Societies Act...	135	1879	42	26
An Act to give to Mortgagees certain powers now commonly inserted in mortgages...		1879	42	20
An Act for the relief of Building, Loan and Savings' Societies and Companies...	137	1880	43	21
An Act to amend the Revised Statutes respecting Mortgages and Sales of Personal Property...	257	1880	43	15
An Act respecting companies incorporated under Imperial Statutes...	250	1880	43	19
An Act to extend the powers of Joint Stock Companies for the erection of Exhibition Buildings...	249	1880	43	18
An Act to extend the powers of Companies incorporated under the Joint Stock Companies Letters Patent Act...	251	1881	44	18
An Act for the incorporation by Letters Patent and the regulation of Timber Slide Companies...	252	1881	19	44
An Act respecting the Credit Foncier Franco-Canadian...	287	1881	44	51
An Act to confer additional powers upon Joint Stock Companies...	291	1882	45	17
An Act respecting returns required from incorporated Companies...	290	1882	45	21

PROVINCE OF QUEBEC.

	PAGE.	YEAR.	VIC.	CAP.
An Act to amend chapter 69 of the Consolidated Statutes for Lower Canada, respecting Building Societies, in providing for the means of their union and fusion...	166	1875	39	61
An Act to amend chapter 69 of the Consolidated Statutes for Lower Canada, respecting Building Societies in the Province of Quebec...	168	1878	41	20

NOVA SCOTIA.

	PAGE.	YEAR.	VIC.	CAP.
An Act for the regulation of Benefit Building Societies	217	1846	12	42
An Act to incorporate the Pictou Permanent Building Society...	228	1879	42	75
An Act to incorporate the Yarmouth Building Society...	230	1880	43	76

NEW BRUNSWICK.

	PAGE.	YEAR.	VIC.	CAP.
An Act for the regulation of Benefit Building Societies...	191	1847	10	83
An Act to revive and continue an Act intituled : An				

[CONTENTS.]

	PAGE.	YEAR.	VIC.	CAP
Act for the regulation of Benefit Building Societies	205	1866	30	22
An Act in amendment of an Act made and passed in the tenth year of the reign of Her Majesty, intituled: An Act for the regulation of Benefit Building Societies and the Act 29th Victoria to revive and continue the same	206	1871	34	56
An Act to incorporate the Saint John Real Estate and Building Company	211	1871	34	57
An Act in further amendment of the Law relating to Benefit Building Societies	215	1880	43	33

PRINCE EDWARD ISLAND.

	PAGE.	YEAR.	VIC.	CAP.
An Act for the regulation of Benefit Building Societies	233	1876	30	37

PROVINCE OF MANITOBA.

An Act, Building Societies, formation of &c.	169	Con. Stat. Man.	9
An Act, The incorporation of Joint Stock Companies by Letters Patent, and their powers	177	"	7
An Act to authorize Corporations and other Institutions incorporated out of this Province, to lend and invest moneys in this Province	350	"	30

BRITISH COLUMBIA.

	PAGE.	YEAR.	VIC.	CAP.
An Ordinance to amend the Law relating to Joint Stock Companies (Con. Stat. 1877)	353	1866	29	37
An Ordinance respecting The Companies Ordinance 1866	355	1869	33	38
An Ordinance to encourage the establishment of Investment and Loan Societies	356	1869	33	147

ANNO-NONO.—VICTORIA REGINA.

9 VIC., CAP. XC.

An Act to encourage the establishment of certain Societies, commonly called Building Societies, in that part of the Province of Canada formerly constituting Upper Canada.

Section.
Preamble; Act 8 Vic. c. 94, cited.
1. When twenty persons in U.C. shall agree to constitute a Building Society, they shall be a corporation for that purpose, after having complied with certain formalities; Shares not to exceed £100 each; Society may make Rules, &c., consistent with the laws of Upper Canada. Proviso: Member not to receive interest until his shares are paid up; Exception.
2. Society may receive a sum of money from any member by way of bonus on any share, without being subject to penalties imposed by the Usury Laws.
3. Society to elect from time to time a Board of Directors; Term of Office; Powers of a majority of Directors; Proviso; Acts of the Directors to be recorded.
4. Rules to declare purposes for which Society is established, &c.; Proviso: To what purposes only the monies of the Society shall be applied.
5. Rules to be recorded in a book kept for that purpose, which shall be open to all members.
6. Rules to be binding on members and officers of the Society; Certified Copies to be evidence; Certiorari taken away.

Section.
7. Rules to be altered, &c., at General Meetings only, and by a certain majority.
8. Rules to specify place of meeting, and powers and duties of members.
9. Directors to appoint Officers of Society, pay Salaries and Expenses, &c.; Officers entrusted with Money to give Security.
10. May take and hold Real Estate, &c.; Mortgaged to Society to secure payments of shares; may proceed on such Mortgages; may invest monies in Public Stocks, &c.
11. Mode of Proceeding when any Member of the Society shall die or become insolvent.
12. Property vested in President and Treasurer of Society for the time being; they may bring suits, &c., concerning such property; continuance of Actions.
13. Secretary to be a competent witness although he be also Treasurer.
14. President, &c., not to be responsible for liabilities of Society.
15. Treasurer to provide Statement of Funds every year; Account to be attested.
16. Interpretation clause.
17. Public Act.

[*18th May, 1846.*]

WHEREAS it is desirable to afford encouragement and protection to the establishment of certain Societies, commonly called Building Societies, for the purpose of raising by small periodical subscriptions a fund to enable the members thereof to obtain unincumbered freehold or leasehold property; And whereas by an Act passed in the eighth year of Her Majesty's reign, certain persons were incorporated as a Society for such purposes in the City of Montreal, by the name and style of the Montreal Building Society, and provisions were made for the conduct and management of that Society, and certain privileges and immunities conferred upon it: And whereas it is expedient to encourage the formation of similar Societies throughout that part of this Province heretofore constituting the Province of Upper Canada, whenever the inhabitants of any particular locality may be desirous of availing themselves of the provisions of this Act ; Be it therefore enacted by the Queen's Most Excellent Majesty, by and with the advice and consent of the Legislative Council and of the Legislative Assembly of the Province of Canada, constituted and assembled by virtue of and under the authority of an Act passed in the Parliament of the United Kingdom of Great Britain and Ireland, intituled An Act to re-unite the Provinces of Upper and Lower Canada, and for the Government of Canada ; and it is hereby enacted by the authority of the same :—

1. That when and so soon as any twenty persons or upwards in that part of this Province of Canada, constituting heretofore the Province of Upper Canada shall have agreed to constitute themselves a Building Society, signed and executed under their respective hands and seals, a declaration of their wish and intention so to constitute themselves such Building Society, and shall have deposited the same with the Clerk of the Peace in the District in which they shall reside, (who for receiving such deposit shall be entitled to receive a fee of two shillings and sixpence) such persons, and such other persons as may afterwards become members of such Society and their several and respective executors, administrators, and assigns, shall be ordained, constituted and declared to be, and shall be a corporation, body corporate and politic, by such name and style as a Building Society as by such declaration so deposited as aforesaid shall have been declared to be the name by which persons so executing the same desire such Society to be known, for the purpose of raising by monthly or other periodical subscriptions of the several members of the said Society, and in shares not exceeding the value of one hundred pounds for each share (such subscriptions not to exceed twenty shillings per month for each share), a stock or fund for the purpose of enabling each member thereof to receive out of the funds of the said Society the amount or value of his share or shares therein to erect or purchase one or more dwelling house or houses or other freehold or leasehold estate, to be secured by way of mortgage or otherwise to the said Society until the amount or value of his share or shares shall have been fully paid to the said Society, with the interest thereon and with all fines and liabilities incurred in respect thereof : and that it shall and may be lawful to and for the several members of such Society, from time to time to assemble together and to make, ordain and constitute such proper and wholesome Rules and Regulations for the government and guidance of the same, as the major part of the members thereof so assembled together deem meet, so as such Rules shall not be repugnant to the express provisions of this Act, or to the general laws of this Province or of Upper Canada ; and to impose and inflict such reasonable fines, penalties and forfeitures upon the several members of the said Society who shall offend against any such Rules, as the majority

of the members may think fit, to be respectively paid to such uses for the benefit of the said Society, as the said Society by such Rules shall direct; and also from time to time to amend and alter such Rules as occasion may require, or annul or repeal the same, and to make new Rules in lieu thereof under such restrictions as are in this Act contained: provided that no member shall receive or be entitled to receive from the funds of such Society any interest or dividend by way of annual or other periodical profit upon any share or shares in the said Society until the amount or value of his share or shares shall have been realized; except on the withdrawal of such member, according to the Rules of the said Society then in force.

2. And be it enacted: That it shall and may be lawful to and for every such Society to have and receive from any member or members such sum or sums of money by way of bonus on any share or shares, for the privilege of receiving the same in advance prior to the same being realized, besides interest for the share or shares so received or any part thereof, without being subject or liable on account thereof to any of the forfeitures or penalties imposed by any Act or Acts of Parliament, or by any Laws in force in that part of the Province heretofore Upper Canada relating to usury.

3. And be it enacted: That every such Society shall and may, from time to time, elect and appoint any number of the members of the said Society to be a Board of Directors, (who shall choose a President and Vice-President), the number and qualification thereof to be declared in the Rules of such Society, and shall and may delegate to such Directors all or any of the powers given by this Act to be executed; and such Directors being so elected and appointed shall continue to act for and during such time as shall be appointed by the Rules of such Society, the powers of such Directors being first declared in and by the said Rules; and in all cases where Directors shall be appointed for any particular purpose, the powers delegated to them shall be reduced to writing and entered in a book by the Secretary or Clerk of the said Society, and a majority of the number of such Directors present at any meeting thereof, shall, at all times, be necessary to concur in any act of such Directors, and they shall, in all things, delegated to them, act for, and in the name of such Society; and all acts and orders of such Directors, under the powers delegated to them, shall have the like force and effect, as the acts and orders of such Society at any General Meeting thereof could, or might have had in pursuance of this Act; Provided always, that the transactions of such Directors shall be entered in a book belonging to such Society, and shall from time to time, and at all times, be subject and liable to the review, allowance and disallowance of such Society, in such manner and form as such Society shall by their General Rules have directed and appointed, or shall in like manner direct and appoint.

4. And be it enacted: That every such Society so established as aforesaid, shall, in or by one or more of their said Rules, declare all and every the intents and purposes for which such Society is intended to be established, and shall also in and by such Rules direct all and

every the uses and purposes to which the money which shall from time to time be subscribed, paid or given to or for the use or benefit of the said Society, or which shall arise therefrom or in anywise, shall belong to the said Society, shall be appropriated and applied, and in what shares or proportions, and under what circumstances, any member of such Society, or other person, shall or may become entitled to the same, or any part thereof: Provided that the application thereof shall not in anywise be repugnant to the uses, intents or purposes of such Society, or any of them to be declared as aforesaid ; and all such Rules during the continuance of the same shall be complied with and enforced ; and the monies so subscribed, paid or given, or so arising to or for the use or benefit of the said Society or belonging thereto, shall not be diverted or misapplied either by the Treasurer or Directors, or any other officer or member of such Society entrusted therewith, under such penalty or forfeiture as such Society shall by any Rule enforce and inflict for such offence.

5. And be it enacted: That the Rules for the management of every such Society shall be entered and recorded in a book to be kept for that purpose, which book shall be open at all seasonable times for the inspection of the members of such Society ; but nevertheless nothing contained herein shall extend to prevent any alteration in or amendment of any such Rules in the whole or in part, or making any new Rules for the management of such Society, in such manner as by the Rules of the said Society shall from time to time be provided.

6. And be it enacted : That all Rules, from time to time, made and in force for the management of such Society, and entered and recorded as aforesaid, shall be binding on the several members and officers of the said Society, and the several contributors thereto and their representatives, and all of whom shall be deemed and taken to have full notice thereof by such entry and record as aforesaid, and the entry of such Rules in the book or books of the said Society as aforesaid, or a true copy of the same, examined with the original, and proved to be a true copy, shall be received as evidence of such Rules, respectively, in all cases : and no *certiorari*, or other legal process shall be brought or allowed to remove any such Rules into any of Her Majesty's Courts of Record.

7. And be it enacted : That no Rule entered as aforesaid shall be altered, recinded or repealed, unless at a General Meeting of the members of such Society, convened by public notice written or printed, signed by the Secretary or President of the said Society, in pursuance of a requisition for that purpose by not less than fifteen of the members of such Society, which requisition shall state the object for which the meeting was called, and shall be addressed to the President and Directors, whereupon each member shall be notified of the proposed alterations, through the Post Office, within fifteen days ; such meeting to consist of not less than one-third of the Shareholders, three-fourths of which meeting must concur in such alterations or repeal.

8. And be it enacted : That the Rules of every such Society shall specify the place or places at which it is intended that the said Society shall hold its meetings, and shall contain provisions with respect to the powers and duties of the members at large, and of such officers as may be appointed for the management of the affairs of the said Society.

9. And be it enacted : That the Directors of every such Society, shall, and may, from time to time, at any of their usual meetings, elect and appoint such person or persons to be officers of the said Society as they think proper, and grant such salaries and emoluments as they may deem fit, and pay such necessary expenses attending the management of the said Society as may be incurred ; and shall, and may, from time to time, elect, when it shall be deemed necessary to carry into execution the purposes of the said Society, for such space of time and for such purposes as shall be fixed and established by the Rules of the said Society, and may from time to time discharge such person or persons, and elect and appoint others in the room of those who shall vacate or die, or be so discharged ; and all and every such officer or other person whatsoever, who shall be appointed to any office in anywise touching or concerning the receipt, management or expenditure of any sum of money collected for the purpose of the said Society, before he shall be admitted to take upon him the execution of any such office or trust, shall become bound in a bond in such form and for such amount as the Directors may determine with two sufficient sureties, for the just and faithful execution of such office or trust, and for rendering a just and true account according to the Rules of the said Society, and in all matters lawful to pay obedience to the same.

10. And be it enacted : That it shall and may be lawful for every such Society to take and hold any real estate, or securities thereon, *bona fide* mortgaged, or assigned to the said Society, either to secure the payment of the shares subscribed for by the members, or to secure the payment of any loans or advances made by, or debts due to such Society, and they may also proceed on such mortgages, assignments or other securities, for the recovery of the monies thereby secured, either at law or in equity, or otherwise, and that such society shall have the power of investing in the names of the President and Treasurer for the time being any surplus funds in the stocks of any of the chartered banks or other public securities of the Province, and that all dividends, interest and proceeds arising therefrom shall be brought to account and applied to and for the use of the said Society, according to the Rules thereof.

11. And be it enacted : That if any person appointed to any office by such Society, and being entrusted with and having in his hands or possession, by virtue of his said office, any monies or effects belonging to such Society, or any deeds or securities relating to the same, shall die or become bankrupt, or insolvent, his heirs, executors, curators, administrators or assigns, or other person, having a legal right, shall, within fifteen days after the demand made by the order of the Directors of such Society or the major part of them assembled at any meeting thereof, deliver over all things belonging to the said Society to such persons as the said Directors shall appoint.

12. And be it enacted : That all real estate, monies, goods, chattles, property, and effects whatever, and all titles, securities for money, or other obligatory instruments and evidences, or monuments, and all other effects whatever, and all rights and claims belonging to or had by such Society, shall be vested in the President and Treasurer of the said Society, for the time being, for the use and benefit of the said Society, and the respective members thereof, their respective executors, administrators or assigns, according to their respective claims and interests, and after the death or removal of any President or Treasurer, shall vest in the succeeding President and Treasurer for the same estate and interest as the former President and Treasurer had therein and subject to the same trusts, without any assignment or conveyance whatever; and also, shall, for all purposes of action or suit, as well criminal as civil, in law or in equity, in anywise touching or concerning the same, be deemed and taken to be, and shall in every such proceeding (when necessary), be stated to be the property of the persons appointed to the offices of President and Treasurer of the said Society for the time being, in the proper names of such President and Treasurer without further description, and such persons shall, and they are hereby authorized to bring or defend, or cause to be brought or defended any action, suit or prosecution, criminal as well as civil, in law or in equity, touching or concerning the property, right or claim aforesaid, of or belonging to or had by the said Society, and in all cases concerning the property, right or claim aforesaid of the said Society, may sue and be sued, plead and be impleaded in their proper names as President and Treasurer of the said Society without other description, and no such suit, action or prosecution shall be discontinued or abated by the death of such persons or their removal from the offices of President and Treasurer, but shall continue in the proper name of the persons commencing the same; any law, usage or custom to the contrary notwithstanding; and the succeeding President and Treasurer shall have the same rights and liabilities, and shall pay or receive like costs as if the action or suit or prosecution had been commenced in their names, for the benefit of or to be satisfied out of the funds of the said Society.

13. And be it enacted: That in all such actions, suits and prosecutions as aforesaid, the Secretary of such Society, shall be a competent witness notwithstanding he may also be Treasurer of the said Society, and that his name may have been used in such action, suit or prosecution as such Treasurer.

14. And be it enacted: That the President, Vice-President, and Directors of every such Society shall, in their private capacity, be exonerated from all responsibility in relation to the liabilities of such Society.

15. And be it enacted: That the rules of every such Society, shall provide that the Treasurer or other principal officer thereof shall once at least in every year, prepare or cause to prepared, a general statement of the funds and effects of or belonging to the said Society, specifying in whose custody or possession the said funds or effects shall then be remaining, together with an account of all and every the various sums of money received and expended by or on account of the said Society since the publication of the preceeding periodical statement, and every such periodical statement shall be attested by two or more members of the said Society appointed Auditors for that purpose, who shall not be Directors, and shall be countersigned by the Secretary or Clerk of the said Society, and every member shall be entitled to receive from the said Society, a copy of such periodical statement without charge.

16. And be it enacted: That the word "Society" in this Act shall be understood to include and to mean Building Society and Institution established under the provisions and authority of this Act; the word "Rules" to include Rules, Orders, By-Laws and Regulations; every word importing the singular number shall extend and be applied to several persons or things, as well as one person or thing, and bodies corporate as well as individual; and every word importing the plural number, shall extend and be applied to one person or thing as well as several persons or things; and every word importing the masculine gender only shall extend and be applied to a female as well as a male; the words "Real Estate" shall extend and apply to unmoveable estate and property generally; and the word "Securities" shall extend and apply to privileges, Mortgages (equitable as well as legal) and incumbrances upon real and unmoveable estate, as well as to other rights and privileges upon personal estate and property: That this Act shall extend to aliens, denizens and females, both to make them subject thereto, and to entitle them to all the benefits given thereby; and that this Act shall be combined in the most beneficial manner for promoting the ends thereby intended.

17. And be it enacted: That this Act shall be deemed a Public Act and shall extend to all Courts of Law or Equity in this Province, and be judicially taken notice of as such by all Judges, Justices and other persons whatsoever without the same being specially shown or pleaded.

CAP. LIII.
An Act respecting Building Societies.

Section.	Section.
1. Societies how incorporated; Powers of Society.	23. May forfeit shares; may expel member; may sue for amount of shares.
2. Members of Society may make Rules,&c. Impose Fines, &c.	24. May sue in Division Court.
3. Except in cases of withdrawal, members not to receive profits on shares, till value of same realized.	25. Society may sell real estate mortgaged in certain cases.
	26. Representatives of officers of Society to deliver over papers and moneys after demand.
4. Society may receive bonus in addition to interest.	27. Property of Society vested in President and Treasurer.
5. Society from time to time to elect Directors.	28. President and Treasurer may bring and defend suits.
6. Powers of Directors to be declared by Rules.	29. Suits not to abate by death or removal from office.
7. Powers of Directors in certain cases to be recorded in books of Society.	30. Secretary of Society a competent witness.
8. Concurrence of majority of Directors necessary.	31. President and Directors relieved of responsibility.
9. Acts of Directors to be binding.	32. Rules to provide that Secretary shall furnish annual statement of funds.
10. Proceedings of Directors to be entered in books of Society.	33. Secretary's statement to be attested by Auditors.
11. Society by rule to declare objects of Society and declare how moneys to be applied.	34. Act extends to aliens, females and bodies corporate.
12. Moneys not to be misapplied under penalties.	35. Interpretation clause.
13. Rules to be recorded in a book.	36. Preamble; 9 V. c. 90; Permanent Societies having fulfilled certain conditions declared to be within this Act; and their subscribers to be members; evidence of membership.
14. Entry of Rules in book, notice to members.	
15. Examined copy of rules entered in book to be evidence.	
16. Rules not to be removed by Certiorari.	37. How By-laws of Permanent Societies may be passed or amended.
17. Rules entered in book not to be altered except at a general meeting.	38. Amount to which Societies may borrow money, limited.
18. Rules to specify time and place r holding meeting.	39. Shareholder whose share is paid up, may receive or invest the amount.
19. Directors to appoint Officers.	
20. Officers appointed to receive moneys to give security.	40. Advances on security of investing on unadvanced shares.
21. Society may take and hold real estate mortgaged by Society for certain purposes.	41. Holding real estate.
	42. Society not bound to see to trusts to which its stock is subject; what receipts shall be sufficient.
22. May invest surplus funds.	

HER Majesty, by and with the advice and consent of the Legislative Council and Assembly of Canada, enacts as follows:

1. In case any twenty or more persons, in Upper Canada, agree to constitute themselves a Building Society, and execute, under their respective hands and seals, a declaration to that effect, and deposit the same with the Clerk of the Peace in the County in which they reside, (who for receiving such deposit shall be entitled to a fee of fifty cents,) such persons, and such other persons as afterwards become members of the Society, and their several and respective executors, administrators and assigns, shall be a corporation, body corporate and politic, as a Building Society, by the name and style mentioned in such declaration, for raising by monthly or other periodical subscriptions of the several members of the Society, in shares not exceeding the value of four hundred dollars for each share, (and in subcriptions not exceeding four dollars per month for each share,) a stock or fund to enable each member to receive out of the funds of the Society the amount or value of his shares therein, for the purpose of erecting or purchasing one or more dwelling house or houses, or other freehold or leasehold estate, or for any other purpose whatsoever, and the amount or value of such shares shall be secured to the Society by mortgage or otherwise on any real estate belonging to the member at the time of his borrowing money from the Society, or on any other real estate acquired by such member, until the amount or value of his shares with the interest thereon, have been fully paid, together with all fines or liabilities incurred in respect thereof. 9 V. c. 90, s. 1—13, 14, V. c. 79, s. 4.

2. The several members of the Society may from time to time assemble together, and make such proper rules for the government of the same as the majority of members so assembled deem meet, so as such rules are not repugnant to the provisions of this Act, or any other law in force in Upper Canada; and they may impose and inflict such reasonable fines, penalties and forfeitures upon the several members of the Society infringing such rules as the majority of the members think fit, and to be respectively paid to such uses, for the benefit of the Society, as the Society by such rules direct; and they may also from time to time amend or rescind such rules, and make new rules in lieu thereof, under such restrictions as are in this Act contained.

3. Except in the case of the withdrawal of a member, according to the rules of the Society then in force, no member shall receive or be entitled to receive from the funds of the Society any interest or dividend by way of annual or other periodical profit upon any share in the Society until the amount or value of his share has been realized.

4. Every such Society may, besides interest, receive from any member a *Bonus* on any share, for the privilege of receiving the same in advance prior to the same being realized, without becoming thereby liable to any forfeitures or penalties imposed by any Laws in force in Upper Canada, relating to Usury. 9 Vic. c. 90, s. 2,--22 V. c. 85, s. 6.

5. Every such Society shall, from time to time, elect and appoint any number of the members of the Society to be a Board of Directors, the number and qualification thereof to be declared in the rules of the Society, and may delegate to such Directors all or any of the powers given by this Act to be executed. 9 V. c. 90, s. 3.

6. The powers of the Directors shall be declared by the rules of the Society, and they shall continue to act during the time appointed by such rules. 9 V. c. 90, s. 3.

7. In case Directors are appointed for any particular purpose, the powers delegated to them shall be reduced to writing and entered in a book by the Secretary or Clerk of the Society. 9 V. c. 90, s. 3.

8. The Directors shall choose a President and Vice President, and they shall in all things delegated to them act for and in the name of such Society, and the concurrence of a majority of the Directors present at any meeting shall at all times be necessary in any Act of the Board. 9 V. c. 90, s. 3.

9. All acts and orders of such Directors, under the powers delegated to them, shall have the like force and effect as the acts and orders of the Society at a General Meeting. 9 V. c. 90, s. 3.

10. The transactions of the Directors shall be entered in a book belonging to the Society, and shall at all times be subject to the review, allowance and disallowance of the Society, in such manner and form as the Society by their general rules direct and appoint. 9 V. c. 90, s. 3.

11. Every such Society shall, in or by one or more of their Rules, declare the objects for which the Society is intended to be established, and thereby direct the purposes to which the money from time to time subscribed to, received by and belonging to the Society, shall be appropriated, and in what shares or proportions and under what circumstances any member of the Society, or other person, may become entitled to the same, or any part thereof. 9 V. c. 90, s. 4.

12. All such Rules shall be complied with and enforced; and the moneys so subscribed to, received by or belonging to the Society, shall not be diverted or misapplied either by the Treasurer or Directors, or any other officer or member of the Society entrusted therewith, under such penalty or forfeiture as the Society by any Rule inflicts for the offence. 9 V. c. 90, s. 4.

13. The Rules for the management of every such Society shall be recorded in a book to be kept for that purpose, and such book shall be open at all seasonable times for the inspection of the members. 9 V. c. 90, s. 5.

14. The rules so recorded shall be binding on the several members and officers of the Society, and the several contributors thereto, and their representatives, and they shall be deemed to have full notice thereof by such record. 9 V. c. 90, s. 6.

15. The entry of the Rules in the books of the Society, or a true copy of the same, examined with the original and proved to be a true copy, shall be received as evidence thereof. 9 V. c. 90, s. 6.

16. Such Rules shall not by *Certiorari* or other legal Process, be removed into any of Her Majesty's Courts of Record. 9 V. c. 90, s. 6.

17. No Rule so recorded as aforesaid shall be altered or rescinded, unless at a General Meeting of the Members, convened by public notice written or printed, signed by the Secretary or President of the Society in pursuance of a requisition for that purpose made by not less than fifteen of the Members, stating the objects for which the meeting is called, and addressed to the President and Directors; and each member of the

Society shall within fifteen days after such requisition, be notified through the Post Office, of the proposed alterations; and such general meeting shall consist of not less than one third of the shareholders, three-fourths of whom must concur in the proposed alterations or repeal. 9 V. c. 90, s. 7.

18. The Rules of the Society shall specify the place or places at which it is intended that the Society shall hold its meetings, and shall contain provisions with respect to the powers and duties of the members at large, and of the officers appointed for the management of its affairs. 9 V. c. 90, s. 8.

19. The Directors shall from time to time, at any of their usual meetings, appoint such persons as they think proper, to be officers of the Society, grant such salaries and emoluments as they deem fit, and pay the necessary expenses attending the management of the Society; and shall from time to time when necessary elect such persons as may be necessary for the purposes of the Society, for the time and for the purpose expressed in the Rules of the Society, and may from time to time discharge such persons, and appoint others in the room of those who vacate, die or are discharged. 9 V. c. 90, s. 9.

20. Every such officer or other person appointed to any office in anywise concerning the receipt of money, shall before entering upon the duties of his office, execute a Bond with two sufficient sureties in such form and for such amount as the Directors determine, for the just and faithful execution of his office, according to the Rules of the Society. 9 V. c. 90, s. 9.

21. Every such Society may take and hold any real estate, or securities thereon, *bonâ fide* mortgaged, or assigned to it, either to secure the payment of the shares subscribed for by its members, or to secure the payment of any loans or advances made by, or debts due to the Society, and may proceed on such mortgages, assignments or other securities, for the recovery of the moneys thereby secured either at law or in equity or otherwise, and generally may pursue the same course, exercise the same powers and take and use the same remedies to enforce the payment of any debt or demand due to the Society as any person, or Body Corporate may by Law take or use for a like purpose.

22. Every such society may, in the names of the President and Treasurer for the time being, invest any surplus funds in the stocks of any of the chartered Banks or other public securities of the Province, and all dividends, interest and proceeds arising therefrom shall be brought to account and be applied to the use of the Society, according to the Rules thereof. 9 V. c. 90, s. 10,—13, 14 V. c. 79, s. 2.

23. Every such Society may declare forfeited to the Society the shares of any member who is in default or who neglects to pay the number of instalments or monthly subscriptions fixed by any stipulation or By-law, and may expel such member from the Society, and the Secretary shall make a minute of such forfeiture and expulsion in the Books of the Society; or instead of such forfeiture and expulsion, the

Society may recover the arrears by an action of debt. 13, 14 V. c. 79, s. 3.

24. If the amount in arrear does not exceed forty dollars the action may be brought in the Division Court of the Division wherein the office of the Society is kept. 13, 14 V. c. 79, s. 3.

25. Whenever any such Society has received from a Shareholder an assignment, mortgage or transfer of any real estate to secure the payment of any advances, and containing an authority to such Society to sell the real estate in case of non-payment of any stipulated number of instalments or sum of money, and to apply the proceeds of such sale to the payment of the advances, interest and other charges due to the Society, such stipulations and agreements shall be valid and binding, and the Society may cause the same to be enforced either by foreclosure or by an action or proceeding in either of Her Majesty's Superior Courts of Common Law, in which action the venue shall be laid in the County in which the lands lie, and the action may be brought in the names of the President and Treasurer of the Society, describing them as such, or in the corporate name of the Society. 13, 14 V. c. 79, s. 1.

26. If any person appointed to an office by the Society and being entrusted with and having in his possession by virtue of his office, any moneys or effects belonging to the Society, or any deeds or securities relating thereto, dies or becomes bankrupt or insolvent, his legal representative, or other person having a legal right, shall within fifteen days after demand made by the order of the Directors of the Society or the major part of them assembled at any meeting thereof, deliver over all things belonging to the Society, to such persons as the Directors may appoint. 9 V. c. 90, s. 11.

27. All real and personal estate, property and effects, and all titles, securities, instruments and evidences, and all rights and claims of or belonging to the Society, shall be vested in the President and Treasurer and their successors in office for the time being for the use of the Society and the respective members thereof, according to their respective claims and interests, and shall, for all purposes of bringing or defending actions or suits civil or criminal, be deemed to be, and shall be stated to be, the property of the President and Treasurer, in the proper names of the President and Treasurer for the time being.

28. The President and Treasurer may bring or defend any action suit or prosecution, criminal or civil, respecting any property, right or claim aforesaid, and may sue and be sued, plead and be impleaded in their proper names as President and Treasurer of the Society without other description.

29. No such suit, action or prosecution shall be discontinued or abated by the death or removal from office of the President or Treasurer, but shall continue in their names; and the succeeding President and Treasurer shall have the same rights and liabilities, and shall pay or receive like costs as if the action, suit or prosecution had been commenced or been defended in their names, for the benefit of or to be satisfied out of the funds of the Society. 9 V. c. 90, s. 12.

80. In all suits and prosecutions, the Secretary of the Society shall be a competent witness, notwithstanding he may also be Treasurer of the Society, and his name used in the suit or prosecution as such Treasurer. 9 V. c. 90, s. 13.

81. The President, Vice-President and Directors of the Society in their private capacity, shall be exonerated from all responsibility in relation to the liabilities of the Society. 9 V. c. 90, s. 14.

82. The rules of the Society shall provide that the Treasurer or other principal Officer thereof shall, once at least in every year, prepare a general statement of the funds and effects of or belonging to the Society, specifying in whose custody or possession, such funds or effects are then remaining, together with an account of all sums of money received or expended by or on account of the Society since the publication of the preceding periodical statement. 9. V. c. 90, s. 15.

83. Every such periodical statement shall be attested by two or more members of the Society not being Directors, appointed Auditors for that purpose, and shall be countersigned by the Secretary or Clerk of the Society, and every member shall be entitled to receive from the Society without charge a copy of such periodical statement.

84. This Act shall for all purposes extend to aliens, denizens and females; and co-partners and corporate bodies may hold shares in any Society incorporated under the provisions of this Act, in the same manner as single individuals; and this Act shall be construed in the most beneficial manner for promoting the ends thereby intended. 13, 14 V. c. 79, s. 4.—9 V. c. 90, s. 16.

85. The word "Society" in the foregoing sections of this Act shall be understood to include and to mean Building Society and Institution established under the provisions and authority of this Act, or any former Act respecting Building Societies; the word "Rules" to include Rules, Orders, By-laws and Regulations; the words "Real Estate" shall extend and apply to immoveable estate and property generally; and the word "securities" shall extend and apply to privileges, mortgages, (equitable as well as legal,) and incumbrances upon real and immovable estate, as well as to other rights and privileges upon personal estate and property. 9 V. c. 90, s. 16.

86. Whereas under the Act passed in the ninth year of Her Majesty's Reign intituled, *An Act to encourage the establishment of certain Societies, commonly called Building Societies, in that part of the Province of Canada formerly constituting Upper Canada,* certain Building Societies have been established called Permanent Building Societies, which have in a great measure superseded those Societies called terminating Building Societies, and are conducted on more certain and equitable principles than the said terminating Building Societies, by enabling persons to become members thereof at any time for investment therein or to obtain the advance of their shares or share by giving security therefor, and to fix and determine with the said Society the time and amount which such members shall repay such advanced share or shares and obtain the release of the said security, without being liable to the contingency of losses or profits in the business of the said Society; And whereas doubts had arisen as to whether such Permanent Building Societies were within the meaning and intention of the said recited Act; Therefore, any Permanent Building Society established under the said hereinbefore recited Act and the amended Act thereto, or established under this Act, after this Act takes effect, and conducted on the principle hereinbefore mentioned, which has fulfilled and observed or which fulfils and observes all the conditions necessary to be fulfilled and observed for the establishment of a Building Society under the said recited Acts, or under this Act, (as the case may be) shall be and the same is hereby declared to be and to have been a Building Society within the meaning and intention of the said recited Acts and of this Act, and to be and to have been entitled to all the powers, benefits and advantages of the said recited Acts and of this Act; and any person or persons who have signed the Rules and Regulations of any such Building Society entered and recorded in a book, as in the fifth section of the said recited Act, passed in the ninth year of Her Majesty's reign and in the thirteenth section of this Act is required, and have subscribed his or their name or names as a shareholder or shareholders for one or more shares, shall, from the time of such signature and subscription, be and be deemed to have been a member or members of such Building Society; and the production of the book containing the rules for the management of such Society, kept as in the fifth section of the said Act and in the thirteenth section of this Act is required, signed by such person and duly witnessed, shall, at all times and for all purposes, be sufficient evidence of membership in such Building Society. 22 V. c. 45, s. 1, (1859.)

37. Any Permanent Building Society may alter, amend, repeal or create any Regulation, Rule or By-law for the working of the said Society at a public meeting of the members of such Society, convened as is directed by the said seventeenth section of this Act, and at which public meeting one third of the members of the said Society, entitled to vote by the Rules of the said Society, and representing not less than two-thirds of the unadvanced Stock of such Society, do, either in writing under their hand or by a vote at such meeting, concur in such alteration, amendment or repeal of such Regulation, Rule or By-law, or in the creation of any new Rule, Regulation or By-law. 22 V. c. 45, s. 2, (1859.)

38. Every such Society, by its Rules, Regulations and By-laws authorized to borrow money, shall not borrow, receive, take or retain, otherwise than in stock and shares in such Society, from any person or persons, any greater sum than three-fourths of the amount of capital actually paid in on unadvanced shares, and invested in real securities by such Society; and the paid in and subscribed capital of the Society shall be liable for the amount so borrowed, received or taken by any Society. 22 V. c. 45, s. 3, (1859.)

39. When any share or shares in any Society have been fully paid up according to the rules of the Society, or have become due and payable to the holder thereof, then and in such case the holder of such

share or shares may either withdraw the amount of his share or shares from the said Society, according to the rules and regulations thereof, or invest the amount of his said share or shares in the Society, and receive therefrom periodically such proportion of the profits made by such Society as may be provided for by a By-law to be passed for the purpose ; and the amount of such share or shares so invested shall become fixed and permanent capital or shares in the said Society not withdrawable therefrom, but transferable in the same manner as other shares in the said Society. 22 V. c. 45, s. 4.

40. Such Society may advance to members on the security of investing on unadvanced shares in the said Society, and may receive and take from any person or persons, or bodies corporate, any Real or Personal Security of any nature or kind whatever as Collateral Security for any advance made to members of the Society. 22 V. c. 45, s. 5.

41. Any Society may hold absolutely Real Estate for the purposes of its place of business, not exceeding the annual value of Six Thousand Dollars. 22 V. c. 45, s. 6.

42. Such Society shall not be bound to see to the execution of any Trust, whether expressed, implied, or constructive, to which any share or shares of its stock may be subject ; and the receipt of the party in whose name any such share or shares stand in the books of the Society, or if such share or shares stand in the name of more parties than one, the receipt of one of the parties shall, from time to time, be a sufficient discharge to the Society for any payment of any kind made in respect of such share or shares, notwithstanding any Trust to which such share or shares may then be subject, and whether or not such Society has had notice of such Trust; and the Society shall not be bound to see to the application of the money paid upon such receipt. **22 V.** c. 45, s. 7, (1859.)

CAP. XXXVIII.

An Act to make further provisions for the management of Permanent Building Societies in Upper Canada.

Section.
Preamble.
1. Directors may close subscription of shares ; Proviso.
2. Members may determine at a general or special meeting to close subscription of shares.
3. Shares to be immediately advanced excepted.

Section.
4. Members may vote by proxy.
5. Quorum of members for altering By-laws.
6. Yearly returns to the Auditor of Public Accounts.
7. Sect. 39 of c. 53, Con. Stat. U. C., amended as to paying up shares in full ; as to borrowing money.
8. Inconsistent provisions repealed.

[*Assented to* 18*th September*, 1865.]

WHEREAS it is expedient to make further provisions for the management of Permanent Building Societies in Upper Canada :

Therefore, Her Majesty, by and with the advice and consent of the Legislative Council and Assembly of Canada, enacts as follows:

1. It shall be lawful for the Directors of any Permanent Building Society in Upper Canada, at any time and from time to time as they may think expedient, by resolution, to close for any specified time, or until further order, the subscription of shares to be held for investment in the Society, and thereafter, until the expiration of such specified time, or until such further order, no new shares shall be subscribed for investment in the Society; Provided always, that such new issue of shares shall be allotted to the then existing shareholders *pro rata*, as nearly as possible without fractions, but in case such new shares be not taken up within thirty days, then the said shares, or the remaining shares shall be sold, and any premium thereon applied to the general benefit of the Society.

2. It shall be lawful for the members entitled to vote, at any time by resolution to be passed at any special or general meeting, for which meeting, notice of such intended resolution shall have been duly given, according to the seventeenth section of chapter fifty-three of the Consolidated Statutes for Upper Canada, to determine that no new shares shall thereafter be subscribed for investment in any such Society; and thereafter no new shares for investment shall at any time be subscribed therein, and the subscription of such shares shall cease for ever.

3. Nothing done under the preceding clauses of this Act shall have the effect of preventing any such Society from creating, as it otherwise might, any share or shares to be immediately advanced to the subscriber or subscribers thereof, or of preventing any person from subscribing, as he otherwise might, for any share or shares, in order immediately to obtain the advance thereof from such Society by giving security therefor.

4. Any member entitled to vote at any meeting of any Permanent Building Society, held under the thirty-seventh section of chapter fifty-three of the Consolidated Statutes for Upper Canada, may be represented and vote at such meeting by his proxy, such proxy being a member of such Society.

5. It shall be lawful at any general meeting, convened under section seventeen of the fifty-third chapter of the Consolidated Statutes for Upper Canada, for two-thirds of the shareholders there present in person, or by proxy, representing not less than one half the amount paid up on investing shares, to alter, repeal or amend any of the rules or by-laws of such Society.

6. It shall be the duty of the Secretary or Treasurer, and the President or Vice-President of every such society, to make yearly returns upon oath, to the Auditor of Public Accounts, of the affairs of such Society, in such manner as may be by him prescribed, stating therein the mode by which the assets of such Society are valued.

7. The thirty-ninth section of chapter fifty-three, above mentioned shall be amended by adding the following proviso thereto: "Provided always, that any share or shares may, at any time, be paid up in full and capitalized at once as permanent stock, and any such share or shares heretofore paid in full or in part, shall be as valid as if the same had been paid by periodical or other subscription: Provided, also, that no such Society hereafter to be established, shall borrow money or receive deposits until not less than one hundred thousand dollars of stock shall have been subscribed, and not less than forty thousand dollars shall have been actually paid thereon."

8. All provisions of all former Acts which may be inconsistent with this Act shall be held and taken to be by this Act amended, so far as may be necessary to render them consistent with this Act.

CAP. LXIX.

An Act respecting Building Societies.

Section.
1. A certain declaration required to be made to constitute a Building Society; Purpose for which such Society shall be constituted; Rules for the government of the Society to be made by its members. Members to receive no profits until the amounts of their shares is realized: Exception.
2. Society may receive a bonus for advance made to members.
3. Appointment of Board of Directors; majority of Directors must concur in all proceedings; minute book of proceedings.
4. Society to declare certain particulars in their rules; application of moneys restricted.
5. Rules to be entered in a book to be open for inspection.
6. Such entry to be deemed sufficient notice and to make rules binding.
7. How only rules may be repealed or amended.
8. Place of meeting, &c., to be specified.
9. Appointment of officers; certain officers to give security for the faithful discharge of their duties.
10. Society may hold real estate hypothecated to them: Investment of surplus funds.
11. Society may make loans on certain conditions.
12. Society may sell property hypothecated to them on non-payment of instalments &c., secured thereby: Actions at law may be brought in the corporate name.
13. Nature of securities upon which society may advance money: Who may be members of Building Societies.

Section.
14. What must be alleged in actions to sell property hypothecated: What evidence will suffice in such actions: Laws in relation to real estate under seizure to apply to proceedings under this Act.
15. Cases in which shares may be declared forfeited.
16. Provision in the event of the death or insolvency of any officer of such society.
17. All the property, &c., of such society to be vested in the society by its corporate name; Pending actions not affected.
18. The Secretary to be a competent witness.
19. Liability of Directors limited.
20. General statement of affairs to be annually prepared by Treasurer.
21. This Act to extend to Permanent Building Societies.
22. Permanent Building Societies having fulfilled the conditions required under this Act to be Building Societies within the meaning thereof.
23. Such societies may amend, &c., their rules, and how
24. To what extent such Society may borrow money.
25. Holders of shares fully paid up may withdraw or invest the amount.
26. Society may loan money on unadvanced shares.
27. Society may hold certain real estate.
28. Society not bound to see to the execution of trusts which any shares may be subject.
29. Nothing in this Act to affect the Montreal Building Society.
30. Interpretation of certain words: Application and construction of this Act.

HER Majesty, by and with the advice and consent of the Legislative Council and Assembly of Canada, enacts as follows:

1. Whenever any twenty persons or upwards in any part of Lower Canada have agreed to constitute themselves a Building Society, and have signed and executed, under their respective hands and seals, a declaration of their intention to become such Building Society, and have deposited the same with the Prothonotary of the Superior Court for the District wherein such Society is to be formed, and to have its principal office or place of business, (who for receiving such deposit shall be entitled to receive a fee of fifty cents) such persons and such other persons as may afterwards become members of such Society, and their several and respective heirs, executors, curators, administrators, successors and assigns, shall be a body corporate and politic, by such name and style, as a Building Society, as by the said declaration is declared:

2. Such Society shall be constituted for the purpose of raising, by monthly or other periodical subscriptions of the several members of the said Society, in shares not exceeding the value of four hundred dollars for each share, (and by subscriptions not exceeding four dollars per month for each share), a stock or fund for enabling each member to receive out of the funds of the Society the amount or value of his share or shares therein, for the purpose of erecting or purchasing one or more dwelling houses, or other freehold or leasehold estate, such advance to be secured by mortgage or otherwise to the said Society until the amount or value of his share or shares is fully paid to the said Society, with the interest thereon, and with all fines or liabilities incurred in respect thereof;

3. The several members of such Society may, from time to time, assemble together, and make, ordain and constitute such proper and wholesome Rules and Regulations for the government and guidance of the same, as to the major part of the members thereof so assembled together seem meet, so as such Rules be not repugnant to the express provisions of this Act, or to the laws in force in Lower Canada; and may impose and inflict reasonable fines, penalties and forfeitures upon members of the Society offending against such Rules, to be respectively paid to such uses for the benefit of the said Society, as the said Society by such Rules shall direct; and may also from time to time amend and alter such Rules as occasion may require, or annul or repeal the same, and make new Rules in lieu thereof, subject to the provisions hereinafter made;

4. But no member shall receive from the funds of any such Society any interest or dividend by way of annual or other periodical profit upon any share in the Society, until the amount or value of his share or shares has been realized; except on the withdrawal of such member according to the Rules of the Society then in force. 12 V. c. 57. s. 1.

2. Every such Society may receive from any member any sum of money by way of *bonus* on any share, for the privilege of receiving the

same in advance prior to its being realized, besides interest for the share so received or any part thereof, without being held thereby to contravene any law relating to usury. *Ibid*, s. 2.

2. Each such Society shall, from time to time, elect and appoint any number of the members of the said Society to be a Board of Directors (who shall choose a President and Vice-President), the number and qualification thereof to be declared in the Rules of such Society; and may delegate to such Directors the execution of all or any of the powers given by this Act; and such Directors being so elected shall continue to act during such time as shall be appointed by the Rules of such Society, the power of such Directors being first declared in and by the said Rules; and in all cases where Directors are appointed for any particular purpose, the powers delegated to them shall be reduced to writing and entered in a book by the Secretary of the Society:

2. A majority of the number of such Directors, present at any meeting thereof must concur in any act of such Directors in order to make such act valid, and they shall, in all things delegated to them, act for and in the name of such Society; and all acts and orders of such Directors, under the powers delegated to them, shall have the like force and effect as the acts and orders of the Society at any general meeting thereof could have had under this Act;

3. But the transactions of the Directors shall be entered in a book belonging to the Society, and shall from time to time and at all times be subject and liable to the review, allowance and disallowance of such Society, in such manner and form as such Society have by their general Rules directed. 12 V. c. 57, s. 3.

4. Every such Society shall, by one or more of their said Rules, declare all and every the interest and purposes for which such Society is established; and shall also in and by such Rules direct all and every the uses and purposes to which the money from time to time subscribed, paid or given to or for the use or benefit of the said Society, or arising therefrom or in anywise belonging to the Society, shall be appropriated and applied;—and in what shares or proportions and under what circumstances any member of such Society, or other person shall become entitled to the same, or any part thereof:

2. But the application of such money shall not in any wise be repugnant to the uses, interests or purposes of such Society, or any of them to be declared as aforesaid ;—and all such Rules during their continuance shall be complied with and enforced; and no such moneys as aforesaid shall be diverted or misapplied either by the Directors or Treasurer, or any other officer or member of the Society entrusted therewith, under such penalty or forfeiture as the Society may, by any Rule, inflict for such offence. *Ibid*, s. 4.

5. The Rules for the management of each such Society shall be entered and recorded in a book to be kept for that purpose, which book shall be open at all seasonable times for the inspection of the members of such Society, but nothing in this section shall prevent any alteration in or amendment of any such Rules in whole or in part, or the making any new Rules for the management of the Society, in such manner as by the Rules of the Society may from time to time be provided. 12 V. c. 57, s. 5.

6. All Rules from time to time made and in force for the management of any such Society and entered and recorded as aforesaid, shall be binding on the several members and officers of the Society, and the several contributors thereto, and their representatives, all of whom shall be held to have full notice thereof by such entry and record as aforesaid; and the entry of such Rules in the book or books of the said Society as aforesaid, or a true copy of the same, examined with the original and proved to be a true copy, shall be received as evidence of such rules respectively, in all cases. 12 V. c. 57, s. 6.

7. No rule entered as aforesaid shall be altered, rescinded or repealed, unless at a general meeting of the members of the Society, convened by public notice written or printed, signed by the Secretary or President of the Society in pursuance of a requisition for that purpose by more than one half of the members of such Society, which requisition shall state the objects for which the meeting is called, and shall be addressed to the President and Directors: whereupon each member shall be notified of the proposed alterations through the post office, within fifteen days; but three-fourths of the members present at such meeting must concur in such alterations or repeal. 12 V. c. 57, s. 7,— 18 V. c. 116, ss. 1 *and* 2.

8. The rules of every such Society shall specify the place or places at which it is intended that the Society shall hold its meetings, and shall contain provisions with respect to the powers and duties of the members at large, and of such officers as may be appointed for the management of the affairs of the Society. 12 V. c. 57, s. 8.

9. The Directors of every such Society shall from time to time at any of their usual meetings, elect and appoint such officers of the Society, and grant such salaries and emoluments as they may deem fit and pay any necessary expenses incurred in the management of the Society; and shall elect such officers for such space of time and for such purposes as shall be fixed and established by the rules of the said Society, and may from time to time discharge them, and appoint others in the room of those who vacate or die or are discharged:

2. Every such officer or other person appointed to any office in any wise concerning the receipt, management or expenditure of any sum of money collected for the purposes of the said Society, shall, before being admitted to take upon him the execution of any such office or trust, enter into a bond in such form and for such amount as the Directors may determine, with two sufficient sureties, for the just and faithful execution of such office or trust, and for rendering a just and true account according to the rules of the said Society for paying obedience to the same and in all matters lawful. 12 V. c. 57, s. 9.

10. Any such Society may take and hold any real estate, or securities thereon, *bonâ fide* mortgaged, assigned or hypothecated to the said Society, either to secure the payment of the shares subscribed for by its members, or to secure the payment of any loans or advances made by, or debts due to such Society, and may also proceed on such mortgages, assignments or other securities, for the recovery of the moneys thereby secured, either at law or in equity or otherwise; and such Society may invest in the names of the President and Treasurer for the time being, any of its surplus funds in the stocks of any of the chartered banks or other public securities of the Province, and all dividends, interest and proceeds arising therefrom shall be brought to account and applied to and for the use of the Society according to the rules thereof. 12 V. c. 57, s. 10.

11. Any such Society may, from time to time, lend and advance to any member or other person, money from and out of its surplus funds, upon the security and mortgage (*hypothèque*) of real estate, and for such period as to the Society or its Directors seems satisfactory or expedient, and may receive therefor such sum of money, by way of bonus, besides interest thereon, as may be agreed upon, without being subject on account thereof to any forfeiture or penalty, and may from time to time vary such investments at their discretion. 20 V. c. 54, s. 1

12. Whenever any such Society has received from any shareholder a mortgage or hypothec, or an assignment or transfer of any real estate belonging to him or her, to secure the payment of any advance, and containing an authority to the Society to sell such real estate in case of non-payment of any stipulated number of instalments or sums of money (as every such Society is hereby authorized to do) and containing also power to the said Society to apply the proceeds of such sale to the payment of the advances, interest and all other charges due to the said Society, and after perfect payment thereof and of all costs and expenses incident thereto, to pay over the balance to the owner of such estate:—such stipulations and agreement shall be valid and binding to all intents and purposes whatsoever, and such Society may cause the same to be enforced by an action or proceeding in the usual course in any law in Lower Canada, having competent jurisdiction, and such action may be brought in the corporate name of any such Society. 14, 15 V. c. 23, s. 1, *and* 18 V. c. 116, s. 3.

13. Every such Society may advance, in the usual manner, moneys on any real estate whatsoever of any member of the said Society, as well for the actual purchase of the same and for the erection of buildings thereon, as generally upon the security of any real estate belonging to any such member at the time of his borrowing such moneys, and may take a mortgage, hypothec or assignment of all such real estate whatsoever in security for such advances, on the same conditions and with the same privileges in all respects as any other real estate by this Act authorized to be mortgaged, hypothecated or assigned; and all securities heretofore taken for moneys advanced in the manner above mentioned, shall be valid and binding on the parties to all intents and purposes whatsoever, as if taken under this Act:

2. All or any person or persons whosoever, whether capitalists or otherwise, may become members of any such society; and co-partners

and corporate bodies may hold shares therein, in the same manner as single individuals. 14, 15 Vic. c. 23, s. 4.

14. In any action or proceeding instituted by any such Society for the purpose of realizing or bringing to sale any property hypothecated, mortgaged or assigned to the Society as aforesaid, it shall not be necessary to set forth the special matters in the declaration,—but it shall be sufficient to allege that the defendant hypothecated, mortgaged or assigned (as the case may be) the real estate, describing the same, to the Society, and that the amount, (or sufficient part of the amount) stipulated by such party to be paid, has become and remains due and owing, whereby by virtue of this Act an action hath accrued to the Society, to have the said estate and property sold :

2. In order to maintain such action, it shall be sufficient, in addition to the customary evidence of the hypothec, mortgage or assignment of such property or estate, to prove by any one witness, whether in the employment of, or a shareholder in such Society or not, or by any other means, that the defendant is in arrear or indebted to the said Society in or exceeding a sum on the accruing of which, by the terms of such hypothec, mortgage, assignment or agreement, the said Society has the right to have the said property or estate sold ; and thereupon the Court shall give judgment for the said amount, and by such judgment order the property to be sold by the Sheriff of the district wherein it lies, after three insertions in the course of four months in the *Canada Gazette ;* and it shall not be necessary for the Sheriff to go through any formality in seizing the said lands or otherwise ;

3. All the laws of Lower Canada, with respect to the protection of immoveable property under seizure, and with respect to the filing of oppositions to the sale of lands or immoveable property, or after such sale, to the payment, return and distribution of the money, to the re-sale of such immoveable property at the *folle enchère* of any purchaser, and to the obtaining possession of any such immoveable property after sale, shall be applicable to the proceedings authorized by this Act ; and the provisions of all laws of Lower Canada regulating the sale of real estate, and the judicial proceedings relative thereto, shall, in so far as applicable and it is not otherwise provided for by this Act, extend to all proceedings to be had under this Act ; and if it be not otherwise herein directed, all such proceedings, in so far as may be, shall be conducted in like manner as proceedings under ordinary writs of execution, and the deed to be given by the Sheriff shall have the like effect as a deed given under an ordinary writ of execution ; except that the Sheriff of the District shall, in addition to his disbursements, be entitled to deduct only one per centum commission from the gross proceeds of the sale. 14, 15 Vic., c. 23, s. 2.

15. Every such Society may forfeit and declare forfeited to the Society, the shares of any member who neglects or is in arrear to pay such number of instalments as may be fixed by any stipulation, or bylaw ; and every such Society may pursue the same course, exercise the same power, and take and use the same remedies to enforce the payment of any debt or demand due to such Society, or any person or body corporate may by law take or use for such purpose. 14, 15 V. c. 23, s 3.

16. If any person appointed to any office by any such Society, and being entrusted with and having in his hands or possession, by virtue of his office, any moneys or effects belonging to such Society, or any deeds or securities relating to the same, dies or becomes bankrupt or insolvent, his heirs, executors, curators, administrators or assigns, or other person having a legal right, shall, within fifteen days after demand made by the order of Directors of such Society or the major part of them, assembled at any meeting thereof, deliver over all things belonging to the said Society, to such persons as the said Directors shall appoint, and shall pay out of the estates, assets or effects of such person, all sums of money remaining due which such person received by virtue of his office, before any of his other debts are paid or satisfied, and all such assets, estates and effects shall be bound to the payment and discharge thereof accordingly; except that the same shall not be paid or satisfied to the prejudice of mortgages or privileges on real estate or of liens or privileges on personal estate only, duly executed previous to the appointment of such officer. 12 V. c. 57, s 11.

17. All real and personal property, moneys, goods, chattels and effects whatever, and all titles, securities for money or other obligatory instruments and evidences or muniments, and all other effects whatever, and all rights and claims belonging to or had by any such Society, shall be vested in the Society by its corporate name and style, declared in the declaration mentioned in the first section of this Act as that under which such Society shall be known;—and shall for all purposes of action or suit, as well criminal as civil, in law as in equity, in anywise touching or concerning the same, be deemed and taken to be, and shall in every such proceeding (when necessary) be stated to be, the property of the Society by the name and style aforesaid, without further description, and by the said name and style the Society may sue and be sued, bring or defend any action, suit or prosecution, criminal as well as civil, in law or in equity, touching or concerning the property, right or claim, of or belonging to the Society, and in all cases concerning any property, right or claim of the said Society, may sue and be sued, plead and be impleaded. 12 V. c. 57, s. 12,—and 18 V. c. 116, s. 3.

2. But nothing in this Act has abated or discontinued or shall abate or discontinue or affect any action, prosecution or proceeding brought on behalf of any such Society by the President and Treasurer thereof; and the same shall be continued in the corporate name of the Society. 18 V. c. 116.

18. In all such actions, suits and prosecutions to which any such Society is a party, the Secretary of such Society shall be a competent witness, notwithstanding he be also Treasurer, and that his name has been used in such action, suit or prosecution as such Treasurer. 12 V. c. 57, s. 13.

19. The President, Vice-President and Directors of every such Society shall in their private capacity be exonerated from all responsibility in relation to the liabilities of such Society. 12 V. c. 57. s. 14.

20. The rules of every such Society shall provide that the Treasurer or other principal officer thereof shall once at least in every year prepare a general statement of the funds and effects of the Society, specifying in whose custody or possession the said funds or effects are then remaining, with an account of every sum of money received and expended by or on account of the Society since the publication of the preceeding periodical statement; and every such periodical statement shall be attested by two or more members of the said Society, appointed Auditors for that purpose, who shall not be Directors and shall be countersigned by the Secretary of the Society, and every member shall be entitled to receive from the said Society a copy of such periodical statement, without charge. 12 V. c. 57, s. 15.

PERMANENT BUILDING SOCIETIES.

21. Permanent Building Societies, enabling persons to become members thereof at any time for investment therein, or to obtain the advance of their shares by giving security therefor, and to fix and determine with any such Society the time and amount as and by which such members shall repay such advanced shares and obtain the release of the said security, without being liable to the contingency of losses or profits in the business of the said Society, may be formed and subsist under this Act. 22 V. (1859) c. 58, *preamble*, s. 1.

22. Any Permanent Building Society established and conducted on the principles hereinbefore mentioned, which has fulfilled and observed the requisite conditions for the establishment of a Building Society under the foregoing provisions of this Act, shall be a Building Society within the meaning of this Act; and any person who has approved the Rules and Regulations of any such Building Society entered and recorded in a book, as in the fifth section required, and has subscribed his name as a shareholder for one or more shares, shall, from the time of such approbation and subscription, be a member of such Building Society; and the production of the book containing the Rules for the management of such Society, kept as in the said section required, signed by such person, or by his duly authorized attorney, and duly witnessed, shall be sufficient evidence of membership in such Building Society. 22 V. (1859) c. 58, s. 1.

23. Any Permanent Building Society may alter, amend, repeal or make any Regulation, Rule or By-law for the working of the Society at a public meeting of the members thereof, duly convened according to this Act and the Rules of such Society. *Ibid*, s. 2.

24. No such Society, by its Rules, Regulations and By-laws authorized to borrow money, shall borrow, receive, take or retain, otherwise than in stock and shares in such Society, from any person or persons, any greater sum than three-fourths of the amount of capital actually paid in on unadvanced shares and invested in real securities by such Society;—and the paid in and subscribed capital of the Society shall be liable for the amount so borrowed, received or taken by any Society. *Ibid*, s. 3.

25. When any share in any such Society has been fully paid up according to the Rules of the Society, or has become due and payable to the holder thereof, the holder of such share may either withdraw the amount of such share from the said Society, according to the Rules and Regulations thereof, or invest the amount of such share in the Society, and receive therefrom, periodically, such proportion of the profits made by such Society as shall be provided for by a By-law to be passed for the purpose; and the amount of such share so invested shall become fixed and permanent capital or shares in the said Society not withdrawable therefrom, but transferable in the same manner as other shares in the said Society. *Ibid*, s. 4.

26. Any such Society may advance to members on the security of investing on unadvanced shares in the said Society, and may receive and take from any personal or body corporate, any real or personal security of any kind whatever as collateral security for any advance made to members of the Society. *Ibid*, s. 5.

27. Any such Society may hold absolutely real estate for the purposes of its place of business, not exceeding the annual value of six thousand dollars. *Ibid*, s. 6.

28. No such Society shall be bound to see to the execution of any trust, whether expressed, implied or constructive, to which any share of its stock is subject; and the receipt of the party in whose name any such share stands in the books of the Society, (or if such share stand in the names of more parties than one, the receipt of one of the parties) shall be a sufficient discharge to the Society for any payment of any kind made in respect of such share, notwithstanding any trust to which such share is then subject, and whether or not the Society has had notice of such trust; and the Society shall not be bound to see to the application of the money paid upon such receipt. 22 V. (1859) c. 58, s. 7.

29. Nothing in this Act shall apply to or affect "The Montreal Building Society," incorporated under the Act eighth Victoria, chapter ninety-four, or in any wise to affect the said Act. 12 V. c. 57, s. 16.

30. In this Act the word "Society" means a Building Society established under this Act; the word "Rules" shall include Rules, Orders, By-laws and Regulations; the words "Real Estate" mean and include immoveable estate and property generally; and the words "Personal Estate" mean and include all Moneys, Goods, Chattels and other property not being real property; and the words "Securities" includes Privileges, Mortgages (equitable as well as legal), *hypothèques* and incumbrances upon real estate, as well as other rights and privileges upon personal estate and property:

2. This Act shall extend to aliens, denizens and females, both to make them subject thereto and to entitle them to all the benefits given thereby;

3. This Act shall be construed in the most beneficial manner for promoting the ends thereby intended. 12 V. c. 57, s. 17.

CAP. L.

An Act to make further provision for the management of Permanent Building Societies carrying on business in the Province of Ontario.

Section.
Preamble.
1. Directors may make or amend By-laws, &c., for the working of the Society: Proviso for confirmation by Shareholders.
2. Liability of Shareholders limited.
3. Society may lend money to others than its members: Proviso, as to rules affecting borrowers.
4. C. S. U. C. c. 53, s, 22 repealed. New section. Society may purchase and sell certain securities.
5. Repayment and recovery of money advanced and interest thereon.
6. C. S. U. C. c. 53, s. 38 repealed. New section. Power to receive money deposits and issue debentures: Proviso, limiting money deposits: Proviso, cash in hands of Society to be deducted. Form of Debentures.
7. Interest to the society may be demanded in advance.
8. Powers of Directors of Society.
9. By-laws and documents of Society, when authentic to be *prima facie* evidence.
10. C. S. U. C. c. 53 s. 42 repealed. New section. Society not bound to see to execution of trusts or application of moneys paid on receipt, &c.
11. C. S. U. C. c. 53 s. 20 repealed. New

Section.
section: Persons in service of Society to furnish security.
12. To what societies only section 6 of this Act shall apply.
13. Amalgamation of two societies.
14. Joint agreement between Directors of Societies proposing to amalgamate or consolidate their stock, &c.
15. To be submitted to stockholders of each society for consideration. Agreement if adopted, to be filed with Sec'y of State.
16. Upon completion of consolidation the new corporation to possess rights, powers, &c., and be subject to duties, &c., of each of united societies.
17. All property and rights vested in new corporation without further act or deed. Proviso, as to rights of creditors, &c., of either of corporations.
18. Auditors and Directors, their appointment, remuneration, &c.
19. Annual statement of Assets and liabilities to be transmitted to the Minister of Finance. Statement to be attested on oath, and may be published. Penalty for non-transmission, Proceedings by Minister of Finance in case of insolvency of a society.
Schedule A.—Form of Debenture and Coupon.

[*Assented to 26th May*, 1874.]

WHEREAS it is expedient to make further provision for the management of Permanent Building Societies carrying on business in the Province of Ontario: Therefore Her Majesty, by and with the advice and consent of the Senate and House of Commons of Canada, enacts as follows:—

1. The Directors of any such Permanent Building Society may, from time to time, alter, amend, repeal or create any regulation, rule or by-law for the working of any such Society: Provided that such action of the Directors shall not have a binding force until confirmed at any general meeting of the shareholders of such Society upon a vote of two-thirds of the capital stock represented at such meeting,—notice being given of the proposed changes, in the notice calling such meeting.

2. No shareholder of any such Society shall be liable for or charged with the payment of any debt or demand due by such Society, beyond the extent of his shares in the capital of such Society not then paid up.

3. Any such Society may lend money in conformity with the laws authorizing the establishment of Building Societies in Canada, and with the by-laws of such Society, to any person or persons or body corporate at such rates of interest as may be agreed upon, without requiring any of such borrowers to become subscribers to the stock or members of the said Society: Provided always, that all borrowers from any such Society shall be subject to all the rules of such Society in force at the time of their becoming borrowers, but not to any other rules.

4. Section twenty-two of chapter fifty-three of the Consolidated Statutes for Upper Canada is hereby repealed, and the following substituted therefor:—

"22. Any such Society may purchase mortgages upon real estate, debentures of municipal corporations, school sections and school corporations, Dominion or Provincial stock or securities, and they may re-sell any such securities as to them shall seem advisable, and for that purpose they may execute such assignments or other instruments as may be necessary for carrying the same into effect; they may also make advances to any person or persons or body corporate upon any of the above mentioned securities at such rate of discount or interest as may be agreed upon."

5. The principal money so advanced on mortgages may be repaid by means of a sinking fund of not less than two per centum per annum, within such time as the Society shall direct and appoint, and as shall be specified in the mortgage or assignment of mortgage to be made of such real estate, and of such revenues, rates, rents, tolls or profits as hereinafter mentioned; and the Society may do all Acts that may be necessary for advancing money, and for recovery and obtaining repayment thereof, and for enforcing payment of all interest accruing therefrom, or any conditions attached to such advance or any forfeiture consequent on the non-payment thereof, and give all necessary and proper receipts, acquittances and discharges for the same, and do, authorize and exercise all acts and powers whatsoever requisite or expedient to be done or exercised in relation to the said purposes.

6. Section thirty-eight of chapter fifty-three of the Consolidated Statutes for Upper Canada is hereby repealed, subject to the provisions of the twelth section of this Act, and the following substituted therefor:—

"38. It shall be lawful for any such Society to receive money on deposit, and also for the Board of Directors of any such Society to issue debentures of such Society for such sums, not being less than one hundred dollars, and in such currency as they may deem advisable, and payable in the Dominion of Canada or elsewhere not less than one year from the issue thereof: Provided always that the aggregate amount of money deposits in the hands of such Society, together with the amount of debentures issued and remaining unpaid, shall not at any time exceed the amount of principal remaining unpaid on the mortgages at such time held by such Society and shall not exceed the amount of capitalized, fixed and permanent stock in such Society, not liable to be withdrawn therefrom, by more than one-third of the total amount of the said capitalized stock : Provided further, that the amount of cash actually in the hands of any such Society, or deposited in any chartered bank, shall be deducted from the sum total of the liabilities which such Society may be authorized to incur as above stated :"

The debentures of such Society may be in the form of Schedule A to this Act or to the like effect.

7. Any such society may, and is hereby empowered to demand and receive in advance the half-yearly interest from time to time acruing on any advances of money made by such Society under and by virtue of this Act.

8. The President, Vice-President and Directors of any such Society shall have and exercise the powers, privileges and authorities set forth and vested in them by this Act and any other Act regulating such Society, subject to the Rules or By-laws of such Society, and they shall be subject to and be governed by such Rules, Regulations and Provisions as are herein contained with respect thereto and by the By-laws of such Society; and the Directors shall and may lawfully exercise all the powers of such Society, except as to such matters as are directed by law to be transacted by a general meeting of such Society. The Directors may use and affix, or may cause to be used and affixed, the seal of such Society to any document or paper which in their judgment may require the same; they may make and enforce the calls upon the shares of the respective shareholders; they may declare the forfeiture of all shares on which such calls are not paid; they may make any payments and advances of money they may deem expedient which are or shall at any time be authorized to be made by or on behalf of such Society, and enter into all contracts for the execution of the purposes of such Society, and for all other matters necessary for the transaction of its affairs; they may generally deal with, treat, sell and dispose of the lands, property and effects of such Society, for the time being, in such manner as they shall deem expedient and conducive to the benefit of such Society as if the same lands, property and effects were held and owned according to the tenure and subject to the liabilities, if any, from time to time affecting the same, not by a body corporate, but by any of Her Majesty's subjects being of full age. They may do and authorize, assent to or adopt all acts required for the due exercise of any further powers and authorities which may hereafter be at any time granted to such Society by the Parliament of Canada for the performance and fulfilment of any conditions or provisions from time to time prescribed by the said Parliament in giving such further powers and authorities or in altering or repealing the same respectively or any of them.

9. All by-laws of any such Society shall be reduced to writing, and shall have affixed thereto the common seal of the Society, and any copy or extract therefrom, certified under the signature of the Secretary or Manager, shall be evidence in all courts of justice in Canada, of such by-laws or extract from them, and that the same were duly made and are in force; and in any action or proceeding at law, criminal or civil or in equity, it shall not be necessary to give any evidence to prove the seal of such Society; and all documents purporting to be sealed with the seal of any such Society, attested by the President, Treasurer or Manager thereof, shall be held *primâ facie* to have been duly sealed with the seal of such Society.

10. Section forty-two of chapter fifty-three of the Consolidated Statutes for Uppper Canada is hereby repealed, and the following substituted therefor:—

"42. Such Society shall not be bound to see to the execution of any trust, whether expressed, implied or constructive, to which any share or shares of its stock, or to which any deposit or any other moneys payable or in the hands of any such Society, may be subject; and the receipt of the party or parties in whose name any such share or shares or monies stand in the books of the Society, shall, from time to time, be sufficient discharge to the Society for any payment of any kind made in respect of such share or shares or moneys, notwithstanding any trust to which the same may then be subject, and whether or not such Society has had notice of such trust; and the Society shall not be bound to see to the application of the money paid upon such receipt."

11. Section twenty of chapter fifty-three of the Consolidated Statutes for Upper Canada is hereby repealed, and the following substituted therefor:

"20. Every such officer or other person appointed to any office in anywise concerning the receipt of money shall furnish security to the satisfaction of the Directors for the just and faithful execution of the duties of his office according to the rules of the Society, and any person entrusted with the performance of any other service, may be required by the Directors to furnish similar security."

12. The sixth section of this Act shall apply only to any such Society having a paid up capital of not less than two hundred thousand dollars in fixed and permanent stock, not liable to be withdrawn therefrom: Provided that all such Societies having a paid up capital exceeding forty thousand dollars may receive deposits to the amount of their paid up capital, and the remaining sections of this Act shall extend and apply to every such Society carrying on business in Ontario, or constituted or incorporated under the provisions of the Acts herein referred to, or of the Consolidated Statutes for Upper Canada, chapter fifty-three, or under any Act of the Legislature of the late Province of Canada, or of the Parliament of Canada: and any rights, powers or privileges of any such Society, contrary to the provisions of this Act, are hereby repealed.

13. It shall be lawful for any such Society to unite, amalgamate, and consolidate its stock, property, business and franchises with the stock, property, business and franchises of any other such Building, Saving or Loan Society, incorporated or chartered, within the Province of Ontario, and to enter into all contracts and agreements therewith, necessary to such union and amalgamation.

14. The Directors of the two Societies proposing to so amalgamate or consolidate as aforesaid, may enter into a joint agreement under the corporate seals of each of the said Corporations, for the amalgamation and consolidation of the said Corporations,—prescribing the terms and conditions thereof, the mode of carrrying the same into effect, the name of the new corporation, the number of the Directors and other officers thereof, and who shall be the first Directors and officers thereof and their places of residence, the number of shares of the capital stock, the amount or par value of each share, and the manner of conveting the capital stock of each of the said Corporations into that of the new Corporation, and how and when and for how long Directors and other Officers of such new Corporation shall be elected, and when elections shall be held,—with such other details as they shall deem necessary to perfect such new organization and the consolidation and amalgamation of the said Corporations, and the after management and working thereof.

15. Such agreement shall be submitted to the stockholders of each of the said Societies at a meeting thereof to be held separately for the purpose of taking the same into consideration; notice of the time and place of such meetings and the object thereof shall be given by written or printed notices, addressed to each shareholder of the said Societies respectively at his last known post office address or place of residence, and also by a general notice to be published in a newspaper published at the chief place of business of such Societies once a week for two successive weeks. At such meetings of stockholders, such agreement shall be considered, and a vote by ballot taken for the adoption or rejection of the same,—each share entitling the holder thereof to one vote, and the said ballots to be cast in person or by proxy; and if two thirds of the votes of all the stockholders of such Corporations shall be for the adoption of such agreement, then that fact shall be certified upon the said agreement by the Secretary of each of such Corporations under the Corporate seals thereof; and if the said agreement shall be so adopted at the respective meetings of the stockholders of each of the said Corporations, the agreement so adopted and the said certicates thereon shall be filed in the office of the Secretary of State of the Dominion of Canada, and the said agreement shall from thence be taken and deemed to be the agreement and Act of consolidation and amalgamation of the said Societies, and a copy of such agreement so filed, and of the certificates thereon, properly certified, shall be evidence of the existence of such new Corporation.

16. Upon the making and perfecting of the said agreement and act of consolidation, as provided in the next preceding section and the filing of the said agreement as in the said section provided, the several Societies, parties thereto, shall be deemed and taken to be consolidated, and to form one Corporation by the name in the said agreement provided, with a common seal, and shall possess all the rights, privileges, and franchises, and be subject to all the disabilities and duties of each of such Corporations so consolidated and united, except as herein otherwise provided.

17. Upon the consummation of such act of consolidation as aforeall and singular the business, property, real, personal and mixed, and all rights and interest appurtenant thereto, all stock, mortgages or other securities, subscriptions, and other debts due on whatever account, and other things in action belonging to such Corporations or either of them, shall be taken and deemed to be transferred to and vested in such new Corporation without further act or deed: Provided however, that all rights of creditors and liens upon the property of either of such Corporations, shall be· unimpaired by such consolidation, and all debts, liabilities and duties of either of the said Corporations, shall thenceforth attach to the new Corporation, and be enforced against it to the same extent as if the said debts, liabilities and duties had been incurred or contracted by it; and provided also that no action or proceeding legal or equitable by or against the said Corporations so consolidated, or either of them, shall abate or be affected by such consolidation, but for all the purposes of such action or proceeding, such Corporation may be deemed still to exist, or the new Corporation may be substituted in such action or proceeding in the place thereof.

18. The choice and removal of the Auditors of the Society, the determination as to the remuneration of the Directors and of the Auditors shall be exercised at general meetings of the Society, and the Auditors shall not necessarily be shareholders: Provided that in case of the death or failure to act of any such Auditor, the Directors may appoint an Auditor in his place; and at all meetings of shareholders of the Society, the shareholders shall have one vote for each share held by them respectively.

19. Such Society shall, on or before the fifteenth day of February in each year, transmit to the Minister of Finance a full and clear statement of their assets and liabilities on the day of the date thereof, and such statement shall contain, in addition to such other particulars as the Minister of Finance may require,—

1st. The amount of stock subscribed;

2nd. The amount paid in upon such stock;

3rd. The amount borrowed for the purposes of investments and the securities given therefor;

4th. The amount invested and secured by mortgage deeds;

5th. The value of real estate under mortgage;

6th. The amount of mortgages over due and in default;

7th. The amount of mortgages payable by instalments:

And such statement shall be attested by the oath before some Justice of the Peace, of two persons, one being the President, Vice-President, Manager or Secretary, and the other the Manager or Auditor of such Society, each of whom shall swear distinctly that he has such quality or office as aforesaid, that he has had the means of verifying, and has verified the statement aforesaid, and found it to be exact and true in every particular, that the property under mortgage has been set down at its true value, to the best of his knowledge and belief; and that the amount of the shares, deposits and debentures issued and outstanding, as he verily believes, is correct; and such statement shall be published by the Minister of Finance, in such manner as he shall think most conducive to the public good ; and for any neglect to transmit such statement in due course of post within five days after the day to which it is to be made up, such Society shall incur a penalty of one hundred dollars per diem; and if the same be not transmitted within one month after the said day, or if it shall appear by the statement that such Society is insolvent, the Minister of Finance may, by a notice in the *Canada Gazette*, declare the business of such Society to have ceased; and if the Minister of Finance shall, in any case, suspect any such statement to be wilfully false, he may depute some competent person to examine the books and enquire into the affairs of such Society and to report to him on oath ; and if by such report it shall appear that such statement was wilfully false, or that such Society is insolvent, or if the person so deputed shall report on oath that he has been refused such access to the books or such information as would enable him to make a sufficient report, the Minister of Finance may, by notice in the *Canada Gazette*, declare the business of such Society to have ceased ; but in any of the cases in which discretionary power is given to the Minister of Finance to declare the business of such Society to have ceased, he may before so doing give notice to such Society and afford the same an opportunity of making any explanation it may be advisable to make; and all expenses attending such periodical statements, and the publication thereof shall be borne by such Society.

SCHEDULE A.

Society.

Debenture No.　　　　　Transferable　　　　　$

Under the authority of an Act of the Parliament of Canada Victoria, Chapter

The President and Directors of the　　　　　Society promise to pay to　　　　　　　　　　or bearer the sum of　　　　　dollars, on the　　　　day of　　　　　, in the year of Our Lord One thousand eight hundred and at the Treasurer's office here, with interest at the rate of　　　per cent. per annum, to be paid half-yearly on presentation of the proper coupon for the same as hereunto annexed, say on the day of　　　　, and the　　　　day of in each year at the office of the Treasurer here (or their agents in　　　　.)

Dated at　　　　, the　　　　day of　　　　, 18 .
For the President and Directors of the　　　　　Society.
C. D.　　　　　　　　　　　　　A. B.
Secretary.

COUPON.

No. 1. $

Half-yearly dividend due   of   18 ,   on
Debenture No.   issued by this Society on the
day of   , 18   for $ at   per cent. per
annum, payable at the office of the Treasurer,   , (or at the
Society's agents   .)

For the President and Directors.
   C. D.   A.B.
   Secretary.

CAP. XLVIII.

An Act to amend the Act thirty-seventh Victoria, chapter fifty, respecting Permanent Building Societies in Ontario.

Section.
Preamble. 37 V., c. 50.
1. Governor in Council may authorize change of name.
2. Notice to be given. Power of Governor.
3. How such change of name shall be proved

Section.
Clerk of the Peace to endorse certificate on declaration. Fee. Penalty for not filing delaration.
4. Change of name not to affect rights.
5. Fees for change of name.

[Assented to 28th April, 1877.]

IN amendment of the Act passed in the thirty-seventh year of Her Majesty's reign, intituled "*An Act to make further provision for the management of Permanent Building Societies carrying on business in the Province of Ontario.*" Her Majesty, by and with the advice and consent of the Senate and House of Commons of Canada, enacts as follows :

1. Where any such Society as mentioned in the said Act thirty-seventh Victoria, chapter fifty, is desirous of changing its name, the Governor-General, upon being satisfied that the change desired is not for any improper purpose and is not otherwise objectionable, may, by Order in Council, change the name of the Society to some other name set forth in the said order.

2. The Society shall give at least four weeks' previous notice in the *Canada Gazette* of the intention to apply for the change of name, and shall state the name proposed to be adopted : in case the proposed name be considered objectionable the Governor in Council may, if he think fit, change the name of the Society to some other unobjectionable name without requiring any further notice to be given.

3. Such change shall be conclusively established by the insertion in the *Canada Gazette* of a notice thereof by the Secretary of State ; and his certificate of such change having been made shall be obtained by the Society, and filed in the office of the Clerk of the Peace of the County with whom is filed the declaration constituting such Society ;

42   Cap. 48.   *Permanent Building Societies, Ont.*   40 VIC.

the Clerk shall, upon payment by the Society of a fee of one dollar therefor, endorse a copy of such certificate upon the said declaration: and the Society shall (under a penalty of two hundred dollars in case of default) within one month after the insertion of the said notice cause the said certificate to be filed, and require the said endorsement to be made as aforesaid.

4. No alteration of its name under this Act shall affect the rights or obligations of any such Society, and all proceedings may be continued or commenced by or against any such Society by its new name that might have been continued or commenced by or against it by its former name.

5. The Governor in Council may establish the fees to be paid on applications for change of name under this Act.

CAP. XLIX.

An Act to amend the "Act to make further provision for the management of Permanent Building Societies carrying on business in the Province of Ontario."

Section.
    Preamble. 37 V., c. 50.
 1. Society having $100,000 paid up, may exercise power under s. 6.
 2. Amount of debenture and deposit debts of Societies limited. Proviso: as to

Section.
    deposits. How liabilities shall be estimated. Proviso: as to Companies now incorporated.
 3. Section 19 of Act 37 Vic., c. 50 amended.
 4. Society what to mean.

[*Assented to* 28*th April*, 1877.]

WHEREAS by section six of the Act passed in the thirty-seventh year of Her Majesty's reign, chapter fifty, as applied by section twelve of the said Act, it is in effect amongst other things enacted, that it shall be lawful for any Permanent Building Society carrying on business in the Province of Ontario and having a paid-up capital of not less than two hundred thousand dollars in fixed and permanent stock, not liable to be withdrawn therefrom, to receive deposits, and also for the Board of Directors of any such Society to issue debentures of such Society ; Provided always, among other conditions, that the aggregate amount of money deposits in the hands of such Society, together with the amount of debentures issued and remaining unpaid, shall not, at any time, exceed the amount of capitalized, fixed and permanent stock in such Society, not liable to be withdrawn therefrom, by more than one-third of the total amount of the said capitalized stock ; And whereas it is expedient that such limitation should be enlarged and that Societies having a fixed and permanent paid-up capital, not liable to be withdrawn, of one hundred thousand dollars should be invested with the powers conferred by section six of the said Act ; Therefore, Her Majesty, by and with the advice and consent of the Senate and House of Commons of Canada, enacts as follows :

1. Notwithstanding anything in the twelfth section of the said Act contained, any Society having a fixed and permanent paid-up capital of one hundred thousand dollars, not liable to be withdrawn, may exercise the powers by the sixth section of the said Act conferred, and the term "such Society" in the said Act and in this Act shall be held to include any such Society as in this section first mentioned.

2. The aggregate amount of money deposits in the hands of any such Society, together with the amount of its debentures issued and remaining unpaid may be equal to but shall not, at any time, exceed double the amount of the unimpaired, capitalized, fixed and permanent stock in such Society, not liable to be withdrawn therefrom : Provided always, that the amount held by any Society on deposit shall not exceed the amount of the paid-up and unimpaired capital of such Society, and that the total liabilities of any such Society shall not at any time exceed the amount of principal remaining unpaid on the mortgages at such time held by such Society; and that in estimating the liabilities of any such Society the amount of cash actually in the hands of such Society or deposited to its credit in any chartered bank, shall be deducted therefrom ; and that in estimating the unimpaired, capitalized, fixed and permanent stock of any such Society, the amount of all loans or advances made by it to its shareholders upon the security of their stock, shall be deducted therefrom : Provided always, that in the event of any Company now incorporated availing itself of the provisions of this Act for the purpose of enlarging its powers to borrow money by debentures, nothing herein contained shall be construed as affecting, or in any wise impairing the right of the holders of debentures issued by the said Company.

3. The nineteenth section of the said Act is hereby amended by adding thereto, immediately after the word "instalments" therein, the figure and words following, that is to say :

8th. The rate or rates of interest at which the mortgages held by the Society have been computed or discounted to ascertain the amount of the principal remaining unpaid thereon.

4. The word "Society" in this Act shall also include and mean "Company."

CAP. XXII.

An Act to amend the law respecting Building Societies carrying on business in the Province of Ontario.

Section.
Preamble.
1. How Permanent Societies in Ontario may make shares thereafter subscribed for permanent capital and not withdrawable

Section.
2. Directors may fix amount payable on subscription or as premiums on such shares, and pay dividends by way of periodical profits. Proviso.

[*Assented to* 10*th May*, 1878.]

HER Majesty, by and with the advice and consent of the Senate and House of Commons of Canada, enacts as follows:—

1. The members of any Permanent Building Society carrying on business in the Province of Ontario, entitled to vote, may, at any time, by a resolution, to be passed by a majority of two-thirds of the votes of such members present or represented by proxy at any special or general meeting, (for which meeting notice of such intended resolution shall be duly given), determine that all shares thereafter subscribed for in such Society shall be fixed and permanent capital and not liable to be withdrawn therefrom; and any share thereafter subscribed for in such Society shall be fixed and permanent capital and not withdrawable therefrom, but transferable in the same manner as other shares in such Society.

2. The Directors of any such Society may fix the amount to be paid on the subscription of any such shares, which amount shall not be less than twenty per cent. on the shares subscribed, and the premium (if any) which shall be paid thereon, and when such premium shall be payable; and it shall be in the discretion of the Directors, from time to time, to call up the balance of any such shares, at such time or times as they think best. And any such Society may, from time to time, pay dividends by way of annual or other periodical profits, upon the amounts paid on such shares. In all other respects such shares shall be subject to the general provisions respecting shares in Permanent Building Societies carrying on business in the Province of Ontario.

CHAP. XLIX.

An Act respecting Building Societies carrying on business in the Province of Ontario.

Section.
Preamble. Sec. 2 of 40 V., c. 49 cited. And its Proviso.
1. Certain words in section 2 of 40 V., c. 49 interpreted.
2. Permanent Building Societies in the Province of Ontario under Dominion laws, may carry on business in the Province of Manitoba and the North-West Territories.
3. And may hold real estate.
4. In case of the transmission of interest in

Section.
any share, &c., otherwise than by transfer, Directors may require a written declaration showing the nature of such transmission.
5. What shall be sufficient justification of Directors for recognizing transmission if by will or intestacy.
6. Provision for case of Directors having reasonable doubts as to legality of any claim to any share, &c.
7. "Society" interpreted.

[*Assented to* 15*th May,* 1879.]

WHEREAS, by the second section of the Act passed in the fortieth year of Her Majesty's reign, chapter forty-nine, it is enacted as follows:—"The aggregate amount of money deposits in the hands of any such Society, together with the amount of its debentures issued and remaining unpaid, may be equal to, but shall not at any time exceed double the amount of the unimpaired, capitalized, fixed and permanent stock in such Society not liable to be withdrawn therefrom: Provided always, that the amount held by any Society on deposit shall not exceed the amount of the paid-up and unimpaired capital of such

Society, and that the total liabilities of any such Society shall not at any time exceed the amount of principal remaining unpaid on the mortgages at such time held by such Society; and that, in estimating the liabilities of any such Society, the amount of cash actually in the hands of such Society or deposited to its credit in any chartered bank, shall be deducted therefrom; and that in estimating the unimpaired, capitalized, fixed and permanent stock of any such Society, the amount of all loans or advances made by it to its shareholders upon the security of their stock shall be deducted therefrom."

And whereas, doubts may arise as to the meaning of the words "liabilities of such Society," where the same occur in the said section;

And whereas, it is expedient to remove such doubts and to amend the said Act:

Therefore Her Majesty, by and with the advice and consent of the Senate and House of Commons of Canada, enacts as follows:—

1. In the said section the words "liabilities of such Society," or "total liabilities of such Society," shall be taken to mean, and are hereby declared to mean, only the liabilities of any such Society to the public, and shall not be taken to include, and it is hereby declared that the same do not include the liability of any such Society to its shareholders in respect of its capital stock, or otherwise to its shareholders as such.

2. Any Permanent Building Society carrying on business in the Province of Ontario, under the laws of the Dominion, having a fixed and permanent capital stock of not less than one hundred thousand dollars, is hereby authorized to carry on business in the Province of Manitoba, or in the North-West Territories, or in any Province that may be formed out of the same; and for such purpose is hereby declared to be a body corporate with all the powers, privileges and liabilities heretofore enjoyed by such Society in the Province of Ontario only.

3. Any such Society may hold, absolutely, real estate for the purposes of or in connection with its place or places of business, not exceeding the annual value of ten thousand dollars; but this section shall not affect any action or suit now pending.

4. If the interest of any person or persons in any share or shares in the capital stock, or in any bond, debenture or obligation of any such Society,—such bond, debenture or obligation not being payable to bearer,—hath become, or shall become transmitted in consequence of the death, or bankruptcy or insolvency of any such holder, or in consequence of the marriage of a female holder or by any other lawful means other than a transfer upon the books of the Society, the Directors shall not be bound to allow any transfer pursuant to such transmission to be entered upon the books of the Society, or to recognize such transmission in any manner until a declaration in writing, shewing the nature of such transmission, and signed and executed by the person or persons claiming by virtue of such transmission, and also executed by the former shareholder, if living and having power to execute the same, shall have been filed with the Manager of the Society, and approved by the Directors; and if such declaration purporting to be signed and executed shall also purport to be made or acknowledged in the presence of a Notary Public, or of a Judge of a Court of Record, or of a Mayor of any city, town or borough or other place, or a British Consul or Vice-Consul, or other accredited representative of the British Government in any foreign country, the Directors may, in the absence of direct actual notice of a contrary claim, give full credit to such declaration, and unless the Directors are not satisfied with the responsibility of the transferee, shall allow the name of the party claiming by virtue of such transmission to be entered in the books of the Society.

5. If such transmission has taken place or shall hereafter take place by virtue of any testamentary act or instrument, or in consequence of an intestacy, the probate of the will, or letters of administration, or act of curatorship, or testament testamentary, or testament dative expede, or other judicial or official document under which the title, whether beneficial or as trustee, or the administration or control of the personal estate of the deceased, shall purport to be granted by any court or authority in the Dominion of Canada, or in Great Britain or Ireland, or any other of Her Majesty's Dominions, or in any foreign country, or an authenticated copy thereof, or official extract therefrom, shall, together with the said declaration, be produced and deposited with the Manager; and such production and deposit shall be sufficient justification and authority to the Directors for paying the amount or value of any dividend, coupon, bond, debenture or obligation or share, or transferring, or consenting to the transfer of any bond, debenture or obligation or share, in pursuance of and in conformity to such probate, letters of administration or other such document as aforesaid.

6. Whenever the Directors shall entertain reasonable doubts as to the legality of any claim to or upon such share or shares, bonds, debentures, obligations, dividends, coupons, or the proceeds thereof, then and in such case it shall be lawful for the Society to file in any one of the superior courts of law, or in the Court of Chancery, in the Province of Ontario, a petition stating such doubts, and praying for an order or judgment adjudicating and awarding the said shares, bonds, debentures or obligations, dividends, coupons or proceeds to the party or parties legally entitled to the same : and such court shall have authority to restrain any action, suit or proceeding against the Society, the Directors or officers thereof, for the same subject matter, pending the determination of the said petition ; and the Society and the Directors and officers thereof shall be fully protected and indemnified by obedience to such order or judgment against all actions, suits, claim, and demands in respect of the matters which shall have been in question in such petition, and the proceedings thereupon : Provides, always, that if the court adjudges that such doubts were reasonable the costs, charges and expenses of the Society in and about such petition and proceedings, shall form a lien upon such shares, bonds, debentures or obligations, dividends, coupons or proceeds, and shall be paid to the said Society before the Society shall be obliged to transfer or assent to the transfer, or to pay such shares, bonds, debentures or obligations, dividends, coupons or proceeds to the party or parties found entitled thereto.

7. The word "Society" in this Act shall also include and mean "Company."

CHAP. XLIII.

An Act for the relief of Permanent Building Societies and Loan Companies.

Section.
Preamble ; 37 V., c. 50.
1. Certain statements transmitted to Minister of Finance to be deemed sufficient under sec. 19 of 37 V., c. 50. as amended by 40 V., sec. 49. Societies which transmitted them indemnified.
2. As to actions for penalties commenced after or before the passing of this Act. Stay of proceedings in suits commenced.
3. Effect on such actions of subsequent receipt by the Minister of a sufficient statement. Exception.
4. Statement not required in case society has ceased to do business or has never done any. Proof of having done no business
5. Section 19 of 37 V., c. 50 as amended by sec. 3 of 40 V., c. 49 repealed, and a new section substituted. Annual statement transmitted to [Minister of

Section.
Finance. What such statement must contain. Particulars as to mortgages. Cash value of investments and how calculated. To be attested on oath and by what officers. And to be published by the Minister of Finance. Penalty for non-transmission. Proceedings by Minister of Finance under Order-in-Council in certain cases of default to transmit statement.
6. Certain statements made in conformity with this Act or under the sections it repeals to be deemed sufficient.
7. Extension of time for making statement, for want of sufficient time to examine it. Proviso. As to statements due on 1st March, 1880.
8. Application of provisions of sections 5 and 7 of this Act. Interpretation.
9. Compliance with this Act by officers to be deemed compliance by company, &c.

[*Assented to 7th May*, 1880.]

WHEREAS, acting under the authority of the Act passed in the thirty-seventh year of Her Majesty's reign, chapter fifty, entituled "*An Act to make further provision for the management of Permanent Building Societies Carrying on business in the Province of Ontario*," the Minister of Finance has, from time to time, furnished to Building, Loan or Saving Societies or Companies in Ontario, on their application, printed forms purporting to be forms of statement in accordance with the provisions of the said Act in that behalf; and whereas, on account of some difference in the language used in the said forms as compared with the language of the said Act, and by reason of affidavits not having been made verifying such statements, doubts have arisen as to whether returns made upon the said forms are a compliance with the said Act, and it is desirable to remove such doubts and to relieve societies whose officers have made their returns upon the said forms from being harassed by suits for penalties under the said Act, and also to further amend the said Act above cited : Therefore Her Majesty by and with the advice and consent of the Senate and House of Commons of Canada, enacts as follows :—

1. Every statement transmitted to the Minister of Finance, at any time previous to the passing of this Act, by any Building, Loan or Saving Society or Company incorporated under chapter fifty-three of the Consolidated Statutes of Upper Canada, or any Act thereby consolidated, or otherwise incorporated, which statement purports to have been filled up according to the said printed forms, or otherwise in substantial compliance with the provisions hereinafter mentioned, whether the same has or has not been attested by oath or affirmation, shall be deemed and taken to be, and to have been a sufficient statement, and in compliance in all respects with the provisions of the nineteenth section of the said Act, intituled *"An Act to make further provision for the management of Permanent Building Societies carrying on business in the Province of Ontario,"* or of the said section as amended by the third section of the Act passed in the fortieth year of Her Majesty's reign, chapter forty-nine, as the case may be, and to have been properly made, filled up and attested according to the provisions of the said Acts, whether such statements were attested or not, or whether or not the said statement or the affidavit verifying the same was transmitted in due time to the said Finance Minister; and every society or company incorporated as aforesaid, the officers of which shall have transmitted such statement, shall be and is hereby indemnified, exonerated, freed and discharged of and from all pecuniary penalties and forfeitures whatsoever (if any) which may have been incurred by such Company or Society by reason of its having neglected to transmit any other or further, or differently attested statement, or to perform the obligations imposed on it by the said Acts or any of them in that behalf.

2. In case any action, suit or proceedings shall, after the passing of this Act, be brought, carried on or prosecuted against any society or company for or on account of any pecuniary penalty or forfeiture whatever incurred or to be incurred by any such neglect, as is intended to be relieved against by this Act, such society or company may plead the general issue, and upon their defence give this Act and the special matter in evidence upon any trial to be had thereupon; and in any action or suit commenced before the passing of this Act or now pending against any society or company for or on account of any such neglect, the court or judge thereof shall on the application of the defendant, order all proceedings in such action or suit to be stayed on payment of the costs thereof to the plaintiff therein, but in default of such application the plaintiff may prosecute such action or suit to judgment.

3. No action brought after the passing of this Act against any society or company incorporated as aforesaid for any past or future failure to comply with the provisions of the said Act, or of the said Act as amended as aforesaid, as the case may be, shall be maintained, if such action was or is commenced at any time subsequent to the receipt by the Minister of Finance of the statement required by the said Act, or of the statement, whether attested as aforesaid or not, declared valid by this Act, unless such action is brought by the Crown, or by the Minister of Justice suing on behalf of the Crown.

4. The provisions of the said nineteenth section of the said Act, intituled " *An Act to make further provision for the management of Permanent Building Societies carrying on business in the Province of Ontario,*" shall not, nor shall those of the said section as amended as aforesaid, be held to apply, or to have applied, to any society or company which has ceased or shall have ceased, to carry on business prior to the year for which the return is or was required, nor to any society or company which, though incorporated, never carried on business ; and upon its being proved that any society or company incorporated as aforesaid did not lend any money, or receive any deposit, or issue any debenture during the year for which it is alleged a return in accordance with such section, or with such section as amended as aforesaid, has not been made, such society or company shall be deemed to have ceased to carry on business within the meaning of this section.

5. The nineteenth section of the said Act passed in the thirty-seventh year of Her Majesty's reign, chaptered fifty, as amended by the third section of the said Act, passed in the fortieth year of Her Majesty's reign, chaptered forty-nine, and the said last mentioned section, are hereby repealed, and the following substituted therefor :

" 19. Such Society shall, on or before the first day of March in
" each year, transmit to the Minister of Finance a full and clear state-
" ment of the Society's assets and liabilities on some day to be stated
" therein ; and such day shall not be more than twelve months prior
" to the said first day of March, or earlier than the end of the last
" preceding financial year of such Society ; and such statement shall
" contain, in addition to such other particulars as the Minister of
" Finance may require, the following :

" (*a*.) The amount of stock subscribed ;

" (*b*.) The amount paid in upon such stock ;

" (*c*.) The amount borrowed for the purposes of investment and
" the securities given therefor ;

" (*d*.) The amount invested and secured by mortgage deeds ;

" (*e*.) Amount of mortgages payable by instalments ;

" (*f*.) The number and aggregate amount of mortgages upon
" which compulsory proceedings have been taken during the past year ;
" and also the value of mortgaged property held for sale, and the
" amount chargeable against it."

" (*g*.) The present cash value of the society's investments on
" mortgages and other securities, and the rate or rates per cent. at
" which the future repayments are discounted in ascertaining such
" present cash value ; which rate or rates shall be at least equal to the
" rate or rates which such mortgages or other securities respectively
" bear, or were originally calculated to yield.

" 2. Such statement shall be attested by the oath (taken before some
" Justice of the Peace, or commissioner for taking affidavits in the
" superior courts) of two persons, one being the president, vice-presid-
" ent, manager or secretary, and the other the manager, secretary or

"auditor of such society, each of whom shall swear distinctly that he
"holds such office as aforesaid, that the statement has been prepared by
"the proper officers of the company, that the deponent believes that it
"has been prepared with due care, and that he believes it to be true, in
"every particular; and such statement shall be published by the
"Minister of Finance in such manner as he thinks most conducive to
"the public good; and for any neglect to transmit such statement in
"due course of post, within five days after the day upon which the
"same should be transmitted, such society shall incur a penalty of fifty
"dollars per diem, but not exceeding in the whole one thousand dollars."

"3. If such statement is not transmitted within a month after the
"said first day of March, or if it appears by the statement that such
"society is not in a condition to justify its continuance in business with
"the powers theretofore possessed by such society, the Minister of
"Finance may, under the authority of, or by order of the Governor-
"General in Council, by a notice in the *Canada Gazette*, declare the
"business of such society to have ceased, so far as regards borrowing
"money, and any other matters mentioned in the Order in Council
"and notice aforesaid."

6. Any statement heretofore made, or which may be hereafter made by any society or company with reference to a financial year of such society or company ending prior to the passing of this Act, shall be deemed sufficient if such return is made, either in accordance with the provisions of the said section nineteen hereinbefore repealed, or of the said section as amended as aforesaid, as the case may be, or in accordance with the provisions of this Act.

7. If any officer of a society or company shall, when called upon to attest the statement required under this Act, find himself unable to make the required affidavit of attestation on account of his having doubts as to the correctness of the statement presented to him for attestation, and further time is needed in order to permit of an examination of the items making up such statement, then, upon application of such officer, or of any one on his behalf, or on behalf of the society or company, made at any time before the sixth day of March of the proper year, the Minister of Finance may enlarge the time for transmitting such statement to a day not later than the first day of May of such year,—and the day so fixed by the said Minister of Finance shall thereupon become the day within five days of which the said statement, attested as required by this Act, shall be transmitted by such society or company to the Minister of Finance, under the like penalties, in case of omission to make the same within such time, as if such day had been inserted in the nineteenth section of the said Act as amended by this Act, in lieu of the first day of March : Provided that the said enlargement of time shall not prevent proceedings being taken under the nineteenth section of the said Act as amended hereby, if the Governor-General in Council shall so order.

2. It shall be sufficient, if the statement required to be furnished on or before the first day of March, one thousand eight hundred and eighty, is transmitted to the Minister of Finance on or before the first

day of May next following, with power to the said Minister of Finance, under the like circumstances, to enlarge such time to a day not later than the first day of June of such year.

8. The provisions contained in section five of this Act, from the figure 19 to the end thereof, and in section seven of this Act, shall apply to every Investment, Loan or Savings Society or Company incorporated by Act of Parliament of Canada, and to every institution or corporation incorporated without the Dominion of Canada and lending and investing money in Canada, and to the officers in Canada of every such society or company, institution or corporation, and to the Minister of Finance with relation to every such society or company, institution or corporation; and for that purpose the word "society" in the said sections shall mean also and include company, institution or corporation, as the case may require.

9. The compliance by or on the part of any such society or company, institution or corporation and its officers with the said provisions, shall be deemed and taken to be a compliance with the provisions of any section of any Act requiring such society or company, institution or corporation to transmit to the Minister of Finance any annual statement or return of its affairs or of its assets and liabilities.

CHAP L.

An Act to make further provision respecting the constituting and management of Building Societies in the Province of Quebec.

Section.
Preamble.
1. Societies may be incorporated by letters patent.
2. Notice to be given and what it must show.
3. Petition for letters patent and what it shall contain.
4. Preliminary conditions to be established. Proof. 37 V., c. 37.
5. What to be recited.
6. Notice of granting letters patent.
7. Dividends. Not to impair capital. Rate limited.
8. Increase of capital stock.
9. Powers of Directors Affixing seal, etc. Calls. Payments and advances. Contracts. Administering property. Further powers. By-laws. Proviso : Conversion of shares may be suspended. Proviso.
10. Society may lend money. Proviso. May purchase hypothecs and make investments. Sinking fund. Sales with right of redemption.
11. Society may hold real property for its own use ; and may acquire such when hypothecated to it. Proviso, for sale in such cases.
12. Society may receive deposits and issue debentures. May pay interest on deposits. Form of debentures. From whom deposits may be received. Proviso. Officers to give security.
13. Provisions as to borrowing money by the Society. 20 per cent. paid up. Amount on debentures limited. Amount on deposit. If they borrow in both ways.

Section.
Calculation of liabilities. Borrowing to be on permanent stock only.
14. Liability of shareholders limited.
15. Society not bound to see to trusts.
16. Provisions for amalgamation of two societies.
17. Joint agreement between Directors of societies proposing to amalgamate or consolidate their stock, etc.
18. To be submitted to stockholders of each society for consideration. Votes on it by ballot. Agreement, if adopted, to be filled with Secretary of State. Proviso, as to proof.
19. Upon completion of consolidation the new corporation to possess rights, powers, etc., of each of united societies.
20. All property and rights vested in new corporation without further act or deed. Proviso.
21. Auditors and Directors, their appointment, remuneration, etc.
22. Annual statement of assets and liabilities to be transmitted to Minister of Finance. What to contain. Statement to be attested on oath, and may be published. Penalty for non-transmission. Proceedings by Minister of Finance, in case of insolvency, or suspected insolvency of a society.
23. Sub-section of s. 1, C. S. L. C., c. 69, repealed.
24. How this Act shall be interpreted. As to existing societies. Proviso, as to borrowing powers. And after 1st July, 1878.

[*Assented to* 28*th April*, 1877.]

WHEREAS it is expedient to make further provisions respecting the constituting and management of Building Societies in the Province of Quebec : Therefore Her Majesty, by and with the advice and consent of the Senate and House of Commons of Canada, enacts as follows :—

1. The Governor in Council may, by letters patent under the Great Seal, grant a charter to any number of persons not less than thirty, who shall present a petition to that effect, constituting such persons and others who may become shareholders in the Society by the said letters patent created, a body corporate and politic, the object of which shall be to provide for its members means of investing their savings, to assist them in acquiring immovable property, or in freeing and improving that which they already possess ; and to offer to borrowers on the security of immovable property, and of public and other securities, easy terms of loan and repayment; and no Building Society shall be established in the said Province without such letters patent.

2. The applicants for such letters patent must give at least one month's previous notice in the *Canada Gazette* of their intention to apply for such charter, stating therein,—

1. The proposed corporate name of the Society;

2. The place or places in the Province of Quebec where its operations are to be carried on, with special mention if there be two or more such places, of some one of them as its chief place of business;

3. The intended amount of its capital stock, which shall in no case be less than two hundred and fifty thousand dollars;

4. The number of shares and amount of each share;

5. The names in full and the address and calling of each of the applicants, with special mention of the names of not less than five nor more than nine of their number, who are to be the first Directors of the Society.

3. At any time, not more than one month after the last publication of such notice, the applicants may petition the Governor-General, through the Secretary of State of Canada, for the issue of such letters patent:

Such petition must recite the facts set forth in the notice, and must further state the amount of stock subscribed for and the names of the subscribers, and also the amount paid in upon the stock of each subscriber:

The aggregate of the stock so taken must be at least the one-half of the total amount of stock of the Society, and such capital stock shall amount to at least two hundred and fifty thousand dollars:

The aggregate so paid in thereon must be at least twenty per cent. for permanent shares and five per cent. for temporary shares:

Such aggregate must have been paid in to the credit of the Society or of trustees therefor, and must be standing at such credit, in some chartered bank or banks in the said Province:

The petition may ask for the embodying in the letters patent, of any provision which otherwise under this Act might be embodied in any by-law of the Company when incorporated.

4. Before the letters patent are issued, the applicants must establish to the satisfaction of the Secretary of State, or of such other officer as may be charged by order of the Governor-in-Council to report thereon, the sufficiency of their notice and petition, the truth and sufficiency of the facts therein set forth, and that the proposed name is not the name of any other known incorporated or unincorporated Society; and to that end, the Secretary of State, or such other officer, may take and keep of record any requisite evidence in writing, by solemn declaration under the Act thirty-seventh Victoria, (1874,) chapter thirty-seven, intituled "*An Act for the Suppression of Voluntary and Extra Judicial Oaths,*" or by oath or affirmation, and may receive and administer every requisite solemn declaration, oath or affirmation.

5. The letters patent shall recite all the material averments of the notice and petition.

6. Notice of the granting of the letters patent shall be forthwith given by the Secretary of State, in the *Canada Gazette*, in the form of Schedule A appended to this Act; and thereupon, from the date of the letters patent, the persons therein named and their successors shall be a body corporate and politic by the name mentioned therein.

7. It shall be the duty of the Directors to declare and pay half-yearly dividends to the permanent shareholders, of such part of the profits of the Society as they shall deem expedient; but no dividend or bonus shall be declared or paid out of the capital stock of the Society, nor shall any dividend exceeding eight per cent. per annum be paid until the Society has a reserve fund equal to at least twenty per cent. on the paid-up permanent capital stock,—all bad and doubtful debts having previous to the calculation of such reserve fund, been first deducted.

8. The capital stock of the Society may be increased from time to time by resolution of the Directors, who may impose such restrictions and conditions respecting the subscription of such new permanent or temporary shares as they may deem expedient—such resolution, however, to be approved by the shareholders at a general meeting called for the purpose, and to remain inoperative until so approved.

9. The Directors of the Society shall exercise all the powers, privileges and authority which are vested in them by this Act and any other Act regulating such Society, subject to the rules or by-laws of such Society, and they shall be subject to and be governed by such rules, regulations and provisions as are herein contained with respect thereto and by the by-laws of such Society; and the Directors may lawfully exercise all the powers of such Society, except as to such matters as are directed by law to be transacted at a general meeting of such Society. The Directors may use and affix, or may cause to be used and affixed, the seal of such Society to any document or paper which in their judgment may require the same; they may make and enforce the calls upon the shares of the respective shareholders; they may declare the forfeiture of all shares on which such calls are not paid; they may make any payments and advances of money they may deem expedient which are or shall at any time be authorized to be made by or on behalf of such Society, and enter into all contracts for the execution of the purposes of such Society, and for all other matters necessary for the transaction of its affairs: they may generally deal with, treat, sell and dispose of the lands, property and effects of such Society, for the time being, in such manner as they shall deem most advantageous, expedient and conducive to the benefit of such Society; they may do and authorize, assent to or adopt, all acts required for the due exercise of any further powers and authorities which may hereafter be, at any time, granted to such Society by the Parliament of Canada.

2. The Directors of any such Society may, from time to time, alter, amend, repeal or create any regulation, rule or by-law for the working of any such Society, and for the investment or application of

its funds: Provided that such action of the Directors shall not have binding force until confirmed at any general meeting of the shareholders of such Society, upon a vote of two-thirds of the capital stock represented at such meeting; notice being given of the proposed changes in the notice calling such a meeting.

3. The Directors may also, by by-law, when they deem it expedient to do so, either suspend for a limited time or until further notice, the right of converting accumulated temporary shares into permanent shares, or may permit such conversion, or make it compulsory upon all the shareholders, on such conditions as they may determine: Provided always, that such by-law shall not have force and effect until it has been confirmed in the manner hereinbefore provided.

10. Any such Society may lend money to any person or persons or body corporate, without requiring any of such borrowers to become subscribers to the stock or members of the said Society: Provided always, that all borrowers from any such Society shall be subject to all the rules of such Society in force at the time of their becoming borrowers, but not to any other rules.

2. The Society may purchase hypothecs on immovable property, debentures of municipal corporations, school sections and school corporations, Dominion or Provincial stock or securities, and they may resell any such securities as to them shall seem advisable, and for that purpose they may execute such assignments or other instruments as may be necessary for carrying the same into effect; they may also make advances to any person or persons or body corporate upon any of the above-mentioned securities, at such rates of discount or interest as may be agreed upon.

3. The principal money so advanced on hypothecs may be repaid by means of a sinking fund of not less than two per centum per annum, within such time as the Society shall direct and appoint, and as shall be specified in the deed of hypothec or of transfer of hypothec to be made of such immovable property.

4. The Society may also make loans to its members and others on the security of immovable property sold to the Society, with right of redemption on such conditions as may be agreed upon.

11. The Society may hold such immovable property as may be necessary for the transaction of their business, not exceeding in yearly value the sum of ten thousand dollars in all, or as, being hypothecated to them, may be acquired by them for the protection of their investments, and may, from to time, sell, hypothecate, lease or otherwise dispose of the same: Provided always, that it shall be incumbent upon the Society to sell any immovable property acquired in satisfaction of any debt within seven years after it shall have fallen to them.

12. It shall be lawful for any such Society to receive money on deposit, and also for the Board of Directors of any such Society to issue debentures of such Society for such sums not being less than one hundred dollars, and in such currency as they may deem advisable, and payable in the Dominion of Canada, or elsewhere, not less than one year from the issue thereof, or to assign, transfer or deposit, by way of pledge or otherwise, for the sums so borrowed, any of the securities or property of the Society, and either with or without power of sale or other special provisions, as the Directors shall deem expedient; and the Society may receive money on deposit, for such periods and at such rate of interest as may be agreed upon, and money so received on deposit shall, for the purposes of this Act, be deemed to be money borrowed by the Society.

2. The debentures of such Society may be in the form of Schedule B to this Act, or to the like effect.

3. And it shall be lawful for the Society to receive deposits from any person or persons whomsoever, whatever be his, her or their status or condition of life, and whether such person or persons be qualified by law to enter into ordinary contracts or not; and to pay any part of or all the principal thereof, and the whole or any part of the interest thereon, to such person or persons respectively, without the authority, aid, assistance or intervention of any person or persons, official or officials being required, any law, usage or custom to the contrary notwithstanding: Provided always, that if the person making any deposit in the Society be not, by the existing laws of the Province of Quebec, authorized to do so, then the total amount of deposits made by such person shall not exceed the sum of two thousand dollars.

4. Every officer or other person appointed to any office under the Society, in any wise concerning the receipt of money, shall furnish security to the satisfaction of the Directors for the just and faithful execution of the duties of his office according to the rules of the Society; and any person entrusted with the performance of any other service, may be required by the Directors to furnish similar security.

13. Provided always,—

1. That the Society shall not borrow money unless at least one hundred thousand dollars of its subscribed capital stock has been paid up.

2. That the Society shall not borrow money unless at least twenty per cent. of its subscribed capital stock has been paid up.

3. That if the Society borrow money solely on debentures or other securities, the aggregate amount of the sums so borrowed shall not at any time exceed four times the amount of its paid up and unimpaired capital, or the nominal amount of its subscribed capital, at the option of the Society;

4. That if the Society borrow by way of deposit, the aggregate amount of the sums so borrowed shall not at any time exceed the aggregate amount of its paid up capital and of its cash actually in hand, or deposited by the Society in any chartered bank or banks in Canada;

5. That if the Society borrow money both by way of debentures or other securities, or by guarantee, as aforesaid, and also by way of deposit, then the aggregate amount of money deposits in the hands of the Society, together with the amount of debentures and other securities issued by it, as aforesaid, shall not at any time exceed the amount of the

principal moneys remaining unpaid on securities then held by the Society, nor shall it exceed the then actually paid up and unimpaired capital of the Society by more than one-third of such capital; but the amount of cash then actually in the hands of the Society, or deposited by them in any chartered bank, or both, shall be deducted from the aggregate amount of the liabilities which the Society has then incurred, as above mentioned, in calculating such aggregate amount for the purposes of this sub-section;

6. That no Building Society shall have power to receive money on deposit, or issue debentures, unless upon the responsibility of its permanent capital stock, and that no accumulating shares, or shares liable to be withdrawn therefrom, shall authorize any such Society to receive deposits or issue debentures to any amount whatever.

14. No shareholder of any such Society shall be liable for or charged with the payment of any debt or demand due by such Society, or held to the payment thereof, beyond the sum not paid up on his shares in the capital of such Society.

15. Such Society shall not be bound to see to the execution of any trust, whether expressed, implied or constructive, to which any share or shares of its stock, or to which any deposit or any other moneys payable or in the hands of any such Society may be subject; and the receipt of the party or parties in whose name any such share or shares or moneys stand in the books of the Society, shall, from time to time, be sufficient discharge to the Society for any payment made in respect of such share or shares or moneys, notwithstanding any trust to which the same may be subject, and whether or not such Society has had notice of such trust; and the Society shall not be bound to see to the application of the money paid upon such receipt.

16. It shall be lawful for the Society to unite, amalgamate and consolidate its stock, property, business and franchises with those of any other society incorporated or chartered to transact a like business, and any other business in connection with such business, or any building, savings or loan company or society heretofore or hereafter incorporated or chartered, or to purchase and acquire the assets of any such company or society, and to enter into all contracts and agreements therewith necessary to such union, amalgamation, consolidation, purchase or acquisition.

17. The Directors of the Society, and of any other such company or society, may enter into a joint agreement under the corporate seals of each of the said corporations for the union, amalgamation or consolidation of the said corporations, or for the purchase and acquisition, by the Society, of the assets of any other such company or society, prescribing the terms and conditions thereof, the mode of carrying the same into effect, the name of the new corporation, the number of the directors and other officers thereof, and who shall be the first directors and officers thereof, the manner of converting the capital stock of each of the said corporations into that of the new corporation, with such other details as they shall deem necessary to perfect such new organi-

zation, and the union, amalgamation and consolidation of the said corporations, and the after management and working thereof,—or the terms and mode of payment for the assets of any other such company or society purchased or acquired by the Society.

18. Such agreement shall be submitted to the shareholders of each of the said corporations at a meeting thereof to be held separately for the purpose of taking the same into consideration. Notice of the time and place of such meetings, and the objects thereof, shall be given by written or printed notices addressed to each shareholder of the said corporations respectively, at his last known post office address or place of residence, and also by a general notice to be published in a newspaper published at the chief place of business of such corporations, once a week, for six successive weeks. At such meetings of shareholders such agreement shall be considered, and a vote by ballot taken for the adoption or rejection of the same, each share entitling the holder thereof to one vote, and the said ballots being cast in person or by proxy; and if two-thirds of the votes of all the shareholders of such corporations shall be for the adoption of such agreement, then that fact shall be certified upon the said agreement, by the secretary of each of such corporations, under the corporate seals thereof; and if the said agreement shall be so adopted at the respective meetings of the shareholders of each of the said corporations, the agreement so adopted and the said certificates thereon shall be filed in the office of the Secretary of State of Canada, and the said agreement shall thenceforth be taken and deemed to be the agreement and act of union, amalgamation and consolidation of the said corporations, or the agreement and deed of purchase and acquisition by the Society, of the assets of such company so selling, as the case may be, and a copy of such agreement so filed, and of the certificates thereon properly certified, shall be evidence of the existence of such new corporation: Provided, nevertheless, that due proof of the foregoing facts shall be laid before the Governor in Council, and, if deemed expedient by the Governor in Council, letters patent shall be issued, and notice thereof duly published by the Secretary of State in the *Canada Gazette*, after which the new corporation may transact business.

19. Upon the making and perfecting of the said agreement and act of consolidation, as provided in the next preceding section, the several societies, parties thereto, shall be deemed and taken to be consolidated and to form one corporation by the name in the said agreement provided, with a common seal, and shall possess all the rights, privileges and franchises of each of such corporations.

20. Upon the consummation of such act of consolidation as aforesaid, all and singular, the business, property, movable and immovable, and all rights and incidents appurtenant thereto, all stock, hypothecs or other securities, subscriptions and other debts, due on whatever account, and other things in action belonging to such corporations or either of them, shall be taken or deemed to be transferred to and vested in such new corporation without further act or deed: Provided however, that all rights of creditors and liens upon the property of either of such corporations shall be unimpaired by such consolidation, and all debts, liabilities and duties of either of the said corporations shall thenceforth attach to the new corporation and be enforced against it to the same extent as if the said debts, liabilities and duties had been incurred or been contracted by it; and provided also, that no action or proceeding, legal or equitable, by or against the said corporations so consolidated, or either of them shall abate or be affected by such consolidation, but for all the purposes of such action or proceeding such corporation may be deemed still to exist; or the new corporation may be substituted in such action or proceeding in the place thereof.

21. The choice and removal of the Auditors of the Society, the determination as to the remuneration of the Directors and o fthe Auditors, shall be exercised at general meetings of the Society, and the auditors shall not necessarily be shareholders: Provided that in case of the death or failure to act of any such Auditor, the Directors may appoint an auditor in his place; and at all meetings of shareholders of the Society the shareholders shall have one vote for each share held by them respectively.

22. Such Society shall, on or before the fifteenth day of February in each year, transmit to the Minister of Finance a full and clear statement of their assets and liabilities on the day of the date thereof, and such statement shall contain, in addition to such other particulars as the Minister of Finance may require—

1st. The amount of stock subscribed;

2nd. The amount paid in upon such stock;

3rd. The amount borrowed for the purposes of investments and the securities given therefor;

4th. The amount invested and secured by hypothecs;

5th. The value of immovable property under hypothec;

6th. The amount of hypothecs overdue and in default;

7th. The amount of hypothecs payable by instalments;

8th. The amount held as deposits:

And such statement shall be attested by the oath, before some Justice of the Peace, of two persons, one being the President, Vice-President, Manager or Secretary, and the other the Manager or Auditor of such Society, each of whom shall swear distinctly that he has such quality or office as aforesaid, that he has had the means of verifying, and has verified the statement aforesaid, and found it to be exact and true in every particular; that the property under mortgage has been set down at its true value, to the best of his knowledge and belief, and that the amount of the shares, deposits, and debentures issued and outstanding, as he verily believes, is correct; and such statement shall be published by the Minister of Finance, in such manner as he shall think most conducive to the public good: and for any neglect to transmit such statement in due course of post within five days after the day to which it is to be made up, such Society shall incur a penalty of one hundred dollars *per diem;* and if the same be not transmitted within one month after the said day, or if it shall appear by the statement that such Society is insolvent, the Minister of Finance may, by a notice in the

Canada Gazette, declare the business of such Society to have ceased: and if the Minister of Finance shall, in any case, suspect any such statement to be wilfully false, he may depute some competent person to examine the books and enquire into the affairs of such Society, and to report to him on oath; and if by such report it shall appear that such statement was wilfully false, or that such Society is insolvent, or if the person so deputed shall report on oath that he has been refused such access to the books, or such information as would enable him to make a sufficient report, the Minister of Finance may, by notice in the *Canada Gazette*, declare the business of such Society to have ceased; but in any of the cases in which discretionary power is given to the Minister of Finance to declare the business of such Society to have ceased, he may before so doing give notice to such Society, and afford the same an opportunity of making any explanation it may be advisable to make; and all expense attending such periodical statements, and the publication thereof, shall be borne by such Society.

23. Subsection one of the first section of chapter sixty nine of the Consolidated Statutes for Lower Canada, intituled "*An Act respecting Building Societies*," is hereby repealed, together with all other provisions of the said Act which are incompatible with this Act.

24. This Act shall apply as well to societies now existing as to societies hereafter incorporated in the manner hereinbefore provided; but it shall not be so construed as to prevent existing societies not having the capital required by this Act to continue their business and operations: Provided however, that any such Society that has not already borrowed money either on deposit or debentures, or both, or otherwise, shall not be allowed to do so until its permanent capital is raised to the amount required by this Act, and in accordance with the provisions thereof, and that any such Society that has borrowed money already shall not from and after the passing of this Act, issue any more debentures, and shall not, from and after the first day of July, one thousand eight hundred and seventy-eight, if it is a Society existing in a city or in an incorporated town, and from and after the first day of July, one thousand eight hundred and seventy-nine if it is a Society existing elsewhere than in a city or incorporated town, borrow or receive money on deposit or otherwise, unless its permanent capital be raised to the amount required by this Act, and according to the provisions thereof.

SCHEDULE A.

Public notice is hereby given that under the Act of the Parliament of Canada   Victoria, chapter   , (1877,) respecting Building Societies, letters patent have been issued under the Great Seal of the Dominion of Canada, bearing date the   day of   incorporating (*here state names, address and calling of each corporator named in the letters patent*) as a Building Society, by the name of (*here state the name of the Society, as in the letters patent*), with a total capital stock of   dollars, (*state here whether the stock is permanent or temporary, or how much thereof is permanent and how much temporary, as the case may be*), divided into   shares of   dollars each.

Dated at the office of the Secretary of State of Canada, this   day of

          A.B.
         Secretary.
       SCHEDULE

SCHEDULE B.

              Society.

Debenture No.   Transferable $

Under the authority of an Act of the Parliament of Canada Victoria, Chapter

The President and Directors of the   Society promise to pay to   or bearer the sum of   dollars, on the   day of   , in the year of Our Lord One thousand eight hundred and   at the Treasurer's office here, with interest at the rate of   per cent. per annum, to be paid half-yearly on presentation of the proper coupon for the same as hereunto annexed, say on the   day of   , and the   day of   in each year at the office of the Treasurer here (or their agents in   .)

Dated at   , the   day of   , 18   .
For the President and Directors of the   Society.
  C. D.   A. B.
  Secretary.

COUPON.

No. 1. $

Half-yearly dividend due   of   18   ,   on Debenture No.   issued by this Society on the   day of   , 18   for $ at   per cent. per annum, payable at the office of the Treasurer, at   , (or at the Society's agents   .)

For the President and Directors.
  C. D.   A.B.
  Secretary.

CAP. XLVIII.

An Act to provide for the Liquidation of the affairs of Building Societies in the Province of Quebec.

Section.
Preamble.
1. Liquidation may be resolved upon at any general meeting after notice. Its effect.
2. Liquidators may then be appointed.
3. President. Quorum. Decision of questions.
4. Powers and duties of liquidators. Proviso. Realization assets, disposing of claims, &c.
5. Division of amounts realized from sale of assets. How made and who to participate in, &c.
6. Members may be paid by transfer of claims. Effect of transfer.
7. As to payment of principal money due to the Society under obligations.
8. Provision when appropriations to members are payable by terms without interest. Proviso. As to amount paid as premiums for appropriation.

Section.
9. Liquidators to obey orders from meetings. And pay over on dismissal.
10. Shareholders may authorize divisions in kind of the property of the Society.
11. Responsibility, remuneration and tenure of liquidator. Removal and filling vacancies.
12. Interim and final reports of liquidators to meetings of shareholders, and dissolution of Society at final meeting. Proviso, as to unknown creditors. Act of Quebec 35 V., c. 5, cited.
13. Cessation of fines.
14. Addresses of shareholders to be left at office.
15. Power to any fifteenth shareholders to call a special meeting for the purposes of this Act.
16 Limitation of application of Act.

[*Assented to* 15*th May,* 1879.]

WHEREAS a large number of persons of limited means have invested their earnings in Building Societies in the Province of Quebec, and on account of a long period of depression such persons are exposed to lose their earnings for want of means to continue the payment of their contributions, and it is expedient to come to their relief by providing a speedy and inexpensive mode of liquidating the affairs of such societies in the said Province. Therefore Her Majesty, by and with the advice and consent of the Senate and House of Commons of Canada, enacts as follows:—

1. Any Building Society in the Province of Quebec may, at any annual general meeting, or at any special general meeting, by a majority or two-thirds of the votes of the members present in person or by proxy at such meeting,—each member being entitled to one vote for every share then held by him,—adopt a resolution for the liquidation of the society's affairs; provided that public notice of such meeting, and of the proposal to liquidate to be made thereat, shall have been given at least fifteen days previously in a French newspaper and in an English newspaper in the locality; and provided also that a special notice, containing the same information as the public notice, shall have been sent by post to each member of the society at least fifteen days before such meeting; and from and after the adoption of such resolution the society shall be deemed to be in liquidation.

2. The shareholders may, at the same meeting, by a majority of the votes given, appoint three or five Liquidators, who shall take the place of the directors then in office, and shall be charged with the duty of liquidating the affairs of the society ; and any director then in office may be appointed a liquidator.

3. The liquidators shall elect one of their number to be their President; and the majority of the liquidators shall form a quorum of the Board of Liquidators ; and every question shall be decided by the majority of the votes of the liquidators present at the meeting of the board at which it is put to the vote ; and the President shall have a casting vote.

4. The liquidators shall have all the powers conferred, and be subject to all the obligations towards the shareholders imposed, by law and by the by-laws of the Society, upon the directors. Nevertheless the Society, shall not transact any business except such as may be requisite for the purpose of accomplishing the liquidation ; and the liquidators shall proceed with diligence to realize all the assets of the Society without any unnecessary sacrifice ; and to that end they may dispose, either by private sale or by auction, of the movable and immovable property of the Society, including the debts due to it, and they may compound and compromise with the Society's debtors, and do whatever they may deem to be advisable in order to the liquidation of the affairs of the Society on the most advantageous terms.

5. After paying the Society's debts, the liquidators shall divide from time to time, and at such times as they shall decide themselves, by way of dividend, what they have realized from the assets. This division shall be made proportionally to the amount paid in by each shareholder ; but no shareholder in arrear on the payment of his calls shall be entitled to participate in the division so long as the other shareholders shall not have been reimbursed in full for the payment to those calls which he shall have neglected to pay ; and every shareholder so in arrear shall be charged with interest at the rate of six per cent. per annum on the amount of his calls due and unpaid, and such interest shall diminish in proportion to the amount which shall be reimbursed to the other shareholders in respect of the same calls.

6. In case it should be resolved to pay some of the members by means of transfers of claims or moneys due to the Society, it shall be lawful for the liquidators to divide the debts due to the Society into several parts, and to transfer a part or parts to different members ; and the debtors of whose debts such tranfers may be made shall suffer such division and pay to the creditors so delegated ;—provided, however, that no debt shall be divided into more then four parts, and that the debtor shall not not be bound to pay elsewhere than at his domicile, if he has any, where the debt was contracted ; and if he has no domicile, then he shall be bound to pay at the domicile or elect domicile of the creditors in the place where the debt was contracted.

7. The principal money due under every obligation executed by any shareholder in favour of the Society, the day of payment of which is undefined, or which is appointed to be paid on the extinction of any class, shall continue to become payable according to the terms of the obligation itself, and of the by-laws of the Society ; but moreover, the liquidators may, from time to time, exact on account of the principal moneys of such obligations the payment of such amounts as may be necessary for the purpose of placing the shareholders on a footing of equality with respect to the final result of the liquidation; but such amounts shall not become payable until after a month's notice to the debtors.

8. In any society or societies where the appropriations obtained by members are repayable to the Society in payments extending over a term of years without interest, then the members having obtained any such appropriation or appropriations, and being bound by obligation or otherwise so to repay the same, shall pay to the said liquidators in addition to the principal sum or sums so received by them, and each of them a sum of money which shall be equivalent to interest at the rate of seven per centum per annum, for the time for which they and each of them shall have had the use of the said principal sum or sums, or any portion thereof;—the said amount so to be payable for interest to be computed from the time each of such members received the principal sum of each appropriation up to the time that he shall have repaid it in full, and in such manner that he shall pay interest for the length of time he shall have had the said sum or sums and each or any portion thereof, on the said sum or sums or on the portion or portions thereof he shall have had and not repaid as the case may be. The total amount of the said interest having been so ascertained the said liquidators shall credit, on account thereof, the said debtor with the amount of weekly subscriptions paid in by him upon the subscription book on which he has obtained any such appropriation, up to the date of the liquidation of such society, and shall apportion the balance into payments to be made at such times as they may fix during and beyond the term granted for the repayment of the principal sum of the said appropriation: provided always, that the said debtor shall not be obliged to pay in any one year, as such interest, any larger sum than the amount which, had the society continued in operation, he would have been bound to pay in such year as subscriptions on the subscription book, on which he obtained such appropriation;

No amount paid by any member as premium or bonus for the obtaining of any appropriation shall be credited on account of or imputed in deduction of the said amount to be paid by him as interest, under the foregoing provisions.

9. The liquidator or liquidators shall give such security and shall receive such remuneration as may be determined upon at a meeting of the shareholders, and shall be at all times bound to obey orders given to them by resolutions adopted at a regular meeting of the members, and may be dismissed at any such meeting; and on their dismissal they shall hand over all the assets of the society, as well as all its books and papers, to their successors, or to any person appointed by such meeting, under penalty of fifty dollars for every day of retention of any such assets, book or papers,—which penalty may be recovered by any member of the society by civil action as a debt, and shall be enforceable by imprisonment until paid.

10. The shareholders in general meeting assembled may authorize the division in kind of the whole or a part of the property of the society, and also the payment in kind of the proportional amount accruing to any shareholder in respect of his shares; they may also authorize the sale in one lot of all the assets of the society, on such terms as they may see fit; they may also authorize the liquidators to purchase for the benefit of the society the rights of any shareholder, and to pay for the same either in money or in kind,—that is to say, with the property of the society.

11. The liquidators shall not be subject to any greater responsibility than the Directors of the Society are subject to by law and by the by-laws of the Society. Their remuneration shall be fixed by the shareholders in general meeting assembled, and they shall be bound to give such security as the shareholders may require. They shall be subject to instructions from the shareholders, in so far as the same may be compatible with the laws and with the by-laws of the society. They may be removed from office by the shareholders at any meeting, and replaced by others; and in the case of any vacancy arising among them, either by death, refusal to act, incapacity, removal from office or otherwise, such vacancy shall be filled by the shareholders at any general meeting; and until any such vacancy has been filled the liquidators remaining in office shall continue to exercise the same powers; but it shall be their duty to call, with all convenient speed, a meeting of the shareholders for the purpose of filling the vacancy.

12. The liquidators shall make a report of the state of the society's affairs to the shareholders at each annual general meeting, and at such other meetings as the shareholders may determine upon for that purpose; and on the occasion of the final liquidation, the liquidators shall make a report to a final meeting of the shareholders, called for that purpose, which report shall be subject to the approval of the meeting; and such meeting shall then have power to dissolve the society and to surrender its charter, which shall thereupon expire and become null and void: and at such final meeting the shareholders may make such orders as they think fit with respect to the custody of the books, papers and records of the Society; provided always that if there remain debts to be paid to unknown creditors, or to creditors to whom payment cannot be made, the liquidators shall deposit the amount in the hands of the Treasurer of the Province of Quebec, under the authority of chapter five of the Acts of the Legislature of the Province of Quebec, passed in the thirty-fifth year of Her Majesty's reign, intituled "An Act respecting Judicial and other Deposits," and of the Acts amending the said Act, and shall, in so doing, comply with the formalities prescribed by the said Acts; and the charter shall not be surrendered until after such deposit has been made.

13. No fine shall be incurred after the day on which liquidation is resolved upon.

14. Every shareholder shall leave his address, in writing, at the Society's office; and every special notice required by this Act shall be sent to such address; and in case any shareholder neglects to conform to the above requirement, such notices shall be addressed to him at his last known place of residence, and if there is none such, then at the place where the Society has its principal office or place of business.

15. Any fifteen shareholders of any Building Society in the Province of Quebec shall have power to call a special general meeting of the shareholders thereof for the purposes of this Act, by giving public notice thereof in conformity with the first section of this Act.

16. This Act shall not apply to permanent shares of any Building Society, if such shares are all paid and converted into unredeemable stock, unless three-fourths of the members present at a meeting held for the purpose of liquidating agree to liquidate.

CHAP. XLIII.

An Act to amend the law respecting the Incorporation of Joint Stock Companies by Letters Patent.

Section.
Preamble.
1. Short title.
2. Interpretation of the words : Company, Undertaking, Loan Company, Real Estate, Shareholder, Manager.
3. Companies formed for certain purposes may be incorporated by letters patent. Exception.
4. Notice to be given in the *Canada Gazette*, and what it shall contain :—name ; purposes ; chief place of business ; capital ; shares ; names, &c., of applicants.
5. Petition for letters patent ; what it shall contain ; a certain amount of stock must be taken ; and a certain amount paid-up thereon. Disposal of amount paid-up. Certain provisions may be inserted in patent.
6. Preliminary conditions to be established ; proof of facts asserted.
7. Facts to be recited in letters patent.
8. Governor may give another corporate name.
9. Notice of issuing letters patent.
10. General corporate powers of such companies.
11. Governor may change name by supplementary patent.
12. Company may obtain change of name.
13. Change not to affect rights or obligations.
14. Company may authorize Directors to apply for extension of powers.
15. Application by Directors. Notice in *Gazette*.
16. Proof to be furnished to Secretary of State. 37 V., c. 37.

Section.
17. Grant of supplementary patent. Notice in *Gazette*.
18. By-law for increase or decrease of number of Directors ; when to be valid.
19. Subdivision of shares.
20. Increase of capital. By-law for that purpose.
21. Reduction of capital ; proviso as to loan companies. By-law for that purpose.
22. Such by-law to be approved by shareholders and confirmed by supplementary letters patent. Liability to creditors not affected.
23. Petition for supplementary letters patent to confirm by-law. By-law, etc., to be produced with petition. Evidence may be taken and kept by Secretary of State.
24. Granting of supplementary letters patent ; notice ; effect of such letters patent.
25. Powers given to the company to be subject to this Act.
26. Board of Directors.
27. Provisional Directors.
28. Qualifications of after Directors ; residence.
29. Election of Directors.
30. Mode and times of election. Yearly Notice. Votes ; proxies ; all calls must have been paid ; majority to decide ; casting vote. Ballot. Vacancies, how filled. President and Vice-President ; officers.
31. Failure to elect Directors, how remedied.
32. Powers and duties of Directors : stock ; dividend ; Directors and officers ; meetings ; fines ; general powers ; con-

firmation of by-laws; proviso: special general meetings; proviso: confirmation of by-laws for sale of stock below par, etc.
33. Evidence of by-laws.
34. Stock deemed personal estate.
35. Allotment of stock.
36. Reference book to be kept and what to contain. Copy of letters patent, by-laws, etc. Names of shareholders. Address. Number of shares. Amounts paid, etc. Names, etc., of Directors. Register of transfers.
37. Books to be open for inspection and taking extracts therefrom.
38. Forfeiture for neglect.
39. Books to be *prima facie* evidence.
40. Penalty for false entries.
41. Transfer of shares valid only after entry.
42. Liabilities of Directors as regards transfers of shares in certain cases; how only a Director may avoid liability.
43. Provision when shares are transmitted otherwise than by transfer; order of Court may be obtained on application; proviso: notice of application; proviso as to costs.
44. Restriction as to transfer.
45. As to transfer by debtor to Company.
46. Transfer by personal representative.
47. Liability of shareholders; when to accrue.
48. Limited to amount unpaid on stock.
49. Trustees, etc., not personally liable.
50. But entitled to vote.
51. Company not to be liable in respect of trusts, etc.
52. Calling in of moneys unpaid on shares.
53. Interest on calls overdue.
54. Payment in advance on shares; interest allowed.
55. Forfeiture of shares for non-payment of calls; proviso: liability of holders continued.
56. Enforcement of payment by calls by action; what only need be alleged and proved and how.
57. Directors indemnified in suits, etc., against the Company; except by their own neglect or default.
58. Dividends not to impair capital.
59. Debts to Company may be deducted from.
60. Officers and agencies of the Company in Canada.
61. Service of process on Company.
62. Use of common seal dispensed with in certain cases.
63. Service of notices upon members.
64. Service of notice by post.
65. Acts of Company's attorney valid.
66. Contracts, etc., when to be binding on Company; proviso: not to issue paper money.
67. Liability of Directors declaring a dividend when Company is insolvent, etc.; how Directors may avoid liability.

68. No loan by Company to shareholders, except by loan companies, liability of Directors.
69. Liability of Directors for wages; limitation of suits, etc.
70. Actions between Company and shareholders.
71. Mode of incorporation, etc., how to be set forth in legal proceedings; proof of incorporation.
72. Forfeiture of charter for non-user.
73. Company subject to future legislation.
74. Fees on letters patent, etc., to be fixed by Governor-in-Council. Amount of fees may be varied. Must be paid before action taken.
75. Winding up Acts to apply.
76. Proofs may be by declaration or affidavit.
77. Certain informalities not to invalidate letters patent.
78. Word "limited" to be inserted after name of Company on all notices, etc.
79. Penalty for contravention of preceding section; penalty on Directors or officers using or authorizing use of seal without "limited" on it.
80. Existing companies may apply for charters under this Act; effect of such charters.
81. Subsisting companies may apply for charters with extended powers.
82. Provisions touching supplementary letters patent to apply.
83. Shares to be paid in cash, except under sub-sec. 5 of sec. 5, or special contract.
84. Prospectus, etc., to specify contracts entered into by Company, with promoters, directors, etc., thereof; or be deemed fraudulent.
85. Issue of bonds, etc., by Company; proviso: limiting amount to be borrowed; further proviso.
86. Agencies in United Kingdom.
87. Full statement of affairs at each meeting for elections.
88. Shares.
89. Powers and business of the Company; making loans and on what securities; powers incident to such loans, and enforcing payment thereof; capital may be employed for such purposes.
90. Company may act as agents and lend money, and recover the same either on their own behalf or as agents for others; powers as such; and may guarantee repayment if they see fit; money of which repayment is guaranteed, to be deemed borrowed.
91. Borrowing powers of Company and security to be given by it; may issue debentures, bonds, etc., for not less than $100 or £20 each.
92. Company may receive moneys on deposit; to be deemed borrowed.
93. Provisions and limitations as to borrowing powers. Amount borrowed by deposit limited. If the Company borrows

solely on debentures, etc. If it borrows in both ways ; proviso as to cash in hand. Proviso as to companies now incorporated.
94. Not to purchase stock in other companies.
95. Power to hold real estate ; proviso as to such estate not held for Company's own use.
96. Company may charge commission.
97. What interest Company may recover ; proviso as to fines.
98. Register of securities.
99. Company may unite with any other like Company.
100. Agreement for such union how made, etc., and what to provide.
101. Must be approved by shareholders of each Company after due notice ; proceedings at meeting ; and if the agreement be adopted ; letters patent may issue to the new company.
102. Effect of the agreement when perfected.
103. Business and rights of both companies invested in new company ; proviso : saving rights of third parties.
104. Annual statement to Minister of Finance and what it must show ; proviso.
105. 32, 33 V., c. 43, repealed ; proviso. Proviso as to pending applications under the said Act.
106. Copies of certain notices to be published by the Company in local paper.
107. Corporations authorized to lend money under 37 V., c. 49, to make returns as if incorporated under this Act.

[*Assented to* 28*th April*, 1877.]

HER Majesty, by and with the advice and consent of the Senate and House of Commons of Canada, enacts as follows :

1. This Act may be cited as "*The Canada Joint Stock Companies' Act*, 1877."

2. The following expressions in this Act, and in all letters patent and supplementary letters patent issued under the same, shall have the meaning hereby assigned to them respectively, unless there is something in the subject or context repugnant to such construction, that is to say :

1. The expression "the Company," means the Company so incorporated by letters patent :

2. The expression "the undertaking" means the business of every kind which the Company is authorized to carry on :

3. The expression "Loan Company" means a company chartered for any of the purposes to which the powers of Loan Companies extend, as hereinafter provided :

4. The expression "real estate," or "land," includes messuages, lands, tenements and hereditaments of any tenure, and all immovable property of every kind :

5. The expression "shareholder" means every subscriber to or holder of the stock in the Company, and includes the personal representatives of the shareholder :

6. The word "Manager" includes the Cashier and Secretary.

3. The Governor-in-Council may, by letters patent under the great seal, grant a charter to any number of persons, not less than five, who shall petition therefor, constituting such persons, and others who may become shareholders in the Company thereby created, a body corporate and politic, for any of the purposes or objects to which the legislative authority of the Parliament of Canada extends, except the construction and working of railways, or the business of banking and the issue of paper money, or insurance.

4. The applicants for such letters patent must give at least one month's previous notice in the *Canada Gazette*, of their intention to apply for the same, stating therein—

1. The proposed corporate name of the Company, which shall not be that of any other known company, incorporated or unincorporated, or any name liable to be confounded therewith, or otherwise on public grounds objectionable ;

2. The purposes within the purview of this Act, for which its incorporation is sought ;

3. The place within the Dominion of Canada, which is to be its chief place of business ;

4. The intended amount of its capital stock,—which, in the case of a loan company, shall not be less than one hundred thousand dollars ;

5. The number of shares and amount of each share ;

6. The names in full and the address and calling of each of the applicants, with special mention of the names of not less than three nor more than fifteen of their number, who are to be the first or Provisional Directors of the Company, and the major part of whom must be resident in Canada.

5. At any time, not more than one month after the last publication of such notice, the applicants may petition the Governor-General, through the Secretary of State of Canada, for the issue of such letters patent :

2. Such petition must recite the facts set forth in the notice, and must further state the amount of stock taken by each applicant, and also the amount paid in upon the stock of each applicant, and the manner in which the same has been paid in, and is held for the Company :

3. The aggregate of the stock so taken must be at least the one-half of the total amount of the stock of the Company :

4. The aggregate so paid in thereon must, if the Company be not a loan company, be at least ten per cent. thereof : if the Company be a loan company the aggregate so paid in thereon must be at least ten per cent. thereof, and must not be less than one hundred thousand dollars :

5. Such aggregate must have been paid in to the credit of the Company, or of trustees therefor, and must be standing at such credit in some chartered bank or banks in Canada, unless the object of the Company is one requiring that it should own real estate,—in which case any part not more than one-half of such aggregate may be taken as being paid in, if *bonâ fide* invested in real estate suitable to such object, duly held by trustees for the Company, and being of the required value over and above all incumbrances thereon :

6. The petition may ask for the embodying in the letters patent of any provision which under this Act, might be made by by-law of the Company incorporated ; and such provision so embodied shall not, unless provision to the contrary be made in the letters patent, be subject to repeal or alteration by by-law.

6. Before the letters patent are issued, the applicants must establish to the satisfaction of the Secretary of State, or of such other officer as may be charged by the Governor-in-Council to report thereon, the sufficiency of their notice and petition, and the truth and sufficiency of the facts therein set forth, and that the proposed name is not the name of any other known incorporated or unincorporated Company; and to that end, the Secretary of State, or such other officer, shall take and keep of record any requisite evidence in writing, by solemn declaration, under the Act thirty-seventh Victoria (1874), chapter thirty-seven, intituled "*An Act for the Suppression of Voluntary and Extra-Judicial Oaths*," or by oath or affirmation.

7. The letters patent shall recite such of the established averments of the notice and petition, as to the Governor may seem expedient.

8. The Governor may, if he think fit, give to the Company a corporate name, different from that proposed by the applicants in their published notice, if the latter is objectionable.

9. Notice of the granting of the letters patent shall be forthwith given by the Secretary of State, in the *Canada Gazette*, in the form of the Schedule A, appended to this Act; and thereupon, from the date of the letters patent, the persons therein named, and their successors, shall be a body corporate and politic by the name mentioned therein.

10. Subject to the special provisions herein contained respecting loan companies, every Company so incorporated may acquire, hold, sell and convey any real estate, requisite for the carrying on of the undertaking of such Company, and shall forthwith become and be invested with all property and rights, real and personal, theretofore held by or for it under any trust created with a view to its incorporation, and with all the powers, privileges and immunities requisite or incidental to the carrying on of its undertaking, as if it were incorporated by a special Act of Parliament, embodying the provisions of this Act and of the letters patent.

11. In case it should be made to appear, to the satisfaction of the Governor in Council, that the name of any Company (whether given by the original or by supplementary letters patent or on amalgamation) incorporate under the provisions of this Act, is the same as the name of an existing incorporated or unincorporated Company, or so similar thereto as to be liable to be confounded therewith, it shall be lawful for the Governor in Council to direct the issue of supplementary letters patent, reciting the former letters and changing the name of the Company to some other name to be set forth in the supplementary letters patent.

12. When a Company incorporated under the provisions of this Act, is desirous of adopting another name, the Governor in Council, upon being satisfied that the change desired is not for any improper purpose, may direct the issue of supplementary letters patent reciting the former letters and changing the name of the company to some other name, to be set forth in the supplementary letters patent.

13. No alteration of its name under the two last preceding sections shall affect the rights or obligations of the Company, and all proceedings may be continued or commenced by or against the Company by its new name that might have been continued or commenced by or against the Company by its former name.

14. The Company may from time to time, by a resolution passed by a vote of at least two-thirds in value of the total shareholders of the Company, at a special general meeting called for the purpose, authorize the Directors to apply for supplementary letters patent extending the powers of the Company to such other purposes or objects, within the purview of this Act, as may be defined in the resolution.

15. The Directors may, at any time within six months after the passing of any such resolution, petition the Governor, through the Secretary of State of Canada, for the issue of such supplementary letters patent;

2. The applicants for such supplementary letters patent must give at least one month's previous notice in the *Canada Gazette* of their intention to apply for the same, stating therein the purposes or objects to which it is desired to extend the powers of the Company.

16. Before such supplementary letters patent are issued, the applicants must establish to the satisfaction of the Secretary of State or of such other officer as may charged by the Governor in Council to report thereon, the due passing of the resolution authorizing the application and the sufficiency of their notice and petition; and to that end the Secretary of State or such other officer, shall take and keep of record any requisite evidence, in writing, by solemn declaration under the Act thirty-seventh Victoria, (1874), chapter thirty-seven, above mentioned, or by oath or affirmation.

17. Upon due proof so made, the Governor in Council may grant supplementary letters patent under the great seal, extending the powers of the Company to all or any of the objects defined in the resolution; and notice thereof shall be forthwith given by the Secretary of State, in the *Canada Gazette*, in the form Schedule C, appended to this Act; and thereupon, from the date of the supplementary letters patent, the undertaking of the Company shall extend to and include the other purposes or objects set out in the supplementary letters patent as fully as if such other purposes or objects were mentioned in the original letters patent.

18. The Company may, by by-law, increase to not more than fifteen, or decrease to not less than three, the number of its directors, or change the Company's chief place of business in Canada; provided that no by-law for either of the said purposes shall be valid or acted upon unless it be sanctioned by a vote of not less than two-thirds in value of the shareholders present in person or represented by proxy, at a general meeting duly called for considering the by-law, nor until a copy of such by-law, certified under the seal of the Company, has been deposited with the Secretary of State, and has also been published in the *Canada Gazette*.

19. The Directors of the Company, other than a Loan Company, may at any time make a by-law subdividing the existing shares into shares of a smaller amount.

20. The Directors of the Company, at any time after the whole capital stock of the Company shall have been taken up and fifty per cent. thereon paid in, but not sooner, may make a by-law for increasing the capital stock of the Company to any amount which they may consider requisite in order to the due carrying out of the objects of the Company:

2. Such by-law shall declare the number of the shares of the new stock; and may prescribe the manner in which the same shall be allotted; and in default of its so doing, the control of such allotment shall be held to vest absolutely in the Directors.

21. The Directors of the Company, at any time, may make a by-law for decreasing the capital stock of the Company to any amount which they may consider sufficient in order to the due carrying out of the undertaking of the Company, and advisable: Provided that the capital stock of a loan Company shall never be decreased to less than one hundred thousand dollars:

2. Such by-law shall declare the number and value of the shares of the stock as so decreased, and the allotment thereof, or the rule or rules by which the same shall be made.

22. But no by-law for increasing or decreasing the capital stock of the Company, or subdividing the shares, shall have any force or effect whatever, until after it shall have been sanctioned by a vote of not less than two-thirds in value of all the shareholders of the Company, at a general meeting of the Company duly called for considering the same, and afterwards confirmed by supplementary letters patent.

2. The liability of shareholders to persons who were, at the time of the reduction of the capital, creditors of the Company, shall remain as though the capital had not been decreased.

23. At any time not more than six months after such sanction of such by-law, the Directors may petition the Governor, through the Secretary of State, for the issue of supplementary letters patent to confirm the same:

2. With such petition they must produce a copy of such by-law, under the seal of the Company, and signed by the President, Vice-President or Secretary, and establish to the satisfaction of the Secretary of State, or of such other officer as may be charged by the Governor-in-Council, to report thereon, the due passage and sanction of such by-law, and the *bonâ fide* character and expediency of the increase or decrease of capital or subdivision of shares thereby provided for;

3. And to that end the Secretary of State, or such officer, shall take and keep of record any requisite evidence in writing, by solemn declaration as above mentioned, oath or affirmation.

24. Upon due proof so made, the Governor-in-Council may grant such supplementary letters patent under the great seal; and notice thereof shall be forthwith given by the Secretary of State in the *Canada Gazette*, in the form of Schedule B, appended to this Act: and thereupon, from the date of the supplementary letters patent, the capital stock of the Company shall be and remain increased or decreased, and the shares shall be subdivided, as the case may be, to the amount, in the manner and subject to the conditions set forth by such by-law; and the whole of the stock, as so increased or decreased, shall become subject to the provisions of this Act, in like manner (so far as may be) as though every part thereof had been or formed part of the stock of the Company originally subscribed.

25. All powers given to the Company by the letters patent or supplementary letters patent shall be exercised, subject to the provisions and restrictions contained in this Act.

26. The affairs of the Company shall be managed by a Board of not less than three nor more than fifteen Directors.

27. The persons named as such, in the letters patent, shall be the Directors of the Company, until replaced by others duly appointed in their stead.

28. No person shall be elected or appointed as a Director thereafter, unless he is a shareholder, owning stock absolutely in his own right, and to the amount required by the by-laws of the Company, and not in arrear in respect of any call thereon; and the major part of the Directors of the Company shall, at all times, be persons resident in Canada.

29. Directors of the Company shall be elected by the shareholders, in general meeting of the Company assembled, at some place within the Dominion of Canada, at such times, in such wise, and for such term, not exceeding two years, as the letters patent, or (in default thereof) the by-laws of the Company, may prescribe.

30. In default only of other express provisions in such behalf, by the letters patent or by-laws of the Company,—

1. Such election shall take place yearly,—all the members of the Board retiring, and (if otherwise qualified) being eligible for re-election:

2. Notice of the time and place for holding general meetings of the Company shall be given at least twenty-one days previously thereto, in some newspaper published in or as near as may be to the place where the chief office or place of business of the Company is situate:

3. At all general meetings of the Company, each shareholder shall be entitled to give one vote for each share then held by him: such votes may be given in person or by proxy,—the holder of any such proxy being himself a shareholder; but no shareholder shall be entitled, either in person or by proxy, to vote at any meeting unless he shall have paid all the calls upon all the shares held by him. All questions proposed for the consideration of the shareholders shall be determined by the majority of votes,—the Chairman presiding at such meeting having the casting vote in case of an equality of votes:

4. Elections of Directors shall be by ballot:

5. Vacancies occurring in the Board of Directors may be filled for the unexpired remainder of the term, by the Board, from among the qualified shareholders of the Company:

6. The Directors shall, from time to time, elect from among themselves a President and, if they see fit, a Vice-President of the Company; and may also name all other officers thereof.

31. If, at any time, an election of Directors be not made, or do not take effect at the proper time, the Company shall not be held to be thereby dissolved; but such election may take place at any general meeting of the Company duly called for that purpose; and the retiring Directors shall continue in office until their successors are elected.

32. The Directors of the Company shall have full power in all things to administer the affairs of the Company, and to make or cause to be made for the Company, any description of contract which the Company may by law enter into; and may, from time to time, make by-laws not contrary to law, nor to the letters patent of the Company, nor to this Act, to regulate the allotment of stock, the making of calls thereon, the payment thereof, the issue and registration of certificates of stock, the forfeiture of stock for non-payment, the disposal of forfeited stock and of the proceeds thereof, the transfer of stock, the declaration and payment of dividends, the number of the Directors, their term of service, the amount of their stock qualification, the appointment, functions, duties and removal of all agents, officers, and servants of the Company, the security to be given by them to the Company, their remuneration and that (if any) of the Directors, the time at which, and place where the annual meetings of the Company shall be held, the calling of meetings, regular and special, of the Board of Directors and of the Company, the quorum, the requirements as to proxies, and the procedure in all things at such meetings, the imposition and recovery of all penalties and forfeitures admitting of regulation by by-law, and the conduct in all other particulars of the affairs of the Company; and may, from time to time, repeal, amend or re-enact the same: but every such by-law, and every repeal, amendment or re-enactment thereof, unless in the meantime confirmed at a general meeting of the Company, duly called for that purpose, shall only have force until the next annual meeting of the Company, and in default of confirmation thereat, shall, at and from that time only, cease to have force: Provided always, that one-fourth part in value of the shareholders of the Company shall, at all times, have the right to call a special meeting thereof for the transaction of any business specified in such written requisition and notice as they may issue to that effect: Provided also, that no by-law for the issue, allotment or sale of any portion of the unissued stock at any greater discount or at any less premium than what has been previously authorized at a general meeting, or for the payment of the President or any Director shall be valid or acted upon until the same has been confirmed at a general meeting.

33. A copy of any by-law of the Company, under their seal, and purporting to be signed by any officer of the Company, shall be received as against any shareholder of the Company as *primâ facie* evidence of such by-law in all courts in Canada.

84. The stock of the Company shall be deemed personal estate, and shall be transmissible as such and shall be transferable, in such manner only, and subject to all such conditions and restrictions as, by this Act or by the letters patent or by-laws of the Company, are or shall be prescribed.

85. If the letters patent, or the supplementary letters patent make no other definite provision, the stock of the Company, or any increased amount thereof, so far as it is not allotted thereby, shall be allotted when and as the Directors, by by-law may ordain.

86. The Company shall cause a book or books to be kept by the Secretary, or by some other officer especially charged with that duty, wherein shall be kept recorded—

1. A copy of the letters patent incorporating the Company, and of any supplementary letters patent, and of all by-laws thereof;

2. The names, alphabetically arranged, of all persons who are or have been shareholders;

3. The address and calling of every such person, while such shareholder;

4. The number of shares of stock held by each shareholder:

5. The amounts paid in and remaining unpaid, respectively, on the stock of each shareholder;

6. The names, addresses and calling of all persons who are or have been Directors of the Company, with the several dates at which each became or ceased to be such Director:

7. A book called the Register of Transfers shall be provided, and in such book shall be entered the particulars of every transfer of shares in the capital of the Company.

87. Such books shall, during reasonable business hours of every day, except Sundays and holidays, be kept open for the inspection of shareholders and creditors of the Company, and their personal representatives, at the office or chief place of business of the Company; and every such shareholder, creditor or representative may make extracts therefrom.

88. Every Company neglecting to keep such book or books as aforesaid, shall forfeit its corporate rights.

89. Such books shall be *primâ facie* evidence of all facts purporting to be thereby stated, in any suit or proceeding against the Company or against any shareholder.

40. Every Director, officer or servant of the Company, who knowingly makes or assists to make any untrue entry in any such book, or who refuses or wilfully neglects to make any proper entry therein, or to exhibit the same, or to allow the same to be inspected and extracts to be taken therefrom, is guilty of a misdemeanor.

41. No transfer of shares, unless made by sale under execution, or under the decree, order or judgment of some competent court in that behalf, shall be valid for any purpose whatever, save only as exhibiting the rights of the parties thereto towards each other, and as rendering the transferee liable *ad interim* jointly and severally with the transferrer to the Company and their creditors,—until the entry thereof has been duly made in such book as aforesaid.

42. No transfer of shares whereof the whole amount has not been paid in shall be made without the consent of the Directors; and whenever any transfer of shares not fully paid in has been made with such consent to a person being apparently of insufficient means to fully pay up such shares, the Directors, jointly and severally, shall be liable to the creditors of the Company, in the same manner and to the same extent as the transferring shareholder, but for such transfer, would have been; but if any Director present when any such transfer is allowed, do forthwith, or if any Director then absent, do within twenty-four hours after he shall have become aware thereof and able so to do, enter on the minute book of the Board of Directors his protest against the same, and do within eight days thereafter publish such protest in at least one newspaper published at, or as near as may be possible to, the office or chief place of business of the Company, such Director may thereby, and not otherwise, exonerate himself from such liability.

43. Whenever the interest in any share or shares of the capital stock of the Company shall be transmitted by the death of any shareholder or otherwise, or whenever the ownership of or legal right of possession in any such share or shares shall change by any lawful means other than by transfer, according to the provisions of this Act, and the Directors of the Company shall entertain reasonable doubts as to the legality of any claim to and upon such share or shares of stock,—then, and in such case, it shall be lawful for the Company to make and file in one of the Superior Courts of law or equity, in the Province in which the head office of the Company is situated, a declaration and petition in writing, addressed to the justices of the court, setting forth the facts and the number of shares previously belonging to the party in whose name such shares stand in the books of the Company, and praying for an order or judgment adjudicating and awarding the said shares to the party or parties legally entitled to the same,—and by which order or judgment the Company shall be guided and held fully harmless and indemnified and released from all and every other claim for the said shares or arising therefrom: Provided always, that notice of such petition shall be given to the party claiming such share or shares, or to the attorney of such party duly authorized for the purpose, who shall, upon the filing of such petition, establish his right to the several shares referred to in such petition; and the delays to plead and all other proceedings in such cases shall be the same as those observed in analogous cases before the said superior courts: Provided also that the costs and expenses of procuring such order and adjudication shall be paid by the party or parties to whom the said shares shall be declared lawfully to belong; and such shares shall not be transferred until such costs and expenses be paid, saving the recourse of such party against any party contesting his right.

44. No share shall be transferable until all previous calls thereon have been fully paid up.

45. The Directors may decline to register any transfer of shares belonging to any member who is indebted to the Company.

46. Any transfer of the share or other interest of a deceased member, made by his personal representative, shall, notwithstanding such personal representative may not himself be a member, be of the same validity as if he had been a member at the time of his execution of the instrument of transfer.

47. Each shareholder, until the whole amount of his shares has been paid up, shall be individually liable to the creditors of the Company to an amount equal to that not paid up thereon; but shall not be pliable to an action therefor by any creditor, before an execution against the Company has been returned unsatisfied in whole or part; and the amount due on such execution, not exceeding the amount unpaid on his shares, as aforesaid, shall be the amount recoverable, with costs, against such shareholder, and any amount so recoverable, being paid by the shareholder, shall be taken as paid on his shares.

48. The shareholders of the Company shall not, as such, be held responsible for any act, default, or liability whatsoever of the Company, or for any engagement, claim, payment, loss, injury, transaction, matter or thing whatsoever, relating to or connected with the Company, beyond the amount unpaid on their respective shares in the capital stock thereof, subject to the provisions of the next preceding section.

49. No person holding stock in the Company as an executor, administrator, tutor, curator, guardian or trustee, shall be personally subject to liability as a shareholder; but the estates and funds in the hands of such person, shall be liable in like manner, and to the same extent, as the testator, or intestate, or the minor, ward or interdicted person, or the person interested in such trust fund would be, if living and competent to act and holding such stock in his own name; and no person holding such stock as collateral security, shall be personally subject to such liability; but the person pledging such stock shall be considered as holding the same and shall be liable as a shareholder accordingly.

50. Every such executor, administrator, curator, guardian or trustee, shall represent the stock in his hands, at all meetings of the Company, and may vote accordingly as a shareholder; and every person who pledges his stock may nevertheless represent the same at all such meetings, and may vote accordingly as a shareholder.

51. The Company shall not be bound to see to the execution of any trust, whether express, implied or constructive, in respect of any share; and the receipt of the shareholder in whose name the same may stand in the books of the Company, shall be a valid and binding discharge to the Company for any dividend or money payable in respect of such share, and whether or not notice of such trust has been given to the Company; and the Company shall not be bound to see to the application of the money paid upon such receipt.

52. The Directors may, from time to time, make such calls upon the members in respect of all moneys unpaid upon their respective shares, as they shall think fit, at such times and places and in such payments or instalments as the letters patent, or this Act, or the by-laws of the Company may require or allow.

53. A call shall be deemed to have been made at the time when the resolution of the Directors authorizing such call was passed; and if a shareholder fails to pay any call due from him, before or on the day appointed for the payment thereof, he shall be liable to pay interest for the same, at the rate of six per cent, per annum, from the day appointed for payment to the time of actual payment thereof.

54. The Directors may, if they think fit, receive from any member willing to advance the same, all, or any part of the amounts due on the shares held by such member, beyond the sums then actually called for; and upon the moneys so paid in advance, or so much thereof as shall, from time to time, exceed the amount of the calls then made upon the shares in respect of which such advance shall be made, the Company may pay interest at such rate, not exceeding eight per cent. per annum, as the member paying such sum in advance and the Directors shall agree upon.

55. If, after such demand or notice as, by the letters patent or by-laws of the Company, may be prescribed, any call made upon any share or shares be not paid within such time as, by letters patent or by-laws, may be limited in that behalf, the Directors, in their discretion, by vote to that effect duly recorded in their minutes, may summarily declare forfeited any shares whereupon such payment is not made, and the same shall thereupon become the property of the Company and may be disposed of as, by the by-laws of the Company or otherwise, they may ordain; but notwithstanding such forfeiture, the holder of such shares at the time of forfeiture shall continue liable to the then creditors of the Company for the full amount unpaid on such shares at the time of forfeiture less any sums which may have been subsequently received by the Company in respect thereof.

56. The Company may, if they see fit, instead of declaring forfeited any share or shares, enforce payment of all calls and interest thereon, by action in any competent court; and in such action it shall not be necessary to set forth the special matter, but it shall be sufficient to declare that the defendant is a holder of one share or more, stating the number of shares, and is indebted in the sum of money to which the calls in arrear amount, in respect of one call or more upon one share or more, (stating the number of calls and the amount of each,) whereby an action hath accrued to the company under this Act; and a certificate under their seal, and purporting to be signed by any officer of the Company, to the effect that the defendant is a shareholder, that such call or calls has or have been made, and that so much is due by him and unpaid thereon, shall be received as against the defendant in all courts as *primâ facie* evidence to that effect.

57. Every Director of the Company, and his heirs, executors and administrators and estate and effects respectively may, with the consent of the Company, given at any general meeting thereof, from time to time, and at all times, be indemnified and saved harmless out of the funds of the Company, from and against all costs, charges and expenses whatsoever which he shall or may sustain or incur in or about any action, suit or proceeding which shall be brought, commenced or prosecuted against him, for or in respect of any act, deed, matter or thing whatsoever, made, done or permitted by him, in or about the execution of the duties of his office; and also from and against all other costs, charges and expenses which he shall sustain or incur, in or about, or in relation to the affairs thereof, except such costs, charges or expenses as shall be occasioned by his own wilful neglect or default.

58. The Company shall not make any dividend whereby their capital will be, in any degree, reduced.

59. The Directors may deduct from the dividends payable to any member all such sums of money as may be due from him to the Company, on account of calls or otherwise.

60. The Company shall, at all times, have an office in the city or town in which their chief place of business shall be, which shall be the legal domicile of the Company in Canada ; and notice of the situation of that office and of any change therein shall be advertised in the *Canada Gazette ;* and they may establish such other offices and agencies elsewhere in the Dominion of Canada, as they may deem expedient.

61. Any summons, notice, order or other process or document required to be served upon the Company, may be served by leaving the same at the said office in the city or town in which their chief place of business may be, with any grown person in the employ of the Company, or on the President or Secretary of the Company, or by leaving the same at the domicile of either of them, or with any grown person of his family or in his employ ; or if the Company have no known office or chief place of business, and have no known President or Secretary, then the court may order such publication as it may deem requisite to be made in the premises and such publication shall be held to be due service upon the Company.

62. Any summons, notice, order or proceeding requiring authentication by the Company may be signed by any Director, manager, or other authorized officer of the Company, and need not be under the common seal of the Company ; and the same may be in writing or in print, or partly in writing and partly in print.

63. Notices requiring to be served by the Company upon the members, may be served either personally or by sending them through the post, in registered letters, addressed to the members at their places of abode as appearing on the books of the Company.

64. A notice or other document served by post by the Company on a member, shall be taken as served at the time when the registered letter containing it would be delivered in the ordinary course of post; to prove the fact and time of service it shall be sufficient to prove that such letter was properly addressed and registered, and was put into the post office, and the time when it was in, and the time requisite for its delivery in the ordinary course of post.

65. Every deed which any person, lawfully empowered in that behalf by the Company as their attorney, signs on behalf of the Company, and seals with his seal, shall be binding on the Company and have the same effect as if it was under the common seal of the Company.

66. Every contract, agreement, engagement or bargain made, and every bill of exchange drawn, accepted or endorsed, and every promissory note and cheque made, drawn or endorsed on behalf of the Company, by any agent, officer or servant of the Company, in general accordance with his powers as such under the by-laws of the Company, shall be binding upon the Company; and in no case shall it be necessary to have the seal of the Company affixed to any such contract, agreement engagement, bargain, bill of exchange, promissory note or cheque, or to prove that the same was made, drawn, accepted or endorsed, as the case may be, in pursuance of any by-law or special vote or order; nor shall the party so acting as agent, officer or servant of the Company be thereby subjected individually to any liability whatsoever to any third party therefor: Provided always, that nothing in this Act shall be constructed to authorize the Company to issue any note payable to the bearer thereof, or any promissory note intended to be circulated as money, or as the note of a bank, or to engage in the business of banking or insurance.

67. If the Directors of the Company declare and pay any dividend when the Company is insolvent, or any dividend the payment of which renders the Company insolvent, or diminishes the capital stock thereof, they shall be jointly and severally liable, as well to the Company as to the individual shareholders and creditors thereof, for all the debts of the Company then existing, and for all thereaftercontracted during their continuance in office, respectively; but if any Director present when such dividend declared do forthwith, or if any Director then absent do within twenty-four hours after he shall have become aware thereof and able so to do, enter on the minutes of the Board of Directors his protest against the same, and within eight days thereafter publish such protest in at least one newspaper published at, or as near as may be possible to, the office or chief place of business of the Company, such Director may thereby, and not otherwise, exonerate himself from such liability.

68. Except only in the case of a loan Company, no loan shall be made by the Company to any shareholder, and if such be made, all Directors and other officers of the Company making the same, or in anywise assenting thereto, shall be jointly and severally liable for the amount of such loan, with interest, to the Company, and also to the creditors of the Company for all debts of the Company then existing, or contracted between the time of the making of such loan and that of the repayment thereof.

69. The Directors of the Company shall be jointly and severally liable to the clerks, laborers, servants and apprentices thereof, for all debts not exceeding six months wages due for service performed for the Company whilst they are such Directors respectively; but no Director shall be liable to an action therefor, unless the Company has been sued therefor within one year after the debt became due, nor yet unless such Director is sued therefor within one year from the time when he ceased to be such a Director, nor yet before an execution against the Company has been returned unsatisfied in whole or in part; and the amount due on such execution shall be the amount recoverable with costs against the Directors.

70. Any description of action may be prosecuted and maintained between the Company and any shareholder thereof; and no shareholder shall, by reason of being a shareholder, be incompetent as a witness therein.

71. In any action or other legal proceeding, it shall not be requisite to set forth the mode of incorporation of the Company, otherwise than mention of it under its corporate name, as incorporated by virtue of letters patent—or of letters patent and supplementary letters patent, as the case may be,—under this Act; and the notice in the *Canada Gazette*, of the issue of such letters patent or supplementary letters patent, shall be *primâ facie* proof of all things thereby declared; and on production of the letters patent or supplementary letters patent themselves, or of any exemplification or copy thereof under the great seal, the fact of such notice shall be presumed; and, save only in any proceeding by *scire facias* or otherwise for direct impeachment thereof, the letters patent or supplementary letters patent themselves, or any exemplification or copy thereof under the great seal, shall be conclusive proof of every matter and thing therein set forth.

72. The charter of the Company shall be forfeited by non-user during three consecutive years at any one time,—or if the Company do not go into actual operation within three years after it is granted; and no declaration of such forfeiture by any Act of Parliament shall be deemed an infringement of such charter.

73. The Company shall be subject to such further and other provisions as Parliament may hereafter deem expedient.

74. The Governor in Council may, from time to time, establish, alter and regulate the tariff of the fees to be paid on application for letters patent and supplementary letters patent under this Act, may designate the department or departments through which the issue thereof shall take place, and may prescribe the forms of proceeding and record in respect thereof, and all other matters requisite for carrying out the object of this Act:

2. Such fees may be made to vary in amount, under any rule or rules,—as to nature of Company, amount of capital, and otherwise,—that may be deemed expedient:

3. No steps shall be taken in any department towards the issue of

82   Cap. 43.   *Incorporation by Letters Patent.*   40 Vic.

any letters patent or supplementary letters patent under this Act, until after the amount of all fees therefor shall have been duly paid.

75. The Company shall be subject to the provisions of any Act for the winding up of Joint Stock Companies, and to the provisions of "*The Insolvent Act of* 1875", and the amendments thereto, relating to incorporated companies.

76. Proof of any matter which may be necessary to be made under this Act may be made by solemn declaration under the Act thirty-seventh Victoria, (1874) chapter thirty-seven, or by affidavit before any Justice of the Peace, or any Commissioner for taking affidavits, to be used in any of the courts in any of the Provinces of the Dominion, or any Notary Public, who are hereby authorized and empowered to administer oaths and receive affidavits and declarations for that purpose.

77. The provisions of this Act relating to matters preliminary to the issue of the letters patent or supplementary letters patent shall be deemed directory only, and no letters patent or supplementary letters patent issued under this Act shall be held void or voidable on account of any irregularity in any notice prescribed by this Act, or on account of the insufficiency or absence of any such notice, or on account of any irregularity in respect of any other matter preliminary to the issue of the letters patent or supplementary letters patent.

78. The Company shall paint or affix, and shall keep painted or affixed, its name, with the word "limited" after the name, on the outside of every office or place in which the business of the Company is carried on, in a conspicuous position, in letters easily legible, and shall have its name with the said word after it, engraven in legible characters on its seal, and shall have its name, with the said word after it, mentioned in legible characters in all notices, advertisements and other official publications of the Company, and in all bills of exchange, promissory notes, endorsements, cheques, and orders for money or goods, purporting to be signed by or on behalf of such Company, and in all bills of parcels, invoices and receipts of the Company.

79. If the Company does not paint or affix, and keep painted or affixed, its name, with the word "limited" after it, in manner directed by this Act, it shall be liable to a penalty of twenty dollars for not so painting or affixing its name, and to a penalty of twenty dollars per day for every day during which such name is not so kept painted or affixed; and every Director and manager of the Company who shall knowingly and wilfully authorize or permit such default shall be liable to the like penalties; and if any Director, manager or officer of such Company, or any person on its behalf, uses or authorizes the use of any seal purporting to be a seal of the Company whereon its name, with the said word "limited" after it, is not so engraven as aforesaid, or issues or authorizes the issue of any notice, advertisement or other official publication of such Company or signs or authorizes to be signed on behalf of such Company any bill of exchange, promissory note, endorsement, cheque, order for money or goods, of issues or authorizes to be issued any bill of parcels, invoice, or receipt of the Company, wherein its name, with the said word after it, is not mentioned in manner aforesaid, he shall be liable to a penalty of two hundred dollars, and shall further be personally liable to the holder of such bill of exchange, promissory note, cheque, or order for money or goods, for the amount thereof, unless the same is duly paid by the Company.

80. Any Company for purposes or objects within the purview of this Act, heretofore incorporated, whether under a special or a general Act, and now being a subsisting and valid corporation, may apply for letters patent under this Act, and the Governor in Council, upon proof that notice of the application has been inserted for four weeks in the *Canada Gazette*, may direct the issue of letters patent incorporating the shareholders of the said Company as a Company under this Act: and thereupon all the rights or obligations of the former Company shall be transferred to the new Company, and all proceedings may be continued or commenced by or against the new Company that might have been continued or commenced by or against the old Company; and it shall not be necessary in any such letters patent to set out the names of the shareholders; and after the issue of the letters patent the Company shall be governed in all respects by the provisions of this Act, except that the liability of the shareholders to creditors of the old Company shall remain as at the time of the issue of the latters patent.

81. Where a subsisting Company applies for the issue of letters patent under this Act, the Governor in Council may, by the letters patent, extend the powers of the Company to such other objects within the purview of this Act as the applicants may desire, and as the Governor in Council may think fit to include in the letters patent, and which have been mentioned in the notice of the application for the same, in the *Canada Gazette*, and may, by the said letters patent, name the first Directors of the new Company, and the letters patent may be to the new Company by the name of the old Company or by another name.

82. All the provisions of this Act touching the obtaining of supplementary letters patent by Companies incorporated hereunder shall, so far as applicable, apply and extend to applications for letters patent under the eightieth and eighty-first sections hereof.

83. Subject to the provisions of sub-section five of section five of this Act, every share in the Company shall be deemed and taken to have been issued and to be held subject to the payment of the whole amount thereof in cash, unless the same shall have been otherwise determined by a contract duly made in writing and filed with the Secretary of State at or before the issue of such shares.

84. Every prospectus of the Company, and every notice inviting persons to subscribe for shares in the Company, shall specify the dates and the names of the parties to any contract entered into by the Company or the promoters, directors or trustees thereof, before the issue of such prospectus or notice, whether subject to adoption by the Directors or the Company or otherwise; and any prospectus or notice not specifying the same shall be deemed fraudulent on the part of the promoters, directors and officers of Company knowingly issuing the same, as regards any person taking shares in the Company on the faith of such prospectus unless he shall have had notice of such contract.

85. In case a by-law authorizing the same is sanctioned by a vote of not less than two-thirds in value of the shareholders then present in person or represented by proxy, at a general meeting duly called for considering the by-law, the Directors may borrow money upon the credit of the Company and issue the bonds, debentures or other securities for any sums borrowed, at such prices as may be deemed expedient or necessary; but no such debentures shall be for a less sum than one hundred dollars: and the Directors may, under the like sanction, hypothecate or pledge the real or personal property of the Company to secure any sums borrowed by the Company: Provided always, that the amount to be borrowed shall not at any time be greater than seventy-five per cent. of the actual paid-up stock of the Company; Provided also, that the limitation by this section made shall not be held to apply to commercial paper discounted by the Company.

86. The Company may have an agency, or agencies, in any city or town in England, Scotland or Ireland.

87. The Directors of every Company shall lay before its shareholders a full and clear printed statement of the affairs and financial position of the Company at or before each general meeting of the Company for the election of Directors.

SECTIONS EIGHTY-EIGHT TO ONE HUNDRED AND FOUR, INCLUSIVE, RELATE TO LOAN COMPANIES ONLY.

88. The capital stock of every Loan Company shall be divided into shares of one hundred dollars each.

89. Any Loan Company may, from time to time, lend and advance money, by way of loan or otherwise, for such periods as they may deem expedient, on any real security, or on the public securities of the Dominion, or of any of the Provinces thereof, or on the security of debentures of any municipal or other corporation, issued under or in pursuance of any statutory authority, and upon such terms and conditions as to the Company shall seem satisfactory or expedient; and may acquire, by purchase or otherwise, any security upon which they are authorized to lend or advance money, and may re-sell the same as they may deem advisable,—with power to do all acts that may be necessary for advancing such sums of money and for receiving and obtaining repayment thereof, and for compelling the payment of all interest (if any) accruing from such sums so advanced, and the observance and fulfilment of any conditions annexed to such advance, and the forfeiture of any term or property consequent on the non-fulfilment of such conditions, or of conditions entered into for delay of payment; and to give receipts, acquittances and discharges for the same, either absolutely and wholly or partially, and to execute such deeds, assignments or other instruments as may be necessary for carrying any such purchase or re-sale into effect; and for all and every, and any of the foregoing purposes, and for every and any other purpose in this Act mentioned or referred to, the Company may lay out and apply the capital and property, for the time being, of the Company, or any part thereof, or any of the moneys authorized to be hereafter raised or received by the Company in addition to their capital for the time being, with power to do, authorize and exercise all acts and powers whatsoever, in the opinion of the Directors of the Company, requisite or expedient to be done or exercised in relation thereto.

90. The Company are hereby empowered to act as an agency association, and for the interest and on behalf of others who may entrust them with money for that purpose, and either in the name of the Company or of such others, to lend and advance money to any person or persons, upon such securities as are mentioned in the last preceding section, or to any body or bodies corporate whomsoever, or to any municipal or other authority, or any board or body of trustees or commissioners whatsoever, upon such terms and upon such security as to the Company shall appear satisfactory, and to purchase and acquire any securities on which they are authorized to advance money, and again to re-sell the same; and the conditions and terms of such loans and advances, and of such purchases and re-sales may be enforced by the Company for their benefit, and for the benefit of the person or persons or corporation for whom such money has been lent and advanced, or such purchase and re-sale made ; and the Company shall have the same power in respect of such loans, advances, purchases and sales as are conferred upon them in respect of loans, advances, purchases and sales made from their own capital : and they may also guarantee the repayment of the principal or the payment of the interest, or both, of any moneys entrusted to the Company for investment, and for all and every or any of the foregoing purposes, may lay out and employ the capital and property, for the time being, of the Company, or any part of the moneys authorized to be raised by the Company, in addition to their capital for the time being, or any moneys so entrusted to them as aforesaid, and may do, assent to, and exercise all acts whatsoever, in the opinion of the Directors of the Company for the time being, requisite or expedient to be done in regard thereto; and moneys of which the repayment of the principal or payment of interest is guaranteed by the Company, shall, for the purposes of this Act, be deemed to be money borrowed by the Company.

91. Subject to the conditions and provisions hereinafter made, the Directors may, from time to time, with the consent af the Company in general meeting, borrow money on behalf of the Company, at such rates of interest as may be lawful under section ninety-seven of this Act, and upon such terms as they may, from time to time, think proper ; and the Directors may, for that purpose, execute any debentures, mortgages, bonds or other intruments, under the common seal of the Company, for sums of not less than one hundred dollars or twenty pounds sterling each, or assign, tranfer or deposit, by way of equitable mortgage or otherwise, for the sums so borrowed, any of the documents of title, deeds, muniments, securities or property of the Company, and either with or without power of sale or other special provisions, as the Directors shall deem expedient.

92. Subject to the conditions and provisions hereinafter made the Directors may, from time to time, with the consent of the Company at a general meeting, receive money on behalf of the Company on deposit for such periods and at such rate of interest as may be agreed upon; and money so received on deposit shall, for the purposes of this Act, be deemed to be money borrowed by the Company.

93. Provided always,—

1. That the Company shall not borrow money unless at least one hundred thousand dollars of its subscribed capital stock has been paid up;
2. That the Company shall not borrow money unless at least twenty per cent. of its subscribed capital stock has been paid up:
3. That if the Company borrow money by way of deposit, under the ninety-second section, the aggregate amount of the sums so borrowed by way of deposit, shall not at any time, whether the Company borrows solely by way of deposit or also in other ways, exceed the aggregate amount of its paid up capital, and of its other cash actually in hand, or deposited by it in any chartered bank or banks in Canada;
4. That if the Company borrow money solely on the debentures or other securities mentioned in the ninety-first section, and by guarantee under the ninetieth section, and not by way of deposit, under the ninety-second section, the aggregate amount of the sums so borrowed shall not, at any time, exceed four times the amount of its paid up and unimpaired capital, or the amount of its subscribed capital, at the option of the Company;
5. That if the Company borrow money both by way of debentures or other securities or by guarantee, as aforesaid, and also by way of deposit, then the aggregate amount of money so borrowed shall not at any time exceed the amount of the principal moneys remaining unpaid on securities then held by the Company, nor shall it exceed double the amount of the then actually paid up and unimpaired capital of the Company; but the amount of cash then actually in the hands of the Company, or deposited by them in any chartered bank, or both, shall be deducted from the aggregate amount of the liabilities which the Company has then incurred, as above mentioned, in calculating such aggregate amount for the purposes of this sub-section:
6. Provided always, that in the event of any Company, now incorporated, availing itself of the provisions of this Act for the purpose of enlarging its powers to borrow money by debentures, nothing herein contained shall be construed as affecting, or in any wise impairing the right of the holders of debentures issued by the said Company.

94. The Company shall not use any of its funds in the purchase of stock in any other incorporated Company.

95. The Company may hold such real estate as may be necessary for the transaction of their business, not exceeding in yearly value the sum of ten thousand dollars in all, or, as being mortgaged or hypothecated to them, may be acquired by them for the protection of their investments, and may, from time to time, sell, mortgage, lease or otherwise dispose of the same: Provided always, that it shall be incumbent upon the Company to sell any real estate acquired in satisfaction of any debt within seven years after it shall have been so acquired, otherwise it shall revert to the previous owner, or his heirs or assigns.

96. The Company when acting as an agency association may charge such commission to the lender or borrower, or both, upon the moneys invested on their behalf as may be agreed upon, or as may be reasonable in that behalf.

97. The Company may stipulate for, take, reserve and exact any rate of interest or discount that may be lawfully taken by individuals, or in the Province of Quebec by incorporated Companies under like circumstances, and may also receive an annual payment on any loan by way of a sinking fund for the gradual extinction of such loan, upon such terms and in such manner as may be regulated by the by-laws of the Company: Provided always, that no fine or penalty shall be stipulated for, taken, reserved or exacted in respect of arrears of principal or interest, which shall have the effect of increasing the charge in respect of arrears beyond the rate of interest or discount on the loan.

98. A register of all securities held by the Company shall be kept; and within fourteen days after the taking of any security an entry or memorial specifying the nature and amount of such security, and the names of the parties thereto, with their proper additions, shall be made in such register.

99. It shall be lawful for the Company to unite, amalgamate and consolidate its stock, property, business and franchises with those of any other Company or Society incorporated or chartered to transact a like business, and any other business in connection with such business, or any Building, Savings or Loan Company or Society heretofore or hereafter incorporated or chartered, or to purchase and acquire the assets of any such Company or Society, and to enter into all contracts and agreements therewith necessary to such union, amalgamation, consolidation, purchase or acquisition.

100. The Directors of the Company, and of any other such Company or Society, may enter into a joint agreement under the corporate seals of each of the said Corporations, for the union, amalgamation or consolidation of the said Corporations, or for the purchase and acquisition by the Company of the assets of any other such Company or Society, prescribing the terms and conditions thereof, the mode of carrying the same into effect, the name of the new Corporation, the number of the Directors and other officers thereof, and who shall be the first Directors and officers thereof, the manner of converting the capital stock of each of the said corporations into that of the new corporation, with such other details as they shall deem necessary to perfect such new organization, and the union, amalgamation and consolidation of the said corporations, and the after management and working thereof, or the terms and mode of payment for the assets of any other such Company or Society purchased or acquired by the Company.

101. Such agreement shall be submitted to the shareholders of each of the said corporations at a meeting thereof to be held separately for the purpose of taking the same into consideration. Notice of the time and place of such meetings, and the objects thereof, shall be given by written or printed notices, addressed to each shareholder of the said corporations respectively, at his last known post office address or place of residence, and also by a general notice to be published in a newspaper published at the chief place of business of such corporations, once a week, for six successive weeks. At such meetings of shareholders such agreement shall be considered, and a vote by ballot taken for the adoption or rejection of the same,—each share entitling the holder thereof to one vote, and the said ballots being cast in person or by proxy; and if two-thirds of the votes of all the shareholders of such corporations shall be for the adoption of such agreement, then that fact shall be certified upon the said agreement by the secretary of each of such corporations, under the corporate seals thereof; and if the said agreement shall be so adopted at the respective meetings of the shareholders of each of the said corporations, the agreement so adopted and the said certificates thereon shall be filed in the office of the Secretary of State of Canada, and the said agreement shall, from thenceforth, be taken and deemed to be the agreement and act of union, amalgamation and consolidation of the said corporations, or the agreement and deed of purchase and acquisition by the Company of the assets of such Company so selling, as the case may be; and a copy of such agreement so filed, and of the certificates thereon properly certified, shall be evidence of the existence of such new corporation; Provided, nevertheless, that due proof of the foregoing facts shall be laid before the Governor in Council, and if deemed expedient by the Governor in Council, letters patent shall be issued and notice thereof duly published by the Secretary of State in the *Canada Gazette*,—after which the new corporation may transact business.

102. Upon the making and perfecting of the said agreement and Act of consolidation, as provided in the next preceding section, the several Societies, parties thereto, shall be deemed and taken to be consolidated, and to form one corporation by the name in the said agreement provided, with a common seal, and shall possess all the rights, privileges and franchises of each of such corporations.

103. Upon the consummation of such Act of consolidation as aforesaid, all and singular the business, property, real, personal and mixed, and all rights and incidents appurtenant thereto, all stock, mortgages or other securities, subscriptions and other debts due on whatever account, and other things in action belonging to such corporations or either of them, shall be taken and deemed to be transferred to and vested in such new corporation without further act or deed : Provided however, that all rights of creditors and liens upon the property of either of such corporations shall be unimpaired by such consolidation, and all debts, liabilities and duties of either of the said corporations shall thenceforth attach to the new corporation, and be enforced against it to the same extent as if the said debts, liabilities and duties had been incurred or contracted by it; and provided also that no action or proceeding, legal or equitable, by or against the said corporations so consolidated, or either of them, shall abate or be affected by such consolidation, but for all the purposes of such action or proceeding such corporation may be deemed still to exist, or the new corporation may be substituted in such action or proceeding in the place thereof.

104. The Company shall transmit on or before the first day of March in each year to the Minister of Finance a statement in duplicate, to the thirty-first day of December inclusive of the previous year, verified by the oath of their President or Vice-President and manager, setting out the capital stock of the Company, and the proportion thereof paid up, the assets and liabilities of the Company, the amount and nature of the investments made by the Company, both on their own behalf and on behalf of others, and the average rate of interest derived therefrom,—distinguishing the classes of securities, and also the extent and value of the lands held by them, under the ninety-fifth section, and such other details as to the nature and extent of the business of the Company as may be required by the Minister of Finance, and in such form and with such details as the said Minister may from time to time require and prescribe : Provided always that in no case shall the Company be bound to disclose the names or private affairs of any person who may have dealings with them.

105. "*The Canada Joint Stock Companies Letters Patent Act,* 1869," is hereby repealed, in so far as regards the formation or incorporation hereafter, by virtue of any of the provisions thereof, of any Company, the incorporation of which is subject to the control of the Parliament of Canada ; but every such Company heretofore incorporated by virtue of that Act or of any of the Acts thereby repealed, shall so remain ; and no provision of such Acts shall, as touching any such Company, be in anywise affected by this Act.

And every application for the incorporation of any Company, the incorporation of which is subject to the control of the Parliament of Canada,—pending at the time of the passing of this Act, under " *The Canada Joint Stock Companies Letters Patent Act,* 1869," may be proceeded with, and the incorporation may be obtained by virtue thereof, as though this Act had not been passed.

106. A copy of every notice of issue of letters patent or supplementary letters patent which, under the provisions of this Act, the Secretary of State is required to insert in the *Canada Gazette,* shall forthwith, after such insertion, be, by the Company to which such notice relates, inserted on four several occasions in at least one newspaper in the county, city or place where the head office or chief agency is established.

107. Every corporation or institution incorporated without the limits of Canada, which has been or may be authorized, under the provisions of the Act passed in the thirty-seventh year of Her Majesty's reign, chaptered forty-nine, to lend and invest money in Canada, shall, by the agent or manager in Canada, make returns to the Minister of

Finance, of all the business done by it in Canada, at the same and in the same manner as if such corporation or institution had been incorporated under the provisions of this Act.

SCHEDULE A.

Public notice is hereby given, that under the *Canada Joint Stock Companies Act*, 1877, letters patent have been issued under the great seal of the Dominion of Canada, bearing date the   day of   incorporating [*here state names, address and calling of each corporator named in the letters patent*], for the purpose of [*here state the undertaking of the Company, as set forth in the letters patent*], by the name of [*here state the name of the Company, as in the letters patent*], with a total capital stock of   dollars, divided into   shares of   dollars.

Dated at the office of the Secretary of State of Canada, this   day of   18

A. B.,
Secretary.

SCHEDULE B.

Public notice is hereby given, that under *The Canada Joint Stock Companies Act*, 1877, supplementary letters patent have been issued under the great seal of the Dominion of Canada, bearing date the   day of   whereby the total capital stock of [*here state the name of the Company*] is increased [*or* decreased, *as the case may be*] from   dollars to   dollars.

Dated at the office of the Secretary of State of Canada this   day of   18

A. B.,
Secretary.

SCHEDULE C.

Public notice is hereby given, that under *The Canada Joint Stock Companies' Act*, 1877, supplementary letters patent have been issued under the great seal of the Dominion of Canada, bearing date the   day of   , whereby the undertaking of the Company has been extended to include [*here set out the purposes or other objects mentioned in the supplementary letters patent*].

Dated at the office of the Secretary of State of Canada this   day of   18

A. B.,
Secretary.

CHAP. XLIX.

An Act to authorize corporations and institutions incorporated without the limits of Canada to lend and invest moneys therein.

Section.
Preamble.
1. British Company incorporated for lending money may be licensed by Secretary of State to carry on its business in Canada. Proviso, real estate to be sold within five years from time of its acquisition by the corporation.
2. Formalities to be observed by licensed corporation before commencing its business in Canada.

Section.
3. Service of process in suits against such licensed corporations and proceedings thereon.
4. Publication of notice of license or of having ceased to carry on business in any place.
5. Evidence on which licenses shall be issued by Secretary of State.
6. Fee for license.

[*Assented to 26th May*, 1874.]

WHEREAS, it would greatly tend to assist the progress of public works and other improvements now going on within the Dominion of Canada if facilities were offered to institutions and corporations incorporated without the Dominion of Canada for the purpose of lending moneys, to lend their money within the Dominion, and with that object it is expedient to confer on such institutions and corporations powers to contract, and also to hold as security lands within the Dominion: Therefore Her Majesty, by and with the advice and consent of the Senate and House of Commons of Canada, enacts as follows:—

1. It shall be lawful for any institution or corporation duly incorporated under the laws of the Parliament of Great Britain and Ireland, for the purpose of lending, on receiving a license from the Secretary of State authorizing it to carry on business within the Dominion of Canada, to transact any loaning business of any description whatsoever within the said Dominion of Canada, in its corporate name, except the business of banking, and to take and hold any mortgages of real estate, and any railway, municipal, or other bonds of any kind whatsoever, on the security of which it may lend its money at any rate of interest not exceeding the rate permissible, on such securities by the Acts incoporating similar Companies in the several Provinces of the Dominion, and whether the said bonds form a charge on real estate within the said Dominion or not, and also to hold such mortgages in its corporate name, and to sell and tranfer the same, and to hold and convey the title to real estate acquired as mortgages or charges: Provided such corporation shall sell or dispose of the real estate so acquired within five years from the time that the mortgage on the said real estate shall have become due and payable under the terms of the instrument creating such mortgage.

2. Every Company obtaining such license as aforesaid shall, before the commencement of such business, file in the office of the Secretary of each Province in which the Company proposes to do business, a certified copy of the charter, Act of Incorporation, or articles of association of such Company, and also a power of attorney to the agent or manager of such Company, in such Province, signed by the President or Managing Director and Secretary thereof, and verified as to its authenticity by the oath of the principal agent or manager of such Company in the Dominion, or by the oath of any person cognizant of the fact necessary for its verification, which power of attorney must expressly authorise such agent or manager as far as respects business done by such agent or manager within such Province to accept process in all suits and proceedings against such Company in the Province for any liabilites incurred by such Company therein, and must declare that service of process on such agent or manager for such liabilities shall be legal and binding on such Company to all intents and purposes whatever, and waiving all claims of error by reason of such service.

3. After such certified copy of the charter and such power of attorney are filed as aforesaid, any process in any suit or proceeding against such Company for any liability incurred in any Province may be served upon such manager or agent in the same manner as process may be served upon the proper officer of any Company incorporated in such Province, and all proceedings may be had thereupon to judgment and execution in the same manner as in proceedings in any civil suit in such Province.

4. Every Company obtaining such license as aforesaid shall forthwith give due notice thereof in the official Gazette and in at least one newspaper in the county, city or place where the principal manager or agent of such Company transacts the business thereof, and shall continue the publication thereof for the space of one calendar month, and the like notice shall be given when such Company shall cease or notify that they cease to carry on business within the Province.

5. The Secretary of State may, if he see fit, issue such license as aforesaid on being furnished with evidence of the due incorporation of the Company (applying for such license) under the laws of the Imperial Parliament of Great Britain and Ireland or of any foreign state, which evidence shall be a certified copy of the charter, Act of incorporation or articles of association of such Company and on being furnished with a power of Attorney from such Company to the person appointed to be the principal agent or manager of such Company within the Dominion, under the seal of such Company and signed by the President or Managing Director and Secretary thereof, and verified by the oath of an attesting witness, expressly authorizing such agent or manager to apply for such license and the fee to be paid by such Company on the issuing of such license shall be twenty dollars.

CHAP. XLII.

An Act relating to interest on moneys secured by mortgage of real estate.

Section.

Preamble.
1. No interest recoverable in certain cases, unless the mortgage contains a certain statement as to principal and interest.
2. No rate recoverable beyond that shewn in such statement.
3. No fine allowed on payments in arrear.

Section.

Proviso: for interest on arrears of interest.
4. Overcharge of fine or interest may be recovered back.
5. Mortgage may be discharged after five years on certain conditions.
6. Act to apply to mortgages made after 1st July, 1880.

[*Assented to 7th May*, 1880.]

WHEREAS it is expedient to make certain provisions concerning interest on moneys secured by mortgage of real estate: Therefore Her Majesty, by and with the advice and consent of the Senate and House of Commons of Canada, enacts as follows:

1. Whenever any principal money or interest secured by mortgage of real estate is by the same made payable on the sinking fund plan, or on any plan under which the payments of principal money and interest are blended, or on any plan which involves an allowance of interest on stipulated repayments, no interest whatever shall be chargeable, payable or recoverable, on any part of the principal money advanced, unless the mortgage contains a statement showing the amount of such principal money and the rate of interest chargeable thereon, calculated yearly or half-yearly, not in advance.

2. Whenever the rate of interest shown in the statement referred to in the next preceding section is less than the rate of interest which would be chargeable by virtue of any other provision, calculation or stipulation in the mortgage, no greater rate of interest shall be chargeable, payable or recoverable on the principal money advanced than the rate shewn in the said statement.

3. No fine or penalty or rate of interest shall be stipulated for, taken, reserved or exacted on any arrear of principal or interest which shall have the effect of increasing the charge on any such arrear beyond the rate of interest payable on principal money not in arrear: Provided always, that nothing in this section contained shall have the effect of prohibiting a contract for the payment of interest on arrears of interest or principal at any rate not greater than the rate payable on principal money not in arrear.

4. In case any sum is paid on account of any interest, fine or penalty not chargeable, payable or recoverable under the foregoing sections, such sums may be recovered back or deducted from any other interest, fine or penalty chargeable, payable or recoverable on the principal.

5. Whenever any principal money or interest secured by mortgage of real estate is not, under the terms of the mortgage, payable till a time more than five years after the date of the mortgage then in case at any time after the expiration of such five years, any person liable to pay or entitled to redeem the mortgage, tenders or pays to the person entitled to receive the money, the amount due for principal money, and interest to the time of payment as calculated under the foregoing sections, together with three months' further interest in lieu of notice, no further interest shall be chargeable, payable or recoverable at any time thereafter on the principal money or interest due under the mortgage.

6. This Act shall apply to all moneys secured by mortgage on real estate executed after the first day of July, in the year of our Lord one thousand eight hundred and eighty.

CAP. CLXIII.

An Act to authorize Corporations and Institutions incorporated out of Ontario to lend and invest moneys therein.

Section.
1. Certain Institutions incorporated by the Parliament of Great Britain or Canada may receive a license to carry on business in Ontario.
2. Property acquired to be re-sold within five years from acquisition.
3. Evidence whereon license may issue.

Section.
4. Fee for license.
5. Notice of Company being licensed.
6. Charter of Company and power of attorney to agent in Ontario to be filed with Provincial Secretary.
7. Service of process on the Company.

HER MAJESTY, by and with the advice and consent of the Legislative Assembly of the Province of Ontario, enacts as follows :—

1. Where any institution or corporation duly incorporated under the laws of the Parliament of Great Britain and Ireland, or of the Dominion of Canada, for the purpose of lending or investing moneys, is authorized by its statute, charter or instrument of incorporation to lend money in this Province, such institution or corporation may apply for and receive a license from the Provincial Secretary authorizing it to carry on business within Ontario, to transact any loaning business of any description whatever (except the business of Banking) within Ontario in its corporate name and to take and hold any mortgages of real estate, and any railway, municipal or other bonds of any kind whatsoever, and on the security of which it may lend its money, and whether the said bonds form a charge on real estate within the said Province or not, and also to hold such mortgages in its corporate name, and to sell and transfer the same at its pleasure, and in all respects to have and enjoy the same powers and privileges with regard to lending its moneys and transacting its business within the said Province as a private individual might have and enjoy, so far as is within the legislative authority of this Province. 39 V. c. 27, s. 1.

2. Such corporation shall sell or dispose of any real estate to which it may acquire a title in fee simple by foreclosure or by the release of the equity of redemption therein, within five years from the date of such foreclosure, and any real estate which is not within the said period disposed of as hereinbefore required shall be forfeited to and become vested in the Crown. 39 V. c. 27, s. 1.

2. The Provincial Secretary may, if he sees fit, issue such license as aforesaid on being furnished with evidence of the due incorporation of the Company applying for such license under the laws of the Imperial Parliament of Great Britain and Ireland, or of the Dominion of Canada, which evidence shall be a certified copy of the charter, Act of incorporation, or articles of association of such Company, and on being furnished with a power of attorney from such Company to the person appointed to be the principal Manager or Agent of such Company within this Province, under the seal of such Company, and signed by the President or Managing Director and Secretary thereof, and verified by the oath of an attesting witness expressly authorizing such Manager or Agent to apply for such license. 39 V. c. 27, s. 5.

4. The fee to be paid by such Company on the issuing of such license, shall be such sum as may be fixed by the Lieutenant-Governor in Council. 39 V. c. 27, s. 5.

5. Every Company obtaining such license as aforesaid shall forthwith give due notice thereof in the *Ontario Gazette* and in at least one newspaper in the County, City or place where the principal Manager or Agent of such Company in the Province transacts the business thereof, for the space of one calendar month, and the like notice shall be given when such Company ceases or notifies that it ceases to carry on business within the Province. 39 V. 3. 27, s. 4.

6. Every Company obtaining such license as aforesaid shall, before the commencement of such business, file in the office of the Provincial Secretary a certified copy of the charter, Act of incorporation, or articles of association of such Company, and also a power of attorney to the Principal Manager or Agent of such Company in the Province of Ontario, signed by the President or Managing Director and Secretary thereof, and verified as to its authenticity by the statutory declaration of the principal Manager or Agent of such Company, or of any person cognizant of the facts necessary for its verification, which power of attorney shall expressly authorize such Manager or Agent, as far as respects business done by such Manager or Agent within the said Province, to accept process in all suits and proceedings against such Company in the Province for any liabilities incurred by such Company therein, and shall declare that service of process on such Manager or Agent for such liabilities shall be legal and binding on such Company to all intents and purposes whatever, and waiving all claims of error by reason of such service. 39 V. c. 27, s. 2.

7. After such certified copy of the charter and such power of attorney are filed as aforesaid, any process in any suit or proceeding against such Company for any liability incurred in the Province may be served upon such Manager or Agent in the same manner as process may be served upon the proper officer of any Company incorporated in the Province, and all proceedings may be had thereupon to judgment and execution in the same manner as in proceedings in any civil suits in the Province. 39 V. c. 27, s. 3.

CHAP. CLXIV.

An Act respecting Building Societies.

Section.
1. Interpretation clause; Society; Rules; Real Estate; Securities.
2. Societies how incorporated. Powers of Society. In forming a Society under this Act, the words "Building" or "Society" may be omitted.
3. Members of Society may make rules, etc., impose fines, etc.
4. Society by rule to declare objects of Society and declare how moneys to be applied.
5. Moneys not to be misapplied under penalties.
6. Rules to be recorded in a book.
7. Entry of rules in books, notice to members.
8. Examined copy of rules entered in book to be evidence.
9. Rules not to be removed by certiorari.
10. Rules entered in book not to be altered except at a general meeting. Quorum of members for altering by-laws.
11. Rules to specify time and place for holding meeting.
12. Society from time to time to elect Directors.
13. Powers of Directors to be declared by rules.
14. Powers of Directors in certain cases to be recorded in books of Society.
15. Concurrence of majority of Directors necessary.
16. Acts of Directors to be binding.
17. Proceedings of Directors to be entered in books of Society.
18. Directors to appoint officers.
19. Persons in service of Society to furnish security.
20. Society may take and hold real estate mortgaged by Society for certain purposes.
21. Society may purchase and sell and lend on certain securities.
22. May forfeit shares. May expel members. May sue for amount of shares.
23. May sue in Division Court.
24. Except in cases of withdrawal, members not to receive profits on share till value of same realized.
25. Society may receive bonus in addition to interest.
26. Society may sell real estate mortgaged in certain cases.
27. Representatives of officers of Society to deliver over papers and moneys after demand.
28. Property of Society vested in President and Treasurer.
29. President and Treasurer may bring and defend suits.

Section.
30. Suits not to abate by death or removal from office.
31. President and Directors relieved from responsibility.
32. Rules to provide that Secretary shall furnish annual statement of funds.
33. Secretary's statement to be attested by auditors.
34. Act extends to aliens, females and bodies corporate.
35. Member or investor in Building Society may nominate a successor; disposition of funds of intestate member; when mistaken payments valid as against the Society.
36. Disposition of proceeds of sale under mortgages.
37. Rights of execution creditors.
38. Preamble; 9 V. c. 90; Permanent Societies having fulfilled certain conditions, declared to be within this Act; and their subscribers to be members; 9 V. c. 90, s 5, C.S.U.C. c. 53, s. 13; evidence of membership.
39. How by-laws of Permanent Societies may be passed or amended.
40. Members may vote by proxy.
41. Amount to which Societies may borrow money, limited.
42. Shareholder whose share is paid up, may receive or invest the amount. As to paid up shares in full. As to borrowing money.
43. Advances on security of investing on unadvanced shares.
44. Directors may close subscription of shares.
45. Members may determine at a general or special meeting to close subscription of shares.
46. Shares to be immediately advanced excepted.
47. Liability of shareholders limited.
48. Holding real estate.
49. Society not bound to see to execution of trusts or application of moneys paid on receipt, etc.
50. Society may lend money to others than its members ; proviso as to rules affecting borrowers.
51. Repayment and recovery of money advanced and interest thereon,
52. Power to borrow money on debentures. Not to exceed their mortgages ; liabilities and principal on mortgages, how estimated. Deductions to be made in estimating the paid-up capital.
53. Reserve Fund.
54. Amount and form of debentures.
55. Notice of intention of Society to avail itself of the increased borrowing powers

Building Societies. Cap. 164. 97

Section.	Section.
56. Directors may make or amend by-laws, etc. Confirmation by shareholders. Alteration at general meeting.	66. Auditors and directors, their appointment, remuneration, etc. Scale of votes.
57. Powers of Directors of Society.	67. Annual statement of assets and liabilities etc., to be transmitted to Provincial Treasurer.
58. Powers of Directors.	
59. By-laws and documents of Society, when authentic and *prima facie* evidence.	68. Statement to be attested on oath, and to be published. Penalty for non-transmission.
60. Amalgamation of Societies.	
61. Joint agreement between Directors proposing to amalgamate, &c.	69. In case of non-transmission, or bad condition of the Society, their power to borrow may be stayed.
62. To be submitted to shareholders of each Society for consideration.	70. Business may be stayed by the Provincial Treasurer on examination and report of false statement, or bad condition or refusal to show books.
63. Vote by ballot to be taken. Agreement, if adopted, to be filed with Provincial Secretary.	
64. Upon completion of consolidation, the new corporation to possess rights, powers, etc., and be subject to duties, etc., of each of united societies.	71. Notice by Treasurer of intent to stay business of Society.
	72. Power to change name.
	73. Notice of intent to change name.
	74. Procedure on change of name.
65. All property and rights vested in new corporation without further act or deed. Proviso, as to rights of creditors, etc., of either of corporations. Proviso as to actions against.	75. Confirmation of all acts done under 37 V. c. 50. (*Dom.*) Changes of name confirmed.
	76. To what Societies this Act applies.

HER MAJESTY, by and with the advice and consent of the Legislative Assembly of the Province of Ontario enacts as follows:—

1. In the construction of this Act,—

(1.) "Society" shall include and mean Building Society and Institution established under the provisions and authority of this Act, or any former Act respecting Building Societies,

(2.) "Rules" shall include rules, orders, by-laws, and regulations;

(3.) "Real Estate" shall extend and apply to immovable estate and property generally; and

(4.) "Securities" shall extend and apply to privileges, mortgages (equitable as well as legal), and incumbrances upon real and immovable estate, as well as to other rights and privileges upon personal estate and property. C. S. U. C. c. 53, s. 35.

2. In case any twenty or more persons agree to constitute themselves a Building Society, and execute, under their respective hands and seals, a declaration to that effect, and deposit the same with the Clerk of the Peace in the County in which they reside (who for receiving such deposit shall be entitled to a fee of fifty cents), such persons, and such other persons as afterwards become members of the Society, and their several and respective executors, administrators and assigns, shall be a corporation, body corporate and politic, as a Building Society, by the name and style mentioned in such declaration, for raising by monthly or other periodical subscriptions of the several members of the Society, in shares not exceeding the value of four hundred dollars for each share (and in subsciptions not exceeding four dollars per month for each share), a stock or fund to enable each member to receive out of the funds of the Society the amount or value of his shares therein, for the purpose of erecting or purchasing one or

7

more dwelling house or houses, or other freehold or leashold estate, or for any other purpose whatsover, and the amount or value of such shares shall be secured to the Society by mortgage or otherwise on any real estate belonging to the member at the time of his borrowing money from the Society, or on any other real estate acquired by such member, until the amount or value of his shares, with interest thereon, have been fully paid, together with all fines or liabilities incurred in respect thereof. C. S. U. C. c. 53, s. 1.

2. In constituting a Building Society under this Act it shall not be necessary that the declaration of agreement to that effect shall refer to, or use the word "Building" or the word "Society," or that the body incorporated under such Act be designated by use of either of either of such words. 39 V. c. 32, s. 28.

3. The several members of the Society may from time to time assemble together, and make such proper rules for the Government of the same as the majority of members so assembled deem meet, so as such rules are not repugnant to the provisions of this Act, or any other law in force in Ontario; and they may impose and inflict such reasonable fines, penalties and forfeitures upon the several members of the Society infringing such rules as the majority of the members think fit, and to be respectively paid to such uses, for the benefit of the Society, as the Society by such rules direct; and they may also from time to time amend or rescind such rules, and make new rules in lieu thereof, under such restrictions as are in this Act contained. C. S. U. C. c. 53, s. 2.

4. Every such Society shall, in or by one or more of their rules, declare the objects for which the Society is intended to be established, and thereby direct the purposes to which the money from time to time subscribed to received by and belonging to the Society, shall be appropriated, and in what shares or proportions and under what circumstances any member of the Society, or other person, may become entitled to the same or any part thereof. C. S. U. C. c. 53, s. 11.

5. All such rules shall be complied with and enforced; and the moneys so subscribed to, received by or belonging to the Society, shall not be diverted or misapplied either by the Treasurer or Directors, or any other officer or member of the Society entrusted therewith, under such penalty or forfeiture as the Society by any rule inflicts for the offence. C. S. U. C. c. 53, s. 12.

6. The rules for the mangement of every such Society shall be recorded in a book to be kept for that purpose, and such book shall be open at all seasonable times for the inspection of the members. C. S. U. C. c. 53, s. 13.

7. The rules so recorded shall be binding on the several members and officers of the Society, and the several contributors thereto, and their representatives, and they shall be deemed to have full notice thereof by such record. C. S. U. C. c. 53, s. 14.

8. The entry of the rules in the books of the Society, or a true copy of the same, examined with the original and proved to be a true copy, shall be received as evidence thereof. C. S. U. C. c. 53, s. 15.

9. Such rules shall not, by *certiorari* or other legal process, be removed into any of Her Majesty's Courts of record. C. S. U. C. c. 53, s. 16.

10. No rule so recorded as aforesaid shall be altered or rescinded, unless at a general meeting of the members, convened by public notice written or printed, signed by the Secretary or President of the Society in pursuance of a requisition for that purpose made by not less than fifteen of the members, stating the objects for which the meeting is called, and addressed to the President and Directors ; and each member of the Society shall, within fifteen days after such requisition, be notified through the Post Office of the proposed alterations.

2. It shall be lawful at any general meeting convened under this section for two-thirds of the shareholders there present in person, or by proxy, representing not less than one-half the amount paid up on investing shares, to alter, repeal or amend any of the rules or by-laws of such Society. C. S. U. C. c. 53, s. 17; 29 V. c. 38, S. 5.

11. The rules of the Society shall specify the place or places at which it is intended that the Society shall hold its meetings, and shall contain provisions with respect to the powers and duties of the members at large, and of the officers appointed for the management of its affairs. C. S. U. C. c. 53, s. 18.

12. Every such Society shall, from time to time, elect and appoint any number of the members of the Society to be a Board of Directors, the number and qualification thereof to be declared in the rules of the Society, and may delegate to such Directors all or any of the powers given by this Act to be executed. C. S. U. C. c. 53, s. 5.

13. The powers of the Directors shall be declared by the rules of the Society, and they shall continue to act during the time appointed by such rules. C. S. U. C. c. 53, s. 6.

14. In case Directors are appointed for any particular purpose, the powers delegated to them shall be reduced to writing and entered in a book by the Secretary or Clerk of the Society. C. S. U. C. c. 53, s. 7.

15. The Directors shall choose a President and Vice-President, and they shall in all things delegated to them act for and in the name of such Society, and the concurrence of a majority of the Directors present at any meeting shall at all times be necessary in any act of the Board. C. S. U. C. c. 53, s. 8.

16. All acts and orders of such Directors, under the powers delegated to them, shall have the like force and effect as the acts and orders of the Society at a general meeting. C. S. U. C. c. 53, s. 9.

17. The transactions of the Directors shall be entered in a book belonging to the Society, and shall at all times be subject to the review, allowance and disallowance of the Society, in such manner and form as the Society by their general rules direct and appoint. C. S. U. C. c. 53, s. 10.

18. The Directors shall from time to time, at any of their usual meetings, appoint such persons as they think proper to be officers of the Society, grant such salaries and emoluments as they deem fit, and pay the necessary expenses attending the management of the Society; and shall from time to time when necessary elect such persons as may be necessary for the purposes of the Society, for the time and for the purpose expressed in the rules of the Society, and may from time to time discharge such persons, and appoint others in the room of those who vacate, die or are discharged. C. S. U. C. c. 53, s. 19.

19. Every officer or other person appointed to any office in anywise concerning the receipt of money shall furnish security to the satisfaction of the Directors for the just and faithful execution of the duties of his office according to the Rules of the Society, and any person entrusted with the performance of any other service may be repaired by the Directors to furnish similar security. 39 V. c. 32, s. 11.

20. Every such Society may take and hold any real estate, or securities thereon, *bona fide* mortgaged or assigned to it, either to secure the payment of the shares subscribed for by its members or to secure the payment of any loans or advances made by, or debts due to the Society, and may proceed on such mortgages, assignments or other securities, for the recovery of the moneys thereby secured, either at Law or in Equity or otherwise, and generally may pursue the same course, exercise the same powers, and take and use the same remedies to enforce the payment of any debt or demand due to the Society, as any person or body corporate may by law take or use for a like purpose. C. S. U. C. c. 53, s. 21.

21. Any such Society may purchase mortgages upon real estate, debentures of Municipal Corporations, or of Public School Corporations, or Dominion or Provincial stock or securities; and may re-sell any such securities as to it seems advisable, and for that purpose may execute such assignments or other instruments as may be necessary for carrying the same into effect; and any such Society may also, in conformity with the laws of Canada, make advances to any person or persons or body corporate upon any of the above mentioned securities at such lawful rates of discount or interest as may be agreed upon. 39 V. c. 32, s. 4. [*See also* 37 V. c. 50, s. 4 (D).]

22. Every such Society may declare forfeited to the Society the shares of any member who is in default, or who neglects to pay the number of instalments or monthly subscriptions fixed by any stipulation or by-law, and may expel such member from the Society, and the Secretary shall make a minute of such forfeiture and expulsion in the books of the Society; or instead of such forfeiture and expulsion, the Society may recover the arrears by an action of debt. C. S. U. C. c. 53, s. 23.

23. If the amount in arrear does not exceed forty dollars, the action may be brought in the Division Court of the division wherein the office of the Society is kept. C. S. U. C. c. 53, s. 24.

24. Except in the case of the withdrawal of a member, according to the rules of the Society then in force, no member shall receive, or be entitled to receive, from the funds of the Society any interest or dividend by way of annual or other periodical profit upon any share in the Society until the amount or value of his share has been realized. C. S. U. C. c. 53, s. 3.

25. Every such Society may, besides interest, receive from any member a bonus on any share for the privilege of receiving the same in advance prior to the same being realized. C. S. U. C. c. 53, s. 4.

26. Wherever any such Society has received from a shareholder an assignment, mortgage or transfer of any real estate to secure the payment of any advances, and containing an authority to such Society to sell the real estate in case of non-payment of any stipulated number of instalments or sum of money, and to apply the proceeds of such sale to the payment of the advances, interest and other charges due to the Society, such stipulations and agreements shall be valid and binding, and the Society may cause the same to be enforced either by foreclosure or by an action or proceeding in either of Her Majesty's Superior Courts of Common Law; and in such action the venue shall be laid in the County in which the lands lie, and the action may be brought in the names of the President and Treasurer of the Society, describing them as such, or in the corporate name of the Society. C.S.U.C. c. 53, s. 25.

27. If any person appointed to an office by the Society, and being entrusted with and having in his possession, by virtue of his office, any moneys or effects belonging to the Society, or any deeds or securities relating thereto, dies or becomes bankrupt or insolvent, his legal representative, or other person having a legal right, shall, within fifteen days after demand made by the order of the Directors of the Society, or the major part of them, assembled at any meeting thereof, deliver over all things belonging to the Society to such persons as the Directors appoint. C. S. U. C. c. 53, s. 26.

28. All real and personal estate, property and effects, and all titles, securities, instruments and evidences, and all rights and claims of or belonging to the Society, shall be vested in the President and Treasurer and their successors in office for the time being, for the use of the Society and the respective members thereof, according to their respective claims and interests, and shall, for all purposes of bringing or defending actions or suits, be deemed to be, and shall be stated to be, the property of the President and Treasurer, in the proper names of the President and Treasurer for the time being. C. S. U. C. c. 53, s. 27.

29. The President and Treasurer may bring or defend any action, suit or prosecution, respecting any property, right or claim aforesaid, and may sue and be sued, plead and be impleaded in their proper names as President and Treasurer of the Society without other description. C. S. U. C. c. 53, s. 28.

30. No such suit, action or prosecution shall be discontinued or abated by the death or removal from office of the President or Treasurer, but shall continue in their names; and the succeeding President and Treasurer shall have the same rights and liabilities, and shall pay or receive like costs as if the action, suit or prosecution had been commenced or been defended in their names, for the benefit of or to be satisfied out of the funds of the Society. C. S. U. C. c. 53, s. 29.

31. The President, Vice-President and Directors of the Society, in their private capacity, shall be exonerated from all responsibility in relation to the liabilities of the Society. C. S. U. C. c. 53, s. 31.

32. The rules of the Society shall provide that the Treasurer or other principal officer thereof shall, once at least in every year, prepare a general statement of the funds and effects of or belonging to the Society, specifying in whose custody or possession such funds or effects are then remaining, together with an account of all sums of money received or expended by or on account of the Society since the publication of the preceding periodical statement. C. S. U. C. c. 53, s. 32.

33. Every such periodical statement shall be attested by two or more members of the Society, not being Directors, appointed Auditors for that purpose, and shall be countersigned by the Secretary or Clerk of the Society, and every member shall be entitled to receive from the Society without charge a copy of such periodical statement. C. S. U. C. c. 53, s. 33.

34. This Act shall for all purposes extend to aliens, denizens and females; and co-partners and corporate bodies may hold shares in any Society incorporated under the provisions of this Act, in the same manner as single individuals; and this Act shall be construed in the most beneficial manner for promoting the ends thereby intended. C. S. U. C. c. 53, s. 34.

35. A member of, or investor in, or depositor with any Building Society having a sum of money in the funds thereof not exceeding two hundred dollars, may from time to time nominate any person or persons (such person or persons being within the Statute of Distributions) as successor or successors at death of such member or depositor, provided that such nomination is made in writing, and duly deposited with the Secretary or Manager of the Society; and upon receiving a statutory declaration of the death of the nominator, the Society shall substitute the name of the nominee on its books in the place of the nominator, or may immediately pay to the nominee the amount due to the deceased member or depositor.

2. If any member, investor or depositor with the Society having in the funds thereof a sum of money not exceeding two hundred dollars, dies intestate and without making any such nomination, then the amount due shall be paid to the person who appears to the Society to be entitled under the Statute of Distributions to receive the same without taking out letters of administration, upon the Society receiving a statutory declaration of death and intestacy, and that the person so claiming is entitled, as aforesaid.

3. Wherever the Society, after the decease of any member or depositor, has paid any such sum of money to the person who at the time appeared to be entitled to the effects of the deceased, under the belief that he died intestate without having appointed any nominee, the payment shall be valid and effectual with respect to any demand from any other person as next of kin or as the lawful representative of such deceased member or depositor against the funds of the Society;

but nevertheless, such next of kin or representative shall have his lawful remedy for the amount of such payment as aforesaid against the person who has received the same. 38 V. c. 18, s. 6.

86. In case of a sale of property mortgaged to the Society, any surplus not exceeding two hundred dollars over and above the amount due to the said Society, and costs, derived from sale under power of sale of any property mortgaged to the said Society, and over and above any claim of an execution creditor as hereinafter provided, where the mortgagor or his assigns died intestate, shall be and is hereby declared to be personal property, whether such sale took place before or after the death of the mortgagor or person entitled to the equity of redemption; except that, in all such cases, the widow of the intestate shall be entitled to a third of such surplus absolutely in satisfaction of her dower, and the Society shall have the like powers as to paying such surplus over without probate, or letters of administration, to such widow and next of kin, according to their respective interests, as is conferred by the thirty-fifth section of this Act upon the Society in case of depositors and members dying intestate. 38 V. c. 18, s. 7.

87. Nothing in the preceding section shall prejudice the right of any execution creditor in respect of any right or lien he may have in respect of such surplus or any portion thereof to the amount of the execution in the hands of the Sheriff. 38 V. c. 18, s. 8.

PERMANENT BUILDING SOCIETIES.

88. Whereas under the Act passed in the ninth year of Her Majesty's reign, entitled *An Act to encourage the establishment of certain Societies, commonly called Building Societies,* in that part of the Province of Canada formerly constituting Upper Canada, certain Building Societies have been established called Permanent Building Societies, which have in a great measure superseded those Societies called Terminating Building Societies, and are conducted on more certain and equitable principles than the said Terminating Building Societies, by enabling persons to become members thereof at any time for investment therein, or to obtain the advance of their shares or share by giving security therefor, and to fix and determine with the said Society the time when and amount at which such members shall repay such advanced share or shares, and obtain the release of the said security, without being liable to the contingency of losses or profits in the business of the said Society: And whereas doubts had arisen as to whether such Permanent Building Societies were within the meaning and intention of the said recited Act; Therefore, any Permanent Building Society established under the said hereinbefore recited Act, and the Acts amending the same or under the fifty-third chapter of the Consolidated Statutes for Upper Canada, or hereafter established under this Act, and conducted on the principle hereinbefore mentioned, which has fulfilled and observed or which fulfils and observes all the conditions necessary to be fulfilled and observed for the establishment of a Building Society under the said recited Acts, or under this Act (as the case may be), shall be and the same is hereby declared to be and to have been a Building Society within the meaning and intention of the said recited Acts and of this Act, and to be and to have been entitled to all the powers, benefits and advantages of the said recited Acts and of this Act; and any person or persons who have signed the rules and regulations of any such Building Society entered and recorded in a book, as in the fifth section of the said recited Act, passed in the ninth year of Her Majesty's reign, and in the thirteenth section of the fifty-third chapter of the Consolidated Statutes for Upper Canada and in the sixth section of this Act is required, and have subscribed his or their name or names as a shareholder or shareholders for one or more shares, shall, from the time of such signature and subscription, be and be deemed to have been a member or members of such Building Society; and the production of the book containing the rules for the management of such Society, kept as aforesaid signed by such person and duly witnessed, shall, at all times and for all purposes, be sufficient evidence of membership in such Building Society. C. S. U. C. c. 53, s. 36.

39. Any Permanent Building Society may alter, amend, repeal or create any regulation, rule or by-law for the working of the said Society, at a public meeting of the members of such Society, convened as is directed by the tenth section of this Act, and at which public meeting one-third of the members of the said Society, entitled to vote by the rules of the said Society, and representing not less than two-thirds of the unadvanced stock of such Society, do, either in writing under their hand or by a vote at such meeting, concur in such alteration, amendment or repeal of such regulation, rule or by-law, or in the creation of any new rule, regulation or by-law. C. S. U. C. c. 53, s. 37.

40. Any member entitled to vote at any meeting of any Permanent Building Society, held under the last preceding section, may be represented and vote at such meeting by his proxy such proxy being a member of such meeting. 29 V. c. 38, s. 4.

41. Except as provided in, and subject to, the fifty-second to fifty-fifth sections, every such Society, by its rules, regulations and by-laws authorized to borrow money, shall not borrow, receive, take or retain, or otherwise than in stock and shares in such Society, from any person or persons, any greater sum than three-fourths of the amount of capital actually paid in on unadvanced shares, and invested in real securities by such Society; and the paid in and subscribed capital of the Society shall be liable for the amount so borrowed, received or taken by any Society. C. S. U. C. c. 53, s. 38.

42. When any share or shares in any Society have been fully paid up according to the rules of the Society, or have become due and payable to the holder thereof, then and in such case the holder of such share or shares may either withdraw the amount of his share or shares from the said Society, according to the rules and regulations thereof, or invest the amount of his said share or shares in the Society, and receive therefrom periodically such proportion of the profits made by such Society as may be provided for by a by-law to be passed for the purpose; and the amount of such share or shares so invested shall become fixed and permanent capital or shares in the said Society, not withdrawable therefrom, but transferable the same manner as other shares in the said Society.

2. Any share or shares may, at any time, be paid up in full and capitalized at once, as permanent stock, and any such share or shares heretofore paid in full, of in part, shall be as valid as if the same had been paid by periodical or other subscription.

3. No such Society hereafter to be established shall borrow money or receive deposits until not less than one hundred thousand dollars of stock has been subscribed, and not less than forty thousand dollars has been actually paid thereon. C. S. U. C. c. 53, s. 39 : 29 V. c. 38, s. 7.

43. Such Society may advance to members on the security of investing on unadvanced shares in the said Society, and may receive and take from any person or persons, or bodies corporate, any real or personal security of any nature or kind whatever as collateral security for any advance made to members of the Society. C.S.U.C. c. 53, s. 40.

44. The Directors of any such Society at any time, and from time as they may think expedient may, by resolution, close for any specified time, or until further order, the subscription of shares to be held for investment in the Society, and thereafter, until the expiration of such specified time, or until such further order, no new shares shall be subscribed for investment in the Society. Such new issue of shares shall be allotted to the then existing shareholders *pro rata*, as nearly as possible without fractions ; but in case such new shares are not taken up within thirty days, then the said shares, or remaining shares, shall be sold, and any premium thereon applied to the general benefit of the Society. 29 V, c, 38, s. 1.

45. The members entitled to vote at any time, may by resolution to be passed at any special or general meeting, (for which meeting notice of such intended resolution shall be duly given,according to the tenth section of this Act,) determine that no new shares shall thereafter be subscribed for investment in any such Society ; and thereafter no new shares for invesment shall at any time be subscribed therein, and the subscription of such shares shall cease for ever. 29 V. c. 38, s. 2.

46. Nothing done under the two next preceding clauses of this Act shall have the effect of preventing any such Society from creating as it otherwise might, any share or shares to be immediately advanced to the subscriber or subscribers thereof, or of preventing any person from subscribing, as he otherwise might, for any share or shares, in order immediately to obtain the advance thereof from such Society by giving security therefor. 29 V. c. 38, s. 3.

47. No shareholder of any such Society shall be liable for or charged with the payment of any debt or demand due by the Society, beyond the extent of his shares in the capital of the Society not then paid up. 39 V., c. 32, s.2. [*See also* 37 V., c. 50, s. 2 (D).]

48. Any society may hold absolutely real estate for the purposes of its place of business, not exceeding the annual value of six thousand dollars. C. S. U. C. c. 53, s. 41.

49. Such Society shall not be bound to see to the execution of any trust, whether expressed, implied or constructive, to which any share or shares of its stock, or to which any deposit or any other moneys payable by or in the hands of any such Society, may be subject; and the receipt of the party or parties in whose name any such share or shares or moneys stand in the books of the Society, shall, from time to time, be sufficient discharge to the Society for any payment of any kind made in respect of such share or shares or moneys, notwithstanding any trust to which the same may then be subject, and whether or not such Society has had notice of such trust; and the Society shall not be bound to see to the application of the money paid upon such receipt. 39 V., c. 32, s. 10. [*See also* 37 V., c. 50, s. 10 (D).]

50. Any such Society may lend money in conformity with the laws of Canada and with the laws authorizing the establishment of Building Societies in Ontario, and the by-laws of such Society, to any person or persons or body corporate, at such lawful rates of interest as may be agreed upon, without requiring any of such borrowers to become subscribers to the stock or members of the said Society : but all borrowers from any such Society shall be subject to all the rules of such Society in force at the time of their becoming borrowers, but not to any other rules. 39 V., c. 32, s.3. [*See also* 37 V., c. 50, s. 3 (D).]

51. The principal money so advanced on mortgages may be repaid by means of a sinking fund of not less than two per centum per annum, within such time as the Society directs and appoints, and is specified in the mortgage or assignment of mortgage to be made of such real estate, and by means of such revenues, rates, rents, tolls or profits as hereinafter mentioned; and the Society may do all acts that may be necessary for advancing money, and for recovering and obtaining repayment thereof, and for enforcing payment of all interest accruing therefrom, or any conditions attached to such advance or any forfeiture consequent on the non-payment thereof, and give all necessary and proper receipts, acquittances and discharges for the same, and do, authorize and exercise all acts and powers whatsoever requisite or expedient to be done or exercised in relation to the said purposes. 39 V., c. 32, s 5. [*See also* 37 V. c. 50, s. 5 (D).]

52. The Board of Directors of any such Society having a paid-up capital of not less than two hundred thousand dollars in fixed and permanent stock not liable to be withdrawn therefrom, may issue debentures of such Society to such an amount as, with all other liabilities of such Society, will be equal to double the amount of the capitalized fixed and permanent stock, not liable to be withdrawn therefrom, and the reserve fund of such Society. 39 V., c. 32, s. 6 ; 40 V.. c. 22, s. 1.

2. The total liabilities of such Society shall not at any time exceed the amount of principal remaining unpaid on the mortgages at such time held by such Society ; and in estimating the liabilities of such Society, the amount of cash actually in the hands of such Society, or deposited in any chartered bank, shall be deducted therefrom ; and in ascertaining the principal remaining unpaid on the mortgages held by any such Society, it shall be incumbent upon such Society to compute or discount such mortgages at rates of interest at least equal to the rates which they respectively bear or were originally calculated to yield. 40 V., c. 22, s. 1.

8. All loans or advances by any Society, to its shareholders upon the security of their stock, shall be deducted from the amount of paid-up capital upon which such Society is authorized to borrow. 40 V., c. 22, s. 1. [*See also* 37 V., c. 50, s. 6 (D).]

53. The reserve fund of any Society shall consist of surplus profits and assets, after full and ample provision has been made for all bad and doubtful debts, and other known contingent deductions. 40 V., c. 22, s. 2.

54. The debentures of such Society shall be for such sums, not being less than one hundred dollars, and in such currency as the Board of Directors may deem advisable, and shall be payable not less than one year from the issue thereof at such place as may be therein mentioned, and may be in the form of the Schedule to this Act, or to the like effect. 39 V., c. 32, s. 6, *part*, and s. 7. [*See also* 37 V., c. 50, s. 6 (D).]

55. In case any Society which has heretofore issued debentures under the Act passed in the thirty-ninth year of Her Majesty's reign, and chaptered thirty-two, desires to avail itself of the increased borrowing powers hereinbefore conferred, it shall be the duty of the Board of Directors of such Society, to leave at the place where such debentures are payable, a copy of the fifty-second to fifty-fifth sections inclusive of this Act, and a printed notice directed to the holders of such debentures, that such Society intends to avail itself of the provisions of said sections, and thereupon any such debenture holder shall at any time within six months after the leaving of such notice, as aforesaid, have the right after giving six months' notice in writing, to demand, and on presentation of his debentures and coupons, to receive payment of such debentures with interest up to the time of payment—such notice in writing to be left, and presentation for payment to be made at the place where such debentures are payable. 40 V., c. 22, s. 3.

56. The Directors of any Permanent Building Society incorporated under this Act, or under any other Act respecting Building Societies within the legislative authority of the Legislature of this Province, may from time to time alter, amend, repeal or create any regulation, rule or by-law for the working of any such Society.

2. Such action of the Directors shall not have a binding force until confirmed at a general meeting of the shareholders of the Society upon a vote of two-thirds of the capital stock represented at such meeting, - notice being given of the proposed changes, in the notice calling the meeting.

3. At such general meeting the shareholders may, by a like vote, alter or amend such proposed regulations, rules or by-laws, and may confirm the same as so altered and amended. 39 V. c. 32, s. 1. [*See also* 37 V. c. 50, s. 1 (D).]

57. The President, Vice-President and Directors of any Permanant Building Society, incorporated as aforesaid, shall have and exercise the powers, privileges and authorities set forth and vested in them by this Act and any other Act regulating such Society, subject to the rules or by-laws of such Society; and they shall be subject to and be governed by such rules, regulations and provisions as are herein contained with respect thereto and by the by-laws of such Society; and the Directors shall and may lawfully exercise all the powers of such Society, except as to such matters as are directed by law to be transacted by a general meeting of such Society. 39 V. c. 32, s. 8, *first part.* [*See also* 37 V. c. 50, s. 8 (D).]

58. The Directors may use and affix, or may cause to be used and affixed, the seal of such Society to any document or paper which in their judgment may require the same; they may make and enforce the calls upon the shares of the respective shareholders; they may declare the forfeiture of all shares on which such calls are not paid; they may make any payments and advances of money they may deem expedient which are authorized to be made by or on behalf of such Society, and enter into all contracts for the execution of the purposes of such Society, and for all other matters necessary for the transaction of its affairs; they may generally deal with, treat, sell and dispose of the lands, property and effects of such Society, for the time being, in such manner as they deem expedient and conducive to the benefit of such Society, as if the same lands, property and effects were held and owned according to the tenure and subject to the liabilities, if any, from time to time affecting the same, not by a body corporate, but by any of Her Majesty's subjects being of full age: they may do and authorize, assent to or adopt, all acts required for the due exercise of any further powers and authorities which may hereafter be at any time granted to such Society by the Legislature for the performance and fulfilment of any conditions or provisions from time to time prescribed by the Legislature in giving such further powers and authorities, or in altering or repealing the same respectively or any of them. 39 V. c. 32, s. 8, *last part.* [*See also* 37 V. c. 50, s. 8 (D).]

59. All by-laws of any such Society shall be reduced to writing, and shall have affixed thereto the common seal of the Society, and any copy or extract therefrom, certified under the signature of the Secretary or Manager, shall be evidence in all civil Courts of Justice in Ontario of such by-laws or extracts from them, and that the same were duly made and are in force; and in any civil action or proceeding at Law or in Equity it shall not be necessary to give any evidence to prove the seal of such Society, and all documents purporting to be sealed with the seal of any such Society, attested by the President, Treasurer or Manager thereof, shall be held *prima facie* to have been duly sealed with the seal of such Society. 39 V. c. 32, s. 9. [*See also* 37 V. c. 50, s. 9 (D).]

60. Any Permanent Building Society incorporated as aforesaid may unite, amalgamate and consolidate its stock, property, business and franchises with the stock, property, business and franchises of any other Building, Saving or Loan Society, incorporated or chartered as aforesaid, and may enter into all contracts and agreements therewith, necessary to such union and amalgamation. 39 V. c. 32, s. 12.

61. The Directors of the two Societies proposing to so amalgamate or consolidate as aforesaid, may enter into a joint agreement, under the corporate seals of each of the said Corporations, for the amalgamation and consolidation of the said Corporations, prescribing the terms and conditions thereof, the mode of carrying the same into effect, the name of the new Corporation, the number of the Directors and other officers thereof, and who shall be the first Directors and officers thereof and their places of residence, the number of shares of the capital stock, the amount of par value of each share, and the manner of converting the capital stock of each of the said Corporations into that of the new Corporation, and how, and when, and for how long Directors and other officers of such new Corporations shall be elected, and when elections shall be held,—with such other details as they deem necessary to perfect such new organization and the consolidation and amalgamation of the said Corporations, and the after management and working thereof. 39 V. c. 32, s. 13.

62. Such agreement shall be submitted to the shareholders of each of the said Societies at a meeting thereof to be held separately for the purpose of taking the same into consideration; notice of the time and place of such meetings and the object thereof shall be given by written or printed notices, addressed to each shareholder of the said Societies respectively at his last known post office address or place of residence, and also by a general notice to be published in a newspaper published at the chief place of business of such Societies once a week for two successive weeks. 39 V. c. 32, s. 14, *first part*.

63. At such meetings of shareholders, such agreement shall be considered, and a vote by ballot taken for the adoption or rejection of the same, and each share shall entitle the holder thereof to one vote, and the said ballots shall be cast in person or by proxy; and if two-thirds of the votes of all the shareholders of such Corporations are for the adoption of such agreement, then that fact shall be certified upon the said agreement by the Secretary of each of such Corporations under the corporate seals thereof; and if the said agreement is so adopted at the respective meetings of the shareholders of each of the said Corporations, the agreement so adopted and the said certificates thereon shall be filed in the office of the Provincial Secretary, and the said agreement shall from thence be taken and deemed to be the agreement and act of consolidation and amalgamation of the said Societies, and a copy of such agreement so filed, and of the certificates thereon, properly certified, shall be evidence of the existence of such new Corporation. 39 V. c. 32, s. 14, *last part*.

64. Upon the making and perfecting of the said agreement and act of consolidation, as provided in the next preceding section, and the filing of the said agreement as in the said section provided, the several Societies parties thereto, shall be deemed and taken to be consolidated, and to form one Corporation by the name in the said agreement provided, with a common seal, and shall possess all the rights, privileges, and franchises, and be subject to all the disabilities and duties of each of such Corporations so consolidated and united, except as herein otherwise provided. 39 V. c. 32, s. 15.

65. Upon the consummation of such act of consolidation as aforesaid, all and singular the business, property, real, personal and mixed, and all rights and interests appurtenant thereto, all stock, mortgages or other securities, subscriptions and other debts due on whatever account, and other things in action belonging to such Corporations or either of them, shall be taken and deemed to be transferred to and vested in such new Corporation without further act or deed.

2. All rights of creditors and liens upon the property of either of such Corporations shall be unimpaired by such consolidation, and all debts, liabilities and duties of either of the said Corporations shall thenceforth attach to the new Corporation, and be enforced against it to the same extent as if the said debts, liabilities and duties had been incurred or contracted by it.

3. No action or proceeding, legal or equitable, by or against the said Corporations so consolidated, or either of them, shall abate or be affected by such consolidation, but for all the purposes of such action or proceeding, such Corporation may be deemed still to exist, or the new Corporation may be substituted in such action or proceeding in the place thereof. 39 V. c. 32, s. 16.

66. The choice and removal of the Auditors of the Society the determination as to the remuneration of the Directors and of the Auditors, shall be exercised at general meetings of the Society; and the Auditors shall not necessarily be shareholders.

2. In case of the death or failure to act of any such Auditor, the Directors may appoint an Auditor in his place, and at all meetings of shareholders of the Society the shareholders shall have one vote for each share held by them respectively. 39 V. c. 32, s. 17.

67. Such Society shall, on or before the fifteenth day of February in each year, transmit to the Provincial Treasurer a full and clear statement of their assets and liabilities on some day to be stated therein, and such day shall not be more than six months prior to the said fifteenth day of February, and such statement shall contain, in addition to such other particulars as the Provincial Treasurer may require, the following:

(*a*) The amount of stock subscribed;

(*b*) The amount paid in upon such stock;

(*c*) The amount borrowed for the purposes of investment and the securities given therefor;

(*d*) The amount invested and secured by mortgage deeds;

(*e*) The amount of mortgages payable by instalments;

(*f*) The number and aggregate amount of mortgages upon which compulsory proceedings have been taken during the past year;

(*g*) The present cash value of the Society's investments on mortgages and other securities, and the rate or rates per cent. at which the future repayments are discounted in ascertaining such present cash value. 39 V. c. 32, s. 18.

68. Such statement shall be attested by the oath, before some Justice of the Peace, of two persons, one being the President, Vice-President, Manager or Secretary, and the other the Manager, Secretary or Auditor of such Society, each of whom shall swear distinctly that he holds such office as aforesaid; that he has had the means of verifying and has verified the statement aforesaid, and found it to be exact and true in every particular; and such statement shall be published by the Provincial Treasurer, in such manner as he thinks most conducive to the public good; and for any neglect to transmit such statement in due course of post within five days after the day upon which the same should be transmitted, such Society shall incur a penalty of one hundred dollars per diem. 39 V. c. 32, s. 19.

69. If such statement is not transmitted within one month after the said fifteenth day of February, or if it appears by the statement that such Society is not in a condition to justify its continuance in business with the powers theretofore possessed by such Society, the Provincial Treasurer may, under the authority of or by order of the Lieutenant-Governor in Council, by a notice in the *Ontario Gazette*, declare the business of such Society to have ceased so far as regards borrowing money and any other matters mentioned in the Order in Council and notice aforesaid. 39 V. c. 32, s. 20.

70. If the Provincial Treasurer, in any case, suspects any such statement to be wilfully false, he may depute some competent person to examine the books and inquire into the affairs of such Society and to report to him on oath; and if by such report it appears that such statement was wilfully false, or that such Society is not in a condition to justify its continuance in business, with the powers theretofore possessed by such Society, or if the person so deputed reports on oath sworn as aforesaid, that he has been refused such access to the books or such information as would enable him to make a sufficient report, the said Treasurer may, under the authority aforesaid, by notice in the *Ontario Gazette*, declare the business of such Society to have ceased, as in the next preceding section provided for. 39 V. c. 32, s. 21.

71. In any of the cases in which discretionary power is given to declare the business of such Society to have ceased, the Treasurer may before so doing give notice to such Society and afford the same an opportunity of making any explanation it may be advisable to make; and all expenses attending such periodical statements and the publication thereof shall be borne by such Society. 39 V. c. 32, s. 22.

72. Where any such Society as mentioned in the fifty-sixth section is desirous of changing its name, the Lieutenant-Governor, upon being satisfied that the change desired is not for any improper purpose, and is not otherwise objectionable, may by Order in Council change the name of the Society to some other name set forth in the said Order. 39 V. c. 32, s. 25.

73. The Society shall give at least four weeks' previous notice in the *Ontario Gazette* of the intention to apply for the change of name, and shall state the name proposed to be adopted; in case the proposed name is considered objectionable, the Lieutenant-Governor in Council may, if he thinks fit, change the name of the Society to some other unobjectionable name, without requiring any further notice to be given. 39 V. c. 32, s. 26.

74. Such change shall be conclusively established by the insertion in the *Ontario Gazette* of a notice thereof by the Provincial Secretary; and his certificate of such change having been made shall be obtained by the Society and filed in the office of the Clerk of the Peace of the County, with whom is filed the declaration constituting such Society; the Clerk shall, upon payment by the Society of a fee of one dollar therefor, endorse a copy of such certificate upon the said declaration; the Society shall (under a penalty of two hundred dollars in case of default), within one month after the insertion of the said notice, cause the said certificate to be filed, and require the said endorsement made as aforesaid.

2. The Lieutenant-Governor in Council may establish the fees to be paid on applications for change of name under this Act. 39 V. c. 32, s. 27.

75. Every debenture, mortgage, bond, deed, agreement or other instrument executed by or to any Building Society, and every other act, deed, matter or thing done in pursuance of the provisions of an Act passed in the Session held in the thirty-seventh year of Her Majesty's reign, by the Parliament of the Dominion of Canada, and intituled "*An Act to make further provision for the management of Permanent Building Societies carrying on business in the Province of Ontario,*" and every rule made thereunder, shall be as valid and effectual as if this Act had been passed on the twenty-sixth day of May, one thousand eight hundred and seventy-four, and such debenture, mortgage, bond, deed, agreement or other instrument had been executed, or such other act, deed, matter or thing had been done or rule made by virtue thereof; and all changes in the corporate name of any existing Building Society incorporated as aforesaid, heretofore made or purported to be made by or in pursuance of any Act of the said Parliament, are hereby confirmed. 39 V. c. 32, s. 23.

76. All the provisions of this Act shall apply to the Societies mentioned in the fifty-sixth section of this Act, and any rights, powers or privileges of any such Society, contrary to the provisions of this Act, are repealed. 39 V. c. 32, s. 24.

[*See also Acts of Canada*, 37 V. c. 50 *and* 40 V c. 48.]

SCHEDULE.

(*Section* 54.)

FORM OF DEBENTURE.

Society.

Debenture No. Transferable $

Under the authority of the Revised Statutes of Ontario, Chapter one hundred and sixty-four.

The President and Directors of the Society promise to pay to or bearer the sum of
on the day of
in the year of our Lord one thousand eight hundred and
at the Treasurer's Office here (*or as the case may be*), with interest at

Building Societies. Cap. 164. 113

the rate of   per cent. per annum, to be paid half-yearly on presentation of the proper coupon for the same as hereunto annexed, say on the   day of   and the   day of in each year, at the office of the Treasurer here (*or as the case may be*).
Dated at   , the   day of   , 18 .
For the President and Directors of the   Society,
C. D.,   A. B.,
Secretary (*or* Manager).   President.

COUPON.

No. 1. $
Half-yearly dividend due   of   18 , on Debenture No.   issued by this Society on the day of   18 , for $ at   per cent. per annum, payable at the office of the Treasurer,   (*as the case may be*).
For the President and Directors.
                                                C. D.,
                                 Secretary (*or* Manager).

CHAP LVIII.

An Act to enlarge and extend the powers of the "Credit Foncier Franco-Canadien."

Section.
Preamble; act of Quebec, 43, 44 V., c. 60.
1. Powers of the corporation; loans on real estate; on bonds and mortgages; loans to corporations; acquisition of claims; purchase of or loans on bonds and debentures of corporations; and public securities.
2. What only may be taken as security; limit of loans and annuities; valuation of property.
3. Local divisions for business purposes of the company; proviso.
4. Branches and agencies.
5. Advisory boards; qualification of members.
6. Managers and agents.
7. Suing and being sued.
8. Rate of interest limited; sinking fund

Section.
for paying off loan.
9. Of what the annuity for paying off shall be composed. Insurance. Payment of annuities.
10. Interest on arrears and costs.
11. Anticipated payments. Indemnity to company in such case.
12. Act 43 V., c. 42 to apply.
13. Power to borrow money and issue bonds of the corporation; interest on bonds.
14. Bonds may be in dollars or francs.
15. Powers as to real estate, amount limited. Power to dispose of; to purchase claims on such property. Term of holding limited.
16. Notices, how published.
17. Annual report to Minister of Finance and what it must show.

[*Assented to* 21*st March*, 1881.]

WHEREAS the Crédit Foncier Franco-Canadien, incorporated by the statute of the Province of Quebec, passed in the session of the Legislature of that Province held in the forty-third and forty-fourth years of Her Majesty's reign, chapter sixty, intituled "*An Act to incor-*

8

porate the *Crédit Foncier Franco-Canadien,*" has prayed for an extension and enlargement of its powers so as to allow it to transact business throughout the Dominion, and it is expedient to grant the prayer of its petition: Therefore Her Majesty, by and with the advice and consent of the Senate and House of Commons of Canada, enacts as follows:—

1. It shall be lawful for the Corporation created and constituted under the name of "Crédit Foncier Franco-Canadien" by the statute of the Province of Quebec, cited in the preamble, to exercise the powers hereinafter mentioned, in every part of the Dominion of Canada:—

1. To lend money as a first charge on mortgage or hypothecation of real estate, either freehold or leasehold, situate within the Dominion of Canada, repayable either at long date by annuities, including an annual payment by way of sinking fund for the gradual extinction of the loan, or at short date with or without progressive sinking of the debt;

2. To lend money upon the hypothecation or security of mortgages or of hypothecary or privileged claims being a first charge on real estate, either freehold or leasehold, situate within the Dominion of Canada, repayable either at long date by annuities, including an annual payment by way of sinking fund for the gradual extinction of the loan, or at short date with or without progressive sinking of the debt;

3. To lend on mortgage or hypothec or otherwise, to municipal and school corporations throughout the Dominion of Canada, and *fabriques* and trustees for the construction or repair of churches, such sums of money as they may be authorized to borrow, repayable either at long date by annuities, including an annual payment by way of sinking fund for the gradual extinction of the loan, or at short date with or without progressive sinking of the debt;

4. To acquire by assignment or transfer bonds and mortgages and hypothecary or privileged claims being a first charge upon real estate, either freehold or leasehold, situate within the Dominion of Canada;

5. To make loans upon, or to purchase bonds or debentures issued by municipal or school corporations in the Dominion of Canada, and by incorporated companies doing business therein, and to sell the same if deemed advisable;

6. To make loans upon, or to purchase bonds and debentures and other public securities of the Dominion of Canada, or of any of the Provinces thereof, and to sell the same if deemed advisable.

2. The Corporation shall accept as security only real estate, either freehold or leasehold, of which the revenues are deemed sufficient.

The amount of each loan shall not exceed one-half of the estimated value of the real estate, either freehold or leasehold, mortgaged or hypothecated therefor; and the annuity which the borrower may oblige himself to pay shall not exceed the net revenue which it may be estimated that the property might yield.

The valuation of property offered as security shall be made on the double basis of the net revenue which it is susceptible of yielding, and of the price which it would bring if sold.

3. For the management of business each Province other than the Province of Quebec shall form a division; but the Board of Management may, if it deems proper, divide each of such Provinces into two or more divisions, and may subsequently re-divide such divisions and form others; and may also divide the Province of Quebec into more than two divisions, and may subsequently subdivide such divisions and form others.

4. A branch office or agency may be established in any division, whenever the Board of Management deem it advisable.

5. The Board of Management may appoint and remove, when it sees fit, an Advisory Board in any division, composed of two or more shareholders, and may delegate to such Advisory Boards such powers for the granting of loans, not exceeding ten thousand dollars, as it may deem desirable. Each member of such Advisory Boards shall be the holder of twenty-five shares, which shall be affected by privilege as security for his good conduct, and shall not be transferable while he remains in office.

6. A manager or agent may be appointed to administer the affairs of the Corporation in each Province or in any division which may be established by the Board of Management; and such managers or agents shall have the powers and be subject to the obligations prescribed from time to time by the Board of Management.

7. The Corporation may sue and be sued, complain and defend in any court of law or equity in the Dominion.

8. The Corporation may stipulate for, exact and take, on all sums loaned, any rate of interest not exceeding six per centum per annum.

When the loan is repayable by way of a sinking fund, the Corporation shall stipulate for, exact and take an annual sum for the gradual extinction of the loan to be determined by the rate of interest and the duration of the loan, and may also stipulate for, exact and take a percentage or commission for cost of management not exceeding one per centum per annum on the principal loaned; but, in such case, such percentage or commission and the interest together must not exceed six per centum per annum on the principal loaned.

9. The annuity in the case of loans contracted with progressive sinking of the debt is composed of:—
1. The interest;
2. The annual sum for the progressive sinking of the debt; and may also include,
3. The percentage or commission for cost of management.

In case it should be stipulated that the insurance of the buildings on the estate mortgaged or hypothecated, may be made in the name of the Corporation and that the annual premiums therefor may be paid through the medium of the Corporation, the annuity may be increased by the amount of the annual premium.

The annuities are to be paid half-yearly at the periods and places fixed by the Board of Management.

10. Every half-yearly instalment of an annuity, and every instalment of interest on loans without a sinking fund, if not paid when due, shall, of right and without any putting in default being necessary, bear interest for the benefit of the Corporation, at the same rate as the loan itself.

11. Debtors of the Corporation shall have the right to discharge their debts before they become due, whether in whole or in part only.

Anticipated payments shall give rise to an indemnity in favour of the Corporation which shall not exceed three months' interest on the capital repaid before coming due, at the rate stipulated for the loan.

12. The provisions of the Act forty-third Victoria, chapter forty-two, shall apply to the Corporation.

13. The Corporation may, from time to time, borrow money to an amount which shall not exceed five times the amount of its paid up and unimpaired capital; and it may, for that purpose, execute, negotiate and issue obligations or bonds or debentures in sums of not less than five hundred francs, French currency, redeemable either at a fixed period or within a definite term by means of drawings with or without premiums or prizes. It may stipulate and pay on the obligations or bonds or debentures which may be issued by it, any rate of interest that may be lawfully taken by individuals at the place where they are issued.

14. Any bond or debenture issued under the provisions of this Act may be issued in the denomination of dollars or francs, and the coupons attached representing the interest on such bonds may correspond to the denomination of the bond to which they are attached.

15. The Corporation may acquire and hold such real estate as may be necessary for offices for the transaction of its business in the several Provinces of the Dominion; but the value of such real estate acquired in each division for such purpose shall not exceed at the time of acquisition the sum of fifty thousand dollars.

It may, from time to time, lease, mortgage, hypothecate, sell or otherwise dispose of or deal with such real estate.

It may also, for the protection of its investments, purchase and hold real estate mortgaged or hypothecated in its favour; but it shall sell or otherwise dispose or such real estate so acquired in payment or for the protection of its claims, within seven years from the acquisition thereof; and may, in the meantime, deal with and manage and may, from time to time, mortgage, hypothecate or lease the real estate so acquired and held.

16. Notices of meetings of shareholders and all other notices required to be published, shall be published in the *Canada Gazette*.

17. The Corporation shall transmit, on or before the first day of March in each year, to the Minister of Finance, a statement in duplicate to the thirty-first day of December inclusive of the previous year, verified by the oath of the President, Vice-President or the Managing Director, setting out the capital stock of the Corporation and the proportion thereof paid up, the number of shares to order and the number to bearer, the assets and liabilities of the Corporation, the amount and nature of the investments and the average rate of interest derived therefrom, the extent and value of the real estate held, the amount and nature of the obligations or bonds or debentures issued and the rate of interest payable thereon, and such other details as to the nature and extent of its business as may be required by the Minister of Finance, and in such form and with such details as he may, from time to time, require and prescribe; but the Corporation shall in no case be bound to disclose the names or private affairs of any persons who may have dealings with it.

CAP. LIX.

An Act to incorporate the *Credit Foncier* of the Dominion of Canada.

Section.
Preamble.
1. Incorporation
2. Objects of the corporation. Loans on hypothec; loans on privileged claims; to certain public bodies. Acquisition of claims; purchase of bonds; loans to Government; issue of bonds.
3. Head office and branches.
4. Duration of corporation.
5. Capital stock and shares; increase.
6. Separate issue of stock, and payments thereon. When to commence business.
7. Founders of the corporation and their privileges.
8. Allotment of increased stock; to be proportionate. Shareholders may unite in order to vote, &c. Regulations to be made by Board of Management.
9. Payment of shares; calls and notice thereof.
10. Interest on arrears.
11. Forfeiture and sale of shares for non-payment; distribution of proceeds.
12. Stock certificates to bearer. Form.
13. Transfer of stock certificates to order.
14. When to bearer.
15. Exchange of certificates.
16. Collective certificate.
17. Payment of dividend to holder of certificate.
18. Liability of shareholders limited.
19. No division of shares.
20. Effect of transfer of certificate.

Section.
21. Provision in case of loss of certificate.
22. Board of management, and how composed.
23. Elected and provisional directors and qualification; term of and proof of qualification. Security.
24. Order of retirement. Vacancies how filled.
25. Allowance for attendance.
26. Meetings of the Board; Voting at meetings of Board. Vote in writing. Decisions.
27. Minutes to be kept.
28. Powers of the Board of management. Loans; terms; calls; annual statements; dividends; agencies; amalgamation; dissolution; rules; issue of bonds; annual report.
29. Deciding upon applications.
30. Local boards may be appointed; their power. Quorum. Agent.
31. Members of board indemnified.
32. Share register.
33. Appointment of Auditors; vacancies; qualification; Sec. 25 to apply.
34. Duties and powers of Auditors.
35. To make annual returns.
36. May call special meetings.
37. Board of management.
38. Management of affairs.
39. Qualification of manager.
40. Manager's duties and powers.
41. Manager's deputy.

118   Cap. 59.   *Crédit Foncier, Dominion of Canada.*   44 Vic.

Section.
42. Suspension of employees.
43. Detailed annual statement.
44. Power to manager to be executed by board. Deposit of duplicate and notice thereof; effect thereof.
45. General meeting and how composed. List of shareholders ; to be open.
46. Proxies.
47. Time and place of general meeting.
48. Special meetings.
49. Calling of meetings and notice to be given.
50. When meeting is constituted.
51. Second meeting if there is no quorum; proceedings to be valid.
52. Officers of the meeting.
53. Proceedings at the meeting. Increase of capital, &c. All matters of interest to corporation.
54. Minutes to be kept.
55. Copies to be evidence.
56. Nature of loans to be made on annuity; repayable.
57. Security to be taken for loans.
58. Loans may not be made on certain property specified; not on mere usufruct; proviso
59. Amount of loan.
60. Rate of interest.
61. What annuity shall include. Sinking fund.
62. When annuities shall be payable.
63. Interest on overdue annuities.
64. No interest recoverable in certain cases, unless the mortgage contains a certain statement as to principal and interest.
65. No rate recoverable beyond that shewn in such statement.
66. Anticipated payments.
67. Certain property to be insured ; policies.
68. No loan below $250.

Section.
69. Loans in Canadian currency.
70. Application of foregoing provisions.
71. Applications for loans.
72. What obligations may be issued.
73. Descriptions of obligations which may be issued.
74. Drawing to be by lot.
75. Numbers drawn to be posted up.
76. Redemption.
77. Cancellation of bonds.
78. When redeemed by anticipated payments.
79. Transfer of bonds.
80. Minimum amount.
81. Interest.
82. Form of obligation.
83. May be in either currency.
84. What it shall contain.
85. Real estate and special obligations.
86. How secured.
87. Recourse of holders.
88. How secured.
89. Powers as to real estate ; must be disposed of within a certain time.
90. Financial year.
91. Detailed annual statement.
92. How distributed ; reserve fund
93. Distribution of remainder.
94. Reserve fund limited ; Its object.
95. Notice of meetings for certain purposes ; Two-third vote requisite.
96. Restriction as to rules.
97. Dissolution of the corporation.
98. When question shall be submitted.
99. Dissolution if capital is impaired.
100. Method of liquidation.
101. Proceedings for organization ; notice. First meeting for election of directors.
102. Publication of notices.
103. Yearly statement to be transmitted to Minister of Finance, and what it must contain.

[*Assented to* 21st *March,* 1881.]

WHEREAS *La société financière de Paris;* the firm of Kohn, Reinach and Company, of Paris, in France, bankers ; W. Betzold, Esquire, of Paris, in France ; Duncan McIntyre, of Montreal, Esquire ; the Honorable J. Rosaire Thibaudeau, Senator of the Dominion of Canada ; the Honorable Matthew Henry Cochrane, Senator of the Dominion of Canada ; Charles D. Rose, of London, England, banker ; the Honorable Peter Mitchell, of Montreal, and Andrew Robertson, of Montreal, merchant, have by their petition prayed for an Act of incorporation for the establishment, by means of a capital to be subscribed in Canada, Germany, France and elsewhere, of an institution of landed credit having for its object to supply real estate owners in the Dominion of Canada, who may desire to borrow upon hypothecary or mortgage securities, with the means of paying their indebtedness by long term annuities, and with the right to issue and negotiate obligations or bonds bearing interest yearly and repayable at par, or with prizes or premiums ; and whereas it is expedient to grant the prayer of their petition: Therefore Her Majesty, by and with the advice and consent of the Senate and House of Commons of Canada, enacts as follows:—

TITLE FIRST.

INCORPORATION OF THE INSTITUTION.

1. A Corporation is hereby created and constituted under the name of the *Crédit Foncier* of the Dominion of Canada.

TITLE SECOND.

OBJECTS OF THE CORPORATION.

2. The objects of the Corporation shall be,—

1. To loan, upon the hypothec or mortgage, to owners of real estate either freehold or leasehold with the Dominion of Canada, sums of money repayable either at long date by annuities, or at short date, with or without a sinking fund;

2. To loan, upon the security of hypothecary, mortgage or priviledged claims affecting immovables, or of the transfer of a mortgage or lien on real estate either freehold or leashold situate in the Dominion of Canada, sums of money payable either at long date by annuities, or at short date, with or without a sinking fund;

3. To loan, upon hypothec, mortgage or otherwise, to municipal and school corporations, to *Fabriques* and trustees for the construction or repair of churches in the said Dominion, such sums of money as they may be authorized to borrow, and repayable either at long date by annuities, or at short date with or without a sinking fund;

4. To acquire by subrogation or transfer, hypothecary, mortgage or privileged claims upon immovables situate in the said Dominion;

5. To purchase bonds or debentures issued by municipal and school corporations in the said Dominion, and by incorporated companies doing business in the said Dominion, and to re-sell the same if deemed advisable;

6. To make loans to the Government of any of the Provinces of the Dominion;

7. To create and negotiate, as representing its operations, obligations or bonds, to an amount which shall not exceed five times the amount of its paid-up and unimpaired capital.

TITLE THIRD.

HEAD OFFICE AND DURATION OF THE CORPORATION.

3. The seat or chief office of the Corporation shall be at Montreal. Branch offices may be established at such other places in the said Dominion as the Board of Management may deem advisable.

4. The duration of the Corporation shall be limited to ninety-nine years, dating from the coming into force of this Act, unless further extended as hereinafter provided.

TITLE FOURTH.

CAPITAL STOCK—SHARES—INSTALMENTS.

5. The Capital stock shall be five million dollars gold, divided into fifty thousand shares of one hundred dollars each. It may be increased by a resolution adopted at a special general meeting.

6. The capital stock shall be composed of issues of ten thousand shares each, of which the first shall be issued at once, on the ten thousand shares composing the first issue, ten per cent. shall be paid on subscription and fifteen per cent. in the month following: the dates of the issues of the remaining forty thousand shares shall be determined by the Board of Management. Holders of shares previously issued shall, within the delay fixed by the Board of Management, be intitled by privilege and in proportion to the stock they hold, to subscribe for the forty thousand shares. The new shares must be paid up in the same proportion as the shares previously issued; the new shares shall not be allotted below par; and the Board of Management shall determine the amount of the subsequent calls, as well as the manner and the delay in which they shall be paid up; the Corporation may commence business whenever one million dollars have been subscribed and twenty-five per cent. thereof has been paid up.

7. The subscribers to the capital stock to the extent of the ten thousand shares mentioned in section six, shall be the founders of the Corporation, and shall, as such, be entitled to the benefits mentioned in sections eight and ninety-three of this Act. Stock certificates shall be given to the founders to establish their rights under the first paragraph of section eight and to facilitate their obtaining their shares of the profits specified in section ninety-three. The Board of Management shall determine the form of such certificates, and the method of their transfer shall be the same as in the case of shares.

8. In the event of the capital stock being increased beyond five million dollars, the founders and holders of shares previously issued shall have a right, by preference, to subscribe for the shares to be issued in the ratio of thirty per cent. for the founders or their representives, and seventy per cent. for the shareholders.

2. The allotment of such seventy per cent. shall be in proportion to the amount of stock held by each shareholder.

3. Such of the shareholders as do not hold sufficient stock to entitle them to at least one share in the new issue may unite together to form the number and to exercise their rights.

4. A resolution of the Board of Management, shall determine the delays and the manner in which the benefit of the above provisions may be claimed.

9. The amount of the shares shall be payable in gold, or its equivalent, at Montreal or such other place or places and at such dates as may be fixed by the Board of Management. After the first call has been paid up there shall be delivered to each shareholder an interim stock certificate bearing one of a series of numbers, upon which all subsequent payments shall be inscribed. The calls shall be made known to the shareholders by means of advertisements inserted, a month beforehand, in the *Canada Gazette* and one or more daily newspaper published in Montreal, and such other place or places as may be determined by the Board of Management.

10. Every sum of money of which the payment is delayed, shall, of right, bear interest, and without a suit at law being necessary, for the benefit of the Corporation, at the rate of six per cent. per annum from the date at which such payment became due.

11. The Board of Management shall have the power to provide by by-law for the forfeiture of stock for the non-payment of calls made thereon, and the disposal of forfeited stock and of the proceeds thereof. The steps hereinabove authorized to be taken shall not prevent the Corporation from having recourse, at the time, to ordinary proceedings at law: the proceeds of the sale, after deducting the costs, shall be applied upon the amount due by the expropriated shareholders, who shall still be liable for the difference, if there be a deficiency, but who shall be entitled to receive the surplus, if there be any.

12. The Corporation may, if they deem it advisable so to do, deliver certificates to bearer, for shares on which forty per cent. is paid up, provided the said shares are held, owned and transferred on the continent of Europe. Certificates to bearer shall be taken from a register with counterfoil; they shall be numbered consecutively and bare the signature of two Directors and the seal of the Corporation.

3. Stock certificates to order shall be negotiable to order by transfer, granted by the seller and accepted by the buyer; when the parties act through an agent, the power of attorney shall be delivered to the Corporation.

14. Certificates to bearer shall be transferred by simple delivery.

15. Any shareholder may claim, in exchange for certificates made payable to bearer, a certificate to his order: the Board of Management shall determine the conditions, the manner, and the cost of effecting such exchange of certificates.

16. The ownership of more than one share, in the name of the bearer, shall be established by a collective certificate.

17. Every share shall give its holder a right in the ownership of the assets of the Corporation and to a share in the profits, in proportion to the number of shares issued. Payment of the dividends upon any share, either to order or to bearer, shall be valid, if made to the holder of the certificate.

18. The shareholders shall be liable only for the amount of their shares; and no call shall be permitted beyond such amount.

19. Every share shall be indivisible, and the Corporation shall recognize but one owner for each share; co-proprietors of a share shall be required to be represented by one and the same person.

20. The rights and obligations appertaining to shares shall follow the certificate into whatever hands it may lawfully pass; the possession of a share shall of right entail compliance with the by-laws or regulations of the corporation and the decisions of general meetings.

21. In the event of any stock certificates to bearer being lost, the Corporation shall not be obliged to replace them or to pay the interest or dividends due thereon, until it has been furnished with satisfactory proof of the loss of such certificates and of the rights of the claimants, and also until all legal formalities have been fulfilled: the Board of Management shall determine the conditions on which certificates to order, which have been lost or mislaid, shall be replaced.

TITLE FIFTH.

MANAGEMENT OF THE CORPORATION.

Section I.—Board of Management.

22. The Corporation shall be managed by a Board of Management, composed of from seven to twenty-one Directors, who shall annually elect from amongst their number, a President and a Vice-President; the number of Directors may, from time to time, be fixed by by-law; until otherwise provided, the Board shall be composed of seven Directors.

23. The Directors shall be appointed at the general meeting of the shareholders; nevertheless, the first Board of Management shall be appointed by the persons mentioned in the preamble, and by those having power and authority to act for the companies therein named. This latter Board shall remain in office for one year; and before entering upon office, each member shall establish that he is possessed of fifty shares. Fifty shares of his stock shall be held by the Corporation as security for his good conduct and management as Director, and shall not be transferable while he remains in office.

24. One-third in number of the Directors shall go out of office every year after the first year; it shall be decided by lot which of the Directors shall retire during the three years next after the first year; and afterwards, they shall retire by seniority: they may always be re-elected: any vacancy occurring among the Directors shall be temporarily filled up by the Board, and the next ensuing general meeting shall definitively elect a successor: a Director appointed in the place of another shall remain in office only during the remainder of his predecessor's term of office.

25. The Directors shall, for every time they are present, receive a counter, of which the value shall be determined by the general meeting.

26. The Board of Management shall meet as often as the interests of the Corporation may require, and at least once a month. The meetings shall be called by the President or Vice-President, or by the Director chosen by the Board to fill his place.

2. No resolution can be adopted unless three of the Directors residing in Canada are present. Directors residing in foreign parts or those who are absent may be represented at the meetings of the Board by proxy given to one of their colleagues. No Director shall, as proxy, have more than three votes at the Board.

3. Directors who are absent may also give their vote in writing by correspondence.

4. All resolutions and by-laws shall be carried by a majority of the votes cast at the meeting; when the votes are equal, the President, Vice-President or presiding Director shall have a casting vote.

27. The proceedings shall be recorded by minutes entered in a register and signed by the President, the Vice-President, or the Director chosen by the Board to fill his place, and the Secretary; copies or extracts of such minutes which are required to be produced in court or elsewhere, shall be certified by the President or Vice-President.

28. The Board of Management shall have full powers for the management of the affairs of the Corporation: it shall pass by-laws for its internal management; it shall appoint and remove the managers, officers and employees of the Corporation, shall determine their powers and fix their fees, salaries and gratuities; it shall also determine the amount of the security which they shall give, and if necessary, authorize it to be repaid; it shall, if need be, authorize the purchase of immovable property in the Dominion of Canada, for the purpose of establishing its offices therein, and the sales of such immovables and those acquired in payment or for the protection of their claims; it shall decide upon—

1. The general conditions on which loans shall be granted;

2. The conditions and terms on which the borrowing powers shall be exercised;

3. Calls upon shares issued and the issue of new shares;

4. The annual statement of accounts to be submitted to the general meeting;

5. The determining the amount of the dividend and of the amounts to be advanced on account thereof;

6. The establishment or closing of branch offices or agencies;

7. The amalgamation of the Corporation with other companies with the consent of a majority of the shareholders at a meeting specially called for the purpose;

8. Its anticipated dissolution;

9. The rules under which the managers shall in general administer the affairs of their respective divisions;

10. The creation and issue of obligations or bonds; the date of their issue; the rate of interest, which shall not exceed that authorized

by law in the Dominion of Canada; the date of the re-payment thereof, the number of drawings (*tirages au sort*) and the amount of the prizes or premiums, the percentage whereof, together with the interest thereon, shall not exceed the rate authorized by law.

11. It shall submit, each year, to the meeting a report upon the accounts and the financial position of the Corporation,—which report shall be printed and distributed to the members at the meeting.

29. The Board of Management shall decide upon applications for loans and other transactions, and grant or refuse them; but it may delegate that power to a committee thereof, for applications which do not exceed twenty thousand dollars.

30. The Board of Management may appoint and remove, when it sees fit, a "Local Board" in each division; such Local Boards shall be composed of not less than three persons; they shall exercise the powers of the Board relating to applications for loans or proposals for the transfer of hypothecary or mortgage claims, the amount of which does not exceed ten thousand dollars Canadian currency; but the Board of Management may further limit the amount of such applications and proposals. No proceedings of the Local Board shall be valid unless a majority of the members are present; the Board may also appoint an agent to act for the Corporation in Europe and may confer upon him such powers as they deem desirable within the scope of their authority.

31. The members of the Board of Management shall not incur any personal or joint and several liability in the performance of their duties; they shall be responsible only for the proper execution of their trust.

32. A register for the transfer of the shares of the Corporation, sold out of Canada, shall be kept in a place to be fixed by the Board of Management; and the officer in charge of such register shall forward a list of transfers effected therein to the office of the Corporation in Montreal, in order that a complete register may be preserved there of all the shares to order in the said Corporation.

Section II.—*The Auditors.*

33. Three auditors shall be appointed by the general meeting. They shall remain in office for one year, and shall be eligible for re-election.

2. In case of the death, absence, illness or retirement of one of the auditors, the remaining auditors shall forthwith elect a successor.

3. Every auditor shall be the holder of at least twenty-five shares and his stock to that extent shall be held by the Corporation as security for his good conduct as auditor, and shall not be transferable while he remains in office.

4. The provisions of section twenty-five of this Act shall apply to the auditors as well as to the Directors.

84. The duty of the auditors shall be to see to the strict observance of the provisions of this Act as to the issue of bonds and otherwise ; they shall be entitled to be present at the meeting of the Board and to give their opinion ; they shall examine the yearly accounts and inventories and certify to their correctness ; the books and accounts, and generally all documents of the Corporation, shall be submitted for their examination, at their request. They may, at any time, examine the cash, securities and vouchers of the Corporation.

35. They shall make an annual return to the general meeting,—which return shall be printed and distributed to the members two weeks previous to the meeting.

36. The auditors shall have the right, when they unanimously decide upon it, to have a special general meeting called.

Section III.—Management in the Dominion.

37. For the transaction of business the Board of Management may form divisions, and may subdivide such divisions and form others.

38. The affairs of each division shall be administered by a manager who may also be a Director.

39. Every manager shall be the holder of at least fifty shares, and his shares to that extent shall be held by the Corporation as security for his good conduct as manager, and shall not be transferable while he remains in office.

40. The duties and powers of the managers shall be such as may be prescribed from time to time by the Board of Management.

41. The manager may, with the permission of the Board of Management, require the assistance of and be represented by a deputy ; but he shall be responsible for all his acts and the consequences thereof : all powers delegated by him shall be special and temporary.

42. The manager may suspend any employee in his office, but he shall refer the matter to the Board of Management, and he shall temporarily replace any employee who may be suspended ; in case of the death, absence or inability to act of any of the employees, he shall provide a temporary substitute.

43. On the first day of January of each year, the manager shall prepare a detailed statement of the operations of the Corporation in his division during the preceding year : such document shall be submitted to the Board of Management, who, after having examined it, shall forward it, with its observations thereon, to the auditors.

44. The President shall, after the appointment of a manager by the Board of Management, execute in duplicate a procuration or power of attorney, countersigned by the Secretary, authorizing him to act, within the limits of his powers, for and in the name of the Corporation ; a duplicate of the procuration shall be deposited in the office of the Secretary of State of Canada, and the latter shall give notice, in the *Canada Gazette*, of such appointment and of the deposit of the procuration. All registrars shall be bound, after such notice, to receive all deeds passed by such manager within the limits of his powers, and before the publication in the *Canada Gazette* of a revocation of the procuration, as sufficient without requiring any proof of his power to act.

TITLE SIXTH.

GENERAL MEETINGS.

45. The general meeting regularly constituted shall represent the whole body of the shareholders; but in order to be entitled to take part in the proceedings of the general meeting, the shareholders must have held the shares they vote upon at least thirty days before the day appointed for the meeting. A list of shareholders, having a right to take part in the general meeting, shall be prepared by the Board of Management, and shall show opposite the name of each shareholder the number of shares which he holds. Such list shall be open to the examination of such shareholders as wish to examine it for at least ten days before the day fixed for the meeting, at the office of the Corporation in Montreal.

46. No one may be represented except by a proxy who is a member of the meeting.

47. The general meeting shall be held before the thirtieth of April in each year, at Montreal, until some other place has been fixed by by-law.

48. Special meetings shall, moreover, be held whenever the Board of Management deems it necessary, or the auditors unanimously require the same.

49. The meetings shall be called at such place and by such notice as may be determined by by-law, and voting may be by ballot.

50. The meeting shall be regularly constituted when one-fourth of the shares forming the capital stock is represented thereat.

51. If the condition provided for in the next preceding section is not fulfilled, the Board of Management shall, a second time, call a general meeting within an interval of at least one month; and in such case the delay between the calling of the meeting and the day on which it shall be held, may be reduced to fifteen days. All the proceedings of members present at the second meeting shall be valid, whatever may be the number of the shares which they represent, but only with respect to the subjects mentioned on the orders of the day drawn up for the first proposed meeting.

52. The officers of the meeting shall be the chairman, two scrutineers and a secretary; the President of the Board of Management shall be, *ex-officio*, the chairman of the meeting; in his default, the meeting shall be presided over by the Vice-President, or, in the absence of both, by a Director designated by the Board; the duties of scrutineer shall be performed by two shareholders elected at the meeting.

53. The report of the Board of Management on the position of the affairs of the Corporation, shall be read to the meeting, as also, if required, the observations of the auditors: the meeting shall approve or reject the annual accounts and shall appoint the Directors and auditors, whenever it is necessary to replace them; it shall take into consideration, when the proposition is submitted to it, the advisability of increasing the capital of the Corporation, and also the rules and regulations for the government of the Corporation, and for the administration and management of its affairs, and also the amendments or additions to be made to them; finally, it shall definitely decide upon all things touching the interests of the Corporation and, by its resolutions, confer upon the Board of Management the necessary powers for such cases as have not been provided for.

54. The proceedings shall be recorded by minutes entered in a special register, and signed by the officers of the meeting.

55. The proof of the proceedings of the general meeting shall, as far as third parties are concerned, be derived from true copies or extracts, certified as such by the President or Vice-President.

TITLE SEVENTH.
OF LOANS AND OTHER TRANSACTIONS.

56. The Corporation may effect hypothecary or mortgage loans of two kinds: the first shall be repayable by annuities calculated so as to extinguish the debt in a space of ten years at the least and fifty years at the most; the second shall be repayable within a period of not more than ten years.

57. The Corporation shall lend to proprietors of immovables only on first hypothec or mortgage,—constituted seignorial rents and equivalent ground rents being alone excepted: loans by which debts already registered are to be repaid, shall be considered as made on first hypothec or mortgage, when by the fact of such payment or subrogation made in favor of the Corporation, the hypothec so created shall be the first charge on the property; in such cases the Corporation shall keep in its possession sufficient funds to meet such payment.

58. Loans may not be effected by the Corporation on the following,—
1. Theatres;
2. Mines and quarries;
3. Undivided immovables or real estate, if the hypothec or mortgage be not established on the whole of such immovables or real estate, with the consent of all the co-proprietors;
4. Immovables of which the usufruct and the mere ownership are not vested in the same person, unless all those having any right in the property consent to the creation of the hypothec. This provision relates to the management only and shall not affect the validity of the hypothec: Provided always, that nothing herein contained shall prevent loans being effected by the Corporation on the security of leasehold property.

59. The amount of the loan shall not exceed one-half of the estimated value of the immovable hypothecated if the same be farm or unimproved property, or two-thirds of the estimated value in the case of property situated in cities or towns.

60. The rate of interest to be charged on all sums loaned, shall be determined by the Board of Management and shall not exceed six per centum per annum, except in the Provinces and Territories west of the Province of Ontario, where interest at the rate of seven per centum per annum may be charged.

61. The annuity, as well of long as of short date loans stipulated in the contract of loan, shall include—
1. Interest;
2. The sinking fund, determined by the rate of interest and the duration of the loan; and may also include—
3. An annual allowance for cost of management, which shall not exceed one per cent. per annum of the principal loaned; but the interest charged together with the charge for management shall not exceed six per cent. to the borrower in all, except in the Provinces and Territories west of the Province of Ontario, where it shall not exceed seven per cent. per annum in all.

62. Annuities shall be payable half-yearly, at the dates fixed by the Board of Management; but when the first instalment is due the borrower shall only pay interest for such part of six months as have elapsed from the time of the effecting of the loan until the payment of such first instalment.

63. Every half-yearly instalment of an annuity, if not paid when due, shall, of right and without any putting in default being necessary, bear interest for the benefit of the Corporation at the same rate as the loan itself.

64. Whenever any principal money or interest secured by mortgage of real estate is, by the same, made payable on the sinking fund plan, or on any plan under which the payments of principal money and interest are blended, or on any plan which involves an allowance of interest on stipulated repayments, no interest whatever shall be chargeable, payable or recoverable, on any part of the principal money advanced, unless the mortgage contains a statement showing the amount of such principal money and the rate of interest chargeable thereon, calculated yearly or half-yearly, not in advance.

65. Whenever the rate of interest shewn in the statement referred to in the next preceding section is less than the rate of interest which would be chargeable by virtue of any other provision, calculation or stipulation in the mortgage, no greater rate of interest shall be chargeable, payable or recoverable on the principal money advanced than the rate shewn in the said statement.

66. Debtors shall be entitled to discharge their debts before they become due, whether in whole or in part only: anticipated payments shall give rise to an indemnity in favour of the Corporation, which shall not exceed three months interest upon the capital repaid before coming due at the rate agreed upon for the loan.

67. Properties liable in whole or in part to destruction by fire shall be insured against fire, at the expense of the borrower; the contract of loan shall contain a transfer of the amount of the policy in case of loss, and the insurance shall be kept up during the entire continuance of the loan. The Corporation may require that the policy of insurance be made out in its name and that the amount of the annual premiums be paid by it; in such case the amount of annuity shall be increased to that extent. Anticipated payments arising from fires shall not carry with them any right to the indemnity authorized by the latter part of section sixty-six.

68. The Corporation shall not loan an amount less than two hundred and fifty dollars, currency of Canada.

69. Loans shall be effected and be repayable in currency of Canada.

70. The rules laid down in this title shall apply to loans made upon the security of hypothecary or mortgage or privileged claims; and those which relate to the rank of the hypothec or mortgage and to the nature and value of the immovables or real estate offered as security, shall also apply in cases of acquisition by means of subrogation or transfer of such claims.

71. The proceedings upon applications for loans shall be regulated by the Board of Management.

TITLE EIGHTH.

BONDS.
Section I.—General Provisions.

72. The Corporation may create and issue bonds or debentures of two kinds: the first shall be created to represent the operations of the Corporation, with the exception of loans to Governments, to municipal or school corporations, *fabriques*, and church trustees, and public securities, and bonds or debentures of municipal and school corporations belonging to the Corporation; they shall be known as "real estate bonds or debentures:" the second shall be created to represent loans to Governments, municipal and school corporations, *fabriques*, and church trustees, and public securities, and bonds or debentures of municipal and school corporations belonging to the Corporation; they shall be known as "special bonds or debentures."

73. The Corporation may issue bonds or debentures of the following kinds, to wit:—

1. Those redeemable at par with a fixed term for redemption, without prizes;

2. Those redeemable with premiums at a fixed term for redemption, without prizes;

3. Those redeemable at par within a definite delay, without any period being fixed for their redemption before such delay, and by means of a drawing of numbers, without prizes;

4. Those redeemable at par with a right to participate in prizes, within a definite delay, without any period being fixed for their redemption before such delay, and by means of a drawing of numbers;

5. Those redeemable with a premium within a definite delay, without any period being fixed for their redemption before such delay, and by means of a drawing of numbers, without prizes;

6. Those redeemable at par with a premium and a right to participate in prizes, within a definite delay, without a period being fixed for their redemption before such delay, and by means of a drawing of numbers:

The Board of Management shall determine the duration of the delay and the date of the drawings.

74. The drawing of the bonds or debentures which are to be repaid shall be effected by lot, in the presence of the Auditors, or of one or more of them.

75. Within eight days from such drawing the numbers drawn shall be posted up in the office of the Corporation at Montreal, and published as may be fixed by by-law.

76. The bonds or debentures designated by lot shall be redeemed on the day indicated in the notice published; from and after such day the interest on such redeemable bonds or debentures shall cease to run.

77. Bonds or debentures redeemed by such drawing of numbers shall be at once cancelled by means of a stamp; they shall be destroyed in the presence of the President or of his representative, and one of the auditors, and a minute of such operations shall be kept of record.

78. Bonds or debentures redeemed by the Corporation by anticipated payments shall at once be stamped with a special stamp, and they may be replaced in circulation only by resolution of the Board of Management; in all cases they shall participate in the drawing of numbers.

79. Bonds or debentures shall be payable either to order or to bearer: obligations payable to order shall be transferable in the same manner as that indicated for the transfer of shares to order, in accordance with the provisions of section thirteen; the Corporation shall not in any case be responsible for the validity of transfers: bonds or debentures payable to bearer shall be transferable by simple delivery.

80. No bond or debenture shall be issued for an amount less than one hundred dollars.

81. The bonds or debentures shall bear interest,—the rate and the date and manner of payment whereof shall be determined by the Board of Management; whatever may be the form of the bonds or debentures the payment of the interest thereon to the holder thereof shall be lawful.

82. The bonds or debentures shall be represented by scrip taken from a register with a counterfoil; they shall be signed by two Directors, and shall bear the seal of the Corporation.

83. Any bond or debenture issued under the provisions of this Act may be issued in the denomination of dollars or francs and the coupons attached representing interest upon such bond may correspond to the denomination of the bond to which they are attached.

84. The interest upon bonds or debentures, the premiums or prizes, and the sinking fund shall be set forth upon the scrip.

Section II.—Real Estate Bonds.

85. The total amount of the real estate and special bonds to be issued shall not exceed five times the amount of the paid up and unimpaired capital of the corporation.

86. The real estate bonds shall be secured by the assets of the Corporation, with the exception of claims specially set apart to secure the redemption of special bonds.

87. Holders of real estate bonds shall have no other recourse, for the recovery of the principal and interest due thereon, than that which they may exercise against the Corporation directly.

Section III—Special Bonds.

88. The special bonds shall be secured by the assets of the Corporation, with the exception of such assets as are set apart to secure the redemption of real estate bonds.

TITLE NINTH.

ACQUISITION OF REAL ESTATE.

89. The Corporation may acquire and possess such real estate as may be necessary for its offices for the administration of its affairs, in the Dominion of Canada, but the value of such real estate, acquired in each division for such purpose, shall not exceed, at the time of such acquisition, the sum of one hundred thousand dollars, Canadian currency; and it may, from time to time, lease, mortgage, hypothecate, sell or otherwise dispose of or deal with such real estate; and it may also, for the protection of its investments, purchase and hold real estate mortgaged or hypothecated in its favour; but it shall sell or otherwise dispose of such real estate so acquired in payment or for the protection of its claims within seven years from the acquisition thereof; and may, in the meantime, deal with and manage, and may, from time to time, mortgage, hypothecate or lease the real estate so acquired and held.

TITLE TENTH.

INVENTORIES AND ANNUAL STATEMENTS OF ACCOUNTS.

90. The Corporation's financial year shall commence on the first of January and end on the thirty-first of December; the first term shall include, in addition to the year current when the Corporation commences its operations, the whole of the following year also.

91. At the end of the financial year, a detailed general statement of the assets and liabilities shall be prepared under the supervision of the Board of Management, and further, a summary statement of the assets and liabilities shall also be prepared every six months; the accounts shall be prepared by the Board of Management, and shall be submitted to the general meeting of the shareholders which shall approve or reject the same.

TITLE ELEVENTH.

DIVISION OF PROFITS, RESERVE FUND AND PROVIDENT FUND.

92. From the annual net profits of the Company a dividend of ten per cent. upon the paid up stock may be distributed to the stockholders, provided the net profits are sufficient to pay such dividend; and of the remainder of such net profits one tenth shall be applied to the foundation of a reserve fund until such fund amounts to one tenth of the paid up capital.

93. The remainder shall be divided among the stockholders and founders, in the proportion of three fourths to the former and one fourth to the latter.

94. When the reserve fund amounts to one-tenth of the capital stock paid up, the percentage of which it is formed shall cease to be set aside; if such reserve is encroached upon, such percentage shall again be set aside. The reserve fund is intended to provide for unforeseen circumstances.

TITLE TWELFTH.

RULES OR REGULATIONS.

95. When the general meeting shall be called upon to vote on the adoption or amendment of any rules or regulations, the notices calling such meeting shall contain a summary mention thereof; the proceedings at such meeting shall not be valid unless carried by two-thirds of the votes, representing at least one-third of the registered shares.

96. The rules or regulations must not be contrary to the laws of the Dominion of Canada, nor to the provisions of this Act.

TITLE THIRTEENTH.

DISSOLUTION AND LIQUIDATION OF THE CORPORATION.

97. The Corporation shall be dissolved at the expiration of the time fixed by section four, unless by resolution of the general meeting, voting in the manner prescribed in the latter part of section ninety-five, its continuance be authorized.

98. The question of the continuance of the Corporation shall be submitted at the latest, to the general meeting of the shareholders held during the course of the year preceding that in which it would otherwise cease to exist.

99. In the event of the Corporation having lost in addition to its reserve fund, one-third of its paid up capital stock, the dissolution and liquidation of the Corporation shall be proceeded with, unless the shareholders consent to pay up the lost capital.

100. When the dissolution and liquidation of the Corporation shall have been decided upon, the general meeting of the shareholders shall determine the method of liquidation to be followed; it shall also appoint liquidators: if the general meeting does not come to any decision on this point, the dissolution and liquidation shall be proceeded with under the laws in force in the Dominion of Canada.

TITLE FOURTEENTH.

ORGANIZATION AND FINAL CONSTITUTION OF THE CORPORATION.

101. The persons mentioned in the preamble may open subscription books for the first issue of shares in the capital stock, at such place and for such time as they may deem advisable; after the closing of the books they shall allot the ten thousand shares, forming the first issue, in such manner as they may deem proper. Notice shall be given to each subscriber of his allotment, by a letter addressed to his place of residence, and sent by post; and within five days from the date at which such letter was sent to his address, each subscriber shall pay into the hands of the person or banking institution designated for that purpose ten per cent. upon the amount of the shares allotted to him, and subscribers who shall so pay ten per cent. shall become shareholders. As soon as the first issue of shares shall have been subscribed for, and ten per cent. upon the amount issued shall have been paid up, the person specially selected for such purpose among those mentioned in the preamble, shall call a general meeting of the shareholders, by public notice published at least ten days before the date of such meeting; and at such meeting the persons mentioned in the preamble and those authorized to represent the Companies therein mentioned shall elect the first Directors; and the meeting itself shall elect the auditors, and thereupon the Corporation shall be duly organized, and may commence its operations.

102. Notices of meetings of shareholders, and all other notices required to be published, shall be published in the *Canada Gazette*.

103. The Corporation shall transmit, on or before the first day of March in each year, to the Minister of Finance, a statement in duplicate to the thirty-first day of December inclusive of the previous year, verified by the oath of the President, the Vice-President, or the Managing Director, setting forth the capital stock of the Corporation and the proportion thereof paid up, the number of shares to order and the number to bearer, the assets and liabilities of the Corporation, the amount and nature of the investments and the average rate of interest derived therefrom, the extent and value of the real estate held, the amount and nature of the obligations or bonds or debentures issued and the rate of interest payable thereon, and such other details as to the nature and extent of its business as may be required by the Minister of Finance, and in such form and with such details as he may, from time to time, require and prescribe; but the Corporation shall in no case be bound to disclose the names or private affairs of any persons who may have dealings with it.

CHAP VII.

An Act to amend the law respecting Building Societies.

Section.
   Preamble.
 1. Power to sell mortgages made to Building Societies. Rights of Assignee.
 2. Subscribed shares may be determined to be fixed capital. Transfer of shares.

Section.
 3. Directors may fix the amount payable on subscription for shares and premiums. Calls. Dividends.
 4. R. S. 164, s. 67, amended.

[*Assented to* 7*th March*, 1878.]

WHEREAS, doubts exist as to whether a Society formed or incorporated under the provisions of chapter one hundred and sixty-four of the Revised Statutes of Ontario, intituled "An Act Respecting Building Societies," or under any former Act respecting Building Societies, has power under the authority of any of the said Acts to sell or dispose of mortgages given or made directly to the Society, and it is expedient to remove such doubts and to grant additional powers to such Societies;

Therefore Her Majesty, by and with the advice and consent of the Legislative Assembly of the Province of Ontario, enacts as follows:—

1. A society formed or incorporated under the provisions of the said recited Act, or under any former Act respecting Building Societies has heretofore had, and any such society and every society hereafter formed or incorporated under the said recited Act, shall hereafter have power and authority to sell, dispose of and assign mortgages given or made directly to it, in like manner as such Society may, under the provisions of the said Act, sell and assign mortgages purchased by it; and the assignee of any such mortgage shall stand in the place of, and be entitled to, and have all the same rights, powers and remedies, and shall be subject to the same obligations and liabilities, under, upon, or in respect to such mortgage as the Society would have been entitled to have had or been subject to if the assignment thereof had not been made.

2. The members of any such society entitled to vote may, at any time, by resolution to be passed at any special or general meeting (for which meeting notice of such intended resolution shall be duly given) determine that all shares thereafter subscribed for in such Society shall be fixed and permanent capital and not liable to be withdrawn therefrom, and any share thereafter subscribed for in such Society shall be fixed and permanent capital and not withdrawable therefrom; such shares shall be transferable in such manner as the By-Laws of the Society may direct, but no such share shall be transferred, while any call thereon is in arrear or until the same has been forfeited for non-payment of calls.

3. The Directors of any such Society may fix the amount to be paid on the subscription of any such shares, and the premium (if any) which shall be paid thereon, and when such premium shall be payable, and it shall be in the discretion of the Directors from time to time to call up the balance of any such shares at such time or times as they shall think best; and any such Society may from time to time pay, notwithstanding that such shares have not been paid in full, or the value thereof been realized, interest or dividend by way of annual or other periodical profits upon the amounts paid on such shares, and in all other respects, such shares shall be subject to the general provisions contained in the said Act.

4. Section sixty-seven of the said Act is amended by striking out the word "six" in the fifth line thereof, and substituting therefor the word "twelve"; by inserting after the word "February" in the same line the words "or earlier than the end of the last preceding financial year of such Society" and by adding to sub-section (*g*) of the said section the words "which rate or rates shall be at least equal to the rate or rates which such mortgages or other securities respectively bear or were originally calculated to yield."

CHAP. XXVI.

An Act to amend the Building Societies Act.

Section.
1. Preamble.
2. Interpretation.
3. Extension of business into various Provinces of the Dominion.
4. R. S. O., c. 164, s. 48 repealed, and new section substituted.
5. Payment in advance of calls.

[*Assented to* 11*th March*, 1879.]

WHEREAS by the Revised Statutes of Ontario, chapter one hundred and sixty-four, section fifty-two, it is enacted as follows:

"The Board of Directors of any such Society having a paid up "capital of not less than two hundred thousand dollars in fixed and per- "manent stock not liable to be withdrawn therefrom may issue deben- "tures of such society to such an amount as with all the other liabilities "of such society will be equal to double the amount of the capitalized "fixed and permanent stock not liable to be withdrawn therefrom and "the reserve fund of such Society:"

And by sub-section two of said section fifty-two it is also enacted that

"The total liabilities of such Society shall not at any time exceed "the amount of principal remaining unpaid on the mortgages at such "time held by such Society, and in estimating the liabilities of such So- "ciety the amount of cash actually in the hands of such Society or de- "posited in any Chartered Bank shall be deducted therefrom."

And whereas doubts may arise as the meaning of the words "liabilities of such Society" where the same occur in the said section fifty-two:—

And whereas it is expedient to remove such doubts and to amend the said Act:

Therefore Her Majesty, by and with the advice and consent of the Legislative Assembly of the Province of Ontario, enacts as follows:—

1. The first sub-section of section fifty-two of chapter one hundred and sixty-four of the Revised Statutes of Ontario, is hereby amended by striking out the word "two," and inserting the word "one" in lieu thereof.

2. In the said section fifty-two the words "liabilities of such Society," or "total liabilities of such Society" shall be taken to mean and are hereby declared to mean only the liabilities of any such Society to the public and shall not be taken to include, and it is hereby declared that the same do not include the liability of any such Society to its shareholders in respect of its capital stock, or otherwise to its shareholders as such.

3. The Directors of any Society or Company incorporated under the said chapter one hundred and sixty-four, or any Act consolidated therein, which shall, under the authority of the Parliament of Canada, and of the Legislature of the Province in which it is proposed that the business of the Society or Company is to be carried on, pass a By-law authorizing its Directors to extend the business of such Society or Company into any of the Provinces of the Dominion, may give effect to such By-law without being liable or responsible as for any breach of trust in so doing.

4. Section forty-eight of said Chapter one hundred and sixty-four is hereby repealed and the following substituted therefor:

"Any Society may hold absolutely real estate for the purposes of or in connection with its place or places of business not exceeding the annual value of ten thousand dollars;" but this section shall not affect any action or suit now pending.

5. No Shareholder shall be entitled to pay on account of his shares in advance of calls where such payments are prohibited by the by-laws of the Society or Company.

CHAP. XXI.

An Act for the relief of Building, Loan and Savings Societies and Companies.

Section.
Preamble.
1. Certain statements confirmed; pleading and evidence; staying proceedings.
2. Actions brought subsequent to receipt of statement by Treasurer not to be maintained; proviso.
3. Statement not required in case society has ceased to do business.
4. R.S.O., c. 164, ss. 67-69 repealed; annual statement of assets and liabilities; state-

Section.
ment to be attested by oath, and to be published; if statement not transmitted, or if it shews that the society is not in a proper condition, power to borrow may be stayed.
5. Certain returns may be made under this Act, or under repealed provisions.
6. Extension of time for making return; proviso.

[*Assented to 5th March*, 1880.]

WHEREAS, acting under the authority of the Act passed in the thirty-ninth year of Her Majesty's reign, intituled "An Act to make further provisions respecting Permanent Building Societies," and of the Act, chapter one hundred and sixty-four of the Revised Statutes of Ontario, intituled, "An Act respecting Building Societies," as amended by the Act passed in the forty-second year of Her Majesty's reign, intituled, "An Act to amend the Building Societies' Act," the Treasurer of Ontario has from time to time furnished to building, loan or savings societies or companies in Ontario, on their application, printed forms purporting to be forms of statement in accordance with the provisions of the said Acts in that behalf, and having printed thereon a form of affidavit of attestation to be made by the officers of the societies attesting such statement; and whereas, on account of some difference in the language used in the said forms as compared with the language of the said Statutes, doubts have arisen as to whether returns and affidavits made upon the said forms are a compliance with the said Acts, and it is desirable to remove such doubts and to relieve societies whose officers have made their returns upon the said forms from being harassed by suits for penalties under the said Acts, and also to further amend the said Revised Statute of Ontario:

Therefore Her Majesty, by and with the advice and consent of the Legislative Assembly of the Province of Ontario, enacts as follows:—

1. Every statement transmitted to the Treasurer of Ontario, at any time previous to the passing of this Act, by any Building, Loan or Savings Society or Company incorporated under chapter one hundred and sixty-four of the Revised Statutes of Ontario, or under chapter fifty-three of the Consolidated Statutes of Upper Canada, or under "The Ontario Joint Stock Companies' Letters Patent Act, 1874," or under chapter one hundred and fifty of the Revised Statutes, or otherwise incorporated, which statement purports to have been filled up and attested according to the said printed forms, or otherwise in substantial compliance with the provisions hereinafter mentioned, shall be deemed

and taken to be, and to have been, a sufficient statement, and in compliance in all respects with the provisions of the eighteenth and nineteenth sections of the said Act, intituled "An Act to make further provision respecting Permanent Building Societies," and with the sixty-seventh and sixty-eighth sections of the said Revised Statute respecting Building Societies, and to have been properly made, filled up and attested according to the provisions of the said Acts, and of the said Act amending the same, whether such attestation was sworn before a justice of the peace, or before a commissioner authorized to take affidavits in the superior courts, or whether or not the said statement was transmitted in due time to the said Treasurer; and every society, or company incorporated as aforesaid, the officers of which shall have transmitted such statement, shall be and is hereby indemnified, exonerated, freed and discharged of and from all pecuniary penalties and forfeitures whatsoever (if any) which may have been incurred by such company or society by reason of its having neglected to transmit any other, or further, or differently attested statement, or to perform the obligations imposed on it by the said Acts, or either of them, in that behalf;

(2) In case any action, suit, or proceedings shall, after the passing of this Act, be brought, carried on, or prosecuted against any society or company for or on account of any pecuniary penalty or forfeiture whatever incurred or to be incurred by any such neglect, as is intended to be relieved against by this Act, such society or company may plead the general issue, and upon their defence give this Act and the special matter in evidence upon any trial to be had thereupon; and in any action or suit commenced before the passing of this Act or now pending, against any society or company for or on account of any such neglect, the court or judge thereof shall order all proceedings in such action or suit to be stayed on payment of the costs thereof to the plaintiff therein.

2. No action brought against any society or company, incorporated, as aforesaid, for any past or future failure to comply with the provisions of the said Acts, or either of them, shall be maintained if such action was or is commenced at any time subsequent to the receipt by the Treasurer of Ontario of the statement and attestation required by the said Acts, or of the statement and attestation declared valid by this Act, unless such action is brought by the Crown, or by the Attorney-General of Ontario suing on behalf of the Crown.

3. Neither the provisions of the said eighteenth and nineteenth sections of the said Act intituled "An Act to make further provision respecting Building Societies," nor the provisions of the sixty-seventh and sixty-eighth sections of the said Revised Statute, either as originally passed or as heretofore amended, or as amended by this Act, shall be held to apply, or to have applied, to any society or company which has ceased, or shall have ceased, to carry on business prior to the year for which the return is or was required, nor to any society or company which, though incorporated, never carried on business; and upon its being proved that any society or company incorporated as aforesaid did not loan any money, or receive any deposit, or issue any debenture, during the year for which it is alleged a return in accordance with such sections has not been made, such society or company shall be deemed to have ceased to carry on business within the meaning of this section.

4. The sixty-seventh section of the said Revised Statute, as amended by the Act passed in the forty-first year of Her Majesty's reign, chaptered seven, and the sixty-eighth and sixty-ninth sections of the said Revised Statute are hereby repealed and the following substituted therefor:—

67. Such society shall, on or before the first day of March in each year, transmit to the Provincial Treasurer a full and clear statement of the society's assets and liabilities on some day to be stated therein, and such day shall not be more than twelve months prior to the said first day of March, or earlier than the end of the last preceding financial year, and such statement shall contain, in addition to such other particulars as the Provincial Treasurer may require, the following:

(a) The amount of stock subscribed;

(b) The amount paid in upon such stock;

(c) The amount borrowed for the purposes of investment and the securities given therefor:

(d) The amount invested and secured by mortgage deeds;

(e) Amount of mortgages payable by instalments;

(f) The number and aggregate amount of mortgages upon which compulsory proceedings have been taken during the past year;

(g) The present cash value of the society's investments on mortgages and other securities, and the rate or rates per cent. at which the future repayments are discounted in ascertaining such present cash value; which rate or rates shall be at least equal to the rate or rates which such mortgages or other securities respectively bear, or were originally calculated to yield.

68. Such statement shall be attested by the oath (taken before some justice of the peace, or commissioner for taking affidavits in the superior courts) of two persons, one being the president, vice-president, manager or secretary, and the other the manager, secretary or auditor of such society, each of whom shall swear distinctly that he holds such office as aforesaid, that the statement has been prepared by the proper officers of the company, that the deponent believes that it has been prepared with due care, and that he believes it to be true in every particular; and such statement shall be published by the Provincial Treasurer in such manner as he thinks most conducive to the public good; and for any neglect to transmit such statement in due course of post, within five days after the day upon which the same should be transmitted, such society shall incur a penalty of fifty dollars per diem, but not exceeding in the whole one thousand dollars.

69. If such statement is not transmitted within one month after the said first day of March, or if it appears by the statement that such society is not in a condition to justify its continuance in business with the powers theretofore possessed by such society, the Provincial Trea-

surer may, under the authority of, or by order of the Lieutenant-Governor-in-Council, by a notice in the *Ontario Gazette*, declare the business of such society to have ceased, so far as regards borrowing money and any other matters mentioned in the order in Council and notice aforesaid.

5. Any statement heretofore made, or which may be hereafter made, by any society or company with reference to a financial year of such society or company ending prior to the passing of this Act, shall be deemed sufficient if such return is made either in accordance with the provisions of this Act, or with the provisions of the said sections hereinbefore repealed.

6. If any officer of a society or company shall, when called upon to attest the statement required under this Act, find himself unable to make the required affidavit of attestation on account of his having doubts as to the correctness of the statement presented to him for attestation, and further time is needed in order to permit of an examination of the items making up such statement, then, upon application of such officer, or of any one on his behalf, or on behalf of the society or company, made at any time before the sixth day of March of the proper year, the Treasurer of Ontario may enlarge the time for transmitting such statement to a day not later than the first day of May of such year, and the day so fixed by the said Treasurer shall thereupon become the day within five days of which the said statement, attested as required by this Act, shall be transmitted by such society or company to the Treasurer of Ontario, under the like penalties, in case of omission to make the same within such time, as if such day had been inserted in the sixty-seventh and sixty-eighth sections of the said Revised Statute as amended by this Act, in lieu of the first day of March; Provided that the said enlargement of time shall not prevent proceedings being taken under the sixty-ninth section of the said Revised Statute, if the Lieutenant-Governor in Council shall so order;

(2) It shall be sufficient if the statement required to be furnished on or before the first day of March, one thousand eight hundred and eighty, is transmitted to the Treasurer of Ontario, on or before the first day of April next following, with power to the said Treasurer under the like circumstances to enlarge such time to a day not later than the first day of May of such year.

CHAP. CXLIX.

An Act containing General Provisions applicable to Joint Stock Companies incorporated by Special Act for certain purposes.

Section.
1. Short title.
2. Meaning of expression "Special Act."
3. Interpretation clause ; Company, Undertaking, Real Estate, Land, Shareholder.
4. To what Companies this Act shall apply. Manufacturing. Buildings for certain purposes. Mineral Springs. Fisheries. Forwarding. Gas or Water. Telegraphs. Works for transmission of timber. Roads, piers, etc. This Act to be incorporated with Special Acts incorporating Joint Stock Companies for the above purposes.
5. How incorporated with Acts for other purposes.
6. General corporate powers of every such Company. Rev. Stat. c. 1.
7. Powers under Special Act to be subject to this Act.
8. Board of Directors.
9. First Directors.
10. Qualification of Directors.
11. Election of Directors.
12. As to elections when not otherwise provided for.
13. Provision in case of failure of election.
14. Powers of Directors.
15. By-laws for divers purposes ; stock ; dividends ; directors ; officers ; annual meetings ; procedure ; penalties ; miscellaneous ; by-laws to be confirmed.
16. Proof of by-laws.
17. Proviso : calling special meetings.
18. Stock to be personally ; transfer.
19. Allotting stock.
20. Calling in instalments.
21. Ten per cent. at least to be called in yearly.
22. Action for calls ; what only need to be alleged and proved.

Section.
23. Forfeiture, for non-payment ; forfeited shares to belong to the Company.
24. Calls must be paid before transfer.
25. Shareholders in arrear not to vote.
26. Books to be kept by the Company ; what to contain.
27. Directors may disallow transfer of stock in certain cases ; their liability if they allow transfers to persons without means ; how Director may exonerate himself.
28. Effect of transfer limited until allowed.
29. Books to be open to shareholders and creditors of Company.
30. Effect as evidence. Penalty for making untrue entries.
31. Forfeiture of rights for not keeping books.
32. Company not bound to see to trusts on shares.
33. Contracts, bills, notes, &c., by the Company, how to be executed ; proviso.
34. As to holding stock in other corporations.
35. Liability of shareholders.
36. Shareholders not liable beyond amount of their stock.
37. As to stock held by persons in a representative capacity.
38. Voting on such stock.
39. Liability of Directors for certain debts of Company. Limitation of actions.
40. Penalty for paying dividends when Company is insolvent, &c. How a Director may exonerate himself.
41. Penalty for lending Company's money to shareholders.
42. Actions between Company and shareholders.
43. Service of process on Company.

HER MAJESTY, by and with the advice and consent of the Legislative Assembly of the Province of Ontario, enacts as follows :

1. This Act may be cited as "*The Ontario Joint Stock Companies General Clauses Act.*"

2. The expression "The Special Act," when used in this Act, shall be construed to mean any Act incorporating a Company for any of the purposes herein mentioned, and with which this Act is incorporated, in manner hereinafter mentioned,—and also all Acts amending such Act. 24 V. c. 18, s. 3.

3. The following words and expressions, both in this and the Special Act, shall have the meanings hereby assigned to them, unless there is something in the subject or context repugnant to such construction, that is to say :

(1.) "The Company" shall mean the Company incorporated by the Special Act ;

(2.) "The undertaking" shall mean the whole of the works and business of whatever kind, which the Company is authorized to under take and carry on ;

(3.) "Real estate" or "land," shall include all real estate messuages, lands, tenements and hereditaments, of any tenure ;

(4.) "Shareholder" shall mean every subscriber to or holder of, stock in the Company, and shall extend to and include the personal representatives of the shareholder. 24 V. c. 18, s. 4.

4. When not otherwise expressly enacted, this Act shall apply to every Joint Stock Company, subject to the Legislative authority of the Legislature of this Province, and incorporated by any Special Act passed since the the eigteenth day of May, 1861, or hereafter, for any of the following purposes :

1. The carrying on of any kind of manufacturing, shipbuilding, mining, mechanical or chemical business ;

2. The erection and maintenance of any building or buildings to to used in whole or part as a Mechanics' Institute, or Public Reading or Lecture Room, or as a place for holding Agricultural or Horticultural Fairs or Exhibitions, or as a place for Educational, Library, Scientific or Religious purposes, or as a Public Hotel, or as a place for Baths and Bath-houses ;

3. The opening and using of Petrolium, Salt or Mineral Springs ;

4. The carrying on of any Fishery or Fisheries in this Province, or the waters thereto adjacent, and the building and equipping of vessels required for such Fishery or Fisheries ;

5. The carrying on of any general forwarding business, and the construction, owning, chartering or leasing of ships, steamboats, wharves, roads, or other property required for the purpose of such forwarding business ;

6. The supplying of any place with Gas or Water, or with both Gas and Water ;

7. The constructing of any line or lines of Telegraph ;

8. The acquiring or constructing, and maintaining of any dam, slide, pier, boom or other work necessary to facilitate the transmission of timber down any river or stream in this Province, and the blasting of rocks, the dredging or removing of shoals or other impediments, or the improving otherwise of the navigation of such streams for such purpose ;

9. The acquiring or constructing, and maintaining, of any plank, macdamized or gavelled road, or of any bridge, pier, wharf, dry dock, or marine railway ;

And this Act shall be deemed to be incorporated with every such Special Act: and all the clauses and provisions of this Act unless they are expressly varied or excepted by any such Special Act, shall apply to the Company thereby chartered, so far as applicable thereto, and shall, as well as the clauses and provisions of every other Act incorporated with such Special Act, form part of such Special Act, and be construed together therewith as forming one Act. 24 V. c. 18, s. 1.

5. For the purpose of incorporating this Act, or any of its provisions with a Special Act for purposes other than aforesaid it shall be sufficient in such Special Act, to enact, that the clauses of this Act, or such of them as in such Act may be particularly designated to that end, shall be incorporated with such Special Act; and thereupon, all such clauses, save in so far as they are expressly varied or excepted by such Special Act, shall be construed as if the same were formally embodied and reproduced therein. 24 V. c. 18, s. 2.

6. Every Company incorporated for any of the above purposes, under any Special Act, shall be a body corporate under the name declared in the Special Act, and may acquire, hold, alienate and convey, any real estate necessary or requisite for the carrying on of the undertaking of such Company, and shall be invested with all the powers, privileges and immunities necessary to carry into effect the intentions and objects of this Act and of the Special Act, and which are incident to such corporation, or expressed or included in "*The Interpretation Act.*" 24 V. c. 18, s. 5.

7. All powers given by the Special Act to the Company shall be exercised subject to the provisions and restrictions contained in this Act. 24 V. c. 18, s. 6.

8. The affairs of every such Company shall be managed by a Board of not less than three, nor more than nine Directors. 24 V. c. 18, s. 7.

9. The persons named as such, in the Special Act, shall be the Directors of the Company, until replaced by others duly named in their stead. 24 V. c. 18, s. 8.

10. No person shall be elected or named as a Director thereafter, unless he is a shareholder, owning stock absolutely in his own right, and not in arrear in respect of any call thereon: And the major part of the after Directors of the Company shall, further, at all times, be persons resident in this Province, and subjects of Her Majesty by birth or naturalization. 24 V. c. 18, s. 9.

11. The after Directors of the Company shall be elected by the shareholders, in general meeting of the Company assembled, at such times, in such wise, and for such term, not exceeding two years, as the Special Act, or, in default thereof, the by-laws of the Company, may prescribe. 24 V. c. 18, s. 10.

12. In default only of other express provisions in such behalf, by the Special Act or by-laws of the Company,—

144   Cap. 149.   *Joint Stock Co'ys, General Clauses.*

1. Such election shall take place yearly, all the members of the Board retiring, and (if otherwise qualified) being eligible for re-election;

2. Notice of the time and place for holding general meetings of the Company shall be given at least ten days previously thereto, in some newspaper published at or as near as may be to the place in which the office or chief place of business of the Compony is;

3. At all general meetings of the Company, every shareholder shall be entitled to as many votes as he owns shares in the Company, and may vote by proxy;

4. Elections of Directors shall be by ballot:

5. Vacancies occurring in the Board of Directors may be filled for the unexpired remainder of the term, by the Board, from among the qualified shareholders of the Company;

6. The Directors shall from time to time elect from among themselves a President of the Company; and shall also name, and may remove at pleasure, all other officers thereof.   24 V. c. 18, s. 11.

13. If at any time an election of Directors is not made or does not take effect at the proper time, the Company shall not be held to be thereby dissolved; but such election may take place at any general meeting of the Company duly called for that purpose; and the retiring Directors shall continue in office until their successors are elected. 24 V. c. 18, s. 12.

14. The Directors of the Company shall have full power in all things to administer the affairs of the Company, and may make or cause to be made for the Company any description of contract which the Company may by law enter into.   24 V. c. 18, s. 13.

15. The Directors may from time to time make by-laws not contrary to law, nor to the Special Act, nor to this Act, to regulate —

(*a*) The allotment of stock, the making of calls thereon, the payment thereof, the issue and registration of certificates of stock, the forfeiture of stock for non-payment, the disposal of forfeited stock and of the proceeds thereof, the transfer of stock ;

(*b*) The declaration and payment of dividends ;

(*c*) The number of the Directors, their term of service, the amount of their stock qualification ;

(*d*) The appointment, functions, duties and removal of all agents, officers and servants of the Company, the security to be given by them to the Company, their remuneration and that (if any) of the Directors ;

(*e*) The time at which and place where the annual meetings of the Company shall be held ;

(*f*) The calling of meetings, regular and special, of the Board of Directors, and of the Company, the quorum, the requirements as to proxies, and the procedure in all things at such meetings ;

(*g*) The imposition and recovery of all penalties and forfeitures admitting of regulation by by-law ; and

(A) The conduct in all other particulars of the affairs of the Company;
and may from time to time repeal, amend or re-enact the same; but every such by-law, and every repeal, amendment or re-enactment thereof, unless in the meantime confirmed at a general meeting of the Company duly called for that purpose, shall only have force until the next annual meeting of the Company, and in default of confirmation thereat, shall, at and from that time only, cease to have force. 24 V., c. 18, s. 13.

16. A copy of any by-law of the Company, under its seal, and purporting to be signed by any officer of the Company, shall be received as *prima facie* evidence of such by-law in all Courts of Law or Equity in this Province. 24 V., c. 18, s. 14.

17. One-fourth part in value of the shareholders of the Company shall at all times have the right to call a special meeting thereof, for the transaction of any business specified in such written requisition and notice as they may issue to that effect. 24 V., c. 18, s. 13.

18. The stock of the Company shall be deemed personal estate, and shall be transferable, in such manner only, and subject to all such conditions and restrictions as by this Act, or by the Special Act or by-laws of the Company, may be prescribed. 24 V., c. 18, s. 15.

19. If the Special Act makes no other definite provisions, the stock thereof shall be allotted, when and as the Directors, by by-law or otherwise, may ordain. 24 V., c. 18, s. 16.

20. The Directors of the Company may call in and demand from the shareholders thereof, respectively, all sums of money by them subscribed, at such time and places, and in such payments or instalments, as the Special Act, or as this Act may require or allow; and interest shall accrue and fall due, at the legal rate for the time being, upon the amount of any unpaid call, from the day appointed for payment of such call. 24 V., c. 18, s. 17.

21. Not less than ten per centum upon the allotted stock of the Company shall, by means of one or more calls, be called in and made payable within one year from the incorporation of the Company; and for every year thereafter, at least a further ten per centum shall in like manner be called in and made payable, until the whole is called in. 24 V., c. 18, s. 18.

22. The Company may enforce payment of all calls and interest thereon, by action in any Court of competent jurisdiction; and in such action it shall not be necessary to set forth the special matter, but it shall be sufficient to declare that the defendant is a holder of one share or more, stating the number of shares, and is indebted in the sum of money to which the calls in arrear amount, in respect of one call or more upon one share or more, stating the number of calls and the amount of each, whereby an action has accrued to the Company under this Act; and a certificate under the seal, and purporting to be signed by any officer, of the Company, to the effect that the defendant is a

shareholder, that such call or calls has or have been made, and that so much is due by him and unpaid thereon, shall be received in all Courts of Law and Equity as *primâ facie* evidence to that effect. 24 V., c. 18, s. 19.

23. If, after such demand or notice as by the Special Act or by-laws of the Company is prescribed, any call made upon any share or shares is not paid within such time as by the Special Act or by-laws is limited in that behalf, the Directors, in their discretion, by vote to that effect, reciting the facts, and duly recorded in their minutes, may summarily forfeit any shares whereon such payment is not made; and the same shall thereupon become the property of the Company, and may be disposed of as by by-laws or otherwise it may ordain. 24 V., c. 18, s. 20.

24. No share shall be transferable, until all previous calls thereon have been fully paid in, or until declared forfeited for non-payment of calls thereon. 24 V., c. 18, s. 21.

25. No shareholder being in arrear in respect of any call shall be entitled to vote at any meeting of the Company. 24 V., c. 18, s. 22.

26. The Company shall cause a book or books to be kept by the Secretary, or by some other officer specially charged with that duty, wherein shall be kept recorded—

1. The names, alphabetically arranged, of all persons who are or have been shareholders;

2. The address and calling of every such person, while such shareholder;

3. The number of shares of stock, held by each shareholder;

4. The amounts paid in, and remaining unpaid, respectively, on the stock of each shareholder;

5. All transfers of stock, in their order as presented to the Company for entry, with the date and other particulars of each transfer, and the date of the entry thereof; and—

6. The names, addresses and calling, of all persons who are or have been Directors of the Company; with the several dates at which each person became or ceased to be such Director. 24 V., c. 18, s. 23.

27. The Directors may refuse to allow the entry in any such book, of any transfer of stock whereof the whole amount has not been paid in; and whenever entry is made in such book, of any transfer of stock not fully paid in, to a person not being of apparently sufficient means, the Directors, jointly and severally, shall be liable to the creditors of the Company, in the same manner and to the same extent as the transferring shareholder, but for such entry, would have been: but if any Director present when such entry is allowed forthwith, or if any Director then absent, within twenty-four hours after he has become aware thereof and able so to do, enters in the minute book of the Board of Directors his protest against the same, and within eight days thereafter causes such protest to be published in at least one newspaper published at, or as near as may be possible to, the office or chief place of business of the Company, such Director may thereby, and not otherwise, exonerate himself from such liability. 24 V., c. 18, s. 24.

24. No transfer of stock shall be valid for any purpose whatever, save only as exhibiting the rights of the parties thereto towards each other, and as rendering the transferee liable *ad interim* jointly and severally with the transferor, to the Company and their creditors,— until entry thereof has been duly made in such book or books. 24 V., c. 18, s. 25.

29. Such books shall, during reasonable business hours of every day, except Sundays and statutory and obligatory holidays, be kept open for the inspection of shareholders and creditors of the Company, and their personal representatives, at the office or chief place of business of the Company; and every such shareholder, creditor or representative may make extracts therefrom. 24 V. c. 18, s. 26.

30. Such books shall be *prima facie* evidence of all facts purporting to be thereby stated, in any suit or proceeding against the Company or against any shareholder. 24 V. c. 18, s. 27.

[*Section* 28 *of* 24 V. c. 18, *is as follows:*

28. Every Director, officer or servant of the Company, who knowingly makes or assists to make any untrue entry in any such book, or who refuses or neglects to make any proper entry therein, or to exhibit the same, or to allow the same to be inspected and extracts to be taken therefrom, shall be guilty of a misdemeanor, and being convicted thereof shall be punished accordingly.]

31. Every Company neglecting to keep such book or books open for inspection as aforesaid, shall forfeit its corporate rights. 24 V. c. 18, s. 29.

32. The Company shall not be bound to see to the execution of any trust, whether express, implied or constructive, in respect of any shares; and the receipt of the shareholder in whose name the same stand in the books of the Company, shall be a valid and binding discharge to the Company for any dividend or money payable in respect of such shares, and whether or not notice of such trust has been given to the Company; and the Company shall not be bound to see to the application of the money paid upon such receipt. 24 V. c. 18, s. 30.

33. Every contract, agreement, engagement or bargain made, and every bill of exchange drawn, accepted or endorsed, and every promissory note and cheque made, drawn or endorsed on behalf of the Company, by any agent, officer or servant of the Company, in general accordance with his powers as such under the by-laws of the Company, shall be binding on the Company; and in no case shall it be necessary to have the seal of the Company affixed to any such contract, agreement, engagement, bargain, bill of exchange, promissory note or cheque, or to prove that the same was made, drawn, accepted or endorsed, as the case may be, in pursuance of any by-law, or special vote or order; nor shall the party so acting as agent, officer or servant of the Company, be thereby subjected individually to any liability whatsoever to any third party, therefor;

2. Nothing in this section shall be construed to authorize the Company to issue any note payable to the bearer thereof, or any promissory note intended to be circulated as money, or as the note of a bank. 24 V. c. 18, s. 31.

34. No Company shall use any of its funds in the purchase of stock in any other corporation, unless in so far as such purchase is specially authorized by the Special Act, and also by the Act creating such other corporation. 24 V. c. 18, s. 32.

35. Each shareholder, until the whole amount of his stock has been paid up, shall be individually liable to the creditors of the Company, to an amount equal to that not paid up thereon; but shall not be liable to an action therefor by any creditor, before an execution against the Company has been returned unsatisfied in whole or in part; and the amount due on such execution shall be the amount recoverable with costs, against such shareholders. 24 V. c. 18, s. 33.

36. The shareholders of the Company shall not as such be held responsible for any Act, default or liability whatsoever, of the Company, or for any engagement, claim, payment, loss, injury, transaction, matter or thing whatsoever, relating to or connected with the Company, beyond the amount of their respective shares in the capital stock thereof. 24 V. c. 18, s. 34.

37. No person holding stock in the Company as an executor, administrator, tutor, curator, guardian or trustee, shall be personally subject to liability as a shareholder, but the estates and funds in the hands of such person, shall be liable in like manner, and to the same extent, as the testator or intestate, or the minor, ward, and interdicted person, or the person interested in such trust fund, would be, if living and competent to act, and holding such stock in his own name; and no person holding such stock as collateral security, shall be personally subject to such liability, but the person pledging such stock shall be considered as holding the same, and shall be liable as a shareholder accordingly. 24 V. c. 18, s. 35.

38. Every such executor, administrator, tutor, curator, guardian or trustee, shall represent the stock in his hands, at all meetings of the Company, and may vote accordingly as a shareholder; and every person who pledges his stock may nevertheless represent the same at all such meetings, and may vote accordingly as a shareholder. 24 V. c. 18, s. 36.

39. The Directors of the Company shall be jointly and severally liable upon any and every written contract or undertaking of the Company on the face whereof the word "*Limited*" or the words "*Limited Liability*" are not distinctly written or printed after the name of the Company where first occurring, and also to the labourers, servants and apprentices of the Company, for all debts not exceeding one year's wages, due for service performed to the Company whilst they are such Directors respectively; but no Director shall be liable to an action upon any such contract or undertaking or for recovery of any such debt, unless the Company has been sued upon or for the same within one year after the same became exigible, nor yet unless such Director is sued thereon or therefor within one year thereafter, nor yet before an execution against the Company has been returned unsatisfied in whole or in part; and the amount due on such execution shall be the amount recoverable, with costs, against the Directors. 24 V. c. 18, s. 39.

40. If the Directors of the Company declare and pay any dividend when the Company is insolvent, or any dividend the payment of which renders the Company insolvent, or diminishes the capital stock thereof, they shall be jointly and severally liable, as well to the Company as to the individual shareholders and creditors thereof, for all the debts of the Company then existing, and for all thereafter contracted during their continuance in office, respectively; but if any Director present when such dividend is declared, forthwith, or if any Director then absent, within twenty-four hours after he has become aware thereof and able so to do, enters on the minutes of the Board of Directors his protest against the same, and within eight days thereafter causes such protest to be published in at least one newspaper published in or as near as may be possible to the place where the office or chief place of business of the Company is, such Directors may thereby, and not otherwise, exonerate himself from such liability. 24 V.c. 18, s. 37.

41. No loan shall be made by the Company to any shareholder, and if such is made, all Directors and other officers of the Company making the same, or in any wise assenting thereto, shall be jointly and severally liable to the Company for the amount of such loan,—and also to third parties, to the extent of such loan with legal interest, for all the debts of the Company contracted from the time of the making of such loan to that of the re-payment thereof. 24 V. c. 18, s. 38.

42. Any description of action may be prosecuted and maintained between the Company and any shareholder thereof. 24 V. c. 18, s. 41.

43. Service of all manner of summons or writ whatever upon the Company, may be made by leaving a copy thereof at the office or chief place of business of the Company, with any grown person in charge thereof, or elsewhere with the President or Secretary thereof; or if the Company has no known office or chief place of business, and has no known President or Secretary, then, upon return to that effect duly made, the Court shall order such publication as it may deem requisite to be made in the premises, for at least one month, in at least one newspaper; and such publication shall be held to be due service upon the Company. 24 V. c. 18, s. 40.

CHAP. CL.

An Act respecting the incorporation of Joint Stock Companies by Letters Patent.

Section.
1. Short title.
2. Interpretation of the words :—" The letters patent," " The supplementary letters patent," " The Company," " The undertaking," " Real estate," " Land," " Shareholder."
3. Companies formed for certain purposes may be incorporated by letters patent.
4. Notice to be given in the Ontario Gazette, and what it shall contain.
5. Petition for letters patent, what it shall contain.
6. Notices for incorporation of companies by the Legislature may in certain cases be accepted as notices for letters patent.
7. Lieutenant-Governor may dispense with notice when capital $3,000 or under.
8. Preliminary conditions, to be established. Proof thereof. Power to take affidavits.
9. Name different from that proposed may be given without further notice.
10. Notice of issuing letters patent. Completion of incorporation.
11. Change of name and supplementary letters patent. Compelling change of name.
12. Change of name. 37 V. c. 35 (O).
13. Certain informalities not to invalidate letters patent.
14. General corporate powers of such companies.
15. Sub-division of shares.
16. Increase of capital. By-law for that purpose.
17. Reduction of capital; by-law for that purpose; liability of shareholders on decrease; such by-laws must be approved by shareholders and confirmed by supplementary letters-patent.
18. Petition for supplementary letters patent; By-law, &c., to be produced with petition; powers of officer charged to report on petition.
19. Granting of supplementary letters patent; notice thereof; effect of such letters patent.
20. Powers by the letters patent to be subject to this Act.
21. Board of Directors.
22. Provisional Directors.
23. Qualifications of Directors.
24. After Directors, to be elected.
25. Mode of election; yearly; notice; votes; ballot; vacancies; President and officers.
26. Failure to elect Directors, how remedied.
27. Change in the number of Directors.

Section.
28. Powers and duties of Directors.
29. By-laws ; stock ; dividends ; Directors ; officers ; meetings ; fines ; conduct of affairs generally ; confirmation of by-laws.
30. Power to issue bonds, debentures, and to grant mortgages.
31. Special meetings.
32. Evidence of by-laws.
33. Stock, personal estate.
34. Allotment of stock.
35. Disposal of stock. Payment to President or Director.
36. Calling in instalments.
37. Calls. Ten per cent within first year.
38. Enforcement of payment of calls, by action.
39. Forfeiture of shares.
40. Restriction as to transfers.
41. Shareholders in arrears not to vote.
42. Record books to be kept and what to contain.
43. Refusal to enter transfer if calls not paid.
44. Transfer valid only after entry.
45. Books to be opened for inspection.
46. Books to be prima facie evidence.
47. Penalty for false entries.
48. Liability for refusal to allow inspection of books.
49. Lists of shareholders and statements of affairs to be made yearly, with other particulars. Contents of statement ; mode of writing same ; verification thereof; posting thereof; deposit with Provincial Secretary ; penalty for default.
50. Company not to be liable in respect of trusts, &c.
51. Contracts, &c. when to be binding on company. Proviso as to notes, banking and insurance.
52. Not to purchase stock in other corporations.
53. Liability of shareholders.
54. Limited to amount of stock.
55. Trustees &c., not personally liable. Mortgages.
56. Trustee, etc., may vote. Mortgagor of stock may vote.
57. Liability of Directors declaring a dividend when Company is insolvent, &c. How a Director may avoid such liability.
58. No loan by Company to shareholder. Except in certain cases.
59. Liability of Directors for wages.
60. Service of process on the Company.

Section.
61. Actions between Company and shareholders.
62. Mode of incorporation, etc., how to be set forth in legal proceedings.
63. Forfeiture of charter for non-user.
64. Fees on letters patent, etc., to be fixed by Order-in-Council.

Section.
65. Subsisting companies may apply under this Act.
66. Subsisting companies may apply for letters patent with extended powers.
67. Proofs may be by affidavit.
68. Winding up Acts to apply.

HER MAJESTY, by and with the advice and consent of the Legislative Assembly of the Province of Ontario, enacts as follows:

1. This Act may be cited as "*The Ontario Joint Stock Companies' Letters Patent Act.*"

2. The following expressions in this Act, and in all letters patent and supplementary letters patent issued under the same, shall have the meaning hereby assigned to them, unless there is something in the subject or context repugnant to such construction, that is to say:

(1.) "The letters patent" shall mean the letters patent incorporating a Company for any purpose contemplated by this Act;

(2.) "The supplementary letters patent" shall mean any letters patent granted for the increasing or reducing of the capital stock of such Company.

(3.) "The Company" shall mean the Company so incorporated by letters patent;

(4.) "The undertaking" shall mean the whole of the works and business of every kind, which the Company is authorized to carry on;

(5.) "Real estate" or "land" shall include all immovable real property of every kind;

(6.) "Shareholder" shall mean every subscriber to, or holder of stock in the Company, and extend to, and include the personal representatives of the shareholder. 37 V. c. 35, s. 2.

3. The Lieutenant-Governor in Council may, by letters patent under the Great Seal, grant a charter to any number of persons, not less than five, who shall petition therefor, constituting such persons and others who may become shareholders in the Company thereby created, a body corporate and politic, for any purposes or objects to which the legislative authority of the Legislature of Ontario extends, except the construction and working of Railways and the business of Insurance. 37 V. c. 35, s. 3.

4. The applicants for such letters patent must give at least one month's previous notice in the *Ontario Gazette*, of their intention to apply for the same, stating therein:

(*a.*) The proposed corporate name of the Company, which shall not be that of any other known Company, incorporated or unincorporated, or any name liable to be unfairly confounded therewith, or otherwise on public ground objectionable;

(*b.*) The object for which its incorporation is sought;

(*c.*) The place or places within the Province of Ontario, where its operations are to be carried on, with special mention if there be two or more such places, of some one of them as its chief place of business:

(*d.*) The amount of its capital stock;
(*e.*) The number of shares and amount of each share;
(*f.*) The names in full and the address and calling of each of the applicants, with special mention of the names of not less than three of their number, who are to be the first Directors of the Company. 37 V. c. 35, s. 4; 39 V. c. 7, s. 25.

5. At any time, not more than one month after the last publication of such notice, the applicants may petition the Lieutenant-Governor, through the Provincial Secretary, for the issue of such letters patent.

2. Such petition must state the facts required to be set forth in the notice, and must further state the amount of stock taken by each applicant, and also the amount, if any, paid in upon the stock of each applicant.

3. The petition must also state whether such amount is paid in cash or by transfer of property, or how otherwise.

4. In case the petition is not signed by all the shareholders whose names are proposed to be inserted in the letters patent, it shall be accompanied by a memorandum of association, signed by all the persons whose names are to be so inserted, or by their attorneys, lawfully authorized in writing, and such memorandum shall contain the particulars required by the next preceding section.

5. The petition may ask for the embodying in the letters patent, of any provision which otherwise under this Act might be embodied in any by-law of the Company when incorporated. 37 V. c. 35, s. 5.

6. Where a notice has been published according to the rules of the Legislative Assembly for an Act incorporating any Company, the incorporation whereof is sought for objects for which incorporation is authorized by this Act, and a Bill has been introduced into the said Assembly in accordance with such notice, and is subsequently thrown out or withdrawn, then in case a petition to the Lieutenant-Governor for the incorporation under this Act of such Company is filed with the Provincial Secretary within one month from the day of the termination of the Session of the Assembly for which the said notice was given, such notice may be accepted in lieu of the notice required by the fourth section. 40 V. c. 8, s. 64.

7. The Lieutenant-Governor may dispense with the publication of the notice mentioned in section four, in any case in which the capital of the proposed Company is three thousand dollars or under; and in such case the petition to the Lieutenant-Governor shall state the particulars mentioned in section four in addition to the particulars mentioned in section five. 40 V. c. 8, s. 65.

8. Before the letters patent are issued, the applicants must establish to the satisfaction of the Provincial Secretary, or of such other officer as may be charged by order of the Lieutenant-Governor in Council to report thereon, the sufficiency of their notice and petition, and that the proposed name is not the name of any other known incorporated or unincorporated Company.

8. The Provincial Secretary, or such other officer, may for the purposes aforesaid, take and keep of record any requisite evidence in writing under oath or affirmation, and he, or any Justice of the Peace, or Commissioner for taking affidavits in any of the Superior Courts, may administer every requisite oath or affirmation. 37 V. c. 35, s. 6.

9. The letters patent shall recite such of the material averments of the notice and petition so established, as the Lieutenant-Governor may find convenient to insert therein, and the Lieutenant-Governor may, if he thinks fit, give to the Company, a corporate name different from the name proposed by the applicants in the published notice; and the objects of the Company as stated in the letters patent may vary from the objects stated in the said notice, provided the objects of the Company as stated in the letters patent, are of a similar character to those contained in the notice published as aforesaid. 40 V. 8, s. 62.

10. Notice of the granting of the letters patent shall be forthwith given by the Provincial Secretary, in the *Ontario Gazette*, in the form of the Schedule A appended to this Act; and from the date of the letters patent the persons therein named and their successors shall be a body corporate and politic by the name mentioned therein. 37 V. c. 35, s. 8.

11. In case it is made to appear that any Company is incorporated under a name the same as, or similar to, that of an existing Company, it shall be lawful for the Lieutenant-Governor in Council to direct the issue of supplementary letters patent reciting the former letters, and changing the name of the Company to some other name to be set forth in the supplementary letters patent; and no such alteration of name shall affect the rights or obligations of the Company; and all proceedings may be continued and commenced by or against the Company by its new name, that might have been continued or commenced by or against the Company by its former name.

2. The Court of Chancery may compel an application under this section whenever a Company improperly assumes the name of, or a name similar to, that of an existing Company. 37 V. c. 35, s. 9.

12. Where a Company heretofore incorporated under *The Ontario Joint Stock Companies Letters Patent Act* 1874, or incorporated under this Act is desirous of adopting another name, the Lieutenant-Governor in Council, upon being satisfied that the change desired is not for any improper purpose, may direct the issue of supplementary letters patent reciting the former letters patent, and changing the name of the Company to some other name set forth in the supplementary letters patent. 38 V. c. 23, s. 5.

13. The provisions of this Act relating to matter preliminary to the issue of the letters patent shall be deemed directory only; and no letters patent issued under this Act shall be held void or voidable, on account of any irregularity in any notice prescribed by this Act, or on account of the insufficiency or absence of any such notice, or on account of any irregularity in respect of any other matter preliminary to the issue of such letters patent. 38 V. c. 23, s. 3.

14. Every Company so incorporated may acquire, hold, alienate and convey real estate subject to any restrictions or conditions in the letters patent set forth, and shall forthwith become and be invested with all rights, real and personal, heretofore held by or for the Company under a trust created with a view to its incorporation, and with all the powers, privileges and immunities requisite to the carrying on of its undertaking, as though the Company had been incorporated by a Special Act of the Legislature, making the Company a body politic and corporate, and embodying all the provisions of this Act, and of the letters patent. 37 V. c. 35, s. 10; 40 V. c. 8, s. 63.

15. The Directors of the Company, if they see fit at any time, may make a by-law sub-dividing the existing shares into shares of smaller amount. 37 V. c. 35, s. 11.

16. The Directors of the Company, if they see fit at any time, after the whole capital stock of the Company has been taken up and fifty per centum thereon paid in, but not sooner, may make a by-law for increasing the capital stock of the Company to any amount which they may consider requisite for the due carrying out of the objects of the Company;

2. Such by-law shall declare the number and value of the shares of the new stock; and may prescribe the manner in which the same is to be allotted; and in default of its so doing, the control of such allotment shall be held to vest absolutely in the Directors. 37 V. c. 35, s. 12.

17. The Directors of the Company, if they see fit at any time, may make a by-law for decreasing the capital stock of the Company to any amount which they may consider sufficient for the due carrying out of the undertaking of the Company, and advisable.

2. Such by-law shall declare the number and value of the shares of the stock as so decreased; and the allotment thereof or the rule or rules by which the same is to be made. 37 V. c. 35, s. 13.

3. The liability of shareholders to persons who were, at the time of the reduction of the capital, creditors of the Company, shall remain as though the capital had not been decreased. 37 V. c. 35, s. 14, (2.)

4. But no by-law for increasing or decreasing the capital stock of the Company, or subdividing the shares, shall have any force or effect whatever, until after it has been sanctioned by a vote of not less than two-thirds in value of the shareholders at a general meeting of the Company duly called for considering the same, and afterwards confirmed by supplementary letters patent. 37 V. c. 35, s. 14, (1.)

18. At any time not more than six months after such sanction of such by-law, the Directors may petition the Lieutenant-Governor, through the Provincial Secretary, for the issue of supplementary letters patent to confirm the same.

2. With such petition they shall produce such by-law, and establish to the satisfaction of the Provincial Secretary, or of such other officer as may be charged by order of the Lieutenant-Governor in Council, to report thereon the due passage and sanction of such by-law, and if the

petition is in respect of increase or decrease of capital, the *bond fide* character of the increase or decrease of capital thereby provided for, and that notice of the application for supplementary letters patent has been inserted for one month in the *Ontario Gazette.*

17a. The directors of any company which has been heretofore incorporated or shall be hereafter incorporated under "The Ontario Joint Stock Companies' Letters Patent Act," or "The Ontario Joint Stock Companies' Letters Patent Act 1874," may make a by-law for creating and issuing any part of the capital stock as preference stock, giving the same such preference and priority, as respects dividends and otherwise over ordinary stock, as may be declared by such by-law. 41 V. c. 8, s. 16. *Joint Stock Companies may issue preferential stock.*

(2) Such by-law may provide that the holders of such preference shares shall have the right to select a certain stated proportion of the board of directors, or may give them such other control over the affairs of the company as may be considered expedient. 41 V. c. 8, s. 16. *Powers to preference share-holders.*

(3) No such by-laws shall have any force or effect whatever until after it has been unanimously sanctioned by the vote of the shareholders, present in person or by proxy at a general meeting of the company, duly called for considering the same, or unanimously sanctioned in writing by the shareholders of such company. 41 V. c. 8, s. 16. *Sanction required as to preference shares.*

(4) All the provisions of The Ontario Joint Stock Letters Patent Act not inconsistent with this Act shall apply to companies who may create and issue preferential stock hereunder; and holders of such stock shall be shareholders within the meaning of the said Act, and shall in all respects possess the rights and be subject to the liabilities of shareholders within the meaning of the said Act, provided, however, that in respect of dividends and otherwise they shall, as against the original or ordinary shareholders, be entitled to the preference given by any by-law as aforesaid. 41 V. c. 8, s. 16. *Ont. Jt. Stk. Letters Patent Act to apply on issue of preference stock. Rights and liabilities of holders.*

(5) Nothing in this section shall affect or impair the rights of creditors of any company. 41 V. c. 8, s. 16. *Rights of creditors continued.*

newspaper published at or as near as may be to the office or chief place of business of the Company;

14. Every Company so incorporated may acquire, hold, alienate and convey real estate subject to any restrictions or conditions in the letters patent set forth, and shall forthwith become and be invested with all rights, real and personal, heretofore held by or for the Company under a trust

report thereon the due passage and sanction of such by-law, and if the petition is in respect of increase or decrease of capital, the *bonâ fide* character of the increase or decrease of capital thereby provided for, and that notice of the application for supplementary letters patent has been inserted for one month in the *Ontario Gazette.*

8. The Provincial Secretary, or such other officer, may for the purposes aforesaid take and keep of record any requisite evidence in writing, under oath or affirmation; and he, or any Justice of the Peace, or Commissioner for taking affidavits in the Superior Courts, may administer every requisite oath or affirmation. 37 V. c. 35, s. 15.

19. Upon due proof so made, the Lieutenant-Governor in Council may grant such supplementary letters patent under the Great Seal; and notice thereof shall be forthwith given by the Provincial Secretary in the *Ontario Gazette*, in the form of the Schedule B appended to this Act; and thereupon, from the date of the supplementary letters patent, the shares shall be subdivided, or the capital stock of the Company shall be and remain increased, or decreased, as the case may be, to the amount, in the manner, and subject to the conditions set forth by such by-law; and the whole of the stock, as so increased or decreased, shall become subject to the provisions of this Act, in like manner (so far as may be) as though every part thereof had formed part of the stock of the Company originally subscribed. 37 V. c. 35, s. 16.

20. All powers given to the Company by the letters patent and supplementary letters patent granted in its behalf, shall be exercised subject to the provisions and restrictions contained in this Act. 37 V. c. 35, s. 17.

21. The affairs of every such Company shall be managed by a Board of not less than three Directors. 39 V. c. 7, s. 25.

22. The persons named as such, in the letters patent, shall be the Directors of the Company, until replaced by others duly appointed in their stead. 37 V. c. 35, s. 19.

23. No person shall be elected or appointed as a Director thereafter, unless he is a shareholder, owning stock absolutely in his own right, and not in arrear in respect of any call thereon. 37 V. c. 35, s. 20.

24. The after Directors of the Company shall be elected by the shareholders in general meeting of the Company assembled at some place within this Province, at such times, in such wise, and for such term, not exceeding two years, as the letters patent, or (in default thereof) the by-laws of the Company may prescribe. 37 V. c. 35, s. 21.

25. In default only of other express provisions in such behalf, by the letters patent or by-laws of the Company;

1. Such election shall take place yearly, all the members of the Board retiring, and (if otherwise qualified) being eligible for re-election;

2. Notice of the time and place for holding general meetings of the Company shall be given at least ten days previously thereto, in some newspaper published at or as near as may be to the office or chief place of business of the Company;

3. At all general meetings of the Company, every shareholder shall be entitled to as many votes as he owns shares in the Company, and may vote by proxy;

4. Elections of Directors shall be by ballot;

5. Vacancies occurring in the Board of Directors may, unless the by-laws otherwise direct, be filled for the unexpired remainder of the term, by the Board, from among the qualified shareholders of the Company;

6. The Directors shall, from time to time, elect from among themselves, a President of the Company; and shall also name, and may remove at pleasure, all other officers thereof. 37 V., c. 35, s. 22.

26. If at any time an election of Directors is not made, or does not take effect at the proper time, the Company shall not be held to be thereby dissolved; but such election may take place at any general meeting of the Company duly called for that purpose; and the retiring Directors shall continue in office until their successors are elected. 37 V., c. 35, s. 23.

27. A company incorporated under this Act may by by-law increase or decrease the number of its Directors, or may change the Company's chief place of business in Ontario.

2. No by-law for either of the said purposes shall be valid or acted upon unless it is sanctioned by a vote of not less than two-thirds in value of the shareholders present, in person or by proxy, at a general meeting duly called for considering the by-law, nor until a copy of such by-law has been certified under the seal of the Company to the Provincial Secretary, and also has been published in the *Ontario Gazette*. 38 V., c. 23, s. 2.

28. The Directors of the Company shall have full power in all things to administer the affairs of the Company; and may make, or cause to be made, for the Company, any description of contract which the Company may by law enter into. 37 V., c. 35, s. 24, *part*.

29. The Directors may, from time to time, make by-laws not contrary to law, or to the letters patent of the Company, or to this Act to regulate—

(*a.*) The allotment of stock; the making of calls thereon; the payment thereof; the issue and registration of certificates of stock; the forfeiture of stock for non-payment; the disposal of forfeited stock and of the proceeds thereof; the transfer of stock;

(*b.*) The declaration and payment of dividends;

(*c.*) The number of the Directors, their term of service, the amount of their stock qualification;

(*d.*) The appointment, functions, duties and removal of all agents, officers and servants of the Company; the security to be given by them to the Company; and their remuneration;

(*e.*) The time at which and place where the annual meetings of the Company shall be held; the calling of meetings, regular and special, of the Board of Directors, and of the Company; the quorum; the requirements as to proxies; and the procedure in all things at such meetings;

(*f.*) The imposition and recovery of all penalties and forfeitures admitting of regulation by by-law; and

(*g.*) The conduct in all other particulars of the affairs of the Company;

and may, from time to time, repeal, amend or re-enact the same; but every such by-law, and every repeal, amendment or re-enactment thereof, unless in the meantime confirmed at a general meeting of the Company, duly called for that purpose, shall only have force until the next annual meeting of the Company; and in default of confirmation thereat, shall, at and from that time only, cease to have force; and in that case no new by-law to the same or like effect shall have any force, until confirmed at a general meeting of the Company. 37 V., c. 35, s. 24, *part.*

80. In case a by-law, authorizing the same, is sanctioned by a vote of not less than two-thirds in value, of the said shareholders, then present in person or by proxy, at a general meeting duly called for considering the by-law, the Directors may borrow money upon the credit of the Company, and issue the bonds, debentures, or other securities of the Company, and may sell the said bonds, debentures, or other securities at such prices as may be deemed expedient or be necessary; but no such debentures shall be for a less sum than one hundred dollars;

2. The Directors may, under the like sanction, hypothecate, mortgage, or pledge the real or personal property of the Company, to secure any sum or sums borrowed for the purposes thereof. 37 V., c. 35, s. 25.

81. One-fourth part in value of the shareholders of the Company shall at all times have the right to call a special meeting thereof, for the transaction of any business specified in such written requisition and notice as they may issue to that effect. 37 V., c. 35, s. 24, *part.*

82. A copy of any by-law of the Company, under its seal, and purporting to be signed by any officer of the Company, shall be received as *prima facie* evidence of such by-law in all Courts of Law or Equity in Ontario. 37 V., c. 35, s. 26.

83. The stock of the Company shall be deemed personal estate, and shall be transferable, in such manner only, and subject to all such conditions and restrictions as by this Act, or by the letters patent or by-laws of the Company, may be prescribed. 37 V., c. 35, s. 27.

84. If the letters patent make no other definite provision, the stock of the Company, so far as it is not allotted thereby, shall be allotted when and as the Directors, by by-law or otherwise ordain. 37 V. c. 35, s. 28.

85. No by-law for the allotment or sale of stock at any greater discount or at any less premium than what has been previously authorized at a general meeting, or for the payment of the President or any Director, shall be valid or acted upon until the same has been confirmed at a general meeting. 37 V. c. 35, s. 24, *part.*

36. The Directors of the Company may call in and demand from the shareholders thereof, respectively, all sums of money by them subscribed, at such times and places, and in such payments or instalments, as the letters patent, or this Act, or the by-laws of the Company require or allow; and interest shall accrue and fall due, at the legal rate for the time being, upon the amount of any unpaid call, from the day appointed for payment of such call. 37 V. c. 35, s. 29.

37. Not less than ten per centum upon the allotted stock of the Company, shall, by means of one or more calls, be called in and made payable within one year from the incorporation of the Company; the residue, when and as the by-laws of the Company direct. 37 V. c. 35, s. 30.

38. The Company may enforce payment of all calls and interest thereon, by action in any Court of competent jurisdiction; and in such action it shall not be necessary to set forth the special matter, but it shall be sufficient to declare that the defendant is a holder of one share or more, stating the number of shares, and is indebted in the sum of money to which the calls in arrear amount, in respect of one call or more upon one share or more, stating the number of calls and the amount of each, whereby an action has accrued to the Company under this Act; and a certificate under the seal, and purporting to be signed by an officer of the Company, to the effect that the defendant is a shareholder, that such call or calls has or have been made, and that so much is due by him and unpaid thereon, shall be received in all Courts of Law and Equity as *prima facie* evidence to that effect. 37 V. c. 35, s. 31.

39. If after such demand or notice as by the letters patent or by-laws of the Company is prescribed, any call made upon any share or shares is not paid within such time as by such letters patent or by-laws may be limited in that behalf, the Directors in their discretion, by vote to that effect, reciting the facts, and duly recorded in their minutes, may summarily forfeit any shares whereon such payment is not made; and the same shall thereupon become the property of the Company, and may be disposed of as by-laws or otherwise the Company may ordain. 37 V. c. 35, s. 32.

40. No share shall be transferable, until all previous calls thereon have been fully paid in, or until declared forfeited for non-payment of calls thereon. 37 V. c. 35, s. 33.

41. No shareholder being in arrear in respect of any call shall be entitled to vote at any meeting of the Company. 37 V. c. 35, s. 34.

42. The Company shall cause a book or books to be kept by the Secretary, or by some other officer especially charged with that duty, wherein shall be kept recorded—

(*a.*) A copy of the letters patent incorporating the Company, and of any supplementary letters patent for increasing or decreasing the capital stock thereof, and of all by-laws thereof;

(*b.*) The names, alphabetically arranged, of all persons who are or have been shareholders;

(*c.*) The address and calling of every such person while such shareholder;

(*d.*) The number of shares of stock held by each shareholder;

(*e.*) The amounts paid in, and remaining unpaid, respectively, on the stock of each shareholder;

(*f.*) All tranfers of stock, in their order as presented to the Company for entry, with the date and other particulars of each transfer, and the date of the entry thereof; and

(*g.*) The names, addresses and calling of all persons who are or have been Directors of the Company; with the several dates at which each person became or ceased to be such Director. 37 V. c. 35, s. 35.

43. The Directors may refuse to allow the entry, into any such book, of any tranfer of stock whereon any call has been made which has not been paid in. 37 V. c. 35, s. 36.

44. No transfer of stock, unless made by sale under execution, shall be valid for any purpose whatever save only as exhibiting the rights of the parties thereto towards each other, and as rendering the transferee liable *ad interim* jointly and severally with the transferor to the Company and their creditors, until the entry thereof has been duly made in such book or books. 37 V. c. 35, s. 37.

45. Such books shall, during reasonable business hours of every day, except Sundays and holidays, be kept open for the inspection of shareholders and creditors of the Company, and their personal representatives, at the office or chief place of business of the Company; and every such shareholder, creditor or representative, may make extracts therefrom. 37 V. c. 35, s. 38.

46. Such books shall be *prima facie* evidence of all facts purporting to be thereby stated, in any suit or proceeding against the Company or against any shareholder. 37 V. c. 35, s. 39.

47. No Director, officer or servant of the Company, shall knowingly make or assist to make any untrue entry in any such book, or shall refuse or neglect to make any proper entry therein; and any person violating the provisions of this section shall, besides any criminal liability which he may thereby incur, be liable in damages for all loss or injury which any person interested may have sustained thereby. 37 V. c. 35, s. 40.

48. Any Director or officer who refuses to permit any person entitled thereto to inspect such book or books, or make extracts therefrom, shall forfeit and pay to the party aggrieved the sum of one hundred dollars; and in case the amount is not paid within seven days after the recovery of judgment, the Court in which the judgment is recovered, or a Judge thereof, may direct the imprisonment of the offender for any period not exceeding three months, unless the amount with costs is sooner paid. 37 V. c. 35, s. 41.

49. Every Company incorporated under this Act shall on or before the first day of February, in every year, make a list in triplicate (verified as hereinafter required) of all persons who on the thirty-first day of December previously, were shareholders of the Company; and such list shall state the names alphabetically arranged, and the addresses and callings of such persons, the amount of stock held by them, and the amount unpaid thereon; and shall also make out a summary, verified as hereinafter required, of the state of the affairs of the Company, on the thirty-first day of December preceding.

2. Such summary shall contain the following particulars:

Firstly, The names and residences and post office addresses of the Directors, Secretary, and Treasurer of the Company;

Secondly, The amount of the capital of the Company and the number of shares into which it is divided;

Thirdly, The number of shares taken from the commencement of the Company up to the thirty-first day of December preceding the date of the summary;

Fourthly, The amount of stock (if any) issued free from call; if none is so issued, this fact to be stated;

Fifthly, The amount issued subject to call;

Sixthly, The amount of calls made on each share;

Seventhly, The total amount of calls received;

Eighthly, The total amount of calls unpaid;

Ninthly, The total amount of shares forfeited;

Tenthly, The total amount of shares which have never been allotted or taken up;

Eleventhly, The total amount for which shareholders of the Company are liable in respect of unpaid stock held by them;

Twelfthly, The said summary may also, after giving the information hereinbefore required, give in a concise form, such further information respecting the affairs of the Company, as the Directors may consider expedient.

3. The said list and summary, and every duplicate thereof required by this Act, shall be written or printed on only one side of the sheet or sheets of paper containing the same.

4. The said list and summary shall be verified by the affidavit of the President and Secretary, and if there are no such officers, or they, or either of them are or is at the proper time, out of this Province, or otherwise unable to make the same, by the affidavit of the President or Secretary and one of the Directors, or two of the Directors, as the case may require; and if the President or Secretary does not make or join in the affidavit, the reason thereof shall be stated in the substituted affidavit.

5. One of the duplicate lists and summaries, with the affidavit of verification, shall be posted in the head office of the Company in Ontario, on or before the second day of February; and the Company shall keep the same so posted, until another list and summary are posted under the provisions of this Act; and the other two triplicate lists and summaries of verification shall be deposited with the Provincial Secretary, on or before the eighth day of February next after the time hereinbefore fixed for making the summary.

6. If any Company makes default in complying with the provisions of this section, such Company shall incur a penalty of twenty dollars for every day during which such default continues, and every Director, Manager or Secretary of the Company, who knowingly and wilfully authorizes or permits such default, shall incur the like penalty. 37 V. c. 35, s. 42.

50. The Company shall not be bound to see to the execution of any trust, whether express, implied or constructive, in respect of any share; and the receipt of the shareholder in whose name the same stands in the books of the Company, shall be a valid and binding discharge to the Company for any dividend or money payable in respect of such share, whether or not notice of such trust has been given to the Company; and the Company shall not be bound to see to the application of the money paid upon such receipt. 37 V. c. 35, s. 43.

51. Every contract, agreement, engagement or bargain made and every bill of exchange drawn, accepted or endorsed, and every promissory note and cheque made, drawn or endorsed on behalf of the Company by any agent, officer or servant of the Company, in general accordance with his powers as such under the by-laws of the Company, shall be binding upon the Company; and in no case shall it be necessary to have the seal of the Company affixed to any such contract, agreement, engagement, bargain, bill of exchange, promissory note or cheque, or to prove that the same was made, drawn, accepted or endorsed, as the case may be, in pursuance of any by-law, or special vote or order; nor shall the party so acting as agent, officer or servant of the Company, be thereby subjected individually to any liability whatsoever to any third party therefor.

2. Nothing in this Act shall be construed to authorize the Company to issue any note payable to the bearer thereof, or any promissory note intended to be circulated as money, or as the note of a bank, or to engage in the business of Banking or Insurance. 37 V. c. 35, s. 44.

52. No Company shall use any of its funds in the purchase of stock in any other corporation, unless expressly authorized by by-law confirmed at a general meeting. 37 V. c. 35, s. 45.

53. Each shareholder, until the whole amount of his stock has been paid up, shall be individually liable to the creditors of the Company, to an amount equal to that not paid up thereon, but shall not be liable to an action therefor by any creditor, before an execution against the Company has been returned unsatisfied in whole or in part; and

the amount due on such execution shall, subject to the provisions of the next section, be the amount recoverable with costs, against such shareholders.

2. Any shareholder may plead by way of defence, in whole or in part, any set-off which he could set up against the Company, except a claim for unpaid dividends, or a salary, or allowance as a President or Director. 37 V. c. 35, s. 46.

54. The shareholders of the Company shall not as such be held responsible for any act, default, or liability whatsover, of the Company, or for any engagement, claim, payment, loss, injury, transaction, matter or thing whatsoever, relating to or connected with the Company, beyond the unpaid amount of their respective shares in the capital stock thereof. 37 V. c. 35, s. 47.

55. No person holding stock in the Company as an executor, administrator, tutor, curator, guardian or trustee, shall be personally subject to liability as a shareholder; but the estates and funds in the hands of such person shall be liable in like manner, and to the same extent, as the testator or intestate or the minor, ward or interdicted person, or the person interested in such trust fund, would be, if living and competent to act and holding such stock in his own name; and no person holding such stock as collateral security, shall be personally subject to such liability, but the person pledging such stock shall be considered as holding the same, and shall be liable as a shareholder accordingly. 37 V. c. 35, s. 48.

56. Every such executor, administrator, tutor, curator, guardian, or trustee, shall represent the stock in his hands, at all meetings of the Company, and may vote accordingly as a shareholder; and every person who pledges his stock may nevertheless represent the same at all such meetings, and may vote accordingly as a shareholder. 37 V. c. 35, s. 49.

57. The Directors of the Company shall not declare or pay any dividend when the Company is insolvent, or any dividend the payment of which renders the Company insolvent, or diminishes the capital stock thereof, but if any Director present when such dividend is declared, forthwith, or if any Director then absent, within twenty-four hours after he has become aware thereof and able so to do, enters on the minutes of the Board of Directors his protest against the same, and within eight days thereafter causes such protest to be published in at least one newspaper published at or as near as may be possible to, the office or chief place of business of the Company, such Director may thereby, and not otherwise, exonerate himself from liability. 37 V. c. 35, s. 50.

58. No loan shall be made by the Company to any shareholder, and if such is made, all Directors and other officers of the Company making the same, or in anywise assenting thereto, shall be jointly and severally liable to the Company for the amount of such loan, and also to third parties, to the extent of such loan with legal interest, for debts of the Company contracted from the time of the making of such loan to that of the repayment thereof: But this section shall not apply to a

Building Society, or to a Company incorporated for the loan of money, in any manner to which the authority of this Legislature, or the meaning of this Act applies. 37 V. c. 35, s. 51.

59. The Directors of the Company shall be jointly and severally liable to the labourers, servants and apprentices thereof, for all debts not exceeding one year's wages due for services performed for the Company while they are such Directors respectively; but no Director shall be liable to an action therefor unless the Company has been sued therefor within one year after the debt became due, nor yet unless such Director is sued therefor within one year from time when he ceased to be such Director, nor yet before an execution against the Company has been returned unsatisfied in whole or in part; and the amount due on such execution shall be the amount recoverable with costs against the Directors. 37 V. c. 35, s. 52.

60. Service of all manner of summons or writ whatever upon the Company, may be made by leaving a copy thereof at the office or chief place of business of the Company, with any grown person in charge thereof, or elsewhere with the President or Secretary thereof; or if the Company has no known office or chief place business, and has no known President or Secretary, then upon return to that fact duly made, the Court shall order such publication as it may deem requisite to be made in the premises, for at least one month, in at least one newspaper; and such publication shall be held to be due service upon the Company. 37 V. c. 35, s. 53.

61. Any description of action may be prosecuted and maintained between the Company and any shareholder thereof. 37 V. c. 35, s. 54.

62. In an action or other legal proceeding, it shall not be requisite to set forth the mode of incorporation of the Company, otherwise than by mention of it under its corporate name, as incorporated by virtue of letters patent, or of letters patent and supplementary letters patent, as the case may be, under this Act; and the letters patent or supplementary letters patent themselves, or any exemplification or copy thereof under the Great Seal, shall be conclusive proof of every matter and thing therein set forth. 37 V. c. 35, s. 55.

63. The charter of the Company shall be forfeited by nonuser during three consecutive years at any one time, or if the Company does not go into actual operation within three years after it is granted; and no declaration of such forfeiture by any Act of the Legislature shall be deemed an infringement of such charter. 37 V. c. 35, s. 56.

64. The Lieutenant-Governor in Council may from time to time establish, alter, and regulate the tariff of the fees to be paid on applications for letters patent and supplementary letters patent under this Act; may designate the Department or Departments through which the issue thereof shall take place; and may prescribe the forms of proceeding and record in respect thereof, and all other matters requisite for carrying out the objects of this Act.

2. Such fees may be made to vary in amount, under any rule or rules—as to nature of Company, amount of capital, and otherwise—that may be deemed expedient.

3. No step shall be taken in any Department towards the issue of any letters patent or supplementary letters patent under this Act, until after all fees therefor have been duly paid. 37 V., c. 35, s. 58.

65. Any Company for purposes or objects within the scope of this Act, heretofore incorporated, whether under a Special or General Act, and now being a subsisting and valid corporation, may apply for letters patent under this Act; and the Lieutenant-Governor-in-Council, upon proof that notice of the application has been inserted for four weeks in the *Ontario Gazette*, may direct the issue of letters patent incorporating the shareholders of the said Company as a company under this Act, and thereupon all the rights or obligations of the former Company shall be transferred to the new Company, and all proceedings may be continued and commenced by or against the new Company, that might have been continued or commenced by or against the old Company, and it shall not be necessary in any such letters patent to set out the names of the shareholders ; and after the issue of the letters patent, the Company shall be governed in all respects by the provisions of this Act, except that the liability of the shareholders to creditors of the old Company shall remain as at the time of the issue of the letters patent. 37 V., c. 35, s. 60.

66. Where a subsisting company applies for the issue of letters patent under the provisions of the preceding section, the Lieutenant-Governor may by the letters patent extend the powers of the Company to such other objects within the scope of this Act as the applicants desire, and as the Lieutenant-Governor thinks fit to include in the letters patent, and may by the said letters patent name the first Directors of the new Company, and the letters patent may be to the new Company by the name of the old Company or by any other name. 38 V., c. 23, s. 1.

67. Proof of any matter which may be necessary to be made under this Act, may be made by affidavit before any Justice of the Peace or Commissioner for taking affidavits, who are hereby authorized and empowered to administer oaths for that purpose. 37 V., c. 35, s. 62.

68. The Company shall be subject to the provisions of any Act of the Legislature for the winding up of Joint Stock Companies. 37 V., c. 35, s. 63.

SCHEDULE "A."

(*Section* 10.)

NOTICE OF GRANTING LETTERS PATENT.

Public notice is hereby given, that under "*The Ontario Joint Stock Companies' Letters Patent Act,*" Letters Patent have been issued under the great seal of the Province of Ontario, bearing date the   day of   incorporating [*here state names, address and calling of each corporator named in the Letters Patent*], for the purpose of [*here state the undertaking of the Company, as set forth in the Letters Patent*], by the name of [*here state the name of the Company in the Letters Patent*], with a total capital stock of   dollars, divided into   shares of   dollars each.

Dated at the office of the Provincial Secretary of Ontario, this   day of

A. B.,
Provincial Secretary.

SCHEDULE "B."

(*Section.* 19.)

NOTICE OF GRANTING SUPPLEMENTARY LETTERS PATENT.

Public notice is hereby given, that under "*The Ontario Joint Stock Companies' Letters Patent Act*," Supplementary Letters Patent have been this day issued under the great seal of the Province of Ontario, bearing date the   day of   whereby the total capital stock of [*here state the name of the Company*] is increased [*or* decreased, *as the case may be*] from   dollars to   dollars   [*or* whereby the capital stock of the Company of   shares of   dollars each is subdivided into   shares of   dollars each.]

Dated at the office of the Provincial Secretary of Ontario, this   day of

A. B.,
Provincial Secretary.

CAP. LXI.

An Act to amend chapter 69 of the Consolidated Statutes for Lower Canada respecting Building Societies, in providing for the means of their union and fusion.

Section
Preamble.
1. Right of amalgamation ; mode ; meetings ; notice ; how published and forwarded ; approval ; effect of the approval.
2. Deed of Union.
3. Deposit of the deed.

Section.
4. Name of the Society amalgamated ; effect of the amalgamation ; rights of the societies dissolved.
5. Pending cases.
6. Interpretation.
7. Act in force.

[*Assented to* 24*th December*, 1875.]

WHEREAS it is expedient to provide for the union or fusion of Building Societies established in this Province, under the provisions of chapter 69 of the Consolidated Statutes for Lower Canada, and with such view to amend such Act : Therefore, Her Majesty, by and with the advice and consent of the Legislature of Quebec, enacts as follows :—

1. It shall be lawful for two or more Building Societies established under the provisions of chapter 69 of the Consolidated Statutes for Lower Canada, to unite and join together to form one corporation, under the name of either of such societies, and to unite their capital, property, business, privileges, hypothecs, warranties, rights, powers and duties, by observing, however, the formalities hereinafter set forth ;

(*a*.) The Directors of each of the societies desirous of meeting, shall fix and establish the terms of union, at one of their respective meetings, held in the ordinary manner, at their respective offices or places of business. When the Directors of each of such societies have settled the terms of union, the Secretary of each shall convene a general meeting of the shareholders of the Society, at the usual place of business of each society, by notice published in the French and English languages, twice in each language, during one month, in two newspapers, if there are two in the city, town, village or municipality, in which is situated the society's place of business, or in the same newspaper, if there is only one published in such locality, and in default of such newspaper there, in any other newspaper published in the neighbourhood ; and a copy of this notice shall be forwarded by mail to the address of each shareholder ;

(*b*.) At such general meeting of the shareholders of each of such societies (which shall be presided over by the Society's President, or in default of him or in his absence, by a person to be selected by the meeting), the draft of union settled and determined by the Directors of such societies respectively, must be approved (if approved it is) by at least two-thirds of the members and shareholders present and each shareholder can be represented by a proxy, provided said proxy is a shareholder ; and at the same time and at same meeting, the resolution motion or by-law approving the draft of union submitted, either absolutely or with such modifications, as the meeting shall determine, shall contain, or shall be an authorization to the President of such society, to sign any deed, document, resolution or by-law necessary to complete definitely the fusion of the societies.

2. When the draft of union shall have been so approved by the meeting of shareholders, the presidents of the societies about to unite (each of which is thereunto authorized by this Act), shall execute either in notarial form or *sous seing privé* (and in the latter case the deed shall be executed in triplicate), a deed of union, in conformity with the draft adopted by the meeting of the shareholders of each of the societies.

3. A copy of the notarial deed, or one of the triplicates, shall be filed in the office of the prothonotary of the district wherein is the head office or principal place of affairs of the Building Society, the name of which is preserved.

Another copy or one of the triplicates shall be filed in the registry office of the registration division, wherein is the head office or principal place of business of the Society, the name of which is kept; and such latter Society shall retain the other triplicate or a copy of the notarial deed, as the case may be, to form part of its archives.

4. After the execution or passing of the deed, the society, the name whereof, shall have been retained for the purposes of the union, shall alone remain in existence, and the other societies united thereto shall be dissolved.

The subsisting Society shall thenceforward become and be possessed, of all the assets and rights of the societies so dissolved; and the shareholders and members of the dissolved societies shall become and be members and shareholders in the subsisting Society, on the terms stipulated in the deed of union.

The rights of creditors of the dissolved societies shall not be in any manner affected by such union, and they may be enforced against the subsisting Society, as the representative of the dissolved societies.

5. No proceedings pending, or judgment rendered against any of the societies united or dissolved, shall be effected by such union or fusion.

Such proceedings may be continued against the subsisting Society, by suit or rule *en reprise d'instance* or by any other procedure permitted by law and any judgment so rendered may be executed against the subsisting Society.

6. The provisions of the Act shall form part of chapter 69 of the Consolidated Statutes for Lower Canada.

7. This Act shall enter into force on the day of the sanction thereof.

CHAP. XX.

An Act to amend Chapter 69 of the Consolidated Statutes for Lower Canada respecting Building Societies in the Province of Quebec.

Section.
C.S.L.C. c. 69, s. 23, amended ; transformation of appropriation shares into permanent shares.

Section.
2. Act in force.

[*Assented to 9th March*, 1878.]

HER Majesty, by and with the advice and consent of the Legislature of Quebec, enacts as follows :

1. Section 23 of chapter 69 of the Consolidated Statutes of Lower Canada is amended by adding thereto the following subsection :

" Any building society carrying on business only in the Province of Quebec, may also, on the authority of the unanimous vote of the appropriation stock holders, given at a similar meeting and of the majority of votes given at such meeting, by all the other members of said society, order the transformation of appropriation shares into permanent shares of the Society, and determine upon what conditions and at what date such transformation shall take place."

2. The present Act shall come into force ninety days after its sanction.

MANITOBA BUILDING SOCIETY.

DIV. IX.

Building Societies, Formation, &c.

Section

346. Certain declaration to be made to constitute a Building Society. Purpose for which such Society shall be constituted. Rules for the government of the Society to be made by its members. Members to receive no profits until the amount of their shares is realized. Exception.
347. Society may receive a bonus for advance made to members.
348. Appointment of Board of Directors. Minute book of proceedings.
349. Society to declare certain particulars in their rules. Application of money restricted.
350. Rules to be entered in a book open for inspection.
351. Such entries to be deemed sufficient notice and to make rules binding.
352. How only rules may be repealed or amended.
353. Place of meeting &c. to be specified.
354. Appointment of officers.
355. Certain officers to give security for the faithful discharge of their duties.
356. Society may hold real estate hypothecated to them. Investments of surplus funds.
357. Society may make loans on certain conditions.
358. Society may sell property hypothecated to them on non-payment of instalments, &c., secured therein; actions at law may be brought in the corporate name.
359. Nature of securities upon which Society may advance money; who may be

Section

members of Building Societies.
360. What evidence will suffice in such actions.
361. Cases in which shares may be declared forfeited.
362. Provisions in the event of the death or insolvency of any officer of such society.
363. All the property, &c., of such Society to be vested in the Society by its corporate name.
364. Liability of members.
365. General statement of affairs to be annually prepared by treasurer.
366. The provisions hereof extended to Permanent Building Societies.
367. Permanent Building Societies having fulfilled the conditions hereby required under to be Building Societies within the meaning thereof.
368. Such Societies may amend their rules and by-laws.
369. To what extent such Society may borrow money.
370. Holders of shares fully paid up may withdraw or invest the amount.
371. Society may loan money on unadvanced shares.
372. Society may hold certain real estate.
373. Society not bound to see to the execution of trusts to which any shares may be subject.
374. Interpretation of certain words.
375. To extend to aliens, denizens and citizens.
376. How cited.

FORMATION OF SOCIETIES, ETC.

346. Whenever any twenty persons or upwards in any part of Manitoba, have agreed to constitute themselves a Building Society, and signed and executed, under their respective hands and seals, a declaration of their intention to become such Building Society, and have therein stated its principal or chief place of business in this Province, and have deposited the same with the prothonotary of the Court of Queen's Bench (who for receiving such deposit shall be entitled to receive a fee of fifty cents), such persons, and such other persons as may afterwards become members of such Society, and their several and respective heirs, executors, curators, administrators, successors and assigns, shall be a body corporate and politic by such name and style as a Building Society, as by the said declaration is declared; and such society shall be constituted for the purpose of raising by monthly or other periodical subscriptions of the several members of the said society, in shares not exceeding the value of four hundred dollars for each share (and by subscriptions not exceeding four dollars per month for each share), a stock or fund for enabling each member to receive out of the funds of the society the amount or value of his share or shares therein, for the purpose of erecting or purchasing one or more dwelling houses, or other freehold or leasehold estate or any such like purpose, such advance to be secured by mortgage or otherwise to the society until the amount or value of his share or shares is fully paid to the society, with interest thereon, and with all fines or liabilities received in respect thereof; and the several members of such society may, from time to time, assemble together and make, ordain and constitute such proper and wholesome rules and regulations for the government and guidance of the same as to a majority of the members thereof so assembled together may seem meet, so as such rules be not repugnant to the express provisions hereof or to law; and may impose and inflict reasonable fines, penalties and forfeitures upon members of the society offending against such rules, to be respectively paid to such uses and the benefit of the said society as the said society by such rules shall direct; and may also, from time to time, amend and alter such rules as occasion may require, or annul or repeal the same, and make new rules in lieu thereof, subject to the provisions hereinafter contained; and no member shall receive from the funds of any such society any interest or dividend by way of annual or other periodical profit upon any share in the society until the amount or value of his share or shares has or have been realized; except on the withdrawal of such member according to the rules of the society then in force. 38 V. c. 21, s. 1.

POWERS—DIRECTORS.

347. Every such society may receive from any member any sum of money by way of bonus on any share for the privilege of receiving the same in advance prior to its being realized, besides interest for the share so received or any part thereof. 38 V. c. 21, s. 2.

348. Each such society shall, from time to time, elect and appoint any number of the members of the said society to be a Board of Directors—(who shall choose a President and Vice-President) the number and qualification thereof to be declared in the rules of such society; and may delegate to such Directors the exercise and execution of all lawful powers, and Directors being so elected shall continue to act during such time as shall be appointed by the rules of such society—the powers of such Directors being first declared in and by the said rules or otherwise; and in all cases where Directors are appointed for any particular purpose, the powers delegated to them shall be reduced to writing and entered in a book by the Secretary of the society; and a majority of the members of such Directors present at any meeting thereof, must concur in any act of such Directors in order to make such act valid; and they shall in all things delegated to them act for and in the name of the society, and all acts and orders of such Directors under the powers delegated to them shall have the like force and effect as the acts and orders of the society at any general meeting thereof could have had; but the transactions of the Directors shall be entered in a book belonging to the society, and shall from time to time, and at all times, be subject and liable to the review, allowance and disallowance to the society, in such manner and form as such society have by their general rules directed. 38 V. c. 21, s. 3.

849. Every such society shall, by one or more of their said rules declare all and every the interests and purposes for which such society is established, and shall also in and by such rules direct all and every the uses and purposes to which the money from time to time subscribed, paid or given to or for the use or benefit of the said society, or arising therefrom, or in anywise belonging to the society, shall be appropriated and applied, and in what shares or proportions and under what circumstances any member of such society, or other person, shall become entitled to the same, or any part thereof; but the application of such money shall not in anywise be repugnant to the uses, interests or purposes of such society, or any of them, to be declared as aforesaid; and all such rules during their continuance, shall be complied with and enforced; and no such moneys as aforesaid shall be diverted or unsupplied either by the Directors or Treasurer, or any other officer or member of the society entrusted therewith, under such penalty or forfeiture as the society may by any rule inflict for such offence. 38 V. c. 21, s. 4.

850. The rules for the management of each such society shall be entered and recorded in a book to be kept for that purpose which book shall be open at all seasonable times for the inspection of the members of such society; but nothing in this section shall prevent any alteration or amendment of any such rules in the whole or in part or the making of any new rules for the management of the society in such manner as by the rules the society may from time to time be provided. 38 V. c. 21, s. 5.

RULES—REGULATIONS.

851. All rules from time to time made and in force for the management of such society and entered and recorded as aforesaid, shall be binding on the several members and officers of the Society, and the several contributors thereto and their representatives, all of whom shall be held to have full notice thereof by such entry and record as aforesaid; and the entry of such rules in the book or books of the said Society as aforesaid or a true copy of the same examined with the original and proved to be a true copy shall be received as evidence of such rules respectively in all cases. 38 V. c. 21, s. 6.

852. No rule entered as aforesaid, shall be altered, rescinded or repealed unless at a general meeting of the members of the Society, convened by public notice written or printed, signed by the Secretary and President of the Society in pursuance of a requisition for that purpose by more than one half of the members of such Society, which requisition shall state the objects for which the meeting is called and all be addressed to the President and Directors; whereupon each member shall be notified of the proposed alterations through the post office, within fifteen days; but three-fourths of the members present at such meeting must concur in such alterations or repeal. 38 V. c. 21, s. 7.

353. The rules of every such society shall specify the place or places at which it is intended that the society shall hold its meetings and shall contain provisions with respect to the powers and duties of the members at large, and of such affairs as may be appointed for the management of the affairs of the society. 38 V. c. 21, s. 8.

354. The Directors of every such society shall, from time to time at any of their usual meetings elect and appoint such officers of the Society and grant such salaries and emoluments as they may deem fit, and pay any necessary expenses incurred in the management of the Society and shall elect such officers for such space of time and for such purposes as shall be fixed and established by the rules of the said Society, and may from time to time, discharge them and appoint others in the room of those who vacate or die or are discharged. 38 V. c. 21, s. 9.

355. Every such officer or other person appointed to any office in any wise concerning the receipt, management or expenditure of any sum of money collected for the purposes of the said Society shall, before being admitted to take upon him the execution of any such office or trust, enter into a bond in such form and for such amount as the Directors may determine with two sufficient securities for the just and faithful execution of such office or trust, and for rendering a just and true account according to the rules of the said Society for paying obedience to the same and in all matters lawful. 38 V. c. 21, s. 9.

356. Any such society may take and hold any real estate or securities thereon *bona fide* mortgaged, assigned or hypothecated to the said society either to secure the payment of the shares subscribed for by its members or to secure the payment of any loans or advances made by or debts due such society and may also proceed on such mortgages, assignments or other securities, for the recovery of the monies thereby secured, either at law or in equity or otherwise; and such society may invest in the names of the President and Treasurer for the time being, any of its surplus funds in the stocks of any of the chartered banks or other public securities of the province; and all dividends, interests and proceeds arising therefrom shall be brought to account and applied to and for the use of the society according to the rules thereof. 38 V. c. 21, s. 10.

POWERS AND AUTHORITY.

357. Any such society may from time to time lend and advance to any member or other person, money from out of its surplus funds, upon the security and mortgage (hypothéque) of real estate and for such period as to the Society or its Directors seem satisfactory or expedient; and may receive therefor such sum of money by way of bonus besides interest thereon as may be agreed upon, without being subject on account thereof to any forfeiture or penalty and may from time to time vary such investments at their discretion. 38 V. c. 21, s. 11.

858. Whenever any such society has received from any shareholder a mortgage, or hypothec, or an assignment or transfer of any real estate belonging to him or her, to secure the payment of any advance, and containing authority to the Society to sell such real estate in case of non-payment of any stipulated number of instalments or sums of money (as every such Society is hereby authorized to do) and containing also power to the said Society, to apply the proceeds of such sale to the payment of the advances, interest and all other charges due to the said Society, and after perfect payment thereof, and of all costs and expenses incident thereto, to pay over the balance to the owner of such estate; such stipulations and agreements shall be valid and binding to all intents and purposes whatsoever, and such Society may cause the same to be enforced by an action or proceeding in the usual course in any court of law in Manitoba, having competent jurisdiction, and such action may be brought in the corporate name of any such Society. 38 V. c. 21, s. 12.

859. Every such Society may advance in the usual manner moneys on any real estate whatsoever of any member of the said Society, as well for the actual purchase of the same, and for the erection of buildings thereon, as generally upon the security of any real estate belonging to any such member at the time of his borrowing such moneys, and may take a mortgage or assignment of all such real estate whatsoever in securities for such advances, on the same conditions and with the same privileges in all respects as any other real estate authorized to be mortgaged or assigned; and all securities theretofore taken for monies advanced in the manner aforesaid, shall be valid and binding on the parties to all intents and purposes whatsoever; and all or any person or persons whatsoever, whether capitalists or otherwise, may become members of any such Society, and co-partners and corporate bodies may hold shares therein in the same manner as single individuals. 38 V. c. 21, s. 13.

ACTIONS AND SUITS.

860. In any action or proceeding instituted by any such society for the purpose of realizing or bringing to sale any property mortgaged or assigned to the Society as aforesaid, it shall not be necessary to set forth the special matters in the declaration, but it shall be sufficient to allege that the defendant mortgaged or assigned (as the case may be) the real estate—describing the same—to the Society, and that the amount (or sufficient part of the amount) stipulated by such party to be paid has become and remains due and owing, whereby an action hath accrued to the Society to have the said estate and property sold; and in order to maintain such action it shall be sufficient, in addition to the customary evidence of the mortgage or assignment of such property or estate, to prove by any one witness, whether in the employment of or a shareholder in, such society or not, or by any other means that the defendant is in arrear and indebted to the said society in, or exceeding, a sum on the accruing of which, by the terms of such mortgage, assignment or agreement, the said Society has the right to have the said property or estate sold, any law to the contrary notwithstanding, and thereupon the court shall give judgment for the said amount, and by such judgment order the property to be sold by the Sheriff, after three insertions in the course of four months in the *Manitoba Gazette*: and it shall not be necessary for the Sheriff to go through any formalities in seizing the lands or otherwise. 38 V. c. 21, s. 14.

361. Every such Society may forfeit and declare forfeited to the Society, the shares of any member who neglects or is in arrear such number of instalments as may be fixed by any stipulation or by-law, and every such society may pursue the same course, exercise the same powers, and take and use the same remedies to enforce the payment of any debt or demand due to such society, as any person or body corporate may by law take or use for such purpose. 38 V. c. 21, s. 15.

362. If any person appointed to any office by any such society, and being entrusted with, and having in his hands or possession by virtue of his office any moneys or effects belonging to such Society, or any deeds or securities relating to the same, dies or becomes bankrupt or insolvent, his heirs, executors, curators, administrators, or assigns, or other persons having a legal right, shall, within fifteen days after demand made by the order of the directors of such society, or the major part of them, assembled at any meeting thereof, deliver over all things belonging to the said society, to such persons as the said directors shall appoint and shall pay out of the estate, assets or effects of such person, all sums of money remaining due which such person received by virtue of his office, before any of his other debts are paid or satisfied, and all such assets, estate and effects shall be bound to the payment and discharge thereof accordingly; except that the same shall not be paid or satisfied to the prejudice of mortgages or privileges on real estate, or of liens or privileges on personal estate only, duly executed previous to the appointment of such officer. 38 V. c. 21, s. 16.

363. All real and personal property, moneys, goods, chattels and effects whatever, and all titles, securities for money or other obligatory instruments and evidences or monuments and all other effects whatever, and all rights and claims belonging to or held by any such Society shall be vested in the Society by its corporate name under which such Society shall be known, and shall for all purposes of action or such as well as criminal as civil, in law as in equity, in anywise touching or concerning the same deemed and taken to be, and shall in every such proceeding (when necessary) be stated to be the property of the Society by the name and style aforesaid without further description and by the said name and style the Society may sue and be sued, bring or defend any action, suit, proceeding or prosecution, criminal as well as civil in law or in equity, touching or concerning the property, right or claim or belonging to the Society and in all cases concerning any property, right or claim of the said Society, may sue and be sued, plead and be impleaded. 38 V. c. 21, s. 17.

ANNUAL STATEMENT.

364. Members of the Society shall not be personally responsible in respect to the liabilities of the Corporation beyond the amount of the sum unpaid on shares. 38 V. c. 21, s. 19.

865. The rules of every such Society shall provide that the Treasurer or other principal officer thereof shall once at least, in every year, prepare a general statement of the funds and effects of the Society, specifying in whose custody or possession the said funds or effects are then remaining with an account of every sum of money received and expended by or on account of the Society, since the publication of the preceding periodical statement; and every such periodical statement shall be attested by two or more members of the Society appointed Auditors for that purpose who shall not be Directors, and shall be countersigned by the Secretary of the Society; and every member shall be entitled to receive from the said Society a copy of such periodical statement without charge. 38 V. c. 21, s. 20.

PERMANENT BUILDING SOCIETIES.

866. Permanent Building Societies enabling persons to become members thereof at any time for investment therein or to obtain the advance of their shares by going security therefor and to fix and determine with any such Society the time and amount at, and by which such members shall repay such advanced shares and obtain the release of the said security without being liable to the contingency of losses or profits in the business of the Society, may be formed and subsist under the provisions hereof. 38 V. c. 21, s. 21.

867. Any Permanent Building Society established and conducted on the principles hereinbefore mentioned which has fulfilled and observed the requisite conditions for the establishment of a Building Society under the provisions hereof shall be a Building Society within the meaning of the provisions herein contained, and any person who has approved the rules and regulations of any such Building Society entered and recorded in a book as hereinbefore required, and has subscribed his name as a shareholder for one or more shares, shall from the time of such approbation and subscription be a member of such Building Society, and the production of the book containing the rules for the management of such Society kept in the manner aforesaid, signed by such person or by his duly authorized attorney and duly witnessed shall be sufficient evidence of membership in such Society. 38 V. c. 21, s. 22.

POWERS OF, &C.

868. Any Permanent Building Society may alter amend, report, or make any regulation, rule or by-law for the working of the Society, at a public meeting of the members thereof, duly convened according to the rules of such Society. 38 V. c. 21, s. 23.

869. No such Society, by its rules, regulations and by-laws, authorized to borrow money, shall borrow, receive, take or obtain, otherwise than in stock and shares in such Society from any person or persons any greater sums than three-fourths of the amount of capital actually paid in on unadvanced shares and invested in real securities by said Society; and the paid in and subscribed capital of the Society shall be liable for the amount so borrowed, received or taken by any Society. 38 V. c. 21, s. 24.

370. When any share in any such Society has been fully paid up according to the rules of the Society, or has become due and payable to the holder thereof, the holder of such share may either withdraw the amount of such share from the said Society according to the rules and regulations thereof, or invest the amount of such share in the Society, and receive therefrom periodically such proportions of the profits made by such Society as shall be provided for by a by-law to be passed for the purpose; and the amount of such share so invested shall become fixed, and permanent capital or shares in the said Society not withdrawable therefrom but transferable in the same manner as other shares in the said Society, 38 V. c. 21, s. 25.

371. Any such Society may advance to members on the security of investing on unadvanced shares in the said Society, and may receive and take any person or body corporate, any real or personal security of any kind whatever as collateral security for any advance made to members of the Society. 38 V. c. 21, s. 26.

372. Any such Society may hold absolutely real estate for the purposes of its place of business, not exceeding the annual value of ten thousand dollars. 38 V. c. 21, s. 27.

373. No such Society shall be bound to see to the execution of any trust, whether expressed, implied or constructive, to which any share of its stock is subject; and the receipt of the party in whose name any such share stands in the books of the Society (or if such share stands in the name of more than one the receipt of one of the parties) shall be sufficient discharge to the Society for any payment of any kind made in respect of such share notwithstanding any trust to which such share is then subject, and whether or not the Society has had notice of such trust; and the Society shall not be bound to see to the application of the money paid upon such receipt. 38 V. c. 21, s. 28.

374. The word "Society" means a Building Society, established under the provisions hereof; the word "Rules" shall include Rules, Orders, By-laws and Regulations; the words "real estate" mean and include a moveable estate and property generally; and the words "personal estate" mean and include all monies, goods, chattels and other property, not being real property; and the word "securities" includes privileges, mortgages (equitable as well as legal) and incumbrances on real estate as well as other rights and privileges upon personal estate and property. 38 V. c. 21, s. 29.

375. The sections in division nine shall extend to aliens, denizens and females both to make them subject thereto and to entitle them to all the benefits therefrom. 38 V. c. 21, s. 29.

376. The sections in division nine of this chapter may be cited as "The Building Society Act of Manitoba."

DIV. VII.

The incorporation of Joint Stock Companies by Letters Patent and their Powers.

Section.

226. Charter may be granted by Lieutenant-Governor in Council. Except railways and insurances.
227. Notice to be given.
228. Petition for the issue of letters patent.
229. Applicants to establish sufficiency of notice and the proposed name or the name of the Company. Evidence to be taken and kept.
230. Letters patent to recite all material averments or notice and petition.
231. Notice of grant to be given in official Gazette by Provincial Secretary. Parties therein named shall be body corporate.
232. Lieutenant-Governor in Council may change name of Company; not to affect rights and obligations of Company.
233. Company may acquire and hold, and be invested with real and personal rights.
234. Directors may make by-laws to subdivide shares.
235. Also to increase capital stock.
237. And to decrease capital stock.
238. Shareholders to sanction increase or decrease of capital stock or sub-division of shares by two-thirds in value vote.
240. Directors may petition Lieutenant-Governor for supplementary letters patent.
241. Lieutenant-Governor (on proof) may grant supplementary letters patent. Notice to be given by Provincial Secretary in Gazette.
242. All powers subject to restrictions and provisions of this Act.
243. Affairs of Company, how managed.
244. Who shall be Directors of the Company.
245. Directors to be shareholders.
246. Directors to be elected.
247. Mode of election.
248. Failure to elect Directors how remedied.
249. Powers and duties of Directors. By-laws Confirmation of By-laws. Special general meeting. Disposal of stock. Payment to President or Director.
250. Power to issue bonds, debentures and other securities.
251. Evidence of by-laws.
252. Stock personal Estate.

Section.

253. Allotment of stock.
254. Calling in instalments.
255. Ten per cent. within first year.
256. Enforcement of payments of calls by action.
257. Forfeiture of shares.
258. Restriction as to transactions.
259. Shareholders in arrear not to vote.
260. Books to be kept and what to contain.
261. Refusal to enter transfer if calls not paid.
262. Transfer valid only after entry.
263. Books to be open for inspection.
264. Books to be *prima facie* evidence.
265. Penalty for false entries.
266. Liability for refusal to allow inspection of books.
267. List of shareholders on statements of affairs to be made yearly, with other particulars; mode of writing the same; verification thereof; posting thereof; deposit with Prov. Sec.; Penalty for default.
268. Company not to be liable in respect of trusts, &c.
269. Contracts when to be binding on Company; proviso as to notes, banking and insurance.
270. Not to purchase stocks in other corporations.
271. Liability of shareholders.
272. Limited amount of stock.
273. Trustees not personally liable; mortgages.
274. Trustees may vote.
275. Liability of Directors declaring a dividend when Company is insolvent, etc.; how a Director may avoid liability.
276. Liability of Directors for wages.
277. Actions between Company and shareholders.
278. Forfeiture of charter for non-user.
279. Future legislation.
280. Fees on letters patent, etc., to be fixed by Order-in-Council.
281. Companies existing or being formed may apply under this Act.
282. Wherein notice given of intention to apply for an Act of Parliament this session.
283. Proofs may be by affidavit.

226. The Lieutenant-Governor in Council may, by letters patent under the great seal of the Province, grant a charter to any number of persons not less than five, who shall petition therefor, constituting such persons and others who may become shareholders in the Company thereby created a body corporate and politic for any purposes or objects to which the legislative authority of the Legislature of Manitoba extends, except the construction and working of railways and the business of insurance, and the buying and selling of lands; provided always, that the capital stock of any such Company shall not at any time exceed the amount of five hundred thousand dollars. 38 V. c. 28, s. 3.

227. The applicant for such letters patent must give at least one month's previous notice in the *Manitoba Gazette* of their intention to apply for the same, stating therein:

(1.) The proposed corporate name of the Company, which shall not be that of any other known Company incorporated or unincorporated, or any name liable to be unfairly confounded therewith, or otherwise on public grounds objectionable;

(2.) The object for which the incorporation is sought;

(3.) The place or places within the Province of Manitoba where its operations are to be carried on, with special mention if there be two or more such places, or some one of them its chief place of business;

(4.) The amount of its capital stock;

(5.) The number of shares, and amount of each share;

(6.) The names in full and the address and calling of each of the applicants, with special mention of the names of not less than three nor more than nine of their number who are to be the first Directors of the Company. 38 V. c. 28, s. 4.

228. At any time not more than one month after the last publication of such notice, the applicants may petition the Lieutenant-Governor, through the Provincial Secretary, for the issue of such letters patent:

(1.) Such petition must state the facts required to be set forth in the notice, and must further state the amount of stock taken by such applicant, and also the amount, if any, paid in upon the stock of each applicant;

(2.) The petition shall also state whether the amount is paid in cash or transfer of property, or how otherwise;

(3.) In case the petition is not signed by all the shareholders whose names are proposed to be inserted in the letters patent, it shall be accompanied by a memorandum of association, signed by all the parties whose names are to be so inserted, or by their attorneys duly authorized in writing, and such memorandum shall contain the particulars required by the next preceding sub-section;

(4.) The petition may ask for the embodying in the letters patent of any provision which otherwise under the provisions hereof might be embodied in any by-law of the Company when incorporated. 38 V. c. 28, s. 5.

229. Before the letters patent are issued, the applicants must establish to the satisfaction of the Provincial Secretary, or of such other officer as may be charged by the Lieutenant-Governor in Council to report thereon, the sufficiency of their notice and petition, and that the proposed name is not the name of any other known incorporated or unincorporated Company;

(1.) And to that end, the Provincial Secretary, or such other officer may take and keep of record any requisite evidence in writing under oath, affirmation or otherwise; and he or any Justice of the Peace or Commissioner for taking affidavits in the Court of Queen's Bench, may administer every requisite oath or affirmation. 38 V. c. 28, s. 6.

280. The letters patent shall recite all the material averments of the notice and petition as so established. 38 V. c. 28, s. 7.

281. Notice of the granting of the letters patent shall be forth with given by the Provincial Secretary in the *Manitoba Gazette* in the form of schedule A in section 284; and from the date of the letters patent the persons therein named and their successors shall be a body corporate and politic by the name mentioned therein. 38 V. c. 28, s. 8.

282. In case it should be made to appear that any Company is incorporated under the same name, or under a name similar to that of an existing Company, it shall be lawful for the Lieutenant-Governor in Council to direct the issue of supplementary letters patent reciting the former letters and changing the name of the Company to some other name to be set forth in the supplementary letters patent; and no such alteration of name shall affect the rights and obligations of the Company; and all proceedings may be continued and commenced by or against a Company by its new name that might have been continued or commenced by or against the Company by its former name; and the Court of Queen's Bench may compel an application under this section whenever a Company improperly assumes the name of or a name similar to, that of any existing Company. 38 V. c. 28, s. 9.

283. Every Company so incorporated may acquire, hold, alienate and convey any real estate requisite for the carrying on of the undertaking of such Company; and shall forthwith become and be invested with all the rights, real and personal, heretofore held by or for the Company under a trust created with a view to its incorporation, and with all the powers, privileges and immunities requisite to the carrying on of its undertaking, as though the Company had been incorporated by a special Act of the Legislature, making the Company a body politic and corporate, and embodying all the provisions herein contained and of the letters patent 38 V. c. 28, s. 10.

284. The Directors of the Company, if they see fit at any time, may make a by-law sub-dividing the existing shares into' shares of a smaller amount. 38 V. c. 28, s. 11.

285. The Directors of the Company, if they see fit at any time, after the whole capital stock of the Company shall have been taken up, and fifty per centum thereon paid in, but not sooner, may make a by-law for increasing the capital stock of the Company to any amount which they may consider requisite to the due carrying out of the objects of the Company. 38 V. c. 28, s. 12.

236. Such by-laws shall declare the number and value of the shares of the new stock; and may prescribe the manner in which the same shall be allotted; and in default of its so doing the control of such allotment shall be held to vest absolutely in the Directors. 38 V. c. 28, s. 12.

237. The Directors of the Company, if they see fit at any time, may make a by-law for decreasing the capital stock of the Company to any amount which they may consider sufficient in order to the due carrying out of the undertaking of the Company, and advisable; but such by-law shall declare the number and value of the shares so decreased and the allotment thereof, or the rule or rules by which the same shall be made. 38 V. c. 28, s. 13.

238. But no by-law for increasing or decreasing the capital stock of the Company, or subdividing the shares, shall have any force or effect whatever until it shall have been sanctioned by a vote of not less than two-thirds in value of the shareholders at a general meeting of the Company, duly called to consider the same, and afterwards confirmed by supplementary letters patent. 38 V. c. 28, s. 14.

239. The liabilities of the shareholders to persons who were, at the time of the reduction of the capital creditors of the Company, shall remain as though the capital had not been decreased. 38 V. c. 28, s. 14.

240. At any time not more than six months after such sanction of such by-law, the Directors may petition the Lieutenant-Governor, through the Provincial Secretary, for the issue of supplementary letters patent to confirm the same:

(1.) With such petition they must produce such by-law and establish to the satisfaction of the Provincial Secretary or of such other officer as may be charged by order of the Lieutenant-Governor in Council to report thereon, the due passing and sanction of such by-law; and if the petition is in respect of increase or decrease of capital, the *bona fide* character of increase or decrease of the capital thereby provided for; and that notice of the application for supplementary letters patent has been inserted for one month in the *Manitoba Gazette;*

(2.) And to that end the Provincial Secretary or such other officer, may take and keep of record any requisite evidence in writing under oath or affirmation, or otherwise; and he or any Justice of the Peace or Commissioner aforesaid, may administer every requisite oath or affirmation. 38 V. c. 28, s. 15.

241. Upon the due proof of the same being so made, the Lieutenant-Governor in Council, may grant such supplementary letters patent under the great seal of the Province; and notice thereof shall forthwith be given by the Provincial Secretary in the *Manitoba Gazette* in the form of schedule B in section 284, and thereupon from the date of the supplementary letters patent the shares shall be subdivided, or the capital stock of the Company shall be and remain increased or decreased, as the case may be, to the amount, in the manner and subject to the conditions set forth by such by-law; and the whole of the stock, as so increased or decreased, shall become subject to the provisions hereof in like manner (so far as may be), as though every part thereof had formed part of the stock of the Company originally subscribed. 38 V. c. 28, s. 16.

242. All powers given to the Company by the letters patent granted in its behalf, shall be exercised subject to the provisions and restrictions herein contained. 38 V. c. 28, s. 17.

243. The affairs of every such Company shall be managed by a Board, of not less than three, nor more than nine Directors. 38 V. c. 28, s. 18.

244. The persons named as such in the letters patent shall be the Directors of the Company, until replaced by others duly appointed in their stead. 38 V. c. 28, s. 19.

245. No person shall be elected or appointed a Director unless he is a shareholder owning stock absolutely in his own right, and not in arrear in respect of any calls thereon. 38 V. c. 28, s. 20.

246. The Directors of the Company shall be elected by the shareholders in general meeting of the Company assembled at some place within the Province at such times, in such wise, and for such terms, not exceeding two years, as the letters patent, or (in default thereof) the by-laws of the Company, may prescribe. 38 V. c. 28, s. 21.

247. In default of other express provisions in such behalf by letters patent or by by-laws of the Company:

(1.) Such election shall take place yearly, all the members of the Board retiring and (if otherwise qualified) being eligible for re-election;

(2.) Notice of the time and place for holding general meetings of the Company shall be given at least thirty days previously thereto, in some newspaper published at or as near as may be to the office or chief place of business of the Company:

(3.) At all the general meetings of the Company every shareholder shall be entitled to as many votes as he owns shares in the Company, and may vote by proxy;

(4.) Elections of Directors shall be by ballot.

(5.) Vacancies occurring in the Board of Directors may, unless the by-laws otherwise direct, be filled for the un-expired remainder of the term, by the Board, from among the qualified shareholders of the Company;

(6.) The Directors shall from time to time, elect from among themselves a President of the Company; and shall also appoint and may remove at pleasure all other officers thereof. 38 V. c. 28, s. 22.

248. If at any time an election of Directors be not made, or do not take effect at the proper time, the Company shall not be held to be thereby dissolved; but such election may take place at any general meeting of the Company duly called for that purpose; and the retiring Directors shall continue in office until their successors are elected. 38 V. c. 28, s. 23.

249. The Directors of the Company shall have full power in all things to administer the affairs of the Company; and may make, or cause to be made for the Company, every description of contract the Company may by law enter into; and may, from time to time, make by-laws, not contrary to law, nor to the letters patent of the Company to regulate the allotment of stock, the making of calls thereon, the payment thereof, the issue of registration of certificates of stock, the forfeiture of stock for non-payment, the disposal of forfeited stock and of the proceeds thereof, the transfer of stock, the declaration and payment of dividends, the number of the Directors, their term of service, the amount of their stock, qualifications, the appointment, functions, duties and removal of all agents, officers and servants of the Company, the security to be given by them to the Company, their remuneration, the time at which, and place where the annual meetings of the Company shall be held, the calling of meetings regular and special of the Board of Directors and of the Company, the quorum, the requirement as to proxies, and to the procedure in all things at such meetings, the imposition and recovery of all penalties and forfeitures admitting of regulation by by-law, and the conduct in all other particulars of the affairs of the Company, and may from time repeal, amend, or re-enact the same; but every such by-law, and every repeal, amendment or re-enactment thereof, unless in the meantime confirmed at a general meeting of the Company duly called for that purpose, shall only have force until the next annual meeting of the Company; and in default of confirmation thereat, shall, at and from that time only, cease to have force, and in that case no new by-law to the same or like effect shall have any force until confirmed at a general meeting of the Company: provided always that one fourth part in value of the shareholders of the Company shall at all times have the right to call a special meeting thereof, for the transaction of any business specified in such written requisition and notice as they may issue to that effect: provided also that no by-law for the allotment or sale of stock at any greater discount; or at any less premium that what has been previously authorized at a general meeting, or for the payment of the President or any Director, shall be valid or acted upon, until the same has been confirmed at a general meeting or special general meeting. 38 V. c. 28, s. 24.

250. In case a by-law, authorizing the same, is sanctioned by a vote of not less than two-thirds in value of the said shareholders, then present in person or by proxy, at a general meeting or a special general meeting duly called for considering the by-law, the Directors may borrow money upon the credit of the Company, and issue the bonds, debentures and other securities of the Company and may sell the said bonds, debentures or other securities at such prices as may be deemed expedient or be necessary: but no such debentures shall be for a less sum than one hundred dollars; and the Directors may, under the like sanction hypothecate, mortgage or pledge the real or personal property of the Company to secure any sum or sums borrowed for the purposes thereof. 38 V. c. 28, s. 25.

251. A copy of any by-law of the Company, under their seal and purporting to be signed by any officer of the Company shall be received as *prima facie* evidence of such by-law of all courts of law or equity in Manitoba. 38 V. c. 28, s. 26.

252. The stock of the Company shall be deemed personal estate, and shall be transferable in such manner only, and subject to all such conditions and restrictions as herein, or in letters patent, or in the by-laws of the Company are contained. 38 V. c. 28, s. 27.

253. If the letters patent make no other definite provision the stock of the Company, so far as it is not allotted thereby, shall be allotted when and as the Directors by by-law or otherwise may ordain. 38 V. c. 28, s. 28.

254. The Directors of the Company may call in and demand from the shareholders thereof respectively, all sums of money by them subscribed, at such times and places, and in such payments or instalments as the letters patent or the provisions hereof, or the by-laws of the Company may require or allow, and interest shall accrue and fall due at the rate of six per centum per annum, upon the amount of any unpaid call, from the day appointed for the payment of such call. 38 V. c. 28, s. 29.

255. Not less than ten per centum upon the allotted stock of the Company shall, by means of one or more calls, be called in and made payable within one year from the incorporation of the Company; the residue when and as the by-laws of the company shall direct. 38 V. c. 28, s. 30.

256. The company may enforce payment of all calls and interest thereon, by action in any competent court; and in such action it shall not be necessary to set forth the special matter, but it shall be sufficient to declare that the defendant is a holder of one share or more, stating the number of shares, and is indebted in the sum of money to which the calls in arrear amount in respect of one call or more upon one share or more, stating the number of calls and the amount of each, whereby an action hath accrued to the Company; and a certificate under their seal, and purporting to be signed by any officer of the Company, to the effect that the defendant is a shareholder, that such call or calls has or have been made, and that so much is due by him and unpaid thereon, shall be received in all courts of law and equity as *prima facie* evidence to that effect. 38 V. c. 28, s. 31.

257. If after such demand or notice as by the letters patent or by-laws of the Company may be prescribed, any call made upon any share or shares be not paid within such a time as by such letters patent or by-laws may be limited in that behalf, the Directors in their discretion, by vote to that effect reciting the facts, the same being duly recorded in their minutes, may summarily forfeit any share or shares whereon such payment is not made; and the same shall thereupon become the property of the Company and may be disposed of as by by-laws or otherwise they shall ordain. 38 V. c. 28, s. 32.

258. No share or shares shall be transferable until all previous calls thereon have been fully paid in, or until declared forfeited for non-payment of calls thereon. 38 V. c. 28, s. 33.

259. No shareholder, being in arrear in respect of any call, shall be entitled to vote at any meeting of the Company. 38 V. c. 29, s. 34.

260. The Company shall cause a book or books to be kept by the Secretary, or by some other officer especially charged with that duty, wherein shall be kept recorded:—

1. A copy of the letters patent incorporating the Company, and any supplementary letters patent for increasing or decreasing the capital stock thereof and of all by-laws thereof;

2. The names, alphabetically arranged, of all persons who are or have been shareholders;

3. The address and calling of every such person while such shareholder;

4. The number of shares of stock held by each shareholder;

5. The amount paid in and remaining unpaid, respectively, on the stock of each shareholder;

6. All transfers of stock in their order as presented to the Company for entry, with the date and other particulars of each transfer, and the date of the entry thereof; and

7. The names, addresses and calling of all persons who are or have been directors of the Company, with the several dates at which each ever became, or ceased to become such director. 38 V. c. 28, s. 35.

261. The directors may refuse to allow the entry into any such book of any transfer of stock whereon any call has been made which has not been paid in. 38 V. c. 28, s. 36.

262. No transfer of stock, unless made by sale under execution, shall be valid for any purpose whatever, save only as exhibiting the rights of the parties thereto towards each other, and as rendering the transferee liable *ad interim*, jointly and severally with the transferer, to the Company and their creditors until the entry thereof has been duly made in such book or books. 38 V. c. 28, s 37.

263. Such books shall, during reasonable business hours every day, except Sundays and holidays, be kept open for the inspection of shareholders and creditors of the Company and their personal representatives, at the office or chief place of business of the Company, and every such shareholder, creditor or representative may make extracts therefrom. 38 V. c. 28, s. 38.

264. Such books shall be *primâ facie* evidence of all facts purporting to be thereby stated, in any suit or proceeding against the Company or against any shareholder. 38 V. c. 28, s. 39.

265. No director, officer, or servant of the Company, shall knowingly make, or assist to make any untrue entry in any such book, or shall refuse or neglect to make any proper entry therein; and any persons violating the provisions of this section shall, besides being punished criminally, be liable in damages for all loss or injury which any person interested may have sustained thereby. 38 V. c. 28, s. 40.

366. Any director or officer refusing to permit any person entitled thereto to inspect such book or books, or make extracts therefrom, shall forfeit and pay to the party aggrieved the sum of one hundred dollars; and in case the amount be not paid within seven days after the recovery of a judgment, the court in which a judgment is recovered, or a judge thereof, may direct the imprisonment of the offender for any period not exceeding three months, unless the amount, with costs, be sooner paid. 38 V. c. 28, s. 41.

367. Every Company incorporated under the provisions hereof shall, on or before the first day of February in every year, make a list in triplicate (verified as is hereinafter required) of all persons who on the 31st day of December previously, were shareholders of the Company, and such list shall state the names, alphabetically arranged, and the addresses and callings of such persons, the amount of stock held by them, and the amount unpaid thereon; and shall also make out a summary, verified as hereinafter required, of the state of the affairs of the Company on the thirty-first day of December preceding, which shall contain the following particulars:—

1. The names and residences and post office addresses of the directors, secretary and treasurer of the Company:

2. The amount of the capital of the Company, and the number of shares into which it is divided;

3. The number of shares taken from the commencement of the Company up to the thirty-first day of December preceding the summary;

4. The amount of stock (if any) issued free from call; if none is issued, this fact to be stated;

5. The amount issued subject to call;

6. The amount of calls made on each share;

7. The total amount of calls received;

8. The total amount of calls unpaid;

9. The total amount of shares forfeited;

10. The total amount of shares which have never been allotted or taken up;

11. The total amount for which shareholders of the Company are liable in respect of unpaid stock held by them, respectively;

12. The said summary may also, after giving the information hereinafter required, give in a concise form such further information respecting the affairs of the Company as the directors may consider expedient;

13. The said list and summary, and every duplicate thereof required by the provisions hereof, shall be written or printed on one side of the sheet or sheets of paper containing the same;

14. The said list and summary shall be verified by the affidavit of the President and Secretary; and if there be no such officers, or they or either of them are or is at the proper time out of the Province, or otherwise unable to make the same, by the affidavit of the President or

186   Div. 7.   *Joint Stock Co'ys by Letters Patent.*

Secretary and one of the Directors, or two of the Directors, as the case may require; and if the President or Secretary do not make or join in the affidavit, the reason thereof shall be stated in the substituted affidavit;

15. One of the duplicate lists and summaries, with the affidavits of verification, shall be posted in the head office of the Company, in Manitoba, on or before the 2nd day of February, and the Company shall keep the same so posted until another list and summary shall be posted, under the provisions hereof; and the other duplicate list and summary, with the affidavit of verification, shall be deposited with the Secretary of the Province of Manitoba, on or before the 8th day of February next after the time hereinbefore fixed for making of the same;

16. If any Company makes default in complying with the provisions of this section, such Company shall incur a penalty of $20 every day during which default continues; and every Director, Manager or Secretary who shall knowingly and wilfully authorize or permit such default shall incur the like penalty. 38 V. c. 28, s. 42.

268. The Company shall not be bound to see to the execution of any trust, whether express, implied or constructive, in respect of any share; and the receipt of the shareholder, in whose name the same may stand in the books of the Company, shall be a valid and binding discharge to the Company for any dividend or money payable in respect of such share, and whether or not notice of such trust has been given to the Company; and the Company shall not be bound to see to the application of the money paid upon such receipt. 38 V. c. 28, s. 43.

269. Every contract, agreement, engagement or bargain made, and every bill of exchange drawn, accepted or endorsed, and every promissory note or cheque drawn or endorsed on behalf of the Company by any agent, officer or servant of the Company, in general accordance with his powers as such officer under the by-laws of the Company or otherwise, shall be binding upon the Company; and in no case shall it be necessary to have the seal of the Company affixed to any such contract, agreement, engagement, bargain, bill of exchange, promissory note or cheque, or to prove that the same was made, accepted or endorsed, as the case may be, in pursuance of any by-law or special vote or order; nor shall the party so acting as agent, officer or servant of the Company be thereby subjected, individually, to any liability whatsoever to any third party therefor; provided always, that nothing herein contained shall be construed to authorize the Company to issue any note payable to the bearer thereof, or any promissory note intended to be circulated as money, or as the note of a bank, or to engage in the business of banking or insurance or buying or selling land as aforesaid. 38 V. c. 28, s. 44.

270. No Company shall use any of its funds in the purchase of stock in any other Corporation, unless expressly authorized by a by-law confirmed at a general meeting. 38 V. c. 28, s. 45.

271. Each shareholder, until the whole amount of his stock has been paid up, shall be individually liable to the creditors of the Company to an amount equal to that not paid up thereon, but shall not be liable to an action therefor by any creditor before an execution against the Company has been returned unsatisfied in whole or in part, and the amount due on such execution shall, subject to the provisions of the next succeeding section, be the amount recoverable, with costs, against such shareholders; provided that any shareholder may plead by way of defence, in whole or in part, any set off which he could set up against the Company except a claim for unpaid dividends, or a salary or allowance as a President or Director. 38 V. c. 28, s. 46.

272. The shareholders of the Company shall not as such be held responsible for any Act, default or liability whatsoever of the Company, or for any engagement, claim, payment, loss, injury, transaction, matter or thing whatsoever, relating to or connected with the Company, beyond the unpaid amount of their respective shares in the capital stock thereof. 38 V. c. 28, s. 47.

273. No person holding stock in the Company as an executor, administrator, tutor, curator, guardian or trustee shall be personally subject to liability as a shareholder; but the estate and funds in the hands of such person shall be liable in like manner, and to the same extent, as the testator or intestate or the minor, ward, or other interested person in such trust fund would be if competent to act and holding such stock in his own name; and no person holding such stock as collateral security shall be personally subject to such liability; but the person pledging such stock shall be considered as holding the same, and shall be liable as a shareholder accordingly. 38 V. c. 28, s. 48.

274. Every such executor, administrator, tutor, curator, guardian or trustee shall represent the stock in his hands at all meetings of the Company, and may vote accordingly as a shareholder; and every person who pledges his stock may nevertheless represent the same at all such meetings and may vote accordingly as a shareholder. 38 V. c. 28, s. 49.

275. The Directors of the Company shall not declare or pay any dividend when the Company is insolvent, or any dividend the payment of which renders the Company insolvent, or diminishes the capital stock thereof; but if any Director present, when such dividend is declared, do forthwith, or if any Director then absent do within twenty-four hours after he shall become aware thereof, and able so to do, enter in the minutes of the Board of Directors his protest against the same, and within eight days thereafter publish the same in at least one newspaper published at or as near as may be possible to, the office or chief place of business of the Company, such Director may thereby, and not otherwise, exonerate himself from liability. 38 V. c. 28, s. 50.

276. The Directors of the Company shall be jointly and severally liable to the labourers, servants and apprentices thereof (excluding the officers of the Company) for all debts not exceeding one year's wages due for services performed for the Company whilst they are such Directors respectively; but no Director shall be liable for an action therefor, unless the Company has been sued therefor within one year after the debt became due, nor yet unless such Director is sued therefor within one year from the time when he ceased to be such Director, nor yet before an execution against the Company has been returned unsatisfied in whole or in part ; and the amount due on such execution shall be the amount recoverable with costs against the Directors. 38 V. c. 28, s. 52.

277. Any description of action may be prosecuted and maintained between the Company and any shareholder thereof. 38 V. c. 28, s. 54.

278. The charter of the Company shall be forfeited by non-user during three consecutive years at one time, or if the Company do not go into actual operation within three years after it is granted ; and no declaration of such forfeiture by any Act of the Legislature shall be deemed an infringement of such charter. 38 V. c. 28, s. 56.

279. The Company shall be subject to such further and other provisions as the Legislature of Manitoba may hereafter deem expedient, in order to secure the due management of its affairs and the protection of its shareholders and creditors. 38 V. c. 28, s. 57.

280. The Lieutenant-Governor in Council may, from time to time, establish, alter and regulate the tariff of the fees to be paid on application for letters patent and supplementary letters patent under the provisions thereof, and he may designate the department or departments through which the issue thereof shall take place, and may prescribe the forms of proceeding and record in respect thereof, and all matters requisite for the carrying out the objects of the provisions herein contained and such fees may be made to vary in amount, under any rule or rules—as to the nature of Company, amount of capital and otherwise—as may be deemed expedient ; and no steps shall be taken in any department towards the issue of any letters patent or supplementary letters patent, under the provisions hereof until the amount of all fees therefor shall have been duly paid. 38 V. c. 28, s. 58.

281. Any company for purposes or objects within the scope of the provisions herein contained heretofore incorporated, whether under Special or General Act, and now being a subsisting and valid corporation, or in respect of which proceedings for incorporation are now being had under which it may hereafter become incorporated, may apply for letters patent under the foregoing provisions ; and the Lieutenant-Governor-in-Council upon proof that notice of the application has been inserted for four weeks in the *Manitoba Gazette*, may direct the issue of letters patent incorporating the shareholders of the said Company as a company under the foregoing provisions, and thereupon all the rights and obligations of the former Company shall be transferred to the new Company and all proceedings may be continued or commenced by, or against the new Company that might have been continued or commenced by, or against the old Company ; and it shall not be necessary in any such letters patent to set out the names of shareholders; and after the issue of the letters patent the Company shall be governed in all repects by the provisions hereof, except that the liability of the shareholders to creditors of the old Company shall remain as at the time of the letters patent. 38 V. c. 28, s. 59.

282. Whereas notice has been duly published according to the rules of the Legislative Assembly that an application would be made to the legislature at its then next session for an Act incorporating any Company, the incorporation whereof is sought for objects for which incorporation is authorized by the provisions hereof, and in contemplation of its passing a notice of an application for incorporation under the forgoing provisions shall not be necessary, and the Lieutenant-Governor-in-Council upon the report of the proper Minister or officer that proof has been furnished, that the other requirements hereinbefore contained have been complied with, may grant a charter of incorporation to such Company; in any application under this section the facts required to be stated in the petition may be verified in any manner that the Provincial Secretary, or other officer charged to report thereon, may deem sufficient, and in such case it shall not be requisite that the petition should be signed by all the shareholders, to be named in the letters patent, or that the memorandum of association or other particulars should be in accordance with the requirements hereinbefore contained. 38 V. c. 28, s. 60.

283. Proof of any matter which may be necessary to be made hereunder, may be by affidavit before any Justice of the Peace or Commissioner for taking affidavits who are hereby authorized and empowered to administer oaths for that purpose; or otherwise as the Provincial Secretary or other officer shall think proper. 38 V. c. 28, s. 61.

284. The following are the Schedules A and B referred to in sections 231 and 241; and the sections in division 7 of this chapter may be cited as "The Manitoba Joint Stock Companies Incorporation Act."

SCHEDULE A.

(*Referred to in section* 231.)

Public notice is hereby given that under the Statute in that behalf, letters patent have been issued under the great seal of the Province of Manitoba, bearing date the   day of   incorporating (*here state the name, address and calling of each corporator named in the letters patent*), for the purpose (*here state the undertaking of the Company, as set forth in the letters patent*), with a total capital stock of   dollars, divided into shares of   each.

Dated at the office of the Provincial Secretary of Manitoba, this   day of

                                              A. B.

                                      Provincial Secretary.

190   Div. 7.   *Joint Stock Co'ys by Letters Patent.*

SCHEDULE B.

(*Referred to in section* 241.)

Public notice is hereby given that under the Statute in that behalf, supplementary letters patent have been this day issued under the great seal of the Province of Manitoba, bearing date the   day of   whereby the total capital stock of (*here state the name of the Company*) is increased (*or* decreased, *as the case may be*), from   dollars to   dollars (*or* whereby the capital stock of the Company of   shares $ each is subdivided into   shares of $ each.)

Dated at the office of the Provincial Secretary of Manitoba, this   day of

A. B.

Provincial Secretary

CHAP. LXXXIII.

An Act for the regulation of Benefit Building Societies.

Sections.
1. Societies, for what purpose established, powers, &c.
2. Bonus &c., when not usurious.
3. Forms of conveyance, how to be made.
4. Rules of Society, to whom submitted &c.
5. To whom submitted if no certificate.
6. Fee to Barrister on submission.
7. Until when Societies not entitled to benefit of Act.
8. When rules to be binding and on whom.
9. When rules not to be altered.
10. What rules to specify.
11. Officers, how appointed, &c.
12. Committees, how appointed, &c.
13. Treasurer, what accounts to render.
14. Conveyance, how made when Trustee out of jurisdiction.
15. Fee, when not allowed.

Section.
16. Executors, &c., when to pay money due society.
17. Effects of societies, in whom vested.
18. Trustees, limitation of responsibility.
19. Payment to next of kin, when.
20. Payment of sums of limited amount.
21. Cases of fraud &c., by whom heard.
22. Rules for settling disputes.
23. References on disputes.
24. What orders and disputes final.
25. Minors, powers of.
26. Annual audits, &c., how made.
27. When members may be witnesses.
28. What sufficient to discharge mortgage.
29. Funds, where not to be invested.
30. When Act extended to all Building Societies.
31. Interpretation clause.
32. When Act may be amended.

SCHEDULE.

[*Passed* 14*th April* 1847.]

WHEREAS certain societies, commonly called Building Societies, have been established in different parts of the United Kingdom of Great Britain, and in the Province of Canada, principally amongst the industrious classes, for the purpose of raising by small periodical subscriptions a fund to assist the members thereof in obtaining a small freehold or leasehold property, and it is expedient to afford encouragement and protection to such Societies, and the property obtained therewith in this province;—

Be it therefore enacted, &c.

1. It shall and may be lawful for any number of persons in this Province to form themselves into and establish societies for the purpose of raising by the monthly or other subscriptions of the several members of such societies, shares not exceeding the value of one hundred and fifty pounds for each share, such subscriptions not to exceed in the whole twenty shillings per month for each share, a stock or fund for the purpose of enabling each member thereof to receive out of the funds of such society the amount or value of his or her share or shares therein, to erect or purchase one or more dwelling house or dwelling houses, or other real or leasehold estate to be secured by way of mortgage to such society until the amount or value of his or her shares shall have been fully paid to such society with the interest thereon and all fines or other payments incurred in respect thereof and to and for the several members of each society from time to time to assemble together and to make, ordain and constitute such proper and wholesome rules and regulations for the government and guidance of the same as to the major part of the members of such society so assembled together and shall seem meet so as such rules shall not be repugnant to the express provisions of this Act and to the general laws of this Province and to impose and inflict such reasonable fines, penalties and forfeitures upon the several members of any such society who shall offend against any such rules as the members may think fit to be respectively paid to such uses for the benefit of such society as such society by such rules shall direct, and also from time to time to alter and amend such rules as occasion shall require or amend or repeal the same, and to make new rules in lieu thereof under such restrictions as are in this Act contained, provided that no member shall receive or be entitled to receive from the funds of such society any interest or dividend by way of annual or other periodical profit upon any shares in such society until the amount or value of his or her share shall have been realized except on the withdrawal of such member according to the rules of such society then in force.

2. It shall and may be lawful to and for any such society to have and receive from any member or members thereof any sum or sums of money by way of bonus on any share or shares for the privilege of receiving the same in advance prior to the same being realized and also any interest for the share or shares so received on any part thereof without being subject or liable on account thereof to any of the forfeitures or penalties imposed by any act or acts of assembly relating to usury.

3. It shall and may be lawful to and for any such society, in and by the rules thereof, to describe the form or forms of conveyance, mortgage, transfer, agreement, bond or other instrument which may be necessary for carrying the purposes of the said society into execution and which shall be specified and set forth in a schedule to be annexed to the rules of such society and duly certified and deposited as hereinafter provided.

4. Two transcripts fairly written on paper or parchment of all rules made in pursuance of this act, signed by three members and countersigned by the Secretary of any such society (accompanied in the case of an alteration or amendment of rules with an affidavit of the Secretary or one of the officers of the said society that the provisions of this Act have been duly complied with) with all convenient speed after the same shall be made, altered or amended and so from time to time after every making, altering or amending thereof shall be submitted to such Barrister at Law as may be appointed by Her Majesty's Attorney General of this Province for the purpose of ascertaining whether the said rules of such society or alteration or amendment thereof are calculated to carry into effect the intention of the parties framing such rules, alterations or amendments and are in conformity to law and to the provisions of this Act, and the said Barrister shall advise with the said Secretary, if required, and shall give a certificate on each side of the said transcripts that the same are in conformity to law and to the provisions of this Act, or point out in what part or parts the said rules are repugnant thereto, and the Barrister for advising as aforesaid and perusing the rules, or alterations or amendments of the rules of each respective society, and giving such certificates as aforesaid, shall demand no further fee than the sum of one guinea, which shall be defrayed by each society respectively; and one of such transcripts, when certified by the said Barrister, shall be returned to the society and the other of such transcripts shall be transmitted by such Barrister to the Clerk of the Peace for the County wherein such society shall be formed, and by him laid before the Justices for such County at the General Sessions of the Peace, or adjournment thereof held next after the time when such transcript shall have been so certified and transmitted to him as aforesaid, and the Justices then and there present are hereby authorized and required, without motion, to allow and confirm the same and such transcript shall be filed by such Clerk of the Peace with the rolls of the Sessions of the Peace in his custody without fee or reward, and all rules, alterations and amendments thereof from the time when the same shall be certified by the said Barrister and shall be binding on the several members and officers of the said society and all persons having interest therein.

5. Provided always, that in case any such Barrister shall refuse to certify all or any of the rules so to be submitted for his perusal and examination it shall then be lawful for any such society to submit the same to the Court of General Sessions of the Peace together with the reasons assigned by the said Barrister in writing for any such rejection or disapproval of any one or more such rules, and the Justices at their said General Sessions shall and may, if they think fit, confirm and allow the same notwithstanding any such rejection or disapproval by any such Barrister.

6. Provided always, that the said Barrister shall be entitled to no further fee for or in respect of any alteration or amendment of any rules upon which one fee has been already paid to the said Barrister within the period of three years; provided also, that if any rules, alterations or amendments are sent to such Barrister accompanied with an affidavit of being a copy of any rules or alterations or amendments of the rules of any other society which shall have been already enrolled under the provisions of this Act the said Barrister shall certify and return the same as aforesaid without being entitled to any fee for such certificate.

7. No such society as aforesaid shall have the benefit of this Act unless all the rules for the management thereof shall be entered in a book to be kept by the Secretary of such society and which book shall be open at all seasonable times for the inspection of the members of such society, but nevertheless nothing contained herein shall extend to prevent any alteration in or amendment of any such rules so entered and deposited and filed as aforesaid, or repealing or amending the same or any of them in the whole or in part or making any new rules for the management of such society in such manner as by the rules of such society shall from time to time be provided, but such new rules or such alterations in, or amendments of former rules or any order annulling or repealing any former rules in the whole or in part shall not be in force until the same respectively shall be entered in such book as aforesaid

and certified when necessary by such Barrister as aforesaid, and until a transcript thereof shall be deposited with such Clerk of the Peace as aforesaid, who shall file and certify the same as aforesaid.

8. All rules from time to time made and in force for the management of such society as aforesaid, and duly entered in such book as aforesaid, and confirmed by the Justices as aforesaid, shall be binding on the several members and officers of such society, and the several contributors thereto, and their representatives all of whom shall be deemed and taken to have full notice thereof by such entry and contribution as aforesaid; and the entry of such rules in such book as aforesaid, or the transcript thereof deposited with such Clerk of the Peace as aforesaid, or a true copy of such transcript, examined with the original, and proved to be a true copy, shall be received as evidence of such rules respectively in all cases, *certiorari* or other legal process shall be brought or allowed to remove any such rules into any Court of Judicature of this Province, and every copy of any such transcript deposited with any Clerk of the Peace as aforesaid, shall be made without fee or reward, except the actual expense of making such copy.

9. No rule confirmed by the Justices of the Peace in manner aforesaid shall be altered, rescinded or repealed unless at a general meeting of the members of such society as aforesaid, convened by public notice, written or printed, signed by the Secretary or President of such society, in pursuance of a requisition for that purpose by seven or more of the members of such society, which said requisition and notice shall be publicly read at the two usual meetings of such society to be held next before such general meeting, for the purpose of such alteration or repeal, unless a committee of such members shall have been nominated for that purpose at a general meeting of the members of such society convened in manner aforesaid, in which case such committee shall have the like power to make such alterations or repeal, and unless such alteration or repeal shall be made with the concurrence and approbation of three-fourths of the members of such society then and there present, or by the like proportion of such committee as aforesaid, if any shall have been nominated for that purpose.

10. The rules of every society formed under the authority of this Act shall specify the place or places at which it is intended such society shall hold its meetings, and contain provisions with respect to the powers and duties of the members at large, and of such committees or officers as may be appointed for the management of the affairs of such society provided always that it shall and may be lawful for any such society to alter their place or places of meeting whenever they may consider it necessary, upon giving notice thereof in writing to the Clerk of the Peace for the County within which such society shall be held, the said notice to be given within seven days before or after such removal, and signed by the Secretary or other principal officer and also by three or more of the members of the said society; and provided that the place or places at which such society intended to hold their meetings shall be situate within the County in which the rules of the said society are enrolled.

11. Every such society shall and may from time to time at any of their usual meetings or by their committee, if any such shall be appointed for that society, elect and appoint such person into the office of Trustee, President, Secretary, Surveyor or Treasurer of such society as they shall think proper and also shall and may from time to time elect and appoint such other officers as shall be deemed necessary to carry into execution the purposes of such society for such space of time and for such purposes as shall be fixed and established by the rules of such society and from time to time to elect and appoint others in the room of those who shall vacate or die and such Trustee, Treasurer, and all and every other officer or other person whatsoever who shall be appointed to any office in any wise touching or concerning the receipt management or expenditure of any sum of money collected for the purpose of any such society before he, she or they shall be admitted to take upon him, her or them the execution of any such office or trust (if required so to do by the rules of such society to which such officer shall belong) shall become bound in a bond according to the form prescribed in the schedule to this Act, annexed with two sufficient sureties for the just and faithful execution of such office or trust and for rendering a just and true account according to the rules of such society and in all matters lawful to pay obedience to the same in such penal sum of money as by the major part of such society at any such meeting as aforesaid shall be thought expedient and to the satisfaction of such society and every such bond to be given by or on the behalf of such Trustee or Treasurer or of any other person appointed to any other office or trust shall be given to the Clerk of the Peace of the County where such society shall be established for the time being without fee or reward and in case of forfeiture it shall be lawful to sue upon such bond in the name of the Clerk of the Peace for the time being for the use of the said society fully indemnifying and saving harmless such Clerk of the Peace from all costs and charges in respect of such suit.

12. Every such society shall and may from time to time elect and appoint any number of the members of such society to be a committee the number thereof to be declared in the rules of every such society, and shall and may delegate to such committee all or any of the powers given by this Act to be executed, who being so delegated shall continue to act as such committee for and during such time as they shall be appointed for such society for general purposes, the powers of such committee being first declared in and by the rules of such society confirmed by the Justices of the Peace at their sessions and filed in the manner hereinbefore directed, and all acts and orders of such committee under the powers so delegated to them shall have the like force and effect as the acts and orders of such society at any general meeting thereof could or might have had in pursuance of this Act, provided always, that the transactions of such committee shall be entered in a book belonging to such society and shall be from time to time and at all times subject and liable to the review, allowance or disallowance and control of such society in such manner and form as such society shall by their general rules confirm by the Justices and filed as aforesaid, have directed and appointed or shall in like manner direct and appoint.

13. Every person who shall have, or receive any part of the moneys, effects or funds of or belonging to any such society or shall in any manner have been or shall be intrusted with the disposal, management or custody thereof or of any securities, books, papers or property relating to the same, his or her executors, administrators and assigns respectively shall upon demand made or notice in writing given or left at the last or usual place of residence of such persons in pursuance of any order of such society or committee to be appointed as aforesaid given in his or her account at the usual meeting of such society or to such committee thereof as aforesaid to be examined and allowed or disallowed by said society or committee thereof and shall on the like demand or notice pay over all the moneys remaining in his or her hands and assign and transfer or deliver all securities and effects, books, papers and property taken or standing in his or her name as aforesaid or being in his or her hands or custody to the Trustee or Treasurer for the time being or to such other person as such society or committee thereof shall appoint, and in case of any neglect or refusal to deliver such account or to pay over such moneys or to assign, transfer or deliver such securities and effects, books, papers and property in manner aforesaid, it shall and may be lawful to and for every such society, in the name of the Trustees or Treasurer or other principal officer thereof as the case may be, to exhibit a petition to the Supreme Court of this Province who shall and may proceed thereon in a summary way and make such order therein upon hearing all parties concerned as to such Court in their discretion shall seem just, which order shall be final and conclusive and all assignments and sales and transfers made in pursuance of such order shall be good and effectual in law to all intents and purposes whatsoever.

14. When, and so often as, any person seized or possessed of any lands, tenements or hereditaments or other property, or any estate or interest therein as a Trustee of any such society, shall be out of the jurisdiction of or not amenable to the process of the Supreme Court of this Province, or shall be idiot, lunatic or of unsound mind or it shall be unknown or uncertain whether he or she be living or dead, or such person shall refuse to convey or otherwise assure such lands, tenements, hereditaments, or property or estate or interest to the person duly nominated as Trustee of such society in their stead, either alone or together with any continuing Trustee as occasion shall require then and in every or any such case it shall be lawful for the Judges of the said Court to appoint such person as to such Court shall seem meet on behalf and in the name of the person seized or possessed as aforesaid to convey, surrender, release, assign or otherwise assure the said lands, tenements, hereditaments or property or real estate or interest to such Trustee so duly nominated as aforesaid and every such conveyance, release, surrender, assignment or assurance shall be as valid and effectual to all intents and purposes as if the person being out of the jurisdiction or not amenable to the process of the said Court, or not known to be alive, or having refused, or as if the person being idiot, lunatic or of unsound mind had been at the time of the execution thereof of sane mind, memory and understanding and had by himself or herself executed the same.

15. No fee, reward, emolument or gratuity whatsoever shall be demanded, taken or received by any officer of such Court for any matter or thing done in such Court in pursuance of this Act and upon the presenting of any such petition it shall be lawful for the Judges of the said Court to assign Counsel learned in the law on behalf of such society who are hereby respectively required to do their duties therein without fee or reward.

16. If any person who may hereafter be appointed to any office in any such society and being entrusted with the keeping of the accounts, or having in his hands or possession, by virtue of his said office or employment, any moneys or effects belonging to such society or any deeds or securities relating to the same shall die or become bankrupt or insolvent or have any execution or attachment or other process issued against his lands, goods, chattels or effects or property or estate, heritable or movable, or make any disposition, assignment or other conveyance thereof for the benefit of his creditors, his heirs, executors, administrators or assigns or other person having legal right, or the Sheriff or other officer executing such process, shall, within forty days after demand made in writing by the order of any such society or committee thereof or the major part of them assembled at any meeting thereof, deliver and pay over all moneys and other things belonging to such society to such person as such society or committee shall appoint and shall pay out of the estates, assets or effects, heritable or movable, of such persons all sums of money remaining due which such person received by virtue of his said office or employment before any other of his debts are paid or satisfied, or before the money directed to be levied by such process as aforesaid or which may be recovered or recoverable under the same is paid over to the party issuing such process and all such assets, lands, goods, chattels, property, estates and effects shall be bound to the payment and discharge thereof accordingly.

17. All real and heritable property, moneys, goods, chattels and effects whatever and all titles, securities for money or other obligatory instruments and evidence or muniments and all other effects whatever and all rights or claims belonging to or had by such society shall be vested in the Trustees or Treasurer of such society for the time being, for the use and benefit of such society and the respective members thereof, their respective executors or administrators, according to their respective claims and interest; and after the death or removal of any Trustee or Treasurer, shall vest in the succeeding Trustee or Treasurer, for the same estate or interest as the former Trustee or Treasurer had therein, and subject to the same trusts, without any assignment or conveyance whatever, and also shall for all purposes of action or suit, as well criminal as civil, in law or in equity, in any wise touching or concerning the same, be deemed and taken to be, and shall in every such proceeding (where necessary) be stated to be the property of the person

appointed to the office of Trustee or Treasurer of such society for the time being, in his or her proper name, without further description; and such person shall, and he or she is hereby respectively authorized to bring or defend or cause to be brought or defended, any action, suit or prosecution, criminal as well as civil, in law or in equity, touching or concerning the property, right or claim aforesaid of or belonging to or had by such society; provided that such person shall have been thereunto duly authorized by the consent of the majority of members present at any meeting of the society or committee thereof; and such person so appointed shall and may in all cases concerning the property, right or claim aforesaid of such society, sue and be sued, plead and be impleaded in his or her proper name as Trustee or Treasurer of such society without other description; and no such suit, action or prosecution shall be discontinued or abated by the death of such person, or his or her removal from the office of Trustee or Treasurer, but the same shall and may be proceeded in by the succeeding Trustee or Treasurer in the proper name of the person commencing the same, any law, usage or custom to the contrary notwithstanding; and such succeeding Trustee or Treasurer shall pay or receive like costs as if the action or suit had been commenced in his or her name for the benefit of or to be reimbursed from the funds of such society.

18. The Trustees or Treasurer, or any officer of any society established under the authority of this Act shall not be liable to make good any deficiency which may arise in the funds of such society unless such person shall have respectively declared by writing, under their hands, deposited and registered in like manner with the rules of such society, that they are willing so to be answerable, and it shall be lawful for each of such persons or for such persons collectively, to limit his, her or their responsibility to such a sum as shall be specified in any such instrument or writing; provided always, that the said Trustee and Trustees or Treasurer, and every the officer of any such society shall be and they are hereby declared to be personally responsible and liable for all moneys actually received by him, her or them, on account of or to or for the use of the said society.

19. Whenever the Trustees of any society established under this Act, at any time after the decease of any member, have paid and divided any sum of money to or amongst any person or persons who shall at the time of such payment appear to such Trustees to be entitled to the effects of any deceased intestate member, the payment of any such sum or sums of money shall be valid and effectual with respect to any demand of any other person or persons as next of kin of such deceased intestate member against the funds of such society, or against the Trustees thereof, but nevertheless such next of kin or representative shall have remedy for such money so paid as aforesaid against the person or persons who shall have received the same.

20. In case any member of any society shall die, who shall be entitled to any sum not exceeding twenty pounds, it shall be lawful for the Trustees or Treasurer, of such society, and they are hereby authorized and permitted, if such Trustees or Treasurer shall be satisfied that no will was made and left by such deceased member, and that no letters of administration will be taken out of the funds, goods, and chattels of such depositor to pay the same at any time after the decease of such member, according to the rules and regulations of the said society; and in the event of there being no rules and regulations made in that behalf, then the said Trustee or Treasurer are hereby authorized and permitted to pay and divide the same to and amongst the person or persons entitled to the effects of the deceased intestate, and that without administration.

21. For the more effectually preventing fraud and imposition on the funds of such societies, if any officer, member or any other person, being, or representing himself or herself to be a member of such society, or the nominee, executor, administrator, or assignee of any member of such Society, or any other person whatever, shall in or by any false representation or imposition, fraudulently obtain possession of the moneys of such Society, or any part thereof, or having in his or her possession any sum of money belonging to such Society, shall fraudulently withold the same, and for which offence no especial provision is made in the rules of such Society, it shall be lawful for any one Justice of the Peace residing within the county within which such Society shall be held, upon complaint made on oath by an officer of such Society, to summon such person against whom such complaint shall be made, to appear at a time and place to be named in such summons, and upon his or her appearance, or in default thereof, upon due proof upon oath of the service of such summons, it shall and may be lawful for any two justices residing within the county aforesaid, to hear and determine the said complaint, according to the rules of the said Society, confirmed as directed by this Act; and upon due proof of such fraud, the said Justices shall convict the said party, and award double the amount of the money so fraudulently obtained or withheld, to be paid to the Treasurer, to be applied by him to the purposes of the Society so proved to have been imposed upon and defrauded, together with such costs as shall be awarded by the said justices, not exceeding the sum of ten shillings; and in case such person against whom such complaint shall be made, shall not pay the sum of money so awarded to the person, and at the time specified in the said order, such justices are hereby required by warrant under their hands and seals, to cause the same to be levied by distress and sale of goods of such person on whom such order shall have been made, or by other legal proceeding, together with such costs as shall be awarded by the said justices, not exceeding the sum of ten shillings, and also the costs and charges attending such distress and sale, or other legal proceeding, returning the overplus (if any) to the owner; and in default of such distress being found, the said justices of the peace shall commit such person so proved to have offended to the Provincial Penitentiary, there to be kept at hard labour for such a period not exceeding three calendar months, as to them shall seem fit; provided nevertheless, that nothing herein contained shall prevent the said Society from proceeding by indictment or complaint against the party complained of; and provided also, that no party shall be proceeded against by indictment or complaint if a previous conviction has been obtained for the same offence under the provisions of this Act.

22. Provision shall be made by one or more of the rules of every such Society, to be confirmed as required by this Act, specifying whether a reference of every matter in dispute between any such Society, or any person acting under them, and any individual member thereof or person claiming on account of any member, shall be made to such of Her Majesty's Justices of the Peace as may act in and for the county in which such Society may be formed, or to arbitrators to be appointed in manner hereinafter directed; and if the matter so in dispute shall be referred to arbitration, certain arbitrators shall be named and elected at the first meeting of such Society, or committee thereof, that shall be held after the enrolment of its rules, none of the said arbitrators being beneficially interested, directly or indirectly, in the funds of the said Society, of whom a certain number, not less than three, shall be chosen by ballot in each such case of dispute, the number of the said arbitrators and mode of ballot being determined by the rules of each Society respectively; the names of such arbitrators shall be duly entered in the Book of the said Society in which the rules are entered as aforesaid; and in case of the death, or refusal, or neglect of any or all of the said arbitrators to act, it shall and may be lawful to and for the said Society or committee thereof, and they are hereby required, at their next meeting, to name and elect one more arbitrator or arbitrators as aforesaid, to act in the place of the said arbitrator or arbitrators so dying or refusing, or neglecting to act as aforesaid; and whatever award shall be made by the said arbitrators, or the major part of them, according to the true purport and meaning of the rules of such Society, confirmed by the Justices according to the directions of this Act, shall be in the form to this Act annexed, and shall be binding and conclusive on all parties and shall be final to all intents and purposes without appeal or being subject to the control of one or more Justices of the Peace and shall not be removed or removeable into any Court of law or restrained or restrainable by the injunction of any Court of equity and should either of the said parties in dispute refuse or neglect to comply with or conform to the decision of the said arbitrators or the major part of them, it shall and may be lawful for any one Justice of the Peace residing within the County within which such Society shall be held, upon good and sufficient proof being adduced before him of such award having been made and of the refusal of the party to comply therewith upon complaint made by or on behalf of the party aggrieved to summon the person against whom such complaint shall be made to appear at a time and place to be named in such summons and upon his or her appearance or in default thereof upon due proof upon oath of the service of such summons any two Justices of the Peace may proceed to make such order thereupon as to them may seem just and if the sum of money so awarded together with the sum for costs not exceeding the sum of ten shillings as to such Justices shall seem meet shall not be immediately paid and such Justices shall by warrant under their hands and seal, cause such sum and costs as aforesaid to be levied by distress or by distresses and sale of the moneys, goods, chattels, securities and effects belonging to the said party or to the said society or other legal proceeding together with all further costs and charges attending such distress and sale or other legal proceeding returning the overplus (if any) to the said party or to the said society or to one of the Trustees or Treasurer thereof and in default of such distress being found or such other legal proceeding being ineffectual then to be levied by distress and sale of the proper goods of the said party or of the said society so neglecting or refusing as aforesaid by other legal proceedings together with such further costs and charges as aforesaid, returning the overplus (if any) to the owner, provided always, that when the rules of any Society provided for a reference to arbitrators of any matter in dispute and it shall appear to any Justice of the Peace on the complaint on oath of a member of any such society or of any person claiming on account of such member that application has been made to such society or the Trustees or Treasurer or other officer thereof for the purpose of having any dispute so settled by arbitration and that such application has not within forty days been complied with or that the arbitrators have neglected or refused to make any award it shall and may be lawful for such Justice to summon the Trustee or Treasurer or other officer of the society or any one of them against whom the complaint is made and for any two Justices to hear and determine the matter in dispute in the same manner as if the rules in the said society had directed that any matter in dispute as aforesaid should be decided by Justices of the Peace anything herein contained to the contrary thereof notwithstanding.

23. If by the rules of any such Society it is directed that any matter in dispute as aforesaid shall be decided by Justices of the Peace, it shall and may be lawful for any such Justices, on complaint being made to him of any refusal or neglect to comply with the rules of such Society by any member or officer thereof, to summon the person against whom such complaint shall be made, to appear at a time and place to be named in such summons, and upon his or her appearance, or in default thereof, upon due proof on oath of the service of such summons, it shall and may be lawful for any two justices to proceed to hear and determine the said complaint, according to the rules of the said Society; and in the case the said justices shall adjudge any sum of money to be paid by such person against whom such complaint shall be made and such person shall not pay such sum of money to the person, and at the time specified by such justices, they shall proceed to enforce their award in the manner hereinbefore directed to be used, in case of any neglect to comply with the decision of the arbitrators appointed under the authority of this Act.

24. Every sentence, order and adjudication of any justices under this Act, shall be final and conclusive to all intents and purposes, and shall not be subject to appeal, and shall not be removed or removable into any Court of Law, or restrained or restrainable by the injunction of any Court of Equity, and no suspension, advocation, or reduction shall be competent.

25. A minor may become a member of any such Society and shall be empowered to execute all instruments, give all necessary acquittances, and enjoy all the privileges, and be liable to all the responsibilities appertaining to members of matured age, notwithstanding his or her incapacity or disability in law to act for himself or herself; Provided always, that such minor be admitted into such Society by and with the consent of his or her parents, masters, or guardians.

26. The rules of every such Society shall provide that the trustees, Treasurer, or other principal officer thereof, shall once in every year at least, prepare or cause to be prepared a general statement of the funds and effects of or belonging to such Society, specifying in whose custody or possession the said funds or effects shall be then remaining, together with an account of all and every the various sums of money received and expended by or on account of the said Society since the publication of the preceding periodical statement; and every such periodical statement shall be attested by two or more members of such Society, appointed Auditors for that purpose, and shall be countersigned by the Secretary of such Society, and every member shall be entitled to receive from the said Society a copy of such periodical statement; on payment of such sum as the rules of such Society may require, not exceeding the sum of sixpence.

27. On the trial of any action, indictment, or other proceeding respecting the property of any Society enrolled under the authority of this Act; or in any proceedings before any Justice of the Peace, any member of such Society shall be a competent witness, and shall not be objected to on account of any interests he may have as such member in the result of such action, indictment or other proceeding.

28. It shall be lawful for the trustees named in any mortgage made on behalf of such societies, or the survivor or survivors of them, for the trustees for the time being, to endorse upon any mortgage or further charge given by any member of such Society to the trustees thereof for moneys advanced by such Society to any member thereof, a receipt for all moneys intended to be secured by such mortgage or further charge, which shall be sufficient to vacate the same, and vest the estate of and in the property comprised in such security, in the person or persons for the time being entitled to the equity of redemption, without it being necessary for the trustees of any such Society to give any re-conveyance of the property so mortgaged, which receipt shall be specified in a schedule to be annexed to the rules of such Society, duly certified and deposited as aforesaid.

29. Nothing herein contained shall authorize any Building Society established under this Act to invest its funds, or any part thereof, in any Savings Bank.

30. All Building Societies hereafter to be established shall be entitled to the protection and benefits of this Act, but no such Society shall be entitled thereto until their rules shall have been certified and deposited in the manner hereinbefore directed by this Act.

21. Wherever in this Act, in describing or referring to any person, the word importing the singular number or the masculine gender only is used, the same shall be understood to include, and shall be applied to several persons or parties, as well as one person or party, and females as well as males, unless there be something in the subject or context repugnant to such construction.

22. This Act may be altered, amended or repealed, at this present or any future session of Assembly.

Schedule referred to in this Act.

FORM OF AWARD.

We, the major part of the arbitrators, duly appointed by the Building Society established at   in the County of   do hereby award and order, that A. B., (specifying by name the party or the officer of the Society) do on the   day of   , pay to C. D. the sum of   (or we do hereby reinstate in, or expel A. B. from the said Society, as the case may be.)

Dated this   day of   , A.D. 18

E. F.

G. H.

FORM OF BOND.

Know all men by these presents, that we, A. B., of   Treasurer (or trustee, etc.,) of the   Building Society established at   in the County of   , and C. D., of   , and G. H., of   (as sureties on behalf of the said A. B.) are jointly and severally bound to E. F, the present Clerk of the Peace for the County of   in the sum of   to be paid to the said E. F., as such Clerk of the Peace or his successor, Clerk of the Peace, of the said County of   for the time being or his certain attorney, for which payment well and truly to be made we jointly and severally bind ourselves and each of us by himself our and each of our heirs, executors and administrators firmly by these Presents.

Sealed with our seals; dated the   day of   in the year of our Lord one thousand eight hundred and

Whereas the above bounden A. B. hath been duly appointed Treasurer (or Trustee, etc.,) of the   Building Society established as aforesaid, and he together with the above bounden C. D. and G. H., as his sureties have entered into the above written bond subject to the condition hereinafter contained. Now, therefore the condition of the above written bond is such that if the said A. B. shall and do justly and faithfully execute his office of Treasurer (or Trustee, etc.,) of the said Society established as aforesaid, and shall and do render a just and true account of all moneys received and paid by him, and shall and do pay over all the moneys remaining in his hands, and assign and transfer or deliver all securities and effects, books, papers and property of, or belonging to the said Society in his hands, or custody to such person or persons, as the said Society shall appoint according to the rules of the said Society together with the proper or legal receipts or vouchers for such payments, and likewise shall and do in all respects well and truly and faithfully perform and fulfil his office of Treasurer (or Trustee, etc.,) to the said Society according to the rules thereof, then the above written bond shall be void and of no effect, otherwise shall be and remain in full force and virtue.

A. B.   [L.S.]
C. D.   [L.S.]
G. H.   [L.S.]

CAP. XXII.

An Act to revive and continue an Act intituled "An Act for the regulation of Benefit Building Societies.

Section.
1. Act 10 Vic. cap. 83, revised.
2. Saint John Building Society, &c., protected by said Act.

Section.
3. Acts done by New Brunswick Benefit Building Society, &c., and Saint John Building Society, &c., when valid.

Passed, 16th April, 1866.

WHEREAS the Act of Assembly made and passed in the tenth year of the reign of Her present Majesty, intituled "An Act for the regulation of Benefit Building Societies, hath by chapter 162, title 49, of the revised Statutes of the promulgation and repeal of Statutes, been repealed; and whereas at the time of the repeal of the said Act "The New Brunswick Building Society and Savings' Fund," was in existence, but has since been closed, and divers mortgages made to the Trustees of the said Society cancelled; and whereas since the repeal of the said Act "The Saint John Building Society and Investment Fund" hath been formed, and hath been in existence four years and upwards; and whereas, as is recited in and by the said repealed Act, it is desirable to afford encouragement and protection to the Societies commonly called Benefit Building Societies, and the property obtained therewith in this Province;—

Be it therefore enacted by the Lieutenant Governor, Legislative Council and Assembly, as follows:—

1. The said Act of Assembly made and passed in the tenth year of the reign of Her present Majesty, intituled, "An Act for the regulation of Benefit Building Societies," shall be and the same is hereby revived and declared to be and continue in full force and operation from the time of the passing of this Act.

2. The Society now established or existing in the City of Saint John, under the name and style of "The Saint John Building Society and Investment Fund" and all Benefit Building Societies hereafter to be established within this Province, shall be entitled to the protection and benefits of the said revised Act.

3. All the proceedings and business transactions of the said "New Brunswick Benefit Building Society and Savings' Fund," and of and connected with the Saint John Building Society and Investment Fund, since the time of the repeal of the said Act hereby revived, (so far as the same shall have been in accordance with the provisions of the said Act,) shall be and shall be held to be and to have been as valid and effectual in all respects as if the said "Act for the regulation of Benefit Building Societies" had not been repealed, but had continued in force until the passing of this Act; and all mortgages cancelled by the acting Trustees of the said "New Brunswick Benefit Building Society and Savings' Fund" in accordance with the rules of the said Society, and the said Act hereby revised, shall be held to have been

duly cancelled and discharged; and the rules and regulations adopted by the members of the said "Saint John Building Society and Investment Fund," (so far as the same shall be in accordance with the terms of the said revived Act,) shall be held to have been, and shall continue and remain in full force and effect; and the officers of the said Society, shall respectively continue until such time as they may be displaced and others appointed in their room, pursuant to the said rules; and all moneys, securities for money, books, writings, property and effects, belonging to, or made or taken in the name of such Society or the Trustees thereof, shall vest in the persons now acting as Trustees of the said "Saint John Building Society and Investment Fund," to the use and for the benefit, and subject to the liabilities of the said Society, and so from time to time in the succeeding Trustees thereof, and the said securities shall in all respects be valid and effectual according to the tenor thereof; and the said "Saint John Building Society and Investment Fund" shall from its commencement be held and taken to have been and from henceforth shall be a valid Benefit Building Society, under the terms of the said Act hereby revived and continued.

CAP. LVI.

An Act in amendment of an Act made and passed in the tenth year of the Reign of Her present Majesty, intituled "An Act for the regulation of Benefit Building Societies and the Act 29th Victoria to revive and continue the same."

Section.
1. Societies how formed and established.
2. Societies may hold real estate, &c.
3. Persons forming such Society to be and continue a corporation.
4. Society to have a corporate seal, and the rights and privileges of a Corporation.
5. Office of Trustees abolished; management of Society vested in Directors
6. What the rules of Society shall specify.
7. Shares classified.
8. When members shall receive interest on his share.
9. When shares may be capitalized.
10. Society may receive money on deposit; Proviso.

Section.
11. Society may prescribe certain forms of conveyance; where conveyance, &c., shall be filed.
12. Society may prescribe terms of insurance entry, sale, &c.
13. Certain existing Societies to receive the benefits of this Act; Proviso.
14. "The Saint John Building Society and Investment Fund" to be a Corporation.
15. "The Provisional Land and Building Society and Savings Fund" to be a Corporation.
16. Inconsistant provisions of former Acts to be deemed amended.

Passed 17th *May*, 1871.

Be it enacted by the Lieutenant Governor, Legislative Council, and Assembly, as follows:—

1. It shall and may be lawful for any number of persons in this Province to form themselves into and establish Societies for raising by subscriptions of the several members of such Societies, in shares not exceeding the value of four hundred dollars for each shares, a stock or fund to enable each member to receive out of the funds of the Society the amount or value of his shares therein, for the purpose of erecting or purchasing one or more dwelling house or houses, or other freehold or leasehold estate, or for any other purposes whatever; and the amount or value of such shares so advanced shall be secured to the Society by mortgage on freehold or leasehold estate of such member, until the amount or value of his shares, with the interest thereon, shall have been fully repaid, as provided by the rules of such Society, together with all fines or liabilities incurred in respect of such shares, as may be provided by such rules.

2. Every such Society now formed or hereafter to be formed shall have the power of purchasing and holding freehold and leasehold estate, of building houses and other structures or erections thereon, and of selling or renting the same, as to such Society or the Directors thereof may be deemed advisable.

3. The persons forming such Society, and all such persons as shall from time to time become, be and continue members thereof, and their several and respective executors, administrators and assigns, shall from the time that the rules of such Society shall be certified or combined, and a transcript thereof filed with the Clerk of the Peace as is provided in the said Act, for the regulation of Benefit Building Societies, be and continue a corporation, body corporate and politic as a Benefit Building Society, by the name and style mentioned in the rules, for the purposes aforesaid.

4. Every such Society shall have a corporate seal, and may receive, take and hold any real and heritable property, lands and tenements, moneys, securities for money, or other obligatory instruments, goods, chattels and effects whatsoever, and give, grant, sell, let, cancel, release or assign the same, and may bring or defend, or cause to be brought or defended any action, suit, prosecution or proceeding at law or in equity, concerning the property, rights or claims of such Society, and shall have generally all the rights, powers and privileges, incident to a corporation by Act of Assembly or otherwise.

5. The offices of Trustee or Trustees in any such Society is hereby abolished; and all real and personal estate, property and effects, and all titles, securities, instruments and evidences, and all rights and claims of or belonging to any such Society, shall vest in the Committee of Management or Directors thereof for the time being, and their successors in office, in the corporate name of such Society, for the use of the Society and the respective members thereof according to their respective claims and interests.

6. The rules of every such Society shall specify the place or places at which it is intended the Society shall hold its meetings, and the name by which it shall be styled and known, (which name and style may be altered in like manner as is provided in the Act for the regulation of Benefit Building Societies, for an alteration of the said rules) and shall contain provisions with respect to the powers and duties

of the members at large, and of the officers appointed for the management of its affairs; but it shall be lawful for any Society, or for the Directors of such Society, to change the place or places of meeting, or establish new places of meeting, upon filing a written notice thereof with the Clerk of the Peace with whom the rules may be filed.

7. There may be three classes of shares in any such Society, viz: monthly investing shares, paid up investing shares and capitalized shares or stock to be regulated respectively by the rules of the Society.

8. No member of any such Society, except in the case of his withdrawal according to the rules of the Society in such case provided shall receive from the funds of the Society any interest or dividend by way of annual or other periodical profit upon any monthly investing or paid up investing share or shares in the Society, until the amount or value of his share or shares has been realized, matured or capitalized as provided for by rule in such case.

9. Any share or shares in any such Society may be capitalized at any time as may be provided for by rule in such case, and such share or shares when so capitalized shall become fixed and permanent capital stock or shares in such Society, not withdrawable therefrom, but transferable in the same manner as other shares in the said Society, or as may be provided by the rule.

10. It shall and may be lawful for any such Society in the rules thereof to provide for the receiving of money on deposit, paying therefor such rate or rates of interest as may be agreed upon, and upon and under such regulations as may be deemed advisable, and to pledge the estate and property, assets and effects, moneys and securities belonging to such Society, as security for the repayment of such moneys or deposits, and the interest thereon; provided that the amount of money on deposit shall in no case exceed three-fourths of the amount of the accrued value of the investing shares and capitalized stock of such Society.

11. Any such Society may in the rules thereof describe the form of conveyance or other instrument required for carrying its purposes into execution, and which may be specified in a schedule to be annexed to the rules of such Society, and certified or confirmed as hereinafter provided; and the Directors of such Society shall file with the Registrar of Deeds for every County wherein any lands secured by way of mortgage to the Society may be situate, a copy of the rules of the Society and of such form or forms annexed thereto: and such Registrar shall receive the same without fee or reward, and shall preserve the same with the Recorder of Deeds for such County.

12. Any such Society may in the rules thereof prescribe the powers, terms and conditions for or relating to the insurance to be made or effected upon the buildings and erections upon any lands or tenements, freehold or leasehold estate, secured to the Society by way of mortgage; and further may prescribe upon what default of payment, or breach of such rules or of the terms of any mortgage, deed or security to the Society or any of them, the lands and premises mortgaged to the Society may be entered upon, and the rents and profits thereof received or distrained for, by such Society, or its agent appointed by the Directors thereof, or may be absolutely sold; and may prescribe and make such powers, terms, provisions and conditions for, or relating to such insurance, entry, distress or sale of any of them, and for indemnity of the purchasers at any such sale, or otherwise in respect of any mortgage security as shall be deemed advisable; and it shall be sufficient in all mortgage deeds or securities made or taken to or by any such Society, to refer therein to such powers, terms, provisions and conditions as prescribed in the said rules, without stating the same in any such security at large; and all the powers, terms, provisions and conditions in the said rules contained with respect to such mortgage-deeds or securities, shall be deemed to be incorporated in the said mortgage deeds and securities, equally as if stated at large therein; and all sales and conveyances made under the same shall be valid and effectual in the premises; and the deed or conveyance of the said Society, executed under its corporate seal, and purporting to be made in pursuance of the said provisions and powers, shall be *prima facie* evidence of the same, and that the same have been duly executed, and that all the proceedings on which such conveyance was founded were rightly had.

13. "The Saint John Building Society and Investment Fund" and "The Provincial Land and Building Society and Savings Fund," established and existing under and by virtue of Act of Assembly 10th Victoria, chapter 83, intituled, An Act for the regulation of Benefit Building Societies, and the Act of Assembly 29th Victoria, chapter 22, intituled, An Act to revive and continue an Act intituled, An Act for the regulation of Benefit Building Societies, shall from henceforth respectively be entitled to the protection and benefits, and shall be established and exist as incorporated Building Societies under the terms of this Act; and all real and personal estate, rights or claims of what nature or kind soever, moneys, securities for money, books, writings, property and effects belonging to the said societies, or made or taken in the name of, or at present vested in the Trustees of the said Societies, shall from henceforth respectively be fully and absolutely vested and remain in the said Saint John Building Society and Investment Fund, and Provincial Land and Building Society and Savings' Fund, incorporated by the terms of this Act, their successors and assigns, for the like uses, trusts and purposes for which the same are at present held by or vested in the said societies respectively, or in the said Trustees: and the said securities shall in all respects be valid and effectual to the said Societies respectively, according to the tenor thereof, and may be sued, prosecuted and proceeded upon as provided by the terms of this Act, in the name of the said Societies respectively, in like manner as if the same had been taken or made in the said name; and all powers of sale, and other powers, rights or privileges therein or thereby given, or reserved or contained, shall and may be exercised in the name or under the corporate seals of the said Societies respectively as the Directors of the same for the time being, or the major part of them present at any meeting, shall direct and appoint, according to the tenor of such powers, rights or privileges respectively; and the rules of the said Societies shall be and continue in full force and effect save and excepting as the same shall be altered by the terms of this Act, until the same shall be rescinded, altered or amended as hereinbefore is provided ; and all suits, actions or prosecutions relating to or in any manner concerning the said societies, which before the passing of this Act could have been sued, brought or had by or against the Trustees of the said Societies, shall from henceforth be sued or brought by or against the said Societies respectively, in their incorporated name, under the terms of this Act; provided that the present Directors of the said Societies respectively shall and may continue to act as Directors thereof until the next annual general meeting of the members of the said Societies held for the election of Directors after the passing of this Act.

14. The said The Saint John Building Society and Investment Fund, shall be and become a Corporation under the style and name of "The Saint John Building Society," and for that purpose shall have all the benefits, rights, privileges and advantages of a corporation established by Act of Assembly or otherwise, subject to the provisions of the Act of Assembly, 10th Victoria, chapter 83, intituled an Act for the regulation of Benefit Building Societies, and an Act of Assembly 29th Victoria, chapter 22, intituled, An Act to revive and continue an Act intituled, An Act for the regulation of Benefit Building Societies.

15. The said The Provincial Land and Building Society and Savings' Fund, shall be and become a Corporation under the style and name of " The Provincial Building Society," and for that purpose shall have all the benefits, rights and privileges and advantages of a Corporation established by Act of Assembly or otherwise, subject to the provisions of the Act of Assembly, 10th Victoria, chapter 83, intituled An Act for the Regulation of Benefit Building Societies, and an Act of Assembly, 29th Victoria, chapter 22, intituled, An Act to revive and continue an Act intituled, An Act for the regulation of Benefit Building Societies.

16. All provisions of all former Acts or amendments of Acts, which may be inconsistent with this present Act, shall be held and taken to be this Act amended so far as may be necessary to render them consistent with this Act.

CAP. LVII.

An Act to incorporate the Saint John Real Estate and Building Society.

Section.	Section.
1. Company incorporated.	11. Production of register to be deemed prima facie evidence.
2. Capital stock.	12. When dividends shall not be paid.
3. First meeting, by whom called.	13. Liability of Company.
4. Qualification of voter.	14. Company may classify shares.
5. Shareholder liable for calls.	15. Class A, shareholders may have preferential interest.
6. Power of Company to levy and collect assessments; how recovered.	16. Preferential interest to class A, how secured.
7. No transfer made until all calls paid.	17. When class B, shares may be granted to holders of class A.
8. What constitutes a discharge to Company.	18. Dividends to be made to class A.
9. In any suit Company need not set forth special matter.	19. Annual and other meetings, when held.
10. On trial, what constitutes sufficient proof.	

[*Passed* 17*th May*, 1871.]

BE IT ENACTED, by the Lieutenant-Governor, Legislative Council, and Assembly, as follows:

1. That John M. Robinson, Thomas B. Buxton, William S. Berton, Frederick P. Robinson, their associates, successors and assigns, be and they are hereby declared to be a body corporate, by the name of "The St. John Real Estate and Building Company," with all the general powers and privileges made incident to corporations by Act of Assembly in this Province, for the purpose of building and erecting houses, buildings and other erections in the city of St. John, and renting and leasing the same, and for the leasing or purchasing of lands in the said city of St. John, and the constructing and maintaining of buildings thereon, as may be necessary, requisite or convenient, and such other works, business and operations as may be incident thereto.

2. The capital stock of the said Corporation shall be fifty thousand dollars of the current money of the Province of New Brunswick, divided into five hundred shares of one hundred dollars each; provided, however, that the said Corporation shall have power to increase the said capital stock to a sum not exceeding the sum of one hundred thousand dollars.

3. That the first meeting of the said Corporation for the organization thereof, may be called by the said Frederick P. Robinson, or in case of his death, neglect or refusal, by any one of the parties named in this Act, at such time and place as he may appoint by publishing notice of the same in any one public newspaper printed and published in the city of St. John, for ten days previous to the day of such meeting.

4. Each and every person owning a share in the capital stock of the said Company shall be a member thereof, and shall be entitled to vote at all meetings of the said Company; and members may give as many votes as they own shares, and may vote by proxy, such proxy being a stockholder and authorized in writing; provided, however, that no member acting as such proxy shall be the proxy of more than one absent stockholder.

5. Each and every shareholder in the said Corporation shall be, and be held liable, to the said Company for each and every call or assessment made; not, however, to exceed in amount the stock subscribed by him, for the purpose of enabling the said Company to pay the debts and engagements of the said Corporation, or for the purposes of or to carry on the operations for which the said Company is incorporated; which call or assessment may be sued for by the said Corporation, and recovered in any Court of Record within the Province.

6. The Company or the Directors, if empowered by the by-laws of the Corporation, shall have power from time to time to levy and collect assessments upon the shares, or upon such of them on which the amount subscribed has not been paid up, of such sums of money as may be deemed necessary for carrying on the business, or for the purpose or operations of the said Company; and whenever any assessment shall be made as aforesaid, it shall be the duty of the Treasurer or Secretary of the said Company to give notice thereof in a public newspaper printed in the city of St. John, requiring payment of the same within not less than thirty days; and if any stockholder shall neglect or refuse to pay to the Treasurer the amount of such assessment upon his shares, or any part of such amount, at the time in such notice prescribed, the same may be either sued for and recovered in the manner provided in the last preceding section, or the Treasurer may advertise all such delinquent shares for sale at public auction, giving at least thirty days' notice of the time and place of such sale by publishing a notice thereof in some one public newspaper published in the city aforesaid; and all shares on which the assessment or any part thereof is not paid, with interest from the time such assessment became due, may be sold to the highest bidder, and after retaining the amount due on such assessment, and all interest due thereon, and all expenses of advertising and selling, the residue (if any) of the moneys for which such shares shall be sold, shall be paid over to the former owner thereof, and a new certificate or certificates of the shares so sold shall be made and delivered to the purchaser or purchasers thereof.

7. No shareholder shall be entitled to transfer or vote upon any share after any call shall have been made in respect thereof, until he or she shall have paid all calls for the time being due on every share held by him or them.

8. The said Company shall not be bound to see to the execution of any trust whatever express, implied or constructive, to which any of the said shares may at any time be subject, and the receipt of the party in whose name any such share shall stand in the books of the said Company, or if it stands in the name of more parties than one, the receipt of any one of the parties in whose name the same shall stand in the register of stockholders, shall from time to time be a sufficient discharge to the said Company for any dividend or other sum of money payable in respect of such share, notwithstanding any trust to which such share may then be subject, and whether or not the said Company shall have had notice of such trust, and notwithstanding the other owner or owners of such share or shares shall not have joined in such receipt, and that the said Company shall not be in any way bound to see to the application of the money paid upon such receipt.

9. In any action or suit to be brought by the said Company against any shareholder to recover any money due for any call, it shall not be necessary to set forth the special matter; but it shall be sufficient for the said Company to declare that the defendant is the holder of one or more shares in the said Company (stating the number of shares), and is indebted to the said Company in the sum of money to which the calls in arrear shall amount, in respect to one call or more upon one share or more, stating the number and amount of each such calls, whereby an action hath accrued to the said Company by virtue of this Act.

10. On the hearing of such action or suit, it shall be sufficient to prove that the defendant, at the time of the making of such call, was the holder of one or more shares, as the case may be, in the said Company, that such call was in fact made, and such notice thereof given as is directed by this Act; and it shall not be necessary to prove the appointment by the Directors by whom such call was made, nor any other matter whatever; and thereupon the said Company shall be entitled to recover what shall be due upon such call, and interest thereon unless it shall appear either that such call exceeds the prescribed amount aforesaid, or that due notice of such call was not given.

11. The production of the register of the shareholders shall be *primâ facie* evidence that the parties whose names are therein entered as owners of shares are shareholders, and of the number and amount of their respective shares.

12. The dividend shall be paid in respect of any share, until all calls and assessments then due and unpaid, in respect of that and every other share held by the person to whom such dividend may be payable, shall have been faithfully paid.

13. The joint stock and property of the said Company shall be responsible for the debts and engagements of the said Company, and the holders of stock in the said Company shall be chargeable in their private and individual capacity for all debts and liabilities of the said Company, in proportion to the stock they respectively hold; provided, however, that in no case shall any one stockholder be liable to pay a sum exceeding the amount of stock actually held by him; provided, nevertheless, that nothing herein contained shall be construed to exempt the joint stock of the said Corporation from being also liable for and chargeable with the debts and engagements of the same.

14. The said Company may, at any meeting of shareholders, set apart any number of the present or future shares of the said Company, to be denominated "class A shares," and all other shares may be designated "class B shares."

15. The shareholders of the said Company, or a majority of them, at any meeting, may from time to time grant to the holders of class A shares a preferential interest or dividend not exceeding seven per cent. per annum, on such terms and conditions as at any such meeting may be imposed.

16. The shareholders of the said Company, or a majority of them, may from time to time subject and charge, in such manner as they see fit, the lands, goods and other property, incomes and profits, present and future of the said Company or such parts thereof as they may think fit to secure the payment or other satisfaction to the holders of class A shares of any interest or dividend aforesaid not exceeding seven per cent. as aforesaid.

17. The shareholders of the said Company or a majority of them, may at any meeting or meetings of the said Company, grant to the holders of paid up "class A shares" or any of them, such number of "class B shares" as the said shareholders or a majority of them may deem proper, and upon such terms and conditions as they may impose.

18. No greater dividend than seven per cent. per annum shall be made to class A shareholders until class B shareholders shall have received full six per cent. per annum interest or dividend on the amount of stock paid up by them, with interest on arrears of such dividends, if any.

19. The time and place of holding annual or semi-annual, and all special or other meetings of the said Corporation, as also the number, iligibility, duties and powers of Directors, officers and servants, their continuance in office, removal or disqualification, the filling up of vacancies, the time and manner of election or appointments, and any and every other matter and thing whatsoever connected with the objects and purposes for which the said Company is incorporated, may be established or regulated by by-laws of the said Company to be made at any meeting of the said Company, or adjournment thereof, which by-laws not inconsistent with this Act of incorporation, they are empowered to make.

CHAP. XXXIII.

An Act in further amendment of the law relating to Benefit Building Societies.

Section.
1. Society authorized to invest funds, Amount to be invested.
2. Rights of investors in Society.
3. By-laws of Society to be submitted to and approved of by Attorney General before going into operation.
4. By-laws to be recorded.
5. General statement of Society to be sent to each shareholder before annual meeting.
6. Liability of shareholders.
7. Meaning of the word "capitalized" defined.
8. When general statement shall be published.
9. Penalty for not mailing general statement to shareholders; Amount.

[*Passed 23rd April*, 1880.]

WHEREAS it is deemed expedient to amend an Act made and passed in the tenth year of the Reign of Her present Majesty, intituled An Act for the regulation of Benefit Building Societies, and all other Acts in amendment thereof, so as to declare more fully and clearly the powers and rights of all such Societies now formed or hereafter to be formed in this Province;—

Be it therefore enacted by the Lieutenant-Governor, Legislative Council, and Assembly, as follows:—

1. From and after the passing of this Act it shall and may be lawful for any Building Society in this Province now formed or hereafter to be formed to invest its funds and moneys in good Dominion, Provincial, County, City or School Debentures, not to exceed however, in the whole, more than twenty per centum of the total amount of the assets of any such Society.

2. For the purpose of declaring more clearly the respective rights of those having funds invested in any such Society, it is hereby declared that deposits and debenture indebtedness shall be a first charge upon the funds and assets of any such Society, and monthly investing and paid-up shares, and capitalized stocks shall rank equally next after deposits and debenture indebtedness.

3. From and after the passing of this Act it shall and may be lawful for any such Society now formed or hereafter to be formed to frame by-laws and ordinance, not contrary to Law, for its guidance and government; and it shall not be necessary for such by-laws and ordinances, or any amendment thereof to be certified by a Barrister appointed by the Attorney General, nor shall it be necessary for the same to be filed with the Clerk of the Peace for the county wherein such Society may carry on its business, any thing in the Act 10th Victoria, chapter 83, or any amendments thereof, to the contrary notwithstanding; but before such by-laws and ordinances and amendments thereof come into force and effect they shall first be submitted to and approved of by the Attorney General of the Province for the time being, which approval of by-laws and amendments thereof shall be published in the *Royal Gazette*, or in a daily newspaper published in the city of St. John, or such weekly newspaper as may be best adapted to that purpose, in the case of Societies whose chief place of business in the Province may be elsewhere than in the city of St. John, for one insertion, and such publication shall be evidence of such approval of such by-laws and amendments thereof; provided always, that nothing herein contained shall effect any by-laws of Building Societies now in force.

4. All such by-laws and ordinances, and amendments thereof, after approval as aforesaid, shall be entered in a book to be kept by such Society for that purpose, and shall be signed by the shareholders and borrowers and of any such Society.

5. The general statement of the funds and effects of such Society, which is by the 28th Section of the said Act and amendments thereto, required to be given to each member of such Society, shall be mailed, prepaid by the the Secretary or Secretary-Treasurer of such Society, addressed to each shareholder of such Society, at least six days before each annual meeting, but non compliance with this section shall not render any such general meeting, or any adjournment thereof, or the proceedings of any such meeting, or any adjourment thereof, invalid or illegal.

6. The joint stock and property of any such Society shall be responsible for the debts and engagements of any such Society; and the holders of stock in any such Society shall be chargeable in their private and individual capacity for all debts and liabilities of any such Society in which they may hold stock, in proportion to the stock they respectively hold; provided however, that in no case shall any one stockholder be liable to pay a sum exceeding the amount of stock actually held by him; provided nevertheless, that nothing herein contained shall be construed to exempt the joint stock of the said Corporation from being also liable and chargeable with the debts and engagements of the same.

7. The word "Capitalized" in the seventh section of the Act chapter fifty six, thirty fourth Victoria, intituled An Act in amendment of an Act made and passed in the tenth year of the Reign of Her present Majesty, intituled An Act for the regulation of Benefit Building Societies, and the Acts 29th Victoria to revive and continue the same, shall be read and understood, for all purposes connected with Benefit Building Societies in this Province, to mean Capital Stock as well as Capitalized Stock.

8. The general statement mentioned in the fifth Section of this Act shall within ten days after the annual meeting of any such Society, be published in a public newspaper published in the city or county in which any such Society may have its chief place of business, and if there shall not be any public newspaper published in any such city or county, then such general statement shall be published in the *Royal Gazette*.

9. If such Secretary or Secretary-Treasurer aforesaid shall not mail such general statement as required by the fifth section of this Act, he shall forfeit and pay a penalty of twenty dollars for each offence, such penalty to be enforced and recovered under the summary convictions Act intituled chapter sixty-two, of the Consolidated Statutes of New Brunswick.

CHAP. XLII.

An Act for the regulation of Benefit Building Societies.

Section.
Preamble.
1. Formation of Building Societies; purposes and regulations thereof; proviso.
2. Bonus on shares and interest.
3. Forms of conveyances transfers, &c.
4. Submission of rules for approval by Governor in Council, &c., &c.
5. Rules to be recorded and to be open to inspection.
6. Force of rules.
7. Alteration of approved rules.
8. Place of meeting, powers of members, officers, &c.
9. Election of officers, filling of vacancies, securities required from officers.
10. Election of Committees; powers; proviso.
11. Accounts between individuals and society.
12. Involuntary conveyances by order of court.
13. Title to real property, monies, &c., vested in officers of Society; institution and defence of suits relative thereto, &c.

Section.
14. Liabilities of officers for deficiency in funds; proviso.
15. Payment of money of deceased intestate members.
16. Payment when sum does not exceed £20.
17. Remedy against persons fraudulently detaining funds of societies; proviso.
18. Rules to be provided for submission of differences to justices of the peace or to arbitration; election of arbitrators, &c., &c.; enforcement of awards, &c., &c.; proviso.
19. Proceedings before justices.
20. Minors may become members.
21. Preparation of general statement.
22. Members competent as witnesses.
23. Discharge of mortgages.
24. Funds not to be invested in savings Banks.
25. Societies hereafter established subject to Act.
26. Construction of terms.
27. Alteration or repeal of Act.

Passed the 31st day of March, A.D., 1849.

WHEREAS certain Societies, commonly called Building Societies, have been established in different parts of the United Kingdom of Great Britain, and in the Provinces of Canada and New Brunswick, principally amongst the industrious classes, for the purpose of raising, by small periodical subscriptions, a fund to assist the members thereof in obtaining Freehold or Leasehold Property; and it is expedient to afford encouragement and protection to such Societies, and the Property obtained therewith, in this Province;

I. Be it therefore enacted, by the Lieutenant-Governor, Council, and Assembly, That it shall and may be lawful for any number of persons in this Province to form themselves into and establish Societies, for the purpose of raising by the monthly or other subscriptions of the several members of such Societies, shares, not exceeding the value of One Hundred and Fifty Pounds for each share; such subscription not to exceed in the whole Twenty Shillings per Month for each share; a Stock or Fund for the purpose of enabling each member thereof to receive out of the funds of such Society the amount or value of his or her share or shares therein, to erect or purchase one or more Dwelling House or Dwelling Houses, or other Real or Household Estate— to be secured by way of mortgage to such Society, until the amount or value of his or her shares shall have been fully repaid to such Society, with the interest thereon, and all fines or other payments incurred in respect thereof;—and to and for the several members of each Society from time to time to assemble together, and to make, ordain and constitute such proper and wholesome Rules and Regulations for the government and guidance of the same, as to the major part of the members of such Society so assembled together shall seem meet— so as such rules shall

15

not be repugnant to the express provisions of this Act, and to the general laws of this Province—and to impose and inflict such reasonable fines, penalties, and forfeitures upon the several members of any such Society who shall offend against any such Rules, as the members may think fit, to be respectively paid to such uses for the benefit of such Society, as such Society by such Rules shall direct; and also, from time to time, to alter and amend such Rules as occasion may require, or annul or repeal the same, and to make new Rules in lieu thereof, under such restrictions as are in this Act contained: Provided, That no member shall receive, or be entitled to receive from the funds of such Society any interest or dividend, by way of annual or other periodical profit, upon any shares in such Society, until the amount or value of his or her share shall have been realized, except on the withdrawal of such member according to the Rules of such Society then in force.

II. And be it enacted, That it shall and may be lawful to and for any such Society to have and receive from any member or members thereof any sum or sums of money by way of bonus or any share or Shares for the privilege of receiving the same in advance, prior to the same being realized, and also any interest for the share or shares so received on any part thereof, without being subject or liable on account thereof to any of the forfeitures or penalties imposed by any Act or Acts of Assembly relating to Usury.

III. And be it enacted, That it shall and may be lawful to and for any such Society, in and by the Rules thereof, to describe the form or forms of Conveyance, Mortgage, Transfer, Agreement, Bond, or other instrument which may be necessary for carrying the purposes of the said Society into execution, and which shall be specified and set forth a Schedule to be annexed to the Rules of such Society and duly certified and deposited as hereinafter provided.

IV. And be it enacted, That Two Transcripts, fairly written on Paper or Parchment, of all Rules made in pursuance of this Act, signed by Three Members, and countersigned by the Secretary of any such Society (accompanied, in the case of an alteration or amendment of Rules, with an affidavit of the Secretary, or one of the officers of said Society, that the provisions of this Act have been duly complied with), shall be submitted to the Governor, Lieutenant-Governor, or Commander in Chief for the time being, and the Executive Council; and one of such Transcripts, when approved by the Governor, Lieutenant-Governor, or Commander in Chief, and Executive Council, with a Certificate of Approval, signed by the Provincial Secretary, shall be returned to the Society, and the other of such Transcripts shall be transmitted by the Society to the Clerk of the Peace for the County wherein such Society shall be formed, and shall be filed by such Clerk of the Peace with the Rolls of the Sessions of the Peace in his custody, without fee or reward; and that all Rules, Alterations and Amendments thereof, from the time when the same shall be certified by the Governor, Lieutenant-Governor, or Commander in Chief for the time being, shall be binding on the several Members and Officers of the said Society, and all persons having interest therein.

V. And be it enacted, That the Rules for the management of every such Society shall be entered and recorded in a book to be kept by the Secretary for that purpose, which book shall be open at all seasonable times for the inspection of the Members of such Society, but nevertheless nothing contained herein shall extend to prevent any alteration in, or amendment of, any such rules in the whole or in part, or make any new Rules for the management of such Society, in such manner as by the Rules of the said Society shall from time to time be provided—which Alterations and Amendments shall nevertheless first receive the approval of the Governor and Council, and be recorded as aforesaid.

VI. And be it enacted, That all Rules from time to time made and in force for the management of such Society as aforesaid, and duly entered on such book as aforesaid, and approved by the Governor, Lieutenant-Governor, or Commander in Chief for the time being as aforesaid, shall be binding on the members and officers of such Society, and the several contributors thereto, and their representatives, all of whom shall be deemed and taken to have full notice thereof by such entry and contribution as aforesaid, and the entry of such Rules in such book as aforesaid, or the Transcript thereof, deposited with such Clerk of the Peace as aforesaid, or a true copy of such Transcript examined with the original and proved to be a true copy, shall be received as evidence of such Rules respectively in all cases, and no Certiorari or other legal process shall be brought or allowed to remove any such Rules into any Court of Judicature of this Province, and every copy of any such Transcript deposited with any Clerk of the Peace as aforesaid, shall be made without any fee or reward except the actual expense of making such copy.

VII. And be it enacted, that no rule approved by the Governor, Lieutenant-Governor, or Commander-in-Chief for the time being, in manner aforesaid shall be altered, rescinded or repealed, unless at a general meeting of the members of such society as aforesaid convened by public notice, written or printed, signed by the Secretary or President of such society, in pursuance of a requisition for that purpose by seven or more of that society which requisition and notice shall be publicly read at the two usual meetings of such society to be held next before such general meeting, for the purpose of such alteration or repeal, unless a committee of such members shall have been nominated for that purpose at a general meeting of the members of such society, convened in manner aforesaid, in which case such committee shall have the like power to make such alterations or repeal, and unless such alterations or repeal shall be made with the concurrence and approbation of three-fourths of the members of such society then and there present, or by the like proportion of such committee as aforesaid, if any shall have been nominated for that purpose.

VIII. And be it enacted, that the rules of any society formed under the authority of this Act shall specify the place or places at which it is intended such society shall hold its meetings, and contain provisions with respect to the powers and duties of the members at large, and of such committee or officers as may be appointed for the management of the affairs of such society. Provided always, that it shall and may be lawful for any such society to alter their place or places of meeting whenever they may consider it necessary, upon giving notice thereof in writing to the Clerk of the Peace for the County within which such society shall be held—the said notice to be given within seven days before or after such removal, and signed Secretary or other principal officer and also by three or more of the members of said society, and provided that the place or places at which such society intend to hold their meetings shall be situate within the County in which the Rules of the said Society are enrolled.

IX. And be it enacted, that every such society shall and may from time to time at any of their usual meetings, or by their committee, if any such shall be appointed for that society, elect and appoint such person into the office of Trustee, President, Secretary, Surveyor or Treasurer of such society as they shall think proper and also shall and may, from time to time, elect and appoint such other officers as shall be deemed necessary to carry into execution the purposes of such Society, for such space of time and for such purposes as shall be fixed and established by the Rules of such Society, and from time to time elect and appoint others in the room of those who shall vacate or die; and such Trustees, Treasurer, and all and every other officer or other person whatever, who shall be appointed to any office in any wise touching or concerning the receipt, management or expenditure of any sum of money collected for the purpose of any such society, before he, she or they shall be admitted to take upon him, her or them, the execution of any such office or trust, if required so to do by the Rule of such Society to which such officer shall belong, shall become bound in a Bond according to the form prescribed in the By-laws, with two sufficient sureties for the just and faithful execution of such office or trust, and for rendering a just and true account, according to the Rules of such Society, and in all matters lawful to pay obedience to the same, in such penal sum of money as by the major part of such Society at any such meeting as aforesaid shall be thought expedient and to the satisfaction of such Society, and that every such Bond to be given by or on behalf of such Trustee or Treasurer, or of any other person appointed to any other office or trust shall be given to the Clerk of the Peace of the County where such Society shall be established for the time being, without fee or reward; and in case of forfeiture it shall be lawful to sue upon such Bond in the name of the Clerk of the Peace for the time being, for the use of the said Society, fully indemnifying and saving himself, such Clerk of the Peace, from all costs and charges in respect of any such suit.

X. And be it enacted, That every such Society shall and may from time to time, elect and appoint any number of the members of such Society to be a Committee, the number thereof to be declared by the rules of every such Society, and shall and may delegate to such Committee all or any of the powers given by this Act to be executed, who being so delegated shall continue to act as such Committee for and during such time as they shall be appointed for such Society for general purposes ; the powers of such Committee being first declared in and by the Rules of such Society, confirmed and filed as aforesaid; and all acts and orders of such Committee under the powers so delegated to them, shall have the like force and effect as the acts and orders of such Society at any General Meeting thereof could or might have had in pursuance of this Act: Provided always, That the transactions of such Committee shall be entered in a Book belonging to such Society, and shall be from time to time, and at all times subject and liable to the review, allowance, or disallowance and control of such Society, in such manner and form as such Society shall by their General Rules, confirmed and filed as aforesaid, have directed and appointed, or shall in like manner direct and appoint.

XI. And be it enacted, That every person who shall have or receive any part of the monies, effects or funds of, or belonging to any such Society, or shall in any manner have been or shall be entrusted with the disposal, management or custody thereof, or of any securities, books, papers or property relating to the same, his or her executors, administrators and assigns respectively shall, upon demand made or notice in writing given, or left at the last or usual place of residence of such person, in pursuance of any order of any such Society or Committee to be appointed as aforesaid, give in his or her account at the usual meeting of such Society, to be examined and allowed or disallowed by such Society, and shall on the like demand and notice pay over all the monies remaining in his or her hands, and assign and transfer or deliver all Securities and Effects, Books, Papers and Property taken or standing in his or her name as aforesaid, and being in his or her hands or custody, to the Trustees or Treasurer for the time being, or to such other person as such Society shall appoint, and in case of any neglect or refusal to deliver such account, or to pay over such monies, or to assign, transfer or deliver such Securities and Effects, Books or Papers and Property in manner aforesaid, it shall and may be lawful to and for every such Society in the name of the Trustee or Treasurer, or other principal officer thereof, as the case may be, to exhibit a Petition to the Supreme Court of this Province, or to a Judge thereof, in vacation, who shall and may proceed thereon in a summary way, and make such Order therein upon hearing all parties concerned, as to such Court in their discretion shall seem just, which Order shall be final and conclusive, and all assignments, sales and transfers made in pursuance of such order shall be good and effectual in law, to all intents and purposes whatsoever.

XII. And be it enacted, That when and so often as any person seized or possessed of any Lands, Tenements or Hereditaments, or other Property, or any Estate or Interest therein as a Trustee of any such Society, shall be out of the jurisdiction of, or not amenable to, the process of the Supreme Court of this Province, or shall be Idiot, Lunatic, or of unsound mind, or it shall be unknown or uncertain whether he or she be living or dead, or such person shall refuse to convey, or otherwise assure such Lands or Tenements, Hereditaments or Property, or Estate or Interest, to the person duly nominated as Trustee of such Society in their stead, either alone, or together with any continuing Trustee, as occasion shall require, then, and in every or any such case, it shall be lawful for the said Court, or one of the Judges thereof in vacation, to appoint such person as to such Court or Judge shall seem meet, on behalf and in the name of the person seized or possessed as aforesaid, to convey, surrender, release, assign, or otherwise assure the said Lands, Tenements, Hereditaments or Property, or Estate, or Interest, to such Trustee so duly nominated as aforesaid; and every such Conveyance, Release, Surrender, Assignment or Assurance, shall be as valid and effectual to all intents and purposes as if the person being out of the jurisdiction or not amenable to the process of the said Court, or not known to be alive, or having refused, or as if the person being Idiot, Lunatic, or of unsound mind, had been at the time of the execution of sane mind, memory and understanding, and had by himself or herself executed the same.

XIII. And be it enacted, that all real and heritable property, monies, goods, chattels and effects whatever, and all titles, securities for money, or other obligatory instruments and evidences or muniments, and all other effects whatever, and all rights or claims belonging to or had by such society, shall be vested in the Trustees or Treasurer of such society for the time being, for the use and benefit of such society and the representative members thereof, their respective executors or Administrators, according to their respective claims and interests; and after the death or removal of any Trustee or Treasurer, shall vest in the succeeding Trustee or Treasurer for the same Estate or Interest, as the former Trustee or Treasurer had therein, and subject to the same Trusts, without any Assignment or Conveyance whatever, and also for all purposes of Action or Suit, as well Criminal as Civil, in Law or in Equity, or in anywise touching or concerning the same, be deemed and taken to be, and shall in every such proceeding (where necessary) be stated to be the property of the person appointed to the office of Trustee or Treasurer of such Society for the time being, in his or her proper name, without further description; and such person shall, and he or she is hereby respectively authorized to bring or defend, or cause to be brought or defended, any Action, Suit or Prosecution, Criminal as well as Civil, in Law or in Equity, touching or concerning the Property, right or claim aforesaid, of or belonging to, or had by such Society—provided that such person shall have been thereunto duly authorized by the consent of the majority of members present at any meeting of the Society or Committee, and such person so appointed shall and may in all cases concerning the Property, right or claim aforesaid of such Society, sue and be sued, plead and be impleaded, in his or her proper name, as Trustee or Treasurer of such Society, without other description; and no Suit, Action or Prosecution, shall be discontinued or abate by the death of such person, or his or her removal from the office of Trustee or Treasurer but the same shall and may be proceeded in by the succeeding Trustee or Treasurer, in the proper name of the person commencing the same, any Law, usage or custom to the contrary notwithstanding; and each succeeding Trustee or Treasurer shall pay or receive like costs as if the action or Suit had been commenced in his or her name, for the benefit of, or to be reimbursed from the Funds of the said Society.

XIV. And be it enacted, That the Trustee or Treasurer, or any officer of any Society established under the authority of this Act, shall not be liable to make good any deficiency which may arise in the Funds of such Society, unless such persons shall have respectively declared by writing under their hands deposited and registered in like manner, with the Rules of this Society that they are willing so to be answerable; and it shall be lawful for each of such persons, or for such persons collectively, to limit his or her responsibility to such sum as shall be specified in any such instrument or writing; Provided always, That the said Trustee and Trustees or Treasurer, and every the officer of any such Society shall be, and they are hereby declared to be personally respo:.sible and liable for all monies actually received by him, her or them on account of, or to, or for the use of the said society.

XV. And be it enacted, That whenever the Trustees of any Society established under this Act at any time after the decease of any member, have paid and divided any sum of money to or amongst any person or persons, who shall at the time of such payment appear to such Trustees to be entitled to the effects of any deceased intestate member—the payment of any such sum or sums of money, shall be valid and effectual with respect to any demand of any other person or persons, as next of kin of such deceased intestate member against the funds of such Society, or against the Trustees thereof, but nevertheless such next of kin or representative shall have remedy for such money so paid as aforesaid, against the person or persons who shall have received the same.

XVI. And be it enacted, That in case any member of any Society shall die, who shall be entitled to any sum not exceeding Twenty Pounds, it shall be lawful for the Trustees or Treasurer of such Society, and they are hereby auhorized and permittted, if such Trustees or Treasurer shall be satisfied that no Will was made and left by such deceased member, and that no Letters of Administration will be taken out of the funds goods and chattels of such depositor, to pay the same at any time, after the decease of such member, according to the Rules and Regulations of said Society, and in the event of there being no Rules and Regulations made in that behalf, then the said Trustees or Treasurer are hereby authorized and permitted to pay and divide the same to and amongst the person or persons entitled to the effects of the deceased intestate, and that without administration.

XVII. An be it enacted, that for the more effectually preventing fraud and impostion on the funds of such Societies, if any officer, member, or any other person, being or representing himself or herself to be a member of such Society, or the nominee, executor, administrator or Assignee of any member of such Society, or any other person whatever shall, in or by any false representation or imposition, fraudulently obtain possession of the monies of such Society, or any part thereof, or having in his or her possession any sum of money belonging to said Society shall fraudulently withhold the same, and for which offence no especial provision has been made in the Rules of such

Society, it shall be lawful for any one Justice of the Peace residing within the county within which such Society shall be held, upon complaint made upon oath by an officer of such Society, to summon such person against whom such complaint shall be made, to appear at a time and place to be named in such summons, and upon his or her appearance, or in default thereof, upon due proof upon oath of the service of such summons, it shall and may be lawful for any two Justices residing within the county aforesaid, to hear and determine the said complaint according to the rules of said Society, confirmed as directed by this Act: and upon due proof of such fraud, the said justices shall commit the said party and award double the amount of money so fraudulently obtained or witheld, to be paid to the Treasurer, to be applied by him to the purposes of the Society so proved to have been imposed upon and defrauded, together with such costs as shall be awarded by the said justices, not exceeding the sum of Ten Shillings; and in case such person against whom such complaint shall be made shall not pay the sum of money so awarded to the person, and at the time specified in the said order, such justices are hereby required, by Warrant under their Hands and Seals, to cause the same to be levied by Distress and Sale of Goods of such person on whom such order shall have been made, or by other legal proceeding, together with such costs as shall be awarded by the said justices, not exceeding the sum of Ten Shillings, and also the costs and charges attending such distress and sale, or other legal proceeding, returning the overplus (if any) to the owner; and on default of such distresss being found, the said justices of the Peace shall commit such person so proved to have offended to the County Gaol for such a period not exceeding Three Calender Months, as to them shall seem fit; Provided nevertheless, that nothing herein contained shall prevent the said Society from proceeding by Indictment or Complaint against the party complained of: And provided also, that no party shall be proceeded against by Indictment or Complaint if a previous conviction has been obtained for the same offence under the provisions of this Act.

XVIII. And be it enacted, that provisions shall be made by one or more of the Rules of every such Society to be confirmed as required by this Act, specifying whether a reference of every matter in dispute between any such Society, or any person acting under them, and any individual member thereof, or persons claiming on account of any member, shall be made to such of Her Majesty's Justices of the Peace as may act in and for the county in which such Society may be formed or to Arbitrators to be appointed in manner hereafter directed, and if the matter so in dispute shall be referred to arbitration, certain Arbitrators shall be named and elected at the first meeting of such Society, or committee thereof that shall be held after the enrolment of its Rules, none of the said arbitrators being beneficially interested, directly or indirectly, in the funds of the said Society of whom a certain number, not less than three shall be chosen by ballot in each such case of dispute—the number of the said arbitrators and mode of ballot being determined by the Rules of each society respectively, the names of such arbitrators shall be duly entered in the book of the said Society in which the Rules are entered as aforesaid; and in case of the death or refusal, or neglect of any or all of the said arbitrators to act, it shall and may be lawful to and for the said Society or committee thereof, and they are hereby required at their next meeting to name and elect one or more arbitrator or arbitrators aforesaid; to act in the place of the said arbitrator or arbitrators so dying, or refusing or neglecting to act as aforesaid; and whatever Award shall be made by the said arbitrators or the major part of them, according to the true purport and meaning of the Rules of such society, confirmed by the Justices according to the directions of this Act, shall be in the form prescribed by the By-Laws, and shall be binding and conclusive on all parties, and shall be final to all intents and purposes, without appeal, or being subject to the control of one or more Justices of the Peace, and shall not be removed or removeable into any Court of Law, or restrained or restrainable by the injuction of any Court of Equity; and should either of the said parties in dispute refuse or neglect to comply with, or conform to, the decision of the said arbitrators, or the major part of them, it shall and may be lawful for any one Justice of the Peace residing within the county within which such society shall be held, upon good and sufficient proof being adduced before him of such award having been made, and of the refusal of the party to comply therewith, upon complaint made by or on behalf of the party aggrieved, to summon the person against whom such complaint shall be made, to appear at a time and place to be named in such summons and upon his or her appearance, or in default thereof, upon due proof upon oath, or the service of such summons, any two Justices of the Peace may proceed to make such order thereupon as to them may seem just; and if the sum of money so awarded, together with a sum for costs, not exceeding the sum of ten shillings, as to such Justices shall seem meet, shall not be immediately paid, then such Justices shall by warrant under their hands and seals cause such sum and costs as aforesaid to be levied by distress or distresses and sale of the monies, goods, chattels, securities and effects belonging to the said party or to the said Society, or other legal proceeding, together with all further costs and charges attending such distress and sale, or other legal proceedings returning the overplus (if any) to the said party or to the said Society, or to one of the Trustees or Treasurer thereof; and in default of such distress being found, or such legal proceeding being ineffectual, then to be levied by distress and sale of the proper goods of the said party, or of the said Society so neglecting or refusing as aforesaid, by other legal proceedings together with such further costs and charges as aforesaid, the overplus (if any) to the owner: Provided always, that when the rules of any Society provide for a reference to arbitrators of any matter in dispute, and it shall appear to any Justice of the Peace on the complaint on oath of a member of any such Society, or of any person claiming on account of such member that application has been made to such Society, or to the Trustee or Treasurer, or other officer thereof, for the purpose of having any dispute so settled by arbitration, and that such application has not within forty days, been complied with, or that the arbitrators have neglected or refused to make any award, it shall and may be lawful for such Justice to summon the Trustees, Treasurer or other officer of the Society, or any of them against whom the complaint is made, and for any two Justices to hear and determine the matter in dispute, in the same manner as if the rules of the said Society had directed that any matter in dispute should be decided by Justice of the Peace anything herein contained to the contrary thereof notwithstanding.

XIX. And be it enacted that if, by the rules of any such Society, it is directed that any matter in dispute as aforesaid, shall be decided by Justices of the Peace it shall and may be lawful for any such Justice on complaint being made to him of any refusal or neglect to comply with the rules of such Society, by any member or officer thereof, to summon the person against whom such complaint shall be made, to appear at a place and time to be named in such Summons, and, upon his or her appearance, or, in default thereof, upon due proof on oath of the service of such Summons it shall and may be lawful for any two Justices to proceed to hear and determine the said complaint according to the rules of the said Society; and in case the said Justices shall adjudge any sum of money to be paid by such person against whom such complaint shall be made; and if such person shall not pay such sum of money to the person, and at the time specified by such Justices, they shall proceed to enforce their award in the manner hereinbefore directed to be used in case of any neglect to comply with the decision of the arbitrators appointed under the authority of this Act.

XX. And be it enacted, That a minor may become a member of any such Society and shall be empowered to execute all instruments, give all necessary acquittances, and enjoy all the privileges and be liable to all the responsibilities appertaining to members of matured age, notwithstanding his or her incapacity or disability in law to act for himself or herself: Provided always, that such minor be admitted into such Society, by and with the consent of his or her parents, masters or guardians.

XXI. And be it enacted, That the rules of every Society shall provide that the Trustees, Treasurer or other principal officer thereof, shall once in every year at least, prepare or cause to be prepared a general statement of the funds and effects of or belonging to such Society, specifying in whose custody or possesion the said funds or effects shall be then remaining together with an account of all and every the various sums of money received and expended by or on account of the said Society since the publication of the preceeding periodical statement, and every such periodical statement shall be attested by two or more members of such Society appointed Auditors for that purpose, and shall be countersigned by the Secretary of such Society; and every member shall be entitled to receive from the said Society a copy of such periodical statement on payment of such sum as the rules of such Society may require not exceeding the sum of sixpence.

XXII. And be it enacted, That on the trial of any action, indictment, or other proceeding respecting the property of any Society enrolled under the authority of this Act, or in proceedings before any

Justice of the Peace, any members of such Society shall be a competent witness and shall not be objected to on account of any interests he may have as such member, in the result of such action, indictment or other proceeding.

XXIII. And be it enacted, That it shall be lawful for the Trustees named in any mortgage made on behalf of such Societies or the survivor or survivors of them or for the Trustees for the time being to endorse upon any mortgage or further charge given by any member of such Society to the Trustees thereof for moneys advanced by such Society to any member thereof a receipt for all moneys intended to be secured by such mortgage or further charge which shall be sufficient to vacate the same, and vest the estate of and in the property comprised in such security in the person or persons for the time being entitled to the equity of redemption without it being necessary for the Trustees of any such Societies to give any reconveyance of the property so mortgaged; which receipt shall be specified in a schedule to be annexed to the rules of such Society, duly certified and deposited as aforesaid.

XXIV. Provided always and be it enacted, That nothing herein contained shall authorize any Building Society established under this Act, to invest its funds or any part thereof in any Savings Bank.

XXV. And it be enacted, That all Building Societies hereafter to be established shall be entitled to the protection and benefit of this Act; but no such Society shall be entitled thereto until their rules shall have been certified and deposited in the manner hereinbefore directed by this Act.

XXVI. And be it enacted, That wherever in this Act in describing or referring to any person, the word importing the singular number or the masculine gender only is used the same shall be understood to include and shall be applied to several persons or parties as well as one person or party, and females as well as males, unless there be something in the subject or context repugnant to such construction.

XXVII. And be it enacted, That this Act may be altered amended or repealed, at the present or any future session of Assembly.

CHAP. LXXV.

An Act to incorporate "The Pictou Permanent Building and Loan Society."

Section.
1. Incorporation.
2. Capital stock.
3. Payment of shares.
4. Corporators.
5. First meeting.
6. Management.

Section.
7. First charge.
8. Society's powers, etc.
9. Non-payment of shares.
10. May hold real estate.
11. Liability of Shareholders to be filed.
12. Copy of by-laws, etc.

[*Passed the* 17*th day of April A. D.* 1879.]

BE IT ENACTED by the Governor, Council, and Assembly, as follows:—

1. Joseph A. Gordon, Alexander J. Patterson, Charles T. Irving, Robert P. Frazer, David Logan, Robert Hockin, Alexander C. Bailie, William W. Glennie, Alexander C. McDonald, William W. McLaren, Charles D. McDonald, and such other persons as may become shareholders in the Society hereby created, their successors and assigns are hereby constituted and declared to be a body corporate and politic, under the name of "The Pictou Permanent Building and Loan Society," for the purposes of encouraging the accumulation of capital by furnishing a safe and remunerative investment to its shareholders, assisting in the acquisition and improvement of real estate in the Province of Nova Scotia by supplying capital on easy terms of re-payment upon the security thereof, and making advances upon and purchasing Dominion, Provincial and Municipal securities and debentures, having the head office of the said Society in the town of Pictou, in the Province of Nova Scotia, and shall have perpetual succession and a corporate seal with power to alter and change the same at pleasure, and may by such name, sue and be sued, implead and be impleaded, in all Courts of law and equity.

2. The capital stock of the said Society, shall be two hundred thousand dollars, divided into two thousand shares of one hundred dollars each, which shall be and hereby are vested in the several persons who shall subscribe for the same; provided always, that it shall and may be lawful for the said Society to increase its capital stock to a sum not exceeding five hundred thousand dollars as a majority of the shareholders at a special general meeting expressly convened for that purpose, on the recommendation of the Directors may order and determine.

3. The shares in said capital stock shall be payable as follows:— A deposit of two dollars on each share to be made when the same shall be subscribed, and the balance to be paid in monthly instalments of one dollar each, the first of said monthly instalments to become due and payable at such time as the Directors to be elected, as hereafter provided, shall order. No call exceeding one dollar per month on each share shall be made. In case any member shall desire to pay the whole amount of his share or shares at any one time, or to pay into the funds of the Society from time to time any amount exceeding the sum due on his share or shares, it shall be lawful for the said Directors, in their discretion, to allow interest for the balance above the amount so due for each clear month, at any rate not exceeding six per cent.

4. For the purpose of organizing the said Society, the following persons named in the first section of this Act, shall be provisional Directors thereof, viz:—Joseph A. Gordon, Alexander J. Patterson, Charles F. Irving, Robert C. Fraser, W. Glennie, Robert Hockin, and Charles D. MacDonald, and five of whom shall constitute a quorum.

5. So soon as the sum of fifty thousand dollars shall have been subscribed, it shall be lawful for the said provisional Directors to call a general meeting of the Society in the town of Pictou, written notice thereof having been mailed to each member at least ten days previous to the time of said meeting. At this meeting the shareholders present, either in person or by proxy, shall proceed to elect seven Directors, a Manager, who shall discharge the duties of Secretary and Treasurer, and a Solicitor, who shall strictly hold office for such length of time and on such terms as may be fixed by the rules and by-laws. The said Directors shall elect from their own number a President and Vice-President. The shareholders shall also at said meeting make and pass rules and by-laws for the regulation of the Society and its business, or may by resolution empower the Directors to do so. These rules and by-laws, when so made, shall have the force of law, and shall be binding upon all who at that time are or may subsequently become shareholders. All officers of the Society shall be residents of the town of Pictou. No shareholder shall be eligible to be a Director unless he hold at least twenty shares in the capital stock of the Society in his own name and for his own use. The Manager and Solicitor must each hold at least ten shares in said capital stock. The Director shall hold the office of Manager and Solicitor.

6. The stock, property, affairs and concerns of the said Society, shall be managed by the said Directors, subject to the rules and by-laws, passed as in the foregoing section provided.

7. The expenses of and in connection with obtaining this Act shall form a first charge upon the funds of the Society.

8. The said Society is hereby empowered to loan and advance its funds to any person or persons, or body corporate, upon the security of real estate within the Province of Nova Scotia, Dominion, Provincial and Municipal securities and debentures, or of shares i the Society itself and on no other security, and to take and receive such rates of interest, and such payments by way of bonus, or in reduction of the principal or such instalments, paying off principal and interest together as may be agreed upon.

9. In case any member shall fail to pay any instalments due on his share or shares, and the time for non-payment thereof, when due, within one month after the same shall be due the Directors may in their discretion either collect the sum so due by legal process in any Court of

competent jurisdiction, or may declare the said share or shares forfeited and after ten days' notice in writing, mailed to the said member may proceed to sell the same at public auction, and after payment from the proceeds of the amount so due, the Society shall pay the balance, if any to the said member.

10. The Society may purchase and hold absolutely real estate to the value of ten thousand dollars ($10,000),and in case it should be necessary for the protection of any investment, may also purchase at sheriff's sale, under foreclose or from the mortgagor, any real estate mortgaged to the Society as security for any loan.

11. The liability of each shareholder for the debts of the Society, shall be limited to the amount of the shares held by him less the amount paid upon the same.

12. As soon as the said Society shall commence business, a copy of the by-laws and list of stockholders, certified by the President and Manager, shall be filed in the office of the Provincial Secretary, at Halifax and thereafter once in every year, and within one month after the regular annual meeting of said Society, there shall be filed in the said office a copy, certified as aforesaid, of the by-laws and list of stockholders, with all additions, alterations and amendments made during the past year, together with a statement of the financial condition of the Society for said past year.

CHAP. LXXVI.

An Act to incorporate the Yarmouth Building and Loan Society.

Section.
  Preamble.
  1. Incorporation.
  2. Rules—confirmation of, etc.
  3. Transfer of property, and management of business.

Section.
  4. Society's powers to loan, etc.
  5. May hold real estate.
  6. Copy of rules to be filed.

[*Passed the* 10*th day of April, A. D.* 1880.]

WHEREAS, on or about the first day of May, A. D. 1876, a society called "The Yarmouth Building and Loan Society," was established at Yarmouth, Nova Scotia, with the objects and for the purpose of the formation of a fund by the payments of its shareholders and moneys to be received on deposit, and the establishment of a safe and profitable investment and savings fund for large and small sums of money, and the making of advances from such fund to members who apply therefor and comply with the rules and regulations of said Society; and whereas, for the more effectual carrying out of the objects and purpose of the said Society, it is desirable that the same should be incorporated, and the rules and regulations thereof as now made be confirmed and rendered valid;

Be it therefore enacted by the Governor, Council and Assembly, as follows:

1. All such persons as are now or may hereafter become shareholders in the said Society according to the rules and regulations thereof, shall be and are hereby constituted and declared to be a body corporate and politic, under the name of "The Yarmouth Building and Loan Society," for the purposes and with the objects as hereinbefore, and in the rules and regulations set forth, and shall have perpetual succession and all the general powers and privileges made incident to a corporation by Act of Assembly or other the Statutes of the Provinces of Nova Scotia.

2. All things heretofore done under the rules and regulations of the Society shall be as legal and valid as if the said rules and regulations had been duly in force. The Society hereby incorporated shall from time to time have power to make rules, regulations and by-laws; provided, however, that the same shall not go into operation until they receive the approval and assent of the Governor in Council.

3. All deeds, mortgages, bonds, securities, writings, property, funds or assets given and made to or for the use of or held by the said Society as now organized, or which such Society is or may be interested in or entitled to, is transferred unto, and shall be deemed to have been given and made to or for the use of and shall vest in, the Society hereby incorporated, in like manner and as fully to all intents and purposes as if the said Society had been heretofore incorporated; and the officers of said Society now appointed shall remain in office until others shall be appointed in accordance with said rules and regulations; and the property, affairs and concerns of the Society hereby incorporated, shall be managed in the manner and names and by the officers, as provided in and by the said rules and regulations, or in such manner as may hereinafter be provided by any new or amended rules and regulations; and all actions, suits or proceedings at law or in equity respecting the funds or assets of or any other matter connected with, the Society hereby incorporated, may be brought, prosecuted, or defended in the name or names of the trustees for the time being of the Society hereby incorporated, as provided by the rules and regulations, or in such name and names and in such manner as may hereinafter be provided in and by any new or amended rules and regulations.

4. The said Society is hereby empowered, and it shall be lawful to loan and advance its funds to any of its shareholders, and to make loans and advances on the unadvanced shares of any shareholder or member of the Society, and to accept real estate situated anywhere in Nova Scotia as security for such loan and advances, and to have, take and receive such rate of interest not exceeding the legal rate, and such payments by way of bonus, or such instalments, paying off principal and interest together, as may be agreed upon; and also to impose and inflict such fines, penalties or forfeiture upon its members or shareholders as is provided in and by the rules and regulations of said Society, or as may hereafter be provided in and by any amended or new rules and regulations thereof.

5. The said Society may purchase and hold absolutely real estate to the value of ten thousand dollars; and, further, in case it should become necessary for the protection of any investment, or loan or advance, may also purchase at sheriff's sale, under foreclosure, or other sale, or from the mortgagor, any real estate mortgaged to the Society as security for any loan or advances; and may sell, mortgage, lease or otherwise dispose the same as may be deemed expedient for the objects of the Society.

6. A copy of the rules and regulations, and a list of the shareholders of the Society, certified by the Secretary, shall be filed in the office of the Registrar of Deeds at Yarmouth, within three months after the passing of this Act, and thereafter once in every year, and within one month after the regular annual meeting of the said Society, there shall be filed in the said office a copy, certified as aforesaid, of the list of Shareholders, with all additional alterations and amendments of the rules and regulations made during the past year, together with a statement of the financial condition of the Society for said past year.

CAP. XXXVII.

An Act for the regulation of Benefit Building Societies.

Section.
Preamble.
I. Societies may be formed, Value of shares, &c., how raised. Object of association. Power to frame and amend rules, impose fines, &c. No dividend until share realized, unless on withdrawal.
II. The rules may prescribe forms of instruments.
III. Two transcripts of rules and amended rules, for the Attorney General to advise thereon and give certificate. His fee. How transcripts disposed of; to be confirmed by Supreme Court and filed. Certified rules to bind Society
IV. On refusing to certify, rules may be submitted by society to Supreme Court.
V. Attorney General's further fees.
VI. Rules must be entered in book to be kept by Secretary and open to members' inspection; nothing to prevent amendments; but not to be in force, until, &c.
VII. And so entered and confirmed by Supreme Court, to be binding. What

Section.
copies, &c., to be evidence. No legal process to remove rules into any Court.
VIII. Confirmed rules to be altered only by special general meeting, or specially appointed committee.
IX. Rules to specify places to hold Society's meeting; how such places to be altered
X. Society may appoint its officers; fill vacancies, etc.; those officers receiving or expending its moneys, to give bond with two sureties under penalty; to whom as obligee; provision in case of forfeiture.
XI. Society may appoint committee and delegate powers; powers delegated to be declared in rules; committee's transactions to be subject to review.
XII Persons receiving moneys or securities, to render account on notice, and pay over moneys to trustee or treasurer; on default, society may petition Supreme Court which will proceed in summary way and make final order.

XIII. Supreme Court may appoint person to convey society's property in place of trustee out of jurisdiction, etc. ; Judges of Supreme Court to appoint persons, etc.
XIV. No fee to officers of the Court; Court to assign counsel.
XV. Society's claims in respect of moneys, etc., in possession of officer, by virtue of his office who shall die or become insolvent, etc., to have priority.
XVI. Property to vest in trustee or treasurer, and on death or removal, in succeeding one without assignment, and in all proceedings to be stated as their property, etc. ; succeeding officer's cost.
XVII. Trustee or treasurer not to be liable for deficiency of funds unless by declared consent; may limit responsibility to a definite sum; liable for moneys actually received.
XVIII. Provision for security of trustees on payment of money to the apparent representatives of members dying intestate.
XIX. Member dying entitled to a sum not exceeding £20, and trustee or treasurer satisfied of intestacy, and that administration will not be taken out, have to pay the same.
XX. Officers or members, &c., fraudulently obtaining society's moneys and no special provision in the rules, proceedings before Justices of the Peace; on conviction, double the amount to be awarded and paid to the treasurer; proceedings in case of non-payment on default of distress found, committed to jail and hard labor.
XXI. Rules to declare whether disputes shall be referred to Justices or to Arbitrators; how arbitrators to be appointed; in case of death, &c.; form of award; which shall be final; on refusal to perform, reference to Justices,

Course of proceeding; Justices will cause them to be levied by distress; how arbitration provision to be enforced against society.
XXII. If rules direct reference of disputes to Justices, course of proceedings to be followed.
XXIII. Minors may become members, with consent of parents, etc.
XXIV. Society may receive bonus for shares advanced and interest.
XXV. Rules to provide for yearly general statements of account; Members to have copies.
XXVI. Members admissable as witnesses in legal proceedings notwithstanding interest.
XXVII. Persons aggrieved by order of Justices may appeal to Supreme Court; course of proceedings; Act of 19 Vic. cap 29.
XXVIII. Future Building Societies to have benefit of Act, on rules being certified, &c.
XXIX. Memorials of mortgagees (form Schedule B) to be executed by mortgagors. Reference to Schedule (B.)
XXX. May be registered—mortgage deed being produced to and endorsed by registrar. Have benefit of Registry Acts.
XXXI. Society not authorized to invest in saving's bank.
XXXII. Interpretation clause.
XXXIII. Letters post free within this island. Provisions. Names to be transmitted to the general post office. Penalties for evasions.
XXXIV. Proof of mortgages and memorials; duty of registrar thereon; award.
Schedule (A); form of trustee or treasurer's bond with sureties, for due execution of office, duly accounting, &c.
Schedule (B); Form of memorial of mortgage.

[*Passed May 11, 1866.*]

WHEREAS certain Societies, commonly called Building Societies, have been established in different parts of the United Kingdom of Great Britain, and in the Provinces of British North America, principally amongst the industrious classes, for the purpose of raising, by small periodical subscriptions, a fund to assist the members thereof in obtaining a small freehold or leasehold property ; and it is expedient to afford encouragement and protection to such societies, and the property obtained therewith in this Island: Be it therefore enacted, by the Lieutenant Governor, Council and Assembly.

I. That it shall and may be lawful for any number of persons in this Island to form themselves into and establish societies for the purpose of raising, by the monthly or other subscriptions of the several members of such societies, shares not exceeding the value of one hundred and fifty pounds for each share; such subscriptions not to exceed in the whole twenty shillings per month for each share, or stock or fund, for the purpose of enabling each member thereof to receive out of the funds of such society the amount or value of his or her share or shares therein, to erect or purchase one or more dwelling house or dwelling houses or other real or leasehold estate, to be secured by way of mortgage to such society until the amount or value of his or her shares shall have been fully repaid to such society, with the interest thereon, and all fines and other payments incurred in respect thereof; and to and for the several members of such society, from time to time, to assemble together and to make, ordain and constitute such wholesome and proper rules and regulations for the government and guidance of the same as to the major part of the member such society, so assembled together, shall seem meet, so as such rules shall not be repugnant to the express provisions of this Act and to the general laws of his Island; and to impose and inflict such reasonable fines, penalties and forfeitures upon the several members of any such society who shall offend against any such rules, as the members may think fit, to be respectively paid to such uses for the benefit of such society, as such society, by such rules, shall direct; and also, from time to time, to alter and amend such rules as occasion shall require, or annul or repeal the same, and to make new rules in lieu thereof, under such restrictions as are in this Act contained; provided that no member shall receive, or be entitled to receive, from the funds of such society, any interest or dividend, by way of annual, or other periodical profit, upon any shares in such society until the amount or value of his or her share shall have been realized, except on the withdrawal of such member, according to the rules of such society then in force.

II. It shall and may be lawful to and for any such society, in and by the rules thereof, to describe to form or forms of conveyance, mortgage, transfer, agreement, bond, or other instrument which may be necessary for carrying the purposes of the said society into execution, and which shall be specified and set forth in a shedule to be annexed to the rules of such society, and duly certified and deposited as hereinafter provided.

III. There shall be made two transcipts, fairly written on paper or parchment, of all rules made in pursuance of this Act, signed by three members, and contersigned by the Secretary of such society, (accompanied, in the case of an alteration or amendment of rules, with an affidavit of the Secretary or one of the officers of the said society, that the provisions of this Act have been duly complied with,) with all convenient speed after the same shall be made, altered or amended; and so, from time to time, after every making, altering or amending thereof, shall be transmitted to her Majesty's Attorney General of this Island, for the purpose of ascertaining whether the said rules of such society, alteration or amendment thereof, are calculated to carry into effect the intention of the parties framing such rules, alterations or amendments, and are in conformity to law and to the provisions of this Act; and that the said Attorney General shall advise with the Secretary, if required, and shall give a certificate on each of the said transcripts, that the same are in conformity to law and to the provisions of this Act, or point out in what parts the said rules are repugnant thereto; and that the Attorney General, for advising as aforesaid, and perusing the rules or alterations, or amendments of the rules of each respective society, and giving such certificates as aforesaid, shall demand no further fee than the sum of one guinea, which shall be defrayed by each society respectively; and one of such transcripts, when certified by the Attorney General, shall be returned to the society, and the other of such transcripts shall be transmitted by the Attorney General to the Supreme Court of Judicature, at Charlottetown, during the term next after the when such transcript shall have been so certified as aforesaid; and the Justices of the said Supreme Court are hereby authorized and required, upon motion of counsel, to allow and confirm the same; and such transcript shall be filed by the prothonotary of the said Court, with the records of the said Supreme Court in his custody, without fee or reward; and that all rules, alterations and amendments thereof, from the time when the same shall be certified by the Attorney General, shall be binding on the several members and officers of the said society, and all persons having interest therein.

IV. In case the Attorney General shall refuse to certify all or any of the rules, so to be submitted for his perusal and examination, it shall then be lawful for any such society to submit the same to the said Supreme Court, together with the reasons assigned by the Attorney General in writing, for any such rejection or disapproval of any one or more such rules; and that the said Supreme Court shall and may, if deemed fit, confirm and allow the same, notwithstanding any such rejection or disapproval by the Attorney General.

V. The Attorney General shall be entitled to no further fee for or in respect of any alteration or amendment of any rules upon which one fee has been already paid to the Attorney General, within the period of three years; provided also, that if any rules, alterations or amendments are sent to the Attorney General, accompanied with an affidavit of being a copy of any rules or alterations or amendments of the rules of any other society which shall have been already enrolled under the provisions of this Act, the Attorney General shall certify and return the same, as aforesaid, without being entitled to any fee for such certificate.

VI. No such society, as aforesaid, shall have the benefit of this Act unless all the rules for the management thereof shall be entered in a book to be kept by the Secretary of such society, and which book shall be open at all seasonable times for the inspection of the members of such society; but, nevertheless, nothing contained herein shall extend to prevent any alteration in or amendment of any such rules, so entered or transmitted and filed as aforesaid or repealing or annulling the same, or any of them, in the whole or in part, or making any new rules for the management of such society, in such manner as by the rules of such society, shall, from to time, be provided; but such new rules or such alterations in or amendments of former rules, or any order annulling or repealing any former rules, in whole or in part, shall not be in force until the same respectively shall be entered in such book, as aforesaid, and certified, when necessary, by the Attorney General, and until a trancript thereof shall be transmitted to the Supreme Court, as aforesaid, and the Prothonotary shall file and certify the same as aforesaid.

VII. All rules from time to time made and in force for the management of such society as aforesaid, and duly entered in such book and confirmed by the said Supreme Court as aforesaid, shall be binding on the several members and officers of such society, and the several contributors thereto and representatives, all of whom shall be deemed and taken to have full notice thereof, by such entry and contribution as aforesaid ; and the entry of such rules in such book as aforesaid, or the transcript thereof, transmitted to the said Supreme Court, and filed with the Prothonotary thereof, aforesaid, or a true copy of such transcript examined with the original, and proved to be a true copy, shall be received as evidence of such rules respectively in all cases ; and no legal process whatever shall be brought or allowed to remove any such rules into any Court of law or equity within this Island ; and every copy of any such transcript, transmitted and filed as aforesaid, shall be made without fee or reward, except the actual expense of making such copy.

VIII. No rule, confirmed by the Supreme Court, as aforesaid, shall be altered, rescinded or repealed, unless at a general meeting of the members of such society, as aforesaid, convened by public note, written or printed, signed by the Secretary or President of such society, in pursuance of a requisition for that purpose by seven or more of the members of such society ; which said requisition and notice shall be publicly read at the two usual meetings of society, to be held next before such general meeting, for the purpose of such alteration or repeal, unless a committee of such members shall have been nominated for that purpose at a general meeting of the members of such society, convened in manner aforesaid ; in which case such committee shall have the like power to make such alterations or repeal, and unless such alterations or repeal shall be made with the concurrence and approbation of three-fourths of the members of such society then and there present, or by the like proportion of such committee as aforesaid, if any shall have been nominated for the purpose.

IX. The rules of every Society formed under the authority of this Act, shall specify the place or places at which it is intended such society shall hold its meetings, and certain provisions with respect to the powers and duties of the members at large, and of such committees or officers as may be appointed for the management of the affairs of such society ; provided always, that it shall and may be lawful for any such society to alter their place or places of meeting whenever they may consider it necessary, upon giving notice thereof in writing to the Supreme Court during the next term before or after such removal, and signed by the Secretary or other principal officer, and also by three or more of the members of the said society ; and which said notice shall be filed in like manner as is hereinbefore directed concerning the said rules, or the alterations or amendments.

X. That every such society shall and may, from time to time, at any of their usual meetings, or by their committee, if any such shall be appointed for that society, elect and appoint such person into the office of trustee, president, secretary, surveyor or treasurer of such society as they shall think proper, and also shall and may, from time to time, elect and appoint such other officers as shall be deemed necessary to carry into execution the purposes of such society for such space of time and for such purposes as shall be fixed and established by the rules of such society, and from time to time to elect and appoint others in the room of those who shall vacate or die; and such trustee, treasurer, and all and every other officer or other person whatever, who shall be appointed to any office, in anywise touching or concerning the receipt, management or expenditure of any sum of money collected for the purpose of any such society, before he, she or they shall be admitted to take upon him, her or them, the execution of any such office or trust, (if required so to do by the rules of such society to which such officer shall belong), shall become bound in a bond according to the form prescribed in the schedule to this Act annexed, marked (A,) with two sufficient sureties, for the just and faithful execution of such office or trust, and for rendering a just and true account according to the rules of such society, and in all matters lawful, to pay obedience to the same in such penal sum of money as by the major part of such society at any such meeting, as aforesaid, shall be thought expedient, and to the satisfaction of such society; and that every such bond to be given by or on behalf of such trustee or treasurer, or of any other person appointed to any other office or trust, shall be given to the keeper of the rolls of the commission of the peace in the country wherein such society shall be established for the time being, without fee or reward; and in case of forfeiture it shall be lawful to sue upon such bond, in the name of such keeper of the rolls of such commission of the peace, for such county, as aforesaid, for the time being, for the use of the said society, fully indemnifying and saving harmless such keeper of the rolls, as aforesaid from all costs and charges in respect of such suit.

XI. Every such society shall and may, from to time, elect and appoint any number of the members of such society to be a committee, the number thereof to be declared in the rules of every such society; and shall and may delegate to such committee all or any of the powers given by this Act to be executed, who, being so delegated, shall continue to act as such committee for and during such time as they shall be appointed, for such society for general purposes, the powers of such committee being first declared in and by the rules of such society confirmed by the Supreme Court, and filed in the manner hereinbefore directed; and all acts and orders of such committee, under the powers so delegated to them, shall have the like force and effect as the acts and orders of such society, at any general meeting thereof, could or might have had in pursuance of this Act: Provided always, that the transactions of such committee shall be entered in a book belonging to such society, and shall be, from time to time, and at all times, subject and liable to the review, allowance or disallowance, or control of such society, in such manner and form as such society shall, by their general rules, confirmed by the Supreme Court and filed as aforesaid, have directed and appointed, or shall in like manner direct and appoint.

XII. Every person who shall have or receive any part of the moneys, effects or funds of or belonging to any such society, or shall in any manner have been or shall be entrusted with the disposal, management or custody thereof, or of any securities, books, papers or property relating to the same, his or her executors, administrators and assigns, respectively, shall, upon demand made, or notice in writing given or left at the last or usual place of residence of such persons, in pursuance of any order of such society or committee to be appointed as aforesaid, give in his or her account at the usual meeting of such society, or to such committee thereof, as aforesaid, to be examined, and allowed or disallowed, by such society or committee thereof; and shall, on the like demand or notice, pay over all the moneys remaining in his or her hands, and assign and transfer, or deliver all securities and effects, books, papers and property taken or standing in his or her name as aforesaid, and being in his or her hands or custody, to the trustee or treasurer for the time being, or to such other person as such society or committee thereof shall appoint; and in case of any neglect or refusal to deliver such account, or to pay over such moneys, or to assign, transfer or deliver such securities and effects, books, papers and property in manner aforesaid, it shall and may be lawful to and for every such society, in the name of the trustee or treasurer or other principal officer thereof, as the case may be, to exhibit a petition to the said Supreme Court, who shall and may proceed thereon in a summary way, and make such order therein, upon hearing all parties concerned, as to such court in their discretion, shall seem just, which order shall be final and conclusive, and all assignments, sales and transfers made in pursuance of such order, shall be good and effectual in law, to all intents and purposes whatsoever.

XIII. When and so often as any person seized or possessed of any lands, tenements or hereditaments, or other property, or any estate or interest therein, as a trustee of any such society, shall be out of the jurisdiction of or not amenable to the process of any of the Court of Law and Equity of this Island, or shall be idiot, lunatic, or of unsound mind, or it shall be unknown or uncertain whether he or she be living or dead, or such person shall refuse to convey or otherwise assure such lands, tenements, hereditaments or property, or estate or interest to the person duly nominated as trustee of such society in their stead, either alone or together, with any continuing trustee, as occasion shall require, then, and in every or any such case, it shall be lawful for the Judges of the said Supreme Court to appoint such person as to such Court shall seem meet, on behalf and in the name of the person seized or possessed as aforesaid, to convey, surrender, release, assign, or otherwise assure the said lands, tenements, hereditaments or property, or estate or interest to such trustee so duly nominated as aforesaid; and every such conveyance, release, surrender, assignment or assurance shall be as valid and effectual to all intents and purposes as if the person being out of the jurisdiction, or not amenable to the process of the said Court, or not known to be alive, or having refused, or as if the person being idiot, lunatic, or of unsound mind, had been, at the time of the execution thereof, of sane mind, memory and understanding, and had, by himself or herself executed the same.

XIV. No fee, reward, emolument or gratuity whatsoever shall be demanded, taken or received by any officer of such Court, for any matter or thing done in such Court in pursuance of this Act; and that, upon the presenting of any such petition, it shall be lawful for the Judges of the said Court to assign counsel learned in the law on behalf of such society, who are hereby respectively required to do their duties therein without fee or reward.

XV. If any person who may hereafter be appointed to any office in any such society, and being instructed with the keeping of the accounts, or having in his hands or possession, by virtue of his said office or employment, any moneys or effects belonging to such society, or any deeds or securities relating to the same, shall die, or become bankrupt or insolvent, or have any execution or attachment, or other process issued against his lands, goods, chattels or effects, or property or estate, heritable or moveable, or make any disposition, assignment, or other conveyance thereof, for the benefit of his creditors, his heirs, executors, administrators, or assigns, or other person having legal right, or the Sheriff or other officer executing such process, shall within forty days after demand made in writing by the order of any such society or committee thereof, or the major part of them assembled at any meeting thereof, deliver and pay over all moneys and other things belonging to such society to such person as such society or committee shall appoint, and shall pay out of the estate, assets or effects, heritable or moveable of such persons, all sums of money remaining due which such person received by virtue of his said office or employment before any other of his debts are paid or satisfied, or before the money directed to be levied by such process as aforesaid, or which may be recovered or recoverable under the same, is paid over to the party issuing such process; and all such assets, lands, goods, chattels, property, estates and effects shall be bound to the payment and discharge thereof accordingly.

XVI. All real and heritable property, moneys, goods, chattels and effects, whatever, and all titles, securities for money, or other obligatory instruments and evidences or muniments, and all other effects whatever, and all rights and claims belonging to or had by such society, shall be vested in the trustees or treasurer of such society for the time being, for the use and benefit of such society and the respective members thereof, their respective executors or administrators, according to their respective claims and interest; and after the death or removal of any trustee or treasurer, shall vest in the succeeding trustee or treasurer for the same estate or interest as the former trustee or treasurer had therein, and subject to the same trusts, without any assignment or conveyance whatever; and also shall, for all purposes of action or suit, as well criminal as civil, in law or in equity, in anywise touching or concerning the same, be deemed and taken to be, and shall in every such proceeding, (when necessary), be stated to be, the property of the person appointed to the office of trustee or treasurer of such society for the time being, in his or her proper name, without further description; and such person shall, and he or she is hereby respectively authorized to bring or defend, or cause to be brought or defended, any action, suit or prosecution, criminal as well as civil, in law or in equity, touching or concerning the property, right or claim aforesaid, of or belonging to or had by such society, provided that such person shall have been thereunto duly authorized by the consent of the majority of members present at any meeting of the society or committee thereof; and such person so appointed, shall and may, in all cases concerning the property, right or claim aforesaid, of such society, sue and be sued, plead and be impleaded, in his or her proper name, as trustee or treasurer of such society, without other description; and no such suit, action or prosecution shall be discontinued or abate by the death of such person, or his or her removal from the office of trustee or treasurer, but the same shall and may be proceeded in by the succeeding trustee or treasurer in the proper name of the person commencing the same, any law, usage or custom to the contrary notwithstanding; and such succeeding trustee or treasurer shall pay or receive like costs as if the action or suit had been commenced in his or her name for the benefit of, or to be reimbursed from the funds of such society.

XVII. The trustee or treasurer, or any officer of any society established under the authority of this Act, shall not be liable to make good any deficiency which may arise in the funds of such society, unless such persons shall have respectively declared, by writing, under their hands, transmitted and registered in like manner with the rules of such society, that they are willing so to be answerable; and it shall be lawful for each of such persons, or for such persons collectively, to limit his, her or their responsibility to such a sum as shall be specified in any such instrument or writing; provided always, that the said trustee and trustees or treasurer, and every the officer of any such society, shall be and they are hereby declared to be, personally responsible and liable for all moneys actually received by him, her or them on account of, or to or for the use of the said society.

XVIII. Whensoever the trustees of any society established under this Act, at any time after the decease of any member, have paid and divided any sum of money to or amongst any person or persons who shall at the time of such payment appear to such trustees to be entitled to the effects of any deceased intestate member, the payment of any such sum or sums of money shall be valid and effectual with respect to any demand of any other person or persons as next of kin of such deceased intestate member against the funds of such society, or against the trustees thereof; but nevertheless, such next of kin or representative, shall have remedy for such money so paid as aforesaid against the person or persons who shall have received the same.

XIX. In case any member of any society shall die, who shall be entitled to any sum not exceeding twenty pounds, it shall be lawful for the trustees or treasurer of such society, and they are hereby authorized and permitted, if such trustees or treasurer shall be satisfied that no will was made and left by such deceased member, and that no letters of administration will be taken out of the funds, goods and chattels of such depositer, to pay the same at any time after the decease of such member, according to the rules and regulations of the said society; and in the event of their being no rules and regulations made in that behalf, then the said trustees or treasurer are hereby authorized and permitted to pay and divide the same to and amongst the person or persons entitled to the effects of the deceased intestate, and that without administration.

XX. For the more effectually preventing fraud and imposition in the funds of such societies, if any officer, member or any other person, being or representing himself or herself to be a member of such society, or the nominee, executor, administrator or assignee of any member of such society, or any other person whatever, shall, in or by any false representation or imposition, fraudulently obtain possession of the moneys of such society, or any part thereof, or having in his or her possession any sum of money belonging to such society, shall fraudulently withold the same, and for which offence no especial provision is made in the rules of such society, it shall be lawful for any one Justice of the Peace residing within the County within which such society shall be held, upon complaint made on oath by an officer of such society, to summon such person against whom such complaint shall be made to appear at a time and place to be named in such summons; and upon his or her appearance, or in default thereof, upon due proof upon oath of the service of such summons, it shall and may be lawful for any two Justices, residing within the County aforesaid, to hear and determine the said complaint according to the rules of the said society, confirmed as directed by this Act; and upon due proof of such fraud, the said Justices shall convict the said party, and award double the amount of money, so fraudulently obtained or withheld, to be paid to the treasurer, to be applied by him to the purposes of the society so proved to have been imposed upon and defrauded, together with such costs as shall be awarded by the said Justices, not exceeding the sum of ten shillings; and in case such person against whom such complaint shall be made, shall not pay the sum of money so awarded to the person and at the time specified in the said order, such Justices are hereby required, by warrant under their hands and seals, to cause the same to be levied by distress and sale of goods of such person on whom such order shall have been made, or by other legal proceeding, together with such costs as shall be awarded by the said justices, not exceeding the sum of ten shillings; and also the costs and charges attending such distress and sale, or other legal proceeding, returning the overplus (if any) to the owner: and in default of such distress being found, the said Justices of the Peace shall commit such person, so proved to have offended, to the County gaol, there to be kept to hard labour for such a period not exceeding three calendar months, as to them shall see fit; provided, nevertheless, that nothing herein contained shall prevent the said society from proceeding by indictment or complaint, against the party complained of; and provided also that no party shall be proceeded against, by indictment or complaint, if a previous conviction has been obtained for the same offence under the provisions of this Act.

XXI. Provision shall be made by one or more of the rules of every such society, to be confirmed as required by this Act, specifying whether a reference of every matter in dispute between any such society or any person acting under them, and any individual member thereof or persons claiming an account of any member, shall be made to such of Her Majesty's Justices of the Peace as may act in and for the County in which such society may be formed, or to arbitrators to be appointed in manner hereinafter directed; and if the matter so in dispute shall be referred to arbitration, certain arbitrators shall be named and elected at the first meeting of such society or committee thereof that shall be held after the enrolment of its rules, none of the said arbitrators being beneficially interested, directly or indirectly, in the funds of the said society, of whom a certain number, not less than three, shall be chosen by ballot, in each such case of dispute, the number of the said arbitrators, and mode of ballot, being determined by the rules of each society respectively; the names of such arbitrators shall be duly entered in the book of the said society in which the rules are entered as aforesaid, and in case of the death, or refusal or neglect of any or all of the said arbitrators to act, it shall and may be lawful to and for the said society, or committee thereof, and they are hereby required, at their next meeting, to name and elect one or more arbitrator or arbitrators, as aforesaid, to act in the place of the said arbitrator or arbitrators so dying, or refusing or neglecting to act as aforesaid; and whatever award shall be made by the said arbitrators, or the major part of them, according to the true purpose and meaning of the rules of such society confirmed by the Supreme Court according to the directions of this Act, shall be in the form of this Act annexed, and shall be binding and conclusive on all parties, and shall be final to all intents and purposes without appeal or being subject to the control of one or more Justices of the Peace, and shall not be removed or removable into any Court of law, or restrained or restrainable by the injunction of any Court of equity; and should either of the said parties in dispute refuse or neglect to comply with or conform to the decision of the said arbitrators, or the major part of them, it shall and may be lawful for any one Justice of the Peace residing within the County within which such society shall be held, upon good and sufficient proof being adduced before him of such award having been made, and of the refusal of the party to comply therewith, upon complaint made by or on behalf of the party aggrieved, to summon the person against whom such complaint shall be made, to appear at a time and place to be named in such summons; and upon his or her appearance, or in default thereof, upon due proof upon oath of the service of such summons, any two Justices of the Peace may proceed to make such order thereupon as to them may seem just; and if the sum of money so awarded, together with a sum for costs not exceeding the sum of ten shillings, as to such Justice shall seem meet, shall not be immediately paid, then such Justices shall, by warrant under their hands and seals, cause such sum and costs, as aforesaid to be levied by distress or by distresses and sale of the moneys, goods, chattels, securities and effects belonging to the said party, or to the said society, or other legal proceeding, together with all future costs and charges attending such distress and sale, or other legal proceeding, returning the overplus (if any) to the said party or to the said society, or to one of the trustees or treasurer thereof; and in default of such distress being found, or such other legal proceedings being ineffectual, then to be levied by distress and sale of the proper goods of the said party, or of the said society, so neglecting or refusing as aforesaid by other legal proceedings, together with such further costs and charges as aforesaid returning the overplus (if any) to the owner; provided always that when the rules of any society provide for a reference to arbitrators of any matter in dispute, and it shall appear to any Justice of the Peace on the complaint on oath of a member of any such society, or of any person claiming on account of such member, that application has been made to such society, or the trustees or treasurer, or other officer thereof, for the purpose of having any dispute so settled by arbitration, and that such application has not, within forty days, been complied with, or that the arbitrators have neglected or refused to make any award, it shall and may be lawful for such Justices to summon the trustee, treasurer or other officer of the society, or any one of them against whom the complaint is made, and for any two Justices to hear and determine the matter in dispute in the same manner as if the rules of the said society had directed that any matter in dispute, as aforesaid should be decided by Justices of the Peace, anything herein contained to the contrary notwithstanding.

XXII. If by the rules of any such society, it is directed that any matter in dispute, as aforesaid shall be decided by Justices of the Peace, it shall and may be lawful for any such Justice, on complaint being made to him of any refusal or neglect to comply with the rules of such society by any member or officer thereto, summon the person against whom such complaint shall be made, to appear at a time and place to be named in such summons, and upon his or her appearance or in default thereof, on due proof upon oath of the service of such summons, it shall and may be lawful for any two Justices to proceed to hear and determine the said complaint according to the rules of the said society; and in case the said Justices shall adjudge any sum of money to be paid by such person against whom such complaint shall be made, and if such person shall not pay such sum of money to the person, and at the time specified by such Justices, they shall proceed to enforce their award in the manner hereinbefore directed, to be used in case of any neglect to comply with the decision of the arbitrators appointed under the authority of this Act.

XXIII. A minor may become a member of any such society, and shall be empowered to execute all instruments, give all necessary acquittances, and enjoy all the privileges and be liable to all the responsibilities appertaining to members of matured age, notwithstanding his or her incapacity or disability in law to act for himself or herself; provided always that such minor be admitted into such society by and with the consent of his or her parents, masters or guardians.

XXIV. It shall be and may be lawful to and for any such society to have and receive, from any member or members thereof any sum or sums, by way of bonus, on any share or shares for the privilege of receiving the same in advance prior to the same being realized, and also any interest for the share or shares so received on any part thereof, without being subject or liable on account thereof to any of the forfeitures or penalties imposed by any of the Act or Acts of the General Assembly of this Island.

XXV. The rules of every such society shall provide that the trustees, treasurer or other principal officer thereof, shall once in every year, at least, prepare, or cause to be prepared, a general statement of the funds and effects of or belonging to such society, specifying in whose custody or possession the said funds or effects shall be then remaining, together with an account of all and every the various sums of money received and expended by or on account of the said society since the publication of the preceding periodical statement, shall be attested by two or more members of such society appointed auditors for that purpose, and shall be countersigned by the secretary of such society; and every member shall be entitled to receive from the said society a copy of such periodical statement on payment of such sum as the rules of such society may require, not exceeding the sum of six pence.

XXVI. On the trial of any action, indictment or other proceeding, respecting the property of any society enrolled under the authority of this Act, or in proceedings before any Justice of the Peace, any member of such society shall be a competent witness, and shall not be objected to on account of any interests he may have as such member in the result of such action, indictment or other proceeding.

XXVII. If any person shall consider himself or herself aggrieved by any sentence, order and adjudication made or given by any such Justices under this Act, it shall and may be lawful for such person to appeal to the next sitting of the Supreme Court of Judicature to be holden in the County in which such Justice or Justices shall have jurisdiction; provided always, that such appeal shall be appealed for, and everything relating thereto shall be had and done in like manner as is appointed for appeals from the judgments of Justices of the Peace, under the provisions of the Act of the Assembly of this Island, passed in the nineteenth year of the reign of Her present Majesty Queen Victoria, Chapter twenty-nine, intituled " An Act to facilitate the performances of the duties of Justices of the Peace with respect to summary convictions and orders;" and in every such appeal the Justices of the said Supreme Court are required to affirm, quash or otherwise vary such sentence, order or ajudication as may seem to them meet, and to enforce judgment in manner and form prescribed by the Act of the twenty-third year of the reign of her present Majesty Queen Victoria, chapter sixteen, intituled "An Act relating to the recovery of Small Debts, and to repeal certain Acts therein mentioned," or by any other Act for the recovery of small debts then in force.

XXVIII. All Building Societies hereafter to be established shall be entitled to the protection and benefit of this Act: but no such society shall be entitled thereto until their rules shall have been certified and deposited in the manner hereinbefore directed by this Act.

XXIX. Every person or persons who shall execute a mortgage, or further charge to the trustees of such society, shall also execute, under his or their hands and seals, a memorial thereof, which memorial shall specify the nature of the instrument, the names and additions of the parties thereto, the day and year when the same bear date, the description of the messuages, lands, tenements, hereditaments and premises comprised in and effected by such mortgage or further charge, the amount of money secured thereby, the amount of and the date when the last instalment is due and payable, whether such instrument contain a power of sale, and when such power of sale may be exercised, and which said memorial shall be in the form prescribed in the schedule to this Act annexed marked (B), or as near thereto as circumstances permit, and which said memorial shall be witnessed by one or more witnesses; provided always, that it shall not in any case be necessary for the wife of any mortgagee, who may have executed any such mortgage or further charge, to execute or join in such memorial.

XXX. The memorial of such mortgage may be registered in the office of the Registrar of Deeds at Charlottetown, upon the oath of the subscribing witness, or the acknowledgment of the parties who have executed the same; and the registrar shall thereupon, and upon the back of each memorial, certify the proof or acknowledgment thereof in the form prescribed in the schedule to this Act annexed, marked (C); provided always, that no memorial be registered by the Registrar of Deeds, as aforesaid, unless the mortgage or further charge referred to in the said memorial be produced to the said Registrar of Deeds, which said mortgage shall be endorsed across the face thereof by the said registrar, in the form of the schedule to this Act annexed, marked (D), and shall be delivered to the party producing the same; and such mortgage or further charge, of which a memorial shall have been so registered, shall in all respects be held to come within the provisions of the Act of the General Assembly, passed in the third year of his late Majesty King William the Fourth, chapter ten, intituled "An Act to regulate the registry of deeds and instruments relating to the title of land," and all other acts relating thereto or affecting the same, as though such mortgage, or further charge, had been duly entered and recorded under the provisions of the said last mentioned Act or Acts; and the Registrar of Deeds shall take and receive for the recording of such memorial and such certificates as aforesaid, the sum of one shilling.

XXXI. Nothing herein contained shall authorize any Building Society, established under this Act, to invest its funds, or any part thereof in any savings' bank.

XXXII. Whenever in this Act, in describing or referring to any person, the word importing the singular number or the masculine gender only is used, the same shall be understood to include and shall be applied to several persons or parties, as well as one person or party, and females as well as males; and the words mortgage and further charge, shall be held to apply to any instrument taken to secure the payment of any sum to such society, unless in all such cases there be something in the subject or context repugnant to such construction.

XXXIII. The officers of any such society shall and may receive and send by the general post from and to places within this island, all letters and packets, having relation to the business of such society, free from the duty of postage, provided that such letters and packets as shall be sent to such officers, be directed to them as such, specifying the office held by such officer, on the covers thereof; and all such let ters and packets as shall be sent by any of the officers, having relation to the business of such society, shall have written or printed on the covers thereof the name of the office held by such officer sending the same, and shall be signed on the outside thereof with the name of such officer (such name to be from time to time transmitted to the general post office at Charlottetown); and such officers are hereby strictly forbidden to subscribe or permit their names to be subscribed to any cover or packet except such as shall have relation to such business; and if such officer shall knowingly cause or permit to be sent under any such cover any letter, paper or writing, or any enclosure having no relation to any such business connected with such society, the officer so offending shall forfeit and pay a sum not exceeding the sum of one hundred pounds, which may be sued for and recovered in Her Majesty's Supreme Court of Judicature, at Charlottetown, and which shall be forfeited to Her Majesty, her heirs and successors; and if any letter, paper or writing, or other enclosure, shall be sent under cover to any of the said officers of such society, the same having no relation to the business of such society, such officer so receiving the same is hereby strictly required to transmit the same forthwith to the Postmaster General, with the covers under which the same shall be sent, in order that the contents thereof may be charged with the full rates of postage.

XXXIV. It shall be lawful for any witness to swear to the execution of any mortgage or further charge, or memorial, or for any mortgagee to acknowledge the execution of any mortgage, further charge, or memorial, before any commissioner appointed for the purpose of taking acknowledgements of deeds; and the registrar of deeds is hereby required to register such memorial, and to endorse such certificate upon every mortgage or further charge so sworn to or acknowledged before any such commissioner.

FORM OF AWARD.

We, the major part of the arbitrators, duly appointed by the society established at　　　　in the County of　　　　do hereby award and order that *A. B.*, (specifying by name the party or the officer of the society), do on the day of　　　　pay to *C. D.* the sum of　　　　; or we do hereby reinstate in or expel *A. B.* from said society as the case may be.)

Dated this　　　　day of　　　　one thousand eight hundred and

E. E.
G. H.

SCHEDULE (A).

Know all men by these presents, that we, *A. B.* of　　　　treasurer (or trustee) of the　　　　society established at　　　　in the County of　　　　and *C. D.* of　　　　and *G. H.* of　　　　(as sureties on behalf of the said *A. B.*) are jointly and severally bound to *J. K.*, the present keeper of the rolls of the Commission of the Peace for　　　　County of in the sum of   to be paid to the said *J. K.*, as such keeper of the rolls, or his successor, keeper of the rolls of the said county for the time being, or his certain attorney, for which payment, well and truly to be made, we jointly and severally bind ourselves, and each of us by himself, our and each of our heirs, executors and administrators, firmly by these presents, sealed with our seals, dated the   day of   in the year of our Lord

Whereas the above bounden *A. B.* hath been duly appointed treasurer (or trustee) of the society established as aforesaid, and he, together with the above bounden *C. D.* and *G. H.*, as his sureties, have entered into the above written bond, subject to the condition hereinafter contained; now, therefore, the condition of the above written bond is such that if the said *A. B.* shall and do justly and faithfully execute his office of treasurer (or trustee) of the said society established as aforesaid, and shall and do render a just and true account of all moneys received and paid by him, and shall and do pay over all the moneys remaining in his hands, and assign and transfer or deliver all securities and effects, books, papers and property, of or belonging to the said society in his hands or custody, to such person or persons as the said society shall appoint, according to the rules of the said society, together with the proper or legal receipts or vouchers for such payments, and likewise shall and do in all respects well and truly and faithfully perform and fulfil his office of treasurer (or trustee, &c.,) to the said society according to the rules thereof, then the above written bond shall be void and of no effect, otherwise shall be and remain in full force and virtue.

Signed, sealed and delivered in the presence of

A. B. [L.S.]
C. D. [L.S.]
G. H. [L.S.]

———

SCHEDULE (B.)

Memorial to be registered pursuant to the statute, of a deed of   mortgage (or further charge) between *A. B.* and *C. D.*, his wife, of the one part, and *E. F., G. H.* and *J. K.*, trustees of the   Benefit Building Society (designating the name of the society), bearing date the   day of   one thousand eight hundred and   by which the said mortgagee thereby conveyed all his right and title (or assigned all his leasehold interest, or further charge, all his right and titles in and to all that tract, piece and parcel of land, situate   to secure the payment of the sum of   pounds, the last instalment of which is   pounds, and will be due on the   day of   one thousand eight hundred and   and which said mortgage (or further charge) contains a power of sale which may be exercised   months after default of any of the conditions in the said mortgage by the mortgagee.

SCHEDULE (C.)

I hereby certify that the within memorial was duly registered on   day of   in the year of our Lord one thousand eight hundred and   at the hour of   of the clock, upon the oath of   (or upon the acknowledgment of the within named   .)

H. Y., Registrar.

SCHEDULE (D.)

I hereby certify that this mortgage was duly proved pursuant to the provisions of the "Benefit Building Society Act," on   day of   in the year of our Lord one thousand eight hundred and   at the hour of   of the clock, upon the oath of   (or upon the acknowledgment of the within named   )

H. Y., Registrar.

CHAP. XVIII.

An Act to extend the powers of Joint Stock Companies for the erection of Exhibition Buildings.

Section
1. Resolution for increase of capital.
2. Resolution to be delivered registrar.
3 Allotment of shares.

Section
4. Calls.
5. Power to borrow.

[*Assented to 5th March*, 1880.]

HER Majesty, by and with the advice and consent of the Legislative Assembly of the Province of Ontario, enacts as follows:

1. Whenever the directors of any company incorporated under the Revised Statute respecting Joint Stock Companies for the erection of Exhibition Buildings, are of opinion that the capital of the company is insufficient for the purposes of the company, they may from time to time pass a resolution authorizing the increase of the capital, and such resolution shall declare the addition number of twenty dollar shares that shall be issued.

2. A copy of the said resolution certified under the hand of the president, and sealed with the seal of the company, shall be delivered to the registrar having the custody of the original instrument of incorporation, or his deputy, who shall attach the same to such original instrument and note thereon the time of the day, and the day of the month, and year of the receipt of the same, and thereupon the authorized capital of the company shall be increased as mentioned in such resolution.

3. The directors may also direct how the said shares shall be allotted, sold or subscribed for, and at what rate of discount or premium the same shall be alloted, sold or subscribed for.

4. Such additional shares may be called in, demanded, and recovered in the same manner and under the penalties as provided or authorized as to the original stock.

5. Every company incorporated as aforesaid may from time to time borrow such moneys as the directors may find requisite for the purposes of the company, from such person or bodies corporate as may be willing to lend the same, and at such lawful rate of interest as may be agreed upon, and may by instrument under the seal of the company secure payment thereof; and the directors may under the authority of a resolution passed by a majority of two-thirds in value of the shareholders present in person or by proxy at a general meeting hypothecate, mortgage, or pledge the real or personal property of the company to secure any sum or sums so borrowed; and the recital of such resolution, passed as aforesaid, in the said instrument shall be *prima facie* evidence of the facts so recited.

CHAP. XIX.

An Act respecting Companies incorporated under Imperial Statutes.

Section.
1. Certain powers, etc., may be granted by Letters Patent to companies incorporated under Imperial Statutes.
2. Copy of Act or other instrument of incorporation to be disposited with Provin-

Section.
cial Secretary.
3. Evidence of incorporation.
4. Matters provided for by R.S.O., c. 136 excepted.

[Assented to 5th March, 1880.]

HER Majesty, by and with the advice and consent of the Legislative Assembly of the Province of Ontario, enacts as follows :

1. In case a corporation, now or hereafter incorporated under the laws of the Imperial Parliament of Great Britain and Ireland, desires to carry on any of its business within the Province of Ontario, the Lieutenant-Governor in Council may, by Letters Patent under the Great Seal of the Province, grant to such company, and such company may thenceforth use, exercise and enjoy within the Province, any powers, privileges and rights set forth in the Letters Patent, as desired in or for carrying on the business of the company, and which it is within the authority of the Lieutenant-Governor in Council to grant to a company under the Ontario Joint Stock Companies' Letters Patent Act.

2. No such Letters' Patent shall be issued until such corporation has deposited in the Office of the Provincial Secretary a true copy of the Act of Parliament, charter or other instrument incorporating the said company, verified in the manner which may be satisfactory to the Lieutenant-Governor in Council.

3. The Letters Patent referring to such Act, charter or other instrument as aforesaid, or a copy of such Act, charter or other instrument aforesaid under the hand of the Provincial Secretary, shall be sufficient evidence, in any proceeding in any court in this Province, of the incorporation of the company.

4. This Act shall not apply to matters provided for by the Revised Statute, chapter one hundred and sixty-three.

CAP. XVIII.

An Act to extend the powers of Companies incorporated under the Joint Stock Companies' Letters Patent Act.

Section.	Section.
1. By-laws to increase capital.	of application to be given.
2. Provision respecting name of companies.	5. This Act to be read as part of R. S. O.,
3. Additional powers which may be granted by Supplementary Letters Patent.	c. 150.
4. Orders in Council may direct what notice	6. R. S. O., c. 150, s. 16, repealed.

[*Assented to 4th March*, 1881.]

HER MAJESTY, by and with the advice and consent of the Legislative Assembly of the Province of Ontario, enacts as follows:—

1. Subject to the provisions of the seventeenth, eighteenth and nineteenth sections of "The Ontario Joint Stock Companies' Letters Patent Act," the directors of any company incorporated under the said Act, at any time after nine-tenths of the capital stock of the company has been taken up, and ten per centum thereon paid in, but not sooner, may, if they see fit, make a by-law for increasing the capital stock of the company to any amount which they consider requisite for the due carrying out of the objects of the company;

(2.) Such by-laws shall declare the number and value of the shares of the new stock, and may prescribe the manner in which the same are to be allotted, and in default of its so doing, the control of such allotment shall be held to rest absolutely in the directors.

2. The name of the Province of Ontario or of some locality therein shall constitute part of the name of every company hereafter incorporated under the said Act.

3. In case a resolution, authorizing an application to the Lieutenant-Governor therefor, is passed by a vote of not less than two-thirds in value of the shareholders present in person or by proxy at a general meeting of the company, duly called for considering the subject of such resolution, the Lieutenant-Governor in Council may from time to time direct the issue of Supplementary Letters Patent to the company, embracing any or all of the following matters:

(1.) Extending the powers of the company to any objects, within the scope of the said Act, which the company may desire;

(2.) Limiting or increasing the amount which the company may borrow upon debentures or otherwise;

(3.) Providing for the formation of a reserve fund;

(4.) Varying any provision contained in the Letters Patent, so long as the alteration desired is not contrary to the provisions of the said Act;

(5.) Making provision for any other matter or thing in respect of which provision might have been made by the original Letters Patent.

4. The Lieutenant-Governor may by Order in Council, to be notified in the *Ontario Gazette*, direct in what cases notices of application for Supplementary Letters Patent shall be given in the *Gazette* or otherwise, and the nature of such notice, and he may in any case dispense with notice.

5. This Act shall be read as part of the said Ontario Joint Stock Companies' Letters Patent Act.

6. The sixteenth section of the said Act is hereby repealed.

CAP. XIX.

An Act for the incorporation by Letters Patent and the regulation of Timber Slide Companies.

Section.
1. Short title.
2. Certain powers may be granted to timber slide companies.
3. R. S. O., c. 153, and this Act to apply to company.
4. When letters patent may be issued.
5. Report to be transmitted to Provincial Secretary by applicants.
6. Rate of dividend may be stated in letters Patent.
7. Limitation of company's existence.
8. Particulars of notice in *Gazette*.
9. Contents of report.
10. Report to be considered by Commissioner of Public Works.
11. By-laws to regulate transmission of timber.
12. Copies of proposed by-laws to be annexed to reports of company.
13. When by-law to come in force.
14. Restrictions as to by-laws.
15. Company not to interfere with property without leave.

Section.
16. Consent to formation of company when required.
17. Recovery of payments made for stockholders.
18. On expiration of Company's existence, property to vest in Her Majesty.
19. Company's existence to continue for the purpose of winding up.
20. Distribution of capital and profits.
21. R.S.O., c. 153, s. 57, amended.
22. Section 72, amended.
23. Section 73 amended.
24. Section 75 amended.
25. Letters patent may limit term of existence of certain companies.
26. Existence of company may be extended by supplementary letters patent.
27. Sections 21, 23 and 24 not to apply to certain companies.
28. R. S. O., c. 153, ss. 1-26 and 29-40 repealed.

[*Assented to 4th March*, 1881.]

HER MAJESTY, by and with the advice and consent of the Legislative Assembly of the Province of Ontario, enacts as follows :—

1. This Act may be cited as " The Timber Slide Companies Act of 1881."

2. In case the Lieutenant-Governor in Council thinks fit, he may confer upon any company which has heretofore been, or shall be hereafter incorporated, under the Ontario Joint Stock Companies' Letters Patent Act, for the purpose of acquiring or constructing and maintaining any dam, slide, pier, boom, or other work, necessary to facilitate the transmission of timber down any river or stream in this Province, or for the purpose of blasting rocks or dredging, or removing shoals or other impediments, or of otherwise improving the navigation of any such river or stream for the said purpose, the powers authorized by the Revised Statute respecting Joint Stock Companies, for the construction of works to facilitate the transmission of Timber down Rivers and Streams, being chapter one hundred and fifty-three of the Revised Statutes.

3. Every such company shall thereupon become subject to all the provisions of the said Revised Statute as amended by this Act, and to the provisions of this Act.

4. The letters patent conferring the powers authorized by this Act shall not be issued to any company until proof has been furnished that one-half of the proposed capital has been subscribed in good faith, and that at least ten per centum thereof (or five per centum of the whole capital) has been paid in to the credit of trustees for the company, and remains at their credit in some one or more of the chartered banks of this Province.

5. The applicants for a charter shall, with their application, transmit to the Provincial Secretary a report to be laid before the Commissioner of Public Works, in case the Provincial Secretary or other officer charged by the Lieutenant-Governor in Council with the duty of reporting thereon shall deem that the other requirements preliminary to the issue of the charter have been duly complied with, and shall also cause a copy of such report to be laid before the municipal council of the county in which such works are proposed to be situated; or if the works are situate in more than one county, then before the municipal councils of the counties in or on the boundaries of which such works proposed to be situated; or if such proposed works are in unsurveyed lands not contained within the bounds of any incorporated county, then before the Commissioner of Public Works alone.

6. The Lieutenant-Governor may, in the letters patent, state a rate of dividend, not exceeding fifteen per centum, which the directors shall be at liberty to pay to the shareholders, if the revenues of the Company otherwise justify such payment, and in such case the Commissioner of Public Works shall, in considering the tolls to be allowed, have regard to such rate, but no such rate shall be so fixed for a longer period than ten years.

7. The existence of any company incorporated under this Act may be limited to such a term of years as is fixed by the letters patent.

8. The notice of application in the *Gazette* need not state the objects of the Company with the same detail as is required in the report, but shall give such a description thereof as will reasonably inform the public of the works to be undertaken.

9. The report shall contain—

(1.) A detailed description of the works to be undertaken, and an estimate of their cost;

(2.) An estimate from the best available sources of the quantity of different kinds of timber expected to come down the river or stream yearly after the works have been completed; and

(3.) A schedule of the tolls proposed to be collected.

10. Thirty days after the said report has been laid before the municipal council, or councils, as the case may be, the Commissioner of Public Works shall consider the said report, and in case he approves of the proposed works, he shall report such approval to the Lieutenant-Governor who may thereupon direct the issue of a charter.

11. Every such company may make by laws, and from time to time alter and amend the same, for the purpose of regulating the safe and orderly transmission of timber over or through the works of the company, and the navigation therewith connected.

12. Copies of the proposed by-laws shall be annexed to the reports required to be made by the company by the fifth section of this Act, and such proposed by-laws with such variations as are made therein by the Commissioner of Public Works at any time before the issue of the letters patent, shall, upon the issue of such letters patent, become the by-laws of the company without further action or adoption by the company, and copies of all new by-laws, and of all amended by-laws, with reference to the said subjects, shall be annexed to the annual reports required by the twenty-seventh section of the said Revised Statute.

13. No such new by-law, or amended by-law, shall have any force until one month after it has been included in such report; but if at the end of one month such by-law has not been disallowed as it may be by the Commissioner of Public Works, it shall have full force and be binding upon the company, and upon all persons using the works, unless the Commissioner in the meantime shall have under his hand enlarged the time for considering the same.

14. No such by-law shall impose any penalties, or shall contain anything contrary to the true meaning and intention of the said Revised Statute, chapter one hundred and fifty-three, or this Act.

15. No such company shall construct any such works over or upon or otherwise interfere with or injure any private property, or the property of the Crown, without first having obtained the consent of the owner, or occupier thereof, or of the Crown, except as hereinafter provided.

16. No such company shall be formed under the provisions of this Act to improve any river or stream, for the improvement of which any other company has been formed either under this Act, or any other Act of the Legislature, or upon which there is constructed any provincial work, without the consent of such other company or of the Lieutenant-Governor in Council respectively, which consent shall be formally expressed in writing, and shall be filed in the office of the Provincial Secretary.

17. In all cases where a shareholder has not paid ten per centum on the share or shares held by him, but some other party pays the same on his behalf, the party so paying may recover the amount as a debt, in any competent court, although not previously authorized to pay the money on behalf of such shareholder.

18. Upon the expiration of the period limited for the existence of the company, if any such period is limited by the letters patent, all the dams, slides, piers, booms and other works constructed by the company, for the transmission of timber down any river or stream, or for the improvement of the navigation of such river or stream, shall become the property of Her Majesty for the public uses of the Province, and the said company, or the shareholders thereof, shall have no right to receive any compensation therefor.

19. Notwithstanding the expiration of the said period, the said company shall continue to exist for the purpose of taking such proceedings as may be requisite for getting in its assets, winding up and settling its affairs, and distributing amongst its shareholders the capital stock or accumulated sinking fund of the said company, and the said company may, for the purposes aforesaid, sue and be sued as if the period of its corporate existence had not expired; but after such period the words "in liquidation" shall be added to the name of the company, and shall be a part of such name.

20. No distribution of capital shall be made under the next preceding section until three years after the expiration of the said period limited as aforesaid for the existence of the said company, but this shall not prevent the distribution amongst the shareholders of the annual profits received from investments, and after the said period the fifty-seventh section of the said Joint Stock Companies' Letters Patent Act shall not apply to the company.

21. The fifty-seventh section of the said Revised Statute, chapter one hundred and fifty-three, is hereby amended by inserting after the word "works," in the eleventh line thereof, the following words:— "and running, driving, booming, towing, sorting, and rafting logs and other timber, and providing an equal annual sinking fund, which, invested at six per centum, shall be sufficient to pay back to the shareholders the amount of their paid-up stock at the end of the time limited for the existence of the company," and by adding to the said section the following words: "unless a higher rate is authorized by the letters patent or by Order-in-Council under the sixth section of this Act."

22. The seventy-second section of the said Revised Statute is hereby amended by inserting after the words "undertaken by them" the following words:—"and mentioned in the report required prior to the incorporation of the company;" and by inserting after the word "situate," in the ninth line thereof, the following words: "or by the Commissioner of Public Works."

23. The seventy-third section of the said Revised Statute is hereby amended by inserting after the word "damage" in the thirteenth line thereof, the following words:—"incurred after the time limited for the existence of the company has expired, or."

24. The seventy-fifth section of the said Revised Statute is amended by adding at the end thereof the following words:—" and in settling the amount to be paid to the company for such works, the amount of the sinking fund accumulated at the time of such valuation towards the payment of the capital stock shall be deducted therefrom."

25. Where a company heretofore incorporated under the said Revised Statute, chapter one hundred and fifty three, or under the Consolidated Statute of Canada, chapter sixty-eight, applies for the issue of letters patent under section sixty-five or section sixty-six of the Ontario Joint Stock Companies' Letters Patent Act, the Lieutenant-Governor may, by the letters patent, confer upon the said company any of the powers authorized by this Act, and may by such letters patent limit the term of existence of the said company, and every such company obtaining letters patent as aforesaid, shall be subject to the provisions of the said Revised Statute, chapter one hundred and fifty-three, as amended by this Act, and to the provisions of this Act.

26. The Lieutenant-Governor may by Supplementary Letters Patent extend the term of existence of any company incorporated for a limited period under this Act, for such a number of years, as by Order-in-Council made previous to the expiry of such period he may direct, and the provisions of this Act having regard to the expiration of the term of existence of a company shall thereupon apply to such term as so extended.

27. Sections twenty-one, twenty-three and twenty-four of this Act shall not apply to any company heretofore incorporated, unless and until such company becomes re-incorporated under the said sixty-fifth section of the Ontario Joint Stock Companies' Letters Patent Act.

28. The first twenty-six sections, and also sections numbered from twenty-nine to forty inclusive, of the said Revised Statute respecting Joint Stock Companies for the construction of works to facilitate the transmission of timber down rivers and streams, are hereby repealed, except as to companies heretofore incorporated under the said Act.

CHAP. XV.

An Act to amend the Revised Statute respecting Mortgages and Sales of Personal Property.

Section.
1. R. S. O., c. 119, s. 7, amended.
2. Sec. 10, repealed; statement to be filed yearly or mortgage invalidated as against creditors.
3. Form of statement and affidavit.
4. Mode of filing and entering affidavit and statement.
5. Sec. 15 repealed.

Section.
6. An authority to take or renew mortgages may be a general one.
7. Sec. 17 amended.
8. Sec. 18 amended.
9. Sec. 19 amended.
10. Time Act to come in force; mode of citation.

[*Assented to 5th March*, 1880.]

HER Majesty, by and with the advice and consent of the Legislative Assembly of the Province of Ontario, enacts as follows:

1. Section seven of the Revised Statute, chapter one hundred and nineteen, respecting Mortgages and Sales of Personal Property, is hereby amended by striking out the words " where the mortgagor or bargainor if a resident in Ontario resides at the time of the execution thereof, or if he is not a resident then in the office of the clerk of the County Court of the county, or union of counties," in the third, fourth, fifth and sixth lines of the said section.

2. Section ten of the said Revised Statute is hereby repealed, and the following substituted therefor:

10. Every mortgage, or copy thereof, filed in pursuance of this Act, shall cease to be valid, as against the creditors of the persons making the same and against subsequent purchasers and mortgagees in good faith for valuable consideration, after the expiration of one year from the filing thereof, unless within thirty days next preceding the expiration of the said term of one year, a statement exhibiting the interest of the mortgagee, his executors, administrators or other assigns, in the property claimed by virtue thereof, and shewing the amount still due for principal and interest thereon, and shewing all payments made on account thereof, is again filed in the office of the clerk of the County Court of the county, or union of counties, wherein such goods and chattels are then situate, with an affidavit of the mortgagee, or one of several mortgagees, or of the assignee or one of several assignees, or of the agent of the mortgagee or assignee, or mortgagees or assignees (as the case may be), duly authorized in writing, for that purpose (a copy of which authority shall be filed therewith), that such statement is true, and that the said mortgage has not been kept on foot for any fraudulent purpose.

3. The statement and affidavit mentioned in the next preceding paragraph may be in the form given in the schedule to this Act, to the like effect.

4. The said statement and affidavit shall be deemed one instrument and be filed and entered in like manner as the instruments mentioned in the said Revised Statute are, by section eight thereof, required to be filed and entered, and the like fees shall be payable for filing and entering the same as are now payable for filing and entering such instruments.

5. Section fifteen of the said Revised Statute is hereby repealed, and the following substituted therefor :

15. Where a mortgage has been renewed under section ten of this Act, the endorsement or entries required by the preceding section to be made need only be made upon the statement and affidavit filed on the last renewal, and at the entries of such statement and affidavit in the said book.

6. An authority for the purpose of taking or renewing a mortgage or conveyance under the provisions of the said Revised Statute may be a general one to take and renew all or any mortgages or conveyances to the mortgagee or bargainee.

7. Section seventeen of the said Revised Statute is hereby amended by striking out all the words in the said section down to and inclusive of the word " but," where it occurs in the fifth line thereof, and substituting therefor the word " when ; " and by adding thereto after the words " County Court," in the ninth line thereof, the words following, " and with the substitution of ten days for five days as the time within which the instrument or a copy thereof shall be registered."

8. Section eighteen of the said Revised Statute is hereby amended by striking out all the words " but," in the fourth line thereof, and substituting therefor the word " when."

9. Section nineteen of the said Revised Statute is hereby amended by striking out all the words in the said section down to and inclusive of the word " but," in the fourth line thereof, and substituting therefor the word " when."

10. This Act shall not come into force until the first day of October next, and may be cited as " The Mortgages and Sales of Personal Property Amendment Act, 1880."

SCHEDULE.

(*Section* 3.)

Statement exhibiting the interest of *C.D.* in the property mentioned in a Chattel Mortgage dated the   day of
18   , made between *A.B.*, of   of the one part, and *C.D.*,
of   of the other part and filed in the office of the clerk of
the county court of the county of   on the
day of   18   and of the amount due for principal and interest thereon, and of all payments made on account thereof.

The said *C.D.* is still the mortgagee of the said property, and has not assigned the said Mortgage (*or* the said *E.F.* is the assignee of the said Mortgage by virtue of an assignment thereof from the said *C.D.* to him, dated the   day of   18   ,) (*or as the case may be*).

No payments have been made on account of the said mortgage (*or the following payments, and no other, have been made on account of the said Mortgage* :

   1880, January 1, Cash received..........$100 00)

The amount still due for principal and interest on the said Mortgage is the sum of   dollars, computed as follows : [*here give the computation.*]

             C. D.

County of   ⎫ I,   of the
  To wit: ⎬   of   in the County
of   the mortgagee named in the Chattel Mortgage mentioned in the foregoing (*or* annexed) statement (*or* assignee of   the mortgagee named in the Chattel Mortgage mentioned in the foregoing [*or* annexed] statement), (*as the case may be*), make oath and say :

 1. That the foregoing (*or* annexed) statement is true.
 2. That the Chattel Mortgage mentioned in the said statement has not been kept on foot for any fraudulent purpose.

  Sworn before me at the   of ⎫
    in the county of   ⎬
this   day of   18   . ⎭

CHAP. CXIX.

An Act respecting Mortgages and Sales of Personal Property.

Section.
1. Mortgages of goods not attended with change of possession, shall be registered, or else be void as against creditors, &c., of the mortgagor, with an affidavit, &c.
2. Contents of affidavit.
4. Unless registered, mortgage void.
5. Sales of goods not attended with delivery shall be registered, or else be void as against creditors, &c., of the vendor.
6. Mortgages of goods to secure advances or to indemnify endorsers, etc., to be valid if duly registered.
7. Chattel Mortgages to be registered in the office of County Clerk.
8. Clerk to enter the same.
9. How to proceed if goods mortgaged are removed to another County.
10. Mortgages of chattels must be periodically renewed, else cease to be valid.
11. Affidavit by whom made.

Section.
12. The Clerk's certificate to be evidence of registration.
13. Certificates for discharging chattel mortgages.
14. Entering certificates of discharge.
15. Where Mortgages have been renewed.
16. Entry of assignment of mortgages.
17. Registration of chattel mortgages in Provisional Judicial Districts.
18. In Territorial Districts.
19. In Temporary Judicial District of Nipissing.
20. Instruments executed before 1 July, 1877.
21. Saving clause.
22. Fees for services.
23. The property to be well described.
24. Who to administer the affidavits.
25. Act not to apply to mortgages or vessels duly registered.

HER Majesty, by and with the advice and consent of the Legislative Assembly of the Province of Ontario, enacts as follows:

REGISTRATION OF CHATTEL MORTGAGES AND SALES OF GOODS WHERE POSSESSION IS UNCHANGED.

1. Every mortgage, or conveyance intended to operate as a mortgage, of goods and chattels, made in Ontario, which is not accompanied by an immediate delivery, and an actual and continued change of possession of the things mortgaged, or a true copy thereof, shall, within five days from the execution thereof, be registered as hereinafter provided, together with the affidavit of a witness thereto, of the due execution of such mortgage or conveyance, or of the due execution of the mortgage or conveyance, of which the copy filed purports to be a copy, and also with the affidavit of the mortgagee or of one of several mortgagees, or of the agent of the mortgagee or mortgagees, if such agent is aware of all the circumstances connected therewith and is properly authorized in writing to take such mortgage (in which case a copy of such authority shall be registered therewith). C. S. U. C. c. 45, s. 1; 40 V. c. 7, Sched. A. (134).

2. Such last mentioned affidavit, whether of the mortgagee or his agent, shall state that the mortgagor therein named is justly and truly indebted to the mortgagee in the sum mentioned in the mortgage, that it was executed in good faith and for the express purpose of securing the payment of money justly due or accruing due and not for the purpose of protecting the goods and chattels mentioned therein against the creditors of the mortgagor, or of preventing the creditors of such mortgagor from obtaining payment of any claim against him. C. S. U. C. c. 45, s. 2.

3. Every such mortgage or conveyance shall operate and take effect upon, from and after the day and time of the execution thereof. 26 V. c. 46, sec. 1.

4. In case such mortgage or conveyance and affidavits are not registered as hereinbefore provided, the mortgage or conveyance shall be absolutely null and void as against creditors of the mortgagor, and against subsequent purchasers or mortgagees in good faith for valuable consideration. C. S. U. C. c. 45, sec. 3.

5. Every sale of goods and chattels, not accompanied by an immediate delivery and followed by an actual and continued change of possession of the goods and chattels sold, shall be in writing, and such writing shall be a conveyance under the provisions of this Act, and shall be accompanied by an affidavit of a witness thereto of the due execution thereof, and an affidavit of the bargainee, or his agent duly authorized in writing to take such conveyance (a copy of which authority shall be attached to such conveyance), that the sale is *bona fide* and for good consideration, as set forth in the said conveyance, and not for the purpose of holding or enabling the bargainee to hold the goods mentioned therein against the creditors of the bargainor, and such conveyance and affidavits shall be registered as hereinafter provided, within five days from the executing thereof, otherwise the sale shall be absolutely void as against the creditors of the bargainor and as against subsequent purchasers or mortgagees in good faith. C.S.U.C. c. 45, s. 4.

6. In case of an agreement in writing for future advances for the purpose of enabling the borrower to enter into and carry on business with such advances, the time of repayment thereof not being longer than one year from the making of the agreement, and in case of a mortgage of goods and chattels for securing the mortgagee repayment of such advances, or in case of a mortgage of goods and chattels for securing the mortgagee against the endorsement of any bills or promissory notes or any other liability by him incurred for the mortgagor, not extending for a longer period than one year from the date of such mortgage, and in case the mortgage is executed in good faith, and sets forth fully by recital or otherwise, the terms, nature and effect of the agreement, and the amount of liability intended to be created, and in case such mortgage is accompanied by the affidavit of a witness thereto of the due execution thereof, and by the affidavit of the mortgagee, or in case the agreement has been entered into, and the mortgage taken by an agent duly authorized in writing to make such agreement and to take such mortgage, and if the agent is aware of the circumstances connected therewith, then, if accompanied by the affidavit of such agent, such affidavit, whether of the mortgagee or his agent, mortgage truly sets forth the agreement entered into parties thereto, and truly states the extent of the liability created by such agreement and covered by such mortgage mortgage is executed in good faith and for the express curing the mortgagee repayment of his advances or of the amount of his liability for the mortgagor, as the case may be, and not for the purpose of securing the goods and chattels therein against the creditors of the mortgagor, nor to prevent such creditors from recovering any claims which they may have against such mortgagor, and in case such mortgage is registered as hereinafter provided, the same shall be as valid and binding as mortgages mentioned in the preceding sections of this Act. C. S. U. C. c. 45, s. 5.

7. The instruments mentioned in the preceding sections shall be registered in the office of the Clerk of the County Court of the County or Union of Counties where the mortgagor or bargainor, if a resident in Ontario, resides, at the time of the execution thereof, or, if he is not a resident, then in the office of the Clerk of the County Court of the County or Union of Counties where the property so mortgaged or sold is at the time of the execution of such instrument; and such clerks shall file all such instruments presented to them respectively for that purpose, and shall endorse thereon the time of receiving the same in their respective offices, and the same shall be kept there for the inspection of all persons interested therein, or intending or desiring to acquire any interest in all or any portion of the property covered thereby. C. S. U. C. c. 45, s. 7.

8. The said Clerks respectively shall number every such instrument or copy filed in their offices, and shall enter in alphabetical order in books to be provided by them, the names of all the parties to such instruments, with the numbers endorsed thereon opposite to each name, and such entry shall be repeated alphabetically under the name of every party thereto. C. S. U. C. c. 45, s. 8.

9. In the event of the permanent removal of goods and chattels mortgaged as aforesaid from the County or Union of Counties in which they were at the time of the execution of the mortgage, to another County or Union of Counties before the payment and discharge of the mortgage, a certified copy of such mortgage, under the hand of the Clerk of the County Court in whose office it was first registered, and under the seal of the said Court, and of the affidavits and documents and instruments relating thereto filed in such office, shall be filed with the Clerk of the County Court of the County or Union of Counties to which such goods and chattels are removed, within two months from such removal, otherwise the said goods and chattels shall be liable to seizure and sale under execution, and in such case the mortgage shall be null and void as against subsequent purchasers and mortgagees in good faith for valuable consideration as if never executed. C. S. U. C. c. 45, s. 9; 40 V. c. 8, s. 2).

RENEWAL OF MORTGAGES.

10. Every mortgage, or copy thereof, filed in pursuance of this Act, shall cease to be valid as against the creditors of the persons making the same, and against subsequent purchasers or mortgagees in good faith for valuable consideration, after the expiration of one year from the filing thereof, unless within thirty days next preceding the expiration of the said term of one year, a true copy of such mortgage, together with a statement exhibiting the interest of the mortgagee in the property claimed by virtue thereof, and a full statement of the amount still due for principal and interest thereon, and of all payments made on account thereof, is again filed in the office of the Clerk of the said County Court of the County or Union of Counties wherein such goods and chattels are then situate, with an affidavit of the mortgagee or of one of several mortgagees or of the assignee, or one of several assignees, or of the agent of the mortgagee or assignee, or mortgagees or assignees, as the case may be, duly authorized in writing for that purpose (which authority shall be filed therewith), stating that such statements are true, and that the said mortgage has not been kept on foot for any fraudulent purpose. C. S. U. C. c. 45, s. 10; 40 V. c. 7, Sched. A. (135).

11. The affidavit required by the tenth section may be made by any next of kin, executor or administrator of any deceased mortgagee, or by any assignee claiming by or through any mortgagee, or any next of kin, executor or administrator of any such assignee; but if the affidavit is made by any assignee, next of kin, executor or administrator of any such assignee, the assignment, or the several assignments through which such assignee claims shall be filed in the office in which the mortgage is filed, at or before the time of such refiling by such assignee, next of kin, executor or administrator of such assignee. 40 V. c. 21, s. 5.

EVIDENCE OF REGISTRATION.

12. A copy of such original instrument or of a copy thereof, so filed as aforesaid, including any statement made in pursuance of this Act, certified by the Clerk in whose office the same has been filed, under the seal of the Court shall be received in evidence in all Courts, but only of the fact that such instruments or copy and statement were received and filed according to the endorsement of the Clerk thereon, and of no other fact; and in all cases the original endorsement by the Clerk made in pursuance of this Act, upon any such instrument or copy, shall be received in evidence only of the fact stated in such endorsement. C. S. U. C. c. 45, s. 11.

DISCHARGE OF MORTGAGES.

13. Where any mortgage of goods and chattels is registered under the provisions of this Act, such mortgage may be discharged, by the filing, in the office in which the same is registered, of a certificate signed by the mortgagee, his executors or administrators, in the form given in the Schedule hereto, or to the like effect. 40 V. c. 21, s. 1.

14. The officer with whom the chattel mortgage is filed, upon receiving such certificate, duly proved by the affidavit of a subscribing witness, shall, at each place where the number of such mortgage has been entered, with the name of any of the parties thereto, in the book kept under section eight of this Act, or wherever otherwise in the said book the said mortgage has been entered, write the words, "*Dis d by certificate number* (stating the number of the certificate)," and to the said entry such officer shall affix his name, and he shall also endorse the fact of such discharge upon the instrument discharged, and shall affix his name to such endorsement. 40 V. c. 21, s. 2.

15. Where a mortgage has been renewed under section ten of this Act, the endorsement or entries required by the preceding section to be made, need only be made upon the copy filed on the last renewal, and at the entries of such copy in the said book. 40 V. c. 21, s. 3.

16. In case any registered chattel mortgage has been assigned, such assignment may, upon proof by the affidavit of a subscribing witness, be numbered and entered in the alphabetical chattel mortgage book, in the same manner as a chattel mortgage, and the proceedings authorized by the three next preceding sections of this Act may and shall be had, upon a certificate of the assignee, proved in manner aforesaid. 40 V. c. 21, s. 4.

MORTGAGES AND SALES OF CHATTELS IN UNORGANIZED DISTRICTS.

17. When the mortgagor or bargainor named in any instrument subject to the provisions of this Act is a resident in a Provisional Judicial District, or if such mortgagor or bargainor is not at the time of the execution of such instrument a resident in Ontario, but the personal property mortgaged or sold is within a Provisional Judicial District, then the provisions of this Act shall apply to such instrument with the substitution of "the Clerk of the District Court" for "the Clerk of the County Court;" but this section shall not apply to any portion of a Territorial District which forms part of a provisional Judicial district. 40 V. c. 24, s. 14.

18. If the mortgagor or bargainor named in any such instrument is resident in a Territorial District, or if such bargainor or mortgagor is not at the time of the execution of such instrument a resident in Ontario, but the personal property mortgaged or sold is within a Territorial District, then the provisions of this Act shall apply to such instrument, with the substitution of "the Clerk of the first Division Court of the District" for the "Clerk of the County Court," and with the substitution of "ten days" for "five days," as the time within which the instrument or a copy thereof shall be registered. 40 V. c. 24, s. 14 (2).

19. If the mortgagor or bargainor named in any such instrument, resident in the Temporary Judicial District of Nipissing, or if such bargainor or mortgagor is not at the time of the execution of such instrument a resident in Ontario, but the personal property mortgaged or sold is within the said Temporary Judicial District, then the provisions of this Act shall apply to such instrument, with the substitution of "the Clerk of the County Court of the County of Renfrew" for "the Clerk of the County Court," and with the substitution of "twenty days," for "five days," as the time within which the instrument or a copy thereof shall be registered. 40 V. c. 24, s. 14 (3).

20. Every instrument executed before the first day of July, one thousand eight hundred and seventy-seven, and which, had it been executed after said day, would require registration under the preceding provisions, shall be registered on or before the first day of January, one thousand eight hundred and seventy-eight, in the manner required by the provisions of this Act, and thereafter every such instrument which under the provisions of this Act, requires renewal shall, unless duly renewed, become void in accordance with the provisions of this Act. 40 V. c. 24, s. 14 (4).

21. Nothing in the four preceding sections shall be used to aid in determining whether or not chapter forty-five of the Consolidated Statutes of Upper Canada was, prior to the first day of July, one thousand eight hundred and seventy-seven, in force in any Territorial, Temporary Judicial, or Provisional Juidicial District. 40 V. c. 24, s. 14 (5).

FEES.

22. For services under this Act the Clerks aforesaid shall be entitled to receive the following fees:

1. For filing each instrument and affidavit, and for entering the same in a book as aforesaid, twenty-five cents;
2. For filing assignment of each instrument and for making all proper endorsements in connection therewith, twenty-five cents;
3. For filing certificate of discharge of each instrument and for making all proper entries and endorsements connected therewith, twenty-five cents;
4. For searching for each paper, ten cents; and
5. For copies of any document with certificate prepared, filed under this Act, ten cents for every hundred words. C. S. U. C. c. 45, s. 14; 40 V. c. 21. s. 6.

MISCELLANEOUS.

23. All the instruments mentioned in this Act, whether for the sale or mortgage of goods and chattels, shall contain such sufficient and full description thereof that the same may be thereby readily and easily known and distinguished. C. S. U. C. c. 45, s. 6.

24. All affidavits and affirmations required by this Act shall be taken and administered by any Judge or Commissioner for taking affidavits in and for the Courts of Queen's Bench or Common Pleas, or a Justice of the Peace, and the sum of twenty cents shall be paid for every oath thus administered. C. S. U. C. c. 45, s. 12.

25. This Act does not apply to mortgages of vessels registered under the provisions of any Act in that behalf. C. S. U. C. c. 45, s. 15.

SCHEDULE.
(*Section* 13.)
FORM OF DISCHARGE OF MORTGAGE.

To the Clerk of the County Court of the County of

I, A. B., of do certify that has satisfied all money due on, or to grow due on a certain chattel mortgage made by to , which mortgage bears date the day of , A.D. , and was registered (*or in case the mortgage has been renewed under section ten, was re-registered.*) in the office of the Clerk of the County Court of the County of , on the , A.D , as No. (*here mention the day and date of registration of such assignment thereof, and the names of the parties, or mention that such mortgage has not been assigned, as the fact may be*); and that I am the person entitled by law to receive the money; and that such mortgage is therefore discharged.

Witness my hand, this day of A.D.
One witness stating residence   A.B.
and occupation.

CHAP. V.

An Act respecting the winding up of Joint Stock Companies.

Section.
1. Short title.
2. Application of Act.
3. "Court;" Power of County Court Judge. "Contributory;" case of death of contributory. "Extraordinary resolution;" "Special Resolution."
4. When companies may be wound up voluntarily; on special resolution; on extraordinary resolution for liabilities.
5. When by order of the court.
6. Time and commencement of winding up; registration of winding up.
8. Consequences on commencing to wind up; extent to which company to exist after commencement of winding up. Transfer of shares; property of company. Liquidators, appointment of; remuneration; security. One liquidator; cesser of powers of liquidators; powers of several liquidators. Appointment of inspectors; revocations; remuneration. Directions as to the disposal of property of the company by liquidation.
9. Description and general power of liquidator; bring actions; carry on business; sell property; sale of debts; draw, &c., bills and notes; take out letters of administration to deceased contributors and collect debts; execute deeds; other things; company's seal.
10. Time for creditors to send in claims may be fixed; liquidators may distribute after expiring of time to creditors to claim.
11. General scheme of liquidation may be authorised and compromises with creditors.
12. Power to compromise with debtors and contributories; take security.
13. Power to accept shares, &c., as a consideration for sale of property to another company. Sale or arrangement by liquidators binding unless a member objects; proceedings on objection. Special resolution not invalid because prior to resolution to wind up. Price payable to objecting member; mode of determining price; arbitration; majority to determine disputes; umpire.
14. Settle list of contributories; shareholders' liability to contribute; case of transfer of shares by shareholder; contributories liable in a representative character to be distinguished in list; when real representatives need not be inserted; list evidence of liability.
15. Settlement of list by the court; procedure on settling list by the court. Certificate of result of settlement.

Section.
16. Provision for administration if personal representative fails to pay.
17. Calls on contributories.
18. Contributories liable to arrest like debtors under Revised Stat. c. 67.
19. Employment of counsel by Liquidators; Liquidators or Inspectors not to purchase assets of Company; deposit in bank by Liquidators; separate deposit account to be kept; withdrawal from account; Liquidators to produce bank pass book at meetings, &c.; Liquidator to produce bank pass book when ordered; Liquidator and inspector to be subject to summary jurisdiction of Court; obedience how enforced.
20. Costs and expenses.
21. Remuneration of liquidators in case no other fixed.
22. Filling vacancies in office of liquidator. General meetings during winding up; annual meetings; liquidators to call meeting of contributories; subsequent meetings; where meetings to be held; one mode of giving notice of meeting; another mode of notice of meeting; voting to be in person or by proxy; scale of votes.
23. Applications to the court; stay of action against company before order to wind up; stay of action after commencement of winding up. Settlement of list of contributories; meetings of contributories may be ordered; chairman; order for delivery by contributories and others of property, &c.; order for payment by contributories; power to order payment into a bank to account of official liquidator; order on contributory to be conclusive evidence, except as to real estate of deceased; inspection of books; examination of persons before Court or Liquidator; production of books, &c.; penalty on person summoned not attending; mode of examination; subpœnas; liens; power of court to assess damages against delinquent directors, &c.
24. Proceedings by contributories at their own expense and for their own benefit only.
25. Filling vacancies in office of liquidator; appointment by Court. Removal of liquidator; case of no liquidator.
26. Rescinding of resolutions, &c., by the Court; confirmation on varying resolutions, &c.; costs.
27. Appeals; security for damages and costs; dismissal of appeal; judgment final.

Section.	Section.
28. Powers of Court to be in addition to other power.	40. Account of winding up to be made by liquidator to a general meeting; return of holding of meeting to be sent to Provincial Secretary. Dissolution of Co.
29. Enforcing of Orders; Powers of County Courts.	
30. County Courts to be auxiliary. Transfer to another Court.	41. Order for Dissolution. Report to Provincial Secretary.
31. Enforcement of order of one Court by another.	42. Penalty on default in reporting by liquidator or in making return.
32. Petition on winding up; course of Court on hearing of petition.	43. Disposition of unclaimed dividends.
33. Stay of proceedings to wind up.	44. Deposit by liquidator after dissolution of moneys with sworn statement. Penalty on omission; Money deposited to lie three years; Disposal of books, &c., after winding up; after five years responsibility as to custody of books, &c., to cease.
34. Rules of procedure in ordinary cases, &c., to apply; amendments.	
35. Language of proceedings, &c.	
36. Books, &c., to be *prima facie* evidence.	
37. Service of subpœnas, &c.	
38. Length of notice of proceedings. Service of notice.	45. Board of county judges to make rules and forms as to proceedings and costs, &c.; allowance or disallowance by court of appeal; practice till allowance of rules, &c.
39. Affidavits, before whom sworn; Courts, &c., to take judicial notice of seals, signatures, &c.	

[*Assented to* 7th *March*, 1878.]

HER Majesty, by and with the advice and consent of the Legislative Assembly of the Province of Ontario, enacts as follows:—

1. This Act may be cited as the "Joint Stock Companies' Winding-up Act."

2. This Act shall apply to all incorporated companies or associations incorporated by the Legislature of the Province of Ontario, or under the authority of Any Act of this Province, and to all companies and associations which were incorporated by the Parliament of the Province of Upper Canada, or of the Province of Canada, or under the authority of any Act of the Province of Canada, whose incorporation and the affairs thereof, in the particulars hereinafter mentioned, are subject to the legislative authority of this Province.

INTERPRETATION.

3. Unless otherwise expressed, or otherwise indicated by the context, the word "Court," as used in this Act, means any county court; and any judge of a county court may either in term time or in vacation exercise all the powers conferred by this Act upon the court;

2. The term "contributory" means every person liable to contribute to the assets of a company under this Act, in the event of the same being wound-up: it shall, also, in all proceedings prior to the final determination of such persons, include any person alleged to be a contributory;

3. If any contributory dies either before or after he has been placed on the list of contributories hereinafter mentioned, his personal representatives, heirs and devisees shall be liable in due course of administration to contribute to the assets of the company in discharge of the liability of such deceased contributory, and such personal representatives, heirs, and devisees shall be deemed to be contributories accordingly;

4. The expression "extraordinary resolution" in this Act means a resolution passed by a majority of not less than three-fourths of such members of the company, for the time being entitled to vote, as may be present in person or by proxy (in cases where, by the Act or charter or instrument of incorporation or the regulations of the company, proxies are allowed), at any general meeting of which notice specifying the intention to propose such resolution has been duly given;

5. The expression "special resolution" in this Act means a resolution passed in the manner necessary for an extraordinary resolution, where the resolution after having been so passed as aforesaid has been confirmed by a majority of such members (entitled according to the Act, charter or instrument of incorporation or the regulations of the company to vote) as may be present in person or by proxy, at a subsequent general meeting, of which notice has been duly given, and held at an interval of not less than fourteen days or more than one month from the date of the meeting at which the resolution was first passed.

WHEN COMPANIES MAY BE WOUND UP.

4. A company may be wound up under the Act:

1. Where the period, if any, fixed for the duration of the company by the Act, charter or instrument of incorporation has expired; or where the event (if any) has occurred, upon the occurrence of which it is provided by the Act or charter or instrument of incorporation that the company is to be dissolved; and the company in general meeting has passed a resolution requiring the company to be wound up;

2. Where the company has passed a special resolution (as hereinbefore defined) requiring the company to be wound up;

3. Where the company (though it may be solvent as respects creditors) has passed an extraordinary resolution (as hereinbefore defined) to the effect that it has been proved to their satisfaction that the company cannot by reason of its liabilities continue its business, and that it is advisable to wind up the same.

5. Where no such resolution has been passed as mentioned in the preceding section, the court may, on the application of a contributory, make an order for winding up, in case the court is of opinion that it is just and equitable that the company should be wound up.

6. A winding up shall be deemed to commence at the time of the passing of the resolution authorizing the winding up, or of making the order directing the winding up.

REGISTRATION.

7. A copy of the resolution or order for winding up, certified by the liquidator, may be registered in the registry office of any county, riding or registration division wherein the company may have any real estate; such resolution or order shall be accompanied by a description of the real estate belonging to the company in the county, and certified by the liquidator to be a correct description; and the registrar shall register the said order and description upon payment to him of a fee of one dollar.

CONSEQUENCES OF COMMENCING TO WIND UP.

2. The following consequences shall ensue upon the commencement of the winding up of a company under the authority of this Act:

(1). The company shall, from the date of the commencement of such winding up, cease to carry on its business, except in so far as may be required for the beneficial winding up thereof; and any transfers of shares, except transfers made to or with the sanction of the liquidators, or any alteration in the status of the members of the company, after the commencement of such winding up, shall be void, but the corporate state and all the corporate powers of the company shall, notwithstanding it may be otherwise provided by the Act charter or instrument of incorporation, continue until the affairs of the company are wound up.

(2.) The property of the company shall be applied in satisfaction of its liabilities; and subject thereto, and to the charges incurred in winding up its affairs, shall (unless it is otherwise provided for by the Act, Charter, or Instrument of Incorporation) be distributed amongst the members according to their right and interests in the company.

(3.) Liquidators shall be appointed for the purpose of winding up the affairs of the company and distributing the property.

(4.) The company, in general meeting, shall appoint such persons or person as the company thinks fit to be liquidators or a liquidator, and may fix the remuneration to be paid to them or to him, and they shall give such security as the contributories or the court may determine.

(5.) If one person only is appointed, all the provisions herein contained in reference to several liquidators shall apply to him.

(6.) Upon the appointment of liquidators, all powers of the directors shall cease, except in so far as the company in general meeting, or the liquidators, may sanction the continuance of such powers.

(7.) Where several liquidators are appointed, every power hereby given may be exercised by such one or more of them as may be determined at the time of the appointment, or at a subsequent meeting, or in default of such determination, by any number not less than two.

(8.) The contributories may at any meeting appoint one or more Inspector or Inspectors, to superintend and direct the proceedings of the Liquidator in the management and winding up of the estate; and in case of an Inspector being appointed, all the powers of the Liquidator shall be exercised subject to the advice and direction of the Inspectors; and the contributories may also at any subsequent meeting held for that purpose, revoke any such appointment; and upon such revocation, or in case of death, resignation or absence from the Province of an Inspector, may appoint another in his stead; and such Inspector may be paid such remuneration as the contributories may determine; and where anything is allowed or directed to be done by the Inspectors, it may or shall be done by the sole inspector, if only one has been appointed.

270 Cap. 5. *Winding up Joint Stock Companies.* 41 Vic.

(9). The contributories may, at any meeting, pass any resolution or order, directing the liquidator how to dispose of the property, real or personal, of the company; and in default of their doing so, the liquidator shall be subject to the directions, orders and instructions which he from time to time receives from the Inspectors, if any, with regard to the mode, terms and conditions on which he may dispose of the whole or any part of the property of the company.

GENERAL POWERS OF LIQUIDATORS.

9. The liquidator may be described in all proceedings by the style of "A.B., the liquidator of" (the particular company in respect of which he is appointed), and shall have power to do the following things:

1. To bring or defend any action, suit or other legal proceeding in the name, and on behalf of, the company;

2. To carry on the business of the company so far as may be necessary for the beneficial winding up of the same;

3. To sell the real and personal property of the company by public auction or private contract, according to the ordinary mode in which such sales are made, with power to transfer the whole property to any person or company, or to sell the same in parcels, and on such terms as shall seem most advantageous; but no sale of the assets *en bloc* shall be made without the previous sanction of the contributories given at a meeting called for that purpose;

4. And in case, after having acted with due diligence in the collection of the debts, the liquidator finds that there remain debts due, the attempt to collect which would be more onerous than beneficial to the estate, he shall report the same to the contributories or inspectors (if any); and, with their sanction, he may sell the same by public auction, after such advertisement thereof as they may order; and pending such advertisements, the liquidator shall keep a list of the debts to be sold, open to inspection at his office, and shall also give free access to all documents and vouchers explanatory of such debts; but all debts amounting to more than one hundred dollars shall be sold separately, except as herein otherwise provided;

5. To draw, accept, make, and endorse any bill of exchange or promissory note in the name and on behalf of the company; and to raise upon the security of the assets of the company, from time to time, any requisite sum or sums of money; and the drawing, accepting, making or endorsing of any such bill of exchange or promissory note as aforesaid, on behalf of the company, shall have the same effect, with respect to the liability of the company, as if such bill or note had been drawn, accepted, made or endorsed by or on behalf of such company in the course of carrying on the business thereof:

6. To take out if necessary, in his official name, letters of administration to any deceased contributory; and to do in his official name any other act which may be necessary for obtaining payment of any money due from a contributory or from his estate, and which act cannot be conveniently done in the name of the company; and in all cases

where he takes out letters of administration, or otherwise uses his official name, for obtaining payment of any money due from a contributory, such money shall, for the purpose of enabling him to take out such letters or recover such money, be deemed to be due to the liquidator himself;

7. To execute in the name of the company all deeds, receipts and other documents;

8. And to do and exercise all other acts and things that may be necessary for the winding up of the affairs of the company and the distribution of its assets; and for such purposes to use when necessary the Company's seal.

10. The liquidator may fix a certain day or certain days on or within which creditors of the Company and others having claims thereon are to send in their claims.

2. Where a liquidator has given such or the like notices of the said day as would be given by the Court of Chancery in an administration suit for creditors and others to send in to an executor or administrator their claims against the estate of a testator or intestate, the liquidator shall, at the expiration of the time named in the said notices, or the last of the said notices, for sending in such claims, be at liberty to distribute the assets of the Company, or any part thereof, amongst the parties entitled thereto, having regard to the claims of which the liquidator has then notice; and the liquidator shall not be liable for the assets or any part thereof so distributed to any person of whose claim such liquidator had not notice at the time of distributing the said assets or a part thereof, as the case may be: but nothing in the present Act contained, shall prejudice the right of any creditor or claimant to follow assets into the hands of the person who may have received the same.

11. The liquidators may, with the sanction of an extraordinary resolution of the company, make such compromise or other arrangement as the liquidators deem expedient, with any creditors, or persons claiming to be creditors, or persons having or alleging to have any claim, present or future, certain or contingent, ascertained or sounding only in damages, against the Company, or whereby the Company may be rendered liable.

12. The liquidators may, with the sanction of an extraordinary resolution of the Company, compromise all calls and liabilities to calls, debts, and liabilities capable of resulting in debts, and all claims, whether present or future, certain or contingent, ascertained or sounding only in damages, subsisting or supposed to subsist between the company and any contributory or other debtor or person apprehending liability to the company, and all questions in any way relating to or affecting the assets of the Company or the winding up of the Company, upon the receipt of such sums, payable at such times, and generally upon such terms, as may be agreed upon; with power for the liquidators to take any security for the discharge of such debts or liabilities, and to give a complete discharge in respect of all or any such calls, debts or liabilities.

13. Where any company is supposed to be or is in the course of

being wound up, and the whole or a portion of its business or property is proposed to be transferred or sold to another company, the liquidators of the first mentioned company, with the sanction of a special resolution of the company by whom they were appointed conferring either a general authority on the liquidators or an authority in respect of any particular arrangement, can receive, in compensation or in part compensation for such transfer or sale, shares or other like interest in such other company, for the purpose of distribution amongst the members of the company which is being wound up, or may, in lieu of receiving cash, shares or other like interests, or in addition thereto, participate in the profits of or receive any other benefit from the purchasing company.

(2.) Any sale made or arrangement entered into by the liquidators in pursuance of this section shall be binding on the members of the Company which is being wound up, subject to this proviso, that if any member of the Company which is being wound up, who has not voted in favor of the special resolution passed by the Company of which he is a member, at either of the meetings held for passing the same, expresses his dissent from any such special resolution, in writing, addressed to the liquidators or one of them, and left at the head office of the Company not later than seven days after the date of the meeting at which such special resolution was passed, such dissentient member may require the liquidators to do one of the following things as the liquidators may prefer, that is to say: (1) Either to abstain from carrying such resolution into effect; or (2) to purchase the interest held by such dissentient member, at a price to be determined in manner hereinafter mentioned, such purchase-money to be paid before the Company is dissolved, and to be raised by the liquidators in such manner as may be determined by special resolution.

(3.) No special resolution shall be deemed invalid for the purposes of this section by reason that it is passed antecedently to or concurrently with any resolution for winding up the Company, or for appointing liquidators;

(4.) The price to be paid for the purchase of the interest of any dissentient member may be determined by agreement; but if the parties dispute about the same, such dispute shall be settled by arbitration;

(5.) For the purpose of such arbitration the liquidator shall appoint one arbitrator, and the dissentient member shall appoint another, and the two arbitrators thus chosen (or in case they disagree, the county judge) shall appoint a third arbitrator;

(6.) The arbitrators thus chosen or any two of them, or the arbitrator of one party and an arbitrator appointed by the county judge (in case of the refusal or neglect of either party to appoint an arbitrator) shall finally determine the matter in dispute;

(7.) In case of the disagreement of two arbitrators, where two only are acting, they may appoint an umpire, whose award shall be conclusive.

LIABILITY OF CONTRIBUTORIES.

14. As soon as may be after the commencement of the winding up of a company, the liquidator shall settle a list of contributories.

2. Every shareholder or member of the company or his representative is liable to contribute the amount unpaid on his shares of the capital, or on his liability to the company or to its members or creditors, as the case may be, under the Act, charter, or instrument of incorporation of the company; and the amount which he is liable to contribute shall be deemed assets of the company, and to be a debt due to the company as payable may be directed or appointed under this Act.

3. Where a shareholder has transferred his shares under circumstances which do not by law free him from liability in respect thereof, or where he is by law liable to the company or its contributories or any of them to an amount beyond the amount unpaid on his shares, he shall be deemed a member of the company for the purposes of this Act, and shall be liable to contribute as aforesaid to the extent of his liabilities to the company or the contributories independently of this Act, and the amount which he is so liable to contribute shall be deemed assets and a debt as aforesaid.

4. The list of contributories shall distinguish between persons who are contributories as being representatives of or liable for others.

5. It shall not be necessary where the personal representative of any deceased contributory is placed on the list to add the heirs or devisees of such contributory; nevertheless such heirs or devisees may be added at any time afterwards.

6. Any list so settled shall be *prima facie* evidence of the liability of the persons named therein to be contributories.

15. The list of contributories may be settled by the Court, in which case the liquidator shall make out and leave at the chambers of the Judge a list of the contributories of the company; and such list shall be verified by the affidavit of the liquidator, and shall, so far as is practicable, state the respective addresses of, and the number of shares or extent of interest to be attributed to, each such contributory, and distinguish the several classes of contributories; and such list may from time to time, by leave of the Judge, be varied or added to by the liquidator.

2. Upon the list of contributories being left at the chambers of the Judge, the liquidator shall obtain an appointment for the Judge to settle the same, and shall give notice in writing of such appointment to every person included in the list, and stating in what character; and for what number of shares, or interest, such person is included in the list; and in case any variation in or addition to such list is at any time made by the liquidator, a similar notice in writing shall be given to every person to whom such variation or addition applies. All such notices shall be served four clear days before the day appointed to settle such list, or such variation or addition.

3. The result of the settlement of the list of contributories shall be stated in a certificate by the Clerk of the Court; and certificates may be made from time to time for the purpose of stating the result of such settlement down to any particular time, or to any particular person, or stating any variation of the list.

16. If any person made a contributory as personal representative of a deceased contributory makes default in paying any sum to be paid by him, proceedings may be taken for administering the personal and real estate of such deceased contributory, or either of such estates, and for compelling payment thereout of the money due.

17. The liquidators may, at any time and before they have ascertained the sufficiency of the assets of the company, call on all or any of the contributories, for the time being settled on the list of contributories to pay, to the extent of their liability, all or any sums the liquidators deem necessary to satisfy the debts and liabilities of the company, and the costs, charges and expenses of winding it up and for the adjustment of the rights of the contributories amongst themselves; and the liquidators may, in making a call, take into consideration the probability that some of the contributories upon whom the call is made, may partly or wholly fail to pay their respective portions of the same.

18. Where a person's name is on the list of contributories or is liable to be placed thereon, he shall be subject in respect of his liability, and on the application of the liquidator, to arrest and imprisonment, like any other debtor; and he shall for that purpose be deemed a debtor to the Company, and a debtor to the liquidator, and his arrest may be by an order of the County Court Judge, whether the amount of his liability exceeds or not the ordinary jurisdiction of the said court; and his being placed on the list of contributories under this Act shall be deemed a judgment, and the liquidator shall be deemed a creditor, within the meaning of the Act respecting Arrest and Imprisonment for Debt; and the said persons shall respectively have the same remedies, and the County Court and Judges and the officers of justice shall in such cases have the same powers and duties (as nearly as may be), as in corresponding cases under the said Act.

LIQUIDATOR'S DUTIES.

19. No Liquidator shall employ any counsel, solicitor, or attorney-at-law without the consent of the Inspectors, or of the contributories.

2. No Liquidator or Inspector shall purchase, directly or indirectly, any part of the stock in trade, debts or assets of any description of the estate.

3. The Liquidator shall deposit at interest in some chartered bank to be indicated by the Inspectors or by the Court all sums of money which he may have in his hands, belonging to the company, whenever such sums amount to one hundred dollars:

4. Such deposit shall not be made in the name of the liquidator generally, on pain of dismissal; but a separate deposit account shall be kept for the company of the moneys belonging to the company, in the name of the Liquidator as such, and of the Inspectors (if any); and such moneys shall be withdrawn only on the joint cheque of the Liquidator and one of the Inspectors, if there be any.

5. At every meeting of the contributories, the liquidators shall produce a bank pass book, showing the amount of deposits made for the company, the dates at which such deposits were made, the amounts

withdrawn and dates of such withdrawals; of which production mention shall be made in the minutes of such meeting, and the absence of such mention shall be *primâ facie* evidence that such pass-book was not produced at the meetings;

6. The Liquidator shall also produce such pass-book whenever so ordered by the Court at the request of the Inspectors or of a contributory, and on his refusal to do so, he shall be treated as being in contempt of court.

7. Every Liquidator or inspector shall be subject to the summary jurisdiction of the Court in the same manner and to the same extent as the ordinary officers of the Court are subject to its jurisdiction; and the performance of his duties may be compelled, and all remedies sought or demanded for enforcing any claim for a debt, privilege, mortgage, lien or right of property upon, in, or to any effects or property in the hands, possession or custody of a Liquidator, may be obtained by an order of the Court on summary petition, and not by any suit, attachment, seizure or other proceeding of any kind whatever; and obedience by the Liquidator to such order may be enforced by such Court under the penalty of imprisonment, as for contempt of Court or disobedience thereto; or he may be removed in the discretion of the Court.

EXPENSES.

20. All costs, charges and expenses properly incurred in the voluntary winding-up of a company, including the remuneration o the liquidators, shall be payable out of the assets of the company in priority to all other claims.

21. In case of there being no agreement or provision fixing the remuneration of a liquidator, he shall be entitled to a commission on the net proceeds of the estate of the company of every kind, after deducting expenses and disbursements, such commission to be of five per cent. on the amount realized, not exceeding one thousand dollars, the further sum of two and a half per cent. on the amount realized in excess of one thousand dollars, and not exceeding five thousand dollars, and a further sum of one and a quarter per cent. on the amount realized in excess of five thousand dollars; which said commission shall be in lieu of all fees and charges for his services.

MEETINGS OF CONTRIBUTORIES.

22. If any vacancy occurs in the office of liquidators appointed by the company, by death, resignation or otherwise, a general meeting for the purpose of filling up such vacancy may be convened by the continuing liquidators, if any, or if none, then by any contributory of the company;

(2.) The liquidators may from time to time, during the continuance of the winding up, summon general meetings of the company for the purpose of obtaining the sanction of the company to special resolution or extraordinary resolution, or for any other purposes they think fit;

(3.) In the event of the winding up continuing for more than one year, the liquidators shall summon a general meeting of the company, at the end of the first year, and of each succeeding year from the commencement of the winding-up, or as soon thereafter as may be convenient; and shall lay before such meeting an account, showing their acts and dealings, and the manner in which the winding-up has been conducted during the preceding year.

(4.) The liquidator shall also call meetings of the contributories whenever required in writing so to do, by the inspector or five contributories, or by the court, and he shall state succinctly in the notice calling any meeting the purpose thereof.

(5.) The contributories may, from time to time, at any meeting, determine where subsequent meetings shall be held ; and in the absence of such a resolution all meetings of the contributories shall be held at the office of the liqdidator or of the company, unless otherwise ordered by the court.

(6.) Notice of any meeting shall for the purposes of this Act be deemed to be duly given, and the meeting to be duly held, whenever such notice is given and meeting held in manner prescribed by the Act, charter or instrument of incorporation, or by the regulations of the Company, or by the Court; or,

(7.) Or, notice of the meeting may be given by publication thereof for at least two weeks in the *Ontario Gazette*, or by such other or additional notice as the court or the inspector or the company may direct, and by also, except where the court otherwise directs, addressing notices of the meeting to the contributories within the Province, of contributories who reside out of the Province; and the said notices shall be posted at least ten days before the day on which the meeting is to take place, the postage being prepaid by the liquidator.

(8.) No contributory shall vote at any meeting unless present personally, or represented by some person having a written authority (to be filed with the liquidator) to act on his behalf at the meeting or generally; and when a poll is taken reference shall be had to the number of votes to which each member is entitled by the Act, charter or instrument of incorporation or the regulations of the company.

ASSISTANCE OF THE COURT.

23. The liquidators or any contributory of the company may apply to the Court to determine any question arising in the matter of such winding-up; or to exercise all or any of the powers following; and the Court, if satisfied that the determination of such question, or the required exercise of power, will be just and beneficial, may accede wholly or partially to such application, on such terms and subject to such conditions as the Court thinks fit; or it may make such other order on such application as the Court thinks just.

2. The Court, at any time after the presentation of a petition for winding up a company and before making an order for winding up the company, may restrain further proceedings in any action, suit, or proceeding against the company (other than under the Insolvent Acts in

force at the time, or any other authority with which this Legislature has no jurisdiction) in and upon such terms as the Court thinks fit.

3. The Court may make an order that no suit, action or other proceeding shall be proceeded with or commenced against the company except with the leave of the Court, and subject to such terms as the Court may impose; but this section does not apply to proceedings under any Act of the Parliament of Canada under its jurisdiction in matters of bankruptcy and insolvency or otherwise; a copy of such order shall forthwith be advertised as the Court may direct.

4. The Court may settle the list of contributories.

5. The Court may direct meetings of the contributories to be summoned, held and conducted in such manner as the Court thinks fit, for the purpose of ascertaining their wishes, and may appoint a person to act as chairman of any such meeting, and to report the result of such meeting to the Court.

6. The Court may require any contributory for the time being settled on the list of contributories, or any trustee, receiver, banker, or agent or officer of the company, to pay, deliver, convey, surrender or transfer forthwith, or within such time as the court directs, to or into the hands of the liquidator, any sum or balance, books, papers, estate, or effects which happen to be in his hands for the time being, and to which the company is *prima facie* entitled.

7. The Court may make an order on any contributory for the time being settled on the list of contributories, directing payment to be made, in manner in the said order mentioned, of any moneys due from him or from the estate of the person whom he represents, to the company, exclusive of any moneys which he or the estate of the person whom he represents may be liable to contribute by virtue of any call made or to be made by the Court in pursuance of this Act.

8. The Court may order any contributory, purchaser or other person from whom money is due to the company to pay the same into any bank appointed for this purpose in any general order made under this Act, or in default of such bank into any bank named in the order, or into any branch of such bank, to the account of the official liquidator instead of to the official liquidator, and such order may be enforced in the same manner as if it had directed payment to the official liquidator.

9. Any order made by the Court in pursuance of this Act upon any contributory shall, subject to the provisions herein contained for appealing against such order, be conclusive evidence that the moneys, if any, thereby appearing to be due, or ordered to be paid, are due; and all other pertinent matters stated in such order are to be taken to be truly stated, as against all persons, and in all proceedings whatsoever, with the exception of proceedings taken against the real estate of any deceased contributory, in which case such order shall only be *prima facie* evidence for the purpose of charging his real estate, unless his heirs or devisees were on the list of contributories at the time the order was made.

10. The Court may make such order for the inspection by the

creditors and contributories of the company of its books and papers as the Court thinks just; and any books and papers in the possession of the company may be inspected in conformity with the order of the Court, but not further or otherwise.

11. The Court may, at any time after the commencement of the winding up of the company, summon to appear before the Court or liquidator any officer of the company, or any other person known or suspected to have in his possession any of the estate or effects of the Company, or supposed to be indebted to the Company, or any person whom the Court may deem capable of giving information concerning the trade, dealings, estate or effects of the Company; and in case of refusal to appear or answer the questions submitted, he may be committed and punished by the judge as for a contempt.

12. The Court may require any such officer or person to produce any books, papers, deeds, writings, or other documents in his custody or power relating to the company.

13. If any person so summoned, after being tendered the fees to which a witness is entitled in the county courts, refuses to come before the Court or liquidator at the time appointed, having no lawful impediment, the Court may cause such person to be apprehended, and brought before the Court or liquidator for examination.

14. The Court or liquidator may examine upon oath, any person appearing, or brought before them in the manner aforesaid concerning the affairs, dealings, estate or effects of company, and may reduce into writing the answers of every such person, and require him to subscribe the same.

15. In any proceeding under this Act, the Court may order a writ of *subpœna ad testificandum*, or of *subpœna duces tecum* to issue, commanding the attendance as a witness of any person within the limits of Ontario.

16. Where any person claims any lien on papers, deeds, or writings or documents produced by him, such production shall be without prejudice to the lien; and the Court shall have jurisdiction in the winding up to determine all questions relating to such lien.

17. Where in the course of winding up any company under this Act, it appears that any past or present director, manager, official or or other liquidator, or any officer of such company has misapplied, or retained in his own hands, or become liable or accountable for any moneys of the company, or been guilty of any misfeasance or breach of trust in relation to the company, the Court may, on the application of any liquidator, or of any contributory of the company, notwithstanding that the offence is one for which the offender is criminally responsible, examine into the conduct of such director, manager, or other officer, and compel him to repay any moneys so misapplied or retained, or for which he has become liable or accountable, together with interest after such rate as the Court thinks just, or to contribute such sums of money to the assets of the company by way of compensation in respect of such misapplication, retainer, misfeasance, or breach of trust, as the Court thinks just.

24. If at any time any contributor who desires to cause any proceeding to be taken which, in his opinion, would be for the benefit of the Company, and the liquidator, under the authority of the contributories or of the inspectors, refuses or neglects to take such proceedings, after being duly required so to do, such contributory shall have the right to obtain an order of the Court authorizing him to take such proceeding in the name of the liquidator or company, but at his own expense and risk, upon such terms and conditions as to indemnity to the liquidator as the Court may prescribe; and thereupon any benefit derived from such proceeding shall belong exclusively to the contributory instituting the same for his benefit, and that of any other contributory who may have joined him in causing the institution of such proceeding; but if, before such order is granted, the liquidator shall signify to the Court his readiness to institute such proceeding for the benefit of the Company, an order shall be made prescribing the time within which he shall do so, and in that case the advantage derived from such proceeding shall appertain to the Company.

25. If any vacancy occurs in the office of liquidator appointed by the company, by death, resignation or otherwise, the company in general meeting may fill up such vacancy;

2. If from any cause there is no liquidator acting, either provisionally or otherwise, the Court may on the application of a contributory, appoint a liquidator or liquidators;

3. The Court may also on due cause shown, remove any liquidator and appoint another liquidator;

4. When there is no liquidator the estate shall be under the control of the Court until the appointment of a new liquidator.

26. Any one or more contributories whose claims in the aggregate exceed five hundred dollars, who may be dissatisfied with the resolutions adopted or orders made by the contributories or the Inspectors, or with any action of the liquidator for the disposal of the property of the company, or any part thereof, or for postponing the disposal of the same, or with reference to any matter connected with the management or winding up of the estate, may, within four clear days after the meeting of the contributories, in case the subject of dissatisfaction is a resolution or order of the contributories, or within four clear days after becoming aware or having notice of the resolution of the inspectors or action of the liquidator where such resolution or action is the subject of dissatisfaction, give to the liquidator notice that he or they will apply to the Court, on the day and at the hour fixed by such notice, and not being later than four clear days after such notice has been given, or as soon thereafter as the parties may be heard before such Court, to rescind such resolutions or orders;

2. The Court, after hearing the inspectors, the liquidators and contributories present at the time and place so fixed, may approve, rescind or modify the said resolutions or orders;

3. In case of the application being refused the party applying shall pay all costs occasioned thereby, and in other cases the costs and expenses shall be at the discretion of the Court.

27. Any party who is dissatisfied with any order or decision of the Court in any proceeding under this Act may appeal therefrom to the Court of Appeal, or to any one of the Judges of the said Court; but any appeal to a single Judge may, in his discretion, be referred, on a special case to be settled, to the full Court, and on such terms in the meantime as he may think necessary and just.

2. No such appeal shall be entertained unless the appellant has, within eight days from the rendering of such final order or judgment, taken proceedings on the said appeal, nor unless within the said time he has made a deposit or given sufficient security before a Judge that he will duly prosecute the said appeal and pay such damages and costs as may be awarded to the respondent.

3. If the party appellant does not proceed with his appeal, as the case may be, according to the law or the rules of practice, the Court, on the application of the respondent, may dismiss the appeal, and condemn the appellant to pay the respondent the costs by him incurred.

4. The judgment of the said Court of Appeal shall be final.

28. Any powers by this Act conferred on the Court shall be deemed to be in addition to, and not in restriction of, any other powers subsisting, either at law or in equity, of instituting proceedings against any contributory, or against any debtor of the company for the recovery of any call or other sums due from such contributory, or against any debtor of the company, for the recovery of any call or other sum due from such contributory or debtor, or his estate, and such proceedings may be instituted accordingly.

29. All orders made by the Court may be enforced in the same manner as orders of such Court made in any suit pending therein, or orders of the Court under the Insolvent Acts in force at the time may be enforced; and for the purposes of this part of the Act, the County Courts and the judges thereof shall, in addition to their ordinary powers, have the same power of enforcing any orders made by it, as the Court of Chancery has in relation to matters within the jurisdiction of that Court; and for the last-mentioned purposes the jurisdiction of the County Court Judge shall be deemed to be co-extensive in local limits with the jurisdiction of the Court of Chancery.

30. The various County Courts of the Province, and the Judges of the said Courts respectively shall be auxiliary to one another for the purposes of this Act; and the winding up of a company, or any matter or proceeding relating thereto, may be transferred from one County Court to another with the concurrence, or by the order or orders, of the two courts, or by an order of a judge of the Court of Appeal.

MATTERS OF PRACTICE.

31. Where any order made by one Court is required to be enforced by another Court, an office copy of the order so made, certified by the clerk of the court which made the same, and under the seal of such Court, shall be produced to the proper officer of the Court required to enforce the same, and the production of such copy shall be sufficient evidence of such order having been made; and thereupon such last-mentioned Court shall take such steps in the matter as may be requisite for enforcing such order in the same manner as if it were the order of the Court enforcing the same.

82. Any application to the Court for winding up of a company under this Act shall be by petition; and the petition may be presented by the company, or by any contributory or contributories of the company.

(2) Upon hearing the petition the Court may dismiss the same, with or without costs, or may adjourn the hearing, conditionally or unconditionally, and may make an interim order, or any other order that it deems just.

83. The Court at any time after an order has been made for winding up a company, may, upon the application by motion of any contributory, and upon proof to the satisfaction of the Court that all proceedings in relation to such winding up ought to be stayed, make an order staying the same, either altogether or for a limited time, on such terms and subject to such conditions as the Court deems fit.

84. The rules of procedure for the time being as to amendments of pleadings and proceedings in the County Court, shall as far as practicable apply to all pleadings and proceedings under this Act; and any Court or liquidator before whom such proceedings are being carried on shall have full power and authority to apply the appropriate rules as to amendments to the proceedings so pending before him; and no pleading or proceeding shall be void by reason of any irregularity or default which can or may be amended or disregarded under the rules and practice of the Court.

85. In every petition, application, motion, or other pleading or proceeding under this Act, the parties may state the facts upon which they rely, in plain and concise language; and to the interpretation thereof, the rules of construction applicable to such language in the ordinary transactions of life shall apply.

86. All books, accounts, and documents of the company and of the liquidator, shall, as between the contributories of the company, be *primâ facie* evidence of the truth of all matters purporting to be therein recorded.

87. All rules, writs of subpœna, orders and warrants issued by any Court in any matter or proceeding under this Act, may be validly served in any part of Ontario upon the party affected or to be affected thereby, and the service of them may be validly made in such manner as is now prescribed for similar services, and the person charged with such service shall make his return thereof under oath.

88. Except when otherwise provided, four clear juridical days' notice of any petition, motion, order or rule shall be sufficient; and service of such notice shall be made in such manner as a similar service in a civil suit.

39. Any affidavit, affirmation or declaration required to be sworn or made under the provisions or for the purposes of this Act, may be sworn or made in Ontario, before the liquidator, or before any liquidator, judge, notary public, commissioner for taking affidavits, or Justice of the Peace; and out of Ontario, before any Judge of a Court of Record, any commissioner for taking affidavits to be used in any Court in Canada, any notary public, the chief municipal officer for any town or city, any British consul or vice-consul, or any person authorized by or under any Statute of the Dominion or of this Province to take affidavits.

2. All Courts, judges, justices, commissioners and persons acting judicially, shall take judicial notice of the seal, or stamp or signature (as the case may be) of any such Court, judge, notary public, commissioner, justice, chief municipal officer, consul, vice-consul, liquidator or other person, attached, appended or subscribed to any such affidavit, affirmation or declaration, or to any other document to be used for the purposes of this Act.

DISSOLUTION OF COMPANY.

40. As soon as the affairs of the company are fully wound up, the liquidators shall make up an account showing the manner in which such winding up has been conducted, and the property of the company disposed of; and thereupon they shall call a general meeting of the company for the purpose of having the account laid before them, and hearing any explanation that may be given by the liquidators; the meeting shall be called by advertisement, specifying the time, place, and object of such meeting; and the advertisement shall be published one month at least previously thereto.

(2.) The liquidator shall make a return to the Provincial Secretary of such meeting having been held, and of the date at which the same was held; which return shall be filed in the office of the Provincial Secretary; and on the expiration of three months from the date of the filing of such return, the company shall be deemed to be dissolved.

41. Or whenever the affairs of the company have been completely wound up, the Court may make an order that the company be dissolved from the date of such order, and the company shall be dissolved accordingly: which order shall be reported by the liquidator to the Provincial Secretary.

42. If the Liquidator makes default in transmitting to the Provincial Secretary the return mentioned in the fortieth section, or in reporting the order (if any) declaring the company dissolved, he shall be liable to a penalty not exceeding twenty dollars for every day during which he is in default.

43. All dividends deposited in a Bank and remaining unclaimed at the time of the dissolution of the Company, shall be left for three years in the bank where they are deposited, and if still unclaimed, shall then be paid over by such Bank, with interest accrued thereon, to the Treasurer of Ontario, and, if afterwards duly claimed, shall be paid over to the persons entitled thereto.

44. Every liquidator shall, within thirty days after the date of the dissolution of the company, deposit in the bank appointed or named as hereinbefore provided for, any other money belonging to the estate then in his hands not required for any other purpose authorized by this Act, with a sworn statement and account of such money, and that the same is all he has in his hands; and he shall be subject to a penalty of not exceeding ten dollars for every day on which he neglects or delays such payment; and he shall be a debtor to Her Majesty for such money, and may be compelled as such to account for and pay over the same.

(2.) The money so deposited shall be left for three years in the bank, and shall be then paid over with interest to the Treasurer of the Province, and if afterwards claimed shall be paid over to the person entitled thereto.

(3.) Where any company has been wound up under this Act and is about to be dissolved, the books, accounts and documents of the company and of the Liquidators may be disposed of in such a way as the Company by an extraordinary resolution directs.

(4.) After the lapse of five years from the date of such dissolution no responsibility shall rest on the Company or the Liquidators, or any one to whom the custody of such books, accounts and documents has been committed, by reason that the same or any of them cannot be made forthcoming to any party or parties claiming to be interested therein.

RULES TO CARRY OUT ACT.

45. The Board of County Judges from time to time shall make, and frame and settle the forms, rules and regulations to be followed and observed in proceedings under this Act, and shall make rules as to the costs, fees and charges which shall or may be had, taken or paid in all such cases by or to attorneys, solicitors or counsel, and by or to officers of courts, whether for the officers or for the Crown, and by or to sheriffs, or other persons whom it may be necessary to provide for, or for any service performed or work done under this Act.

(2.) The Board of County Judges or any three of them, shall under their hands, certify to the Chief Justice of the Court of Appeal, all Rules and Forms made under this Act and the Judges of the said Court (of whom the said Chief Justice shall be one) may approve of, disallow, or amend any such Rules or forms; and the Rules and Forms so approved of (with or without amendment, as the case may be) shall have the same force and effect as if they had been made and included in this Act.

(3.) Until such forms, rules and regulations are so approved and subject to any which shall be approved, the practice under this Act shall in cases not hereinbefore provided for, be the same (as nearly as may be), as under the Insolvent Acts for the time being in force in this Province.

CHAP. XX.

An Act to give Mortgagees certain powers now commonly inserted in Mortgages.

Section.
1. Powers incident to mortgages.
2. Receipts for purchase money sufficient discharges.
3. Notice before sale.
4. Improper sale not to defeat title of purchaser.
5. Form of notice.
6. Registration of notice.

Section.
7. Affidavit for registration; certified copy of registered notice to be evidence.
8. Application of purchase money.
9. Conveyance to the purchaser.
10. Owner of charge may call for title deeds and conveyance of legal estate.
11. Taxation of costs.
12. Provisions as to sale, etc., not to apply in certain cases.

[*Assented to* 11th *March,* 1879.]

HER Majesty, by and with the advice and consent of the Legislative Assembly of the Province of Ontario, enacts as follows:—

1. Where any principal money is secured or charged by deed hereafter executed on any hereditaments of any tenure, or on any interest therein, the person to whom such money shall, for the time being, be payable, his executors, administrators and assigns, shall, at any time after the expiration of six months from the time when such principal money shall have become payable, according to the terms of the deed, or after any interest on such principal money shall have been in arrear for six months, or after any omission to pay any premium or any insurance which, by the terms of the deed, ought to be paid by the person entitled to the property subject to the charge, have the following powers, to the same extent (but no more) as if they had been in terms conferred by the person creating the charge, namely:

1. A power to sell, or concur with any other person in selling, the whole or any part of the property by public auction or private contract, subject to any reasonable conditions he may think fit to make, and to rescind or vary contracts for sale, or buy in and re-sell the property, from time to time, in like manner.

2. A power to insure, and keep insured, from loss or damage by fire, the whole or any part of the property (whether affixed to the freehold or not) which is in its nature insurable, and to add the premiums paid for any such insurance to the principal money secured at the same rate of interest.

2. Receipts for purchase money given by the person or persons exercising the power of sale hereby conferred, shall be sufficient discharges to the purchaser, who shall not be bound to see to the application of such purchase money.

3. No such sale as aforesaid shall be made until after three months' notice in writing has been given to any subsequent encumbrancer, and to the person entitled to the property subject to the charge and to such encumbrance, the notice to be given either personally or at his usual or last place of residence in this Province, which notice may be given at any time after any default in making a payment provided for by the deed.

(2.) In case of the death of the person entitled subject to the charge, and of his interest therein passing to infant heirs or devisees, the notice shall be given as aforesaid to his executors or administrators, as well as to his heirs or devisees, as the case may be.

(3.) The notice for an infant heir is to be served upon his guardian, and is also to be served upon the infant himself, if over the age of twelve years.

4. But when a sale has been effected in professed exercise of the powers hereby conferred, the title of the purchaser shall not be liable to be impeached on the ground that no case had arisen to authorize the exercise of such power, or that such power has been improperly or irregularly exercised, or that no such notice as aforesaid has been given; but any person damnified by any such unauthorized, improper, or irregular exercise of such power, shall have his remedy against the person selling.

5. The notice of sale may be in the following form or to the following effect:

I hereby require you on or before the   day of   18   , (*a day not less than three calendar months from the service of the notice, and not less than six calendar months after the default*) to pay off the principal money and interest secured by a certain indenture, dated the   day of   18   and expressed to be made between (*here state parties and describe mortgage property*) which said mortgage was registered on the   day of   (*and if the mortgage has been assigned, add:* and has since become the property of the undersigned). And I hereby give you notice that the amount due on the said mortgage for principal, interest, and costs respectively, is as follows: (*set the same forth*).

And unless the said principal money and interest and costs are paid on or before the said   day of   I shall sell the property comprised in the said indenture under the authority of the Act entitled "An Act to give to mortgagees certain powers now commonly inserted in mortgages." Dated the   day of   18   .

6. The notice of sale of lands may be registered in the registry office of the registration division in which the lands are situate, in the same manner as any other instrument affecting the land, and such registration shall have the same effect, and the duties of the registrar in respect of the same shall be as in the case of any other registered instrument, and the fee to be paid such registrar for registering the same shall be fifty cents.

7. The affidavit for the purpose of registering the notice shall be by the person who served the same, and shall prove the time, place, and manner of such service, and also that the copy delivered to the registrar is a true copy of the notice served.

(2.) A copy of any such registered notice and affidavit, certified under the hand and seal of office of the registrar, shall in all cases be received as *prima facie* evidence of the facts therein stated.

8. The money arising by any sale effected as aforesaid shall be applied by the person receiving the same as follows: first, in payment of all the expenses incident to the sale or incurred in any attempted sale; secondly, in discharge of all interest and costs then due in respect of the charge in consequence whereof the sale was made; and thirdly, in discharge of all the principal moneys then due in respect of such charge; and the residue of such money shall be paid to the subsequent encumbrancers according to their priorities, and the balance to the person entitled to the property subject to the charge, his heirs, executors, administrators, or assigns, as the case may be.

9. The person exercising the power of sale hereby conferred shall have power by deed to convey or assign to and vest in the purchaser the property sold, for all the estate and interest therein, which the person who created the charge had power to dispose of.

10. At any time after the power of sale hereby conferred shall have become exercisable, the person entitled to exercise the same shall be entitled to demand and recover, from the person entitled to the property subject to the charge, all the deeds and documents in his possession or power relating to the same property, or to the title thereto, which he would have been entitled to demand and recover if the same property had been conveyed, appointed, surrendered, or assigned to and were then vested in him for all the estate and interest which the person creating the charge had power to dispose of; and where the legal estate shall be outstanding in a trustee, the person entitled to a charge created by a person equitably entitled, or any purchaser from such person, shall be entitled to call for a conveyance of the legal estate to the same extent as the person creating the charge could have called for such a conveyance if the charge had not been made.

11. The mortgagee's costs may, without any order, be taxed by the Master in Chancery or Local Master, at the instance of any party interested.

12. So much of this Act as provides for a power to sell shall not apply in the case of a deed which contains a power of sale; and so much of this Act as provides a power to insure shall not apply in the case of a deed which contains a power to insure, nor shall this Act apply to any deed which contains a declaration that this Act is not to apply thereto.

CAP. LI.

An Act respecting the Credit Foncier Franco-Canadien.

Section.
Preamble.
1. Powers to be exercised by Credit Foncier in Ontario.
2. Security to be taken.
3. Power to form divisions of Province for purposes of business.
4. Branch offices.

Section.
5. Corporation may sue and be sued in Ontario.
6. Appointment and duties of managers.
7. Official seal.
8. President to execute a procuration to manager to act for corporation.
9. Power to acquire real estate necessary for offices

[Assented to 4th March, 1881.]

WHEREAS the Credit Foncier Franco-Canadien, incorporated by the statute of the Legislature of the Province of Quebec, passed in the 43rd and 44th year of Her Majesty's reign, and chaptered sixty, has prayed that the power of transacting the business of loaning money or otherwise, in the Province of Ontario, be conferred upon it; and it is expedient to grant the prayer of the said petition;

Therefore Her Majesty, by and with the advice and consent of the Legislative Assembly of the Province of Ontario, enacts as follows:—

1. It shall be lawful for the corporation created and constituted under the name of Credit Foncier Franco-Canadien, by the statute of the Legislature of the Province of Quebec, cited in the preamble hereto, to exercise the powers hereinafter mentioned in the Province of Ontario;

(1) To lend money as a first charge on bond and mortgage on real estate situate within the Province of Ontario, repayable either at long date by annuities or at short date, with or without progressive sinking of the debt;

(2) To lend money upon the hypothecation of bonds and mortgages, being a first charge on real estate situate within the Province of Ontario, repayable either at long date by annuities or at short date, with or without progressive sinking of the debt;

(3) To lend on mortgage or otherwise to municipal or school corporation in the Province of Ontario, such sums of money as they may be authorized to borrow, repayable either at long date by annuities or at short date, with or without progressive sinking of the debt;

(4) To acquire by assignment, bonds and mortgages being a first charge upon real estate situate in the Province of Ontario;

(5) To purchase bonds or debentures issued by municipal or school corporations in the Province of Ontario, and by incorporated companies doing business in the Province, and to sell the same if deemed advisable;

(6) To make loans upon or purchase public securities of this Province, and sell the same if deemed advisable.

2. The said corporation shall accept as security only real estate of which the revenues are deemed sufficient;

(1) The amount of each loan shall not exceed one half of the estimated value of the real estate mortgaged therefor, and the annuity which the borrower may oblige himself to pay shall not exceed the net revenue which it may be estimated that the property might yield;

(2) The valuation of property offered as security shall be made on the double basis of the net revenue which it is susceptible of yielding and of the price which it would bring if sold.

3. For the transaction of the business of the said corporation the board of management provided for by the said statute of the Legislature of the Province of Quebec, may, if it deems proper, divide the Province of Ontario into two or more divisions, and may subsequently re-divide such divisions and form others.

4. A branch office or agency may be established in the city of Toronto, and at such other places in the Province of Ontario as the said board of management may deem advisable.

5. The said corporation may sue and be sued, complain and defend, in any court of law or equity in the Province of Ontario;

(1) Service of process may be made upon the said corporation at its branch offices or agencies in the Province of Ontario; and if the corporation have no known branch office or agency in the Province, then, upon return to that effect, the Court may order service by publication, by a notice to be given for one month in the *Ontario Gazette*, and such publication shall be held to be due service upon the said corporation.

6. A manager or agent may be appointed to administer the affairs of the said corporation in the Province of Ontario, or in any division thereof which may be established by the said board of management, and when a manager is appointed he shall have the powers conferred and be subject to the obligations imposed upon managers by the statute constituting the said corporation, except as otherwise by this Act provided.

7. Such corporation may commit to the custody of such manager or agent for the time being, an official seal for the purpose of executing in this Province, such deeds and instruments as may be necessary in carrying out the objects of the corporation therein; and such seal, from time to time, may withdraw, alter or renew, and such seal shall be deemed and taken to be the corporate seal of such corporation for the execution of all instruments within this Province, and every deed, conveyance, lease, assignment of mortgage, discharge of mortgage or other written instrument of any kind purporting to be under the corporate seal of the said corporation, or under the aforesaid official seal entrusted to such manager or agent, shall be receivable in evidence as *primâ facie* proof in any court of law or equity in any legal or equitable proceeding of a civil nature in this Province, and also for the purposes of the Registry Act," that such deed, conveyance, lease, assignment, of mortgage, discharge of mortgage, or other written instrument has been duly executed by such corporation, without any further proof of the said corporate or official seal, or of either of them, or of the appointment, official character, or signature of the person or persons purporting to have affixed such seal or seals, or to have acted as such manager or agent.

8. The president of said corporation shall, after the appointment of any such manager, execute in duplicate a procuration countersigned by the secretary of said corporation, authorizing such manager to act within the limits of his powers, for and in the name of the corporation;

(1) A duplicate of the procuration shall be deposited in the office of the Provincial Secretary, and the latter shall give notice in the *Ontario Gazette* of such appointment, and of the deposit of the procuration;

(2) All registrars and all Courts in the Province of Ontario shall after such notice, receive all deeds passed by the manager within the limits of his powers, and before the publication in the *Ontario Gazette* of a notice of the revocation of the procuration, as sufficient, without requiring any proof of his power to act.

9. The said corporation may acquire and hold such real estate as may be necessary for its offices for the transaction of its business in the Province of Ontario, but the value of the real estate acquired for such purpose, shall not at any time exceed the sum of one hundred thousand dollars: it may, from time to time, lease, mortgage, sell or otherwise dispose of such real estate; it may also, for the protection of its investments, purchase and hold real estate mortgaged in its favor, but it shall sell, or otherwise dispose of, such real estate so acquired in payment, or for the protection of its claims, within seven years from the acquisition thereof; meantime it may, from time to time, mortgage or lease the real estate so acquired and held.

CHAP. XXI.

An Act respecting returns required from Incorporated Companies.

Section.	Section.
1. No action for default in making return to be brought after receipt of return by proper officer; proviso.	3. When R. S. O., c. 150, s. 49, not to apply.
2. Limitation of amount of penalty.	4. "Return"—meaning of.

[*Assented to 4th March*, 1881.]

HER MAJESTY, by and with the advice and consent of the Legislative Assembly of the province of Ontario, enacts as follows:—

1. No action brought against any incorporated company which is required, or whose directors or officers are required, to make a return to the Government of Ontario, or to any officer or department thereof, or brought against any director or officer of such company, either under the provisions of the "Ontario Joint Stock Companies' Letters Patent Act," or under any other Act, for not duly making a return in accordance with the requirements of any such Act, or for any default in respect of the mode of dealing with such return shall be maintained if such action is or was commenced subsequent to the receipt by the proper officer or department of the said Government of the return, for the non-making of which, or with reference to which such action is brought, or subsequent to the receipt by such officer or department of a return for a later year: Provided the return made is, except in respect of the time at which the same is made, in substantial compliance with the requirements of the Act under which it is or was made as aforesaid, and is duly verified in accordance with the provisions of such Act, unless such action is brought by the Crown, or by the Attorney-General of Ontario sueing on behalf the Crown.

2. The entire amount of the penalty or penalties to be recovered against any company, or the directors or officers thereof, in respect of any default or defaults in complying with any of the requirements of the forty-ninth section of the said Ontario Joint Stock Companies' Letters Patent Act, or in complying with the requirements, in respect of the making of returns, of any other Act up to the time at which such action is brought shall not in the whole exceed one thousand dollars, and in case several actions are brought, either against the company or against its directors or officers, the court or a judge thereof may give such directions as may appear just, either for consolidating such actions or staying the later action or actions, or any of the said actions, upon such terms as may be deemed fitting, and so much of any Act as authorizes the recovery of any greater penalty is hereby repealed.

3. The forty-ninth section of the said Revised Statute shall not be held to apply or to have applied to any company until the first day of February next after the first thirty-first day of December, after such company has been organized, or has gone into actual operation, whichever shall first happen, and shall not be held to apply to any company which has ceased to carry on business ; and upon its being proved that any company to which this Act applies did not transact any business (other than the payment of taxes or the making of a return) during the year for which it is alleged a return in accordance with the requirements of law has not been made such company shall be deemed to have ceased to carry on business within the meaning of this section.

4. The word "Return" where used in this Act shall include any list, statement or other information required to be furnished to the Government of Ontario, or to any officer of department thereof, by any incorporated company.

CHAP. XVII.

An Act to confer additional powers upon Joint Stock Companies.

Section.
1. Short title.
2. Provisions as to companies authorized to act as trustee, etc.
3. Application of R. S. O., c. 150, ss. 65, 66.
4. Letters Patent for certain purposes may be granted to companies incorporated under special Acts.
5. Application of R. S. O., c. 150, ss. 17-19, and of 44 Vic. c. 18, s. 1.
6. Application of Second Part of Act.
7. Meaning of "special resolution."
8. Authority given by special resolution.
9. Resolution for reduction of capital.
10. Notice of resolution.
11. When resolution may be carried into effect.
12. Provision as to companies which have resolved on a reduction of capital before the passing of this Act.

Section.
13. Liability of officers for payments improperly made under resolution.
14. Liability of shareholders for moneys received under resolution.
15. Restriction on insurance companies, etc.
16. Distribution of assets by companies whose capital is not divided into shares.
17. Resolution to reduce par value of shares not to affect amount payable on such shares.
18. Notice of reduction of par value of shares.
19. Where capital reduced advertisements of company to state same as reduced.
20. R. S. O., c. 170, s. 1, repealed. Not less than ten persons may form a cemetery company.
21. Sec. 2, amended.
22. Winding up of cemetery companies.

[*Assented to 10th March, 1882.*]

HER MAJESTY, by and with the advice and consent of the Legislative Assembly of the Province of Ontario, enacts as follows :

1. This Act may be cited as " The Joint Stock Companies' Act, 1882."

FIRST PART.

2. Wherever any company incorporated under any special Act or under " The Ontario Joint Stock Companies' Letters Patent Act " is authorized to execute the office of executor, administrator, trustee,

receiver, assignee, guardian of a minor, or committee of a lunatic, then in case the Lieutenant-Governor in Council shall approve of such company being accepted by the High Court of Justice as a Trusts Company for the purposes of such court, the said court, or any judge thereof, and every other court or judge having authority to appoint such an officer may, if the court or judge think fit, with the consent of the company, appoint such company to exercise any of the said offices in respect of any estate, or person, under the authority of such court, or judge, or may grant to such company probate of any will in which such company is named an executor; but no company which has issued, or has authority to issue, debentures shall be approved as aforesaid.

(2) Notwithstanding the provisions of the sixty-sixth section of the Chancery Act, or any provision of any other Act requiring that security, or security of any special character, shall be taken, it shall not be requisite for any court, or judge, appointing any such company approved as aforesaid, or for any court granting probate to such company as executor, to require the said company to give any security for the due performance of its duty as such executor, administrator, trustee, receiver, assignee, guardian or committee.

(3) The Lieutenant-Governor in Council may revoke the approval given under this section, and no court, or judge, after notice of such revocation, shall appoint any such company to be an administrator, trustee, receiver, assignee, guardian, or committee, unless such company gives the like security for the due performance of its duty as would be required from a private person.

(4) The liability of the said company to persons interested in an estate held by the said company as executor, administrator, trustee, receiver, assignee, guardian, or committee as aforesaid, shall be the same as if the said estate had been held by any private person in such capacities respectively, and its powers shall be the same.

(5) The High Court, if it deems necessary, may from time to time appoint a suitable person to investigate the affairs and management of such company, who shall report thereon to such court, and regarding the security afforded to those by or for whom its engagements are held, and the expense of such investigations shall be defrayed by the said company; or the court may, if it deems necessary, examine the officers or directors of the said company under oath as to the security aforesaid.

(6) The Lieutenant-Governor may also from time to time, when he deems it expedient, appoint an inspector to examine the affairs of the said company, and report to him on the security afforded to those by and for whom its engagements are held as aforesaid; and the expense of such investigation shall be borne by the said company.

(7) Every court into which money is paid by parties, or is brought by order or judgment, may by order direct the same to be deposited with any such company that may agree to accept the same, and the company may pay any lawful rate of interest on such moneys as may be agreed upon, and when no special arrangement is made, interest shall be allowed by the company at the rate of not less than three per centum annually.

(8) Every such company may invest any trust moneys in its hands in any securities in which private trustees may by law invest trust moneys, and may also invest such moneys (a) in the public stock funds or Government securities of any of the Provinces of the Dominion, or in any securities guaranteed by the United Kingdom of Great Britain and Ireland, or by the Dominion, or by any of the said Provinces; (b) in the bonds or debentures of any municipal corporation in any of the said Provinces.

Provided that such company shall not in any case invest the moneys of any trust in securities prohibited by the trust, and shall not invest moneys intrusted to it by any court in a class of securities disapproved of by the court.

3. The sixty-fifth and sixty-sixth sections of the Joint Stock Companies' Letters Patent Act shall apply to any company which may have been incorporated after the passing of the said Act, or may be hereafter incorporated, for any purpose or object within the scope of the said Act, or within the scope of the said Act as such Act has been or may be hereafter amended, so long as the company applying for re-incorporation is at the time of its application a subsisting and valid corporation; and the said sections shall be construed as if the provisions of this section had been contained in the said Act at the time of the passing thereof.

4. Where any company has been heretofore incorporated by a special Act, for purposes or objects within the scope of the said Joint Stock Companies' Letters Patent Act, then, in case a resolution authorizing an application to the Lieutenant-Governor therefor is passed by a vote of not less than two-thirds in value of the shareholders present, in person or by proxy, at a general meeting of the company, duly called for considering the subject of such resolution, the Lieutenant-Governor in Council may from time to time direct the issue of Letters Patent to the company embracing any or all of the following matters:

(a) Extending the powers of the company to any objects within the scope of the said Letters Patent Act, which the company may desire;

(b) Limiting or increasing the amount which the company may borrow upon debentures or otherwise;

(c) Providing for the formation of a reserve fund;

(d) Varying any provision contained in the special Act, so long as the alteration is not contrary to the provisions of the said Letters Patent Act;

(e) Making provision for any other matter or thing in respect of which provision might have been made had the company been incorporated under the said Letters Patent Act.

(2) No power to execute the office of executor, administrator, trustee, receiver, assignee, guardian of a minor, or committee of a lunatic, shall be conferred under this section upon any company which has authority to issue debentures; and no company, incorporated under the Joint Stock Companies' Letters Patent Act, with power to execute such office, shall issue debentures.

(3) The list and summary required by the forty-ninth section of the said Joint Stock Companies Letters Patent Act shall hereafter be only

required in duplicate, and one of the duplicate lists and summaries shall be deposited with the Provincial Secretary within the time by the said section limited and the other shall be kept posted in the manner required by the said Act.

5. The seventeenth, eighteenth, and nineteenth sections of the said Joint Stock Companies' Letters Patent Act, and the first section of the Act passed in the forty-fourth year of Her Majesty's reign, intituled " An Act to extend the powers of Companies incorporated under the Joint Stock Companies' Letters Patent Act," shall apply to every company which has been heretofore incorporated by a special Act for purposes or objects within the scope of the said Joint Stock Companies' Letters Patent Act.

(2) Where application is made to the Lieutenant-Governor for the issue of Supplementary Letters Patent confirming a by-law increasing or decreasing the capital stock of the company, or subdividing the shares, and the capital of such company, or such capital as increased, does not exceed three thousand dollars, the Lieutenant-Governor may dispense with the insertion in the *Ontario Gazette* of a notice of such application.

SECOND PART.

6. The second part of this Act shall apply to every company and association whose incorporation and the affairs thereof, in the particulars hereinafter mentioned are under the authority of the Legislature of Ontario, where the shareholders or members of the company are entitled to the profits of the business of such company.

7. The expression " special resolution " shall have in such part the same meaning as it has in " The Joint Stock Companies' Winding-up Act " (1878).

8. Where a company has passed a special resolution authorizing any of the acts hereinafter allowed, the directors and officers may act in accordance with the terms of such resolution, subject to the provisions of this Act.

9. The company may by such resolution direct that proceedings be taken to distribute the proceeds of all the assets of the company amongst the shareholders after payment of the debts of the company, or that proceedings be taken to reduce the capital :

(1) Either by paying off the shares of such persons as may elect to be paid off at a rate fixed by such resolution, or to be determined in accordance with a plan therein specified ;

(2) Or by paying off a certain fixed proportion of all the shares.

10. The company shall thereupon give notice (Form A) of such resolution in the *Ontario Gazette* and in some newspaper published in the city of Toronto, and in some other newspaper published where the chief place of business of the company in Ontario is situate, if any newspaper is published in such place.

(2) Such notice shall also state that after some day to be therein named, and which shall not be earlier than three months from the first publication of such notice in the *Gazette*, the company will act upon such resolution.

(3) Such notice shall also call upon all creditors of the company to file their claims against the company forthwith, whether such claims are or are not then due.

(4) Where the company has no place of business in Ontario, or its chief place of business is in Toronto, it will be sufficient if the notice is published in the *Gazette* and in one Toronto newspaper.

(5) The said notice shall be published in the *Gazette* and in each of the said newspapers (where publication in more than one is required) at least six times during the said period of three months, and in computing such six times no two publications shall be counted which occur in the same week.

11. Upon the arrival of the day appointed, or so soon thereafter as conveniently may be, the officers of the said company may act in accordance with the terms of the said resolution: Provided (1) either that the company has no creditors, and a statement (Form B) upon the oath or solemn affirmation of the chief executive officer and of the treasurer of the company stating their belief of this fact, is filed with the clerk of the county or district court of the county or district where the chief office of the company is situated; (2) or the consent of the company's creditors to the resolution being acted upon has been procured in writing, and a statement under oath or solemn affirmation of the said officers, containing the particulars set forth in Form C appended to this Act, is filed with the said clerk.

12. Provided always, that where any such company has before the passing of this Act, at a general meeting of the shareholders thereof called and held as prescribed by section ten of chapter one hundred and sixty-four of the Revised Statutes of Ontario (with notice that the meeting was called for the purpose of considering the resolution hereinafter mentioned), unanimously passed a resolution that proceedings should be taken for the reduction of the capital of the company, by paying off a certain fixed proportion of all the shares, the officers of the company may (after the passing of this Act), act in accordance with the terms of such resolution, provided the company has no creditors, and that (a statement in form B, upon the oath or solemn affirmation of the chief executive officer and of the treasurer of the company, stating their belief of this fact, is filed with the clerk of the county or district court of the county or district where the chief office of the company is situate).

13. No officer of any such company shall make or authorize any payment by virtue of such resolution until one or other of the said statements has been filed as aforesaid, or without the consent of every creditor of the company, so long as to his knowledge any debt, whether the same is due or not, or any accrued liability of the company remains unsatisfied, and any officer who violates the provisions of this section shall, besides being subject to such criminal punishment as is authorized for his offence, be liable personally for the amount of such unsatisfied claim or accrued liability to the creditor or other person entitled to claim from the company.

14. Every shareholder receiving any moneys under any such resolution shall, to the extent of the moneys so received, remain liable for any debts or liabilities of the company then in fact existing, and upon the winding up of such company by judicial process, every such person, his executors or administrators, may be required to contribute to that extent towards the payment of any such debts or liabilities after the other assets of the company have been exhausted; but no executor or administrator shall be held so liable unless at the time he receives notice of the assessment, he has in his hands assets applicable thereto or subsequently receives such assets.

15. No insurance or guarantee company, or other company carrying on business of a like nature, shall pay off any part of its capital stock under this Act until every policy, and that every instrument having the effect of a policy, given by such company has expired, or been terminated, and, in the case of such a company, this fact shall be stated in the statement (Form B or C) filed as aforesaid.

16. Any company or association of such a character that the members thereof are entitled to the profits accruing from its business, may, notwithstanding its capital is not divided into shares, take the proceedings authorized by this Act in order to distribute the proceeds of all the assets of the company among its members, but no such company or association shall pass any resolution for any of the other purposes contemplated by the ninth section of this Act.

17. Where the capital of any company has become impaired and the shareholders pass a special resolution to reduce the par value of the shares of such company, such shares shall thereupon be reduced in accordance with the terms of such resolution, provided that such resolution shall not in any wise affect the amount still remaining payable upon the shares, but the same amount shall, except as to a double or other additional liability, continue to be payable in respect of every share as if such resolution had not been passed; and in case by virtue of the charter or Act of incorporation of such company or of any general or other Act affecting the same, a double, or other additional, liability is cast upon the shareholders, the same proportional liability shall continue, that is to say, if the liability was a double liability, the shareholders shall, as to new creditors, be liable for double the amount of the stock at its reduced value, and in like manner for any other proportion, but in respect of persons who are creditors at the time of such reduction the liability of the shareholders shall continue as if such reduction had not taken place.

18. Wherever a reduction is had under the preceding section a notice thereof (Form D) shall be published at least once a week for six weeks in the manner hereinbefore provided as to notice A.

19. Where any company, acting under the provisions of this Act has reduced its capital, every advertisement, circular, or other document thereafter issued by such company, or any of its officers, containing a statement of the capital of the company shall state such capital at the amount to which it has been reduced.

JOINT STOCK CEMETERY COMPANIES.

20. Section one of the Act respecting Cemetery Companies, chapter one hundred and seventy of the Revised Statutes, is hereby repealed, and the following substituted therefor:

(1.) Any number of persons, not less than ten, may form themselves into a company for the purpose of establishing one or more public cemeteries: Provided always that such cemetery or cemeteries be without the limits of any incorporated village, town, or city.

21. Section two of the said Act respecting Cemetery Companies is amended by striking out the word "twenty," in the first line thereof, and substituting the word "ten" therefor.

22. In case any company which has been or may be hereafter incorporated under the Revised Statutes respecting Cemetery Companies, or under the Act passed in the forty-third year of Her Majesty's reign, intituled "An Act respecting the incorporation of Cemetery Companies by Letters Patent," should, either on account of the burial of bodies in the locality being prohibited by the municipal authorities, or for any other reason, desire to be wound up, then, if no lot has been sold for the purpose of burial, or if such lots have been sold, then with the written consent of all the persons to whom lots have been sold, or of their heirs, or in case any such heir is a minor or insane, then with the assent of the heirs who are of full age and who are of sound mind, the company may be wound up, under the provisions of the ninth section of this Act, or proceedings may be taken to have the company wound up, under the "Joint Stock Companies' Winding-up Act."

(2) All the real and personal property of such company may thereupon be sold by the officers of the company, or by the liquidators, and the proceeds, after payment of all claims against the company, distributed amongst the shareholders. The property so sold shall be freed and discharged from all trusts arising on account of their having been held for the purposes of a cemetery or cemetery company, but nothing herein contained shall be construed to authorize a distribution amongst shareholders of the proceeds of lands devised or conveyed by way of gift to the company, in trust for the purposes of a cemetery, but the proceeds of such lands shall be applied to such municipal or charitable purposes as the donor of the lands, if he is then living, or if he is dead as the Lieutenant-Governor in Council or the High Court of Justice, may direct.

(3) Sections twenty-five, twenty-six, twenty-seven and thirty-one of the Ontario Joint Stock Companies' Letters Patent Act, shall apply to all companies incorporated under the said Act respecting the incorporation of Cemetery Companies by Letters Patent.

SCHEDULE OF FORMS.

FORM A.

[*Section* 10.]

Notice is hereby given that the [*insert name of Company*] has by a special resolution passed by the shareholders of the said company, resolved to [*set out the substance of the resolution*].

The company will act upon the said resolution upon the day of   next.

All creditors of the company are hereby required to file their claims against the company forthwith, whether such claims are or are not now due.

A. B.
Secretary.

Date &c.

FORM B.

[*Sections* 11, 12, *and* 15, *First Method.*]

I, *A. B.*, of the   in the County of   make oath and say [*or* solemnly affirm, *as the case may require*],

1. I am the [*here insert title of office*] of the [*name of company,*] and I am the Chief Executive Officer of the said company, and, as such officer have the supervision and management of the business of the said company.

2. I verily believe the said company is not indebted to any person or persons, or to any company, association or corporation whatsoever, and I verily believe that no person, company, association or corporation has any right of action whatever against the said [*name of company*].

[*In the case of insurance or guarantee companies, or other company carrying on business of a like nature, the following paragraph is to be added :*]

3. Every policy, and every instrument having the effect of a policy, given by the said company has expired or been terminated.

Sworn &c.

N. B.—*The statement by the Treasurer of the company will be identical with the above, except as to the paragraph setting forth the office held.*

FORM C.

[*Sections* 11 *and* 15, *Second Method.*]

I, *C. D.*, of the   in the County of   make oath and say [*or* solemnly affirm, *as the case may require*],

1. I am the [*here insert title of office*] of the [*name of company*],

and I am the Chief Executive Officer of the said company, and, as such officer, have the management and supervision of the business of the said company.

2. I verily believe that the said company is not indebted to any person or persons, or to any company, association, or corporation whatsoever, except those whose names appear in the schedule which is hereto annexed, and every such person, company and association has consented in writing, to the following resolution being acted upon, that is to say [*here set out the resolution*].

3. I verily believe that no person, company, association or corporation, except such as are named in the said schedule, has any right of action whatever against the said company.

[*In the case of insurance or guarantee companies, or other company carrying on business of a like nature, the following paragraph is to be added:*]

4. Every policy, and every instrument having the effect of a policy, given by the said company, has expired or been terminated.

Sworn &c.

N. B.—The statement by the Treasurer of the company will be identical with the above, except as to the paragraph setting forth the office held.

FORM D.

[*Section 18.*]

Notice is hereby given that the [*name of company*], has by a special resolution passed by the shareholders of the said company, reduced the capital of the company from $ to $, and has reduced the par value of each share of the said company from $ to $

A. B.,
Secretary.

Date &c.

CHAP. I.

An Act respecting the Canadian Pacific Railway.

Section.
Preamble. Preference of Parliament for construction by a company. Greater part still unconstructed. Contract entered into.
1. Contract approved.
2. Charter may be granted. Publication and effect of charter.
3. Certain grants of money and land may be made to the company chartered. Conversion of money grant authorized.
4. Certain materials may be admitted free of duty.
5. Company to have possession of completed portions. Conveyance thereof to company when the contract is performed.
6. Security may be taken for operation.

SCHEDULE.
1. Interpretation.
2. Security to be given by the company.
3. Eastern and central sections to be constructed by company described; Standard of railway and provision in case of disagreement as to conformity to it.
4. Commencement and regular progress of the work; period for completion.
5. As to portion made by Government.
6. Government to construct portions now under contract within periods fixed by contract.
7. Completed railway to be property of company; transfer of portions constructed by Government; company to operate the railway forever.
8. Company to equip portions transferred to them.
9. Subsidy in money and land; apportionment of money; and of land; when to be paid or granted; option of company to take terminable bonds; provision as to materials for construction delivered by company in advance; option of the company during a certain time to substitute payment of interest on certain bonds instead of issuing land grant bonds; deposit of proceeds of sale of such bonds; payments by company out of such deposits; payment by delivery of bonds; sinking fund; alteration in apportionment of money grant in such case.
10. Grant of land required for railway purpose; admission of certain materials free of duty; sale of certain material to company by Government.
11. Provision respecting land grant; case of deficiency of land on line of railway provided for; selection in such case with consent of Government.
12. As to Indian title.

Section.
13. Location of railway between terminal points.
14. Power to construct branches; lands necessary for the same.
15. Restriction as to competing lines for a limited period.
16. Exemption from taxation in N. W. territories.
17. Land-grant bonds; their nature and conditions of issue by the company; deposit with Government; for what purposes and on what conditions; if the company make no default in operating railway; in case of such default.
18. Provision if such bonds are sold faster than lands are earned by the company and deposit on interest with Government, and payments by Government to company; lands to be granted subject to such bonds.
19. Company to pay expenses.
20. If land bonds are not issued one-fifth of land to be retained as security; how to be disposed of; substitution of other securities.
21. Company to be incorporated as by schedule A.
22. Railway Act to apply; exceptions.

SCHEDULE A.
1. Certain persons incorporated; corporate name.
2. Capital stock and shares; paid up shares.
3. Substitution of company as contractors; and when; effect of such substitution; notice in Canada Gazette; further instalment to be paid up; and rest of $5,000,000.
4. Necessary franchises and powers granted; proviso.
5. First directors of the Company; number limited; majority to be British subjects; powers and term of office.
6. Qualification of directors; alteration of number; ballot.
7. Quorum; proviso; three must be present.
8. Executive committee; president to be one.
9. Chief place of business; other places; places for service of process, &c.; how to be notified; service of process thereat; and if company fail to appoint places.
10. First and other annual meeting; notice.
11. Special general meetings notice; place.
12. Provision if a meeting be necessary before notice as aforesaid can be given; notices in such case; meetings always valid if all shareholders or their proxies are present.
13. Limitation as to votes and proxies.

Section.

14. And as to calls.
15. Line and gauge of railway; and certain branches; commencement and completion; other branches; name of railway.
16. Company may construct lines of telegraph or telephone, and work them and collect tolls; subject to Con. Stat. Can., c. 67, ss. 14, 15, 16; as to future inventions.
17. Application of 42 V., c. 9.
18. Exceptions as to such application; as to lands of the Crown required; plans and book of reference; deviations from line on plan; deposit of plan, &c.; and of branches; copies thereof; registration thereof.
19. Company may take materials from public lands; and a greater extent for stations &c.
20. Limit of reduction of tolls by Parliament under 42 V., c. 9, s. 17, extended; reduction by Governor in Council extended in like manner.
21. Restriction as to transfers of stock; advances on, by company forbidden.
22. Transfer or transmission to new shareholders subject to veto of directors until completion of contract; proviso; as to transfer by a firm to a partner; note of transfer to be made and for what purpose.
23. Certain other provisions of 42 V, c. 9, not to apply.
24. Company to afford reasonable facilities to and from certain other railway companies; as to rates of carriage traffic in such cases; reservation as to purchasers of land, and emigrants. Contrary agreements void.
25. Company may purchase or acquire by lease or otherwise certain other railways or amalgamate with them; and borrow to a limited amount on bonds in consequence; not to affect prior mortgages.
26. Company may have docks, &c., and run vessels on any navigable water their railway touches.
27. By-laws may provide for certain purposes; must be confirmed at next general meeting.

Section.

28. Amount of bonds limited; mortgages for securing the same on all the property of the company; proviso; in case land grant bonds have been issued under section 30; evidence of mortgage and what conditions the bonds may contain; remedies of holders in default of payment; right of voting may, in such case, be transferred to bondholders; cancellation of shares deprived of voting power; enforcing conditions; further provisions under mortgage deed; provision in case of change of ownership, &c., of railway, in such case; increase of borrowing power if no land grant bonds are issued.
29. Provision if such bonds are issued before completion of railway.
30. Provisions as to issue of land grant mortgage bonds; evidence of mortgage and conditions; name of and how dealt with.
31. Issue of bonds in place of land grant bonds under agreement with Government; to include franchise as well as property of company; section 28 to apply.
32. Facilities for issue of mortgage bonds as to seal and signatures.
33. "Working expenses" defined.
34. Currency on which bonds may be issued; price and conditions of sale; may be exchanged for inscribed stock, &c.
35. Bonds need not be registered; mortgage deed how deposited; and agreement under s. 36; certified copies.
36. Agreement with bondholders, &c., for restricting issues; effect thereof.
37. Company may issue guaranteed or preferred stock to a limited amount; not to affect the privilege of bondholders; voting.
38. Contracts, bills, &c., by its agents to bind the company; proof thereof non-liability of such agent; proviso; as to notes.
39. Reports to Government.
40. Publication of notices.
41. Form of deeds, &c., to the company; Form; obligation of the grantor.

[Assented to 15th February 1881.]

WHEREAS by the terms and conditions of the admission of British Columbia into Union with the Dominion of Canada, the Government of the Dominion has assumed the obligation of causing a Railway to be constructed, connecting the seaboard of British Columbia with the Railway system of Canada;

And whereas the Parliament of Canada has repeatedly declared a preference for the construction and operation of such Railway by means of an incorporated Company aided by grants of money and land, rather than by the Government, and certain Statutes have been passed to enable that course to be followed, but the enactments therein contained have not been effectual for that purpose;

And whereas certain sections of the said Railway have been constructed by the Government, and others are in course of construction, but the greater portion of the main line thereof has not yet been commenced or placed under contract, and it is necessary for the developement of the North-West Territory and for the preservation of the good faith of the Government in the performance of its obligations, that immediate steps should be taken to complete and operate the whole of the said Railway;

And whereas, in conformity with the expressed desire of Parliament, a contract has been entered into for the construction of the said portion of the main line of the said Railway, and for the permanent working of the whole line thereof, which contract with the schedule annexed has been laid before Parliament for its approval and a copy thereof is appended hereto, and it is expedient to approve and ratify the said contract, and to make provision for the carrying out of the same;

Therefore Her Majesty, by and with the advice and consent of the Senate and House of Commons of Canada, enacts as follows:—

1. The said contract, a copy of which with schedule annexed, is appended hereto, is hereby approved and ratified, and the Government is hereby authorized to perform and carry out the conditions thereof, according to their purport.

2. For the purpose of incorporating the persons mentioned in the said contract, and those who shall be associated with them in the undertaking, and of granting to them the powers necessary to enable them to carry out the said contract according to the terms thereof the Governor may grant to them in conformity with the said contract, under the corporate name of the Canadian Pacific Railway Company, a charter conferring upon them the franchises, privileges and powers embodied in the schedule to the said contract and to this Act appended, and such charter, being published in the *Canada Gazette*, with any Order or Orders in Council relating to it, shall have force and effect as if it were an Act of the Parliament of Canada, and shall be held to be an Act of incorporation within the meaning of the said contract.

3. Upon the organization of the said Company, and the deposit by them, with the Government, of one million dollars in cash or securities approved by the Government, for the purpose in the said contract provided, and in consideration of the completion and perpetual and efficient operation of the Railway by the said Company, as stipulated in the said contract, the Government may grant to the Company, a subsidy of twenty-five million dollars in money, and twenty-five million acres of land, to be paid and conveyed to the Company in the manner and proportions, and upon the terms and conditions agreed upon in the said contract, and may also grant to the Company the land for right of way, stations, and other purposes, and such other privileges as are provided for in the said contract. And in lieu of the payment of the said money subsidy direct to the Company, the Government may convert the same, and any interest accruing thereon, into a fund for the payment to the extent of such fund, of interest on the bonds of the Company, and may pay such interest accordingly; the whole in manner and form as provided for in the said contract.

4. The Government may also permit the admission free of duty, of all steel rails, fish plates, and other fastenings, spikes, bolts and nuts, wire, timber, and all material for bridges to be used in the original construction of the said Canadian Pacific Railway, as defined by the Act thirty-seventh Victoria, chapter fourteen, and of a telegraph line in connection therewith, and all telegraphic apparatus required for the first equipment of such telegraph line, the whole as provided by the tenth section of the said contract.

5. Pending the completion of the eastern and central sections of the said railway as described in the said contract, the Government may also transfer to the said Company the possession and right to work and run the several portions of the Canadian Pacific Railway as described in the said Act thirty-seventh Victoria, chapter fourteen, which are already constructed, and as the same shall be hereafter completed; and upon the completion of the said eastern and central sections the Government may convey to the Company, with a suitable number of station buildings, and with water service (but without equipment), those portions of the Canadian Pacific Railway constructed, or agreed by the said contract to be constructed by the Government, which shall then be completed; and upon completion of the remainder of the portion of the said railway to be constructed by the Government, that portion also may be conveyed by the Government to the Company, and the Canadian Pacific Railway defined as aforesaid shall become and be thereafter the absolute property of the Company; the whole, however, upon the terms and conditions, and subject to the restrictions and limitations contained in the said contract.

6. The Government shall also take security for the continuous operation of the said railway during the ten years next subsequent to the completion thereof in the manner provided by the said contract.

SCHEDULE.

THIS CONTRACT AND AGREEMENT MADE BETWEEN HER MAJESTY THE QUEEN, acting in respect of the Dominion of Canada, and herein represented and acting by the Honorable SIR CHARLES TUPPER, K.C.M.G., Minister of Railways and Canals, and George Stephen and Duncan McIntyre, of Montreal, in Canada, John S. Kennedy of New York, in the State of New York, Richard B. Angus and James J. Hill, of St. Paul, in the State of Minnesota, Morton, Rose & Co., of London, England, and Kohn, Reinach & Co., of Paris, France.

Witnesses:

That the parties hereto have contracted and agreed with each other as follows, namely:—

1. For the better interpretation of this contract, it is hereby

declared that the portion of Railway hereinafter called the Eastern section, shall comprise that part of the Canadian Pacific Railway to be constructed, extending from the Western terminus of the Canada Central Railway, near the East end of Lake Nipissing, known as Callander Station, to a point of junction with that portion of the said Canadian Pacific Railway now in course of construction extending from Lake Superior to Selkirk on the East side of Red River; which latter portion is hereinafter called the Lake Superior section. That the portion of said Railway, now partially in course of construction, extending from Selkirk to Kamloops, is hereinafter called the Central section; and the portion of said Railway now in course of construction, extending from Kamloops to Port Moody, is hereinafter called the Western section. And that the words "the Canadian Pacific Railway," are intended to mean the entire Railway, as described in the Act 37th Victoria, chap. 14. The individual parties hereto, are hereinafter described as the Company; and the Government of Canada is hereinafter called the Government.

2. The contractors immediately after the organization of the said Company, shall deposit with the Government $1,000,000 in cash or approved securities, as a security for the construction of the Railway hereby contracted for. The Government shall pay to the Company interest on the cash deposited at the rate of four per cent. per annum, half-yearly, and shall pay over to the Company the interest received upon securities deposited, the whole until default in the performance of the conditions hereof, or until the repayment of the deposit, and shall return the deposit to the Company on the completion of the railway, according to the terms hereof, with any interest accrued thereon.

3. The Company shall lay out, construct and equip the said Eastern section, and the said Central section, of a uniform gauge of 4 feet 8½ inches; and in order to establish an approximate standard whereby the quality and the character of the Railway and of the materials used in the construction thereof, and of the equipment thereof may be regulated, the Union Pacific Railway of the United States as the same was when first constructed, is hereby selected and fixed as such standard. And if the Government and the Company should be unable to agree as to whether or not any work done or materials furnished under this contract are in fair conformity with such standard, or as to any other question of fact, excluding questions of law, the subject of disagreement shall be from time to time referred to the determination of three referees, one of whom shall be chosen by the Government, one by the Company, and one by the two referees so chosen, and such referees shall decide as to the party by whom the expense of such reference shall be defrayed. And if such two referees should be unable to agree upon a third referee, he shall be appointed at the instance of either party hereto, after notice to the other, by the Chief Justice of the Supreme Court of Canada. And the decision of such referees, or of the majority of them, shall be final.

4. The work of construction shall be commenced at the eastern extremity of the Eastern section not later than the first day of July next, and the work upon the Central section shall be commenced by the Company at such point towards the eastern end thereof on the portion of the line now under construction as shall be found convenient and as shall be approved by the Government, at a date not later than the 1st May next. And the work upon the Eastern and Central sections, shall be vigorously and continuously carried on at such rate of annual progress on each section as shall enable the Company to complete and equip the same and each of them, in running order, on or before the first day of May, 1891, by which date the Company hereby agree to complete and equip the said sections in conformity with this contract unless prevented by the Act of God, the Queen's enemies, intestine disturbances, epidemics, floods, or other causes beyond the control of the Company. And in case of the interruption or obstruction of the work of construction from any of the said causes, the time fixed for the completion of the railway shall be extended for a corresponding period.

5. The Company shall pay to the Government the cost, according to the contract, of the portion of railway, 100 miles in length, extending from the city of Winnipeg westward, up to the time at which the work was taken out of the hands of the contractor and the expenses since incurred by the Government in the work of construction, but shall have the right to assume the said work at any time and complete the same, paying the cost of construction as aforesaid so far as the same shall then have been incurred by the Government.

6. Unless prevented by the Act of God, the Queen's enemies, intestine disturbances, epedimics, floods or other causes beyond the control of the Government, the Government shall cause to be completed the said Lake Superior section, by the dates fixed by the existing contracts for the construction thereof; and shall also cause to be completed the portion of the said Western section now under contract, namely, from Kamloops to Yale, within the period fixed by the contracts therefor, namely, by the thirtieth day of June, 1885; and shall also cause to be completed, on or before the first day of May, 1891, the remaining portion of the said Western section, lying between Yale and Port Moody, which shall be constructed of equally good quality in every respect with the standard hereby created for the portion hereby contracted for. And the said Lake Superior section, and the portions of the said Western section now under contract, shall be completed as nearly as practicable according to the specifications and conditions of the contracts therefor, except in so far as the same have been modified by the Government prior to this contract.

7. The Railway constructed under the terms hereof shall be the property of the Company; and pending the completion of the Eastern and Central sections, the Government shall transfer to the Company the possession and right to work and run the several portions of the Canadian Pacific Railway already constructed or as the same shall be completed. And upon the completion of the Eastern and Central sections, the Government shall convey to the Company, with a suitable number of station buildings and with water service but without equipment), those portions of the Canadian Pacific Railway constructed or to be constructed by the Government which shall then be completed; and upon completion of the remainder of the portion of railway to be constructed by the Government, that portion shall also be conveyed to the Company, and the Canadian Pacific Railway shall become and be thereafter the absolute property of the Company. And the Company shall thereafter and forever efficiently maintain, work and run the Canadian Pacific Railway.

8. Upon the reception from the Government of the possession of each of the respective portions of the Canadian Pacific Railway, the Company shall equip the same in conformity with the standard herein established for the equipment of the sections hereby contracted for, and shall thereafter maintain and efficiently operate the same.

9. In consideration of the premises, the Government agree to grant to the Company a subsidy in money of $25,000,000, and in land of 25,000,000 acres, for which subsidies the construction of the Canadian Pacific Railway shall be completed and the same shall be equipped, maintained, and operated,—the said subsidies respectively to be paid and granted as the work of construction shall proceed, in manner and upon the conditions following, that is to say:

a. The said subsidy in money is hereby divided and appropriated as follows, namely :—

CENTRAL SECTION.

Assumed at 1,350 miles—
1st —900 miles, at $10,000 per mile........ $9,000,000
2nd.—450   "   13,333   "   6,000,000
                                         ———— $15,000,000

EASTERN SECTION.

Assumed at 650 miles, subsidy equal to $15,384.61 per mile 10,000,000˙
                                                            ————
                                                            $25,000,000

And the said subsidy in land is hereby divided and appropriated as follows, subject to the reserve hereinafter provided for :—

CENTRAL SECTION.

1st. —900 miles at 12,500 acres per mile....11,250,000
2nd.—450   "   " 16,666.66 "   "   7,500,000
                                              ———— 18,750,000

EASTERN SECTION.

Assumed at 650 miles, subsidy equal to 9,615.35 acres per
mile 6,250,000
                                              ————
                                              25,000,000

b. Upon the construction of any portion of the railway hereby contracted for, not less than 20 miles in length, and the completion thereof so as to admit of the running of regular trains thereon, together with such equipment thereof as shall be required for the traffic thereon, the

Government shall pay and grant to the Company the money and land subsidies applicable thereto, according to the division and appropriation thereof made as hereinbefore provided; the Company having the option of receiving in lieu of cash, terminable bonds of the Government, bearing such rate of interest, for such period and nominal amount as may be arranged, and which may be equivalent according to actuarial calculation to the corresponding cash payment, the Government allowing four per cent, interest on moneys deposited with them.

c. If at any time the Company shall cause to be delivered on or near the line of the said railway, at a place satisfactory to the Government, steel rails and fastenings to be used in the construction of the railway, but in advance of the requirements for such construction, the Government, on the requisition of the Company, shall, upon such terms and conditions as shall be determined by the Government, advance thereon three-fourths of the value thereof at the place of delivery. And a proportion of the amount so advanced shall be deducted according to such terms and conditions from the subsidy to be thereafter paid, upon the settlement for each section of 20 miles of railway, which proportion shall correspond with the proportion of such rails and fastenings which have been used in the construction of such sections.

d. Until the first day of January, 1882, the Company shall have the option, instead of issuing land grant bonds as hereinafter provided, of substituting the payment by the Government of the interest (or part of the interest) on bonds of the Company mortgaging the railway and the lands to be granted by the Government, running over such term of years as may be approved by the Governor in Council, in lieu of the cash subsidy hereby agreed to be granted to the Company or any part thereof; such payments of interest to be equivalent according to actuarial calculation to the corresponding cash payment, the Government allowing four per cent, interest on moneys deposited with them; and the coupons representing the interest on such bonds shall be guaranteed by the Government to the extent of such equivalent. And the proceeds of the sale of such bonds to the extent of not more than $25,000,000; shall be deposited with the Government, and the balance of such proceeds shall be placed elsewhere by the Company, to the satisfaction and under the exclusive control of the Government; failing which last condition the bonds in excess of those sold shall remain in the hands of the Government. And from time to time as the work proceeds the Government shall pay over to the Company: firstly, out of the amount so to be placed by the Company, and, after the expenditure of that amount, out of the amount deposited with the Government, sums of money bearing the same proportion to the mileage cash subsidy hereby agreed upon, which the net proceeds of such sale (if the whole of such bonds are sold upon the issue thereof) or, if such bonds be not all then sold, the net proceeds of the issue, calculated at the rate at which the sale of part of them shall have been made, shall bear to the sum of 25,000,000. But if only a portion of the bond issue be sold, the amount earned by the Company according to the proportion aforesaid, shall be paid to the Company, partly out of the bonds in the hands of the Government, and partly out of the cash deposited with

308   Cap. 1.   *Canadian Pacific Railway.*   44 Vic.

the Government, in similar proportions to the amount of such bonds sold and remaining unsold respectively ; and the Company shall receive the bonds so paid as cash at the rate at which the said partial sale thereof shall have been made. And the Government will receive and hold such sum of money towards the creation of a sinking fund for the redemption of such bonds, and upon such terms and conditions, as shall be agreed upon between the Government and the Company.

e. If the Company avail themselves of the option granted by clause *d*, the sum of $2,000 per mile for the first eight hundred miles of the Central section shall be deducted *pro rata* from the amount payable to the Company in respect of the said eight hundred miles, and shall be appropriated to the remainder of the said Central section.

10. In further consideration of the premises, the Government shall also grant to the Company the lands required for the road bed of the railway, and for its stations, station grounds, workshops, dock ground and water frontage at the termini on navigable waters, buildings, yards, and other appurtenances required for the convenient and effectual construction and working for the railway, in so far as such land shall be vested in the Government. And the Government shall also permit the admission free of duty, of all steel rails, fish plates and other fastenings, spikes, bolts and nuts, wire, timber and all material for bridges, to be used in the original construction of the railway, and of a telegraph line in connection therewith, and all telegraphic apparatus required for the first equipment of such telegraph line ; and will convey to the Company, at cost price, with interest, all rails and fastenings bought in or since the year 1879, and other materials for construction in the possession of or purchased by the Government, at a valuation ; such rails, fastenings and materials not being required by it for the construction of the said Lake Superior and Western sections.

11. The grant of land hereby agreed to be made to the Company, shall be so made in alternate sections of 640 acres each, extending back 24 miles deep, on each side of the railway, from Winnipeg to Jasper House, in so far as such lands shall be vested in the Government,—the Company receiving the sections bearing uneven numbers. But should any of such sections consist in a material degree of land not fairly fit for settlement, the Company shall not be obliged to receive them as part of such grant, and the deficiency thereby caused and any further deficiency which may arise from the insufficient quantity of land along the said portion of railway, to complete the said 25,000,000 acres, or from the prevalence of lakes and water stretches in the sections granted (which lakes and water stretches shall not be computed in the acreage of such sections), shall be made up from other portions in the track known as the fertile belt, that is to say, the land lying between parallels 49 and 57 degrees of north latitude, or elsewhere at the option of the Company, by the grant therein of similar alternate sections extending back 25 miles deep on each side of any branch line or lines of railway to be located by the Company, and to be shown on a map or plan thereof deposited with the Minister of Railways; or of any common front line or lines agreed upon between the Government and the Company,—the conditions hereinbefore stated as to lands not fairly fit for settlement to be applicable to such additional grants. And the Company may with the consent of the Government, select in the North-West Territories any tract or tracts of land not taken up as a means of supplying or patrially supplying such deficiency. But such grants shall be made only from lands remaining vested in the Government.

12. The Government shall extinguish the Indian title affecting the lands herein appropriated, and to be hereafter granted in aid of the railway.

13. The Company shall have the right, subject to the approval of the Governor in Council, to lay out and locate the line of the railway hereby contracted for, as they may see fit, preserving the following terminal points, namely: from Callander station to the point of junction with the Lake Superior station; and from Selkirk to the junction with the western section at Kamloops by way of the Yellow Head Pass.

14. The Company shall have the right, from time to time to lay out, construct, equip, maintain and work branch lines of railway from any point or points along their main lines of railway, to any point or points within the territory of the Dominion. Provided, always, that before commencing any branch they shall first deposit a map and plan of such branch in the Department of Railways. And the Government shall grant to the Company the lands required for the road bed of such branches, and for the stations, station grounds, buildings, workshows, yards and other appurtenances requisite for the efficient construction and working of such branches, in so far as such lands are vested in the Government.

15. For 20 years from the date hereof, no line of railway shall be authorized by the Dominion Parliament to be constructed South of Canadian Pacific Railway, from any point at or near the Canadian Pacific Railway except such line shall run South West, or to the Westward of South West: nor to within fifteen miles of Latitude 49. And in the establishment of any new Province in the North West Territories, provision shall be made for continuing such prohibition after such establishment until the expiration of the said period.

16. The Canadian Pacific Railway, and all stations and station grounds, work shops, buildings, yards and other property, rolling stock and appurtenance required and used for the construction and working thereof, and the capital stock of the Company, shall be forever free from taxation by the Dominion, or by any Province hereafter to be established, or by any Municipal Corporation therein; and the lands of the Company, in the North West Territories, until they are either sold or occupied, shall also be free from such taxation for 20 years after the grant thereof from the Crown.

17. The Company shall be authorized by their Act of incorporation to issue bonds, secured upon the land granted and to be granted to the Company, containing provisions for the use of such bonds in the acquisition of lands, and such other conditions as the Company shall see fit, such issue to be for

310　Cap. 1.　　　*Canadian Pacific Railway.*　　　44 Vic.

$25,000,000. And should the Company make such issue of land grant bonds, then they shall, deposit them in the hands of the Government, and the Government shall retain and hold one-fifth of such bonds as. security for the due performance of the present contract in respect of the maintenance and continuous working of the railway by the Company, as herein agreed, for ten years after the completion thereof, and the remaining $20,000,000 of such bonds shall be dealt with as hereinafter provided. And as to the said one-fifth of the said bonds, so long as no default shall occur in the maintenance and working of the said Canadian Pacific Railway, the Government shall not present or demand payment of the coupons of such bonds, nor require payment of any interest thereon. And if any of such bonds so to be retained by the Government shall be paid off in the manner to be provided for the extinction of the whole issue thereof, the Government shall hold the amount received in payment thereof as security for the same purposes as the bonds so paid off, paying interest thereon at four per cent. per annum so long as default is not made by the Company in the performance of the conditions hereof. And at the end of the said period of ten years from the completion of the said railway, if no default shall then have occurred in such maintenance and working thereof, the said bonds, or if any of them shall then have been paid off, the remainder of said bonds and the money received for those paid off, with accrued interest, shall be delivered back by the Government to the Company with all the coupons attached to such bonds. But if such default should occur, the Government may thereafter require payment of interest on the bonds so held, and shall not be obliged to continue to pay interest on the money representing bonds paid off; and while the Government shall retain the right to hold the said portion of the said land grant bonds, other securities satisfactory to the Government may be substituted for them by the Company by agreement with the Government.

18. If the Company shall find it necessary or expedient to sell the remaining $20,000,000 of the land grant bonds or a larger portion of one dollar for each acre of land then earned by the Company, they shall be allowed to do so, but the proceeds thereof, over and above the amount to which the Company shall be entitled as herein provided, shall be deposited with the Government. And the Government shall pay interest upon such deposit half-yearly, at the rate of four per cent. per annum, and shall pay over the amount of such deposit to the Company from time to time as the work proceeds, in the same proportions, and at the same times and upon the same conditions as the land grant — that is to say ; the Company shall be entitled to receive from the Government out of the proceeds of the said land grant bonds, the same number of dollars as the number of acres of the land subsidy which shall then have been earned by them, less one fifth thereof, that is to say, if the bonds are sold at par, but if they are sold at less than par, then a deduction shall be made therefrom corresponding to the discount at which such bonds are sold. And such land grant shall be conveyed to them by the Government, subject to the charge created as security for the said land grant bonds, and shall remain subject to such charge till relieved thereof in such manner as shall be provided for at the time of the issue of such bonds.

19. The company shall pay any expenses which shall be incurred by the Government in carrying out the provisions of the last two preceding clauses of this contract.

20. If the Company should not issue such land grant bonds, then the Government shall retain from out of each grant to be made from time to time, every fifth section of the lands hereby agreed to be granted, such lands to be so retained as security for the purposes, and for the length of time, mentioned in section eighteen hereof. And such lands may be sold in such manner and at such prices as shall be agreed upon between the Government and the Company, and in that case the price thereof shall be paid to, and held by the Government for the same period, and for the same purposes as the land itself, the Government paying four per cent. per annum interest thereon. And other securities satisfactory to the Government may be substituted for such lands or money by agreement with the Government.

21. The company to be incorporated, with sufficient powers to enable them to carry out the foregoing contract, and this contract shall only be binding in the event of an Act of incorporation being granted to the Company in the form hereto appended as Schedule A.

22. The Railway Act of 1879, in so far as the provisions of the same are applicable to the undertaking referred to in this contract, and in so far as they are not inconsistent with or contrary to the provisions of the Act of incorporation to be granted to the Company, shall apply to the Canadian Pacific Railway.

In witness whereof the parties hereto have executed these presents at the City of Ottawa, this twenty-first day of October, 1880.

```
        (Signed)    CHARLES TUPPER,
                        Minister of Railways and Canals.
           "        GEO. STEPHEN,
           "        DUNCAN McINTYRE,
           "        J. S. KENNEDY,
           "        R. B. ANGUS,
           "        J. J. HILL,
                        Per pro. Geo. Stephen.
           "        MORTON, ROSE & Co.
           "        KOHN, REINACH & Co.,
                        By P. Du P. Grenfell.
```

Signed in presence of F. Braun,
   and Seal of the Department
   hereto affixed by Sir Charles
   Tupper, in presence of
       (Signed)   F. Braun.

SCHEDULE A, REFERRED TO IN THE FOREGOING CONTRACT.

INCORPORATION.

1. George Stephen, of Montreal, in Canada, Esquire; Duncan McIntyre, of Montreal, aforesaid, Merchant; John S. Kennedy, of New York, in the State of New York, Banker; the firm of Morton, Rose and Company, of London, in England, Merchants; the firm of Kohn, Reinach and Company, of Paris, in France, Bankers; Richard B. Angus, and James J. Hill, both of St. Paul, in the State of Minnesota, Esquires; with all such other persons and corporations as shall become shareholders in the Company hereby incorporated, shall be and they are hereby constituted a body corporate and politic, by the name of the "Canadian Pacific Railway Company."

2. The capital stock of the Company shall be twenty-five million dollars, divided into shares of one hundred dollars each, which shares shall be transferable in such manner and upon such conditions as shall be proved by the by-laws of the Company; and such shares, or any part thereof, may be granted and issued as paid-up shares for value *bonâ fide* received by the Company, either in money at par or at such price and upon such conditions as the board of directors may fix, or as part of the consideration of any contract made by the Company

3. As soon as five million dollars of the stock of the Company have been subscribed, and thirty per centum thereof paid up, and upon the deposit with the Minister of Finance of the Dominion of one million dollars in money or in securities approved by the Governor in Council, for the purpose and upon the conditions in the foregoing contract provided, the said contract shall become and be transferred to the Company, without the execution of any deed or instrument in that behalf; and the Company shall, thereupon become and be vested with all the rights of the contractors named in the said contract, and shall be subject to, and liable for, all their duties and obligations, to the same extent and in the same manner as if the said contract had been executed by the said Company instead of by the said contractors; and thereupon the said contractors, as individuals, shall cease to have any right or interest in the said contract, and shall not be subject to any liability or responsibility under the terms thereof otherwise than as members of the corporation hereby created. And upon the performance of the said conditions respecting the subscription of stock, the partial payment thereof, and the deposit of one million dollars to the satisfaction of the Governor in Council, the publication by the Secretary of the State in the *Canada Gazette*, of a notice that the transfer of the contract to the Company has been effected and completed shall be conclusive proof of the fact. And the Company shall cause to be paid up, on or before the first day of May next, a further instalment of twenty per centum upon the said first subscription of five million dollars, of which call thirty days notice by circular mailed to each shareholder shall be sufficient. And the Company shall call in, and cause to be paid up, on or before the 31st day of December, 1882, the remainder of the said first subscription of five million dollars.

4. All the franchises and powers necessary or useful to the Company to enable them to carry out, perform, enforce, use, and avail themselves of, every condition, stipulation, obligation, duty, right, remedy, privilege, and advantage agreed upon, contained or described in the said contract, are hereby conferred upon the Company. And the enactment of the special provisions hereinafter contained shall not be held to impair or derogate from the generality of the franchises and powers so hereby conferred upon them.

DIRECTORS.

5. The said George Stephen, Duncan McIntyre, John S. Kennedy, Richard B. Angus, James J. Hill, Henry Stafford Northcote, of London, aforesaid, Esquires, Pascoe du P. Grenfell, of London, aforesaid, Merchant, Charles Day Rose, of London, aforesaid, Merchant, and Baron J. de Reinach, of Paris, aforesaid, Banker, are hereby constituted the first directors of the Company, with power to add to their number, but so that the directors shall not in all exceed fifteen in number; and the majority of the directors, of whom the President shall be one, shall be British subjects. And the Board of Directors so constituted shall have all the powers hereby conferred upon the directors of the Company, and they shall hold office until the first annual meeting of the shareholders of the Company.

6. Each of the directors of the Company, hereby appointed, or hereafter appointed or elected, shall hold at least two hundred and fifty shares of the stock of the Company. But the number of directors to be hereafter elected by the shareholders shall be such, not exceeding fifteen, as shall be fixed by by-law, and subject to the same conditions as the directors appointed by, or under the authority of, the last preceding section; the number thereof may be hereafter altered from time to time in like manner. The votes for their election shall be by ballot.

7. A majority of the directors shall form a quorum of the board; and until otherwise provided by by-law, directors may vote and act by proxy such proxy to be held by a director only; but no director shall hold more than two proxies, and no meeting of directors shall be competent to transact business unless at least three directors are present thereat in person, the remaining number of directors required to form a quorum being represented by proxies.

8. The board of directors may appoint from out of their number an Executive Committee, composed of at least three directors, for the transaction of the ordinary business of the Company, with such powers and duties as shall be fixed by the by-laws; and the President shall be *ex officio* a member of such committee.

9. The chief place of business of the Company shall be at the City of Montreal, but the Company may, from time to time, by by-law, appoint and fix other places within or beyond the limits of Canada at which the business of the Company may be transacted, and at which the directors or shareholders may meet, when called as shall be determined by the by-laws. And the Company shall appoint and fix by by-law, at least one place in each Province or Territory through which the Railway shall pass, where service of process may be made upon the Company, in respect of any cause of action arising within such Province or Territory, and may afterwards, from time to time, change such place by by-law. And a copy of any by-law fixing or changing any such place, duly authenticated as herein provided, shall be deposited by the Company in the office, at the seat of Government of the Province or Territory to which such by-law shall apply, of the Clerk or Prothonotary of the highest, or one of the highest, courts of civil jurisdiction of such Province or Territory. And if any cause of action shall arise against the Company within any Province or Territory, and any writ or process be issued against the Company thereon out of any court in such Province or Territory, service of such process may be validly made upon the Company at the place within such Province or Territory so appointed and fixed; but if the Company fail to appoint and fix such place, or to deposit, as hereinbefore provided, the by-law made in that behalf, any such process may be validly served upon the Company, at any of the stations of the said Railway within such Province or Territory.

SHAREHOLDERS.

10. The first annual meeting of the shareholders of the Company, for the appointment of directors, shall be held on the second Wednesday in May, one thousand eight hundred and eighty-two, at the principal office of the Company, in Montreal ; and the annual general meeting of shareholders, for the election of directors and the transaction of business generally, shall be held on the same day in each year thereafter at the same place unless otherwise provided by the by-laws. And notice of each of such meetings shall be given by the publication thereof in the *Canada Gazette* for four weeks, and by such further means as shall, from time to time, be directed by the by-laws.

11. Special general meetings of the shareholders may be convened in such manner as shall be provided by the by-laws. And except as hereinafter provided, notice of such meetings shall be given in the same manner as notices of annual general meetings, the purpose for which such meeting is called being mentioned in the notices thereof; and, except as hereinafter provided, all such meetings shall be held at the chief place of business of the Company.

12. If at any time before the first annual meeting of the shareholders of the Company, it should become expedient that a meeting of the directors of the Company, or a special general meeting of the shareholders of the Company, should be held, before such meeting can conveniently be called, and notice thereof given in the manner provided by this Act, or by the by-laws, or before by-laws in that behalf have been passed, and at a place other than at the chief place of business of the Company in Montreal before the enactment of a by-law authorizing the holding of such meeting elsewhere; it shall be lawful for the President or for any three either of directors or of shareholders, or of both, to be held at the city of London in England, at times and places respectively, to be stated in the notices to be given of such meetings respectively. And notices of such meetings may be validly given by a circular mailed to the ordinary address of each director or shareholder as the case may be, in time to enable him to attend such meeting, stating in general terms the purpose of the intended meeting. And in the case of a meeting of shareholders, the proceedings of such meeting shall be held to be valid and sufficient, and to be binding on the Company in all respects, if every shareholder of the Company be present thereat in person or by proxy, notwithstanding that notice of such meeting shall not have been given in manner required by this Act.

13. No shareholder holding shares upon which any call is over due and unpaid shall vote at any meeting of shareholders. And unless otherwise provided by the by-laws, the person holding the proxy of a shareholder shall be himself a shareholder.

14. No call upon unpaid shares shall be made for more that twenty per centum upon the amount thereof.

RAILWAY AND TELEGRAPH LINE.

15. The Company may lay out, construct, acquire, equip, maintain and work a continous line of railway, of the gauge of four feet eight and one-half inches ; which railway shall extend from the terminus of the Canada Central Railway near Lake Nipissing, known as Callander Station, to Port Moody in the Province of British Columbia; and also, a branch line of railway from some point on the main line of railway to Fort William on Thunder Bay ; and also the existing branch line of railway from Selkirk in the Province of Manitoba to Pembina in the said Province ; and also other branches to be located by the Company from time to time as provided by the said contract,—the said branches to be of the gauge aforesaid : and the said main line of railway, and the said branch lines of railway, shall be commenced and completed as provided by the said contract ; and together with such other branch lines as shall be hereafter constructed by the said Company, and any extension of the said main line of railway that shall be hereafter be constructed or acquired by the Company, shall constitute the line of railway hereinafter called THE CANADIAN PACIFIC RAILWAY.

16. The Company may construct, maintain and work a continous telegraph line and telephone lines throughout and along the whole line of the Canadian Pacific Railway, or any part thereof, and may also construct or acquire by purchase, lease or otherwise, any other line or lines of telegraph connecting with the line so to be constructed, along the line of the said railway, and may undertake the transmission of messages for the public by any such line or lines of telegraph or telephone, and collect tolls for so doing ; or may lease such line or lines of telegraph or telephone, or any portion thereof ; and, if they think proper to undertake the transmission of messages for hire, they shall be subject to the provisions of the fourteenth, fifteenth and sixteenth sections of chapter sixty-seven of the Consolidated Statutes of Canada. And they may use any improvement that may hereafter be invented (subject to the rights of patentees) for telegraphing or telephoning, and any other means of communication that may be deemed expedient by the Company at any time hereafter.

POWERS.

17. "*The Consolidated Railway Act,* 1879," in so far as the provisions of the same are applicable to the undertaking authorized by this charter, and in so far as they are not inconsistent with or contrary to the provisions hereof, and save and except as hereinafter provided, is hereby incorporated herewith

18. As respects the said railway, the seventh section of "*The Consolidated Railway Act,* 1879," relating to POWERS, and the eight section thereof relating to PLANS AND SURVEYS, shall be subject to the following provisions :—

a. The Company shall have the right to take, use and hold the beach and land below high water mark, in any stream, lake, navigable water gulf or sea, in so far as the same shall be vested in the Crown and shall not be required by the Crown, to such extent as shall be required by the Company for its railway and other works, and as shall be exhibited by a map or plan thereof deposited in the office of the Minister of Railways. But the provisions of this sub-section shall not apply to any beach or land lying East of Lake Nipissing except with the approval of the Governor in Council.

b. It shall be sufficient that the map or plan and book of reference for any portion of the line of the railway not being within any district or county for which there is a Clerk of the peace, be deposited in the office of the Minister of Railways of Canada; and any omission, mis-statement or erroneous discription of any lands therein may be corrected by the Company, with the consent of the Minister and certified by him; and the Company may then make the railway in accordance with such certified correction.

c. The eleventh sub-section of the said eighth section of the Railway Act shall not apply to any portion of the railway passing over ungranted lands of the Crown, or lands not within any surveyed township in any Province ; and in such places, deviations not exceeding five miles from the line shown on the map or plan as aforesaid, deposited by the Company, shall be allowed, without any formal correction or certificate ; and any further deviation that may be found expedient may be authorized by the order of the Governor in Council, and the Company may then make their railway in accordance with such authorized deviation.

d. The map or plan and book of reference of any part of the main line of the Canadian Pacific Railway made and deposited in accordance with this section, after approval by the Governor in Council, and of any branch of such railway hereafter to be located by the said Company in respect of which the approval of the Governor in Council shall not be necessary, shall avail as if made and deposited as required by the said "*Consolidated Railway Act*, 1879," for all the purposes of the said Act, and of this Act; and any copy of, or extract therefrom, certified by the said Minister or his deputy, shall be received as evidence in any court of law in Canada.

e. It shall be sufficient that a map or profile of any part of the completed railway, which shall not lie within any county or district having a registry office, be filed in the office of the Minister of Railways.

19. It shall be lawful for the Company to take from any public lands adjacent to or near the line of the said railway, all stone, timber, gravel and other materials which may be necessary or useful for the construction of the railway; and also to lay out and appropriate to the use of the Company, a greater extent of lands, whether public or private, for stations, depots, workshops, buildings, side-tracks, wharves, harbours and roadway, and for establishing screens against snow, than the breadth and quantity mentioned in "*The Consolidated Railway Act*, 1879,"—such greater extent taken, in any case being allowed by the Government, and shown on the maps or plans deposited with the Minister of Railways.

20. The limit to the reduction of tolls by the Parliament of Canada provided for by the eleventh sub-section of the 17th section of "*The Consolidated Railway Act*, 1879," respecting TOLLS, is hereby extended, so that such reduction may be to such an extent that such tolls when reduced shall not produce less than ten per cent. per annum profit on the capital actually expended in the construction of the railway, instead of not less than fifteen per cent. per annum profit, as provided by the said sub-section; and so also that such reduction shall not be made unless the net income of the Company, ascertained as described in said sub-section, shall have exceeded ten per cent. per annum instead of fifteen per cent. per annum as provided by the said sub-section. And the exercise by the Governor in Council of the power of reducing the tolls of the Company as provided by the tenth sub-section of said section seventeen is hereby limited to the same extent with relation to the profit of the Company, and to its net revenue, as that to which the power of Parliament to reduce tolls is limited by said sub-section eleven as hereby amended.

21. The first and second sub-sections of section twenty two of "*The Consolidated Railway Act*, 1879," shall not apply to the Canadian Pacific Railway Company; and it is hereby enacted that the transfer of shares in the undertaking shall be made only upon the books of the Company in person or by attorney, and shall not be valid unless so made; and the form and mode of transfer shall be such as shall be, from time to time, regulated by the by-laws of the Company. And the funds of the Company shall not be used in any advance upon the security of any of the shares or stock of the Company.

22. The third and fourth sub-sections of said section twenty two of "*The Consolidated Railway Act*, 1879," shall be subject to the following provisions, namely, that if before the completion of the railway and works under the said contract, any transfer should purport to be made of any stock or share in the Company, or any transmission of any share should be effected under the provisions of said sub-section four, to a person not already a shareholder in the Company, and if in the opinion of the Board it should not be expedient that the person (not being already a shareholder) to whom such transfer or transmission shall be made or effected should be accepted as a shareholder, the Directors may by resolution veto such transfer or transmission; and thereafter, and until after the completion of the said railway and works under the said contract, such person shall not be, or be recognized as a shareholder in the Company; and the original shareholder, or his estate, as the case may be, shall remain subject to all the obligations of a shareholder in the Company, with all the rights conferred upon a shareholder under this Act. But any firm holding paid-up shares in the Company may transfer the whole or any of such shares to any partner in such firm having already an interest as such partner in such shares, without being subject to such veto. And in the event of such veto being exercised, a note shall be taken of the transfer or transmission so voted in order that it may be recorded in the books of the Company after the completion of the Railway and works as aforesaid; but until such completion, the transfer or transmission so vetoed shall not confer any rights, nor have any effect of any nature or kind whatever as respects the Company.

23. Sub-section sixteen of section nineteen, relating to PRESIDENT AND DIRECTORS, THEIR ELECTION AND DUTIES; sub-section two of section twenty-four, relating to BY-LAWS NOTICES &c., subsections five and six of section twenty-eight, relating to GENERAL PROVISIONS, and section ninety-seven, relating to RAILWAY FUND, of "*The Consolidated Railway Act,* 1879," shall not, nor shall any of them apply to the Canadian Pacific Railway or to the Company hereby incorporated.

24. The said Company shall afford all reasonable facilities to the Ontario Pacific Junction Railway Company, when their railway shall be completed to a point of junction with the Canada Pacific Railway; and to the Canada Central Railway Company, for the receiving forwarding and delivering of traffic upon and from the railways of the said Companies, respectively, and for the return of carriages, trucks and other vehicles; and no one of the said Companies shall give or continue any preference or advantage to, or in favour of either of the others, or of any particular description of traffic, in any respect whatsoever; nor shall any one of the said Companies subject any other thereof, or any particular description of traffic, to any prejudice or disadvantage in any respect whatsoever: and any one of the said Companies which shall have any terminus or station near any terminus or station of either of the others, shall afford all reasonable facilities for receiving and forwarding all the traffic arriving by either of the others, without any unreasonable delay, and without preference or advantage, or prejudice or disadvantage, and so that no obstruction may be offered in the using of such railway as a continuous line of communication, and so that all reasonable accommodation may, at all times, by the means aforesaid, be mutually afforded by and to the said several railway companies; and the said Canadian Pacific Railway Company shall receive and carry all freight and passing traffic shipped to or from any point on the railway of either of the said above named railway companies passing over the Canada Pacific Railway or any part thereof, at the same mileage rate and subject to the same charges for similar services, without granting or allowing any preference or advantage to the traffic coming from or going upon one of such railways over such traffic coming from or going upon the other of them, reserving, however, to the said Canadian Pacific Railway Company the right of making special rates for purchasers of land, or for immigrants or intending immigrants which special rates shall not govern or affect the rates of passenger traffic as between the said Company and the said two above named Companies or either of them. And any agreement made between any two of the said companies contrary to the foregoing provisions, shall be unlawful, null and void.

25. The Company under the authority of a special general meeting of the shareholders thereof, and as an extension of the railway hereby authorized to be constructed, may purchase or acquire by lease or otherwise, and hold and operate, the Canada Central Railway, or may amalgamate therewith and may purchase or acquire by lease or otherwise and hold and operate a line or lines of railway from the city of Ottawa to any point at navigable water on the Atlantic seaboard or to any intermediate point, or may acquire running powers over any railway now constructed between Ottawa and any such point or intermediate point. And the Company may purchase or acquire any such railway subject to such existing mortgages, charges or liens thereon as shall be agreed upon, and shall possess with regard to any lines of railway so purchased, or acquired, and becoming the property of the Company, the same powers as to the issue of bonds thereon, or on any of them, to an amount not exceeding twenty thousand dollars per mile, and as to the security for such bonds, as are conferred upon the Company by the twenty-eighth section hereof, in respect of bonds to be issued upon the Canadian Pacific Railway. But such issue of bonds shall not affect the right of any holder of mortgages or other charges already existing upon any line of railway so purchased or acquired; and the amount of bonds hereby authorized to be issued upon such line of railway shall be diminished by the amount of such existing mortgages or charges thereon.

26. The Company shall have power and authority to erect and maintain docks, dockyards, wharves, slips and piers at any point on or in connection with the said Canadian Pacific Railway, and at all the termini thereof on navigable water, for the convenience and accommodation of vessels and elevators; and also to acquire, and work elevators; and to acquire, own, hold, charter, work, and run, steam and other vessels for cargo and passengers upon any navigable water, which the Canadian Pacific Railway may reach or connect with.

BY-LAWS

27. The by-laws of the Company may provide for the remuneration of the president and directors of the Company, and of any executive committee of such directors; and for the transfer of stock and shares; the registration and inscription of stock, shares, and bonds, and the transfer of registered bonds, and the payment of dividends and interest at any place or places within or beyond the limits of Canada; and for all other matters required by the said contract or by this Act to be regulated by by-laws: but the by-laws of the Company made as provided by law shall in no case have any force or effect after the next general meeting of shareholders, which shall be held after the passage of such by-laws, unless they are approved by such meeting.

BONDS.

28. The Company, under the authority of a special general meeting of the shareholders called for the purpose, may issue mortgage bonds to the extent of ten thousand dollars per mile of the Canadian Pacific Railway for the purposes of the undertaking authorized by the present Act; which issue shall constitute a first mortgage and privilege upon the said railway, constructed or acquired, and to be thereafter acquired including rolling stock, and plant, and upon its tolls and revenues (after deduction from such tolls and revenues of working expenses), and upon the franchises of the Company; the whole as shall be declared and described as so mortgaged in any deed of mortgage as hereinafter provided. Provided always, however, that if the Company shall have issued, or shall intend to issue land grant bonds under the provisions of the thirtieth section hereof, the lands granted and to be granted by the Government to the Company may be excluded from the operation of such mortgage and privilege: and provided also that such mortgage and privilege shall not attach upon any property which the Company are hereby, or by the said contract, authorized to acquire or receive from the Government of Canada until the same shall have been conveyed by the Government to the Company but shall attach upon such property, if so declared in such deed, as soon as the same shall be conveyed to the Company. And such mortgage and privilege may be evidenced by a deed or deeds of mortgage executed by the Company, with the authority of its shareholders expressed by a resolution passed at such special general meeting; and any such deed may contain such description of the property mortgaged by such deed, and such conditions respecting the payment of the bonds secured thereby and of the interest thereon, and the remedies which shall be enjoyed by the holders of such bonds or by any trustee or trustees for them in default of such payment, and the enforcement of such remedies, and may provide for such forfeitures and penalties, in default of such payment, as may be approved by such meeting; and may also contain, with the approval aforesaid, authority to the trustee or trustees, upon such default, as one of such remedies, to take possession of the railway and property mortgaged, and to hold and run the same for the benefit of the bondholders thereof for a time to be limited by such deed, or to sell the said railway and property, after such delay, and upon such terms and conditions as may be stated in such deed; and with like approval any such deed may contain provisions to the effect that upon such default and upon such other conditions as shall be described in such deed, the right of voting possessed by the shareholders of the Company, and by the holders of preferred stock therein, or by either of them, shall cease and determine, and shall thereafter appertain to the bondholders, or to them and to the holders of the whole or of any part of the preferred stock of the Company, as shall be declared by such deed ; and such deed may also provide for the conditional or absolute cancellation after such sale of any or all of the shares so deprived of voting power, or of any or all of the preferred stock of the company, or both ; and may also, either directly by its terms, or indirectly by reference to the by-laws of the Company, provide for the mode of enforcing and exercising the powers and authority to be conferred and defined by such deed, under the provisions hereof. And such deed, and the provisions thereof made under the authority hereof, and such other provisions thereof as shall purport (with like approval) to grant such further and other powers and privileges to such trustee or trustees and to such bondholders, as are not contrary to law or to the provisions of this Act, shall be valid and binding. But if any change in the ownership or possession of the said Railway and property shall, at any time, take place under the provisions hereof, or of any such deed, or in any other manner, the said Railway and property shall continue to be held and operated under the provisions hereof, and of "*The Consolidated Railway Act*, 1879," as hereby modified. And if the Company does not avail itself of the power of issuing bonds secured upon the land grant alone as hereinafter provided, the issue of bonds hereby authorized may be increased to any amount not exceeding twenty thousand dollars per mile of the said Canadian Pacific Railway.

29. If any bond issue be made by the Company under the last preceding section before the said railway is completed according to the said contract, a proportion of the proceeds of such bonds, or a proportion of such bonds if they be not sold, corresponding to the proportion of the work contracted for then remaining incomplete, shall be received by the Government, and shall be held, dealt with and, from time to time, paid over by the Government to the Company upon the same conditions, in the same manner and according to the same proportions as the proceeds of the bonds, the issue of which is contemplated by subsection *d.* of Clause 9 of the said contract, and by the thirty-first section hereof.

30. The Company may also issue mortgage bonds to the extent of twenty five million dollars upon the lands granted in aid of the said railway and of the undertaking authorized by this Act ; such issue to be made only upon similar authority to that required by this Act for the issue of bonds upon the railway ; and when so made such bonds shall constitute a first mortgage upon such lands, and shall attach upon them when they shall be granted, if they are not actually granted at the time of the issue of such bonds. And such mortgages may be evidence by a deed or deeds of mortgage to be executed under like authority to the deed of securing the issue of bonds on the railway ; and such deed or deeds under like authority may contain similar conditions and may confer upon the trustee or trustees named thereunder and upon the holders of the bonds secured thereby, remedies, authority, power and privileges and may provide for forfeitures and penalties, similar to those which may be inserted and provided for under the provisions of this Act in any deed securing the issue of bonds on the railway, together with such other provisions and conditions not inconsistent with law or with this Act as shall be so authorized. And such bonds may be styled Land Grant Bonds, and they and the proceeds thereof shall be dealt with in the manner provided in the said contract.

31. The Company may in the place and stead of the said land grant bonds, issue bonds under the twent-eight section hereof, to such amount as they shall agree with the Government to issue, with the interest guaranteed by the Government as provided for in the said contract; and such bonds to constitute a mortgage upon the property of the Company and its franchises acquired and to be thereafter acquired —including the main line of the Canadian Pacific Railway, and the branches thereof hereinbefore described, with the plant and rolling stock thereof acquired and to be thereafter acquired, but exclusive of such other branches thereof and of such personal property as shall be excluded by the deed of mortgage to be executed as security for such issue. And the provisions of the said twenty-eighth section shall apply to such issue of bonds, and to the security which may be given for the payment thereof, and they and the proceeds thereof shall be dealt with as hereby and by the said contract provided.

32. It shall not be necessary to affix the seal of the Company to any mortgage bond issued under the authority of this Act; and every such bond issued without such seal shall have the same force and effect, and be held, treated and dealt with by all courts of law and of equity as if it were sealed with the seal of the company. And if it is provided by the mortgage deed executed to secure the issue of any bonds, that any of the signatures to such bonds or to the coupons thereto appended may be engraved, stamped or lithographed thereon, such engraved, stamped or lithographed signatures shall be valid and binding on the Company.

33. The phrase "working expenses" shall mean and include all expenses of maintenance of the railway, and of the stations, buildings, works and conveniencies belonging thereto, and of the rolling and other stock and moveable plant used in the working thereof, and also all such tolls, rents or annual sums as may be paid in respect of the hire of engines, carriages or waggons let to the Company; also, all rents, charges, or interest on the purchase money of lands belonging to the Company, purchased but not paid for, or not fully paid for; and also all expenses of and incidental to working the railway and the traffic thereon, including stores and consumable articles; also rates, taxes, insurance and compensation for accidents or losses; also all salaries and wages of persons employed in and about the working of the railway and traffic, and all office and management expenses, including directors' fees, agency, legal and other like expenses.

34. The bonds authorized by this Act to be issued upon the railway or upon the lands to be granted to the Company, or both, may be so issued in whole or in part in the denomination of dollars, pounds sterling, or francs, or in any or all of them, and the coupons may be for payment in denominations similar to those of the bond to which they are attached. And the whole or any of such bonds, may be pledged, negotiated or sold upon such conditions and at such price as the Board of Directors shall from time to time, determine. And provision may be made by the by-laws of the Company, that after the issue of any bond, the same may be surrendered to the Company by the holder thereof, and the Company may, in exchange therefor, issue to such holder inscribed stock of the Company, which inscribed stock may be registered or inscribed at the chief place of business of the Company or elsewhere, in such manner, with such rights, liens, privileges and preferences, at such place, and upon such conditions, as shall be provided by the by-laws of the Company.

35. It shall not be necessary, in order to preserve the priority, lien, charge, mortgage or privilege, purporting to appertain to or be created by any bond issued or mortgage deed executed under the provisions of this Act, that such bond or deed shall be enregistered in any manner, or in any place whatever. But every such mortgage deed shall be deposited in the office of the Secretary of State, of which deposit notice shall be given in the *Canada Gazette*. And in like manner any agreement entered into by the Company, under section thirty-six of this Act, shall also be deposited in the said office. And a copy of any such mortgage deed, or agreement, certified to be a true copy by the Secretary of State or his Deputy, shall be received as *primâ facie* evidence of the original in all courts of justice, without proof of the signatures or seal upon such original.

36. If, at any time, any agreement be made by the Company with any persons intending to become bondholders of the Company, or be contained in any mortgage deed executed under the authority of this Act, restricting the issue of bonds by the Company, under the powers conferred by this Act, or defining or limiting the mode of exercising such powers, the Company, after the deposit thereof with the Secretary of State as hereinbefore provided, shall not act upon such powers otherwise then as defined, restricted and limited by such agreement. And no bond thereafter issued by the Company, and no order, resolution or proceeding thereafter made, passed or had by the Company, or by the Board of Directors, contrary to the terms of such agreement, shall be valid or effectual.

37. The Company may, from time to time, issue guaranteed or preferred stock, at such price, to such amount, not exceeding ten thousand dollars per mile, and upon such conditions as to the preferences and privileges appertaining thereto, as shall be authorized by the majority in value of the shareholders present in person or represented by proxy at any annual meeting or at any special general meeting thereof called for the purpose,—notice of the intention to propose such issue at such meeting being given in the notice calling such meeting. But the guarantee or preference accorded to such stock shall not interfere with the lien, mortgage and privilege attaching to bonds issued under the authority of this Act. And the holders of such preferred stock

shall have such power of voting at meetings of shareholders, as shall be conferred upon them by the by-laws of the Company

EXECUTION OF AGREEMENTS.

38. Every contract, agreement, engagement, scrip certificate or bargain made, and every bill of exchange drawn, accepted or endorsed, and every promissory note and cheque made, drawn or endorsed on behalf of the Company, by any agent, officer or servant of the Company, in general accordance with his powers as such under the by-laws of the Company, shall be binding upon the company ; and in no case shall it be necessary to have the seal of the Company affixed to any such bill, note, cheque, contract, agreement, engagement, bargain, or scrip certificate, or to prove that the same was made, drawn, accepted or endorsed as the case may be, in pursuance of any by-law or special vote or order; nor shall the party so acting as agent, officer or servant of the Company be subjected individually to any liability, whatsoever, to any third party thereof ; Provided always, that nothing in this Act shall be construed to authorize the Company to issue any note payable to the bearer thereof, or any promissory note intended to be circulated as money, or as the note of a bank, or to engage in the business of banking or insurance.

GENERAL PROVISIONS.

39. The Company shall, from time to time, furnish such reports of the progress of the work, with such details and plans of the work, as the Government may require.

40. As respects places not within any Province, any notice required by "*The Consolidated Railway Act,* 1879," to be given in the "Official Gazette" of a Province, may be given in the *Canada Gazette.*

41. Deeds and conveyances of land to the Company for the purposes of this Act, (not being letters patent from the Crown) may, in so far as circumstances will admit, be in the form following, that is to say :—

"Know all men by these presents, that I. A. B., in consideration of   paid to me by the Canadian Pacific Railway Company, the receipt whereof is hereby acknowledged, grant, bargain, sell and convey unto the said The Canadian Pacific Railway Company, their successors and assigns, all that tract or parcel of land (*describe the land*) to have and to hold the said land and premises unto the said Company, their successors and assigns for ever.

"Witness my hand and seal, this   day of   one thousand eight hundred and

"Signed, sealed and delivered   }   A.B.   [L.S.]
in presence of   }

" C. D.
" E. F."

or in any other form to the like effect. And every deed made in accordance herewith shall be held and construed to impose upon the vendor executing the same the obligation of guaranteeing the Company and its assigns against all dower and claim for dower and against all hypothecs and mortgages and against all liens and charges whatsoever and also that he has a good, valid and transferable title thereto.

REPEAL OF DUTIES ON PROMISSORY NOTES.

45 VICTORIA, CHAPTER 1.

An Act to repeal the duty on Promissory Notes, Drafts and Bills of Exchange.

Section.
Preamble.
1. Duty repealed after 4th March, 1882.
Proviso: as to rights acquired and

Section.
things done before the said repeal, and for redemption of unused stamps.

[*Assented to 3rd March*, 1882.]

HER Majesty, by and with the advice and consent of the Senate and House of Commons of Canada, enacts as follows:—

1. No duty shall be payable on any promissory note, draft or bill of exchange, made, drawn or accepted in Canada after the fourth day of March, in the present year, one thousand eight hundred and eighty-two; and from and after the said day the Act passed in the forty-second year of Her Majesty's reign, and intituled "*An Act to amend and consolidate the laws respecting duties imposed on promissory notes and bills of exchange*," shall be repealed: Provided always, that all Acts or enactments repealed by the said Act shall remain repealed, and that all things lawfully done, and all rights acquired under the said Act or any Act repealed by it, shall remain valid, and all penalties incurred under them or any of them, may be enforced and recovered, and all proceedings commenced under them or any of them may be continued and completed, as if this Act had not been passed: and provided also, that all unused stamps lawfully issued under the said Acts or any of them for the payment of any duty hereby repealed, shall, after the said day and until the thirtieth day of June, one thousand eight hundred and eighty-two, be received at their cost to the holder thereof at the time of the passing of this Act, in payment of any money payable to Her Majesty for the public uses of Canada, or in exchange for postage stamps of like face value.

CHAP. XXIII.

An Act respecting Insolvent Banks, Insurance Companies, Loan Companies, Building Societies, and Trading Corporations.

Section.

Preamble.
1. Application of Act. As to railways, &c.
2. Application of certain sections. The same.
3. Definition of "Insurance Co.," "Trading Co."
4. "Court."
5. "Official Gazette."
6. "Company."
7. "Province."
8. "Contributory."
9. When a company shall be deemed insolvent.
10. When a company shall be deemed unable to pay its debts.
11. Time to elapse after demand.
12. When winding up commences.
13. Application to court for winding up order.
14. Power of court on the application.
15. If company opposes application; court may adjourn the proceedings and order enquiry.
16. Duty of company and its officers if enquiry is ordered.
17. Duty of the court after report on enquiry.
18. Actions against Co. may be restrained.
19. Company to cease business; transfers of shares void; corporate state continues.
20. After winding up order, actions against Co. stayed.
21. Executions, etc. against Co. void.
22. Court may stay winding up proceedings.
23. Wishes of creditors, &c., how ascertained, Court may require proof.
24. Liquidator to be appointed.
25. An incorporated company may be appointed liquidator.
26. Additional liquidators:
27. Quorum.
28. Security.
29. If no liquidator.
30. Provisional liquidator.
31. Resignation or removal of liquidator.
32. Remuneration of liquidator.
33. Description of liquidator.
34. Duties of liquidator after appointment.
35. Powers of liquidators; suits; business of company; sale of property; general acts; proving in bankruptcy, &c.; drawing or indorsing bills, &c., and raising funds; general powers.
36. When solicitor may be appointed.
37. Debts, &c., due to the company may be compromised.
38. Powers of directors to cease.

Section.

39. Moneys to be deposited in bank.
40. A separate deposit account to be kept.
41. Bank book to be produced at meetings.
42. And on order of court.
43. Liquidator subject to summary jurisdiction of Court; remedies against estate obtained by summary order and not by suit, &c.
44. Balance on hand by liquidator after final winding up to be deposited; penalty for neglect.
45. If not claimed to be paid to Receiver-General.
46. List of contributories.
47. List of contributories must distinguish between those in their own right and those in a representative capacity.
48. Liability of shareholders or their representatives.
49. Liability after transfer of shares.
50. Nature of liability of a contributory.
51. Trustee, &c., of company may be ordered to pay over balance and deliver up books, &c.
52. Court may order debtors of company to pay.
53. When calls may be made on contributories; proviso; proviso.
54. Contributory may be ordered to pay into Court.
55. Distribution of surplus.
56. Contributory about to abscond, &c., may be arrested, and his papers, &c., may be seized.
57. Books, &c., of company are *primâ facie* evidence as between contributories.
58. Court may allow inspection by creditors, &c., of company's books, &c.
59. Contributory to vote personally or by written proxy.
60. What debts may be proved against the company; law of set-off to apply.
61. Distribution of property of company!
62. When creditors must send in claims.
63. After expiration of time for sending in claims, assets may be distributed.
64. Creditors may be compromised with.
65. Duty of creditors holding security; security by negociable instruments.
66. If the security be a mortgage on real estate or a ship; if there are subsequent claims.
67. Duty of liquidator if a secured claim is filed.
68. Rank, &c., on dividend sheet.
69. No lien by judgment and execution: this provision not to apply to lien for costs

Section.

70. Claim or dividend may be objected to; answers and replies; further proceedings consequent upon objection; further powers of Court.
71. Gratuitous contracts, &c., when to be void; contracts injuring or obstructing creditors.
72. When contracts with consideration shall be voidable.
73. As to contracts made in fraud or to obstruct or delay creditors.
74. Securities given by company for payment when void.
75. Payments by Co. when to be void; proviso.
76. As to debts of Co. transferred to contributories.
77. How the powers of the Court may be exercised; in Ontario.
78. Appeals; proviso; proviso; proviso; further appeal; in N.W.T.
79. Practice; security on appeal; and time for limited.
80. If not proceeded with, appeal may be dismissed.
81. Witnesses' attendance, how secured.
82. Persons having information may be examined; if person summoned refuses to attend; Proviso, as to questions of lien on papers.
83. Examination to be on oath; refusal to answer, to be contempt.
84. Officer of Company, &c., mis-applying money may be compelled to repay.
85. Officer of Company, &c., destroying, &c., books, &c., of Company guilty of misdemeanor.
86. Various provincial Courts to be auxiliaries to one another.
87. Order of one Court may be enforced by another.
88. Rules of procedure as to amendments to apply.
89. Before whom affidavits may be made.
90. Judicial notice of seals, &c.
91. Unclaimed dividends to be paid to Receiver General.
92. Powers conferred on Court by this Act are in addition to the other powers of the Court.
93. Costs payable out of estate.
94. Payment of costs in cases of deficiency of assets.
95. Court may direct criminal proceedings against certain officers of the Company.
96. Persons giving false evidence liable as for perjury.
97. Judges may make rules.
98. Until rules are made, present procedure to apply.
99. Provision as to winding up order in case of a Bank.
100. Chairman of meeting.
101. Scale of votes.
102. Chairman to report result of vote.
103. Case of failure to appoint liquidators.
104. Reservation of dividends on outstanding notes.
105. What is sufficient notice to holders of notes; in Quebec.
106. What is sufficient notice to certain policyholders.
107. As to deposit held by Receiver-General.
108. As to holders of policies by life insurance on which no claim has accrued; proviso, if the policy be cancelled.
109. Statement of creditors to be prepared by the liquidator and certain claims collocated without proof; proviso, for contestation; Copy of statement to be filed with superintendent of insurance and notice thereof given.
110. As to claims accruing after the winding up order, but within 30 days thereof.
111. If the holder gives notice of willingness to accept insurance in another company; proviso.
112. Report to Superintendent of Insurance.
113. What publication of notice sufficient.
114. As to deposit held by Receiver-General.
115. As to policies on which no claim has accrued at time of winding up order; proviso, as to cancellation of policy.
116. Statement to be made by liquidators under sect. 114; proviso; copy to be filed with Superintendent of Insurance; notice to each creditor.
117. If a claim accrues after the winding up order, but within 30 days thereof.
118. If within 30 days the holder signifies his willingness to accept insurance in another company.
119. Report to Superintendent of Insurance.

Assented to 17th May, 1882.

HER Majesty, by and with the advice and consent of the Senate and House of Commons of Canada, enacts as follows: —

APPLICATION OF ACT.

1. This Act applies to incorporated Banks including Savings Banks, incorporated Insurance Companies, Loan Companies having borrowing powers, Building Societies having a capital stock, and which are insolvent or in process of being wound up either under a general or a special Act and which, on petition as in this Act set forth, by its shareholders, or creditors, assignees or liquidators, ask to be brought within and under the provisions of this Act.

(a). This Act does not apply to railway or telegraph companies, or to building societies that have not a capital stock.

2. The provisions of sections thirteen to ninety-eight inclusive, of this Act are in the case of a bank (not including a savings bank) subject to the provisions, changes and modifications contained in sections ninety-nine to one hundred and five inclusive.

(a) The provisions of section thirteen to ninety-eight inclusive of this Act are in the case of an Insurance Company subject to the provisions, changes and modifications contained in sections one hundred and six to one hundred and nineteen inclusive.

INTERPRETATION.

3. An insurance company within the meaning of this Act is a company carrying on, either as a mutual or a stock company, the business of insurance whether life, fire, marine (ocean or inland waters), accident, guarantee or otherwise.

(a) A trading company within the meaning of this Act is a company (except railway and telegraph companies,) carrying on business similar to that carried on by apothecaries, auctioneers, bankers, brokers, brickmakers, builders, carpenters, carriers, cattle or sheep salesmen, coach proprietors, dyers, fullers, keepers of inns, taverns, hotels, saloons or coffee houses, lime burners, livery stable keepers, market gardeners, millers, miners, packers, printers, quarrymen, sharebrokers, shipowners, shipwrights, stockbrokers, stock-jobbers, victuallers, warehousemen, wharfingers, persons using the trade of merchandise by way of bargaining, exchange, bartering, commission, consignment or otherwise, in gross or by retail, or by persons who, either for themselves, or as agents or factors for others, seek their living by buying and selling or buying and letting for hire goods or commodities, or by the manufacture, workmanship or the conversion of goods or commodities, or trees,

4. Unless otherwise expressed or indicated by the context the word "court" means in the Province of Ontario, the High Court of Justice; in the Province of Quebec, the Superior Court; in the Province of Nova Scotia, the Supreme Court; in the Province of New Brunswick, the Supreme Court; in the Province of Prince Edward Island, the Supreme Court; in the Province of British Columbia, the Supreme Court; in the Province of Manitoba, the Court of Queen's Bench; and in the North West Territories and the district of Keewatin, such court or magistrate or other judicial authority as may be designated from time to time by proclamation of the Governor in Council, published in the *Canada Gazette.*

5. "Official Gazette" means both the *Canada Gazette* and the Gazette published under the authority of the Government of the Province, Territory or District where the proceedings for the winding up of the business of the company are being carried on, or used as the official means of communication between the Lieutenant-Governor and the people, and if no such Gazette is published, then it means any newspaper published in the the Province, Territory or district, which may be designated by the court for publishing the notices required by this Act.

6. "Company" includes any corporation subject to the provisions of this Act.

7. "Province" includes Territory and District.

8. "Contributory" means a person liable to contribute to the assets of a company under this Act; it also includes in all proceedings prior to the final determination of the contributories, a person alleged to be a contributory.

WHEN COMPANY DEEMED INSOLVENT.

9. A company is deemed insolvent—

(*a*.) If it is unable to pay its debts as they become due;

(*b*.) If it calls a meeting of its creditors for the purpose of compounding with them;

(*c*.) If it exhibits a statement shewing its inability to meet its liabilities;

(*d*.) If it has otherwise acknowleged its insolvency;

(*e*.) If it assigns, removes or disposes of, or is about or attempts to assign, removes or dispose of, any of its property with intent to defraud, defeat, or delay its creditors, or any of them;

(*f*.) If, with such intent, it has procured its money, goods, chattels, land or property to be seized, levied on or taken under or by any process or execution.

(*g*.) If it has made any general conveyance or assignment of its property for the benefit of its creditors, or if, being unable to meet its liabilities in full, it makes any sale of conveyance of the whole or the main part of its stock in trade or assets, without the consent of its creditors, or without satisfying their claims;

(*h*.) If it permits any execution issued against it, under which any of its chattels, land or property are seized, levied upon or taken in execution, to remain unsatisfied till within four days of the time fixed by the sheriff or officer for the sale thereof, or for fifteen days after such seizure.

10. A company is deemed to be unable to pay its debts as they become due

(*a*.) Whenever a creditor by assignment or otherwise, to whom the company is indebted in a sum exceeding two hundred dollars then due has served on the company, in the manner in which process may legally be served on it in the place where the service is made, a demand in writing requiring the company to pay the sum so due, and the company has for the space of time hereinafter mentioned neglected to pay such sum, or to secure or compound for the same to the satisfaction of the creditor.

11. The space of time above referred to it as follows:—In the case of a Bank, ninety days; in all other cases, sixty days next succeeding the service of the demand.

12. The winding up of the business of a company is deemed to commence at the time of the service of the notice of presentation of the petition for winding up.

PROCEEDINGS FOR WINDING UP ORDER.

13. When a company becomes insolvent a creditor for the sum of two hundred dollars may, after four days notice of the application to the company, apply by petition to the court in the Province where the head office of the company is situated, or if they be no head office in Canada then in the Province where its chief place or one of its chief places of business is situated, for an order that the business of the company be wound up. Such order is hereinafter called a "winding up order."

14. The court may make the order applied for, may dismiss the petition with or without costs, may adjourn the hearing conditionally or unconditionally, or make any interim or other order that it deems just.

15. If the company opposes the application on the ground that it has not become insolvent within the meaning of this Act, or that its suspension or default was only temporary, and was not caused by any deficiency in its assets, and shows reasonable cause for believing that such opposition is well founded, the court, in its discretion, may, from time to time, adjourn the proceedings upon such application for a time not exceeding six months, from the time of the application : and may order an accountant, or other person to enquire into the affairs of the company and to report thereon within a period not exceeding thirty days from the date of such order.

16. Upon the service of such order it is the duty of the company, and of the president, directors, managers, officers and employees thereof, and of every other person having possession or knowledge of any asset, book or record thereof, to exhibit to the accountant or other person so named as aforesaid, the books of account of the company, together with all inventories, papers and vouchers referring to the business of the company, or of any person therewith ; and generally to give all such information as may be required by such accountant or other person as aforesaid, in order to form a just estimate of the affairs of the company and any refusal on the part of the president, directors, managers or employees of the company to give such information, is a contempt of the court, and is punishable by fine or imprisonment, or by both, at the discretion of the court.

17. Upon receiving the report of the person ordered to enquire into the affairs of the company, and after hearing such persons, being shareholders or creditors of the company as may desire to be heard thereon, the court may either refuse the application or make the winding up order.

18. The court may at any time after the presentation of a petition for a winding up order and before making the order, upon the application of the company, or of any creditor or contributory, restrain further proceedings in any action, suit or proceeding against the com- upon such terms as the Court thinks fit.

PROCEEDINGS AFTER WINDING UP ORDER.

19. The company, from the making of the winding up order must cease to carry on its business, except in so far as may, in the opinion of the liquidator, be required for the beneficial winding up thereof. Any transfers of shares, except transfers made to or with the sanction of the liquidators, under the authority of the court, or any alteration in the status of the members of the company, after the com- mencement of such winding up, are void, but the corporate state and all the corporate powers of the company, notwithstanding it may be other- wise provided by the Act, charter or instrument of incorporation, con- tinue until the affairs of the company are wound up.

20. When the winding up order is made, no suit, action or other proceeding shall be proceeded with or commenced against the company except with leave of the court and subject to such terms as the court may impose.

21. Any attachment, sequestration, distress or execution put in force against the estate or effects of the company after the making of the winding up order is void.

22. The court may, at any time after the winding up order is made, upon the application of any creditor or contributory, and upon proof to the satisfaction of the court, that all proceedings in relation to the winding up ought to be stayed, make an order staying the same, either altogether or for a limited time, on such terms and subject to such conditions as it deems fit.

23. The court may, as to it may seem just, as to all matters re- lating to the winding up, have regard to the wishes of the creditors, contributories, shareholders or members, as proved to it by any sufficient evidence, and may, if it thinks it expedient, direct meetings of the creditors, contributories, shareholders or members to be summoned, held and conducted in such manner as the court directs, for the purpose of ascertaining their wishes, and may appoint a person to act as chair- man of any such meeting, and to report the result of such meeting to the court ; in the case of creditors, regard is to be had to the amount of debt due to each creditor, and in the case of shareholders or members to the number of votes conferred on each shareholder or member by the law or regulations of the company. The court may prescribe the mode of preliminary proof of creditors' claims for the purpose of the meeting.

LIQUIDATORS.

24. The winding up order must appoint a liquidator or more than one liquidator of the estate and effects of the company ; but no such liquidators shall be appointed unless a previous notice be given to the creditors, contributories, shareholders or members in the manner and form prescribed by the court.

25. An incorporated company may be appointed liquidator to the goods and effects of a company under this Act; and in case an incorporated company is so appointed, it may act through one or more of its principal officers to be appointed by the court.

26. The court may, if it thinks fit after the appointment of one or more liquidators, appoint additional liquidators.

27. If more than one liquidator be appointed, the court may declare whether any act to be done by a liquidator, is to be done by all or any one or more of the liquidators.

28. The court may also determine what security is to be given by a liquidator on his appointment.

29. If at any time there be no liquidator, all the property of the company shall be deemed to be in the custody of the court.

30. The court may, at any time after the presentation of the petition and before the first appointment of a liquidator, appoint provisionally a liquidator of the estate and effects of the company.

31. A liquidator may resign or be removed by the court on due cause shown. A vacancy in the office of liquidator is filled by order of the court.

32. The liquidator is to be paid such salary or remuneration by way of percentage or otherwise as the court directs, upon such notice to the creditors, contributories, shareholders or members, as the court may order. If there be more than one liquidator the remuneration is to be distributed amongst them in such proportions as the court directs.

33. In all proceedings connected with the company a liquidator is to be described as the "liquidator of the (name of company)," and not by his individual name only.

34. The liquidator upon appointment must take into his custody or under his control, all the property, effects and choses in action to which the company is intitled—he must perform such duties in reference to winding up the business of the company as are imposed by the court or by this Act.

35. The liquidator has power with the sanction of the court, and upon such previous notice to the creditors, contributories, shareholders or members, as the court may order,—

(*a*). To bring or defend any action, suit or prosecution or other legal proceeding civil or criminal, in his own name as liquidator or in the name or on behalf of the company as the case may be;

(*b*). To carry on the business of the company as far as may be necessary to the beneficial winding up of the same;

(*c*). To sell the real and personal and heritable and movable property, effects and choses in action of the company, by public auction or private contract, with power to transfer the whole thereof to any person or company, or to sell the same in parcels;

(*d*). To do all acts and to execute in the name and on behalf of the company all deeds, receipts and other documents, and for that purpose to use, when necessary, the company's seal;

(*e*.) To prove, rank, claim, and draw dividends in the matter of the bankruptcy, insolvency or sequestration of any contributory, for any balance against the estate of such contributory, and to take and receive dividends in respect of such balance in the matter of bankruptcy or sequestration as a separate debt due from such bankrupt or insolvent and ratably with the other separate creditors.

(*f*.) To draw, accept, make and endorse any bill of exchange or promissory note in the name and on the behalf of the company; also to raise upon the security of the assets of the company; from time to time, any requisite sum or sums of money; and the drawing, accepting, making or endorsing of every such bill of exchange or promissory note as aforesaid on behalf of the company as if such bill or note had been drawn, accepted, made or endorsed by or on behalf of such company in the course of carrying on the business;

(*g*.) To do and execute all such other things as may be necessary for winding up the affairs of the company and distributing its assets.

36. The liquidator may, with the sanction of the court, appoint a solicitor or law agent to assist him in the performance of his duties.

37. The liquidator may, with the sanction of the court, compromise all calls and liabilities to calls, debts and liabilities capable of resulting in debts, and all claims, whether present or future, certain or contingent, ascertained or sounding only in damages, subsisting or supposed to subsist between the company and any contributory or other debt or or person apprehending liability to the company, and all questions in any way relating to or affecting the assets of the company or the winding up of the company upon the receipt of such sums, payable at such times, and generally upon such terms, as may be agreed upon; with power for the liquidator to take any security for the discharge of such debts or liabilities, and to give a complete discharge in respect of all or any such calls, debts or liabilities.

38. Upon the appointment of the liquidator, all the powers of the directors cease, except in so far as the court or the liquidator may sanction the continuance of such power.

39. The liquidator must deposit at interest in some chartered bank or Post office Savings Bank or other Government savings bank to be indicated by the court, all sums of money which he may have in his hands belonging to the company, whenever and so often as such sums amount to one hundred dollars.

40. Such deposit must not be made in the name of the liquidator generally, on pain of dismissal; but a separate account must be kept for the company of the moneys belonging to the company in the name of the liquidator as such.

41. At every meeting of the contributories or creditors or shareholders or members the liquidator must produce a bank pass book.

showing the amount of the deposits made for the company, the dates at which such deposits were made, the amount withdrawn and dates of such withdrawal; of which production mention must be made in the minutes of such meeting; the absence of such mention is *prima facie* evidence that such pass book was not produced at the meeting.

42. The liquidator must also produce such pass book whenever so ordered by the court, and on his refusal to do so, he may be treated as being in contempt of court.

43. The liquidator is subject to the summary jurisdiction of the court in the same manner and to the same extent as the ordinary officers of the court are subject to its jurisdiction ; and the performance of his duties may be compelled, and all remedies sought or demanded for enforcing any claim for a debt, privilege, mortgage, lien or right of property upon, in or to any effects or property in the hands, possession or custody of a liquidator, may be obtained by an order of the court on summary petition, and not by any suit, attachment, seizure, or other proceeding of any kind whatever ; and obedience by the liquidator to such order may be enforced by such court under the penalty of imprisonment, as for contempt of court or disobedience thereto ; and he may be removed in the discretion of the court.

44. The liquidator must, within three days after the date of the final winding up of the business of the company, deposit in the bank appointed or named as hereinbefore provided for, any other money belonging to the estate then in his hands not required for any other purpose authorized by this Act, with a sworn statement and account of such money, and that the same is all he has in his hands ; he is subject to a penalty not exceeding ten dollars, and not less than ten per cent. per annum interest upon the sums in his hands for every day on which he neglects or delays such payment ; he is a debtor to Her Majesty for such money, and may be compelled as such to account for and pay over the same.

45. The money so deposited must be left for three years in the bank subject to be claimed by those entitled thereto, and must be then paid over with the interest to the Receiver General of Canada, and if afterwards claimed is to be paid over to the person entitled thereto.

CONTRIBUTORIES.

46. As soon as may be after the winding up of a company, the court shall settle a list of contributories.

47. The list of contributories is to distinguish between persons who are contributories in their own right and persons who are contributories as being representatives of or being liable for the debts of others ; it is not necessary, where the personal representative of any deceased contributory, is placed on the list to add the heirs or devisees of such contributory, nevertheless such heirs or devisees may be added as and when the court thinks fit.

48. Every shareholder or member of the company or his representative is liable to contribute the amount unpaid on his shares of the capital, or on his liability to the company or to its members or creditors, as the case may be, under the Act, charter or instrument of incorporation of the company or otherwise; and the amount which he is liable to contribute is deemed an asset of the company, and is a debt due to the company payable as may be directed or appointed under this Act.

49. Where a shareholder has transferred his shares under circumstances which do not by law free him from liability in respect thereof, or where he is by law liable to the company or its members or creditors, as the case may be, to an amount beyond the amount unpaid on his shares, he is deemed a member of the company for the purposes of this Act, and is liable to contribute as aforesaid to the extent of his liabilities to the company or its members or creditors independently of this Act, and the amount which he is so liable to contribute is deemed an asset and a debt as aforesaid.

50. The liability of any person to contribute to the assets of a company under this Act, in the event of the business of same being wound up, creates a debt accruing due from such person at the time when his liability commenced, but payable at the time or respective times when calls are made as hereinafter mentioned for enforcing such liability; in the case of bankruptcy or insolvency of any contributory, the estimated value of his liability to future calls, as well as calls already made, may be proved against his estate. Provided, however, that no call is to compel payment of a debt before the maturity thereof.

51. The court may, at any time after making a winding up order, require any contributory for the time being settled on the list of contributories as trustee, receiver, banker or agent or officer of the company, to pay, deliver, convey, surrender or transfer forthwith, or within such time as the court directs, to or into the hands of the liquidator, any sum or balance, books, papers, estate or effects which happen to be in his hands for the time being, and to which the company is *primâ facie* entitled.

52. The court may, at any time after making a winding up order, make an order on any contributory for the time being settled on the list of contributories, directing payment to be made, in manner in the said order mentioned, of any moneys due from him, or from the estate of the person whom he represents to the company exclusive of any money which he or the estate of the person whom he represents may be liable to contribute by virtue of any call made or to be made in pursuance of this Act.

53. The court may, at any time after making a winding up order, and either before or after it has ascertained the sufficiency of the assets of the company, make calls on and order payment thereof by all or any of the contributories for the time being settled on the list of contributories, to the extent of their liability, for payment of all or any sums it deems necessary to satisfy the debts and liabilities of the company, and the costs, charges, and expenses of winding up, and for the adjustment of the rights of the contributories amongst themselves, and it may, in making a call, take into consideration the probability that

some of the contributories upon whom the same is made may partly or wholly fail to pay their respective portions of the same. Provided, however, that no call is to compel payment of a debt before the maturity thereof; Provided also that the extent of the liability of any contributory is not to be increased by anything in this section contained.

54. The court may order any contributory, purchaser, or other person from whom money is due to the company to pay the same into some chartered bank or Post Office Savings Bank or other Government Savings Bank, to the account of the court instead of to the liquidator, and such order may be enforced in the same manner as if it had directed payment to the liquidator.

55. The court is to adjust the rights of the contributories among themselves, and distribute any surplus that may remain among the parties entitled thereto.

56. The court may, at any time before or after it has made a winding up order, upon proof being given that there is reasonable cause for believing that any contributory or any past or present director, manager, officer or employee of the company is about to quit Canada, or otherwise abscond, or to remove or conceal any of his goods or chattels, for the purpose of evading payment of calls, or for avoiding examination in respect of the affairs of the company, cause such person to be arrested, and his books, papers, moneys, securities for moneys, goods and chattels, to be seized, and him and them to be safely kept until such time as the court may order.

57. Where the business of a company is being wound up, under this Act, all books, of the company and of the liquidators shall, as between the contributories of the company, be *primâ facie* evidence of the truth of all matters purporting to be therein recorded.

58. Where a winding up order has been made, the court may make such order for the inspection by the creditors, shareholders, members and contributories of the company of its books and papers as the court thinks just; and any books and papers in the possession of the company may be inspected in conformity with the order of the court but not further or otherwise.

59. No contributory or creditor or shareholder or member can vote at any meeting unless present personally or represented by some person having a written authority (to be filed with the chairman or liquidator) to act on his behalf at the meeting or generally.

CREDITORS' CLAIMS.

60. When the business of a company is being wound up under this Act, all debts payable on a contingency, and all claims against the company, present or future, certain or contingent, ascertained or sounding only in damages, are admissible to proof against the company,— a just estimate being made, as far as is possible, of the value of all such debts or claims as may be subject to any contingency or sound only in damages, or for some other reason do not bear a certain value.

2. The law of set-off as administered by the courts, whether of law or equity, shall apply to all claims upon the estate of the company, and to all proceedings for the recovery of debts due or accruing due to the company at the commencement of the winding-up, in the same manner and to the same extent as if the business of the company were not being wound up under this Act.

61. The property of the company must be applied in satisfaction of its liabilities and the charges incurred in winding up its affairs; and unless it is otherwise provided by law or by the Act, charter or instrument of incorporation, any property or assets remaining must be distributed amongst the members according to their rights and interests in the company.

62. The court may fix a certain day or certain days on within which creditors of the company and others having claims thereon are to send in their claims.

63. Where the liquidator has given such notices of the said day as may be ordered by the court the liquidator shall at the expiration of the time named in the said notices, or the last of the said notices, for sending in such claims, be at liberty to distribute the assets of the company or any part thereof, amongst the parties entitled thereto, having regard to the claims of which the liquidator has then notice; and the liquidator is not liable for the assets or any part thereof so distributed to any person of whose claim the liquidator had not notice at the time of distributing the said assets or a part thereof, as the case may be.

64. The liquidator may, with the sanction of the court, make such compromise or other arrangement as the liquidator may deem expedient with creditors or persons claiming to be creditors, or persons having or alleging themselves to have any claim, present or future, certain or contingent, ascertained or sounding only in damages against the company, or whereby the company may be rendered liable.

65. If a creditor holds security upon the estate of the company, he must specify the nature and amount of such security in his claim, and must therein on his oath put a specified value thereon; and the liquidator, under the authority of the court, may either consent to the retention of the property and effects constituting such security or on which it attaches, by the creditor, at such specified value, or he may require from such creditor an assignment and delivery of such security, property and effects at such specified value, to be paid by him out of the estate so soon as he has realized such security, together with interest on such value from the date of filing the claim till payment; and in such case the difference between the value at which the security is retained and the amount of the claim of such creditor, is to be the amount for which he may rank as aforesaid; and if a creditor holds a claim based upon negotiable instruments upon which the company is only indirectly or secondarily liable, and which is not mature or exigible, such creditor is considered to hold security within the meaning of this section, and must put a value on the liability of the party primarily

liable thereon as being his security for the payment thereof; but after the maturity of such liability and its non-payment he is entitled to amend and re-value his claim.

66. If the security consists of a mortgage upon ships or shipping or upon real estate or of a registered judgment binding real estate and excepted from the operation of section sixty-nine of this Act, the property mortgaged or bound can only be assigned and delivered to the creditor, subject to all previous mortgages, judgments, hypothecs and liens thereon, holding rank and priority before his claim, and upon his assuming and binding himself to pay all such previous mortgages, judgments, hypothecs and liens, and upon his securing the estate of the company to the satisfaction of the liquidator against any claim by reason of such previous mortgages, judgments, hypothecs and liens; and if there be mortgages, judgments, hypothecs and liens thereon, subsequent to those of such creditor, he can only obtain the property by consent of the subsequently secured creditors; or upon their filing their claims specifying their security thereon as of no value, or upon his paying them the value by them placed thereon; or upon his securing the estate of the company to the satisfaction of the liquidator against any claim by reason of such subsequent mortgages, judgments, hypothecs and liens.

67. Upon a secured claim being filed, with a valuation of the security, it is the duty of the liquidator to procure the authority of the court to consent to the retention of the security by the creditor, or to require from him an assignment and delivery thereof.

68. In the preparation of the dividend sheet due regard must be had to the rank and privilege of every creditor, but no dividend can be allotted or paid to any creditor holding security upon the estate of the company for his claim, until the amount for which he can rank as a creditor upon the estate as to dividends therefrom, be established as herein provided.

69. No lien or privilege upon either the personal or real estate of the company is created for the amount of any judgment debt, or of the interest thereon, by the issue or delivery to the sheriff of any writ of execution, or by levying upon or seizing under such writ the effects or estate of the company; nor is any lien, claim or privilege, created upon the personal or real estate of the company, or upon any debts due or accruing or becoming due to the company by the filing or registering of any memorial or minute of judgment, or by the issue or making of any attachment or garnishee order or other process or proceeding, whether such writ, memorial minute, levy, seizure, attachment, garnishee order or other process of proceeding has been or be issued or made before or after the passing of this Act, if before the payment over to the plaintiff of the moneys actually levied, paid or received under such writ, memorial, minute, attachment, garnishee order or other process or proceeding, the winding up of the business of the company has commenced; but this section does not affect any lien, or privilege for costs, which the plaintiff possesses under the law of the Province in which such writ, attachment garnishee order or other process or proceeding may have been issued; nor so far as regards real estate of the company does it affect judgments registered at least thirty days before the passing of this Act, in any province where the registration of judgment creates a lien.

70. Any creditor or contributory or shareholder or member may object to any claim filed with the liquidator or to any dividend declared. If a claim or a dividend be objected to, the objections must be filed in writing with the liquidator, together with evidence of the previous service of a copy thereof on the claimant. The claimant has six days to answer the objections or such future time as the court may allow. The contestant has three days to reply or such further time as the court may allow. Upon the completion of the issues upon the objections the liquidator must transmit to the court all necessary papers relating to the contestation. The court must then, on the application of either party, fix a day for taking evidence upon the contestation and hearing and determining the same. The court may make such order as may seem proper as to the payment of the costs of the contestation by either party or out of the estate of the company. If, after a claim or dividend has been duly objected to, claimant does not answer the objections, the court may, on the application of the contestant, make an order barring the claim or correcting the dividend, or may make such other order in reference thereto as may appear right.

The court may, should the interests of justice seem to require it, order the person objecting to a claim of dividend to give security for the costs of the contestation within a limited time, and may, in default, dismiss the contestation or stay proceedings thereon upon such terms as the court may think just.

FRAUDULENT PREFERENCES.

71. All fratuitous contracts or conveyances or contracts without consideration or with a merely nominal consideration respecting either real or personal estate made by a company with respect to whose business a winding up order under this Act is afterwards made, with or to any person whatsoever, whether such person be its creditor or not, within three months next preceding the commencement of the winding up or at any time afterwards—and all contracts by which creditors are injured, obstructed or delayed, made by a company unable to meet its engagements and with respect to whose business a winding up order under this Act is afterwards made, with a person knowing such inability or having probable cause for believing such inability to exist or after such inability is public and notorious whether such persons be its creditor or not,—are presumed to be made with intent to defraud its creditors.

72. A contract or a conveyance for a consideration, respecting either real or personal estate, by which creditors are injured or obstructed, made by a company unable to meet its engagements with a person ignorant of such inability, whether such person be its creditor or not, and before such inability has become public and notorious, but within thirty days next before the commencement of the winding up of the business of such company, under this Act, or at any time afterwards, is voidable, and may be set aside by any court of competent jurisdiction, upon such terms as to the protection of such persons from actual loss or liability by reason of such contract, as the court may order.

73. All contracts, or conveyances made and acts done by a company respecting either real or personal estate, with intent fraudulently to impede, obstruct or delay its creditors in their remedies against it, or with intent to defraud its creditors, or any of them, and so made, done and intended with the knowledge of the person contracting or acting with the company, whether such person be its creditor or not, and which have the effect of impeding, obstructing, or delaying the creditors of their remedies, or of injuring them or any of them, are prohibited and are null and void.

74. If any sale, deposit, pledge or transfer be made of any property real or personal by a company in contemplation of insolvency under this Act, by way of security for payment to any creditor; or if any property real or personal, movable or immovable, goods, effects, or valuable security, be given by way of payment by such company to any creditor whereby such creditor obtains or will obtain an unjust preference over the other creditors, such sale, deposit, pledge, transfer or payment is null and void ; and the subject thereof may be recovered back for the benefit of the estate by the liquidator, in any court of competent jurisdiction ; and if the same be made within thirty days next before the commencement of the winding up under this Act, or at any time afterwards, it is presumed to have been so made in contemplation of insolvency.

75. Every payment made within thirty days next before the commencement of the winding up under this Act by a company unable to meet its engagements in full, to a person knowing such inability, or having probable cause for believing the same to exist, is void, and the amount paid may be recovered back by the liquidator by suit in any court of competent jurisdiction: Provided always, that if any valuable security be given up in consideration of such payment, such security or the value thereof, must be restored to the creditor upon the return of such payment.

76. When a debt due or owing by the company, has been transferred within the time and under the circumstances in the next preceding section mentioned, or at any time afterwards to a contributory who knows or has probable cause for believing the company to be unable to meet its engagements or in contemplation of its insolvency under this Act, for the purpose of enabling such contributory to set up by way of compensation or set off the debt so transferred, such debt cannot be set up by way of compensation or set off against the claim upon such contributory.

77. The powers conferred by this Act upon the court may, subject to the appeal hereinafter provided for, be exercised by a single judge thereof, and such powers may be exercised in chambers either during term or in vacation.

2. In the Province of Ontario such powers may, subject to an

appeal to a judge, according to the ordinary practice, be exercised by the master, referee or other officer who under the practice or procedure of the court, presides in chambers. Such master, referee or other officer may refer to a judge any application or matter pending before him.

APPEAL.

78. A person dissatisfied with an order or decision of the court in any proceeding under this Act may, by leave of a judge of the court, appeal therefrom as follows:—

In Ontario to the Court of Appeal;
In Quebec to the Court of Queen's Bench;
In the other provinces, to the full court.

Provided that, in the question to be decided on the appeal, future rights are involved or the decision is likely to affect other cases of a similar nature in the winding up proceedings, or,—

Provided, when the appeal is to a court other than the Supreme Court of Canada, the amount involved in the appeal exceeds five hundred dollars; or,—

Provided, when the appeal is to the Supreme Court of Canada, the amount involved in the appeal exceeds two thousand dollars.

A further appeal to the Supreme Court of Canada by leave of a judge of said Supreme Court may be had from the judgment of the said Court of Appeal, Queen's Bench, or full court, as the case may be.

In the North-West Territories a person dissatisfied with an order or decision of the court in any proceeding under this Act may by leave of a judge of the Supreme Court of Canada appeal therefrom to the Supreme Court of Canada.

79. All appeals are to be regulated as far as possible according to the practice in other cases of the court appealed to;

Provided always, that no such appeal can be entertained unless the appellant has, within fourteen days from the rendering of the order or decision, or within such further time as the court appealed from may allow, taken proceedings on the appeal, nor unless within the said time he has made a deposit or given sufficient security according to the practice of the court appealed to, that he will duly prosecute the said appeal and pay such damages and costs as may be awarded to the respondent.

80. If the party appellant does not proceed with his appeal according to the law or the rules of practice, as the case may be, the court appealed to on the application of the respondent may dismiss the appeal with or without costs.

MISCELLANEOUS.

81. In any proceeding or contestation under this Act, the court may order a writ of *subpœna testificandum* or of *subpœna duces tecum* to issue, commanding the attendance as a witness of any person within the limits of Canada.

82. The court may, after it has made a winding up order, summon before it or before any person to be named by it, any officer of the company or person known or suspected to have in his possession any of the estate or effects of the company, or supposed to be indebted to the company, or any person whom the court may deem capable of giving information concerning the trade, dealings, estate or effects of the company; and the court may require any such officer or person to produce any books, papers, deeds, writings, or other documents in his custody or power relating to the company; and if any person so summoned, after being tendered a reasonable sum for his expenses, refuses without lawful excuse to attend at the time appointed, the court may cause such person to be apprehended, and brought up for examination; nevertheless, in cases where any person claims any lien on papers, deeds or writings or documents produced by him, such production shall be without prejudice to such lien. The court has jurisdiction in the winding up to determine all questions relating to such lien.

83. The court or the person so named may examine upon oath, either by word of mouth or upon written interrogatories, any person appearing or brought up in manner aforesaid concerning the affairs, dealings, estate or effects of the company, and may reduce into writing the answers of any such person, and require him to subscribe the same. If such person without lawful excuse refuses to answer the questions put to him, he is liable to be punished as for contempt of court.

84. Where, in the course of the winding up of the business of a company under this Act, it appears that any past or present director, manager, liquidator, employee, or officer of such company, has misapplied or retained in his own hands or become liable or accountable for any moneys of the company, or been guilty of any misfeasance or breach of trust in relation to the company, the court may, on the application of any liquidator, or of any creditor or contributory of the company, notwithstanding that the offence is one for which the offender is criminally responsible, examine into the conduct of such director, manager, liquidator, officer or employee, and compel him to repay any moneys so misapplied or retained, or for which he has become liable or accountable, together with interest after such rate as the court thinks just, or to contribute such sums of money to the assets of the company by way of compensation in respect of such misapplication, retainer, misfeasance or breach of trust, as the court thinks fit.

85. If any person destroys, mutilates, alters or falsifies any books, papers, writings or securities, or makes or is privy to the making of any false or fraudulent entry in any register, book of account or other document belonging to the company, the business of which is being wound up under this Act, with intent to defraud or deceive any person, every person so offending shall be deemed to be guilty of a misdemeanor, and upon being convicted shall be liable to imprisonment in the penitentiary for any term not less than two years, or to be imprisoned in any gaol or place of confinement for any term less than two years, with or without hard labor.

86. The various courts of the Provinces, and the judges of the said courts respectively, shall be auxiliary to one another for the pur-

poses of this Act: the winding up of the business of the company or any matter or proceeding relating thereto may be transferred from one court to another with the concurrence, or by the order or orders, of the two courts, or by an order of the Supreme Court of Canada.

87. Where any order made by one court is required to be enforced by another court, an office copy of the order so made certified by the clerk or other proper officer of the court which made the same, and under the seal of such court, must be produced to the proper officer of the court required to enforce the same; the production of such copy is sufficient evidence of such order having been made; and thereupon such last mentioned court is to take such steps in the matter as may be requisite for enforcing such order in the same manner as if it were the order of the court enforcing the same.

88. The rules of procedure for the time being as to amendments of pleadings and proceedings in the court, apply as far as practicable to all pleadings and proceedings under this Act; and any court before whom such proceedings are being carried on has full power and authority to apply the appropriate rules as to amendments of the proceedings. No pleading or proceeding is void by reason of any irregularity or default which can or may be amended or disregarded under the rules and practice of the court.

89. Any affidavit, affirmation or declaration required to be sworn or made under the provisions or for the purposes of this Act, may be sworn or made in Canada before a liquidator, judge, notary public, commissioner for taking affidavits, or justice of the peace; and out of Canada, before any judge of a court of record, any commissioner for taking affidavits to be used in any court in Canada, any notary public, the chief municipal officer for any town or city, any British consul or vice-consul, or any person authorized by or under any statute of the Dominion or of any Province to take affidavits.

90. All courts, judges, justices, commissioners and persons acting judicially, are to take judicial notice of the seal, or stamp or signature (as the case may be) of any such court, judge, notary public, commissioner, justice, chief, municipal officer, consul, vice-consul, liquidator or other person, attached, appended or subscribed to any such affidavit, affirmation or declaration, or to any other document to be used for the purposes of this Act.

91. All dividends deposited in a bank and remaining unclaimed at the time of the final winding up of the business of the company, are to be left for three years in the bank where they are deposited, subject to the claim of the party entitled thereto, and if still unclaimed, are then to be paid over by such bank, with interest accrued thereon, to the Receiver General of Canada, and, if afterwards duly claimed, are to be paid over to the persons entitled thereto.

92. Any powers by this Act conferred on the court are in addition to, and not in restriction of, any other powers subsisting either at law or in equity, of instituting proceedings against any contributory, or the estate of any contributory, or against any debtor of the company for the recovery of any call or other sums due from such contributory or debtor, or his estate; and such proceedings may be instituted accordingly.

93. All costs, charges, and expenses properly incurred in the winding up of a company, including the remuneration of the liquidator, are payable out of the assets of the company in priority to all other claims.

94. The court may, in the event of the assets being insufficient to satisfy the liabilities, make an order as to the payment out of the estate of the company of the costs, charges and expenses incurred in winding up any company in such order of priority as the court thinks just.

95. Where a winding up order is made, if it appear in the course of such winding up that any past or present director, manager, officer or member of such company has been guilty of any offence in relation to the company for which he is criminally responsible, the court may, on the application of any person interested in such winding up, or of its own motion, direct the liquidator to institute and conduct a prosecution or prosecutions for such offence, and may order the costs and expenses to be paid out of the assets of the company.

96. If any person, upon any examination upon oath or affirmation authorized under this Act, or in any affidavit, deposition or solemn affirmation in or about the winding up of the business of a company under this Act, or otherwise in or about any matter arising under this Act, wilfully and corruptly gives false evidence, he is, upon conviction, liable to the penalties of wilful perjury.

97. In Ontario, the Judges of the High Court of Justice; in Quebec, the Judges of the Court of Queen's Bench; and in the other provinces the Judges of the Court, or a majority of the judges in each case, of whom the chief justice shall be one; from time to time may make, and frame, and settle the forms, rules and regulations to be followed and observed in proceedings under this Act and may make rules as to the costs, fees and charges which shall or may be had, taken or paid in all such cases by or to attorneys, solicitors or counsel, and by or to officers of courts, whether for the officers or for the Crown, and by or to sheriffs, or other persons whom it may be necessary to provide for, or for any service performed or work done under this Act.

98. Until such forms, rules and regulations are made the various forms, and procedures, including the tariff of costs, fees, and charges in cases under this Act, unless otherwise specially provided, are, as nearly as may be, to be the same as those of the court in other cases.

THE PROVISIONS OF SECTIONS 99 TO 105 INCLUSIVE APPLY TO BANKS ONLY NOT INCLUDING SAVINGS BANKS.

99. In the case of a bank the application for a winding up order must be made by a creditor for a sum of not less than one thousand dollars, and the court must, before making the order, direct a meeting of the shareholders of the bank to be summoned, held and conducted as the court directs for the purpose of ascertaining their wishes as to the appointment of liquidators.

100. The court may appoint a person to act as chairman of the meeting, and in default of such appointment the president of the bank or other person who usually presides at a meeting of the shareholders shall preside.

101. In taking a vote at such a meeting, regard is to be had to the number of votes conferred by law or by the regulation of the bank on each shareholder present or represented at such meeting.

102. The chairman of the meeting must report the result thereof to the court, and if a winding up order be made three liquidators must be appointed and they must be chosen from among those nominated by the shareholders.

103. If no one has been so nominated, the three liquidators must be chosen by the court, if less than three have been nominated the requisite additional liquidator or liquidators must be chosen by the court.

104. It is the duty of the liquidators to ascertain as nearly as may be the amount of notes of the bank intended for circulation and actually outstanding, and to reserve until the expiration of at least two years after the date of the winding up order, or until the last dividend, in case that is not made till after the expiration of the said time, dividends, on such part of such amount in respect of which claims may not be filed ; and if claims have not been filed and dividends applied for in respect of any part of the said amount before the period herein limited the dividends so reserved are to form the last or part of the last dividend.

105. Publication in the *Canada Gazette* and in the Official *Gazette* of each Province of Canada and in two newspapers issued at or nearest the place where the head office of a bank is situate, of notice of any proceeding of which under this Act creditors should be notified, is sufficient notice to holders of bank notes in circulation. If the head office be situated in the Province of Quebec one newspaper is to be published in English and one in French.

THE PROVISIONS OF SECTIONS 106 TO 119 ? INCLUSIVE APPLY ONLY TO LIFE INSURANCE COMPANIES, AND ALSO APPLY TO INSURANCE COMPANIES DOING LIFE AND OTHER INSURANCE, IN SO FAR AS RELATES TO THE LIFE INSURANCE BUSINESS OF SUCH COMPANIES.

106. Publication in the *Canada Gazette* and in the official *Gazette* of each Province of Canada, and in two newspapers issued at or nearest the place where the head office in Canada of an insurance company is situate, of notice of any proceeding of which under this Act creditors should be notified, is sufficient notice to holders of policies or contracts of insurance in respect of which no notice of claim has been received.

107. Notwithstanding the provisions of the statutes in that behalf respecting insurance, any deposit held by the Receiver General for policy holders and any assets vested in trustees pursuant to the said statutes must be applied and distributed under this Act, among the persons entitled to claim thereon according to their rights established by the said statutes respecting insurance.

108. The holder of a policy or contract of life insurance on which no claim has accrued at the time the winding up order is made, is entitled to claim as a creditor for the full net value, at the date of the winding up order, of the policies or contract calculated on the basis mentioned in section sixteen of the *The Consolidated Insurance Act*, 1877, less any amount previously advanced by the company on the security of the policy or contract: Provided always that whenever the company or the liquidator or the holder of the policy or contract of insurance exercises any right which it or he may have to cancel the policy or contract, the holder is entitled to claim as a creditor for the sum which under the terms of the policy or contract is due to him upon such cancellation.

109. The liquidator must, without the filing of any claim, notice or evidence, or the taking of action by any person, make a statement of all the persons appearing by the books and records of the officers of the company, to be creditors or claimants under the one hundred and eighth section hereof, and of the amounts due to each such person thereunder; every such person must be collocated and ranked as and be entitled to the rights of a creditor or claimant for such amount, without filing any claim, notice or evidence, or taking any action: Provided always, that any such collocation may be contested by any person interested, and that any person not collocated or dissatisfied with the amount for which he is collocated, may file his own claim. A copy of such statement certified by the liquidator must forthwith, after the making of such statements, be filed in the office of the Superintendent of Insurance at Ottawa, and notice such filing must forthwith be given by the liquidator by notice in the *Canada Gazette* and in the official *Gazette* of each Province of Canada and in two newspapers issued at or nearest the place where the head office in Canada of the company is situate, and the liquidator must also forthwith send by mail, prepaid, a notice of such filing to each creditor named in the statement addressed to the address in Canada of such creditor as far as known, and in the case of foreign creditors addressed to the address of their representatives or agents in Canada as far as known.

110. The holder of a policy or contract of life insurance upon which a claim accrues after the date of the winding up order and before the expiration of thirty days after the filing in the office of the Superintendent of Insurance of the statement referred to in the one hundred and ninth section hereof, is entitled to claim as a creditor for the full net amount of such claim—less any amount previously advanced by the company on the security of the policy or contract—and the said statement and the dividend sheet must, if necessary, be amended accordingly; no claim which accrues after the expiration of the thirty days above mentioned can rank upon the estate unless and until they be sufficient to pay all creditors in full.

111. If before the expiration of the thirty days above mentioned the holder of a policy or contract of life insurance on which a claim has not accrued, signifies in writing to the liquidator his willingness to accept an insurance in some other company for the amount which can be secured by the dividend on his claim to which such holder may be or become entitled, then the liquidator is empowered, with the sanction of the court, to effect for such holder an insurance to the amount aforesaid in another company or companies approved of by the Superintendent of insurance, and to devote to that purpose the dividend on his claim to which such holder may be or become entitled: Provided, however, that such insurance is to be effected only as part of a general scheme for the assumption by some other company or companies of the whole or part of the outstanding risks and liabilities of the insolvent company.

112. If the company be licensed under the Acts respecting Insurance, it is to be the duty of the liquidator to report to the Superintendent of Insurance once in every six months, or oftener as the superintendent may require, on the condition of the affairs of the company, with such further particulars as the superintendent may require.

THE PROVISIONS OF SECTIONS 113 TO 119 INCLUSIVE, APPLY ONLY TO INSURANCE COMPANIES OTHER THAN LIFE INSURANCE COMPANIES, AND ALSO APPLY TO INSURANCE COMPANIES DOING LIFE AND OTHER INSURANCE, IN SO FAR AS RELATES TO THE INSURANCE BUSINESS OF SUCH COMPANIES WHICH IS NOT LIFE INSURANCE BUSINESS.

113. Publication in the *Canada Gazette*, and in the Official *Gazette* of each Province of Canada, and in two newspapers issued at or nearest the place where the head office of an insurance company is situate, of notice of any proceeding of which under this Act creditors should be notified, is sufficient notice to holders of policies or contracts of insurance in respect of which no notice of claim has been received.

114. Notwithstanding the provisions of the statutes in that behalf respecting insurance, any deposit held by the Receiver General for policy holders, and any assets vested in trustees pursuant to said statutes must be applied and distributed under this Act, among the persons entitled to claim thereon under the said statutes respecting insurance.

115. Holders of policies or contracts of insurance on which no claim has accrued at the time the winding up order is made, are entitled to claim as creditors for a part of the premium paid, proportionate to the period of their policies or contracts respectively unexpired at the date of the winding up order. No claim which accrues after the winding up order is made can rank upon the estate.

Provided always that whenever the company or the liquidator or the holder of the policy or contract of insurance exercises any right which it or he may have to cancel the policy or contract, the holder is entitled to claim as a creditor for the sum which under the terms of the policy or contract is due to him upon such cancellation.

116. The liquidator must, without the filing of any claim, notice or evidence, or the taking of any action by any person, make a statement of all the persons appearing by the books and records of the officers of the company, to be creditors or claimants under the section one hundred and fourteenth hereof, and of the amounts due to each such person thereunder; every such person must be collocated and ranked as and be entitled to the rights of a creditor or claimant for such amount, without filing any claim, notice or evidence, or taking any action : Provided always, that any such collocation may be contested by any person interested, and that any person not collocated or dissatisfied with the amount for which he is collocated, may file his own claim. A copy of such statement certified by the liquidator must forthwith, after the making of such statement, be filed in the office of the Superintendent of Insurance at Ottawa, and notice of such filing must be forthwith given by the liquidator by notice in the *Canada Gazette*, and in the Official *Gazette* of each Province of Canada, and in two newspapers issued at or nearest the place where the head office in Canada of the company is situate. And the liquidator must also forthwith send by mail prepaid, a notice of such filing to each creditor named in the statement, addressed to the address in Canada of such creditor as far as known, and in the case of foreign creditors addressed to the address of their representatives or agents in Canada as far as known.

117. The holder of policy or contract of insurance other than life insurance, upon which a claim accrues after the date of the winding up order, and before the expiration of thirty days after the filing in the office of the Suprintendent of Insurance of the statement referred to in the one hundred and fifteenth section hereof, is entitled to claim as a creditor for the full net amount of such claim ; and the said statement and the dividend sheet must, if necessary, be amended accordingly. No claim which accrues after the expiration of the thirty days above mentioned, can rank upon the estate unless and until there be sufficient to pay all creditors in full.

118. If before the expiration of the thirty days above-mentioned, the holder of a policy or contract of insurance other than life insurance, signifies in writing to the liquidator his willingness to accept an insurance in some other company or companies in lieu of the insurance policy or contract of the insolvent company, then the liquidator is empowered, with the sanction of the court, to effect for such holder an insurance in another company or companies approved of by the Superintendent of Insurance, and to devote to that purpose the dividend on his claim to which such holder may be or become entitled, or such of the assets of the insolvent company as the court may sanction. Provided, however, that such insurance is to be effected only as part of a general scheme for the assumption by some other company or companies, of the whole or part of the outstanding risks and liabilities of the insolvent company.

119. If the company be licensed under the Acts respecting insurance, it is to be the duty of the liquidator to report to the Superintendent of Insurance once in every six months, or oftener as the Superintendent may require, on the condition of the affairs of the company, with such further particulars as the Superintendent may require.

CHAP. XXIV.

An Act to further amend the law respecting Building Societies and Loan and Savings Companies carrying on business in the Province of Ontario.

[*Assented to* 17*th May*, 1882.]

Preamble.	
1. Power to increase capital and shares by a vote of two-thirds in value of shareholders, and to make provisions res-	pecting such increased capital ; Proviso as to allotment of new shares.
	2. Proviso as to new shares not paid up in full.

WHEREAS it is expedient to make better provision for the increase of the permanent capital of Building Societies and Loan and Savings Companies carrying on business in Ontario, and for the enabling of such companies to obtain capital from beyond the limits of the Province : Therefore Her Majesty, by and with the advice and consent of the Senate and House of Commons of Canada, enacts as follows :

1. Any Permanent Building Society or Loan and Savings Company carrying on business in the Province of Ontario may, at any time, and from time to time, by resolution to be passed by a vote of not less than two-thirds in value of all the shareholders of the Company given in person or by proxy, at any general or special meeting of the Company duly called for considering the same, increase the fixed and permanent capital of such Society or Company, by the issue of new stock of such amount and to be divided into shares of such respective amounts and in such currency, and subject to such rules, regulations, privileges and conditions in all respects, and especially with regard to the amount to be paid on the subscription of any such shares and the time at which the balance shall be called up, and to the dividends to be paid thereon, as by the said resolution may be directed, or, if no directions be given, as the Directors may think expedient : Provided always, that such new issue of shares shall be allotted to the then existing shareholders *pro ratâ*, as nearly as possible without fractions, but in case such new shares be not taken up within thirty days, then the said shares, or remaining shares, shall be disposed of as the Directors may, from time to time, determine :

2. Provided further that, with respect to any new shares issued under the provisions of this Act which have not been paid up in full, the holder thereof shall, in respect thereof, be entitled only to as many votes, at general or special meetings of the Society or Company as the amount paid up on such new shares held by him would represent in fully paid up shares of the Society or Company, issued irrespective of this Act.

CAP. XXX.

An Act to author'ze Corporations an other Institutions incorporated out of this Province to lend and invest moneys in this Province.

Section.

Preamble.
1. Any institution incorporated under the laws of Great Britain may receive license from Provincial Secretary to carry on business in Manitoba, and may have certain powers; provided such corporation shall sell any real estate acquired by foreclosure within five years from date of such foreclosure.
2. Certified copy of charter to be filed, also power of attorney, signed, &c; declaration.

Section.

3. Process may be served upon officer of company incorporated in Province.
4. Due notice to be given in *Official Gazette*, etc., of such license.
5. Provincial Secretary may issue license on evidence of due incorporation under laws of Great Britain, &c.
6. License may be obtained by foreign company approved by Governor-in-Council; power of corporation.

WHEREAS it would greatly tend to assist the progress of public improvements now going on within the Province of Manitoba, if facilities were afforded to institutions and corporations incorporated out of the Province of Manitoba for the purpose of lending money, to lend money within the Province, and with that object in view, it is expedient to confer on such institutions and corporations powers to contract, and also to hold as security, lands within the Province of Manitoba: therefore,

Her Majesty, by and with the advice and consent of the Legislative Assembly of Manitoba enacts as follows:

1. Where any institution or corporation duly incorporated under the laws of the Parliament of Great Britain and Ireland, or of the Dominion of Canada, or of the laws of the late Province of Canada or any of the Provinces of Canada, for the purpose of lending or investing moneys, may apply for and receive a license from the Provincial Secretary, authorizing it to carry on business within the Province of Manitoba, to transact any loaning business of any description whatever within the said Province of Manitoba in its corporate name, except the business of banking, and to take and hold any mortgages of real estate and any railway municipal or other bonds of any kind whatsoever, and on the security of which may lend its money, and whether the said bonds form a charge on real estate within the said Province or not, and also to hold such mortgages in its corporate name and to sell and transfer the same at its pleasure, and in all respects to have and enjoy the same powers and privileges with regard to lending its moneys and transacting its business within the said Province as a private individual might have and enjoy, so far as may be within the legislative authority

of this Province; provided such corporation shall sell or dispose of any real estate to which it may acquire a title in fee simple by foreclosure or by the release of the equity of redemption therein within five years from the date of such foreclosure, and any real estate which may not within the said period have been disposed of as herein required, shall be forfeited to and become vested in the Crown, 40 V., c. 15, s. 1 ; 43 V., c. 19, s. 1.

2. Every company obtaining such license as aforesaid shall before the commencement of such business file in the office of the Provincial Secretary of Manitoba a certified copy of the charter, act of incorporation or articles of association of such company, and also a power of attorney to the principal agent or manager of such company in the said Province of Manitoba, signed by the president or managing director and secretary thereof and verified as to its authenticity by the statutory declaration of the principal agent or manager of such company or of any person cognizant of the facts necessary for its verification ; which power of attorney must expressly authorize such agent or manager within the said Province to accept process in all suits and proceedings against such company in the Province, for any liabilities recovered by such company therein, and must declare that service of process on such agent or manager for such liabilities shall be legal and binding on such company to all intents and purposes whatever, and waiving all claims of error by reason of such service. 40 V., c. 15, s. 2.

3. After such certified copy of the charter and such power of attorney are filed as aforesaid, any process in any suit or proceeding against such company for any liability may be served upon such manager or agent in the same manner as process may be served upon the proper officer of any company incorporated in the Province, and all proceedings may be had thereupon to judgment and execution in the same manner as in proceedings in any civil suit in the Province. 40 V., c. 15, s. 3.

4. Every company obtaining such license as aforesaid shall forthwith give due notice thereof in the *Manitoba Gazette*, and in at least one newspaper in the county, city or place where the principal manager or agent of such company in the Province transacts the business thereof, for the space of one month, and the like notice shall be given when such company shall cease, or notify that they cease, to carry on business within the Province. 40 V., c. 15, s. 4.

5. The Provincial Secretary of Manitoba may, if he sees fit, issue such license as aforesaid, on being furnished with evidence of the due incorporation of the company applying for such license under the laws of the Imperial Parliament of Great Britain and Ireland, or of the Dominion of Canada, or the laws of the late Province of Canada or any of the Provinces of the Dominion of Canada, which evidence shall be a certified copy of the charter, act of incorporation or articles of association of such company, and on being furnished with a power of attorney from such company to the person appointed to be the principal agent

or manager of such company within the Province, under the seal of such company and signed by the president or managing director and secretary thereof, and verified by oath of an attesting witness expressly authorizing such agent or manager to apply for such license, and the fee to be paid by such company on the issuing of such license shall be such sum as may be fixed by the Lieutenant-Governor in Council. 43 V., c. 15, s. 2.

6. Any corporation or institution duly incorporated under the laws of Great Britain and Ireland, or of the Dominion of Canada, or of the late Province of Canada, or any of the Provinces of the Dominion of Canada, duly authorized to carry out or effect any of the purposes or objects to which the legislative authority of the Legislature of Manitoba extends, may obtain a license from the Proincial Secretary with the approval of the Lieutenant-Governor in Council authorizing it to carry on its business within the Province of Manitoba, on compliance with the provisions with regard to such license of this Act; and such corporation or institution shall thereupon have the same powers and privileges in Manitoba as if the same were incorporated for the purposes thereof under the provisions of a statute of the Province of Manitoba. 43 V., c. 19, s. 3.

CHAP. XXXVII.

An Ordinance to Amend the Law relating to Joint Stock Companies

Section
Preamble.
1. Repeal of B. C. Joint Stock Co's Act, and Mining Joint Stock Ordinance, 1864.
2. Imperial Act the Companies' Act, 1862—in force.
3. The expression, "the Court," shall mean the Supreme Court of Civil Justice of British Columbia. Judge thereof to have powers of Lord Chancellor.
4. Power to execute deeds out of the United Kingdom.
5. Fees payable same as those in England
6. Colonial Secretary to be substituted for Board of Trade. A.D., 1866.
7. Public notices, how given.

8. Mining Companies formed here may be incorporated by obtaining certificate of registration from a Gold Commissioner
9. Requirements as to registration of Companies' Act, 1862, and part IX. shall apply to all incorporated companies. (Vide part VII. of Gold Mining Ordinance, 1867.)
10. Except to Companies registered under the Gold Mining Ordinance, 1865 (Vide part VII. of Gold Mining Ordinance, 1867.)
11. General orders and rules of 25th November, 1862, in force here. A.D., 1866
12. Short title.

[*Assented to 8th March* 1866.]

WHEREAS it is expedient that the laws relating to the incorporation, regulation, and winding up of trading companies and other associations should be consolidated and amended:

Be it therefore enacted by the Governor of British Columbia, by and with the advice and consent of the Legislative Council thereof as follows:

1. The "British Columbia Joint Stock Companies' Act" and the Mining Joint Stock Companies' Ordinance, 1864," are hereby repealed.

2. An Act of the Imperial Parliament, passed in the session of Parliament, holden in the 25th and 26th years of the reign of Her Majesty Queen Victoria, chapter 89, intituled "The Companies Act, 1862," shall, from and after the passing of this Ordinance be and have, as far as practicable, and save as hereinafter altered and modified, the force of law in this colony.

3. The expression "The Court" as used therein, shall instead of the interpretation given thereto in clause 81 of such Act, mean the Supreme Court of Civil Justice of British Columbia, and any Judge of such last mentioned Court shall have and exercise all the powers in and by the said Act conferred upon the Lord Chancellor and Vice-Chancellor.

4. The power given to Companies to empower any person as their attorney to execute deeds on their behalf in any place not situate in the United Kingdom, shall apply to the execution of deeds in this colony, and such authority shall include a power to Companies in this colony, to empower an attorney to execute deeds on their behalf in the United Kingdom.

5. All fees payable under this Ordinance shall be the same as those payable under "The Companies' Act, 1862" provided, however, that such shall be collected in the ordinary way and not by stamps, and be paid into the Treasury of this colony to the use of Her Majesty, her heirs and successors.

CHAP. CXLVII.

An Ordinance to encourage the establishment of Investment and Loan Societies.

Section.

Preamble.
1. Societies—how incorporated; power to hold lands; evidence of incorporation; date of incorporation; liability of members.
2. Societies to have different names.
3. Who shall be a member of any society.
4. Members of Society may make rules; impose fines; amend or rescind rules.
5. Society shall, by rule, declare objects of society; how money to be appropriated.
6. Rules to specify time and place of holding meeting, and define powers and duties of members and officers.
7. Election of directors.
8. Powers of directors to be declared by rules.
9. Rules to provide that Treasurer shall furnish annual statement of funds; statement to be attested by auditors.
10. Rules to be recorded in a book; copy of rules to be certified by the Registrar of Joint Stock Companies.
11. Rules so recorded to be binding on members.
12. Examined copy of rule to be evidence.
13. Rules not to be altered, except at a special general meeting; meeting to consist of one-third of shareholders, representing not less than two-thirds of unadvanced stock, and majority consent in writing; rules not to be deemed altered until alteration assented to by Registrar of Joint Stock Companies; members to be notified of proposed alterations.
14. Shareholder whose share is paid up, may receive or invest the amount; permanent stock transferable only.
15. Except in cases of withdrawal, members not to receive profits in shares other than in permanent stock until maturity.
16. Society may limit number of shares, and may charge a premium on new shares.
17. Shares may be forfeited; members may be expelled.
18. Transfer of share of deceased member valid.
19. Society may sue members.
20. In certain cases, powers of Directors to be recorded in books of Society.
21. Election of President and Vice-President; concurrence of majority of Directors necessary; quorum to be present.

Section.

22. Proceedings of Directors to be entered in books of Society.
23. Acts of Directors to be binding.
24. Directors at meeting to appoint officers; to remove officers for incompetence or misbehaviour.
25. Officers appointed to receive money to give security.
26. Society may become absolute owner by foreclosure of any property mortgaged to it.
27. In certain cases, society may proceed in mortgage by sale, &c.
28. After default for three months successively, society may sell property held in mortgage.
29. Representatives of deceased officers of Society to deliver over papers and moneys after demand.
30. Ordinance to extend to aliens, &c., but no *feme coverte* or infant to be a Director.
31. How society may invest surplus funds.
32. Amount society may borrow limited.
33. Real estate for place of business.
34. Society not bound to see to trust to which its stock is subject; what receipt sufficient.
35. To whom funds of society may be advanced; value of building placed on property, with money advanced by society, may be estimated in appraising its value, if a bond is given securing its erection.
36. No loan to be made to a director; any director receiving a loan to pay a fine of ten times the amount received.
37. Recovery of fine.
38. Officers who receive a bribe or commission to procure a loan, to incur a penalty of $500.
39. Directors to be liable for debts, if dividend is declared when the society is known by them to be insolvent.
40. Conditions to be observed before profits divided.
41. When the assets of Society to be valued, and accounts are to be audited; return to be made to Colonial Secretary.
42. Penalty on default in making return.
43. Examination of affairs of society by Inspector, approved by the Governor.
44. Powers of Inspector.
45. Result of examination, how dealt with.
46. Power of society to appoint inspector.

1869.   *Investment and Loan Societies.*   Cap. 147.   357

Section.	Section.
47. Official copy of report of inspectors to be evidence.	53. In case of joint owners of a share, on whom notice to be served.
48. Recovery of penalties other than those provided for in sec. 37.	54. How notice to be advertised.
49. Application of penalties.	55. Provision as to winding up of company.
50. Service of notice by Company.	56. Who may draw notes, bills of exchange or receipts for a society.
51. Notices, &c., how served on society.	57. Method of appointing attorney.
52. Document—how to be served by post on society.	58. Differences may be referred to arbitration.
	59. Interpretation clause.
	60. Short title.

[*Assented to* 20*th August,* 1869.]

WHEREAS it is expedient that encouragement should be given to the establishment of societies having for their object the accumulation of money in this Colony, and the investment thereof;

Be it enacted by the Governor of British Columbia, with the advice and consent of the Legislative Council thereof, as follows:—

1. In case any twenty or more persons agree to constitute themselves into a society under this Ordinance, and execute under their respective hands and seals a declaration to that effect, and deposit the same with the Registrar of Joint Stock Companies (who shall grant his certificate thereof, and for the granting of such certificate and recovering and registering such declaration shall be entitled to a fee of five dollars) such persons and such other persons as afterwards become members of the society, and their several and respective executors, administrators and assigns, shall be a corporation body corporate and politic under this Ordinance, with the power to hold lands as hereinafter mentioned, by the name and style mentioned in such declaration, for raising by periodical subscriptions in sums not exceeding ten dollars per month, or otherwise, of or from the several members of the society, in shares (not exceeding the value of five hundred dollars for each share) a stock or fund for investment on real security in Great Britain or Ireland, British Columbia or any other of Her Majesty's possessions, and for enabling persons to become members of such society at any time, either for investment of capital therein or to obtain the advance of their shares or share by giving security therefor without being liable to the contingency of losses or entitled to participate in the profits in the business of the said society; and the certificate of the Registrar of Joint Stock Companies of such declaration as aforesaid having been deposited, shall be conclusive evidence of the incorporation of the society in such certificate mentioned. The date of such certificate shall be the date of incorporation of the society; and the liability of the members shall be limited to the payment of the amount unpaid on the shares held by them respectively.

2. No society shall be incorporated under the provisions of this Ordinance under a name identical with that by which a subsisting society is already incorporated, or so nearly resembling the same as to be calculated to deceive. (No. 165, Revised Statutes, sec. 2.)

3. Every person who shall have signed the rules of any society incorporated under the provisions of this Ordinance shall be deemed to be a member of the society. (No. 165, Revised Statutes, sec. 3.)

4. The several members of the society holding unadvanced shares thereon, may from time to time assemble together and make such proper rules for the government of the society as the majority of the members so assembled may deem meet, so as such rules are not repugnant to the provisions of this Ordinance, or any Act or other Ordinance then in force in British Columbia; and they may impose and inflict such reasonable fines, penalties and forfeitures upon the several members of the society infringing such rules as such majority of the members think fit, to be respectively paid to such uses for the benefit of the society as the society by such rules direct; and they may also from time to time amend or rescind such rules, and make new rules in lieu thereof, under such restrictions as are in this Ordinance contained.

5. Every such society shall in or by one or more of their rules declare the objects for which the society is intended to be established, and thereby direct the purposes to which the money from time to time subscribed to, received by or belonging to the society shall be appropriated, and in what shares or proportions and under what circumstances any member of the society or other person may become entitled to the same or any part thereof.

6. The rules of the society shall specify the place or places at which it is intended that the society shall hold its meetings, and shall contain provisions with respect to the powers and duties of the members at large and of the officers appointed for the management of its affairs.

7. Every such society shall from time to time select and appoint any number of the members of the society to be a board of directors, the number and qualification thereof to be declared in the rules of the society, and may delegate to such directors all or any of the powers given by this Ordinance to be executed.

8. The powers of the directors shall be declared by the rules of the society and they shall continue to act during the time appointed by such rules and until others are appointed.

9. The rules of the society shall provide that the treasurer or other principle officers thereof shall once at least in every year prepare a general statement of the funds and effects of or belonging to the society, and the value of such effects, specifying in whose custody or possession such funds or effect are then remaining, together with an account of all sums of money received or expended by or on account of the society since the publication of the proceeding periodical statement, every such periodical statement shall be attested by two or more members of the society, not being directors, who shall be elected auditors for that purpose by the shareholders, and shall be countersigned by the secretary or clerk for the society, and every member shall be entitled to receive from the society without charge a copy of such periodical statement.

10. The rules for the management of every such society shall be recorded in a book kept for that purpose, and such book shall be open at all reasonable times for the inspection of the members, and a copy of such rules shall be registered by the Registrar of Joint Stock Companies, and certified by him before they shall be binding on the society.

11. The rules so recorded shall be binding on the several members and officers of the society and the several contributors thereto and their representatives, and they shall be deemed to have full notice thereof by such record.

12. The entry of the rules in the books of the society or a true copy of the same examined with the original and proved to be a true copy shall be received as evidence thereof.

13. No rules so recorded as aforesaid shall be altered or rescinded, nor shall any rule be created except at a general meeting of the members convened by public notice, written or printed, signed by the secretary or president of the society in pursuance of a requisition for that purpose, made by not less than fifteen of the members, stating the objects for which the meeting is called, and addressed to the president and directors; and unless such general meeting do consist of not less than one-third of the shareholders present in person or by proxy, representing not less than two-thirds of the unadvanced stock of such society, and the majority of such members present as aforesaid do, in writing under their hand, concur in such alteration or repeal of such rule, or in the creation of any new rule; and no such rule shall be deemed to have been altered, repealed or created until alteration, repeal or creation shall have been assented to by the Registrar of Joint Stock Companies in writing under his hand. Each member of the society shall within fifteen days after the receipt of such requisition by the president or treasurer be notified by circular of the proposed alterations, repeal or addition.

14. When any share or shares in the capital of any society has or have become due and payable to the holder thereof, he may either withdraw the amount of such share or shares from the said society according to the rules and regulations thereof, or invest the amount of his said share or shares as fixed or permanent stock of the society and receive therefrom periodically such proportion of the profits made by such society as may be provided for by the rules of the society. The moneys invested in fixed and permanent stock may not be withdrawn therefrom but may be transferred in the same manner as other shares in the same society.

15. Except in the case of the withdrawal of a member according to the rules of the society then in force, no member shall receive or be entitled to receive from the funds of the society in respect of any share which is not invested as permanent stock, any interest or dividend by way of annual or other periodical profit upon share in the society until after the expiration of the term for which such share was originally granted, or such shorter period as under the rules of the society, may have been substituted therefor.

16. Every such society may from time to time limit the number of shares to be granted, and except in cases provided for in section fourteen, may charge a premium on any new share.

17. Every such society may, after reasonable notice in writing declare forfeited to the society the shares of any member who is in default, or who neglects to pay the number of instalments or monthly subscriptions fixed by any stipulation or by-law, and may expel such members from the society, and the secretary shall make a minute of such forfeiture and expulsion in the books of the society.

18. Any transfer of the share or other interest of a deceased member of any society, under this Ordinance, made by his personal representative, shall, notwithstanding such personal representative may not himself be a member, be of the same validity as if he had been a member at the time of the execution of the instrument of transfer. (No. 165, Revised Statues, sec. 4.)

19. In case any payment, either on account of subscriptions, instalments, fines, or for expenses in relation to any security or otherwise is due or payable to any such society from any member thereof, the same may be recovered by action or suit in the usual manner.

20. In case a sub-committee of directors is appointed for any particular purpose, the powers delegated to them shall be reduced to writing, and entered in a book by the Secretary or clerk of the Society.

21. The Directors shall choose a President and Vice-President, and they shall, in all things delegated to them, act for and in the name of the Society; and the concurrence of a majority of the Directors present at any meeting shall at all times be necessary in any act of the Board; and no business shall be transacted at any meeting of Directors, unless a quorum of Directors, as prescribed by the rules, be present thereat.

22. The transactions of the Directors shall be entered in a book belonging to the Society, and shall at all times be subject to the review of the Society in such manner and form as the Society by their general rules shall direct and appoint.

23. All acts and orders of such Directors, under the powers delegated to them, shall have the like force and effect as the acts and orders of the Society at the general meeting.

24. The Directors shall, from time to time, at any of their usual meetings, appoint such persons as they shall think proper to be officers of the Society, grant such salaries and emoluments as they deem fit, and pay the necessary expenses attending the management of the Society; and shall from time to time, when necessary, elect such persons as may be necessary for the purposes of the Society, for the time and for the purpose expressed in the rules of the Society, and shall, from time to time, for incompetence or misbehaviour, discharge such persons and appoint others in the room of those who vacate, die or are discharged.

25. Every such officer or other person appointed to any office in anywise concerning the receipt of money shall, before entering upon the duties of his office, execute a bond, with two sufficient sureties, in such form and for such amount as the Directors determine, for the just and faithful execution of his office, according to the rules of the Society.

26. Every such society may take and hold any property or securities thereon, *bonâ fide* mortgaged or assigned to it, either to secure the payment of the shares subscribed for by its members, or to assume the payment of any debts due to the said Society, and may become the absolute owner thereof by foreclosure.

27. Whenever any such society has received from a member an assignment, mortgage or transfer of any property to secure the payment of any advance made by, or debt due to such society, and containing an authority to such society to sell such property, in case of non-payment of any stipulated number of instalments or sums of money, and to apply the proceeds of such sale to the payment of the advances, interest and other charges due to the society, such stipulations and agreements shall be valid and binding, and the society may cause the same to be enforced; and may proceed on any such security for the recovery of the moneys thereby secured, either at law or in equity, or otherwise, and generally may also pursue the same course, exercise the same powers, and take and use the same remedies to enforce the payment of any debt or demand due to the Society, as any person or body corporate may by law take or use for a like purpose.

28. In case of default being made in payment of any sum of money secured, or intended to be secured by any deed of security taken by any such society or any part of any such sum, for the space of three months successively, after any or either of the days or times at which the same became payable, it shall be lawful for such society to offer the property comprised in any such deed of security, or any part or parts of such property, for sale by public auction, and either together or in parcels.

29. If any person appointed to an office by the Society, and being intrusted with and having in his possession, by virtue of his office, any moneys or effects belonging to the Society, or any deeds or securities relating thereto, dies or becomes bankrupt or insolvent, his legal representative or other person having a legal right, shall, within fifteen days after demand made by the orders of the Directors of the Society or the major part of them assembled at any meeting thereof, deliver over all things belonging to the Society to such person or persons as the Directors appoint.

30. This Ordinance shall extend to aliens, denizens, females, co-partners, and corporate bodies. *Femes covertes* and infants may hold shares in any society incorporated under this Ordinance, in the same manner as male adults, and for the purpose of dealing with such shares shall be considered as *femes soles*, or male adults, respectively; and this Ordinance shall be construed in the most beneficial manner for promoting the ends thereby intended—but no *feme coverte* or infant shall be a director of any such society.

31. Every such society may invest any surplus funds in the stock of any chartered bank in, or other public security of the colony; and all dividends, interest, and proceeds arising therefrom shall be brought to account and be applied to the use of the society, according to the rules thereof.

32. Every such society by its rules, regulations or by-laws authorized to borrow money, shall not borrow, receive, take or retain otherwise than in stock and shares in such society, from any person or persons any greater sum than three-fourths of the amount of capital actually paid in on unadvanced shares, and invested in securities or in property by such society; and the whole of the property and capital of the society shall be liable for the amount so borrowed, received or taken by any such society.

33. Any such society may hold absolutely real estate for the purposes of its place of business, not exceeding the annual value of three thousand dollars in any one place, exclusive of the improvements which may be made by any such society thereon.

34. Such society shall not be bound to see to the execution of any trust, whether expressed, implied or constructive, to which any share or shares of its stock may be subject, and the receipt of the party in whose name any such share or shares stand in the books of the society, or if such share or shares stand in the names of more parties than one, the receipt of one of the parties shall from time to time be a sufficient discharge to the society for any payment of any kind made in respect of such share or shares, notwithstanding any trust to which such share or shares may then be subject, and whether or not such society has had notice of such trust, and the society shall not be bound to see to the application of the money paid upon such receipt.

35. Such society may advance to members, other than any or either of the directors thereof, on the security of unadvanced shares in permanent stock of the said society or of real property, any portion of the funds of such society not exceeding the amount in value of such unadvanced shares or of such real property, and may receive and take from any person or persons, or bodies corporate, any collateral, further or additional security for any advances made as aforesaid : Provided that it is agreed that any building or other permanent improvement shall be placed on any such real property as aforesaid, with the moneys or any portion thereof to be advanced by such society, the value of such building or permanent improvement may be estimated in appraising the value of such real property, if a bond is given to such society for the purpose of securing the erection of such building or the making of such permanent improvement. [No. 165, Revised Statutes, sec. 5.]

36. No portion of the funds of any society established under this Ordinance shall be advanced to any or either of the directors of such society, nor to nor for his nor their use, upon any security or otherwise ; and should any advance be made contrary to the spirit of this Ordinance the director or directors receiving the same shall forfeit to the said society a sum equal to ten times the amount so advanced, and shall cease to be a director of such society.

37. Every such forfeit or fine may be recovered before a Stipendiary Magistrate of British Columbia in a summary way, by warrant of distress of the goods and chattels of such director or directors. In case of default of payment of such forfeit or fine and of the insufficiency of such distress, such director or directors shall be liable to imprisonment for a term not exceeding twelve calendar months, at the discretion of the Magistrate who shall have issued the warrant of distress.

88. In case any director or directors, the secretary and treasurer, or secretary or treasurer or clerk of any such society shall take, charge or receive any bribe, commission or gratuity for negotiating any loan from or procuring any advance to be made by such society, such person or persons shall incur a penalty of five hundred dollars, and shall upon conviction thereof be removed from office and forfeit to the society all his or their interest in such society.

89. If the directors of any such society shall declare any dividend when the society is known by them to be insolvent, or any dividend the payment of which would to their knowledge render it insolvent, they shall be jointly and severally liable to the extent of the aggregate amount of the dividend so declared, for all the debts of the company then existing, and for all that shall be thereafter contracted so long as they shall respectively continue in office: Provided always, that if any of the directors shall be absent at the time the dividend or dividends shall be so declared, or shall object thereto, and shall forthwith file their objection in writing with the secretary or clerk of the society, they shall be exempt from the said liability.

10. Inasmuch as the stability of societies established under this Ordinance will depend in great measure on the valuation of the assets of such societies and the division of the profits from time to time found or declared to have been made by such societies, no such societies shall be at liberty to divide any of the profits found or declared to have been made by such society, until the principal upon which such profits have been computed, and are so found and declared, or are intended to be so found and declared shall have been sanctioned or approved of by such officer as the Governor or officer administering the Government may from time to time appoint, who shall be entitled to a fee of fifteen dollars for granting a certificate of approval; and if any dividend shall be paid on or in respect of any share in the capital of such society, before such principal as aforesaid shall have been sanctioned or approved as aforesaid, each of the directors who shall not have objected thereto, and shall not have filed his objection in writing with the secretary or clerk of the society before any such payment, shall incur a penalty of five hundred dollars. (As amended by No. 165, Revised Statutes, sec. 7.)

11. In the month of December in each year the assets of the society shall be valued and the accounts audited; and on or before the 14th day of the month of January then following, a return duly verified by the declarations of the auditor and treasurer, shall be made to the Colonial Secretary, in which shall be stated in a tabular form :—

The name of the society;

The nominal capital;

The actual capital;

The number of unadvanced shares held in accumulating stock and the amount paid thereon;

The amount of permanent stock not deposited as security for moneys advanced by the society;

The amount borrowed or received on deposit;

The nature of the presumed assets, with a concise statement of the securities in a tabular form;

The losses and expenses during the year;

The profits devisable per share;

And such other information as the Governor or officer administering the Government shall from time to time, by notice published in the Government *Gazette*, order or require;

42. If any society established under this Ordinance, makes default in making a return to the Colonial Secretary, in compliance with the foregoing directions, such society shall incur a penalty not exceeding twenty-five dollars for every day during which such default continues.

43. Upon the application of one-fifth in value of the holders of unadvanced shares in any society established under this Ordinance, the Governor or officer administering the Government may appoint one or more inspectors to examine into the affairs of the society, and to report thereon in such manner as he may direct.

44. It shall be the duty of all officers and agents of the society to produce for the examination of the inspectors all books and documents in their custody or power. Any inspector may examine upon oath the officers and agents of the society, in relation to its business, and may administer such oath accordingly. If any officer or agent refuses to produce any such book or document, or to answer any question relating to the affairs of the society, he shall incur a penalty not exceeding twenty-five dollars in respect of such offence.

45. Upon the conclusion of the examination, the inspectors shall report their opinion to the Colonial Secretary. Such report shall be written or printed, as the Colonial Secretary directs. A copy shall be forwarded by the Colonial Secretary to the registered office of the society, and a further copy shall at the request of the shareholders, upon whose application the inspection was made, be delivered to them, or to any one or more of them. All expenses of and incidental to any such examination as aforesaid, shall be defrayed by the shareholders upon whose application the inspectors were appointed.

46. Any society registered under this Ordinance may in a general meeting appoint inspectors for the purpose of examining into the affairs of the society. The inspectors so appointed shall have the same powers and perform the same duties as inspectors appointed by the Governor or officer administering the Government with this exception, that instead of making their report to the Colonial Secretary, they shall make the same in such manner and to such persons as the society in general meeting directs, and the officers and agents of society shall incur the same penalties in case of any refusal to produce any book or document or to answer any questions as they would have incurred if such inspectors had been appointed by the Governor.

47. A copy of the report of any inspectors appointed under this Ordinance authenticated by the seal of the society into whose affairs they have made inspection, shall be admissable as evidence in any legal proceeding.

48. All offences under this Ordinance other than those provided for by sec. 37 of this Ordinance, made punishable by any penalty, may be prosecuted summarily before two or more Justices, in manner directed by an Act passed in Session, holden in the eleventh and twelfth years of the reign of Her Majesty Queen Victoria, Cap. 43, intituled: "An Act to facilitate the performance of the duties of Justices of the Peace out of Session, within England and Wales, with respect to summary convictions and orders."

49. The Justices imposing any penalty under this Ordinance may direct the whole or any part thereof to be applied in or towards payment of the costs of the proceedings, or in towards the rewarding the person on whose information, or at whose suit such penalty has been recovered, and subject to such directions, all penalties shall be paid to the Treasurer of the colony, and shall be carried to the credit and form part of the revenue of the colony.

50. Notices requiring to be served by the Company upon shareholders, may be served either personally, or by leaving the same, or sending them through the post office in a letter addressed to the shareholders at their registered places of abode.

51. Any summons, notice, order or other document required to be served upon any such society, may be served on the President, Vice-President or Secretary, or by leaving the same and sending a copy thereof through the post, in a pre-paid letter addressed to the society at their registered office. (No. 165, Revised Statutes, s. 11.)

52. Any document to be served by post on any such society, shall be posted in such time as to permit of its being delivered in due course of delivery within the period (if any) prescribed for the service thereof, and in proving service of such document, it shall be sufficient to prove that such document was properly directed, and that it was sent as a prepaid letter into the post office. (No. 165, Revised Statutes, s. 12.)

53. All notices directed to be given by the societies shall, with respect to any share to which persons are jointly entitled to, be given to whichever of the said persons is named first in the register of the societies, and notice so given shall be sufficient notice to all proprietors of such share.

54. All notices required by this Ordinance to be given by advertisement, shall be advertized in a newspaper circulating in the city or district in which the registered office of the society is situated.

55. The provisions of any Ordinance or Act for the time being in force in British Columbia, relating to the winding up of companies, shall apply to all societies incorporated under this Ordinance.

56. A promisssory note, or bill of exchange, or a receipt or other acknowledgment for money deposited with the Society, at interest, shall be deemed to have been made, drawn, endorsed or given on behalf of the Society, if made, drawn, accepted, endorsed or given in the name of the Society, by the President or Vice-President and the Treasurer of the Society. (No. 165, Revised Statutes, s. 8.)

57. Any such society may, by instrument in writing, under its common seal, empower any person—in respect of any specified matter—as its attorney, to execute deeds on its behalf, and every deed signed by such attorney, on behalf of the society and under its seal, shall be binding on the society, and have the same effect as if it were under the common seal of the society. (No. 165, Revised Statutes, s. 9.)

58. Any such society may, from time to time, by writing, under its common seal, agree to refer, and may refer, to arbitration any existing or future difference, question or other matter whatsoever in dispute between itself and any other society, company or person, in like manner as if it were incorporated under "the Companies' Ordinance, 1869," and the societies parties to the arbitration may delegate to the person or persons to whom the reference is made, power to settle any terms or to determine any matter capable of being lawfully settled or determined by the societies themselves, or by the directors or other managing body of such societies. (No. 165, Revised Statutes, s. 10.)

59. The word "society," in the foregoing sections of this Ordinance, shall be understood to include and to mean any society, company or institution established under the provisions and authority of this Ordinance; the word rules to include rules, orders, by-laws and regulations; and whenever in this Ordinance, in describing or referring to any person or party, matter or thing, any word importing the masculine gender or singular number is used, the same shall be understood to include and shall be applicable to several persons and parties, as well as one person or party, and females as well as males, and bodies corporate as well as individuals, and several matters and things as well as one matter or thing, unless it otherwise be provided, or there be something in the subject or context repugnant to such construction. The term "real property," shall include chattels real as well as real estate.

60. This Ordinance may be cited, for all purposes, as "the Investment and Loan Societies' Ordinance, 1869."

BANKS AND BANKING.

The Act thirty-fourth Victoria, chapter five, intituled, "An Act relating to Banks and Banking," with the amendments made by subsequent Acts * incorporated with it so as to form one Act.

Section.
Preamble.
1. Charters continued to 1st July, 1881. And to 1st of July, 1891.
2. To what banks the Act applies.
3. Matters to be provided for in special Act.
4. Branches and agencies.
5. Increase of capital.
6. How to be allotted.
7. Conditions previous to commencing business by new banks.
8. Amount and denomination of bank notes; Notes to be first charge on assets.
9. Redemption of notes. Payments in Dominion Notes.
10. Dividend not to impair capital; Capital lost to be made up.
11. Dividend limited unless there is a certain reserve.
12. Lists of shareholders to be laid before Parliament.
13. Monthly returns to Government; How attested; Special returns may be called for.
14. Part of reserve to be in Dominion Notes.
15. Exemption from bank tax.
16. Supply of Dominion notes.
16a Offices of redemption at certain cities; Proviso; under 34 V., c. 6, s. 19.
17. Subscription and transfer of stock in United Kingdom.
18. Payment of shares; Proviso.
19. Shares and transfer thereof; Sale of shares under execution.
20. List of transfers to be kept.
21. Transmission of shares otherwise than by transfer; how authenticated; Proviso; Proviso.
22. Transmission by marriage of female shareholder.
23. Transmission by decease.
24. Further provision in such case.
25. Provision in case of doubt as to person entitled; Proviso; Proviso.
26. Bank not bound to see to trusts; Executors and trustees not personally liable; Exception.

Section.
27. Votes on shares; Renewal of proxies.
28. By-laws may be made; Qualification of director; Election; Discounts to directors; Certain by-laws continued.
29. Special general meetings.
30. Board of directors; Notice; Proxies; Vacancies; Election of president, &c.
30a Sections 27, 29 and 30 explained.
31. Provision in case of failure of election.
32. Quorum, &c.
33. General powers of directors; Proviso; Proviso.
34. Calls, and how enforced by action; Proviso.
35. Calls, and how enforced by forfeiture; Proviso.
36. Statement to be laid before annual meeting.
37. Inspection of books, &c.
38. Dividends.
39. Real estate for occupation.
40. Business of the bank defined.
41. Mortgages as additional security.
42. Purchase of land under execution, &c.
43. Absolute title may be acquired; Proviso.
44. Power of sale, &c.
44a. As to advance for building ships.
45. Interpretation of various terms.
46. Warehouse receipts may be taken as collateral security; Proviso; exchange of warehouse receipts for bill or lading and vice versa.
47. When warehouseman, &c., is also the owner; sale of goods on non-payment of debt.
48. As to goods manufactured from articles pledged.
49. Prior claim of the bank over unpaid vendor.
50. Notice to be given before sale of goods pledged as aforesaid.
51. Lien of bank on stock for overdue debts; provision as to collateral security; provision may be varied.
52. No penalty for usury; recital; no restraint to be sever on ground of usury; as to minors or holders.

* 35 V., c. 8 36 V., c. 43; 38 V., c. 17; 40 V., c. 14 42 V., c. 45; 43 V., c. 22 and 44 V., c. 9.

Banks and Banking.

Section.
53. Collection fees.
54. Agency fees.
54a Deposits may be received from persons unable to contract; proviso, amount limited; bank not bound to see to trusts in relation to such deposits.
54b Non-juridical days.
55. Bonds, notes, &c., how and by whom to be signed; proviso.
56. Notes may be signed by machinery.
57. Suspension for ninety days to constitute insolvency.
58. Liability of shareholders in case of insufficiency of assets; calls in such case; proviso: as to directors; proviso: as to banks *en commandite*.
59. Liability of shareholders who have transferred their stock.
60. Embezzlement of bonds, &c., felony.
61. Fraudulent preference, a misdemeanor.
62. Making false statements in returns, a misdemeanor.
63. Refusal to make calls under s. 58, a misdemeanor.
64. Giving false receipts by warehousemen, &c., a misdemeanor.
65. False statements in receipts under s. 46, a misdemeanor.
66. Offences by members of a partnership.
66a Unauthorized use of title "Bank," a misdemeanor.
67. Punishment for misdemeanor.
68. Chartered Banks only to issue notes for circulation; What shall be deemed such notes.
69. How notices shall be given.
70. Bank to be subject to any future winding up Act; and any general Bank Act.
72. What sections shall apply to Bank of B. N. A.
73. How certain Banks may come under this Act.
74. Capital of Bank of N. S. may be reduced.

Section.
75. What provisions shall apply to La Banque du Peuple; Proviso.
76. Certain Acts repealed, 33 V., c. 11; 31 V., c. 11, as to certain Banks; 42 V., c. 45, ss. 3, 4, 5 & 6, as to numbering shares; C.S.C., c. 55.
77. Saving pending cases.

SCHEDULE A.

1. When contracts with agents to be valid.
2. When agents to be deemed owners.
3. What contracts for lien valid.
4. Must be *bona fide*.
5. Antecedent debt not to authorize lien.
6. *Bona fide* transactions with agents bind owners.
7. Documents of title defined.
8. Agents possessed of, to be deemed entrusted, &c.
9. Contracts for a lien founded thereon valid.
10. *Bona fide* loans or advances, when deemed authorized.
11. What contracts to be so considered.
12. Payments, when deemed advances.
13. Possession *prima facie* evidence of ownership.
14. Other liability of agents not to be affected.
15. Consequences of dereliction; misdemeanor
16. Aiders, &c.
17. When agent not liable criminally.
18. Conviction not admissible in evidence.
19. Admissions under oath not admissible in evidence against the party.
20. Owners may redeem goods pledged.
21. Remedy of owner against the estate of an agent bankrupt.
22. Interpretation clause.
23. This Act not to affect transactions prior to 28th July, 1847.
24. Act to relate to 28th July, 1847.

SCHEDULE B.

Banks whose charters are continued.

WHEREAS it is desirable that the provisions relating to the Incorporation of Banks, and the laws relating to Banking, should be embraced as far as practicable in one general Act; Therefore Her Majesty, by and with the advice and consent of the Senate and House of Commons of Canada, enacts as follows:—

1. The Charters or Acts of Incorporation of the several Banks enumerated in the Schedule B to this Act (including any amendments thereof now in force) are continued as to their Incorporation, the amount of capital stock, the amount of each share of such stock, and the chief place of business of each respectively, until the first day of July in the year of our Lord one thousand eight hundred and eighty-one, subject to the right of any such Bank to increase its capital stock in the manner hereinafter provided; and as to other particulars this Act shall form and be the Charters of the said Banks respectively, until the first day of July, 1881, and the provisions thereof shall apply to each of them respectively, and their present Charters shall be repealed, except only as to the matters for which the said Charters are above continued until the day last aforesaid; and

2. The said Charters or Acts of Incorporation of the several Banks mentioned in the Schedule B to this Act, to all which this Act applies, are hereby continued and shall remain in force, subject to the provisions of this Act, until the first day of July, in the year of our Lord one thousand eight hundred and ninety-one, except in so far as they or any of them may be or become forfeited or void under the terms thereof or of this Act, or any other Act, passed or to be passed in that behalf, by non-performance of the conditions of such Charters respectively, insolvency or otherwise. 34 V., c. 5, s. 1, and 43 V., c. 22, s. 11.

2. The provisions of this Act shall apply to any Bank to be hereafter incorporated (which expression in this Act includes any Bank incorporated by any Act passed in the present Session or in any future Session of the Parliament of Canada), whether this Act is specially mentioned in its Act of Incorporation or not, as well as to all Banks and their branches in any part of Canada (except where otherwise expressly mentioned) whose Charters are hereby continued, but not to any other, unless extended to it under the special provisions hereinafter made. 34 V., c. 5, s. 2.

3. The capital stock of any new Bank, the amount of each share, the name of the Bank, and the place where its chief office shall be situate, shall be declared in the Act of Incorporation of any Bank to be hereafter incorporated. 34 V., c. 5, s. 3.

GENERAL REGULATIONS.

4. The Bank may open branches or agencies and offices of discount and deposit and transact business at any place or places in the Dominion. 34 V., c. 5, s. 4.

5. The capital stock of the Bank may be increased, from time to time, by the shareholders at any annual general meeting, or any general meeting specially called for that purpose; and such increase may be agreed on by such proportions at a time as the shareholders shall determine, and shall be decided by the majority of the votes of the shareholders present at such meeting in person or represented by proxy. 34 V., c. 5, s. 5.

6. Any of the original unsubscribed capital stock, or the increased stock of a Bank, shall, when the directors so determine, be allotted to the then shareholders of the Bank *pro rata*, and at such rate as shall be fixed by the directors, provided always that no fraction of a share shall be so allotted; and any of such allotted stock as shall not be taken up by the shareholder to whom such allotment has been made, within three months from the time when notice of the allotment has been mailed to his address, may be opened for subscription to the public, in such manner and on such terms as the directors shall prescribe. 34 V., c. 5, s. 6.

7. No Bank to be hereafter incorporated, unless it be otherwise provided by its Charter, shall issue notes or commence the business of

Banking until five hundred thousand dollars of capital have been *bonâ fide* subscribed and one hundred thousand dollars have been *bonâ fide* paid up, nor until it shall have obtained from the Treasury Board a certificate to that effect, which certificate shall be granted by the Treasury Board when it is proved to their satisfaction that such amounts of capital have been *bonâ fide* subscribed and paid respectively; and if at least two hundred thousand dollars of the subscribed capital of such Bank has not been paid up before it shall have commenced business, such further amount as shall be required to complete the said sum shall be called in and paid up within two years thereafter, and it shall not be necessary that more than two hundred thousand dollars of the stock of any bank, whether incorporated before or after the passing of this Act, be paid up within any limited period from the date of its incorporation. 34 V., c. 5, s. 7.

8. The amount of notes intended for circulation, issued by the Bank and outstanding at any time, shall never exceed the amount of its unimpaired paid up capital: No such note for a sum less than five dollars, or for any sum not being a multiple of five dollars, shall be issued or re-issued by the Bank, and all notes for a less sum than five dollars, or not being such multiple as aforesaid, heretofore issued shall be called in and cancelled as soon as may be practicable. 34 V., c. 5, s. 8; *as amended by* 43 V., c. 22, s. 12.

2. The payment of the notes issued by the Bank and intended for circulation, then outstanding, shall be the first charge upon the assets of the Bank in case of its insolvency. 43 V., c. 22, s. 12.

9. The Bank shall always receive in payment its own notes at par at any of its offices and whether they be made payable there or not; but shall not be bound to redeem them in specie or Dominion notes at any place other than where they are made payable; the place or one of the places at which the notes of the Bank shall be made payable shall always be its chief seat of business. 34 V., c. 5, s. 9.

2. The Bank when making any payment shall, on the request of the person to whom the payment is to be made, pay the same, or such part thereof not exceeding fifty dollars as such person may request, in Dominion notes for one or for two dollars each, at the option of the receiver. 43 V., c. 22, s. 12.

10. No dividend or bonus shall ever be made so as to impair the paid-up capital, and if any dividend or bonus be so made, the directors knowingly and wilfully concurring therein, shall be jointly and severally liable for the amount thereof, as a debt due by them to the Bank; and if any part of the paid up capital be lost, the directors shall, if all the subscribed stock be not paid up, forthwith make calls upon the shareholders to an amount equivalent to such loss; and such loss (and the calls, if any) shall be mentioned in the return then next made by the Bank to the Government; provided that in any case where the capital has been impaired as aforesaid, all net profits shall be applied to make good such loss. 34 V., c. 5, s. 10.

11. No division of profits, either by way of dividends or bonus, or both combined, or in any other way, exceeding the rate of eight per cent. per annum, shall be paid by the Bank, unless after paying the same, it shall have a rest or reserved fund equal to at least twenty per cent. of its paid up capital, deducting all bad and doubtful debts before calculating the amount of such rest. 34 V., c. 5, s. 11.

12. Certified lists of the shareholders (or of the principal partners, if the Bank be *en commandite*), with their additions and residences, and the number of shares they respectively hold, shall be laid before Parliament every year, within fifteen days after the opening of the Session. 34 V., c. 5, s. 12.

13. Monthly returns shall be made by the Bank to the Government in the following form, and shall be made up within the first ten days of each month, and shall exhibit the condition of the Bank on the last juridical day of the month preceding; and such monthly returns shall be signed by the chief accountant, and by the president or vice-president, or the director (or, if the Bank be *en commandite*, the principal partner) then acting as president, and by the manager, cashier, or other principal officer of the Bank at its chief seat of business:—

RETURN of the Liabilities and Assets of the
on the   day of   A.D. 18

Capital authorized .... $
Capital subscribed .... $
Capital paid up .... $

LIABILITIES.

1. Notes in circulation .... $
2. Dominion Government deposits payable on demand
3. Dominion Government deposit payable after notice or on a fixed day ....
4. Deposits held as security for the execution of Dominion Government contracts and for Insurance Companies ....
5. Provincial Government deposits payable on demand
6. Provincial Government deposits payable after notice or on a fixed day ....:....................
7. Other deposits payable on demand ....
8. Other deposits payable after notice or on a fixed day
9. Loans from or deposits made by other Banks in Canada secured ....
10. Loans from or deposits made by other Banks in Canada unsecured ....
11. Due to other Banks in Canada ....
12. Due to agencies of the Bank, or to other Banks or Agencies in foreign countries ....
13. Due to Agencies of the Bank, or to other Banks or Agencies in the United Kingdom ....
14. Liabilities not included under foregoing heads ...

$

ASSETS.

1. Specie..
2. Dominion Notes..............................
3. Notes of and checks on other Banks ....
4. Balances due from other Banks in Canada........
5. Balances due from Agencies of the Bank, or from other Banks or Agencies in foreign countries..
6. Balances due from Agencies of the Bank, or from other Banks or Agencies in the United Kingdom
7. Dominion Government debentures or stock.......
8. Provincial, British or Foreign or Colonial public securities other than Canadian ....
9. Loans to the Government of the Dominion.......
10. Loans to Provincial Governments ....
11. Loans, Discounts or advances for which stock, bonds or debentures of Municipal or other Corporations, or Dominion, Provincial, British or Foreign or Colonial public securities other than Canadian, are held as collateral securities..............
12. Loans, discounts or advances on current account to Municipal Corporations.....................
13. Loans, discounts or advances on current account to other Corporations........................
14. Loans to or deposits made in other Banks secured.
15. Loans to or deposits made in other Banks unsecured.
16. Other current loans, discounts and advances to the public ....
17. Notes and bills discounted overdue and not specially secured ....
18. Other overdue debts not specially secured........
19. Notes and bills discounted overdue and other overdue debts secured by mortgage or other deed on real estate, or by deposit of or lien on stock, or by other securities.........................
20. Real estate, the property of the Bank (other than the Bank premises).........................
21. Mortgages on real estate sold by the Bank.......
22. Bank premises................................
23. Other assets not included under the foregoing heads

$

Aggregate amount of loans to and liabilities, direct or indirect, of directors, and firms or partnerships in which they or any of them have any interest, $

Average amount of specie held during the month, $

Average amount of Dominion Notes held during the month, $

I declare that the above Return has been prepared under my directions, and is correct according to the Books of the Bank.

E. F.,
Chief Accountant.

We declare that the foregoing return is made up from the books of the Bank, and that to the best of our knowledge and belief it is correct, and shews truly and clearly the financial position of the Bank; and we further declare that the Bank has never at any time during the period to which the said return relates, held less than forty per cent. of its cash reserves in Dominion Notes.

(*Place*) this   day of
A. B., *President.*
C. D., *General Manager.*

In addition to the returns specified in this section, the Minister of Finance shall also have power to call for special Returns from any particular Bank, whenever, in his judgment, the same are necessary in order to a full and complete knowledge of its condition. 34 V., c. 5, s. 13, *as amended by* 43 V., c. 22, s. 4.

14. The Bank shall always hold, as nearly as may be practicable, one-half of its cash reserves in Dominion Notes, and the proportion of such reserves held in Dominion Notes shall never be less than forty per cent. thereof. 34 V., c. 5, s. 14, *as amended by* 43 V., c. 22, s. 3.

15. Every Bank to which this Act applies shall be exempt from the tax now imposed on the average amount of its notes in circulation, to which other Banks will continue liable, and from the obligation to hold any portion of its capital in Government Debentures or Debentures of any kind. 34 V., c. 5, s. 15.

16. The Receiver General shall make arrangements as may be necessary for ensuring the delivery of Dominion Notes to any Bank, in exchange for an equivalent amount of specie, at the several offices at which Dominion Notes will be redeemable, in the cities of Toronto, Montreal, Halifax and St. John (N.B.), respectively. 34 V., c. 5, s. 16.

16*a*. The Governor may, in his discretion, establish branch offices of the Receiver General's Department at Winnipeg, Charlottetown and Victoria, respectively, or any of them, for the redemption of Dominion Notes, or may make arrangements with any chartered bank or banks for the redemption thereof at the said cities, in like manner as he may now do at the cities of Montreal, Toronto, Halifax and St. John (N.B.), and under like provisions: Provided that any Assistant Receiver General appointed, at any of the said cities, under the Act of the thirty-fourth Victoria, chapter six, shall be an agent for the issue and redemption of such notes. 43 V., c. 13, s. 1.

INTERNAL REGULATIONS.

Shares and Shareholders.

17. Books of subscription may be opened, and shares of the capital stock of the Bank may be made transferable, and the dividends accruing thereon may be made payable, in the United Kingdom of Great Britain and Ireland, in like manner as such shares and dividends are respectively made transferable and payable at the head office of the Bank; and to that end the Directors may, from time to time, determine the proportion of the shares which will be so transferable in the United Kingdom, and make such rules and regulations, and prescribe such forms, and appoint such agent or agents, as they may deem necessary. 34 V, c. 5, s. 17.

18. The shares of the capital stock shall be paid in by such instalments, and at such times and places as the Directors shall appoint, and executors, administrators and curators paying the instalments upon the shares of deceased shareholders shall be and are respectively indemnified for paying the same; Provided always, that no share or shares shall be held to be lawfully subscribed for, unless a sum equal to at least ten per centum on the amount subscribed for be actually paid at the time or within thirty days after the time of subscribing. 34 V., c. 5, s. 18.

19. The shares of the capital stock of the Bank shall be held and adjudged to be personal estate, and shall be assignable and transferable at the chief place of business of the Bank or at any of its branches which the Directors shall appoint for that purpose, and according to such form as the Directors shall prescribe; but no assignment or transfer shall be valid unless it be made and registered and accepted by the party to whom the transfer is made, in a book or books to be kept by the Directors for that purpose, nor until the person or persons making the same shall, if required by the Bank, previously discharge all his, her or their debts or liabilities to the Bank, which may exceed in amount the remaining stock, if any, belonging to such person or persons valued at the then current rate; and no fractional part or parts of a share, or less than a whole share shall be assignable or transferable.

When any share of the said capital stock shall have been sold under a writ of execution, the officer by whom the writ shall have been executed shall, within thirty days after the sale, leave with the cashier, manager, or other officer of the Bank, an attested copy of the writ, with the certificate of such officer endorsed thereon, certifying to whom the sale has been made, and thereupon (but not till after all debts and liabilities of the holder or holders of the share to the Bank, and all liens existing in favor of the Bank thereon, shall have been discharged as hereinafter provided), the President, Vice-President, Manager or Cashier of the Bank shall execute the transfer of the share so sold to the purchaser: and such transfer being duly accepted, shall be, to all intents and purposes, as valid and effectual in law as if it had been executed by the holder or holders of the said share—any law or usage to the contrary notwithstanding. 42 V, c. 45, s. 1. (*Substituted for* 34 V., c. 5, s. 19.)

20. A list of all transfers of shares registered each day in the books of the Bank, showing the parties to such transfers and the number of shares transferred in each case, shall be made up at the end of each day and kept at the chief office of the bank for the inspection of its shareholders. 34 V., c. 5, s. 20.

21. If the interest in any share or shares in the capital stock becomes transmitted in consequence of the death or bankruptcy or insolvency of any shareholder, or in consequence of the marriage of a female shareholder, or by any other lawful means than by a transfer according to the provisions of this Act, such transmission shall be authenticated by a declaration in writing, as hereinafter mentioned, or in such other manner as the Directors of the Bank shall require, and every such declaration shall distinctly state the manner in which and the party to whom such shares shall have been transmitted, and shall be by such party made and signed; and every such declaration shall be by the party making and signing the same acknowledged before a Judge of a Court of Record, or before the Mayor, Provost or Chief Magistrate of a city, town, borough, or other place, or before a Public Notary, where the same shall be made and signed; and every declaration so signed and acknowledged shall be left with the Cashier, Manager or other officer or agent of the Bank, who shall thereupon enter the name of the party entitled under such transmission in the Registry of shareholders; and until such transmission shall have been so authenticated no party or person claiming by virtue of any such transmission shall be entitled to receive any share of the profits of the Bank, or to vote in respect of any such share or shares: Provided always, that every such declaration and instrument as by this and the following section of this Act is required to perfect the transmission of a share or shares in the Bank which shall be made in any other country than Canada, or some other of the British colonies in North America, or in the United Kingdom of Great Britain and Ireland, shall be further authenticated by the British Consul or Vice-Consul, or other the accredited representative of the British Government in the country where the declaration shall be made, or shall be made directly before such British Consul or Vice-Consul or other accredited representative: and provided also, that nothing in this Act contained shall be held to debar the Directors, Cashier or other officer or agent of the Bank from requiring corroborative evidence of any fact or facts alleged in any such declaration. 34 V., c. 5, s. 21.

22. If the transmission of any share of the capital stock be by virtue of the marriage of a female shareholder, the declaration shall be accompanied by a copy of the register of such marriage, or other particulars of the celebration thereof, and shall declare the identity of the wife with the holder of such share, and shall be made and signed by such female shareholder and her husband: and it shall be competent to them to include therein a declaration to the effect that the share transmitted is the sole property, and under the sole control of the wife, that she may receive and grant receipts for the dividends and profits accruing in respect thereof, and dispose of and transfer the share itself, without requiring the consent or authority of her husband: and such declaration shall be binding upon the Bank and the parties making the same, until the said parties shall see fit to revoke it by a written notice to that effect to the Bank; and further, the omission of a statement in any such declaration, that the wife making the same is duly authorized by her husband to make the same, shall not cause the declaration to be deemed either illegal or informal: any law or usage to the contrary notwithstanding. 34 V., c. 5, s. 22.

23. If the transmission have taken place by virtue of any testamentary instrument, or by intestacy, the probate of the will, or any letters of administration, or act of curatorship, or an official extract therefrom, shall, together with such declaration, be produced and left with the Cashier, or other officer or agent of the Bank, who shall, thereupon, enter the name of the party entitled under such transmission, in the register of shareholders. 34 V., c. 5, s. 23.

24. If the transmission of any share or shares of the capital stock of the Bank be by the decease of any shareholder, the production to the Directors and the deposit with them of any authenticated copy of the probate of the will of the deceased shareholder, or of letters of administration of his estate granted by any Court in the Dominion having power to grant such probate or letters of administration, or by any prerogative, diocesan or peculiar Court or authority in England, Wales, Ireland, or any British Colony, or of any testament testamentary or testament dative, expede in Scotland, or, if the deceased shareholder shall have died out of Her Majesty's dominions, the production to and deposit with the Directors of any authenticated copy of the probate of his or her will or letters of administration of his or her property, or other documents of like import granted by any Court or authority having the requisite power in such matters, shall be sufficient justification and authority to the Directors for paying any dividend, or transferring, or authorising the transfer of any share or shares, in pursuance of and in conformity to such probate, letters of administration, or other such document as aforesaid. 34 V., c. 5, s. 24.

25. Whenever the interest in any share or shares of the capital stock of the Bank shall be transmitted by the death of any shareholder or otherwise, or whenever the ownership of or legal right of possession in any such share or shares shall change by any lawful means other than by transfer, according to the provisions of this Act, and the Directors of the Bank shall entertain reasonable doubts as to the legality of any claim to and upon such share or shares of stock, then, and in such case, it shall be lawful for the Bank to make and file in one of the Superior Courts of Law or Equity in the Province in which the Head Office of the Bank is situated, a declaration and petition in writing, addressed to the Justices of the Court, setting forth the facts and the number of shares previously belonging to the party in whose name such shares stand in the books of the Bank, and praying for an order or judgment adjudicating and awarding the said shares to the party or parties legally entitled to the same, and by which order or judgment the Bank shall be guided and held fully harmless and indemnified and released from all and every other claim for the said shares or arising therefrom: Provided always, that notice of such petition shall be given to the party claiming such share or shares, or to the attorney of such party duly authorized for the purpose, who shall, upon the filing of such petition, establish his right to the several shares referred to in such petition; and the delays to plead and all other proceedings in such cases shall be the same as those observed in analogous cases before the said Superior Courts: Provided also, that the costs and expenses of procuring such order and adjudication shall be paid by the party or parties to whom the said shares shall be declared lawfully to belong, and such shares shall not be transferred until such costs and expenses be paid, saving the recourse of such party against any party contesting his right. 34 V., c. 5, s. 25.

26. The Bank shall not be bound to see to the execution of any trust, whether expressed, implied or constructive, to which any of the shares of its stock shall be subject, and the receipt of the party in whose name any such share shall stand in the books of the Bank, or, if it stands in the name of more parties than one, the receipt of one of the parties shall be a sufficient discharge to the Bank for any dividend or any other sum of money payable in respect of such share, unless express notice to the contrary has been given to the Bank; and the Bank shall not be bound to see to the application of the money paid upon such receipt, whether given by one of such parties or all of them. 34 V., c. 5, s. 26.

2. No person holding stock in any Bank as executor, administrator, guardian or trustee, of or for any person named in the books of the Bank as being so represented by him or her, shall be personally subject to any liabilities as a stockholder, but the estate and funds in his or her hands shall be liable in like manner and to the same extent as the testator, intestate, ward or person interested in such trust-funds would be, if living and competent to hold the stock in his or her own name; and if the trust be for a living person, such person shall also himself or herself be liable as a shareholder; but if such testator, intestate, ward or person so represented is not so named in the books of the Bank, the executor, administrator, guardian, or trustee shall be personally liable in respect of such stock, as if he or she held it in his or her own name as owner thereof. 43 V., c. 22, s. 2.

27. Each shareholder in the Bank shall, on all occasions on which the votes of the shareholders are to be taken, have one vote for each share held by him for at least thirty days before the time of meeting. Shareholders may vote by proxy, but no person but a shareholder shall be permitted to vote or act as such proxy; and no Manager, Cashier, Bank Clerk, or other subordinate officer of the Bank shall vote either in person or by proxy, or hold a proxy for that purpose. All questions proposed for the consideration of the said shareholders shall be determined by the majority of their votes; the Chairman elected to preside at any such meeting of the said shareholders shall vote as a shareholder only, unless there be a tie, in which case (except as to the election of a Director) he shall have a casting vote: and where two or more persons are joint holders of shares, it shall be lawful that one only of such joint holders be empowered by letter of attorney from the other joint holder or holders, or a majority of them, to represent the said shares, and vote accordingly; and in all cases when the votes of the shareholders are taken the voting shall be by ballot. 34 V., c. 5, s. 27; *and see s. 30a as to payment of calls.*

2. No appointment of a proxy to vote at any meeting of the shareholders of the Bank shall be valid for that purpose, unless made or renewed in writing within the three years next preceding the time of such meeting. 43 V., c. 22, s. 12.

28. The shareholders in the Bank shall have power to regulate by by-law the following matters incident to the management and administration of the affairs of the Bank, viz: the qualification and number of the directors, which shall not be less than five nor more than ten, and the quorum thereof; the method of filling up vacancies in the Board of Directors whenever the same may occur during each year; and the time and proceedings for the election of directors, in case of a failure of any election on the day appointed for it:—the remuneration of the President, Vice-President and other directors; and the closing of the transfer book during a certain time not exceeding fifteen days, before the payment of each semi-annual dividend:—Provided that no director shall hold less than three thousand dollars of the stock of the Bank, when the paid up Capital thereof is one million dollars or less, nor less than four thousand dollars of stock when the paid up Capital thereof is over one million and does not exceed three millions, nor less than five thousand dollars of stock when the paid up Capital thereof exceeds three millions; the Directors shall be elected annually by the shareholders and shall be eligible for re-election; Provided that the foregoing provisions, touching Directors, shall not apply to a Bank *en commandite*, which shall in these matters be governed by the provisions of its Charter. The shareholders (or if the Bank be *en commandite*, the principal partners), may also regulate by by-law the amount of discounts or loans which may be made to Directors (or if the Bank be *en commandite* to the principal partners), either jointly or severally, or to any one firm or person, or to any shareholder or to corporations ; Provided that until it is otherwise ordered by bylaw under this section, the by-laws of the Bank on any matter which can be regulated by by-law under this section, shall remain in force, except as to any provision fixing the qualification of Directors at an amount less than that hereby prescribed: and no person shall be a director unless he possesses the number of shares hereby required or such greater number as may be required by any by-law in that behalf. 34 V., c. 5, s. 28.

29. Any number not less than twenty-five of the shareholders of the Bank who together may be proprietors of at least one-tenth of the paid up capital stock of the Bank, by themselves or by their proxies, or the Directors of the bank, or any four of them, shall have power at any time to call a special general meeting of the shareholders of the Bank, to be held at their usual place of meeting upon giving six weeks' previous public notice, specifying in such notice the object or objects of such meeting ; and if the object of any such special general meeting be to consider of the proposed removal of the President, or Vice-President, or of a Director or Directors of the said Bank for maladministration or other specified and apparently just cause, then if a majority of the votes of the shareholders of such meeting be given for such removal, a Director or Directors to replace him or them shall be elected or appointed in the manner provided in the by-laws of the Bank, or if there be no by-laws providing therefor, then by the shareholders at such meeting ; and if it be the President or Vice-President who shall be removed, his office shall be filled up by the Directors (in the manner provided in case of a vacancy occurring in the office of President or Vice-President) who shall choose or elect a Director to serve as such President. 34 V., c. 5, s. 29. *And see s. 30a, as to payment of calls..*

President and Directors.

80. The stock, property, affairs and concerns of the Bank shall be managed by a Board of Directors, the number to be fixed as herein provided, who shall choose from among themselves a President and Vice-President; the Directors shall be natural born or naturalized subjects of Her Majesty, and shall be elected on such day in each year as may be or may have been appointed by the charter or by any by-law of the Bank, and at such time of the day and at such place where the head office of the Bank is situate, as a majority of Directors for the time being shall appoint; and public notice shall be given by the Directors, by publishing the same at least four weeks in a newspaper of the place where the said head office is situate, previous to the time of holding such election; and the election shall be held and made by such of the shareholders of the Bank as have paid all calls made by the Directors, and as shall attend for the purpose in their own proper persons or by proxy, and all elections for Directors shall be by ballot, and the said proxies shall only be capable of being held and voted upon by shareholders then present, and the persons, to the number fixed by by-law, as hereinbefore provided, who have the greatest number of votes at any election, shall be Directors; provided that if it should happen at any election that two or more persons have an equal number of votes, and the election or non-election of one or more of such persons as a Director or Directors depends on such equality, then the Directors who shall have had a greater number, or the majority of them, shall determine which of the said persons so having an equal number of votes shall be the Director or Directors, so as to complete the full number; and in case of a vacancy occurring in the number of Directors, such vacancy shall be filled in the manner provided by the by-laws, but the non-filling of the vacancy shall not vitiate the acts of a quorum of the remaining Directors; and if the vacancy so created shall be that of a President or Vice-President, the Directors, at the first meeting after completion of their number, shall from among themselves, elect a President or Vice-President, who shall continue in office for the remainder of the year. And the said Directors, as soon as may be after the said election, shall proceed in like manner to elect by ballot two of their number to be President and Vice-President; Provided always, that no person shall be eligible to be or continue a Director, unless he shall hold, in his name and for his own use, stock in the said Bank to the amount hereinbefore provided. 34 V., c. 5, s. 30. *And see s.* 30a *as to payment of calls.*

80a. It is the true intent and meaning of sections twenty-seven, twenty-nine and thirty of this Act, that no shareholder in any Bank to which those sections apply has any right to vote, either in person or by proxy, on any question proposed for the consideration of the shareholders of such Bank at any meeting of such shareholders, or in any case where the votes of the shareholders of such Bank are taken, without having paid all calls made by the Directors which have then become due and payable. 40 V., c. 44.

31. In case it should happen that an election of Directors should not be made on any day when it ought to have been made, the Corporation shall not for that cause be deemed to be dissolved, but it shall be lawful on any other day to hold and make an election of Directors in such manner as shall have been provided by the by-laws made by the shareholders in that behalf; and the Directors then in office shall remain so until a new election shall be made. 34 V., c. 5, s. 31.

32. At all meetings of the Directors of the Bank not less than three of them shall constitute a board or quorum for the transaction of business; and at the said meetings the President, or in his absence, the Vice-President, or in their absence, one of the Directors present to be chosen *pro tempore*, shall preside; and the President, Vice-President, or President *pro tempore* so presiding, shall vote as a Director, and if there be an equal division on any question, shall have a casting vote. 34 V., c. 5, s. 32.

33. The Directors for the time being, or a majority of them shall have power to make such by-laws and regulations (not repugnant to the provisions of this Act or the laws of the Dominion of Canada) as to them shall appear needful and proper touching the management and disposition of the stock, property, estate and effects of the Bank, and touching the duties and conduct of the officers, clerks, and servants employed therein, and all such other matters as appertain to the business of a Bank, and shall also have power to appoint as many officers, clerks and servants for carrying on the said business, and with such salaries and allowances as to them may seem meet; and they may also appoint a Director or Directors for any branch of the Bank: Provided always, that before permitting any cashier, officer, clerk or servant of the Bank to enter upon the duties of his office, the Directors shall require him to give bond or other security to the satisfaction of the Directors, for the due and faithful performance of his duties; Provided also, that all by-laws of the Bank lawfully made before the passing of this Act, as to any matter respecting which the Directors can make by-laws under this section (including any by-laws for establishing a guarantee fund for the employees of the Bank) shall remain in force until they are repealed or altered by others made under this Act. 34 V. c. 5, s. 33.

34. The Directors shall have power to make such calls of money from the several shareholders for the time being upon the shares subscribed for in the Bank by them respectively, as they may find necessary, and in the corporate name of the Bank to sue for, recover and get in all such calls, or to cause and declare such shares to be forfeited to the Bank in case of non-payment of any such call; and an action may be brought to recover any money due on any such call, and it shall not be necessary to set forth the special matter in the declaration, but it shall be sufficient to allege that the defendant is holder of one share or more, as the case may be, in the capital stock of the Bank and is indebted to the Bank for a call or calls upon such share or shares, in the sum to which the call or calls amount, as the case may be, stating the amount and number of such calls, whereby an action hath accrued to the Bank to recover the same from such defendant by virtue of this Act ; and it shall be sufficient to maintain such action, to prove by any one witness, (a shareholder being competent) that the defendant, at the time of making any such call, was a shareholder in the number of shares alleged, and to produce the by-law or resolution of the Directors making and prescribing such call, and to prove notice thereof, given in conformity with such by-law or resolution ; and it shall not be necessary to prove the appointment of the Directors or any other matter whatsoever; provided that such calls shall be made at intervals of not less than thirty days, and upon notice to be given at least thirty days prior to the day on which such call shall be payable : and no such call shall exceed ten per cent. of each share subscribed. 34 V., c. 5, s. 34.

35. Provided also, that if any shareholder or shareholders refuse or neglect to pay any or either of the instalments upon his, her, or their shares of the said capital stock at the time or times appointed by such call, as aforesaid, such shareholder or shareholders shall incur a forfeiture to the use of the Bank of a sum of money equal to ten per centum on the amount of such shares ; and, moreover, it shall be lawful for the Directors of the Bank (without any previous formality other than thirty days' public notice of their intention), to sell at public auction the said shares, or so many of the said shares as shall, after deducting the reasonable expenses of the sale, yield a sum of money sufficient to pay the unpaid instalments due on the remainder of the said shares and the amount of forfeitures incurred upon the whole ; and the President, or Vice-President, manager or cashier, of the Bank shall execute the transfer to the purchaser of the shares of stock so sold ; and such transfer being accepted, shall be as valid and effectual in law as if the same had been executed by the original holder or holders of the shares of stock thereby transferred : Provided always, that nothing in this section contained shall be held to debar the Directors, or the shareholders at a general meeting, from remitting either in whole or in part, and conditionally or unconditionally, any forfeiture incurred by the non-payment of instalments as aforesaid, or to prevent the Bank from enforcing the payment of any call or calls by suit in lieu of declaring the same forfeited. 34 V., c. 5, s. 35.

36. At every annual meeting of the shareholders for the election of Directors, the out-going Directors shall submit a clear and full statement of the affairs of the Bank, containing on the one part the amount of the capital stock paid in, the amount of notes of the Bank in circulation and net profits made, the balances due to other Banks and institutions, and the cash deposited in the Bank, distinguishing deposits bearing interest from those not bearing interest and on the other part, the amount of the current coin, the gold and silver bullion, and the amount of Dominion Notes in the vaults of the Bank, the balances due to the Bank from other Banks and institutions, the value of the real and other property of the Bank, and the amount of debts owing to the Bank, including and particularizing the amounts so owing upon bills of exchange, discounted notes, mortgages, and other securities,—thus exhibiting on the one hand the liabilities of, or the debts due by the Bank, and on the other hand the assets and resources thereof; and the said statement shall also exhibit the rate and amount of the last dividend declared by the Directors, the amount of reserved profits at the time of declaring the said dividend, and the amount of debts due to the Bank, overdue and not paid, with an estimate of the loss which will probably accrue thereon. 34 V., c. 5, s. 36.

37. The books, correspondence and funds of the Bank shall at all times be subject to the inspection of the Directors; but no shareholder not being a Director shall be allowed to inspect the accounts of, any person dealing with the Bank. 34 V., c. 5, s. 37.

38. It shall be the duty of the Directors of the Bank to make half-yearly dividends of so much of the profits of the Bank as to the majority of them may seem advisable, and not inconsistent with the provisions of sections ten and eleven of this Act; and to give public notice of the payment of such dividends at least thirty days previously. 34 V., c. 5, s. 38.,

POWERS AND OBLIGATIONS OF THE BANK.

Loans, Interest, Advances on Warehouse Receipts, &c.

39. The Bank shall have the power to acquire and hold real and immovable estate for its actual use and occupation, and the management of its business, and to sell or dispose of the same, and other property to acquire in its stead, for the same purposes. 34 V., c. 5, s. 39.

40. The bank shall not, either directly or indirectly, lend money or make advances upon the security, mortgage or hypothecation of any lands or tenements, or of any ships or other vessels, nor upon the security or pledge of any share or shares of the capital stock of the Bank, or of any goods, wares or merchandise, except as authorized in this Act; nor shall the Bank, either directly or indirectly, deal in the buying and selling or bartering of goods, wares or merchandise, or engage or be engaged in any trade whatever, except as a dealer in gold and silver bullion, bills of exchange, discounting of promissory notes and negotiable securities, and in such trade generally as appertains to the business of Banking; nor shall the bank, either directly or indirectly purchase or deal in any share or shares of the capital stock of the Bank, except where it is necessary to realize upon any such share or shares held by the Bank as security for any pre-existing and matured debt. 34 V., c. 5, s. 40, *as amended by* 38 V., c. 17, s. 1.

41. The Bank may take, hold and dispose of mortgages and hypothèques upon personal as well as real property, by way of additional security for debts contracted to the Bank in the course of its business; and the rights, powers and privileges which the Bank is hereby declared to have or to have had in respect of real estate mortgaged to it, shall be held and possessed by it, in respect of any personal estate which may be mortgaged or hypothecated to it. 34 V., c. 5, s. 41.

42. The Bank may purchase any lands or real estate offered for sale under execution or in insolvency or under the order or decree of a

Court of Equity as belonging to any debtor of the Bank, or exposed to sale by the Bank under a power of sale given to it for that purpose, in cases where, under similar circumstances, an individual could so purchase, without any restriction as to the value of the lands which it may so purchase, and may acquire a title thereto as any individual purchasing at sheriff's sale or under a power of sale, in like circumstances, could do, and may take, have, hold and dispose of the same at pleasure. 34 V., c. 5, s. 42, *as amended by* 43 V., c. 22, s. 5.

43. The Bank may acquire and hold an absolute title in or to land mortgaged to it as security for a debt due or owing to it, either by obtaining a release of the equity of redemption in the mortgaged property, or by procuring a foreclosure in any Court of Chancery or of Equity, or by other means whereby, as between individuals, an equity of redemption can by law be barred, and may purchase and acquire any prior mortgage or charge on such land : Provided always, that no Bank shall hold any real or immovable property howsoever acquired, except such as shall be required for its own use, for any period exceeding seven years from the date of the acquisition thereof. 34 V., c. 5, s. 43, *as amended by* 43 V., c. 22, s. 6.

44. Nothing in any Charter, Act or law shall be construed as ever having prevented or as preventing the Bank from acquiring and holding an absolute title to and in any such mortgaged lands, whatever the value thereof may be, or from exercising or acting upon any power of sale contained in any mortgage given to it or held by it, authorizing or enabling it to sell or convey away any lands so mortgaged. 34 V., c. 5, s. 44.

***44a.** Any Bank advancing money in aid of the building of any ship or vessel, shall have the same right of acquiring and holding security upon such ship or vessel while building and when completed, either by way of mortgage, hypothec, hypothecation, privilege or lien thereon, or purchase, or transfer thereof, as individuals have in the province wherein such ship or vessel is being built, and for that purpose shall be authorized to avail itself of all such rights and means of obtaining and enforcing such security, and shall be subject to all such obligations, limitations and conditions, as are by the law of such province conferred or imposed upon individuals making such advances. 35 V., c. 8, s. 7.

45. For the purpose of this Act, the words "goods, wares and merchandise," when used herein, shall be held to comprise, in addition to the things usually understood thereby, timber, deals, boards, staves, saw-logs, and other lumber, petroleum, crude oil, and all agricultural produce and other articles of commerce ; and the words " warehouse receipt " when used herein shall be held to mean any receipt given by any person, firm or company for any goods, wares or merchandize in his or their actual, visible and continued possession, as bailee or bailees, in good faith, and not as of his or their own property, and shall comprise receipts from any person who is the keeper of any harbour, cove,

---

* This section applies only to the Provinces of Ontario, Quebec, Nova Scotia and New Brunswick.

pond, wharf, yard, warehouse, shed, storehouse, tannery, mill or other place in Canada, for goods, wares or merchandise being in the place or in one or more of the places so kept by him, whether such person is engaged in other business or not, and shall also comprise specifications of timber. The words "bill of lading," when used herein, shall comprise all receipts for goods, wares or merchandize, accompanied by an obligation to transport the same from the place where they were received to some other place, whether by land or water, or partly by land and partly by water, and by any mode of carriage whatever; and the words "ship" or "shipment" shall be held to mean the delivery of any article for transport as aforesaid. 43 V., c. 22. s. 7. (*Substituted for* 34 V., c. 5, s. 45.) *But see s. 47 as to case where the owner is himself a warehouseman, &c.*

46. The Bank may acquire and hold any warehouse receipt or bill of lading as collateral security for the payment of any debt incurred in its favor in the course of its banking business; and the warehouse receipt or bill of lading so acquired shall vest in the Bank, from the date of the acquisition thereof, all the right and title of the previous holder or owner thereof, or of the person from whom such goods, wares and merchandize were received or acquired by the Bank if the warehouse receipt or bill of lading is made directly in favor of the Bank instead of to the previous holder or owner of such goods, wares and merchandize. And if the previous holder of such warehouse receipt or bill of lading be the agent of the owner of the goods, wares and merchandize mentioned therein, within the meaning of the fifty-ninth chapter of the Consolidated Statutes of the late Province of Canada (which is contained in Schedule "A" appended to this Act, and which, as respects such meaning shall apply to all the Provinces of Canada), then the Bank shall be vested with all the right and title of the owner thereof, subject to his right to have the same re-transferred to him, if the debt as security for which they are held by the Bank. be paid: Provided always, that the Bank shall not acquire or hold any warehouse receipt or bill of lading to secure the payment of any bill, note or debt, unless such bill, note or debt be negotiated or contracted at the time of the acquisition thereof by the Bank, or upon the understanding that such warehouse receipt or bill of lading would be transferred to the Bank, but such bill, note or debt may be renewed or the time for the payment thereof extended without affecting such security. And on shipment of any goods, wares and merchandize for which a Bank holds a warehouse receipt, it may surrender such receipt and receive a bill of lading in exchange therefor; or on the reception of any goods, wares and merchandize for which it holds a bill of lading, it may surrender such bill of lading, store such goods, wares and merchandize, and take a warehouse receipt therefor; or ship them or part of them, and take another bill of lading therefor. 43 V., c. 22, s. 7. (*Substituted for* 34 V., c. 5, s. 46.)

47. If any person granting a warehouse receipt or bill of lading is engaged in the calling, as his ostensible business, of keeper of a yard, cove, wharf or harbour, or of warehouseman, miller, saw-miller, maltster, manufacturer of timber, wharfinger, master of a vessel, or other carrier by land or by water, or by both, curer or packer of meat, tanner, dealer in wool, or purchaser of agricultural produce, and is at the same time the owner of the goods, wares and merchandize mentioned in such warehouse receipt or bill of lading, any such warehouse receipt or bill of lading, and the right and title of the Bank thereto and to the goods, wares and merchandize mentioned therein, shall be as valid and effectual as if such owner, and the person making such warehouse receipt, or bill of lading, were different persons.

2. In the event of the non-payment at maturity of any debt secured by a warehouse receipt or bill of lading, the Bank may sell the goods, wares and merchandize mentioned therein, or so much thereof as will suffice to pay such debt with interest and costs returning the overplus, if any, to the person from whom such warehouse receipt or bill of lading, or the goods, wares and merchandize mentioned therein, as the case may be, were acquired; but such power of sale shall be subject to the provisions hereinafter made. 43 V., c. 22, s. 7. (*Substituted for* 34 V., c. 5, s. 47.)

48. If any miller, maltster, or packer or curer of pork grants a warehouse receipt for any cereal grains or hogs which may be manufactured into flour or malt, pork, bacon or hams, respectively, while held thereunder, such warehouse receipt shall vest in any Bank which shall be or become the lawful holder thereof, all the right and title to such manufactured article, which such Bank acquired under such warehouse receipt to the article so manufactured and described in such warehouse receipt, and the Bank shall continue to hold the same and all such right and title, for the same purposes and upon the same conditions as those upon which it previously held such material. 43 V., c. 22, s. 7. (*Substituted for* 34 V., c. 5, s. 48.)

49. All advances made on the security of any bill of lading or warehouse receipt, shall give and be held to give to the Bank making such advances a claim for the repayment of such advances on the goods, wares or merchandize therein mentioned, or into which they have been converted, prior to and by preference over the claim of any unpaid vendor, any law, usage or custom to the contrary notwithstanding. 43 V., c. 22, s. 7. (*Substituted for* 34 V., c. 5, s. 49.)

50. No sale without the consent in writing of the owner, of any timber, boards, deals, staves, saw-logs or other lumber, shall be made under this Act until, nor unless, notice of the time and place of such sale shall have been given by a registered letter, mailed in the post office to the last known address of the pledger thereof, at least thirty days prior to the sale thereof; and no goods, wares or merchandize, other than timber, boards, deals, staves, saw-logs or other lumber, shall be sold by the Bank under this Act without the consent of the owner, until, or unless, notice of the time and place of sale has been given by a registered letter, mailed in the post office to the last known address of the pledger thereof, at least ten days prior to the sale thereof; and every such sale of any article mentioned in this section, without the consent of the owner, shall be made by public auction after a notice thereof by advertisement, stating the time and place there f, in at least two

newspapers published in or nearest to the place where the sale is to be made; and if such sale be in the Province of Quebec, then at least one of such newspapers shall be a newspaper published in the English language, and one other such newspaper shall be a newspaper published in the French language. 43 V., c. 22, s. 7. (*Substituted for* 34 V., c. 5, s. 50.)

51. The Bank shall not make loans or grant discounts on the security of its own stock, but shall have a privileged lien for any debt or liability for any debt to the Bank, on the shares and unpaid dividends of the debtor or party so liable, and may decline to allow any transfer of the shares of such debtor or party until such debt is paid, and if such debt is not paid when due the Bank may sell such shares, after notice has been given to the holder thereof, of the intention of the Bank to sell the same, by mailing such notice in the post office to the last known address of such holder, at least thirty days prior to such sale; and upon such sale being made, the President, Vice-President, Manager or Cashier shall execute a transfer of such shares to the purchaser thereof in the usual transfer book of the Bank, which transfer shall vest in such purchaser all the rights in or to such shares which were possessed by the holder thereof, with the same obligation of warranty on his part as if he were the vendor thereof, but without any warranty from the Bank or by the officer of the Bank executing such transfer;

And nothing in this Act contained shall prevent the Bank from acquiring and holding as collateral security for any advance by or debt to the Bank, or for any credit or liability incurred by the Bank to or on behalf of any person (and either at the time of such advance by, or the contracting of such debt to the Bank, or the opening of such credit, or the incurring of such liability, by the Bank), Dominion, Provincial, British, or Foreign public securities, or the stock, bonds, or debentures of Municipal or other Corporations except Banks; and such stock, bonds, debentures, or securities, may in case of default to pay the debt for securing which they were so acquired and held, be dealt with, sold and conveyed, in like manner and subject to the same restrictions as are herein provided in respect of stock of the Bank on which it has acquired a lien under this Act; this provision may, however, be departed from or varied by any agreement between the Bank and the owner of such stock, bonds, debentures or securities, made at the time at which such debt was incurred, or if the time of payment of such debt has been extended, then by an agreement made at the time of such extension. 43 V., c. 22, s. 8. (*Substituted for* 34 V., c. 5, s. 51.)

52. The Bank shall not be liable to incur any penalty or forfeiture for usury: and may stipulate for, take, reserve or exact any rate of interest or discount not exceeding seven per centum per annum, and may receive and take in advance any such rate, but no higher rate of interest shall be recoverable by the Bank: any rate of interest whatever may be allowed by the Bank upon money deposited with it. 34 V., c. 5, s. 52.

*2. And whereas in some of the Provinces of Canada, laws may be in force imposing penalties on parties other than Banks, for taking, or stipulating, or paying more than a certain rate of interest, and doubts may arise as to the effect of such laws in certain cases, as to parties other than the Bank, to negotiable securities discounted, or otherwise acquired and held by any Bank, — therefore it is declared and enacted that no promissory note, bill of exchange, or other negotiable security, discounted by, or endorsed or otherwise assigned to any Bank to which this section applies, shall be held to be void, usurious, or tainted by usury, as regards such Bank or any maker, drawer, acceptor, indorser, or indorsee thereof, or other party thereto, or *bona fide* holder thereof, nor shall any party thereto be subject to any penalty or forfeiture, by reason of any rate of interest taken, stipulated or received by such Bank, on or with respect to such promissory note, bill of exchange, or other negotiable security, or paid or allowed by any party thereto to another in compensation for, or in consideration of the rate of interest taken or to be taken thereon by such Bank,—but no party thereto, other than the Bank, shall be entitled to recover or liable to pay more than the lawful rate of interest in the Province where the suit is brought, nor shall the Bank be entitled to recover a higher rate than seven per cent. per annum; and no innocent holder of or party to any promissory note, bill of exchange, or other negotiable security, shall in any case be deprived of any remedy against any party thereto, or liable to any penalty or forfeiture, by a reason of any usury or offence against the laws of any such Province respecting interest, committed in respect of such note, bill or negotiable security, without the complicity or consent of such innocent holder or party. 35 V., c. 8, s. 2.

53. The Bank may, in discounting at any of its places of business, branches, agencies or offices of discount and deposit, any note, bill, or other negotiable security or paper payable at any other of its own places or seats of business, branches, agencies or offices of discount and deposit in Canada, receive or retain in addition to the discount, any amount not exceeding the following rates per centum, according to the time it has to run, on the amount of such note, bill or other negotiable security or paper, to defray the expenses attending the collection thereof; that is to say: under thirty days, one-eighth of one per cent.—thirty days or over, but under sixty days, one-fourth of one per cent.—sixty days and over, but under ninety days, three eighths of one per cent.—ninety days and over one-half of one per cent. 34 V., c. 5, s. 53.

54. The Bank may, in discounting any note, bill or other negotiable security or paper, *bona fide* payable at any place in Canada different from that at which it is discounted and other than one of its own places or seats of business, branches, agencies or offices of discount and deposit in Canada, receive and retain in addition to the discount thereon, a sum not exceeding one half of one per centum on the amount thereof, to defray the expenses of agency and charges in collecting the same. 34 V., c. 5, s. 54.

* This applies only to the Provinces of Ontario, Quebec, Nova Scotia and New Brunswick.

*54a. It shall be lawful for any Bank to which this Act applies, (including the Bank of British North America, and La Banque du Peuple) to receive deposits from any person or persons whomsoever, whatever be his, her, or their age, status or condition in life, and whether such person or persons be qualified by law to enter into ordinary contracts or not ; and from time to time to repay any or all of the principal thereof, and to pay the whole or any part of the interest thereon, to such person or persons respectively, without the authority, aid, assistance, or intervention of any person or persons, official or officials, being required, unless before such repayment the money so deposited in and repaid by the Bank, be lawfully claimed as the property of some other party, in which case it may be paid to the depositor with the consent of the claimant, or to the claimant with the consent of the depositor, any law, usage, or custom to the contrary notwithstanding :—Provided always, that if the person making any deposit, as aforesaid, could not, under the law of the Province where the deposit is made, deposit and withdraw money in and from a Bank without this section, then and in that case the total amount of deposits to be received from such person on deposit shall not at any time exceed the sum of five hundred dollars;

2. No such Bank shall be bound to see to the execution of any trust whether expressed, implied, or constructive, to which any deposit made under the authority of this section may be subject ; and, except only in the case of lawful claim by some other party before repayment, the receipt of the person in whose name any such deposit stands, or, if it stand in the name of two persons the receipt of one, and if in the names of more than two persons, the receipt of a majority of such persons, shall be a sufficient discharge to all concerned for the payment of any money payable in respect of such deposit, notwithstanding any trust to which such deposit may then be subject, and whether or not the Bank sought to be charged with such trust (and with whom the deposit may have been made), had notice thereof ; and no such Bank shall be bound to see to the application of the money paid upon such receipt, any law or usage to the contrary notwithstanding. 35 V., c. 8, ss. 3 and 4.

54b. In all matters relating to bills of exchange and promissory notes, the following and no other shall be observed as legal holidays, or non-juridical days, that is to say :—

1. In the Provinces of Ontario, New Brunswick and Nova Scotia.—
Sunday.
New Year's Day.
Good Friday.
Christmas Day.
The birthday (or the day fixed by Proclamation for the celebration of the birthday) of the reigning Sovereign.

✢ The first day of July, Dominion day, and if that day is a Sunday, then the second day of July, under the same name.

---

* This section applies only to the provinces of Ontario, Quebec, Nova Scotia and New Brunswick.

✢ Dominion Day is a non-juridical day throughout the Dominion, under 42 V., c. 47.

Any day appointed by Proclamation for a public holiday or for a general fast, or a general thanksgiving throughout the Dominion ; and the day next following New Year's Day and Christmas Day, when these days respectively fall on Sunday.

And in the Province of Quebec the same days shall be observed as legal holidays, with the addition of,—

The Epiphany.
The Annunciation.
The Ascension.
Corpus Christi.
St. Peter and St. Paul's Day.
All Saints' Day
Conception Day.

2. And in any one of the said Provinces of the Dominion any day appointed by proclamation of the Lieutenant-Governor of such Province for a public holiday or for a fast or thanksgiving within the same.

3. And with regard to bills of exchange and promissory notes, whenever the last day of grace falls on a legal holiday or non-juridical day in the Province where any such bill or note is payable, then the day next following not being a legal holiday or non-juridical day in such province shall be the last day of grace as to such bill or note. 35 V., c. 8, s. 8, and 42 V., c. 47.

Bank Notes, Bonds, &c.

55. The bonds, obligations and bills obligatory or of credit of the Bank under its corporate seal and signed by the President or Vice-President and countersigned by a Cashier or Assistant Cashier, which shall be made payable to any person or persons, shall be assignable by endorsement thereon ; and bills or notes of the Bank signed by the President, Vice-President, Cashier or other officer appointed by the Directors of the Bank to sign the same, promising the payment of money to any person or persons, his, her or their order, or to the bearer, though not under the corporate seal of the Bank, shall be binding and obligatory on it in like manner and with the like force and effect as they would be upon any private person, if issued by him in his private or natural capacity, and shall be assignable in like manner as if they were so issued by a private person in his natural capacity ; Provided always, that nothing in this Act shall be held to debar the Directors of the Bank from authorizing or deputing from time to time any Cashier, Assistant-Cashier or officer of the Bank, or any Director other than the President or Vice-President, or any Cashier, Manager or Local Director of any branch or office of discount and deposit of the Bank, to sign the bills of the Bank intended for general circulation, and payable to order or to bearer on demand. 34 V., c. 5, s. 55.

56. All Bank notes and Bills of the Bank whereon the name or name of any person or persons entrusted or authorized to sign such note or bill on behalf of the Bank, shall or may become impressed by machinery provided for that purpose by or with the authority of the Bank, shall be and shall be taken to be good and valid to all intents and purposes, as if such notes and bills had been subscribed in the proper handwriting of the person or persons entrusted or authorized by the Bank to sign the same respectively, and shall be and be deemed and taken to be Bank notes and bills within the meaning of all laws and statutes whatever, and shall and may be described as Bank bills or notes in all indictments and civil or criminal proceedings whatsoever, any law, statute or usage to the contrary notwithstanding. 34 V., c. 5, s. 56.

And see sub-section 2 of section 8 as to preferential payment of notes of the Bank in case of insolvency

INSOLVENCY.

57. Any suspension by the Bank of payment of any of its liabilities as they accrue, in specie or Dominion notes, shall, if it continues for ninety days, constitute the Bank insolvent and operate a forfeiture of its Charter, so far as regards the issue or re-issue of notes and other Banking operations ; and the Charter shall remain in force only for the purpose of enabling the Directors or the assignee or assignees, or other legal authority (if any be appointed in such manner as may by law be provided) to make the calls mentioned in the next following section of this Act and to wind up its business ; And any such assignee or assignees or other legal authority shall, for such purposes, have all the powers of the Directors. 34 V., c. 5, s. 57.

58. In the event of the property and assets of the Bank becoming insufficient to pay its debts and liabilities, the shareholders of the Bank shall be liable for the deficiency so far as that each shareholder shall be so liable to an amount (over and above any amount not paid up on their respective shares) equal to the amount of their shares respectively ; and if any suspension of payment in full in specie or Dominion notes, of all or any of the notes or other liabilities of the Bank shall continue for six months, the Directors may and shall make calls on such shareholders, to the amount they may deem necessary to pay all the debts and liabilities of the Bank, without waiting for the collection of any debts due to it or the sale of any of its assets or property ; such calls shall be made at intervals of thirty days and upon notice to be given thirty days at least prior to the day on which such call shall be payable ; and any such call shall not exceed twenty per cent. on each share, and payment thereof may be enforced in like manner as for calls on unpaid stock, and the first of such calls shall be made within ten days after the expiration of the said six months ; and any failure on the part of any shareholder liable to such call to pay the same when due, shall operate a forfeiture by such shareholder of all claim in or to any part of the assets of the Bank, such call and any further call thereafter being nevertheless recoverable from him as if no such forfeiture had been incurred : Provided always, that nothing in this section contained shall be construed to alter or diminish the additional liabilities of the Directors hereinbefore mentioned and declared : Provided also, that if the Bank be *en commandite* and the principal partners are personally liable, then, in case of any such suspension, such liability shall at once accrue and may be enforced against such principal partners, without waiting for any sale or discussion of the property or assets of the Bank, or other preliminary proceedings whatever, and the provision respecting calls shall not apply to such Bank. 34 V., c. 5, s. 58.

59. Persons, who having been shareholders in the Bank, have only transferred their shares or any of them to others or registered the transfer thereof within one month before the commencement of the suspension of payment by the Bank, shall be liable to calls on such shares under the next preceding section, as if they had not transferred them, saving their recourse against those to whom they were transferred; and any assignee or other officer or person appointed to wind up the affairs of the Bank, in case of its insolvency, shall have the powers of the Directors with respect to such calls: Provided that if the Bank be *en commandite*, the liability of the principal partners and of the *commanditaires* shall continue for such time after their ceasing to be such as may be provided in the Charter of the Bank, and the foregoing provisions with respect to the transfer of shares or calls shall not apply to such Bank. 34 V., c. 5, s. 59.

OFFENCES AND PENALTIES.

60. If any Cashier, Assistant Cashier, Manager, Clerk or servant of the Bank, secretes, embezzles or absconds with any bond, obligation, bill obligatory or of credit, or other bill or note, or any security for money, or any money or effects entrusted to him as such Cashier, Assistant Cashier, Manager, Clerk or Servant, whether the same belong to the said Bank or belong to any person or persons, body or bodies politic or corporate, or institution or institutions, and be lodged with the said Bank, the said Cashier, Assistant Cashier, Manager, Clerk or Servant, so offending and being thereof convicted in due form of law, shall be deemed guilty of felony, and shall be punished by imprisonment at hard labour in the penitentiary for any term not less than two years, or by imprisonment in any gaol or place of confinement for any term less than two years, in the discretion of the Court. 34 V., c. 5, s. 60.

61. If any President, Vice-President, Director, Principal Partner *en commandite*, Manager, Cashier or other officer of the Bank wilfully gives or concurs in giving any creditor of the Bank any fraudulent, undue or unfair preference over other creditors, by giving security to such creditor or by changing the nature of his claim or otherwise howsoever, he shall be guilty of misdemeanor, and shall further be responsible for all damages sustained by any party by such preference. 34 V., c. 5, s. 61.

62. The making of any wilfully false or deceptive statement in any account, statement, return, report or other document respecting the affairs of the Bank, shall, unless it amounts to a higher offence, be a misdemeanor, and any and every President, Vice-President, Director, Principal Partner *en commandite*, Auditor, Manager, Cashier, or other officer of the Bank preparing, signing, approving or concurring in such statement, return, report or document, or using the same with intent to deceive or mislead any party, shall be held to have wilfully made such false statement, and shall further be responsible for all damages sustained by such party in consequence thereof. 34 V., c. 5, s. 62.

63. Any Director refusing to make or enforce, or to concur in making or enforcing any call under the fifty-eighth section of this Act, shall be deemed guilty of a misdemeanor and shall be personally responsible for any damages suffered by such default. 34 V., c. 5, s. 63.

64. If any miller, warehouseman, master of a vessel, forwarder, carrier, wharfinger, keeper of a cove, yard, harbour or other place for storing timber, deals, staves, boards or other lumber, curer or packer of pork, or dealer in wool, factor, agent or other person, or any clerk or person in his employ, knowingly and wilfully gives to any person any writing purporting to be a receipt for, or an acknowledgment of any cereal grain, timber, deals, staves, boards or other lumber, or other goods, wares, merchandize or property, as having been received in his warehouse, vessel, cove, wharf or other place, or in any such place, about which he is employed, or as having been in any other manner received by him or the person in or about whose business he is employed, before the goods or property named in such receipt, acknowledgment or writing have been actually so received by or delivered to him or his employer, with the intent to mislead, deceive, injure or defraud any person or persons whomsoever, although such person or persons may be then to him unknown ; or if any person knowingly and wilfully accepts or transmits or uses any such false receipt, acknowledgment or writing, the person giving and the person accepting, transmitting or using such false receipt, acknowledgment or writing, shall severally be guilty of a misdemeanor. 34 V., c. 5, s. 64.

65. The wilfully making any false statement in any such receipt, acknowledgment or certificate as in the forty-sixth section of this Act mentioned, or the wilfully alienating or parting with, or not delivering to the holder or indorsee any cereal grain, goods, wares or merchandize mentioned in such receipt, acknowledgment or certificate, contrary to the undertaking therein expressed or implied, shall be a misdemeanor. 34 V., c. 5, s. 65.

66. If any offence in either of the two next preceding sections mentioned be committed by the doing of anything in the name of any firm, company or copartnership of persons, the person by whom such thing is actually done, and any person who connives at the doing thereof shall be deemed guilty of the offence, and not any other person. 34 V., c. 5, s. 66.

66a. Any person, firm or company assuming or using the title of " Bank " without being authorized so to do by this Act, or by some other Act in force in that behalf, shall be guilty of a misdemeanor. 43 V., c. 22, s. 10.

67. Any person convicted of a misdemeanor under this Act shall, on conviction, be liable to be imprisoned in any gaol or place of confinement for any term not exceeding two years, in the discretion of the Court before which the conviction shall be had. 34 V., c. 5, s. 67.

68. No private person or party, except a chartered Bank, shall issue or re-issue, make, draw, or endorse any bill, bond, note, check or other instrument, intended to circulate as money, or to be used as a substitute for money, for any amount whatever, under a penalty of four hundred dollars, to be recovered with costs, in any court having civil jurisdiction to the amount, by any party who will sue for the same; and one-half of such sum shall belong to the party suing for the same, and the other half to Her Majesty, for the public uses of the Dominion.

The intention to pass any such instrument as money, shall be presumed, if it be made for the payment of a less sum than twenty dollars, and be payable either in form or in fact to the bearer thereof, or at sight or on demand, or at less than thirty days thereafter, or be overdue or be in any way calculated or designed for circulation, or as a substitute for money; unless such instrument be a check on some chartered Bank, paid by the maker directly to his immediate creditor, or a promissory note, bill of exchange, bond or other undertaking, for the payment of money paid or delivered by the maker thereof to his immediate creditor, and be not designed to circulate as a substitute for money. 34 V., c. 5, s. 68.

NOTICES.

69. The several public notices by this Act required to be given, shall be given by advertisement in one or more of the newspapers published at the place where the Head Office of the Bank is situate, and in the *Canada Gazette* or such other *Gazette* as shall be generally known and described as the *Official Gazette* for the publication of official documents and notices emanating from the Civil Government of the Dominion. 34 V., c. 5, s. 69.

FUTURE LEGISLATION.

70. The Bank shall be subject to such provisions of any general or special winding up Act to be passed by Parliament as may be declared to apply to Banks; and no special Act which Parliament may deem it right to pass for winding up the affairs of the Bank in case of its insolvency, shall be deemed an infringement of its rights or of the privileges conferred by its charter. 34 V., c. 5, s. 70.

71. The Bank shall always be subject to any general provisions respecting Banks which Parliament may deem necessary for the public interest. 34 V., c. 5, s. 71.

SPECIAL PROVISIONS AS TO CERTAIN BANKS.

72. The Bank of British North America, which, by the terms of its present charter, is to be subject to the general laws of the Dominion, with respect to Banks and Banking, shall not issue or re-issue in Canada, any note for a less sum than five dollars or for any sum not being a multiple of five dollars, and any such note of the said Bank outstanding shall be called in and redeemed as soon as practicable; and the provisions contained in the ninth, twelfth, thirteenth, fourteenth, fifteenth, sixteenth, forty-fifth, forty-sixth, forty-seventh, forty-eighth, forty-ninth, fiftieth, fifty-first, fifty-second, fifty-third, fifty-fourth, fifty-fourth (a), fifty-fourth (b), fifty-sixth, sixtieth, sixty-first, sixty-second, sixty-fourth, sixty-fifth, sixty-sixth, sixty-seventh, sixty-ninth, and seventy-first sections of this Act, and in the second subsection of the eighth, and in the second subsection of the twenty-seventh sections thereof shall apply to the said Bank; those contained in the other sections shall not apply to it. 34 V., c. 5, s. 72, *as amended by* 35 V., c. 8., 40 V., c. 54, *and* 43 V., c. 22.

73. This Act shall not apply to any now existing Bank not mentioned in the schedule B thereunto annexed (except the Bank of British North America to the extent aforesaid and La Banque du Peuple to the extent hereinafter mentioned) unless the Directors of such Bank shall, by special resolution, apply to the Treasury Board, that the provisions of this Act may be extended to such Bank, nor unless the Treasury Board allows such application, and upon publication in the *Official Gazette* of such resolution, and of the minute of the Treasury Board thereon, allowing such application, such Bank shall come under the provisions of this Act. 34 V., c. 5, s. 73.

74. In pursuance of the application made by the Bank of Nova Scotia in that behalf, it shall be lawful for the shareholders of the said Bank, at any special general meeting called for the purpose, and by a by-law to be passed thereat, to reduce the capital and shares of the said Bank by an amount not exceeding thirteen per cent. thereof respectively, and the shares and capital shall thereafter be reckoned at the amount to which they shall be so reduced. 34 V., c. 5, s. 74.

75. All the provisions of this Act except those contained in sections one, two, three, five, six, seven, twenty-seven, twenty-nine, thirty, thirty-one, thirty-two, thirty-three, thirty-five, thirty-six, thirty-seven, fifty-seven, fifty-eight, fifty-nine, sixty-three, seventy, seventy-two, seventy-three, and seventy-four, and so much of section twenty-eight, as is declared not to apply to Banks *en commandite* shall apply to La Banque du Peuple: Provided that wherever the word "Directors" is used in any of the sections which apply to the said Bank it shall be read and construed as meaning the principal partners or members of the corporation of the said Bank: and so much of the Act incorporating the said Bank or of any Act amending or continuing it as may be inconsistent with any section of this Act applying to the said Bank or which makes any provision in any matter provided for by the said sections other than such as is hereby made is hereby repealed. 34 V., c. 5, s. 75,

REPEALING AND SAVING CLAUSES.

76. The Act passed in the thirty-third year of Her Majesty's reign, chaptered eleven, and intituled, *An Act respecting Banks and Banking*, is hereby repealed, and the Act passed in the thirty-first year of Her Majesty's reign, and intituled, *An Act respecting Banks*, is hereby repealed in so far as respects Banks to which this Act applies, including the Bank of British North America and La Banque du Peuple, and shall cease to apply to them after the passing of this Act (or after they respectively come under its provisions, if they are now existing Banks and not mentioned in the Schedule B), except as to rights theretofore acquired under or offences committed against it. 34 V., c. 5, s. 76.

2. Sections three, four, five and six of the Act passed in the forty-second year of Her Majesty's reign, chaptered forty-five, and intituled "*An Act to amend the Act relating to Banks and Banking and the Acts amending the same*," and chapter fifty five of the Consolidated Statutes of the late Province of Canada, intituled "*An Act respecting Banks and freedom of Banking*," are hereby repealed, except as to rights acquired, offences committed, or liabilities incurred before the passing of this Act. 43 V., c. 22, s. 9.

77. Nothing in this Act contained shall affect any case pending when it shall come into force, but such case shall be decided as if this Act had not been passed. 34 V., c. 5, s. 77.

SCHEDULE A.

CONSOLIDATED STATUTES OF CANADA, CHAPTER 59.

An Act respecting the protection of Persons who receive Assignments and enter into Contracts in relation to Goods entrusted to Agents.

HER Majesty, by and with the advice and consent of the Legislative Council and Assembly of Canada, enacts as follows:—

1. Any person may contract for the purchase of goods with any agent entrusted with the possession thereof, or to whom the same may be consigned, and may receive and pay for the same to such agent, and such contract and payment shall be binding upon the owner of the goods notwithstanding the purchaser has notice that he is contracting only with an agent.

2. Any agent entrusted with the possession of goods or of the documents of title thereto shall be deemed the owner thereof for the following purposes, that is to say:

1. To make a sale or contract, as in the first clause mentioned;

2. To entitle the consignee of goods consigned by such agent to a lien thereon for any money or negotiable security advanced or given by him to or for the use of such agent, or received by the agent for the use of the consignee, in like manner as if such agent was the true owner of the goods;

3. To give validity to any contract or agreement by way of pledge (*gage*) lien or security *bonâ fide* made with such agent, as well for an original loan, advance or payment made upon the security of the goods or documents, as for any further or continuing advance in respect thereof; and

4. To make such contract binding upon the owner of the goods and on all other persons interested therein, notwithstanding the person claiming such pledge or lien had notice that he was contracting only with an agent.

3. In case any person has a valid lien and security on any goods or document of title or negotiable security in respect of a previous advance upon a contract with an agent,—and in case he delivers up the same to such agent upon a contract for the pledge (*gage*), lien or security of other goods or of another document or security by such agent delivered to him in exchange, to be held upon the same lien as the goods, documents or security so delivered up,—then such new contract, if *bonâ fide*, shall be deemed a valid contract made in consideration of a present advance of money within this Act, but the lien acquired under such new contract on the goods, document or security deposited in exchange, shall not exceed the value of the goods, documents or security so delivered up and exchanged.

4. Such contracts only shall be valid as are herein mentioned, and such loans, advances and exchanges only shall be valid as are made *bona fide* and without notice that the agent making the same has no authority so to do, or that he is acting *mala fide* against the owner of the goods.

5. No antecedent debt owing from any agent entrusted as aforesaid, shall authorize any lien (*gage*) or pledge in respect of such debt, nor shall it authorize such agent to deviate from any express orders or authority received from his principal.

6. All *bona fide* loans, advances and exchanges as aforesaid (though made with notice of the agent not being the owner, but without notice of his acting without authority), shall bind the owner and all other persons interested in the goods, document or security, as the case may be.

7. Every bill of lading, warehouse keeper's or wharfinger's receipt or order for delivery of goods, every bill of inspection of pot or pearl ashes, and every other document used in the ordinary course of business, as proof of the possession or control of goods, or authorizing or purporting to authorize either by endorsement or by delivery, the possessor of such document to transfer or receive goods thereby represented, shall be deemed a document of title within this Act.

8. Any agent entrusted as aforesaid and possessed of any such document of title, whether derived immediately from the owner of the goods or obtained by reason of the agent having been entrusted with the possession of the goods or of any document of title thereto, shall be deemed to be entrusted with the possession of the goods represented by such document of title.

9. All contracts pledging or giving a lien upon any such document of title shall be deemed a pledge (*gage*) of and lien upon the goods to which it relates, and the agent shall be deemed the possessor of the goods or documents of title whether the same be in his actual custody or be held by any other person for him or subject to his control.

10. When any loan or advance is *bona fide* made to any agent entrusted with and in possession of goods or documents of title as aforesaid on the faith of any contract in writing to consign, deposit, transfer or deliver such goods or documents of title, and the same are actually received by the person making the loan or advance, either at the time of the contract or at a time subsequent thereto, without notice that the agent is not authorized to make the pledge or security, such loan or advance shall be deemed a loan or advance upon the security of the goods or documents of title within this Act.

11. Every contract, whether made direct with the agent as aforesaid, or with any clerk or other person on his behalf shall be deemed a contract with such agent.

12. Every payment, whether made by money, bills of exchange or other negotiable security, shall be deemed an advance within this Act.

13. Every agent in possession of goods or documents as aforesaid shall, for the purposes of this Act, be taken to be entrusted therewith by the owner, unless the contrary be shewn in evidence.

14. Nothing herein contained shall lessen, alter or affect the civil responsibility of any agent for the breach of any duty or contract or the non-fulfilment of his orders or authority, in respect of any such contract, agreement, lien or pledge (*gage*) as aforesaid.

15. In case any agent entrusted as aforesaid, contrary to or without the authority of his principal, for his own benefit and in violation of good faith, makes, by way of pledge (*gage*), lien and security, any consignment, deposit, transfer or delivery of any goods or documents of title so entrusted to him, or contrary to or without such authority, for his own benefit and in violation of good faith, accepts any advance on the faith of any contract to consign, deposit, transfer or deliver such goods or documents of title, such agent shall be deemed guilty of a misdemeanor, and being convicted thereof, shall be sentenced to suffer such punishment by fine or imprisonment in the common gaol for any term not exceeding two years, or by both, as the Court awards.

16. Every clerk or other person who knowingly and wilfully acts and assists in making any such consignment, deposit, transfer or delivery, or in accepting or procuring such advance as aforesaid, shall be guilty of a misdemeanor, and shall be liable, at the discretion of the Court, to any of the punishments which the Court may award, as herein last mentioned.

17. No such agent shall be liable to any prosecution for consigning, depositing, transferring or delivering any such goods or documents of title, in case the same are not made a security for or subject to the payment of any greater sum of money than at the time was justly due and owing to the agent from his principal, together with the amount of any bills of exchange drawn by or on account of his principal, and accepted by such agent.

18. The conviction of any agent as aforesaid shall not be received in evidence in any action at law, or suit in equity against him.

19. No oath, or admission under oath, by an agent entrusted as aforesaid, made previously to his being indicted for the offence, in consequence of the compulsory process of a Court of Law, Equity

or Admiralty in an action, suit or proceeding *bona fide* instituted by a party aggrieved, nor any disclosure made by him in an examination or in a deposition before any Commissioner of Bankrupts, shall be used in evidence in any prosecution against the agent in respect of any act done by him as aforesaid.

20. Nothing herein contained shall prevent the owner from redeeming any goods or documents of title pledged as aforesaid, at any time before the same have been sold, upon repayment of the amount of the lien thereon or restoration of the securities in respect of which the lien exists, and upon payment or satisfaction to the agent of any sum of money for or in respect of which such agent is entitled to retain the goods or documents, by way of lien against such owner; or shall prevent the owner from recovering from the person with whom any goods or documents have been pledged, or who has any lien thereon, any balance or sum of money remaining in his hands as the produce of the sale of the goods, after deducting the amount of the lien under the contract.

21. In case of the bankruptcy of any such agent, and in case the owner of the goods redeems the same, he shall, in respect of the sum paid by him on account of the agent for such redemption, be held to have paid the same for the use of such agent before his bankruptcy, or in case the goods have not been so redeemed, the owner shall be deemed a creditor of the agent for the value of the goods so pledged at the time of the pledge, and may in either case prove for or set-off the sum so paid, or the value of such goods, as the case may be.

22. In construing this Act, the word "person" shall be taken to designate a body corporate or company as well as an individual ; and the word "goods" shall be taken to include all personal property of whatever nature or kind soever, and the word "shipped" shall be taken to mean the carriage of goods, whether by land or by water.

23. Nothing herein contained shall give validity to, or in any wise affect any contract, agreement, lien, pledge (*gage*), or other act, matter, or thing made or done before the twenty-eighth of July, 1847, or destroy or diminish any other right, recourse or remedy not contrary or repugnant to this Act which might be enforced according to the Laws of Upper or Lower Canada.

24. This Act shall relate to and from the twenty-eighth July, one thousand eight hundred and forty-seven, and as respects all transactions and things since that day within the scope and meaning hereof, shall be construed and applied as if it had been passed on that day. 43 V., c. 22, *Schedule A*.

SCHEDULE B.

BANKS WHOSE CHARTERS ARE CONTINUED BY THIS ACT.

1. The Bank of Montreal.
2. The Quebec Bank.
3. La Banque du Peuple.
4. The Consolidated Bank.

5. Molsons Bank.
6. The Bank of Toronto.
7. The Ontario Bank.
8. The Eastern Townships Bank.
9. La Banque Nationale.
10. La Banque Jacques Cartier.
11. The Merchants' Bank of Canada.
12. The Union Bank of Lower Canada.
13. The Canadian Bank of Commerce.
14. The Mechanics' Bank.
15. The Dominion Bank.
16. The Merchants' Bank of Halifax.
17. The Bank of Nova Scotia.
18. The Bank of Yarmouth.
19. The Bank of Liverpool.
20. The Exchange Bank of Canada.
21. La Banque Ville Marie.
22. The Standard Bank of Canada.
23. The Bank of Hamilton.
24. The Halifax Banking Company.
25. The Maritime Bank of the Dominion of Canada.
26. The Federal Bank of Canada.
27. La Banque d'Hochelaga.
28. The Stadacona Bank.
29. The Imperial Bank of Canada.
30. The Pictou Bank.
31. La Banque de St. Hyacinthe.
32. The Bank of Ottawa.
33. The Bank of New Brunswick.
34. The Exchange Bank of Yarmouth.
35. The Union Bank of Halifax.
36. The People's Bank of Halifax—43 V., c. 22, *Schedule B*.
37. La Banque de St. Jean. 44 V., c. 9.

DUTIES ON PROMISSORY NOTES.

42 VICTORIA, CHAPTER 17.

An Act to amend and consolidate the law respecting Duties imposed on Promissory Notes and Bills of Exchange.

Section.
- Preamble.
1. Acts repealed; 31 V., c. 9; 33 V., c. 13; 37 V., c. 47; 41 V., c. 10; Proviso; saving things lawfully done under them.
2. Interpretation; "Bank;" "Broker;" "Instrument."
3. Act 41 V., c. 7, to apply to duties under this Act.
4. Duties on Notes, Drafts and Bills; the duties; as to interest.
5. What shall be deemed instruments liable to duty.
6. Instruments exempted from duty; Con. Stat. Can., c. 55.
7. No duty under certain Acts, on notes, &c., made after 1st February, 1868.
8. No duty on bills drawn and payable out of Canada.
9. Exemption of notarial instruments.
10. How the duties shall be paid; by adhesive stamps; by stamped paper and stamps; cancelling adhesive stamps; the same; penalty for non-compliance with this section.
11. By whom the stamps shall be affixed; penalty for default; if the paper be stamped.
12. Penalty for not affixing the proper stamps at the proper time; presumption in suits for penalty; proviso in favor of innocent holders.
13. Innocent holder of unstamped or insufficiently stamped note, &c., may make it valid by payment of double duty, &c.

Section.
14. Provisions for validity by payment of double duty extended to bills, &c., drawn out of but payable in Canada.
15. When single duty may be paid on such bills, &c.
16. As to suits in which lost or destroyed bills, &c., form the ground of complaint or defence.
17. In what case only penalty shall be enforced as to unstamped bills, &c., after payment or settlement thereof.
18. As to bills, &c., found among effects of deceased persons.
19. Unstamped bills, &c., admissible in evidence in criminal cases.
20. Stamped paper may be prepared; device; redemption of spoiled stamps or stamped paper.
21. Adhesive stamps, device to express value.
22. Sale and distribution of stamped paper and stamps.
23. Governor-in-Council may make regulations to meet doubtful cases.
24. Punishment for forging stamps or having instruments for forging; term of imprisonment; such offence to be forgery.
25. Penalty on bank or broker making, buying or taking note not duly stamped.
26. Penalty for affixing stamps already used.
27. Penalty incurred on each instrument, though several be made on the same day.
28. Recovery of penalties not otherwise provided for.

[*Assented to* 15*th May*, 1879.]

HER Majesty, by and with the advice and consent of the Senate and House of Commons of Canada, enacts as follows:—

1. The Acts thirty-first Victoria, chapter nine, thirty-third Victoria, chapter thirteen, thirty-seventh Victoria, chapter forty-seven, except section one, and forty-first Victoria, chapter ten, are hereby repealed: Provided always, that all Acts or enactments repealed by any of the said Acts shall remain repealed, and that all things lawfully done under them or any of them shall remain valid, and all penalties incurred under them or any of them may be enforced and recovered, and all proceedings commenced under them or any of them may be continued and completed under this Act, which shall not be construed as a new law but as a consolidation and continuation of the repealed enactments with and subject to the amendments hereby made.

2. In this Act the word "Bank" means and includes any chartered bank, and any banking institution, and any branch or agency thereof:

The word "Broker" means and includes any broker or person by repute doing the business of brokerage:

The word "Instrument" means and includes any promissory note, bill of exchange or part thereof, draft or order upon which a duty is payable under this Act.

3. The duties imposed by this Act shall be duties within the meaning and purview of the Act passed in the now last session, intituled, "*An Act to provide for the better auditing of the Public Accounts*," and the proceeds of the said duties shall form part of the Consolidated Revenue Fund of Canada.

4. Upon and in respect of every promissory note, draft or bill of exchange, for an amount not less than twenty-five dollars, made, drawn or accepted in Canada, previous to and from and after the passing of this Act, there shall be levied, collected and paid to Her Majesty, for the public uses of the Dominion, the duties hereinafter mentioned, that is to say :—

- On each such promissory note, and on each such draft or bill of exchange, a duty of one cent, if such note, bill or draft, amounts to but does not exceed twenty-five dollars,—a duty of two cents if the amount thereof exceeds twenty-five but does not exceed fifty dollars,—and a duty of three cents if the amount thereof exceeds fifty dollars but is less than one hundred dollars ;
- On each such promissory note, and on each such draft or bill of exchange for one hundred dollars or more, executed singly, a duty of three cents for the first hundred dollars of the amount thereof, and a further duty of three cents for each additional hundred dollars or fraction of a hundred dollars of the amount thereof ;
- On each such draft or bill of exchange executed in duplicate, a duty of two cents on each part for the first hundred dollars of the amount thereof, and a further duty of two cents for each additional hundred dollars or fraction of a hundred dollars of the amount thereof ;
- On each such draft or bill of exchange executed in more than two parts, a duty of one cent on each part for the first hundred dollars of the amount thereof, and a further duty of one cent for each additional hundred dollars or fraction of hundred dollars of the amount thereof ;
- And any interest made payable at the maturity of any bill, draft or note, with the principal sum, shall be counted as part of the amount thereof.

5. Every bill, draft, order or instrument—

For the payment of any sum of money by a bill or promissory note, whether such payment be required to be made to the bearer or to order;

Every document usually termed a letter of credit, or whereby any person is entitled to have credit with, or to receive from or draw upon any person for any sum of money;

And every receipt for money, given by any bank or person, and entitling the person paying such money, or the bearer of such receipt, to receive the like sum from any third person,—

Shall be deemed a bill of exchange or draft chargeable with duty under this Act.

6. Every bill of exchange, draft or order drawn by any officer of Her Majesty's Commissariat, or by any other officer in Her Majesty's Imperial or Provincial Service, in his official capacity, or any acceptance or indorsement by such officer on a bill of exchange drawn out of Canada, or any draft of or on any bank payable to the order of any such officer in his official capacity, as aforesaid, or any note payable on demand to bearer issued by any chartered bank in Canada, or by any bank issuing such note under the Act, chapter fifty-five of the Consolidated Statutes of the late Province of Canada, intituled "*An Act respecting Banks and freedom of Banking,*" shall be free from duty under this Act; and—

Any cheque, if the same shall be payable on demand,—

Any post office money order, or order on any post office savings bank, and—

Any municipal debenture or coupon of such debenture—shall be free of duty under this Act.

7. No duty shall be payable under the Act of the legislature of the late Province of Canada, passed in the session held in the twenty-seventh and twenty-eighth years of Her Majesty's reign, chapter four, or under the Act of the said legislature, passed in the twenty-ninth year of Her Majesty's reign, chapter four, on any promissory note, draft or bill of exchange made, drawn or accepted, upon or after the said first day of February, one thousand eight hundred and sixty-eight; but to all promissory notes, drafts or bills of exchange made, drawn or accepted in the late Province of Canada, or in the Province of Quebec or Ontario, before the said day, and to all offences committed and penalties incurred in respect thereof, the said Acts shall continue to apply.

8. Notwithstanding anything in this Act contained, no bill of exchange drawn and payable outside of the Dominion of Canada shall be invalid, nor shall the maker or any owner or holder of any such bill be subject to any penalty in consequence of no stamp or stamps of this Dominion being affixed to such bill.

9. Neither this Act nor any of the Acts hereby repealed shall be construed to require or to have required that any stamp be impressed on or affixed to any instrument executed *en brevet* or otherwise before a notary in his official capacity.

10. The duty on any such promissory note, draft, bill of exchange or part thereof, shall be paid by making it upon paper stamped in the manner hereinafter provided, to the amount of such duty, or—

By affixing thereto an adhesive stamp or adhesive stamps of the kind hereinafter mentioned, to the amount of such duty, or—

By making the instrument on stamped paper, and, where the amount in the instrument is in excess of the amount represented by the stamp on the instrument, by affixing thereto adhesive stamps for the portion of the duty to which the instrument is liable in excess of what is represented by the stamped paper:

In either case the adhesive stamps shall be cancelled by writing thereon the signature or part of the signature or the initials of the maker or drawer, or of the witness attesting the signature of the maker or endorser of the instrument, or in the case of a draft or bill made or drawn out of Canada of the acceptor or first indorser in Canada, or some integral or material part of the instrument so as (as far as may be practicable) to identify each stamp with the instrument to which it is attached, and to show that it has not before been used, and to prevent its being thereafter used for any other instrument, or—

The person affixing such adhesive stamp, or the witness attesting the same shall, at the time of affixing the same, write or stamp thereon the date at which it was affixed; and such stamp shall be held *prima facie* to have been affixed at the date stamped or written thereon:

And if no integral or material part of the instrument nor any part of the signature or initials of the maker, drawer, witness or acceptor or first indorser or witness in Canada be written thereon, nor any date be so stamped or written thereon, or if the date do not agree with that of the instrument, such adhesive stamp shall be of no avail; and any person wilfully writing or stamping a false date on any adhesive stamp shall incur a penalty of one hundred dollars for each such offence.

11. The stamp or stamps required to pay the duty hereby imposed shall, in the case of any promissory note, draft or bill of exchange made or drawn within Canada, and not made upon paper stamped to the amount of the duty, be affixed by the maker or drawer thereof, and in the case of any draft or bill of exchange drawn out of Canada, by the acceptor thereof or the first endorser thereof in Canada; and such maker or drawer, acceptor or first indorser, failing to affix such stamp or stamps at the time of making, drawing, accepting or indorsing such note, draft or bill, or affixing stamps of insufficient amount, shall thereby incur a penalty hereinafter imposed; and the duty payable on such instrument, or the duty by which the stamps affixed fall short of the proper amount, shall be doubled, stamps upon the paper being deemed to be affixed thereto for all the purposes of this Act; and any deficiency in the amount of the stamp on the paper may be made up by adhesive stamps.

12. If any person in Canada makes, draws, accepts, indorses, signs, becomes a party to, or pays any promissory note, draft or bill of exchange, chargeable with duty under this Act, before the duty or double duty as the case may be) has been paid, by affixing thereto the proper stamp or stamps, (or by making it on stamped paper or by both) such person shall thereby incur a penalty of one hundred dollars, and save only in the case of payment of double duty, as in the next section provided, such instrument shall be invalid and of no effect in law or in equity, and the acceptance, or payment, or protest thereof, shall be of no effect ; and in suing for any such penalty, the fact that no part of the signature of the party charged with neglecting to affix the proper stamp or stamps, or his initials is or are written over the stamp or stamps affixed to any such instrument, or that no date, or a date that does not correspond with the time when the duty ought to have been paid, is written or marked on the stamp or stamps, shall be *prima facie* evidence that such party did not affix it or them as required by this Act: but no party to or holder of any such instrument shall incur any penalty by reason of the duty thereon not having been paid at the proper time, and by the proper party or parties, provided that at the time it came into his hands it had affixed to it stamps to the amount of the duty apparently payable upon it, that he had no knowledge that they were not affixed at the proper time, and by the proper party or parties, and that he pays the double or additional duty as in the next section provided, as soon as he acquires such knowledge.

13. Any holder of such instrument, including banks and brokers, may pay double duty by affixing to such instrument a stamp or stamps to the amount thereof or to the amount of double the sum by which the stamps affixed fall short of the proper duty, and by writing his initials on such stamp or stamps, and the date on which they were affixed ; and where, in any suit or proceeding in law or equity, the validity of any such instrument is questioned by reason of the proper duty thereon not having been paid at all, or not paid by the proper party, or at the proper time, or of any formality as to the date or erasure of the stamps affixed having been omitted, or a wrong date placed thereon, and it appears that the holder thereof, when he became such holder, had no knowledge of such defects, such instrument shall be held to be legal and valid, if it shall appear that the holder thereof paid double duty, as in this section mentioned, so soon as he acquired such knowledge, even although such knowledge shall have been acquired only during such suit or proceeding; and if it shall appear in any such suit or proceeding to the satisfaction of the court or judge, as the case may be, that it was through mere error or mistake, and without any intention to violate the law on the part of the holder, that any such defect as aforesaid existed in relation to such instrument, then such instrument or any indorsement or transfer thereof, shall be held legal and valid, if the holder shall pay the double duty thereon as soon as he is aware of such error or mistake : but no party who ought to have paid duty thereon shall be released from the penalty by him incurred as aforesaid.

14. The provisions whereby validity may be given to bills of exchange, drafts and promissory notes when drawn or made within Canada, by the payment of double duty thereon, shall for the same purposes and to the same effect, extend to such instruments when drawn or made without Canada but payable in Canada, when stamps to the amount of double duty upon such instruments shall be affixed and cancelled in the same mode as stamps in payment of double duty are affixed and cancelled to such instruments when made or drawn within Canada.

15. It shall be sufficient in the case of any bill of exchange, draft or promissory note drawn or made without Canada but payable within Canada, in order to comply with the law, for any bank, broker, holder or party to such instrument, at the time of the acceptance or indorsation thereof, to affix thereto and cancel the proper single stamps therefor; and the date of cancellation to be marked thereon shall be the true date of such cancellation, and such date need not agree with the date of the instrument.

16. In the case of a suit to recover upon, or a defence of set-off upon a lost or destroyed bill of exchange, draft or promissory note, where there is no evidence that such instrument had been properly stamped, and when the validity of the instrument in question is contested on the ground of insufficient stamps or want of stamps, the Court having cognizance of the suit may, at any stage of the proceeding, in order to give validity to the same, allow double stamps for the requisite amount to be affixed to the record, or to any other paper or proceeding in the cause, and cancelled by or on behalf of the party interested in maintaining the validity of the instrument, plaintiff or defendant, as the case may be.

17. After a note or instrument requiring to be stamped under this Act has been settled or paid, no penalty shall be enforced against any party thereto, or against any person or corporation who had been the holder thereof, by reason of such note or instrument having been insufficiently stamped, or the stamps thereon insufficiently effaced ; unless it be proved, that the party from whom a penalty is demanded, was aware before, or at the date of the maturity of such note or instrument, of the defect in the stamping thereof, or in the effacing of the stamps thereon, and did not thereupon affix double stamps thereto, in the manner provided by this Act. And the reception of such note or instrument by any party to such note or instrument, or by the holder thereof, whether such holder be a corporation or not, or by any employee or agent of such party or holder, shall not be evidence sufficient to justify a conviction or such penalty.

18. In the case of a bill of exchange, draft or promissory note found amongst the securities of a deceased person, unstamped, it shall be sufficient, in order to give validity thereto, for the executor or administrator, to affix and cancel double stamps thereon, with the date of such cancellation and with the initials of the party cancelling the same.

19. Every instrument liable to stamp duty shall be admitted in evidence in any criminal proceeding, although it may not have the stamp required by law impressed thereon or affixed thereto.

20. The Governor in Council may, from time to time, direct stamped paper to be prepared for the purposes of this Act, of such kinds and bearing respectively such device as he thinks proper, and may defray the cost thereof out of any unappropriated moneys forming part of the Consolidated Revenue Fund ; but the device on each stamp shall express the value thereof,—that is to say the sum at which it shall be reckoned in payment of the duties imposed by this Act.

2. And the Governor-in-Council may, from time to time, make and repeal or alter regulations for redeeming spoiled stamped paper, by the issue of new stamped paper or stamps of equal value in exchange therefor ; but no such stamped paper shall be so redeemed unless when presented in quantities at one time representing a value of not less than five dollars.

21. The Governor-in-Council may, from time to time, direct stamps to be prepared for the purposes of this Act, of such kinds and bearing respectively such device as he thinks proper, and may defray the cost thereof out of any unappropriated moneys forming part of the Consolidated Revenue Fund ; but the device on each stamp shall express the value thereof,— that is to say, the sum at which it shall be reckoned in payment of the duties hereby imposed.

22. The Minister of Inland Revenue may appoint any Postmasters, Collectors of Inland Revenue, or other officers of the Government to be the distributors of stamps and stamped paper under this Act, and may authorize any other person to purchase stamps from such distributors to sell again ; and the Governor-in-Council may fix the remuneration to be allowed to such distributors, and the discount to be made to persons so purchasing to sell again ; but such discount shall in no case exceed five per cent. on the value of such stamps, and shall not be allowed on any quantity less than one hundred dollars.

23. The Governor-in-Council may make such further regulations as he may deem necessary for carrying this Act into effect, and may, by an Order-in-Council, declare that any kind or class of instruments as to which doubt may arise, is or is not chargeable with any and what duty under this Act according to the true meaning thereof ; and any Order-in-Council made under this Act may be explained, amended or repealed by any other such order of later date ; and any Order-in-Council under this Act shall be published, and may be proved in the manner provided by the "*Act to amend and consolidate the Acts respecting the Customs*" as to Orders-in-Council under that Act.

24. If any person forges, counterfeits or imitates, or procures to be forged, counterfeited or imitated, any stamp or stamped paper, issued or authorized to be used for the purposes of this Act, or by means whereof any duty hereby imposed may be paid, or any part or portion of any such stamp,—or knowingly uses, offers, sells or exposes to sale, any such forged, counterfeited or imitated stamp,—or engraves, cuts, sinks or makes any plate, die or other thing whereby to make or imitate such stamp or any part or portion thereof, except by permission of the Minister of Inland Revenue, or some officer or person who, under an Order-in-Council in that behalf, may lawfully grant such permission,—

or has possession of any such plate, die or other thing, without such permission,—or, without such permission, uses or has possession of any such plate, die or thing lawfully engraved, cut or made,—or tears off or removes from any instrument, on which a duty is payable under this Act, any stamp by which such duty has been wholly or in part paid,— or removes from any such stamp any writing or mark indicating that it has been used for or towards the payment of any such duty—such person shall be guilty of felony, and shall, on conviction, be liable to be imprisoned in the penitentiary for any term not exceeding twenty-one years; and every such offence shall be forgery, and punishable in the manner in which that crime is punishable by the laws of Canada.

25. Notwithstanding anything herein contained, any bank or any broker who makes, draws or issues or negotiates, presents for payment, or pays, or takes, or receives, or becomes the holder of any instrument not duly stamped, either as a deposit, or in payment, or as a security, or for collection or otherwise, knowing the same not to be duly stamped, and who does not immediately on making, drawing, issuing, negotiating or presenting for payment, or paying, or taking, or receiving or becoming the holder of such instrument, affix thereto and cancel the proper stamps within the meaning of this Act, shall incur a penalty of five hundred dollars for every such offence; and shall not be entitled to recover on such instrument, or to make the same available for any purpose whatever, and any such instrument shall be invalid and of no effect in law or equity.

26. If any person wilfully affixes to any promissory note, draft or bill of exchange, any stamp which has been previously affixed to any other, or used for the purpose of paying any duty under this Act, or any other Act, or which has been in any way previously written upon or defaced, such person shall be guilty of a misdemeanour, and shall thereby incur a penalty of five hundred dollars.

27. The penalties hereinbefore imposed shall be incurred in respect of each such promissory note, draft or bill of exchange, on which the duty or double duty hereby imposed is not paid as aforesaid, or to which a stamp previously used has been fraudulently affixed, whatever be the number of such instruments executed, accepted, paid or delivered, or offences committed on the same day; and a separate penalty to the full amount shall be incurred by each person committing such offence, whatever be the number of such persons.

28. The penalties imposed by the foregoing sections of this Act, shall be recoverable in the manner prescribed by "*The Interpretation Act,*" in cases where penalties are imposed and the recovery is not otherwise provided for.

Private and other Acts, and Amendments thereto, Relating to Building Societies.

ABBREVIATIONS—Que. before the figures, dates, &c., denotes that the Statute has been passed by the Quebec Legislature ; Ont., for Ontario Legislature. Where neither of the foregoing abbreviations occur, the Statutes have been passed by the Dominion Government. When date is followed by (1), or (2), it denotes that the Act was passed in first or second Session of the year.

Anglo-Canadian Mortgage and Investment Co. (Limited) 1874, Cap. 105 (To transfer the securities of) to Omnium Securities Co. (Limited) Ont., 44th Vic., Cap. 49.

Brockville Mutual Building Society, Ont., 42 Vic., Cap. 83.

British American Investment Co., 1860, Cap. 129.

British American Land Co. (Act respecting Loans by) 39 Vic., Cap. 56.

British Canadian Loan & Investment Co. (Limited) 1876, Cap. 57 ; 1877, Cap. 76.

Building Societies generally : Con. Stat. L. C., Cap. 69 ; Con. Stat. U.C., Cap. 53.—1865, Cap. 38 (being the first to enact an annual return to the Auditor of Public Accounts, upon oath) 1874, Cap. 50 (to issue debentures) 1877, Cap. 50 ; 1878, Cap. 22 ; 1879, Caps. 48 and 49.   Que.—1875 (2) Cap. 61 ; 1878 (1) Cap. 20 (Sec. 1 repealed by 1877, Cap. 50, Sec. 23) 1882, 45 Vic., Cap. 24.

KEY TO ABOVE—1878, Cap. 22, applies to the Province of Ontario only ; 1879, Cap. 48, refers to the liquidation of B.S. in Quebec, and the appointment of liquidators : Cap. 49 concerns Ontario ; Que., 1878 (1) Cap. 20, amends Sec. 23 of Con. Stat. L. C., Cap. 69, and authorizes the transformation of appropriation shares into permanent shares. Act to come into force 90 days after sanction.—Sec. 2.

Canada Agricultural Loan Assn., 1860, Cap. 130 ; 1861, Cap. 107 ; 1863 (2) Cap. 48.

Canada Company, 1864, Cap. 100.

Canada Improvement Co., 1872, Cap. 110.

Canada Investment & Agency Co., 1874, Cap. 99.

Canada Investment & Guarantee Co. (Limited) 1875, Cap. 63.

Canada Landed Credit Co., 1866, Cap. 125. To authorize an addition to capital, and other purposes, Ont., 38 Vic., Cap. 73. To extend powers, 39 Vic., Cap. 97. An Act to amend Acts relating to Can. Landed Cr. Co., 1882, 45 Vic., Cap. 110—further amended, 45 Vic., Cap. 72, Ont.

Canada Landed Proprietors' Loan Co., Que., 1875 (1) Cap. 82.

Canada Mortgage Agency (Limited) Ont., 44 Vic., Cap. 50.

Canada Provident Association (An Act to incorporate the) 1882, 45 Vic., Cap. 107; Que., 1875 (2) Cap. 61, concerns union or fusion of Building Societies.

Canada Permanent Building & Savings Society, to change name to Canada Permanent Loan & Savings Co., 1874, Cap. 100; Ont., Cap. 94, 39 Vic.

Canadian Loan & Investment Co., 1866, Cap. 126.

Canadian Securities Co. (Limited) 1877, Cap. 79.

Colonial Building & Investment Association, 1874, Cap. 103.

Companies incorporated under Imperial Statutes (An Act respecting) 1880, 43-44 Vic. Cap. 38.

Crédit-Foncier (Dominion of Canada) 44 Vic., Cap. 59.

Crédit-Foncier Franco-Canadien, Ont., 44 Vic., Cap. 51; 44 Vic., Cap. 58.

Crédit-Foncier (Lower Canada) 1863 (2) Cap. 46; 1864, Cap. 81.

Crédit-Foncier du Bas-Canada, 1873, Cap. 102; 1874, Cap. 97; Que., 1875 (2) Cap. 64.

Crédit-Foncier Franco-Canadien (An Act to incorporate) Que. 1880, 43-4 Vic., Cap. 60.

Defective Letters Patent Remedy, 38 Vic., Cap. 13. Amended, Ont., 39 Vic., Cap. 7, S. 25, Sub-sec. 18; further amended, Ont., 45 Vic., Cap. 17. Que., amended, 1881, 44-45 Vic., Cap. 11.

Dominion Building Society to change name to Dominion Mortgage Loan Co., 1877, Cap. 80.

Dominion Homestead Building Society, Que., 1871, Cap. 38.

Eastern Township Land & Improvement Co., Que., 1875 (1) Cap. 83.

Eastern Townships Colonization and Credit Company, incorporated, Que., 1880, 44-45 Vic., Cap. 61.

England and Canada Mortgage Security Co., 1876, Cap. 58.

English Loan Company— Act amended—Ont., 43 Vic., Cap. 76.

Farmers' Loan & Savings Co., 1874, Cap. 102.

Freehold Loan & Savings Co., 1873, Cap. 104.

Glasgow Canadian Land & Trust Co. (Limited) 1873, Cap. 105.

Hochelaga (Société de Construction du Comté de) 1878, Cap. 41.

Act to confirm Act of Dom. Parlt., 41 Vic., Cap. 41; Que., 1880, 43-44 Vic., Cap. 57.

Home Savings and Loan Co. (Limited) 1879, Cap. 55.

Huron & Erie Savings and Loan Society (to change name) Ont., 39 Vic., Cap. 95.

Iberville (Société Permanente de Construction du District de) Que., 1872, Cap. 78; Dom., 1879, Cap. 76.

Imperial Guarantee & Loan Society, 1872, Cap. 107.

Imperial Statutes respecting Companies incorporated under 1880, 43-44 Vic., Cap. 39.

Imperial Loan & Investment Co., 1875, Cap. 62.

Insolvent Banks, Insurance Companies, Loan Companies, Building Societies, Building Societies & Trading Corporations (An Act respecting) 1882, 45 Vic., Cap. 23.

Joint Stock Companies' Clauses Act, 1869, Cap. 12; Que., 1868, Cap. 24; 1869, Cap. 42. To amend, Que., 1881, 44-45 Vic., Cap. 12.

Joint Stock Co's incorporated by letters patent, 1869, Cap. 13; repealed by 1877, Cap. 43 ; now called " The Canada Joint Stock Companies' Act, 1877."

La Société de Construction St. Jacques, An Act to confirm Act of Federal Parliament, 40 Vic., Cap. 81; 1880, 43-44 Vic., Cap. 58.

Landed Credit Co's to return list of shareholders to Parliament, 1871, Cap. 7, Sec. 37.

Loan Companies (Foreign) authorized to do business in Ontario ; Ont., 39 Vic., Cap. 27.

Loan & Landed Credit Co., 1872, Cap. 109. Privileges confirmed, Que., 1880, 43-44 Vic., Cap. 59.

Loan & Mortgage Co., Quebec, 1875 (2) Cap. 63 ; 1876, Cap. 27, Sec. 15.

London and Canadian Loan & Agency Co. (Limited) 1863 (2) Cap. 50; 1872, Cap. 108 ; 1873, Cap. 107; 1876, Cap. 60; 1879, Cap. 75.

London & Ontario Investment Co. (Limited) 1876, Cap. 62; 1877, Cap. 78.

Manitoba & North-West Loan Co. (Limited) 1879, Cap. 74.

Maritime Savings and Loan Society incorporated, 39 Vic., Cap. 66.

Midland Land Co. (Act to amend) 45 Vic., Cap. 77.

Montreal Building Association : Que., 1868, Cap. 41 ; 1878 (1) Cap. 53. (Name changed to Montreal Investment & Building Co.)

Montreal Board of Real Estate Agents incorporated, 1881, 44-45 Vic., Cap. 68.

Montreal Building Society, incorporated under an Act passed by the

Legislative Assembly, 8 Vic., Cap. 91; made permanent, 1866 (1) Cap. 26.

Montreal Canadian Building Society, Que., 1866, Cap. 40.

Montreal Credit Co., 1874, Cap. 96; Que., 1871, Cap. 36; 1872, Cap. 62.

Montreal District Permanent Building Society of 1863 (1) Cap. 28; 1872, Cap. 109, changes name to Loan & Landed Credit Co.

Montreal (French-Canadian Artisans' Society of) Que., 1876, Cap. 68.

Montreal Investment Association, 1865, (1) Cap. 42; 1873, Cap. 103.

Montreal Investment & Building Co., 1878, Cap. 42; Que., 1878 (1) Cap. 53.

Montreal Investment Trust (An Act to incorporate) 1880, 43-44 Vic., Cap. 39.

Montreal Land Co., Que., 1876, Cap. 70.

Montreal Loan & Landed Credit Co., 1872, Cap. 109.

Montreal Loan & Mortgage Co., Que., 1875 (2) Cap. 63; 1876, Cap. 27, Sec. 14.

Montreal Permanent Building Society, name changed to The Montreal Loan & Mortgage Co., Que., 1875 (2) Cap. 63.

National Investment Co. of Canada (Limited) 1876, Cap. 61; 1877, Cap. 77.

Ottawa Loan & Investment Co., 1874, Cap. 104; 1879, Cap. 71.

Ontario Trust Co., an Act to amend, &c., 45 Vic., Cap. 78.

Permanent Building Societies in Ontario, 1874, Cap. 50; 1877, Caps. 48 and 49; 1878, Cap. 22. (*Vide* Building Societies.)

Peterborough Real Estate Investment Co., Limited (Charter granted), 41 Vic.

Provincial Loan Co., changed name, 39 Vic., Cap. 65; Que., 38 Vic. (2) and 39 Vic.

Société de Prêts et Placements de 1878, Cap. 34; replaces Société de Construction Mutuelle.

Scottish Canadian Loan Co., 1876 (2), Cap. 59.

Security, Loan and Savings Co., 1876 (2), Cap. 64.

St. Jacques (Société de Construction) 1877, Cap. 81.

St. Maurice Lumber and Land Co., Que., 1869, Cap. 65.

St. Pierre Land & Manufacturing Co., Que., 1875 (1) Cap. 84.

Toronto House Building Association, Act to amend and to change name, &c., to The Land Security Co., 45 Vic., Cap. 80.

Trust and Loan Company of Upper Canada, for facilitating conveyance of lands in Canada through their Commissioners or Attorneys, 1862, Cap. 72 ; amending Acts relating to, &c., and enlarging the powers of Co., 1882, 45 Vic., Cap. 111.

Union Loan & Savings Co., 1876 (2), Cap. 63.

United States Corporations may hold lands in Quebec for their occupation or business prosecution only, Que., 1872, Cap. 25.

Western Canada Loan & Savings Co., 1874, Cap. 101 ; to change name Ont., 39 Vic., Cap. 96.

INDEX.

	YEAR.	PAGE.
A brief review of the progress of Building Societies and Loan Companies for the past 18 years, their increase, &c. (Preface)	1882	3
Alphabetically arranged Table of Acts and Amendments passed by the Dominion Parliament, and Legislatures of Ontario and Quebec		408
Banks and Banking, Acts relating to, &c., compiled by Wm. Wilson .. .. (Dom. of Can.)	1880	367
Banks, Insurance Companies, Loan Companies, Building Societies, and Trading Corporations insolvent (Dom. of Can.)	1882	326

UPPER CANADA.

	YEAR.	PAGE.
Benefit Building Societies. (See Building Societies.)		
Building Societies in Upper Canada, first Act passed retained..	1846	9
Building Societies, An Act respecting..	1859	16
Building Societies, Permanent, in Upper Canada, to make further provisions for..	1865	23

LOWER CANADA.

		PAGE.
Building Societies, An Act respecting..	..69 Con. St.	25

DOMINION OF CANADA.

	YEAR.	PAGE.
Building Societies, Permanent, To make further provisions for, carrying on business in the Province of Ontario.. ..	1874	34
Building Societies—To amend 37 Vic., Cap. 50, respecting Permanent Building Societies in Ontario..	1877	41
Building Societies, Permanent, An Act to amend the Act to make further provision for the management of, in Ontario..	1877	42
Building Societies, to make further provision for the regulation of, in Province of Quebec	1877	52
Building Societies To amend the law relating to Building Societies in Ontario ..	1878	43
Building Societies Respecting the carrying on business in Ontario	1879	44

414 INDEX.

	YEAR.	PAGE.
Building Societies, to provide for the liquidation of, in the Province of Quebec	1879	62
Building Societies, Permanent, and Loan Companies, An Act for the relief of	1880	47
Building Societies and Loan and Savings Companies carrying on business in the Province of Ontario	1882	349

ONTARIO LEGISLATURE.

		PAGE.
Building Societies, Respecting	..R.Stat.O.	97

	YEAR.	PAGE.
Building Societies, To amend the law respecting	1878	134
Building Societies—To amend the Act	1879	135
Building Societies, Loan and Savings Societies and Companies, for the relief of	1880	137

QUEBEC LEGISLATURE.

	YEAR.	PAGE.
Building Societies, to amend Cap. 69, Con. Stat. Lower Canada, providing for their union and fusion	1875	166
Building Societies in the Province of Quebec, An Act respecting	1878	168

NOVA SCOTIA LEGISLATURE.

	YEAR.	PAGE.
Building Societies, Benefit, for the regulation of..	1846	217
Building Society, Pictou, to incorporate	1879	228
Building Society, Yarmouth, to incorporate..	1880	230

NEW BRUNSWICK LEGISLATURE.

	YEAR.	PAGE.
Building Societies, Benefit, for the regulation of..	1847	191
Building Societies, Benefit, to revive and continue an Act intituled: An Act for the regulation of	1866	205
Building Societies, Benefit, in amendment of an Act made and passed in the tenth year of the reign of Her Majesty, and an Act, 29th Vic., to revive and continue the same	1871	206
Building Society, St. John Real Estate and, to incorporate	1871	211
Building Societies, in further amendment of the Law relating thereto	1880	215

PRINCE EDWARD ISLAND LEGISLATURE.

	YEAR.	PAGE.
Building Societies, Benefit, for the regulation of..	1876	233

INDEX. 415

MANITOBA LEGISLATURE.

		PAGE.
Building Societies, formation of, &c.	9 Con. Stat.	169

		YEAR.	PAGE.
Canadian Pacific Railway, respecting (Dom. of Can.)	1881	300
Companies incorporated under the Joint Stock Companies' Letters Patent Act—to extend their powers.. (Ont. Leg.)	1881	211

BRITISH COLUMBIA LEGISLATURE.

	YEAR	PAGE
Companies' Ordinance, 1866, Ordinance respecting ..	1869	355

	YEAR	PAGE
Corporations and Institutions incorporated without to lend and invest money in Canada.. .. .. .. (Dom. of Can.)	1874	91
Corporations and Institutions incorporated out of Ontario to lend and invest moneys therein .. .. (Ont. Leg.) 163 R. Stat. O.		94
Corporations and other Institutions incorporated out of this Province to lend and invest money therein, To authorize .. .. .. (Leg. of Man.) 30 Con. Stat. Man.		350
Credit Foncier Franco-Canadian, To enlarge and extend the powers of .. .. (Dom. of Can.)	1881	113
Credit Foncier Franco-Canadian, Respecting the ..(Ont. Leg.)	1881	287
Credit Foncier of the Dominion of Canada, To incorporate .. .. (Dom. of Can.)	1881	117
Duties imposed on Promissory Notes and Bills of Exchange, To amend and consolidate the law respecting (Dom. of Can.)	1879	400
Establishment of Investment and Loan Societies, Ordinance to encourage .. .. .. (Leg. of B C.)	1869	356
Exhibition Buildings, To extend the powers of Joint Stock Companies for the erection of .. (Ont. Leg.)	1880	249
Imperial Statutes, Respecting Companies incorporated under (Ont. Leg.)	1880	250
Incorporated Companies, Respecting returns required from .. (Ont. Leg.)	1882	290
Interest and Moneys secured by Mortgage on Real Estate, Relating to (Dom. of Can.)	1882	93
Joint Stock Companies, by Letters Patent, incorporation, and to amend the law respecting (Dom. of Can.)	1877	66
Joint Stock Companies, Containing general provisions, incorporated by special Act and for certain purposes (Ont. Leg.) 150 R Stat O		141

                                                                              PAGE
Joint Stock Companies—respecting the incorporation by Letters
    Patent .. .. (Ont. Leg.) 150 R.Stat.O. 150
                                                             YEAR. PAGE
Joint Stock Companies, Respecting the winding up of (Ont. Leg.) 1878 266
Joint Stock Companies' Amendments.. .. .. (Ont. Leg.) 1878 154½
Joint Stock Companies, To extend the powers of, for the erection
    of Exhibition buildings.. .. .. (Ont. Leg.) 1880 249
Joint Stock Companies, To extend the powers of Companies
    incorporated under the Letters Patent Act.. (Ont. Leg.) 1881 251
Joint Stock Companies, The incorporation of, by Letters Patent,
    and regulation of Timber Slide Companies.. (Ont. Leg.) 1881 252
Joint Stock Companies, To confer additional powers
    upon .. .. (Ont. Leg.) 1882 291
Joint Stock Companies, The incorporation of, by Letters Patent,
    and their powers   .. (Leg. of Man.) 7 Con. Stat. Man. 177
                                                             YEAR. PAGE.
Joint Stock Companies, An Ordinance to amend the law relating
    to .. ..(British Columbia Leg.) 1866 353
Mortgages and Sales of Personal Property, An Act respect-
    ing .. ..(Ont. Leg.) 119 R. Stat. Ont. 260
                                                             YEAR PAGE.
Pacific Railway, Canadian, respecting.. .. (Dom. of Can.) 1881 300
Permanent Building Societies. (See Building Societies.)
Picton Permanent Building Society, To incorporate 1879 228
                                            (Nova Scotia Leg.)
Promissory Notes, Drafts, and Bills of Exchange, To repeal the
    duty on .. .. (Dom. of Can.) 1882 325
Returns required from incorporated Companies, Respecting .. 1882 290
                                            (Ont. Leg.
Revised Statutes Amendments .. .. .. (Ont. Leg.) 1878 154½
Revised Statutes respecting Mortgages and Sales of Personal
    Property, To amend 1880 257
St. John Real Estate and Building Company, To incorporate 1871 211
                                            (Leg. N. B.)
Timber Slide Companies, For the incorporation and regulation
    of   (Ont. Leg.) 1881 252
To give to Mortgagees certain powers now commonly inserted
    in Mortgages 1879 284
To amend the Revised Statutes respecting Mortgages and Sales
    of Personal Property   1880 257
Yarmouth Building Society, To incorporate (Nova Scotia Leg.) 1880 230

www.ingramcontent.com/pod-product-compliance
Lightning Source LLC
Chambersburg PA
CBHW030546300426
44111CB00009B/875